About the Cover Image

Detail of a Procession, Fresco from the Palace of Knossos, ca. 1500 B.C.E.

These two young men, carrying vessels containing wine or oil, were part of an ancient ceremonial procession on the island of Crete, as depicted in frescoes dating to about 1500 B.C.E. These frescoes, uncovered in a huge palace complex in the early twentieth century, featured hundreds of men and women, some bearing gifts, as well as two priestesses and a goddess figure. The palace and its frescoes are striking expressions of an early civilization, called Minoan, that flourished on Crete between roughly 2000 and 1375 B.C.E. This civilization was known for the sophistication and exuberance of its art and architecture, for the size and complexity of its major city of Knossos, for the prominence of female figures in its religion, and for a network of international connections that included Egypt and the Middle East, the islands of the Aegean Sea, and Greece.

Detail of a procession, from the palace of Knossos, ca. 1500 B.C.E. (fresco painting), Minoan / © Sylvie Allouche / Bridgeman Images

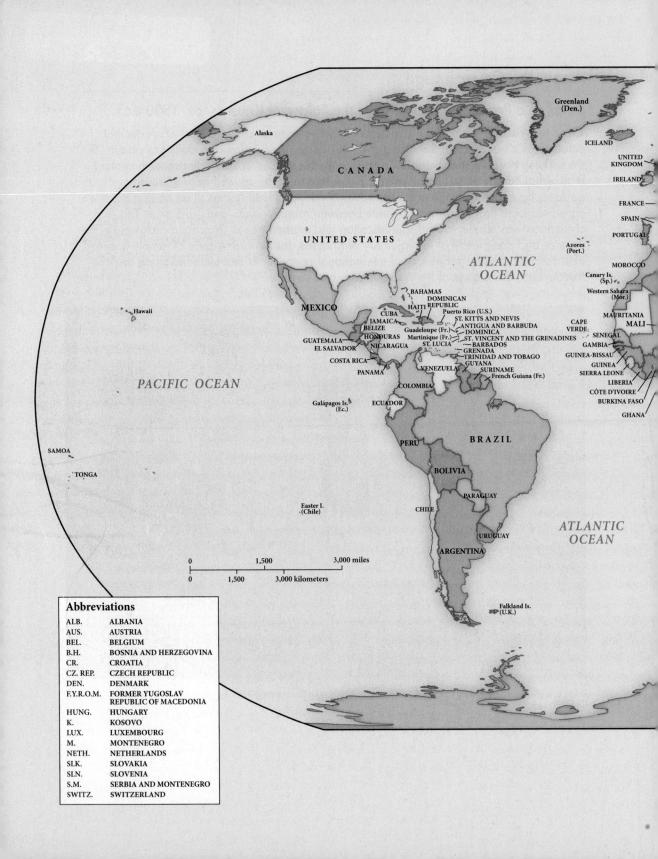

Greenland
(Den.)

ICELAND

UNITED
KINGDOM

IRELAND

FRANCE

SPAIN

PORTUGAL

Azores
(Port.)

MOROCCO

Canary Is.
(Sp.)

Western Sahara
(Mor.)

MAURITANIA

MALI

CAPE
VERDE

SENEGAL

GAMBIA

GUINEA-BISSAU

GUINEA

SIERRA LEONE

LIBERIA

CÔTE D'IVOIRE

BURKINA FASO

GHANA

Alaska

CANADA

UNITED STATES

ATLANTIC
OCEAN

Hawaii

MEXICO

BAHAMAS

DOMINICAN
REPUBLIC

HAITI

CUBA

JAMAICA

BELIZE

GUATEMALA

HONDURAS

EL SALVADOR

NICARAGUA

COSTA RICA

PANAMA

Puerto Rico (U.S.)

ST. KITTS AND NEVIS

ANTIGUA AND BARBUDA

Guadeloupe (Fr.)

DOMINICA

Martinique (Fr.)

ST. VINCENT AND THE GRENADINES

ST. LUCIA

BARBADOS

GRENADA

TRINIDAD AND TOBAGO

GUYANA

VENEZUELA

SURINAME

French Guiana (Fr.)

COLOMBIA

PACIFIC OCEAN

Galápagos Is.
(Ec.)

ECUADOR

PERU

BRAZIL

BOLIVIA

PARAGUAY

SAMOA

TONGA

Easter I.
(Chile)

CHILE

URUGUAY

ATLANTIC
OCEAN

ARGENTINA

Falkland Is.
(U.K.)

0		1,500		3,000 miles

0	1,500		3,000 kilometers	

Abbreviations

ALB.	ALBANIA
AUS.	AUSTRIA
BEL.	BELGIUM
B.H.	BOSNIA AND HERZEGOVINA
CR.	CROATIA
CZ. REP.	CZECH REPUBLIC
DEN.	DENMARK
F.Y.R.O.M.	FORMER YUGOSLAV REPUBLIC OF MACEDONIA
HUNG.	HUNGARY
K.	KOSOVO
LUX.	LUXEMBOURG
M.	MONTENEGRO
NETH.	NETHERLANDS
SLK.	SLOVAKIA
SLN.	SLOVENIA
S.M.	SERBIA AND MONTENEGRO
SWITZ.	SWITZERLAND

ARCTIC OCEAN

NORWAY
SWEDEN
FINLAND
ESTONIA
DEN.
LATVIA
LITHUANIA
NETH. POLAND BELARUS
GERMANY
BEL. CZ. REP.
LUX. SLK.
AUS. HUNG.
SWITZ. CR.
SLN. ROMANIA
ITALY B.H. BULGARIA
M.F.Y.R.O.M.
ALB. GREECE
MALTA

UKRAINE
MOLDOVA

RUSSIAN FEDERATION

GEORGIA
ARMENIA
TURKEY AZERBAIJAN

KAZAKHSTAN

MONGOLIA

UZBEKISTAN KYRGYZSTAN
TURKMENISTAN TAJIKISTAN

N. KOREA
S. KOREA

JAPAN

PACIFIC OCEAN

TUNISIA
CYPRUS
ISRAEL
SYRIA LEBANON
IRAQ
West Bank
Gaza
Strip
JORDAN KUWAIT
BAHRAIN

IRAN

AFGHANISTAN

PAKISTAN

BHUTAN
NEPAL

CHINA

TAIWAN

ALGERIA

LIBYA

EGYPT

SAUDI
ARABIA
QATAR
UNITED ARAB
EMIRATES

OMAN

INDIA

BANGLADESH
MYANMAR
(BURMA)

VIETNAM
LAOS

Mariana Is.
(U.S.)

MARSHALL
IS.

Guam
(U.S.)

NIGER

CHAD

SUDAN

ERITREA

YEMEN

DJIBOUTI

THAILAND

CAMBODIA

PHILIPPINES

NIGERIA
BENIN
TOGO
CAMEROON
CENTRAL
AFRICAN REP.

SOUTH
SUDAN

ETHIOPIA

SOMALIA

MALDIVES

SRI
LANKA

BRUNEI

PALAU

FEDERATED STATES
OF MICRONESIA

NAURU

KIRIBATI

EQ. GUINEA
GABON
SÃO
TOME
&
PRINCIPE

CONGO

DEM. REP. OF
THE CONGO
BURUNDI

RWANDA UGANDA
KENYA

TANZANIA

COMOROS

SEYCHELLES

INDIAN OCEAN

MALAYSIA

SINGAPORE

INDONESIA

PAPUA
NEW
GUINEA

SOLOMON
IS.

TUVALU

ANGOLA

ZAMBIA

MALAWI

MADAGASCAR

MAURITIUS

EAST
TIMOR

VANUATU

FIJI

NAMIBIA
BOTSWANA

ZIMBABWE

AUSTRALIA

New Caledonia
(Fr.)

SOUTH
AFRICA

MOZAMBIQUE
SWAZILAND
LESOTHO

NEW
ZEALAND

Tasmania
(Aust.)

ANTARCTICA

Ways of the World

A Brief Global History with Sources

VOLUME 1

Through the Fifteenth Century

Ways of the World

A Brief Global History with Sources

FOURTH EDITION

Robert W. Strayer

The College at Brockport: State University of New York

Eric W. Nelson

Missouri State University

bedford/st.martin's
Macmillan Learning
Boston | New York

FOR EVELYN RHIANNON WITH LOVE

For Bedford/St. Martin's

Vice President, Editorial, Macmillan Learning Humanities:
Edwin Hill
Program Director for History: Michael Rosenberg
Senior Program Manager for History: William J. Lombardo
History Marketing Manager: Melissa Rodriguez
Director of Content Development, Humanities: Jane Knetzger
Senior Developmental Editor: Heidi L. Hood
Senior Content Project Manager: Christina M. Horn
Workflow Project Supervisor: Joe Ford
Production Supervisor: Robin Besofsky
Senior Media Project Manager: Michelle Camisa
Media Editor: Tess Fletcher
Editorial Assistant: Stephanie Sosa
Copy Editor: Susan Zorn
Indexer: Leoni Z. McVey
Editorial Services: Lumina Datamatics, Inc.
Composition: Lumina Datamatics, Inc.

Cartographer: Mapping Specialists, Ltd.
Photo Editor: Christine Buese
Photo Researcher: Bruce Carson
Permissions Editor: Eve Lehmann
Design Director, Content Management: Diana Blume
Text Design: Lisa Buckley
Cover Design: William Boardman
Printing and Binding: LSC Communications

Cover Image: top, Fragment with wrestling lions and harpies, early 12th century (silk lampas with supplementary discontinuous metal-wrapped patterning wefts), Spanish School (12th century)/Museum of Fine Arts, Boston, Massachusetts, USA/Helen and Alice Colburn Fund and Harriet Otis Cruft Fund/Bridgeman Images; bottom, Detail of a procession, from the palace of Knossos, ca. 1500 B.C.E. (fresco painting), Minoan/© Sylvie Allouche/Bridgeman Images

1   2   3   4   5   6   23   22   21   20   19   18

For information, write: Bedford/St. Martin's, 75 Arlington Street, Boston, MA 02116

ISBN 978-1-319-10972-1 (Combined Edition)
ISBN 978-1-319-10975-2 (Volume 1)
ISBN 978-1-319-10978-3 (Volume 2)

Acknowledgments

Text acknowledgments and copyrights appear at the back of the book on page 544, which constitutes an extension of the copyright page. Art acknowledgments and copyrights appear on the same page as the art selections they cover.

Preface

About *Ways of the World*

Ways of the World is an intentionally brief global history of the human experience that focuses on the big pictures of world history, using examples selectively rather than cluttering the narrative with endless details. It repeatedly highlights issues of change, of comparison, and of connection among culturally different peoples, both in the narrative text and in the book's innovative primary and secondary source features.

The main title of the book, *Ways of the World*, evokes three dimensions of its distinctive character and outlook, all of them based on our experience as teachers and scholars. The first is **diversity** or **variation**, for the "ways of the world," or the ways of being human in the world, have been many and constantly changing. This book seeks to embrace the global experience of humankind, both in its common features and in its vast diversity, while noticing the changing location of particular centers of innovation and wider influence.

Second, the title *Ways of the World* invokes major **panoramas**, **patterns**, or **pathways** in world history rather than a highly detailed narrative, which can often overwhelm students. Thus, most chapters are organized in terms of broad global or transregional themes, illustrated by a limited number of specific examples.

A third implication of the book's title lies in a certain **reflective quality** that appears in the Big Picture essays that introduce each Part, in the Reflections section at the end of each chapter, and periodically in the narrative itself. This dimension of the book offers many opportunities for pondering larger questions about how historians operate, about the dilemmas they face in reconstructing the human journey, and about the relationship of the past to the present.

These elements of *Ways of the World* find expression repeatedly in what we call the **four Cs** of world history: context, change, comparison, and connection. The first "C," **context**, refers to the larger frameworks within which particular historical figures, events, societies, and civilizations take shape. In our telling of the human past, context is central, for in world history nothing stands alone. Like Russian nesting dolls, every story finds a place in some more inclusive narrative. European empires in the Americas, for example, take on new meaning when they are understood as part of a global process of imperial expansion that included the growth of the Inca, Russian, Chinese, and Ottoman empires at the same time.

The second "C," large-scale **change**, both within and especially across major regions of the world, represents another prominent emphasis in *Ways of the World*. Examples include the peopling of the planet, the emergence of "civilization," the linking of Eastern and Western hemispheres in the wake of Columbus's voyages, the Industrial Revolution, and many other significant changes during the course of human history. The flip side of change, of course, is continuity, implying a focus on what persists over long periods of time. And so *Ways of the World* seeks to juxtapose these contrasting elements of human experience. While civilizations have changed dramatically over time, some of their essential features — cities, states, patriarchy, and class inequality, for example — have long endured.

A third "C" involves frequent **comparison**, bringing several regions or cultures into our field of vision at the same time. It means constantly asking "what's the difference?" Thus this book makes comparisons between the Agricultural Revolution in the Eastern and Western hemispheres; between the beginnings of Buddhism and the early history of Christianity and Islam; between the Russian and Chinese revolutions; and between feminism in the Global North and the Global South. These and many more comparisons frequently punctuate our account of the global past.

The final "C" emphasizes **connections**, networks of communication and exchange that increasingly shaped the character of the societies that participated in them. In our account of the human story, world history is less about what happened within particular civilizations or cultures than about the processes and outcomes of their meetings with one another. Cross-cultural encounters then become one of the major motors of historical transformation. Examples include the clash of the ancient Greeks and the Persians; the long-distance commercial networks that linked the Afro-Eurasian world; the numerous cross-cultural interactions spawned by the spread of Islam; the trans-hemispheric Columbian exchange of the early modern era; and the more recent growth of a thoroughly entangled global economy.

These emphases have remained at the heart of *Ways of the World* since its initial publication in 2008. But the book has also changed, grown, and matured. Originally a brief account of the global past by a single author, Robert Strayer, it has acquired a fine co-author in Eric Nelson from Missouri State University.

Along the way, it also began to combine a brief narrative text with thematically based sets of primary sources followed by paired secondary sources at the end of each chapter. What has emerged is a new kind of book for the world history survey, one that enables students to "do history," using the kind of evidence that historians work with. Each of the **Working with Evidence** primary source collections now includes both documents and images and is organized around a particular theme, issue, or question that derives from the chapter narrative. As the title of these features suggests, they enable students to "work with evidence" and thus begin to understand the craft of historians as well as their conclusions. They include brief headnotes that provide context for the sources, and they are accompanied by a series of probing Doing History questions appropriate for in-class discussion and writing assignments. Furthermore, Working with Evidence is now followed by a new **Historians' Voices** secondary source feature that presents two brief extracts from scholarly works, aligned with the theme of the Working with Evidence feature. Thus it can be used in conjunction with that feature or assigned on its own.

Further changes in the book have derived from new scholarship in the rapidly expanding field of World History. Thus we have increasingly integrated issues of gender, the environment, and technology into this account of the human journey. Coverage of particular areas of the world, such as Southeast Asia, Latin America, and Pacific Oceania, has likewise been strengthened. This fourth edition in particular has completely reimagined our treatment of the past century in a more global fashion, moving beyond the cold war framework of earlier editions. And over time the book has more often highlighted individual people and particular events, which sometimes get lost in the broad sweep of world history. Finally, *Ways of the World* has acquired a very substantial electronic and online presence with an impressive array of innovative pedagogical and learning aids.

These changes remind us that textbooks are not fixed and finished compilations of what happened in the past. Rather, such books develop as they respond to new technologies, to new historical research, and to the evolving political, social, and economic conditions of the contemporary world. As authors, we are acutely aware of how much debate and controversy lie behind many of the issues that are explored in *Ways of the World*. This book, then, is a snapshot of our current understanding of World History, shaped by the particular time (the early twenty-first century) and place (the United States) in which it was composed. Such a book written fifty years ago, or in contemporary China, Nigeria, Iran, or Brazil, or in the mid-twenty-first century, would surely be very different. Thus *Ways of the World* can and should be criticized, assessed, and argued with, not simply accepted as a definitive account of the global past.

What Else Is New in the Fourth Edition?

In this new edition, *Ways of the World* continues to change, most notably in a **revision of Part 6**, which deals with the past century. Previously the several chapters of that Part were organized regionally and in terms deriving from the cold war: the Western capitalist world, the communist world, and the third world of developing countries. But with the cold war now more than a quarter of a century in the past, it seemed appropriate to reorganize our treatment of the past century in more global terms. We have done so by distinguishing between major events or milestones and longer-term historical processes. Thus the first two chapters of Part 6, Chapters 20 and 21, focus on milestone events such as the world wars, revolutions, the cold war, decolonization, the demise of communism, and much more. With these "milestones" of the past century in mind, Chapters 22 and 23 turn to the larger and perhaps even more consequential processes occurring beneath the surface of major public events. Chapter 22 treats the enormous acceleration of technological innovation as a decisive driver of a deeply interconnected world economy and of pervasive social change. Chapter 23 then turns the spotlight on the explosive growth of human numbers, on the movement of many people to cities and to new lives abroad, and on the cultural transformations that accompanied modern life during the past century. The chapter—and the book—conclude by examining the enormous and continuing impact of human activity on the entire biosphere, which represents by far the most significant long-term process of this new era and the most critical challenge of the next century.

Another new element in this fourth edition is a feature titled **Controversies**, intended to highlight the debates that accompany so many historical inquiries. These Controversies, which appear in one chapter of each Part of the book, explore debates about key historical issues: when history begins; the origins of major religious traditions; the nature of empires; the idea of the Atlantic world; why the Industrial Revolution began in Europe; and the concept of globalization. We believe these brief essays will counteract any remaining notion of a textbook as an authoritative, encyclopedia-like tome to be assimilated, while conveying an understanding of World History as a frequently contested conversation.

Furthermore, the **Working with Evidence** primary source collections that accompany each chapter now incorporate both documents and images, many of them new to this edition. Thus the visual sources illustrating Pompeii in Chapter 5 are now enriched with a collection of graffiti inscriptions deriving from that ancient Italian city. And the documents that reflect the rise of fascism in Chapter 20 are now combined with propaganda posters and images showing how those ideas were visually presented to the public.

The new **Historians' Voices** feature now supplies a range of secondary sources for students to consider. In Chapter 9, for example, two prominent scholars, Francis Robinson and Karen Armstrong, explore the significance of the life of Muhammad. And in Chapter 22, Peter Stearns and Merry Wiesner-Hanks, both major world historians, offer assessments of global feminism during the past century. Historians' Voices has also been added to the book's companion source reader *Thinking through Sources for Ways of the World*, which is available as a print supplement or online in LaunchPad, adding another dimension to these alternate source collections.

The book's features are rounded out by the popular **Zooming In** essays, which were new to the third edition and call attention to particular people, places, and events, situating them in a larger global context. Appearing once in each chapter, Zooming In addresses topics such as Göbekli Tepe and monumental construction before agriculture, Trung Trac and resistance to the Chinese empire, gunpowder, the end of the Byzantine Empire, feminism and nationalism in Java, the Cuban Revolution, and many more.

A number of pedagogical aids in *Ways of the World* have also been updated or enhanced. New **Landmarks** visual timelines for each Part and each chapter allow students to see at a glance what was happening in various regions of the world during the same period of time. Many of the maps included in this fourth edition now feature a **Mapping History** exercise accompanied by two levels of questions. The first requires students to read the map carefully, and the second asks them to interpret its implications.

Promoting Active Learning

As all instructors know, students can often "do the assignment" or read the required chapter and yet have little understanding of it when they come to class. The problem, frequently, is passive studying—a quick once-over, perhaps some highlighting of the text—but little sustained involvement with the material. A central pedagogical problem in all teaching is how to encourage more active, engaged styles of learning. We want to enable students to manipulate the information of the book, using its ideas and data to answer questions, to make comparisons, to draw conclusions, to criticize assumptions, and to infer implications that are not explicitly disclosed in the text itself.

Ways of the World seeks to promote active learning in various ways. Most obviously, the source-based features in the book itself (Working with Evidence and the new Historians' Voices) and those in the companion reader *Thinking through Sources for Ways of the World* (also available on LaunchPad) invite students to engage actively with documents and images alike, assisted by abundant questions to guide that engagement.

In addition, whenever an instructor assigns the **LaunchPad e-book** (which can be bundled for free with the print book), students have at their disposal all the resources of the print text, including its special features and its primary and secondary sources. But they also gain access to **LearningCurve**, an online adaptive learning tool that helps students actively rehearse what they have read and foster a deeper understanding and retention of the material. With this adaptive quizzing, students accumulate points toward a target score as they go, giving the interaction a game-like feel. Feedback for incorrect responses explains why the answer is incorrect and directs students back to the text to review before they attempt to answer the question again. The end result is a better understanding of the key elements of the text. Instructors who actively assign LearningCurve report that their students come to class prepared for discussion and their students enjoy using it. In addition, LearningCurve's reporting feature allows instructors to quickly diagnose which concepts students are struggling with so they can adjust lectures and activities accordingly.

Further opportunities for active learning are available with the special online activities accompanying *Thinking through Sources for Ways of the World* in LaunchPad. When required by instructors, the wrap-around pedagogy that accompanies the sources virtually ensures active learning. LaunchPad is thus a rich asset for instructors who want to support students in all settings, from traditional lectures to "flipped" classrooms.

For instructors who need a mobile and accessible option for delivering adaptive quizzing with the narrative alone, Macmillan's new **Achieve Read & Practice** e-book platform offers an exceptionally easy-to-use and affordable option. This simple product pairs the Value Edition—a two-color narrative-only text (no sources)—with the power of LearningCurve's quizzing, all in a format that is mobile-friendly, allowing students to complete their assignments on the bus or in the library.

Another aspect of the book important for the promotion of active learning involves the stimulation of curiosity. A **contemporary vignette** opens each chapter with a story that links the past and the present to show the continuing resonance of history in the lives of contemporary people. Chapter 6, for example, begins by describing the inauguration in 2010 of Bolivian president Evo Morales at an impressive ceremony at Tiwanaku, the center of an ancient Andean empire, thus emphasizing the continuing cultural significance of this ancient civilization in contemporary Bolivian culture. At the end of each chapter, a short **Reflections** section raises provocative, sometimes quasi-philosophical, questions about the craft of the historian and the unfolding of the human story. We believe that these brief essays can motivate our students' curiosity, stimulate their own pondering, and provide grist for the mill of vigorous class discussions.

A further technique for encouraging active learning lies in the provision of frequent contextual markers. Student readers need to know where they are going and where they have been. Thus Part-opening **Big Picture essays** preview what follows in the subsequent chapters, while a **chapter outline** suggests what is coming in each chapter. A new **Landmarks** visual timeline, providing a chronological overview of major events and processes, appears at the beginning of each Part and each chapter. **Snapshot boxes** present succinct glimpses of particular themes, regions, or time periods, adding some trees to the forest of world history. A **list of terms** at the end of each chapter invites students to check their grasp of the material. As usual with books published by Bedford/St. Martin's, a **rich illustration program** provides striking visual markers that enhance the narrative.

Active learning also means approaching the text with something to look for, rather than simply dutifully completing the assignment. *Ways of the World* provides such cues in abundance. A **Seeking the Main Point** question helps students focus on the central theme of the chapter. Each chapter also has at least one **Practicing Historical Thinking** question that invites students to reflect on what they have learned to that point in the chapter. A series of **Guided Reading Questions in the margins**, with labels such as "change," "comparison," or "connection," allows students to read the adjacent material with a clear purpose in mind. **Big Picture Questions** at the end of each chapter deal with matters not directly addressed in the text. Instead, they provide opportunities for integration, comparison, analysis, and sometimes speculation. New **Mapping History** exercises invite students to read maps carefully and to interpret their implications.

Teaching History in the Digital Age

Because the teaching of history is changing rapidly, we have created online inter-active complements for *Ways of the World* via Macmillan's premier learning platform, **LaunchPad**, an intuitive and interactive e-book and course space. Free when packaged with the print book or available at a low price when used on its own, LaunchPad grants students and instructors access to a wealth of online tools and resources built specifically for this text to enhance reading comprehension and promote in-depth study. LaunchPad's course space and interactive e-book are ready to use "as is," or they can be edited and customized with your own material and assigned right away.

Developed with extensive feedback from history instructors and students, LaunchPad for *Ways of the World* includes the complete narrative and special features of the print book plus the companion reader, *Thinking through Sources for Ways of the World*, and **LearningCurve**, an adaptive learning tool designed to get students to read before they come to class. With **an expanded set of source-based questions in the test bank and in LearningCurve**, instructors now have more ways to test students on their understanding of sources and narrative in the book. The addition of the **new Bedford Document Collections modules in LaunchPad** means instructors have a flexible repository of discovery-oriented primary source projects to assign. This makes LaunchPad for *Ways of the World* a one-stop shop for working with sources and thinking critically in a multitude of modes.

LaunchPad also includes additional **primary source online activities** for each chapter of the *Thinking through Sources* companion reader. These activities supply a distinctive and sophisticated pedagogy of self-grading exercises that help students not only understand the sources but also think critically about them. More specifically, a short **quiz after each source** offers students the opportunity to check their understanding of materials that often derive from quite distant times and places. Some questions focus on audience, purpose, point of view, limitations, or context, while others challenge students to draw conclusions about the source or to compare one source with another. And a **Draw Conclusions from the Evidence activity** challenges students to assess whether a specific piece of evi-dence drawn from the sources supports or challenges a stated conclusion. Collec-tively these assignments create an active learning environment where reading with a purpose is reinforced by immediate feedback and support. This feedback for each rejoinder creates an active learning environment where students are rewarded for reaching the correct answer through their own process of investigation.

More broadly, in this interactive learning environment, students will enhance their ability to build arguments and to practice historical reasoning. Thus, this LaunchPad pedagogy does for skill development what LearningCurve does for content mastery and reading comprehension.

LaunchPad also provides a simple, user-friendly platform for individual instructors to add their own voice, materials, and assignments to the text, guiding their students' learning outside of the traditional classroom setting. Available with training and support, LaunchPad can help take history teaching and learning into a new era.

For instructors who need a mobile and accessible option for delivering adaptive quizzing with the narrative alone, Macmillan's new **Achieve Read & Practice** e-book platform offers an exceptionally easy-to-use and affordable option. This simple product pairs the Value Edition—a two-color narrative-only text (no sources)—with the power of LearningCurve's quizzing, all in a format that students can use wherever they go. Available for the first time with this edition, Achieve Read & Practice's interactive e-book, adaptive quizzing, and gradebook are built with an intuitive interface that can be read on mobile devices and are fully accessible and available at an affordable price.

To learn more about the benefits of LearningCurve, LaunchPad, Achieve Read & Practice, and the different versions to package with these digital tools, see the Versions and Supplements section on page xix.

"It Takes a Village"

In any enterprise of significance, "it takes a village," as they say. Bringing *Ways of the World* to life in this new edition, it seems, has occupied the energies of several villages. Among the privileges and delights of writing and revising this book has been the opportunity to interact with our fellow villagers.

We are grateful to the community of fellow historians who contributed their expertise to this revision. For this edition, they include Andreas Agocs, University of the Pacific; Tonio Andrade, Emory University; Monty Armstrong, Cerritos High School; Melanie Bailey, Piedmont Virginia Community College; Djene Bajalan, Missouri State University; Anthony Barbieri-Low, University of California, Santa Barbara; Christine Bond, Edmond Memorial High School; Mike Burns, Concordia International School, Hanoi; Elizabeth Campbell, Daemen College; Theodore Cohen, Lindenwood University; Bradley Davis, Eastern Connecticut State University; Denis Gainty, Georgia State University; Duane Galloway, Rowan-Cabarrus Community College; Jay Harmon, Houston Christian High School; Michael Hunt, University of North Carolina at Chapel Hill; Ane Lintvedt, McDonogh School; Aran MacKinnon, Georgia College and State University; Harold Marcuse, University of California, Santa Barbara; Merritt McKinney, Volunteer State Community College; Erin O'Donnell, East Stroudsburg University; Sarah Panzer, Missouri State University; Charmayne Patterson, Clark Atlanta University; Dean Pavlakis, Carroll College; Chris Peek, Bellaire High School; Tracie Provost, Middle Georgia State University; Masako Racel, Kennesaw State University; and Eddie Supratman, Arkansas State University-Beebe.

We also offer our gratitude to reviewers of earlier editions: Maria S. Arbelaez, University of Nebraska–Omaha; Veronica L. Bale, Mira Costa College; Christopher Bellitto, Kean University; Monica Bord-Lamberty, Northwood High School; Stanley Burstein, California State University–Los Angeles; Ralph Croizier, University of

Victoria; Gregory Cushman, the University of Kansas; Edward Dandrow, University of Central Florida; Peter L. de Rosa, Bridgewater State University; Carter Findley, Ohio State University; Amy Forss, Metropolitan Community College; Denis Gainty, Georgia State University; Steven A. Glazer, Graceland University; Sue Gronewald, Kean University; Andrew Hamilton, Viterbo University; J. Laurence Hare, University of Arkansas; Michael Hinckley, Northern Kentucky University; Bram Hubbell, Friends Seminary; Ronald Huch, Eastern Kentucky University; Elizabeth Hyde, Kean University; Mark Lentz, University of Louisiana–Lafayette; Kate McGrath, Central Connecticut State University; C. Brid Nicholson, Kean University; Donna Patch, Westside High School; Jonathan T. Reynolds, Northern Kentucky University; James Sabathne, Hononegah High School; Christopher Sleeper, Mira Costa College; Ira Spar, Ramapo College and Metropolitan Museum of Art; Kristen Strobel, Lexington High School; Michael Vann, Sacramento State University; Peter Winn, Tufts University; and Judith Zinsser, Miami University of Ohio.

The fine people at Bedford/St. Martin's (Macmillan Learning) have provided a second community sustaining this enterprise and the one most directly responsible for the book's fourth edition. It would be difficult for any author to imagine a more supportive and professional publishing team. Our chief point of contact with the Bedford village has been Heidi Hood, our development editor. She has coordinated the immensely complex task of assembling a new edition of the book and has done so with great professional care, with timely responses to our many queries, and with sensitivity to the needs and feelings of authors, even when she found it necessary to decline our suggestions.

Others on the team have also exhibited that lovely combination of personal kindness and professional competence that is so characteristic of the Bedford way. Editorial director Edwin Hill, program director Michael Rosenberg, and program manager William Lombardo have kept an eye on the project amid many duties. Christina Horn, our content project manager, managed the process of turning a manuscript into a published book and did so with both grace and efficiency. Editorial assistant Stephanie Sosa has efficiently and thoughtfully directed the revision of the *Thinking through Sources* companion reader and handled countless other project details. Operating behind the scenes in the Bedford village, a series of highly competent and always supportive people have shepherded this revised edition along its way. Photo researcher Bruce Carson identified and acquired the many images that grace this new edition of *Ways of the World* and did so with a keen eye and courtesy. Copy editor Susan Zorn polished the prose and sorted out our many inconsistent usages with a seasoned and perceptive eye. Melissa Rodriguez has overseen the marketing process, while Bedford's sales representatives have reintroduced the book to the academic world. Media editor Tess Fletcher supervised the development of supplements and media products to support the book, and William Boardman ably coordinated research for the lovely covers that mark *Ways of the World*. Eve Lehmann conducted the always-difficult negotiations surrounding permissions with more equanimity than we could have imagined.

A final and much smaller community sustained this project and its authors. It is that most intimate of villages that we know as a marriage. Sharing that village with me (Robert Strayer) is my wife, Suzanne Sturn. It is her work to bring ideas and people to life onstage, even as I try to do so between these covers. She knows how I feel about her love and support, and no one else needs to. And across the street, I (Eric Nelson) would also like to thank two other residents of this village: my wife, Alice Victoria, and our little girl, Evelyn Rhiannon, to whom this new edition is dedicated. Without their patience and support, I could not have become part of such an interesting journey.

To all of our fellow villagers, we offer deep thanks for an immensely rewarding experience. We are grateful beyond measure.

Robert Strayer, La Selva Beach, California
Eric Nelson, Springfield, Missouri

Versions and Supplements

Adopters of *Ways of the World* and their students have access to abundant print and digital resources and tools, the acclaimed *Bedford Series in History and Culture* volumes, and much more. The LaunchPad course space for *Ways of the World* provides access to the narrative as well as a wealth of primary sources and other features, along with assignment and assessment opportunities at the ready. Achieve Read & Practice supplies adaptive quizzing and our mobile, accessible Value Edition e-book in one easy-to-use, affordable product. See below for more information, visit the book's catalog site at **macmillanlearning.com**, or contact your local Bedford/St. Martin's sales representative.

Get the Right Version for Your Class

To accommodate different course lengths and course budgets, *Ways of the World* is available in several different versions and formats to best suit your course needs. The comprehensive *Ways of the World* includes a full-color art program and a robust set of features. Offered now for the first time, *Ways of the World,* Value Edition, offers a trade-sized two-color option with the full narrative and selected art and maps at a steep discount. The Value Edition is also offered at the lowest price point in loose-leaf format, and these versions are available as e-books. To get the best values of all, package a new print book with LaunchPad or Achieve Read & Practice at no additional charge to get the best each format offers. LaunchPad users get a print version for easy portability with an interactive e-book for the full-feature text and course space, along with LearningCurve and loads of additional assignment and assessment options; Achieve Read & Practice users get a print version with a mobile, interactive Value Edition e-book plus LearningCurve adaptive quizzing in one exceptionally affordable, easy-to-use product.

- **Combined Volume** (Chapters 1–23): available in paperback, Value, loose-leaf, and e-book formats and in LaunchPad and Achieve Read & Practice
- **Volume 1: To the Fifteenth Century** (Chapters 1–12): available in paperback, Value, loose-leaf, and e-book formats and in LaunchPad and Achieve Read & Practice
- **Volume 2: Since the Fifteenth Century** (Chapters 12–23): available in paperback, Value, loose-leaf, and e-book formats and in LaunchPad and Achieve Read & Practice

As noted below, any of these volumes can be packaged with additional titles for a discount. To get ISBNs for discount packages, visit **macmillanlearning.com** or contact your Bedford/St. Martin's representative.

Assign LaunchPad—an Assessment-Ready Interactive E-book and Course Space

Available for discount purchase on its own or for packaging with new books at no additional charge, LaunchPad is a breakthrough solution for history courses. Intuitive and easy to use for students and instructors alike, LaunchPad is ready to use as is and can be edited, customized with your own material, and assigned quickly. LaunchPad for *Ways of the World* includes Bedford/St. Martin's high-quality content all in one place, including the full interactive e-book and the companion reader *Thinking through Sources for Ways of the World*, plus LearningCurve adaptive quizzing, guided reading activities designed to help students read actively for key concepts, auto-graded quizzes for each primary source, and chapter summative quizzes. Through a wealth of formative and summative assessments, including the adaptive learning program of LearningCurve (see the full description ahead), students gain confidence and get into their reading before class. Through the Bedford Document Collections for World History (see full description ahead), embedded within LaunchPad, instructors get a flexible set of primary source projects ready to assign. These features, plus additional primary source documents, video sources and tools for making video assignments, map activities, flashcards, and customizable test banks, make LaunchPad an invaluable asset for any instructor.

LaunchPad easily integrates with course management systems, and with fast ways to build assignments, rearrange chapters, and add new pages, sections, or links, it lets teachers build the courses they want to teach and hold students accountable. For more information, visit **launchpadworks.com**, or to arrange a demo, contact us at **historymktg@macmillan.com**.

Assign LearningCurve So Your Students Come to Class Prepared

Students using LaunchPad or Achieve Read & Practice receive access to LearningCurve for *Ways of the World*. Assigning LearningCurve in place of reading quizzes is easy for instructors, and the reporting features help instructors track overall class trends and spot topics that are giving students trouble so they can adjust their lectures and class activities. This online learning tool is popular with students because it was designed to help them rehearse content at their own pace in a nonthreatening, game-like environment. The feedback for wrong answers provides instructional coaching and sends students back to the book for review. Students answer as many questions as necessary to reach a target score, with repeated chances to revisit material they haven't mastered. When Learning-Curve is assigned, students come to class better prepared.

Achieⅴe
READ & PRACTICE

Assign Achieve Read & Practice So Your Students Can Read and Study Wherever They Go

Available for discount purchase on its own or for packaging with new books at no additional charge, Achieve Read & Practice is Bedford/St. Martin's most affordable digital solution for history courses. Intuitive and easy to use for students and instructors alike, Achieve Read & Practice is ready to use as is and can be assigned quickly. Achieve Read & Practice for *Ways of the World* includes the Value Edition interactive e-book, LearningCurve formative quizzing, assignment tools, and a gradebook. All this is built with an intuitive interface that can be read on mobile devices and is fully accessible and available at a discounted price so anyone can use it. Instructors can set due dates for reading assignments and LearningCurve quizzes in just a few clicks, making it a simple and affordable way to engage students with the narrative and hold students accountable for course reading so they will come to class better prepared. For more information, visit **macmillanlearning.com/ ReadandPractice**, or to arrange a demo, contact us at **historymktg@macmillan.com**.

▷ iClicker

iClicker, Active Learning Simplified

iClicker offers simple, flexible tools to help you give students a voice and facilitate active learning in the classroom. Students can participate with the devices they already bring to class using our iClicker Reef mobile apps (which work with smartphones, tablets, or laptops) or iClicker remotes. We've now integrated iClicker with Macmillan's LaunchPad to make it easier than ever to synchronize grades and promote engagement—both in and out of class. iClicker Reef access cards can also be packaged with LaunchPad or your textbook at a significant savings for your students. To learn more, talk to your Macmillan Learning representative or visit us at **www.iclicker.com**.

Take Advantage of Instructor Resources

Bedford/St. Martin's has developed a rich array of teaching resources for this book and for this course. They range from lecture and presentation materials and assessment tools to course management options. Most can be found in LaunchPad or can be downloaded or ordered at **macmillanlearning.com**.

Bedford Coursepack for Blackboard, Canvas, Brightspace by D2L, or Moodle. We can help you integrate our rich content into your course management system. Registered instructors can download coursepacks that include our popular free resources and book-specific content for *Ways of the World*. Visit **macmillanlearning.com** to find your version or download your coursepack.

Instructor's Resource Manual. The instructor's manual offers both experienced and first-time instructors tools for presenting textbook material in engaging ways. It includes content learning objectives, annotated chapter outlines, and strategies for teaching with the textbook, plus suggestions on how to get the most out of LearningCurve and a survival guide for first-time teaching assistants.

Guide to Changing Editions. Designed to facilitate an instructor's transition from the previous edition of *Ways of the World* to this new edition, this guide presents an overview of major changes as well as of changes in each chapter.

Online Test Bank. The test bank includes a mix of fresh, carefully crafted multiple-choice, matching, short-answer, and essay questions for each chapter. Many of the multiple-choice questions feature a map, an image, or a primary source excerpt as the prompt. All questions appear in Microsoft Word format and in easy-to-use test bank software that allows instructors to add, edit, re-sequence, filter by question type or learning objective, and print questions and answers. Instructors can also export questions into a variety of course management systems.

The Bedford Lecture Kit: *Lecture Outlines, Maps, and Images.* Look good and save time with *The Bedford Lecture Kit*. These presentation materials include fully customizable multimedia presentations built around chapter outlines that are embedded with maps, figures, and images from the textbook and are supplemented by more detailed instructor notes on key points and concepts.

Print, Digital, and Custom Options for More Choice and Value

For information on free packages and discounts up to 50%, visit **macmillanlearning .com**, or contact your local Bedford/St. Martin's sales representative.

NEW *Thinking through Sources for Ways of the World*, Fourth Edition. Designed to accompany *Ways of the World*, each chapter of this reader contains approximately five to eight written and visual primary sources organized around a particular theme, issue, or question. Each of these projects is followed by a related **Historians' Voices** secondary source feature that pairs two brief excerpts from historians who comment on some aspect of the topics covered in the primary sources. *Thinking through Sources for Ways of the World* provides a broad selection of over 140 primary source documents and images as well as editorial apparatus to help students understand the sources. This companion reader is an exceptional value for students and offers plenty of assignment options for instructors. Available free when packaged with the print text and included in the LaunchPad e-book with auto-graded quizzes for each source. In LaunchPad each chapter of the reader includes special primary source online activities—self-graded exercises that challenge students to assess whether a specific piece of evidence drawn from the sources supports or challenges a conclusion related to a guiding question. Also available on its own as a downloadable e-book.

NEW Bedford Select for History. Create the ideal textbook for your course with only the chapters you need. Starting from one of our Value Edition history texts, you can rearrange chapters, delete unnecessary chapters, select chapters of primary sources from *Thinking through Sources for Ways of the World* and add document projects from the Bedford Document Collections, or choose to improve your students' historical thinking skills with the Bedford Tutorials for History. In addition, you can add your own original content to create just the book you're looking for. With Bedford Select, students pay only for material that will be assigned in the course, and nothing more. Order your textbook every semester, or modify from one term to the next. It is easy to build your customized textbook, without compromising the quality and affordability you've come to expect from Bedford/St. Martin's.

NEW The Bedford Document Collections for World History. Found in the LaunchPad for *Ways of the World* and available to customize the print text, this collection provides a flexible repository of discovery-oriented primary source projects ready to assign. Each curated project—written by a historian about a favorite topic—poses a historical question and guides students through analysis of the sources. Examples include "The Silk Road: Travel and Trade in Pre-Modern Inner Asia," "The Spread of Christianity in the Sixteenth and Early Seventeenth Centuries," "The Singapore Mutiny of 1915: Understanding World War I from a Global Perspective," and "Living through Perestroika: The Soviet Union in Upheaval, 1985–1991." For more information, visit **macmillanlearning.com**.

NEW The Bedford Document Collections for World History Print Modules. Choose one or two document projects from the collection (see above) and add them in print to a Bedford/St. Martin's title, or select several to be bound together in a custom reader created specifically for your course. Either way, the modules are affordably priced. For more information, contact your Bedford/St. Martin's representative.

NEW Bedford Tutorials for History. Designed to customize textbooks with resources relevant to individual courses, this collection of brief units, each 16 pages long and loaded with examples, guides students through basic skills such as using historical evidence effectively, working with primary sources, taking effective notes, avoiding plagiarism and citing sources, and more. Up to two tutorials can be added to a Bedford/St. Martin's history survey title at no additional charge, freeing you to spend your class time focusing on content and interpretation. For more information, visit macmillanlearning.com/historytutorials.

The Bedford Series in History and Culture. More than 100 titles in this highly praised series combine first-rate scholarship, historical narrative, and important primary documents for undergraduate courses. Each book is brief, inexpensive, and focused on a specific topic or period. Recent titles in the series include *Apartheid in South Africa: A Brief History with Documents* by David M. Gordon; *Politics and Society in Japan's Meiji Restoration: A Brief History with Documents* by Anne Walthall and M. William Steele; and *The Congo Free State and the New Imperialism: A Brief History with Documents* by Kevin Grant. For a complete list of titles, visit macmillan learning.com. Package discounts are available.

Rand McNally Atlas of World History. This collection of almost 70 full-color maps illustrates the eras and civilizations in world history from the emergence of human societies to the present. Free when packaged.

The Bedford Glossary for World History. This handy supplement for the survey course gives students historically contextualized definitions for hundreds of terms—from *abolitionism* to *Zoroastrianism*—that they will encounter in lectures, reading, and exams. Free when packaged.

Trade Books. Titles published by sister companies Hill and Wang; Farrar, Straus and Giroux; Henry Holt and Company; St. Martin's Press; Picador; and Palgrave Macmillan are available at a 50% discount when packaged with Bedford/St. Martin's textbooks. For more information, visit macmillanlearning.com/tradeup.

A Pocket Guide to Writing in History. Updated to reflect changes made in the 2017 *Chicago Manual of Style* revision, this portable and affordable reference tool by Mary Lynn Rampolla provides reading, writing, and research advice useful to students in all history courses. Concise yet comprehensive advice on approaching typical history assignments, developing critical reading skills, writing effective history papers, conducting research, using and documenting sources, and avoiding plagiarism—enhanced with practical tips and examples throughout—has made this slim reference a best seller. Package discounts are available.

A Student's Guide to History. This complete guide to success in any history course provides the practical help students need to be successful. In addition to introducing students to the nature of the discipline, author Jules Benjamin teaches a wide range of skills, from preparing for exams to approaching common writing assignments, and explains the research and documentation process with plentiful examples. Package discounts are available.

Brief Contents

Preface   ix
Versions and Supplements   xix
Working with Primary Sources   xlv
Prologue: From Cosmic History to Human History   xlix

PART 1   **First Things First: Beginnings in History** TO 600 B.C.E.   2

THE BIG PICTURE Turning Points in Early World History   2

1   First Peoples; First Farmers: Most of History in a Single Chapter TO 3500 B.C.E.   9

2   First Civilizations: Cities, States, and Unequal Societies 3500 B.C.E.–600 B.C.E.   53

PART 2   **Continuity and Change in the Second-Wave Era** 600 B.C.E.–600 C.E.   92

THE BIG PICTURE The Globalization of Civilization   92

3   State and Empire in Eurasia / North Africa 600 B.C.E.–600 C.E.   99

4   Culture and Religion in Eurasia / North Africa 600 B.C.E.–600 C.E.   141

5   Society and Inequality in Eurasia / North Africa 600 B.C.E.–600 C.E.   187

6   Commonalities and Variations: Africa, the Americas, and Pacific Oceania 600 B.C.E.–1200 C.E.   227

PART 3   **Civilizations and Encounters during the Third-Wave Era** 600–1450   268

THE BIG PICTURE Patterns and Processes of the Third-Wave Era   268

7   Commerce and Culture 600–1450   275

8   China and the World: East Asian Connections 600–1300   317

9   The Worlds of Islam: Afro-Eurasian Connections 600–1450   357

10 The Worlds of Christendom: Contraction, Expansion, and Division 600–1450   403

11 Pastoral Peoples on the Global Stage: The Mongol Moment 1200–1450   449

12 The Worlds of the Fifteenth Century   493

Notes   538
Acknowledgments   544
Glossary   545
Index   553

Contents

Preface   ix

Versions and Supplements   xix

Maps   xl

Features   xlii

Working with Primary Sources   xlv

Prologue: From Cosmic History to Human History   xlix

The History of the Universe ▪ The History of a Planet ▪ The History of the Human Species . . . in a Single Paragraph ▪ Why World History? ▪ Context, Change, Comparison, and Connection: The Four Cs of World History

PART 1

First Things First: Beginnings in History TO 600 B.C.E.   2

THE BIG PICTURE Turning Points in Early World History   2

The Emergence of Humankind ▪ The Globalization of Humankind ▪ The Revolution of Farming and Herding ▪ The Turning Point of Civilization ▪ Time and World History

LANDMARKS IN WORLD HISTORY (to ca. 600 B.C.E.)   6

1   First Peoples; First Farmers: Most of History in a Single Chapter TO 3500 B.C.E.   9

Out of Africa: First Migrations   10
Into Eurasia ▪ Into Australia ▪ Into the Americas ▪ Into the Pacific

Paleolithic Lifeways   19
The First Human Societies ▪ Economy and the Environment ▪ The Realm of the Spirit ▪ Settling Down: The Great Transition

Breakthroughs to Agriculture   26
Common Patterns ▪ Variations

The Globalization of Agriculture   33
Triumph and Resistance ▪ The Culture of Agriculture

Social Variation in the Age of Agriculture   37
Pastoral Societies ▪ Agricultural Village Societies ▪ Chiefdoms

photo: © De Agostini Picture Library/AGE Fotostock

Reflections: The Uses of the Paleolithic   41

Second Thoughts   42
What's the Significance? ▪ Big Picture Questions ▪ Next Steps: For
Further Study

LANDMARKS FOR CHAPTER 1   11

CONTROVERSIES Debating the Timescales of History   12

ZOOMING IN Göbekli Tepe: Monumental Construction before Agriculture   25

WORKING WITH EVIDENCE The Australian Dreamtime   44

Source **1.1** Understanding Creation: *Yhi Brings Life to the World*,
Oral tradition recorded in 20th century   44

Source **1.2** The Rainbow Serpent: *The Rainbow Serpent Awakens*,
Oral tradition recorded in 20th century   46

Source **1.3** Explaining the World in Aboriginal Rock Art: *Namondjok
and the Lightning Man*   47

Source **1.4** Understanding Death: *How Death Came: The Purukapali
Myth*, Oral tradition recorded in 20th century   48

Source **1.5** Hunting in Aboriginal Rock Art: *Aboriginal Hunters*   49

HISTORIANS' VOICES Australian Aboriginal Culture   51

Voice **1.1** Dale Kerwin on the Economic and Social Life of
Aboriginal Australians, 2012

Voice **1.2** Barbara West on Aboriginal Dreamtime Cosmology, 2010

2 First Civilizations: Cities, States, and Unequal Societies 3500 B.C.E.–600 B.C.E.

2 First Civilizations: Cities, States, and
Unequal Societies 3500 B.C.E.–600 B.C.E.   53

Something New: The Emergence of Civilizations   54
Introducing the First Civilizations ▪ The Question of Origins ▪ An Urban
Revolution

The Erosion of Equality   65
Hierarchies of Class ▪ Hierarchies of Gender ▪ Patriarchy in Practice

The Rise of the State   69
Coercion and Consent ▪ Writing and Accounting ▪ The Grandeur of Kings

Comparing Mesopotamia and Egypt   74
Environment and Culture ▪ Cities and States ▪ Interaction and Exchange

Reflections: "Civilization": What's in a Word?   81

Second Thoughts   82
What's the Significance? ▪ Big Picture Questions ▪ Next Steps: For
Further Study

LANDMARKS FOR CHAPTER 2   55

ZOOMING IN Caral, a City of Norte Chico   58

WORKING WITH EVIDENCE Indus Valley Civilization   84

   Source 2.1 Cityscape of Mohenjo Daro: *Wall Painting of Mohenjo
      Daro Reconstruction*, 20th century   84

   Source 2.2 A Seal from the Indus Valley: *A Humped Cattle Seal from
      Mohenjo Daro*, 19th century B.C.E.   85

   Source 2.3 Man from Mohenjo Daro: *Statue of an Elite Man*,
      3rd millennium B.C.E.   86

   Source 2.4 Cart and Oxen from Mohenjo Daro: *Stone Model of a
      Cart Pulled by Two Oxen*, ca. 2400 B.C.E.   87

   Source 2.5 Dancing Girl: *An Indus Valley Girl*, ca. 2500 B.C.E.   88

HISTORIANS' VOICES The State . . . or Its Absence . . . in the Indus Valley   91

   Voice 2.1 Gregory Possehl on Indus Valley Civilization in Context,
      2002

   Voice 2.2 Jonathan Kenoyer on Political Life in the Indus Valley, 1998

PART 2

Continuity and Change in the Second-Wave Era

600 B.C.E.–600 C.E.   92

THE BIG PICTURE The Globalization of Civilization   92

LANDMARKS IN WORLD HISTORY (ca. 600 B.C.E.–ca. 600 C.E.)   96

3 State and Empire in Eurasia / North Africa

600 B.C.E.–600 C.E.   99

Empires and Civilizations in Collision: The Persians and the Greeks   102
The Persian Empire ▪ The Greeks ▪ Collision: The Greco-Persian
Wars ▪ Collision: Alexander and the Hellenistic Era

Comparing Empires: Roman and Chinese   111
Rome: From City-State to Empire ▪ China: From Warring States to
Empire ▪ Consolidating the Roman and Chinese Empires ▪ The Collapse
of Empires

Intermittent Empire: The Case of India   125

Reflections: Enduring Legacies of Second-Wave Empires   128

Second Thoughts   129
What's the Significance? ▪ Big Picture Questions ▪ Next Steps: For
Further Study

LANDMARKS FOR CHAPTER 3   101

ZOOMING IN Trung Trac: Resisting the Chinese Empire   116

photo: Museum of Qin Figures,
Lintong, Xi'an, Shaanxi, China/
Laurent Lecat/akg-images

WORKING WITH EVIDENCE Perceptions of Outsiders in the Ancient World   130

Source 3.1 A Greek Historian on Persia: Herodotus, *The Histories*,
mid–5th century B.C.E.   130

Source 3.2 A Greek Goldsmith Depicts the Scythians: *Scythian Cup*,
Crimea, 4th century B.C.E.   131

Source 3.3 A Roman Historian on the Germans: Tacitus, *Germania*,
1st century C.E.   133

Source 3.4 A Roman Depiction of Sarmatians: *Scene from Trajan's
Column, Rome*, 107–113 C.E.   134

Source 3.5 A Chinese Historian on the Xiongnu: Sima Qian,
Records of the Grand Historian, ca. 100 B.C.E.   135

HISTORIANS' VOICES Early Sources on Foreign Cultures   138

Voice 3.1 Stephen Gosch and Peter Stearns on Travelers' Accounts
as Historical Sources, 2008

Voice 3.2 Jerry Bentley on the Idea of "Barbarian," 1993

4 Culture and Religion in Eurasia / North Africa 600 B.C.E.–600 C.E.

141

China and the Search for Order   142
The Legalist Answer ▪ The Confucian Answer ▪ The Daoist Answer

Cultural Traditions of Classical India   148
South Asian Religion: From Ritual Sacrifice to Philosophical
Speculation ▪ The Buddhist Challenge ▪ Hinduism as a Religion of
Duty and Devotion

Toward Monotheism: The Search for God in the Middle East   155
Zoroastrianism ▪ Judaism

The Cultural Tradition of Classical Greece: The Search for a
Rational Order   159
The Greek Way of Knowing ▪ The Greek Legacy

The Birth of Christianity . . . with Buddhist Comparisons   164
The Lives of the Founders ▪ The Spread of New Religions ▪ Institutions,
Controversies, and Divisions

Reflections: Religion and Historians   173

Second Thoughts   174
What's the Significance? ▪ Big Picture Questions ▪ Next Steps: For
Further Study

LANDMARKS FOR CHAPTER 4   143

CONTROVERSIES Debating Religion and the Axial Age   162

ZOOMING IN Perpetua, Christian Martyr   168

WORKING WITH EVIDENCE Representations of the Buddha   176

   Source 4.1 A Greco-Indian Buddha: *The Temptation of the Buddha*   176

   Source 4.2 A Classical Indian Buddha: *An Indian Buddha*   178

   Source 4.3 The Reputation of the Buddha in Ancient Buddhist Stories:
       The Greater Discourse to Sakuludayin, ca. 1st century B.C.E.   179

   Source 4.4 A Korean Bodhisattva of Compassion: *A Bodhisattva of
       Compassion: Avalokitesvara with a Thousand Arms*   180

   Source 4.5 The Buddha and the Outcast: *Sunita the Outcaste*   181

   Source 4.6 A Chinese Buddha: *The Chinese Maitreya Buddha*   182

HISTORIANS' VOICES On the Buddha   184

   Voice 4.1 John Strong on the Context of the Buddha's Life, 2001

   Voice 4.2 Karen Armstrong on the Buddha and Biography, 2001

5 Society and Inequality in Eurasia / North
    Africa 600 B.C.E.–600 C.E.   187

Society and the State in China   188
   An Elite of Officials ▪ The Landlord Class ▪ Peasants ▪ Merchants

Class and Caste in India   193
   Caste as Varna ▪ Caste as Jati ▪ The Functions of Caste

Slavery: The Case of the Roman Empire   198
   Slavery and Civilization ▪ The Making of Roman Slavery

Comparing Patriarchies   204
   A Changing Patriarchy: The Case of China ▪ Contrasting Patriarchies:
   Athens and Sparta

Reflections: What Changes? What Persists?   212

Second Thoughts   213
   What's the Significance? ▪ Big Picture Questions ▪ Next Steps: For
   Further Study

LANDMARKS FOR CHAPTER 5   189

ZOOMING IN The Spartacus Slave Revolt   202

WORKING WITH EVIDENCE Pompeii as a Window on the Roman World   215

   Source 5.1 Terentius Neo and His Wife: *An Elite Couple of Pompeii,*
       1st century C.E.   216

   Source 5.2 A Pompeii Banquet: *A Dinner with Friends,* 1st century C.E.   217

   Source 5.3 From a Pompeii Tavern: *An Evening Out at a Pompeii Bar,*
       1st century C.E.   218

   Source 5.4 The Graffiti of Pompeii: *The Graffiti of Pompeii,* 1st century C.E.   219

   Source 5.5 Household Religion in Pompeii: *A Household Shrine from
       Pompeii,* 1st century C.E.   220

   Source 5.6 Mystery Religion in Pompeii: *An Initiation Ritual,*
       1st century C.E.   222

HISTORIANS' VOICES On Pompeii   224
    Voice 5.1   Mary Beard on the Artifacts of Pompeii, 2017
    Voice 5.2   Andrew Wilson and Miko Flohr on the Economy
              of Pompeii, 2017

6 Commonalities and Variations: Africa, the Americas, and Pacific Oceania 600 B.C.E.–1200 C.E.   227

Continental Comparisons   228
Civilizations of Africa   231
    Meroë: Continuing a Nile Valley Civilization ▪ Axum: The Making of a
    Christian Kingdom ▪ Along the Niger River: Cities without States
Civilizations of Mesoamerica   237
    The Maya: Writing and Warfare ▪ Teotihuacán: The Americas' Greatest City
Civilizations of the Andes   242
    Chavín: A Pan-Andean Religious Movement ▪ Moche: A Civilization of the
    Coast ▪ Wari and Tiwanaku: Empires of the Interior
Alternatives to Civilization   247
    Bantu Africa: Cultural Encounters and Social Variation ▪ North America:
    Ancestral Pueblo and Mound Builders ▪ Pacific Oceania: Peoples of the Sea
Reflections: Deciding What's Important: Balance in the Writing of
    World History   258
Second Thoughts   259
    What's the Significance? ▪ Big Picture Questions ▪ Next Steps: For
    Further Study

LANDMARKS FOR CHAPTER 6   229
ZOOMING IN The Lord of Sipan and the Lady of Cao   244
WORKING WITH EVIDENCE Axum and the World   260
    Source 6.1 The Making of an Axumite Empire: *Inscription on a Stone*
                Throne, 2nd or 3rd century C.E.   260
    Source 6.2 The Columns of Axum: *An Axumite Monument*, late 3rd or
                early 4th century C.E.   261
    Source 6.3 The Coming of Christianity to Axum: Rufinus, *On the*
                Evangelization of Abyssinia, late 4th century C.E.   262
    Source 6.4 Axum and the Gold Trade: Cosmas, *The Gold Trade of*
                Axum, 6th century C.E.   264
    Source 6.5 Axum Gold Coin: *A "Christian Coin" from Axum*   265
HISTORIANS' VOICES Christian Axum   267
    Voice 6.1   Erik Gilbert and Jonathan Reynolds on the Transregional
              Nature of Early Christianity, 2004

photo: © Peter M. Wilson/Alamy

Voice 6.2   Christopher Ehret on the Role of Trade in the Coming of
Christianity to Axum, 2002

PART 3

Civilizations and Encounters during the Third-Wave Era 600–1450   268

THE BIG PICTURE Patterns and Processes of the Third-Wave Era   268
Third-Wave Civilizations ▪ The Ties That Bind: Transregional Interaction in
the Third-Wave Era

LANDMARKS IN WORLD HISTORY (ca. 600 c.e.–ca. 1450)   272

7 Commerce and Culture 600–1450   275

Silk Roads: Exchange across Eurasia   278
The Growth of the Silk Roads ▪ Goods in Transit ▪ Cultures in
Transit ▪ Disease in Transit

Sea Roads: Exchange across the Indian Ocean   285
Weaving the Web of an Indian Ocean World ▪ Sea Roads as a Catalyst for
Change: Southeast Asia ▪ Sea Roads as a Catalyst for Change: East Africa

Sand Roads: Exchange across the Sahara   295
Commercial Beginnings in West Africa ▪ Gold, Salt, and Slaves: Trade and
Empire in West Africa

**An American Network: Commerce and Connection in the Western
Hemisphere**   300

Reflections: Economic Globalization—Ancient and Modern   302

Second Thoughts   303
What's the Significance? ▪ Big Picture Questions ▪ Next Steps:
For Further Study

LANDMARKS FOR CHAPTER 7   277

ZOOMING IN The Arabian Camel   296

WORKING WITH EVIDENCE Travelers' Tales and Observations   305
Source 7.1 A Chinese Buddhist in India: Xuanzang, *Record of the Western
Regions,* 7th century c.e.   305
Source 7.2 A European Christian in China: Marco Polo, *The Travels
of Marco Polo,* 1299   307
Source 7.3 A European Artist Depicts Asia: *The Marvelous Races of the
East,* ca. 1410   309
Source 7.4 A Moroccan Diplomat in West Africa: Leo Africanus,
The History and Description of Africa, 1526   310

photo: Martha Avery/Getty
Images

Source 7.5   A Korean World Map: *The Honkōji Copy of the Kangnido Map, Korea,* 15th century   312

HISTORIANS' VOICES On Travel Writers   315

Voice 7.1   John Larner on Whether Polo Really Traveled to China, 1999

Voice 7.2   Natalie Zemon Davis on Leo Africanus's Audiences, 2006

8 China and the World: East Asian Connections 600–1300

317

Together Again: The Reemergence of a Unified China   318
A "Golden Age" of Chinese Achievement ▪ Women in the Song Dynasty

China and the Northern Nomads: A Chinese World Order in the Making   326
The Tribute System in Theory ▪ The Tribute System in Practice ▪ Cultural Influence across an Ecological Frontier

Coping with China: Comparing Korea, Vietnam, and Japan   331
Korea and China ▪ Vietnam and China ▪ Japan and China

China and the Eurasian World Economy   338
Spillovers: China's Impact on Eurasia ▪ On the Receiving End: China as Economic Beneficiary

China and Buddhism   341
Making Buddhism Chinese ▪ Losing State Support: The Crisis of Chinese Buddhism

Reflections: Why Do Things Change?   345

Second Thoughts   346
What's the Significance? ▪ Big Picture Questions ▪ Next Steps: For Further Study

LANDMARKS FOR CHAPTER 8   319

ZOOMING IN Gunpowder   322

WORKING WITH EVIDENCE China's Scholar-Officials   348

Source 8.1   Scholar-Officials and the Emperor: *Scholars Gathering in a Bamboo Garden,* 12th century   348

Source 8.2   A Gathering of Scholars: *Scholars of the Liuli Hall,* late 13th century   349

Source 8.3   A Solitary Scholar: Ma Yuan, *On a Mountain Path in Spring,* early 13th century   350

Source 8.4   Tang Dynasty Poetry   351
Li Po, *The Mountain and Me,* 8th century
Li Po, *Drinking Alone with the Moon,* 8th century
Wang Wei, *My Retreat at Mount Zhongnan,* 8th century
Du Fu, *A View of Taishan,* 8th century

Source 8.5 Scholar-Officials at Play: Gu Hongzhong, *The Night Revels of Han Xizai*, 10th century   353

HISTORIANS' VOICES Assessing China's Scholar-Officials   355

Voice 8.1 Jacques Garnet on the "Learned Culture" of Song Dynasty China, 1996

Voice 8.2 David Hinton on "Public Service" and "Mountain Seclusion," 2005

9 The Worlds of Islam: Afro-Eurasian Connections 600–1450

357

The Birth of a New Religion   358
The Homeland of Islam ▪ The Messenger and the Message ▪ The Transformation of Arabia

The Making of an Arab Empire   365
War, Conquest, and Tolerance ▪ Conversion ▪ Divisions and Controversies ▪ Women and Men in Early Islam

Islam and Cultural Encounter: A Four-Way Comparison   376
The Case of India ▪ The Case of Anatolia ▪ The Case of West Africa ▪ The Case of Spain

The World of Islam as a New Civilization   383
Networks of Faith ▪ Networks of Exchange

Reflections: Past and Present: Choosing Our History   388

Second Thoughts   389
What's the Significance? ▪ Big Picture Questions ▪ Next Steps: For Further Study

LANDMARKS FOR CHAPTER 9   359

ZOOMING IN Mullah Nasruddin, the Wise Fool of Islam   372

WORKING WITH EVIDENCE The Islamic World in the Seventh Century   391

Source 9.1 Depicting Muhammad with the Angel Gabriel: *Muhammad and the Angel Gabriel*, ca. 1307   391

Source 9.2 Muhammad in Jerusalem: Aqa Mirak, *The Night Journey of Muhammad*, 16th century   393

Source 9.3 Victory in Mecca: Mir Havand, *The Cleansing of the Kaaba*, ca. 1590   395

Source 9.4 Conflict and Division: The Emergence of Shia Islam: Ali ibn Husayn, *Poem*, ca. 680   397

Source 9.5 Conquest   397
Text of Thomas the Presbyter, 640
Pact of Ibn Muslama and the People of Tiflis, 653

Source 9.6 Governing an Empire: Caliph Ali, *Letter to Malik Ashtar*, 658   398

HISTORIANS' VOICES Assessing the Prophet Muhammad   401

  Voice 9.1 Francis Robinson on Western Attitudes to Muhammad, 1996

  Voice 9.2 Karen Armstrong on Muslim Devotion to the Prophet, 1992

10 The Worlds of Christendom: Contraction, Expansion, and Division 600–1450

    403

Christian Contraction in Asia and Africa   404
Asian Christianity ▪ African Christianity

Byzantine Christendom: Building on the Roman Past   409
The Byzantine State ▪ The Byzantine Church and Christian
Divergence ▪ Byzantium and the World ▪ The Conversion of Russia

Western Christendom: Rebuilding in the Wake of Roman
Collapse   415
Political Life in Western Europe ▪ Society and the Church ▪ Accelerating
Change in the West ▪ Europe Outward Bound: The Crusading Tradition

The West in Comparative Perspective   428
Catching Up ▪ Pluralism in Politics ▪ Reason and Faith

Reflections: Remembering and Forgetting: Continuity and Surprise
in the Worlds of Christendom   435

Second Thoughts   436
What's the Significance? ▪ Big Picture Questions ▪ Next Steps: For
Further Study

LANDMARKS FOR CHAPTER 10   405

ZOOMING IN Cecilia Penifader, an English Peasant and Unmarried Woman   422

WORKING WITH EVIDENCE The Remaking of Western Europe   438

  Source 10.1 The Conversion of Clovis: Gregory of Tours, *History of the
Franks*, late 6th century   438

  Source 10.2 Advice on Dealing with "Pagans": Pope Gregory, *Advice to the
English Church*, 601   439

  Source 10.3 Pagan Art and Christian Texts: *Lindisfarne Gospel*, 698–721   440

  Source 10.4 Germanic Law: *Burgundian Code*, ca. 474 C.E.   442

  Source 10.5 Charlemagne's Palace Chapel: *Aachen Palace Chapel*,
completed 805 C.E.   444

HISTORIANS' VOICES The Legacy of Rome   447

  Voice 10.1 Blockmans and Hoppenbrouwers on the End of Roman
Civilization, 2014

  Voice 10.2 Cunliffe on Charlemagne, 2008

photo: From "Grandes Chroniques
de France," 1375–1379/
Bibliothèque Municipale, Castres,
France/Bridgeman Images

11 Pastoral Peoples on the Global Stage: The Mongol Moment 1200–1450   449

The Long History of Pastoral Peoples   450
The World of Pastoral Societies ▪ Before the Mongols: Pastoralists in History

Breakout: The Mongol Empire   457
From Temujin to Chinggis Khan: The Rise of the Mongol Empire ▪ Explaining the Mongol Moment

Encountering the Mongols in China, Persia, and Russia   464
China and the Mongols ▪ Persia and the Mongols ▪ Russia and the Mongols

The Mongol Empire as a Eurasian Network   470
Toward a World Economy ▪ Diplomacy on a Eurasian Scale ▪ Cultural Exchange in the Mongol Realm ▪ The Plague: An Afro-Eurasian Pandemic

Reflections: Changing Images of Pastoral Peoples   478

Second Thoughts   479
What's the Significance? ▪ Big Picture Questions ▪ Next Steps: For Further Study

LANDMARKS FOR CHAPTER 11   451

ZOOMING IN A Mongol Failure: The Invasion of Japan   460

CONTROVERSIES Debating Empire   474

WORKING WITH EVIDENCE Perceptions of the Mongols   481

Source 11.1 The Self-Perception of Mongol Rulers   481
Chinggis Khan, *Letter to Changchun*, 1219
The Secret History of the Mongols, ca. 1240

Source 11.2 Picturing Khubilai Khan   483
Liu Guandao, *Khubilai on a Hunt*, 1280
Marco Polo and Khubilai Khan, 15th century
Khubilai Khan in Council with His Courtiers and Scribes, 1590

Source 11.3 A Persian View of the Conquest of Bukhara: Juvaini, *The History of the World Conqueror*, 1219   487

Source 11.4 A European View of Mongol Life: William of Rubruck, *Journey to the Land of the Mongols*, ca. 1255   488

HISTORIANS' VOICES Assessing the Mongol Impact   491
Voice 11.1 Jack Weatherford on the Mongols in World History, 2004
Voice 11.2 Paul S. Ropp on the Mongol Impact on China's Economy, 2010

photo: Moghul court painting, ca.1596/Pictures from History/ Bridgeman Images

12 The Worlds of the Fifteenth Century   493

Societies and Cultures of the Fifteenth Century   494
Paleolithic Persistence: Australia and North America ▪ Agricultural Village
Societies: The Igbo and the Iroquois ▪ Pastoral Peoples: Central Asia and
West Africa

Civilizations of the Fifteenth Century: Comparing China
and Europe   499
Ming Dynasty China ▪ European Comparisons: State Building and
Cultural Renewal ▪ European Comparisons: Maritime Voyaging

Civilizations of the Fifteenth Century: The Islamic World   508
In the Islamic Heartland: The Ottoman and Safavid Empires ▪ On the
Frontiers of Islam: The Songhay and Mughal Empires

Civilizations of the Fifteenth Century: The Americas   514
The Aztec Empire ▪ The Inca Empire

Webs of Connection   521

After 1500: Looking Ahead to the Modern Era   522

Reflections: What If? Chance and Contingency in World History   525

Second Thoughts   525
What's the Significance? ▪ Big Picture Questions ▪ Next Steps: For
Further Study

LANDMARKS FOR CHAPTER 12   495

ZOOMING IN 1453 in Constantinople   510

WORKING WITH EVIDENCE Islam and Renaissance Europe   527
Source 12.1 Portrait of Mehmed II: Gentile Bellini, *Portrait of
Mehmed II*, ca. 1480   528
Source 12.2 Machiavelli on the Turkish State: Niccolò Machiavelli,
The Prince, 1513   529
Source 12.3 Venetian Trade in the Middle East: *The Venetian Ambassador
Visits Damascus,* 1511   531
Source 12.4 Greek and Islamic Philosophers in Renaissance Art: *Aristotle
and Averroes,* 1483   533
Source 12.5 A Papal Call for Crusade: Pope Clement VI, *Call for Crusade,*
September 30, 1343   535

HISTORIANS' VOICES Christian/Muslim Relations during the Renaissance   537
Voice 12.1 Jerry Brotton on the Role of Cross-cultural Exchange
in the European Renaissance, 2002
Voice 12.2 Bernard Lewis on Hostility between Christians and
Muslims, 1995

Notes	538
Acknowledgments	544
Glossary	545
Index	553
About the Authors	last book page

Maps

MAP 1.1   The Global Dispersion of Humankind   14

MAP 1.2   Migration of Austronesian-Speaking Peoples   19

MAP 1.3   The Global Spread of Agriculture and Pastoralism   28

MAP 1.4   The Fertile Crescent   31

SPOT MAP   Bantu Migration   34

MAP 2.1   First Civilizations   56

MAP 2.2   Mesopotamia   75

MAP 2.3   An Egyptian Empire   80

MAP 3.1   The Persian Empire   103

MAP 3.2   Classical Greece and Its Colonies   105

MAP 3.3   Alexander's Empire and Successor States   109

MAP 3.4   The Roman Empire   113

MAP 3.5   Classical China   118

MAP 3.6   Empire in South Asia   125

SPOT MAP   Ancient Israel   158

MAP 4.1   The Spread of Early Christianity and Buddhism   170

SPOT MAP   The Yellow Turban Rebellion   192

SPOT MAP   The Rebellion of Spartacus   203

MAP 6.1   Africa in the Second-Wave Era   232

MAP 6.2   Civilizations of Mesoamerica   238

MAP 6.3   Civilizations of the Andes   242

MAP 6.4   North America in the Second-Wave Era   250

MAP 6.5   Pacific Oceania   254

MAP 7.1   The Silk Roads   278

MAP 7.2   The Sea Roads   286

MAP 7.3   Southeast Asia, ca. 1200 C.E.   290

SPOT MAP   The Swahili Coast of East Africa   294

MAP 7.4   The Sand Roads   298

MAP 7.5   The American Web   301

MAP 8.1   Tang and Song Dynasty China   320
MAP 8.2   Korean Kingdoms, ca. 500 C.E.   332
MAP 8.3   Vietnam   333
MAP 8.4   Japan   335
MAP 8.5   The World of Asian Buddhism   342

MAP 9.1   Arabia at the Time of Muhammad   360
MAP 9.2   The Arab Empire and the Initial Expansion of Islam, 622–900 C.E.   366
MAP 9.3   The Growing World of Islam, 900–1500   377
MAP 9.4   The Sultanate of Delhi   378
MAP 9.5   The Ottoman Empire by the Mid-Fifteenth Century   379
MAP 9.6   West Africa and the World of Islam   381

MAP 10.1   The Byzantine Empire   410
MAP 10.2   Western Europe in the Ninth Century   417
MAP 10.3   Europe in the Middle Ages   420
MAP 10.4   The Crusades   426

SPOT MAP   The Xiongnu Empire   455
SPOT MAP   The Seljuk Empire   456
SPOT MAP   The Almoravid Empire   457
MAP 11.1   The Mongol Empire   458
MAP 11.2   Trade and Disease in the Fourteenth Century   472

MAP 12.1   Asia in the Fifteenth Century   501
MAP 12.2   Europe in 1500   503
MAP 12.3   Africa in the Fifteenth Century   506
MAP 12.4   Empires of the Islamic World   509
MAP 12.5   The Americas in the Fifteenth Century   515
MAP 12.6   Religion and Commerce in the Afro-Eurasian World   523

Features

CONTROVERSIES

Debating the Timescales of History   12
Debating Religion and the Axial Age   162
Debating Empire   474

HISTORIANS' VOICES

Australian Aboriginal Culture   51
The State . . . or Its Absence . . . in the Indus Valley   91
Early Sources on Foreign Cultures   138
On the Buddha   184
On Pompeii   224
Christian Axum   267
On Travel Writers   315
Assessing China's Scholar-Officials   355
Assessing the Prophet Muhammad   401
The Legacy of Rome   447
Assessing the Mongol Impact   491
Christian/Muslim Relations during the Renaissance   537

MAPPING HISTORY

MAP 1.1   The Global Dispersion of Humankind   14
MAP 1.3   The Global Spread of Agriculture and Pastoralism   28
MAP 2.1   First Civilizations   56
MAP 2.3   An Egyptian Empire   80
MAP 3.3   Alexander's Empire and Successor States   109
MAP 3.4   The Roman Empire   113
MAP 4.1   The Spread of Early Christianity and Buddhism   170
MAP 6.1   Africa in the Second-Wave Era   232
MAP 6.5   Pacific Oceania   254
MAP 7.2   The Sea Roads   286
MAP 7.4   The Sand Roads   298
MAP 8.1   Tang and Song Dynasty China   320
MAP 8.5   The World of Asian Buddhism   342

MAP 9.2   The Arab Empire and the Initial Expansion of Islam,
           622–900 C.E.   366
MAP 9.3   The Growing World of Islam, 900–1500   377
MAP 10.3   Europe in the Middle Ages   420
MAP 10.4   The Crusades   426
MAP 11.1   The Mongol Empire   458
MAP 11.2   Trade and Disease in the Fourteenth Century   472
MAP 12.1   Asia in the Fifteenth Century   501
MAP 12.6   Religion and Commerce in the Afro-Eurasian World   523

SNAPSHOT

The History of the Universe as a Cosmic Calendar   Prologue
Writing in Ancient Civilizations   72
World Population during the Age of Agricultural Civilization   94
Thinkers and Philosophies of the Second-Wave Era   166
Social Life and Duty in Classical India   195
Continental Population in the Second-Wave Era and Beyond   230
Economic Exchange Along the Silk Roads   280
Economic Exchange in the Indian Ocean Basin   288
Chinese Technological Achievements   339
Key Achievements in Islamic Science and Scholarship   387
European Borrowing   429
Varieties of Pastoral Societies   452
World Population Growth, 1000–2000   524

WORKING WITH EVIDENCE

The Australian Dreamtime   44
Indus Valley Civilization   84
Perceptions of Outsiders in the Ancient World   130
Representations of the Buddha   176
Pompeii as a Window on the Roman World   215
Axum and the World   260
Travelers' Tales and Observations   305
China's Scholar-Officials   348
The Islamic World in the Seventh Century   391
The Remaking of Western Europe   438
Perceptions of the Mongols   481
Islam and Renaissance Europe   527

ZOOMING IN

Göbekli Tepe: Monumental Construction before Agriculture   25
Caral, a City of Norte Chico   58
Trung Trac: Resisting the Chinese Empire   116
Perpetua, Christian Martyr   168
The Spartacus Slave Revolt   202
The Lord of Sipan and the Lady of Cao   244
The Arabian Camel   296
Gunpowder   322
Mullah Nasruddin, the Wise Fool of Islam   372
Cecilia Penifader, an English Peasant and Unmarried Woman   422
A Mongol Failure: The Invasion of Japan   460
1453 in Constantinople   510

Working with
Primary Sources

Two sets of primary sources accompany each chapter of *Ways of the World*. **Working with Evidence** collections appear at the end of each chapter in the book, while *Thinking through Sources* sets are available either as a print supplement or in LaunchPad—the interactive course space for this text. Both collections typically feature written sources, such as inscriptions, letters, diaries, law codes, official records, and sacred texts, alongside visual sources—paintings, sculptures, engravings, photographs, posters, cartoons, buildings, and artifacts. Both collections are followed by a pair of secondary sources—short extracts from the writings of modern historians, archeologists, and other scholars. Collectively these sources provide an opportunity for you to practice the work of historians in a kind of guided "history laboratory." In working with this evidence, you are "doing history," much as students conducting lab experiments in chemistry or biology courses are "doing science."

Since each feature explores a theme of a particular chapter, the chapter narrative itself provides a broad context for analyzing these sources. Furthermore, brief introductions to each feature and to each document or image offer more specific context or background information, while questions provide things to look for as you examine each source. Other more integrative questions offer a focus for using those sources together to probe larger historical issues. What follows are a few more specific suggestions for assessing these raw materials of history.

Working with Documents

Written sources or documents are the most common type of primary source that historians use. For example, a number of ancient religious texts are sampled in the Working with Evidence feature of Chapter 4, while the documents in Chapter 13 present ideas about political authority in Mughal India, France, and the Inca Empire.

Analysis of such documents usually begins with the basics:

- Who wrote the document?
- When and where was it written?
- What type of document is it (for example, a letter to a friend, a political decree, an exposition of a religious teaching)?

Sometimes the document itself will provide answers to these questions. On other occasions, you may need to rely on the introductions.

Once these basics have been established, a historian is then likely to consider several further questions that situate the document in its particular historical context:

- Why was the document written, for what audience, and under what circumstances?
- What point of view does it reflect? What other views or opinions is the document arguing against? Can you get a sense of the larger conversation in which this document is participating?

Inspiration and intention are crucial factors that shape the form and content of a source. For instance, one might examine a document differently depending on whether it was composed for a private or a public readership, or whether it was intended to be read by a small elite or a wider audience.

Still another level of analysis seeks to elicit useful information from the document.

- What material in the document is believable, and what is not?
- What might historians learn from this document?
- What can the document tell us about the individual who produced it and the society from which he or she came?

In all of this, historical imagination is essential. Informed by knowledge of the context and the content of the document, your imagination will help you read it through the eyes of its author and its audience. You should ask yourself: how might this document have been understood at the time it was written? But in using your imagination, you must take care not to read into the documents your own assumptions and understandings. It is a delicate balance, a kind of dance that historians constantly undertake. Even documents that contain material that historians find unbelievable can be useful, for we seek not only to know what actually happened in the past but also to grasp the world as the people who lived that past understood it. And so historians sometimes speak about reading documents "against the grain," looking for meanings that the author might not have intended to convey.

Working with Images

Visual sources derive from the material culture of the past—religious icons or paintings that add to our understanding of belief systems, a family portrait that provides insight into presentations of self in a particular time and place, a building or sculpture that reveals how power and authority were displayed in a specific empire. These kinds of evidence represent another category of primary source material that historians can use to re-create and understand the past. But such visual sources can be even more difficult to interpret than written documents. The ideas that animated the creators of particular images or artifacts are often not obvious. Nor are the meanings they conveyed to those who viewed or used them. The lovely images from the ancient Indus River valley civilization contained in the Working with Evidence feature for Chapter 2, for example, remain enigmatic although still engaging to twenty-first-century viewers. Propaganda posters, frequently used in the source features for Volume 2, convey vividly how various groups or governments understood their own times. Despite the difficulties of interpretation, visual sources can provide insights not offered by written documents.

To use visual sources, we must try as best we can to see these pieces of evidence through the eyes of the societies that produced them and to decode the symbols and other features that imbue them with meaning. Thus context is, if anything, even more crucial for analyzing visual evidence than it is for documents. For example, understanding artistic depictions from the life of Muhammad, featured in Chapter 9, depends heavily on some knowledge of Islamic history and culture. A set of basic questions, similar to those you would ask about a written document, provides a starting point for analyzing visual sources:

- When and where was the image or artifact created?
- Who made the image or artifact? Who paid for or commissioned it? For what audience(s) was it intended?
- Where was the image or artifact originally displayed or used?

Having established this basic information about the image or artifact, you may simply want to describe it, as if to someone who had never seen it before.

- If the source is an image, who or what is depicted? What activities are shown? How might you describe the positioning of figures, their clothing, hairstyles, and other visual cues?
- If the source is an object or building, how would you describe its major features?

Finally, you will want to take a stab at more interpretive issues, making use of what you know about the context in which the visual source was created.

- What likely purpose or function did the image or artifact serve?
- What message(s) does it seek to convey?

- How could it be interpreted differently depending on who viewed or used it?
- What are the meanings of any symbols or other abstract features in the visual source?
- What can the image or artifact tell us about the society that produced it and the time period in which it was created?

Beyond analyzing particular sources, you will be invited to draw conclusions from sets of related sources—both visual and written—that address a central theme in the chapter. What can you learn, for example, about the life of Chinese elites from the sources in Chapter 8? And what do the images and documents in the Working with Evidence feature of Chapter 15 disclose about the reception of Christianity in various cultural settings?

Alongside these primary sources, the **Historians' Voices** features offer you the opportunity to consider how contemporary scholars make historical arguments and draw sound conclusions. While primary sources—documentary and visual alike—are the foundation for all historical accounts, students and scholars gain further perspective from reading the analysis of modern experts who use their deep knowledge of the sources to examine and explain the past. Immersing yourself in documents, images, and the writings of modern scholars allows you to catch a glimpse of the messiness, the ambiguity, the heartaches, and the achievements of history as it was lived and as it has been recorded.

Using these sources effectively, however, is no easy task. In fact, the work of historians might well be compared with that of Sisyphus, the ancient Greek king who, having offended the gods, was condemned to eternally roll a large rock up a mountain, only to have it ceaselessly fall back down. Like Sisyphus, historians work at a mission that can never be completely successful—to recapture the past before it is lost forever in the mists of time and fading memory. The evidence available is always partial and fragmentary. Historians and students of history alike are limited and fallible, for we operate often at a great distance—in both time and culture—from those we are studying. And we rarely agree on important matters, divided as we are by sex, nationality, religion, race, and values, all of which shape our understandings of the past.

Despite these challenges, scholars and students have long found their revisiting of the past a compelling project—intensely interesting, personally meaningful, and even fun—particularly when working with "primary" or "original" sources, which are the building blocks of all historical accounts. Such sources are windows into the lives of our ancestors, though these windows are often smudged and foggy. We hope that working with the evidence contained in these sources will enrich your own life as you listen in on multiple conversations from the past, eavesdropping, as it were, on our ancestors.

Prologue
From Cosmic History to Human History

History books in general, and world history textbooks in particular, share something in common with those Russian nested dolls in which a series of carved figures fit inside one another. In much the same fashion, all historical accounts take place within some larger context, as stories within stories unfold. Individual biographies and histories of local communities, particularly modern ones, occur within the context of one nation or another. Nations often find a place in some more encompassing civilization, such as the Islamic world or the West, or in a regional or continental context such as Southeast Asia, Latin America, or Africa. And those civilizational or regional histories in turn take on richer meaning when they are understood within the even broader story of world history, which embraces humankind as a whole.

In recent decades, some world historians have begun to situate that remarkable story of the human journey in the much larger framework of both cosmic and planetary history, an approach that has come to be called "big history." It is really the "history of everything" from the big bang to the present, and it extends over the enormous, almost unimaginable timescale of some 13.8 billion years, the current rough estimate of the age of the universe.[1]

The History of the Universe

To make this vast expanse of time even remotely comprehensible, some scholars have depicted the history of the cosmos as if it were a single calendar year (see Snapshot). On that cosmic calendar, most of the action took place in the first few milliseconds of January 1. As astronomers, physicists, and chemists tell it, the universe that we know began in an eruption of inconceivable power and heat. Out of that explosion of creation emerged matter, energy, gravity, electromagnetism, and the "strong" and "weak" forces that govern the behavior of atomic nuclei. As gravity pulled the rapidly expanding cosmic gases into increasingly dense masses, stars formed, with the first ones lighting up around 1 to 2 billion years after the big bang, or the end of January to mid-February on the cosmic calendar.

Hundreds of billions of stars followed, each with its own history, though following common patterns. They emerge, flourish for a time, and then collapse and die. In their final stages, they sometimes generate supernovae, black holes, and pulsars — phenomena at least as fantastic as the most exotic of earlier creation stories. Within the stars, enormous nuclear reactions gave rise to the elements that are reflected in the periodic table known to all students of chemistry. Over eons, these stars came together in galaxies, such as our own Milky Way, which probably emerged in March or early April, and in even larger structures called groups, clusters, and superclusters. Adding to the strangeness of our picture of the cosmos is the recent and controversial notion that perhaps 90 percent or more of the total mass of the universe is invisible to us, consisting of a mysterious and mathematically predicted substance known to scholars only as "dark matter."

The contemplation of cosmic history has prompted profound religious or philosophical questions about the meaning of human life. For some, it has engendered a sense of great insignificance in the face of cosmic vastness. In disputing the earth- and human-centered view of the cosmos, long held by the Catholic Church, the eighteenth-century French thinker Voltaire wrote: "This little globe, nothing more than a point, rolls in space like so many other globes; we are lost in this immensity."[2] Nonetheless, human consciousness and our awareness of the mystery of this immeasurable

SNAPSHOT The History of the Universe as a Cosmic Calendar

Big bang	January 1	13.7 billion years ago
Stars and galaxies begin to form	End of January / mid-February	12 billion years ago
Milky Way galaxy forms	March / early April	10 billion years ago
Origin of the solar system	September 9	4.7 billion years ago
Formation of the earth	September 15	4.5 billion years ago
Earliest life on earth	Late September / early October	4 billion years ago
Oxygen forms on earth	December 1	1.3 billion years ago
First worms	December 16	658 million years ago
First fish, first vertebrates	December 19	534 million years ago
First reptiles, first trees	December 23	370 million years ago
Age of dinosaurs	December 24–28	66 to 240 million years ago
First human-like creatures	December 31 (late evening)	2.7 million years ago
First agriculture	December 31: 11:59:35	12,000 years ago
Birth of the Buddha / Greek civilization	December 31: 11:59:55	2,500 years ago
Birth of Jesus	December 31: 11:59:56	2,000 years ago

Adapted from Carl Sagan, *The Dragons of Eden* (New York: Random House, 1977), 13–17.

universe render us unique and generate for many people feelings of awe, gratitude, and humility that are almost religious. As tiny but knowing observers of this majestic cosmos, we have found ourselves living in a grander home than ever we knew before.

The History of a Planet

For most of us, one star, our own sun, is far more important than all the others, despite its quite ordinary standing among the billions of stars in the universe and its somewhat remote location on the outer edge of the Milky Way galaxy. Circling that star is a series of planets, formed of leftover materials from the sun's birth. One of those planets, the third from the sun and the fifth largest, is home to all of us. Human history—our history—takes place not only on the earth but also as part of the planet's history.

That history began with the emergence of the entire solar system about two-thirds of the way through the history of the universe, some 4.7 billion years ago, or early September on the cosmic calendar. Geologists have learned a great deal about the history of the earth: the formation of its rocks and atmosphere; the movement of its continents; the collision of the tectonic plates that make up its crust; and the constant changes of its landscape as mountains formed, volcanoes erupted, and erosion transformed the surface of the planet. All of this has been happening for more than 4 billion years and continues still.

The most remarkable feature of the earth's history—and so far as we know unrepeated elsewhere—was the emergence of life from the chemical soup of the early planet. It happened rather quickly, only about 600 million years after the earth itself took shape, or late September on the cosmic calendar. Then for some 3 billion years, life remained at the level of microscopic single-celled organisms. According to biologists, the many species of larger multicelled creatures—all of the flowers, shrubs, and trees as well as all of the animals of land, sea, and air—have evolved in an explosive proliferation of life-forms over the past 600 million years, or since mid-December on the cosmic calendar. The history of life on earth has, however, been periodically punctuated by massive die-offs, at least five of them, in which very large numbers of animal or plant species have perished. The most widespread of these "extinction events," known to scholars as the Permian mass extinction, occurred around 250 million years ago and eliminated some 96 percent of living species on the planet. That catastrophic diminution of life-forms on the earth has been associated with massive volcanic eruptions, the release of huge quantities of carbon dioxide and methane into the atmosphere, and a degree of global warming that came close to extinguishing all life on the planet. Much later, around 66 million years ago, another such extinction event decimated about 75 percent of plant and animal species, including what was left of the dinosaurs. Most scientists now believe that it was caused primarily by the impact of a huge asteroid that landed near the Yucatán Peninsula off the coast of southern Mexico, generating enormous earthquakes, tsunamis, fireballs, and a cloud of toxic dust and debris. Many scholars believe we are currently in the midst of a sixth extinction event, driven, like the others, by major climate change, but which, unlike the others, is the product of human actions.

So life on earth has been and remains both fragile and resilient. Within these conditions, every species has had a history as its members struggled to find resources, cope with changing environments, and deal with competitors. Egocentric creatures that we are, however, human beings have usually focused their history books and history courses entirely on a single species—our own, *Homo sapiens*, humankind. On the cosmic calendar, *Homo sapiens* is an upstart primate whose entire history occurred in the last few minutes of December 31. Almost all of what we normally study in history courses—agriculture, writing, civilizations, empires, industrialization—took place in the very last minute of that cosmic year. The entire history of the United States occurred in the last second.

Yet during that very brief time, humankind has had a career more remarkable and arguably more consequential for the planet than any other species. At the heart of human uniqueness lies our amazing capacity for accumulating knowledge and skills. Other animals learn, of course, but for the most part they learn the same things over and over again. Twenty-first-century chimpanzees in the wild master much the same set of skills as their ancestors did a million years ago. But the exceptional communication abilities provided by human language allow us to learn from one another, to express that learning in abstract symbols, and then to pass it on, cumulatively, to future generations. Thus we have moved from stone axes to lasers, from spears to nuclear weapons, from "talking drums" to the Internet, from grass huts to the pyramids of Egypt, the Taj Mahal of India, and the skyscrapers of modern cities.

This extraordinary ability has translated into a human impact on the earth that is unprecedented among all living species.[3] Human populations have multiplied far more extensively and have come to occupy a far greater range of environments than has any other large animal. Through our ingenious technologies, we have appropriated for ourselves, according to recent calculations, some 25 to 40 percent of the solar energy that enters the food chain. We have recently gained access to the stored solar energy of coal, gas, and oil, all of which have been many millions of years in the making, and we have the capacity to deplete these resources in a few hundred or a few thousand years. Other forms of life have felt the impact of human activity, as numerous extinct or threatened species testify. Human beings have even affected the atmosphere and the oceans as carbon dioxide and other emissions of the industrial age have warmed the climate of the planet in ways that broadly resemble the conditions that triggered earlier extinction events. Thus human history has been, and remains, of great significance, not for ourselves alone, but also for the earth itself and for the many other living creatures with which we share it.

The History of the Human Species . . . in a Single Paragraph

The history of our species has occurred during roughly the last 200,000–300,000 years, conventionally divided into three major phases, based on the kind of technology that was most widely practiced. The enormously long Paleolithic age, with its gathering and hunting way of life, accounts for 95 percent or more of the time that humans have occupied the planet. People utilizing a stone-age Paleolithic technology initially settled every major landmass on the earth and constructed the first human societies (see Chapter 1). Then beginning about 12,000 years ago with the first Agricultural Revolution, the domestication of plants and animals increasingly became the primary means of sustaining human life and societies. In giving rise to agricultural villages and chiefdoms, to pastoral communities depending on their herds of animals, and to state- and city-based civilizations, this agrarian way of life changed virtually everything and fundamentally reshaped human societies and their relationship to the natural order. Finally, around 1750 a quite sudden spurt in the rate of technological change, which we know as the Industrial Revolution, began to take hold. That vast increase in productivity, wealth, and human control over nature once again transformed almost every aspect of human life and gave rise to new kinds of societies that we call "modern."

Here then, in a single paragraph, is the history of humankind—the Paleolithic era, the agricultural era, and, most recently and briefly, the modern industrial era. Clearly this is a big picture perspective, based on the notion that the human species as a whole has a history that transcends any of its particular and distinctive cultures. That perspective—known variously as planetary, global, or world history—has become increasingly prominent among those who study the past. Why should this be so?

Why World History?

Not long ago—in the mid-twentieth century, for example—virtually all college-level history courses were organized in terms of particular civilizations or nations. In the United States, courses such as Western Civilization or some version of American History served to introduce students to the study of the past. Since then, however, a set of profound changes has pushed much of the historical profession in a different direction.

The world wars of the twentieth century, revealing as they did the horrendous consequences of unchecked nationalism, persuaded some historians that a broader view of the past might contribute to a sense of global citizenship. Economic and cultural globalization has highlighted both the interdependence of the world's peoples and their very unequal positions within that world. Moreover, we are aware as never before that our problems—whether they involve economic well-being, global warming, disease, or terrorism—respect no national boundaries. To many thoughtful people, a global present seemed to call for a global past. Furthermore, as colonial empires shrank and new nations asserted themselves on the world stage, these peoples also insisted that their histories be accorded equivalent treatment with those of Europe and North America. An explosion of new knowledge about the histories of Asia, Africa, and pre-Columbian America erupted from the research of scholars around the world. All of this has generated a "world history movement," reflected in college and high school curricula, in numerous conferences and specialized studies, and in a proliferation of textbooks, of which this is one.

This world history movement has attempted to create a global understanding of the human past that highlights broad patterns cutting across particular civilizations and countries, while acknowledging in an inclusive fashion the distinctive histories of its many peoples. This is, to put it mildly, a tall order. How is it possible to encompass within a single book or course the separate stories of the world's various peoples? Surely it must be something more than just recounting the history of one civilization or culture after another. How can we distill a common history of humankind as a whole from the distinct trajectories of particular peoples? Because no world history book or course can cover everything, what criteria should we use for deciding what to include and what to leave out? Such questions have ensured no end of controversy among students, teachers, and scholars of world history, making it one of the most exciting fields of historical inquiry.

Context, Change, Comparison, and Connection: The Four Cs of World History

Despite much debate and argument, most scholars and teachers of world history would probably agree on four major emphases of this remarkable field of study. The first lies in the observation that in world history, nothing stands alone. Every event, every historical figure, every culture, society, or civilization gains significance from its inclusion in some larger framework. This means that **context** is central to world history and that contextual thinking is the essential skill that world history teaches. And so we ask the same question about every particular occurrence: where does it fit in the larger scheme of things?

A second common theme in world history involves **change** over time. Most often, it is the "big picture" changes—those that affect large segments of humankind—that are of greatest interest. How did the transition from a gathering and hunting economy to one based on agriculture take place? How did cities, empires, and civilizations take shape in various parts of the world? What impact did the growing prominence of Europe have on the rest of the world in recent centuries? A focus on change provides an antidote to a persistent tendency of human thinking that historians call "essentialism." A more common term is "stereotyping." It refers to our inclination to define particular groups of people with an unchanging or essential set of characteristics. Women are nurturing; peasants are conservative; Americans are aggressive; Hindus are religious. Serious students of history soon become aware that every significant category of people contains endless divisions and conflicts and that those human communities are constantly in flux. Peasants may often accept the status quo, except of course when they rebel, as they frequently have. Americans have experienced periods of isolationism and withdrawal from the world as well as times of aggressive engagement with it. Things change.

But some things persist, even if they also change. We should not allow an emphasis on change to blind us to the continuities of human experience.

A recognizably Chinese state has operated for more than 2,000 years. Slavery and patriarchy persisted as human institutions for thousands of years until they were challenged in recent centuries, and in various forms they exist still. The teachings of Buddhism, Christianity, and Islam have endured for centuries, though with endless variations and transformations.

A third element that operates constantly in world history books and courses is that of **comparison**. Whatever else it may be, world history is a comparative discipline, seeking to identify similarities and differences in the experience of the world's peoples. What is the difference between the development of agriculture in the Middle East and in Mesoamerica? Was the experience of women largely the same in all patriarchal societies? Why did the Industrial Revolution and a modern way of life evolve first in Western Europe rather than somewhere else? What distinguished the French, Russian, and Chinese revolutions from one another? Describing and, if possible, explaining such similarities and differences are among the major tasks of world history. Comparison has proven an effective tool in efforts to counteract Eurocentrism, the notion that Europeans or people of European descent have long been the primary movers and shakers of the historical process. That notion arose in recent centuries when Europeans were in fact the major source of innovation in the world and did for a time exercise something close to world domination. But comparative world history sets this recent European prominence in a global and historical context, helping us to sort out what was distinctive about the development of Europe and what similarities it bore to other major regions of the world. Puncturing the pretensions of Eurocentrism has been high on the agenda of world history.

A fourth emphasis within world history, and in this book, involves the interactions, encounters, and **connections** among different and often distant peoples. Focusing on cross-cultural connections — whether those of conflict or more peaceful exchange — represents an effort to counteract a habit of thinking about particular peoples, states, or cultures as self-contained or isolated communities. Despite the historical emergence of many separate and distinct societies, none of them developed alone. Each was embedded in a network of relationships with both near and more distant peoples.

Moreover, these cross-cultural connections did not begin with Columbus. The Chinese, for example, interacted continuously with the nomadic peoples on their northern border; generated technologies that diffused across all of Eurasia; transmitted elements of their culture to Japan, Korea, and Vietnam; and assimilated a foreign religious tradition, Buddhism, that had originated in India. Though clearly distinctive, China was not a self-contained or isolated civilization. Thus world history remains always alert to the networks, webs, and encounters in which particular civilizations or peoples were enmeshed.

Context, change, comparison, and connection — all of them operating on a global scale — represent various ways of bringing some coherence to the multiple and complex stories of world history. They will recur repeatedly in the pages that follow.

A final observation about this account of world history: *Ways of the World*, like all other world history textbooks, is radically unbalanced in terms of coverage. Chapter 1, for example, takes on some 95 percent of the human story, well over 200,000 years of our history. By contrast, the last century alone occupies four entire chapters. In fact, the six major sections of the book deal with progressively shorter time periods, in progressively greater detail. This imbalance owes much to the relative scarcity of information about earlier periods of our history. But it also reflects a certain "present mindedness," for we look to history, always, to make sense of our current needs and circumstances. And in doing so, we often assume that more recent events have a greater significance for our own lives in the here and now than those that occurred in more distant times. Whether you agree with this assumption or not, you will have occasion to ponder it as you consider the many and various "ways of the world" that have emerged in the course of the human journey and as you contemplate their relevance for your own journey.

Ways of the World

A Brief Global History with Sources

PART 1

First Things First: Beginnings in History

to 600 B.C.E.

Chapter 1 First Peoples; First Farmers: Most of History in a Single Chapter, to 3500 B.C.E.

Chapter 2 First Civilizations: Cities, States, and Unequal Societies, 3500 B.C.E.–600 B.C.E.

THE BIG PICTURE

Turning Points in Early World History

Human beings have long been inveterate storytellers, and so too are contemporary historians. They tell stories about individuals, communities, nations, civilizations, and, in the case of world history, about humankind as a whole. All tellers of stories—ancient and modern alike—have to decide where to begin their accounts and what major turning points in those narratives to highlight. For world historians seeking to tell the story of "all under Heaven," as the Chinese put it, four major "beginnings," each of them an extended historical process, have marked the initial stages of the human journey.

The Emergence of Humankind

The first large-scale process in the human story lies in biological evolution. According to archeologists and anthropologists, the evolutionary line of descent leading to *Homo sapiens* separated from that of chimpanzees, our closest primate relatives, some 5 to 6 million years ago, and it happened in eastern and southern Africa. There, perhaps twenty or thirty different species emerged, all of them members of the Homininae (or hominid) family of human-like creatures. What they all shared was bipedalism, the ability to walk upright on two legs. Over time, these hominid species changed. Their brains grew larger; they began to make and use simple stone tools; some started to eat meat, at least occasionally; eventually they learned to control fire. By 1 million years ago, some hominid species, especially *Homo erectus*, began to migrate out of Africa, and their remains have been found in various parts of Eurasia.

But all of these earlier hominid species finally died out, except one: *Homo sapiens*, ourselves. With a remarkable capacity for symbolic language that permitted the accumulation and transmission of learning, our species too appeared first in Africa and quite recently, probably no more than 250,000 years ago. For a long time, all of the small number of *Homo sapiens* lived in Africa, but sometime after 100,000 years ago, they too began to migrate out of Africa onto the Eurasian landmass, then to Australia, and ultimately into the Western Hemisphere and the Pacific islands.

The Globalization of Humankind

This amazing journey represents the second major turning point in the human story. Our ancient ancestors — small in stature, not fast on foot, and armed with a very limited technology of stone tools — were able to adapt to almost every environmental setting on the planet. The phase of human history during which these initial migrations took place is known to scholars as the Paleolithic era. The word "Paleolithic" literally means the "old stone age," but it refers more generally to a gathering, hunting, and fishing way of life, before agriculture allowed people to grow crops or raise animals deliberately. Lasting until roughly 12,000 years ago, and in many places much longer, the Paleolithic era represents over 95 percent of the time that human beings have inhabited the earth. Although often neglected by historians and history textbooks, this long period of the human experience merits greater attention and is the focus of the initial sections of Chapter 1.

The Revolution of Farming and Herding

Then, a third process began to completely reshape the human experience. Around 12,000 years ago, human communities in parts of the Middle East, Asia, Africa, and the Americas began the laborious process of domesticating animals and selecting seeds to be planted. This momentous accomplishment, often called the Agricultural Revolution, surely marks the single most significant and enduring transformation of our history. Now our species learned to exploit and manipulate particular organisms, both plant and animal. Farming and raising animals allowed for a substantial increase in human numbers and over many centuries generated a profound transformation of the environment. Forests were felled, arid lands irrigated, meadows plowed, and mountains terraced. Increasingly, the landscape reflected human intentions and actions.

The Turning Point of Civilization

The most prominent and powerful human communities to emerge from this Agricultural Revolution were those often designated as "civilizations," more complex societies that were based in bustling cities and governed by formal states. Their emergence in Eurasia, Africa, and the Americas marked the fourth major transformation in human history. Because almost all of the world's people now live in such societies, states and cities have come to seem almost natural. In world history terms, however, their appearance is quite recent. Not until several thousand years *after* the beginning of agriculture did the first cities and states emerge, around 3500 B.C.E. Well after 1000 C.E., substantial numbers of people still lived in communities without any state or urban structures. Nonetheless, people living in state- and city-based societies or civilizations have long constituted the most powerful and innovative human communities on the planet. They have given rise to empires of increasing size, enduring cultural and religious traditions, new technologies, sharper class and gender inequalities, new conceptions of masculinity and femininity, and large-scale warfare. The earliest of these civilizations provide the focus of Chapter 2.

Time and World History

Reckoning time is central to all historical study, for history is essentially the story of change over time. Recently it has become standard in the Western world to refer to dates prior to the birth of Christ as B.C.E. (before the Common Era), replacing the earlier B.C. (before Christ) usage. This convention is an effort to become less Christian-centered and Eurocentric in our use of language, although the chronology remains linked to the birth of Jesus. Similarly, the time following the birth of Christ is referred to as C.E. (the Common Era) rather than A.D. (*Anno Domini*, Latin for "year of the Lord"). Dates in the more distant past are designated in this book as B.P. (before the present), or simply as so many "years ago." Of course, these conventions are only some of the many ways that human societies have charted time, and they reflect the global dominance of Europeans in recent centuries. But the Chinese frequently dated important events in terms of the reign of particular emperors, while Muslims created a new calendar beginning with Year 1, marking Muhammad's forced relocation from Mecca to Medina in 622 C.E. As with so much else, the ways we represent change over time reflect the cultures in which we have been born and the historical experience of our societies.

World history frequently deals with very long periods of time, often encompassing many millennia or centuries in a single paragraph or even in a single sentence. This panoramic perspective provides context, a big picture framework in which we can situate particular events, societies, and individual experiences. Doing so allows us to discern patterns and trends that may be invisible from the viewpoint of a local community, a single nation, or one civilization. In the narrative that follows, there will be plenty of particulars—events, places, people—but always embedded in some larger setting that heightens their significance.

Landmarks in World History (to ca. 600 B.C.E.) *(All dates are B.C.E.)*

27,000	26,000	25,000	24,000	23,000	22,000	21,000	20,000	19,000	18,000	17,000	16,000	15,000

AFRICA

◄ **250,000–200,000** Emergence of *Homo Sapiens*

◄ **100,000–70,000** Earliest evidence of human symbolic behavior

◄ **100,000–60,000** Human migration out of Africa into Eurasia

EURASIA

◄ **70,000** Human entry into Asia

◄ **45,000** Human entry into Europe

◄ **35,000** Earliest female figurines from Germany

◄ **33,000–15,000** Paleolithic cave art in Europe

▪ **25,000** Extinction of Neanderthals

THE AMERICAS AND PACIFIC OCEANIA

◄ **60,000–40,000** Human entry into Australia

◄ **30,000** Extinction of large mammals in Australia

◄ **30,000–15,000** Human entry into the Americas

14,000　13,000　12,000　11,000　10,000　9000　8000　7000　6000　5000　4000　3000　2000　1000

14,000–8000
Harvesting of wild grains
in northeastern Africa

4000
Domestication of donkey
in northeastern Africa

3500–3000
Beginnings of
Egyptian civilization

8000–4000
Cattle-based pastoral
societies in Africa

3400–3200
Nubian kingdom
of Ta-Seti

3000–1000
Agricultural breakthroughs
in sub-Saharan Africa

3000–2000
Beginning of Bantu migrations

1259
Treaty ending conflict between
Egypt and the Hittites

1000–500
Ironworking in sub-Saharan Africa

14,000–8000
Global warming and end of last Ice Age

6000
Early chiefdoms in Mesopotamia

10,000
Göbekli Tepe: monumental
Paleolithic construction

5400 Wine making in Iran

4000 Domestication of horses

10,000–8000
Earliest agricultural
revolutions

3500–3000 Beginnings of
Mesopotamian civilization

2200–2000
Beginnings of Chinese, Indian, and Central
Asian civilizations

11,000
Clovis culture in North America

3000–1800 Norte Chico
civilization in Peru

9000
Extinction of various large
mammals in North America

3000–2000
Domestication of potatoes, quinoa,
and manioc in the Andes

1500
Human entry into Pacific Oceania

1400–800
Lapita culture in Melanesia

4000–3000
Domestication of corn in Mexico

1200
Olmec civilization in
Mesoamerica

7

First Peoples; First Farmers

Most of History in a Single Chapter

to 3500 B.C.E.

Out of Africa: First Migrations
  Into Eurasia
  Into Australia
  Into the Americas
  Into the Pacific
Paleolithic Lifeways
  The First Human Societies
  Economy and the Environment
  The Realm of the Spirit
  Settling Down: The Great Transition
Breakthroughs to Agriculture
  Common Patterns
  Variations
The Globalization of Agriculture
  Triumph and Resistance
  The Culture of Agriculture
Social Variation in the Age of Agriculture
  Pastoral Societies
  Agricultural Village Societies
  Chiefdoms
Reflections: The Uses of the Paleolithic

"We do not want cattle, just wild animals to hunt and water that we can drink."[1] That was the view of Gudo Mahiya, a prominent member of the Hadza people of northern Tanzania, when he was questioned in 1997 about his interest in a settled life of farming and cattle raising. The Hadza represent one of the very last peoples on earth to continue a way of life that was universal among humankind until 10,000 to 12,000 years ago. In 2014, only about 1,300 Hadza survived, and of these just several hundred still made a living by hunting game, collecting honey, digging up roots, and gathering berries and fruit. Almost certainly, Gudo Mahiya's way of life is doomed, as farmers, cattle herders, governments, missionaries, and now tourists push the Hadza toward extinction. The likely disappearance of the Hadza people and their culture is among the final chapters of a very long story in which gathering, hunting, and fishing peoples have been unsuccessfully on the defensive against more numerous and powerful neighbors for 10,000 years. ■

Nonetheless, that way of life sustained humankind for more than 95 percent of our time on the earth. During countless centuries, human beings successfully adapted to a wide variety of environments without benefit of deliberate farming or animal husbandry. Instead, our early ancestors wrested a livelihood by gathering wild foods such as berries, nuts, roots, and grain; by scavenging dead animals; by hunting live animals; and by fishing. Known to scholars as "gathering and hunting" peoples, they were foragers or food collectors

« Paleolithic Art The rock art of gathering and hunting peoples has been found in Africa, Europe, Australia, and elsewhere. This image from the San people of southern Africa represents aspects of their outer life in the form of wild animals and hunters with bows as well as the inner life of their shamans during a trance, reflected in the elongated figures with both human and animal features.

rather than food producers. Because they used stone rather than metal tools, they also have been labeled Paleolithic, or Old Stone Age, peoples.

Then, around 12,000 years ago, an enormous transformation began to unfold as a few human societies—in Eurasia, Africa, and the Americas alike—started to practice the deliberate cultivation of plants and the domestication of animals. This Agricultural or **Neolithic** (New Stone Age) **Revolution** marked a technological breakthrough of immense significance, with implications for every aspect of human life. This chapter, dealing with the long **Paleolithic era** and the initial transition to an agricultural way of life, represents most of human history—everything, in fact, before the advent of urban-based civilizations, which began only 5,500 years ago.

And yet history courses and history books often neglect this long phase of the human journey and instead choose to begin the story with the early civilizations of Egypt, Mesopotamia, China, and elsewhere. Some historians identify "real history" with writing and so dismiss the Paleolithic and Neolithic eras as largely unknowable because their peoples did not write. (See Controversies: Debating the Timescales of History, page 12.) Others, impressed with the rapid pace of change in human affairs in more recent times, assume that nothing much of real significance happened during the long Paleolithic era—and that no change meant no history.

But does it make sense to ignore the first 200,000 years or more of human experience? The achievements of Paleolithic peoples—the initial settlement of the planet, the creation of the earliest human societies, the beginnings of reflection on the great questions of life and death—surely deserve our attention. And the breakthrough to agriculture arguably represents the single most profound transformation of human life in all of history. Our grasp of the human past is incomplete—massively so—if we choose to disregard the Paleolithic and Neolithic eras.

SEEKING THE MAIN POINT

What arguments does this chapter make for paying serious attention to human history before the coming of "civilization"?

Out of Africa: First Migrations

The first 150,000 years or more of human experience was an exclusively African story. Around 200,000 to 250,000 years ago, in the grasslands of eastern and southern Africa, *Homo sapiens* first emerged, following in the footsteps of many other hominid or human-like species before it. Time and climate have erased much of the record of these early people, and Africa has witnessed much less archeological research than other parts of the world. Nonetheless, scholars have turned up evidence of distinctly human behavior in Africa long before its appearance elsewhere. Africa, almost certainly, was the place where the "human revolution" occurred, where "culture," defined as learned or invented ways of living, became more important than biology in shaping behavior.

What kinds of uniquely human activity show up in the early African record?[2] In the first place, our ancient African ancestors began to create new technologies as stone blades and points fastened to shafts replaced the earlier hand axes; tools made

Landmarks for Chapter 1*

| 75,000 B.P. | 60,000 | 45,000 | 30,000 | 15,000 | 1 |

THE WORLD

250,000–200,000
Earliest *Homo sapiens*

16,000–10,000
End of the last Ice Age

12,000–4,000
Earliest agricultural revolutions

10,000
Human population of 6 million

AFRICA

100,000
Earliest evidence of human ritual activity: South Africa

100,000–60,000 Beginning of human
migration out of Africa

16,000
Collection of wild grains

8,000
Domestication of the donkey

4,000–3,000
Domestication of sorghum

EURASIA

70,000
Human entry into East Asia

45,000 Human entry into Europe

35,000–17,000
Cave art in Europe

12,000–10,000
Agricultural Revolution in the Fertile Crescent

6,000–5,000
Domestication of horses

THE AMERICAS

30,000–15,000
Human entry into the Americas

13,000–11,000
Clovis culture in North America

11,000
Extinction of large mammals in North America

6,000–5,000
Beginning of domestication of corn in southern Mexico

4,000–3,000
Domestication of potatoes in Andes region

OCEANIA

60,000–40,000
Human entry into Australia (first use of boats)

30,000
Extinction of large mammals in Australia

3,500–1,000
Austronesian migration to Pacific islands (and Madagascar)

1,000–800
Human entry into New Zealand (last major region to receive human settlers)

*All dates are B.P. or Before the Present, and all dates are approximate.

Debating the Timescales of History

So when does world history begin? And does it matter?

If "world history" refers to the story of humankind, professional historians until recently were largely in agreement that history began with writing, for as one book published in 1898 put it, "No documents, no history."[3] While humans clearly existed before writing—some 200,000 years, in fact—historians viewed their pasts as almost completely unrecoverable from the few physical remains that survived. They described these earlier peoples as prehistoric or "before history" and left their study to archeology and what was later called paleoanthropology. But writing emerged only about 5,500 years ago, and even then was limited to a few places. Furthermore, until the last several centuries writing was confined largely to elites, who wrote primarily about "the wars they fought, the literature they wrote, and the gods they worshipped."[4] Thus an understanding of the human journey based only on written records was massively skewed and incomplete.

From the mid-twentieth century onward, increasingly accurate and affordable scientific techniques—including radio-carbon dating, DNA testing, and advances in linguistics and archeology—allowed scholars to date artifacts and the movements of human populations that occurred tens or even hundreds of thousands of years ago. A much clearer understanding of early human history emerged as scholars were able to trace chronologically such crucial developments as the spread of our species across the planet and the dissemination of bronze-working technologies. The world before writing no longer seemed so

unrecoverable, and many scholars—historians, archeologists, and others—broadened the definition of "history" to incorporate not only peoples of the distant past but also the lives of those who had left no written record. While large gaps in our knowledge persisted, the new techniques opened up windows into the past that had been mostly shut before.

Even as historians debated the extent to which the "prehistory" of our species should or could be incorporated into historical accounts, a related question emerged about how—or whether—to locate all of human history within some greater context. Over the past several decades, some historians have begun to integrate the human story into the much larger frameworks of planetary and cosmic evolution, an approach that has come to be called "big history." Remarkable advances in the natural sciences—astronomy, geology, and evolutionary biology—suggest that the cosmos as a whole has a history, as do the stars, the solar system, the planets, including the earth, and life itself. They have a history because they have changed over time, for change is the fundamental feature of all historical accounts.

Such understandings have caused some to conclude that human history can be fully understood only if contextualized in the changing patterns of the cosmos. As the historian William McNeill has written, "Human beings, it appears, do indeed belong to the universe and share its unstable, evolving character . . . what happens among human beings and what happens among the stars looks to be part of a grand, evolving story."[5] Supporters of this view assert that big history "offers a powerful way

from bones appeared, and so did grindstones. Settlements were planned around the seasonal movement of game and fish. Patterns of exchange over a distance of almost 200 miles indicate larger networks of human communication. The use of body ornaments, beads, and pigments as well as possible planned burials suggests the kind of social and symbolic behavior that has characterized human activity ever since. The earliest evidence for this kind of human activity comes from the Blombos Cave in South Africa, where excavations in 2008 uncovered a workshop for the processing of ochre (a naturally occurring earth pigment with a red, yellow, or brown color) dating to around 100,000 years ago, well before such behavior surfaced elsewhere in the world.

of understanding the place of our own species, *homo sapiens,* within the universe. By doing so it helps us to understand better what human history is all about."[6]

But not all historians agree with this perspective. Some critics of "big history" argue that its almost unimaginable timescales, measured in billions or many millions of years, leave too little room for the human story, reducing it to insignificance. The types of problems or questions that have long occupied professional historians, such as the legacies of the Chinese warring states period or World War I, are worthy of little more than a mention in big history timescales. Others complain that the careful reading and analysis of documents have been replaced by scientific forms of inquiry. Is "big history," they ask, really history at all?

Whatever one may think of these debates, big history represents the latest chapter in a remarkable rethinking of when world history begins. At the turn of the twentieth century few historians could conceive of history beginning more than 6,000 years ago, but by the early twenty-first century some argue that the human story finds its most appropriate place in a process that began over thirteen billion years earlier.

Clearly the timescales of human history matter, because they shape the questions we ask and the techniques of inquiry that we employ. If we seek to understand the ups and downs of civilizations over the past five millennia, written records are essential. Without them, we would know little about the evolution of Buddhism, the rise and fall of empires, the Industrial Revolution, and much more. But if we want to know something of the process by which humans came to occupy almost every environmental niche on the earth, then written

records are of little help, because almost all of that process took place long before writing was invented anywhere. So we must rely on DNA analysis, carbon dating, and linguistics.

Finally, when historians turn to the cosmic or "big history" timescale, they are motivated by still other concerns. For David Christian, one of the leading practitioners of "big history," that grand scale of things offers a "creation myth" for our times, a coherent and scientifically informed explanation of the origins and evolution of our universe and the place of humankind within it.[7] For those more philosophically or spiritually inclined, the "big history" outlook raises profound questions about the relationship of human history to the larger narrative of cosmic and planetary evolution. Does the human experiment represent the story of just one more species thrown up by the ceaseless transformations of the web of life on this planet? Or is human consciousness distinctive, representing perhaps the cosmos becoming aware of itself? In these perspectives the human story is solidly anchored within the unfolding of the universe, the geological transformations of the planet, and the evolution of life on the earth.

QUESTIONS TO CONSIDER

1. How might your understanding of world history change if you subscribed to the idea that history began with writing, began with the emergence of our species, or began at the start of the universe?

2. In what specific ways have advancements in science affected how historians understand world history?

The development and spread of human culture were highly uncertain and took place amid immense obstacles. Around 70,000 years ago an enormous volcanic eruption on the island of Sumatra in present-day Indonesia resulted in a cooler and drier global climate and, scholars speculate, something close to human extinction. But human numbers recovered, growing slowly to perhaps 500,000 by 30,000 years ago and then to 6 million by 10,000 years ago.[8] As this recovery took shape, sometime between 100,000 and 60,000 years ago, human beings began their long trek out of Africa and into Eurasia, Australia, the Americas, and, much later, the islands of the Pacific, where they encountered vastly different environments (see Map 1.1). Much of this long journey occurred during the difficult climatic conditions of the

MAPPING HISTORY

Map 1.1 The Global Dispersion of Humankind

With origins in Africa perhaps 250,000 years ago, members of our species (*Homo sapiens*) have migrated to every environmental setting on the planet over the past 100,000 years.

EUROPE

(45,000 years ago)

ASIA

(70,000 years ago)

(100,000 years ago)

AFRICA

PACIFIC OCEAN

Equator

(3,500 years ago)

(1,500 years ago)

(40,000–60,000 years ago)

AUSTRALIA

INDIAN OCEAN

(1,000 years ago)

NEW ZEALAND

Ice sheet (20,000 years ago)
Land bridges (20,000 years ago)
Human expansion (dates for earliest human occupation)

ANTARCTICA

READING THE MAP: Trace the routes of human migration and settlement from the point where our species first left Africa. In what order were the regions of the world settled, and how long did it take for that settlement to unfold?

INTERPRETING THE MAP: Identify those regions where humans settled last. What geographic factors may have delayed the settlement of these regions?

last Ice Age (at its peak around 20,000 years ago), when thick ice sheets covered much of the Northern Hemisphere. The Ice Age did give these outward-bound human beings one advantage, however: the amount of water frozen in northern glaciers lowered sea levels around the planet, creating land bridges among various regions that were separated after the glaciers melted. Britain was then joined to Europe; eastern Siberia was connected to Alaska; and parts of what is now Indonesia were linked to mainland Southeast Asia.

Into Eurasia

Human migration out of Africa led first to the Middle East and from there to Asia about 70,000 years ago and to Europe about 45,000 years ago. Among the most carefully researched areas of early human settlement in Eurasia are those in southern France and northern Spain. There, around 35,000 to 17,000 years ago, Paleolithic peoples left a record of their world in hundreds of cave paintings depicting bulls, horses, and other animals, brilliantly portrayed in colors of red, yellow, brown, and black. Images of human beings, impressions of human hands, and various abstract designs sometimes accompanied these cave paintings.

Guided Reading Question

■ **CHANGE**
What was the sequence of human migration across the planet?

Farther east, archeologists have uncovered still other remarkable Paleolithic adaptations to Ice Age conditions. Across the vast plains of Central Europe, Ukraine, and Russia, new technologies emerged, including bone needles, multilayered clothing, weaving, nets, storage pits, baskets, and pottery. Partially underground dwellings constructed from the bones and tusks of mammoths compensated for the absence of caves and rock shelters. All of this suggests that some of these people had lived in more permanent settlements, at least temporarily abandoning their nomadic journeys. Associated with these Eastern European peoples were numerous female figurines, the oldest of which was uncovered in 2008 in Germany and dated to at least 35,000 years ago. Carved from stone, antlers, mammoth tusks, or, occasionally, baked clay, these so-called **Venus figurines** depict the female form, often with exaggerated breasts, buttocks, hips, and stomachs. Similar figurines have been found all across Eurasia, raising any number of controversial questions. (See the image of the Willendorf Venus, page 23.) Does their widespread distribution suggest a network of human communication and cultural diffusion over a wide area? If so, did they move from west to east or vice versa? What do they mean in terms of women's roles and status in Paleolithic societies?

Into Australia

Early human migration to Australia, perhaps 60,000 years ago, came from Indonesia and involved another first in human affairs—the use of boats. Over time, people settled in most regions of this huge continent, though quite sparsely. Scholars estimate the population of Australia at about 300,000 in 1788, when the first Europeans arrived. Over tens of thousands of years, the peoples of Australia had developed perhaps 250 languages; learned to collect a wide variety of bulbs, tubers, roots, seeds, and cereal grasses; and become proficient hunters of large and small animals, as well as birds, fish, and other marine life. A relatively simple technology, appropriate to a gathering and hunting economy, sustained Australia's Aboriginal people into modern times.

Accompanying Aboriginals' technological simplicity and traditionalism was the development of an elaborate and complex outlook on the world, known as the **Dreamtime**. (See Working with Evidence, page 44, for more on the Dreamtime.) Expressed in endless stories, in extended ceremonies, and in the evocative rock art of the continent's peoples, the Dreamtime recounted the beginning of things: how ancestral beings crisscrossed the land, creating its rivers, hills, rocks, and waterholes; how various peoples came to inhabit the land; and how they related to animals and to one another. In this view of the world, everything in the natural order was a vibration, an echo, a footprint of

Australian Rock Art: The Rainbow Serpent Associated with creation, fertility, and social harmony, the Rainbow Serpent has figured prominently in Australian Aboriginal mythology and in its rock art. See a story associated with the Rainbow Serpent in Working with Evidence, Source 1.2. (Prisma by Dukas Presseagentur GmbH/Alamy)

these ancient happenings, which linked the current inhabitants intimately to particular places and to timeless events in the past.

The journeys of the Dreamtime's ancestral beings reflect the networks of migration, communication, and exchange that linked the continent's many Paleolithic peoples. Far from living as isolated groups, they had long exchanged particular stones, pigments, materials for ropes and baskets, wood for spears, feathers and shells for ornaments, and an addictive psychoactive drug known as *pituri* over distances of hundreds of miles. Songs, dances, stories, and rituals likewise circulated. Precisely how far back in time these networks extend is difficult to pinpoint, but it seems clear that Paleolithic Australia, like ancient Europe, was both many separate worlds and, at the same time, one loosely connected world.

Into the Americas

The earliest settlement of the Western Hemisphere occurred much later than that of Australia, for it took some time for human beings to penetrate the frigid lands of eastern Siberia, which was the jumping-off point for the move into the Americas. Experts continue to argue about precisely when the first migrations occurred (somewhere between 30,000 and 15,000 years ago), about the route of migration (by land across the Bering Strait or by sea down the west coast of North America), about how many separate migrations took place, and about how long it took to penetrate to the tip of South America. Some DNA evidence suggests a possible separate migration by sea from Pacific Polynesia.

Whenever the earliest migrations occurred, one of the first clearly defined and widespread cultural traditions in the Americas is associated with people who made a distinctive projectile point, known to archeologists as a Clovis point. Scattered all over North America, **Clovis culture** first emerged around 13,000 years ago and spread rapidly across much of North America. Scattered bands of Clovis people ranged over this huge area, camping along rivers, springs, and waterholes, where large animals congregated. Although they certainly hunted smaller animals and gathered many wild plants, Clovis men show up in the archeological record most dramatically as hunters of very large mammals, such as mammoths and bison. Killing a single mammoth could provide food for many weeks or, in cold weather, for much of the winter. The wide distribution of Clovis point technology suggests yet again a regional pattern of cultural diffusion and at least indirect communication over a large area.

Then, rather abruptly, by roughly 11,000 years ago, all trace of the Clovis culture disappeared from the archeological record at about the same time that many species of large animals, including the mammoth and several species of horses and camels, also became extinct. Did the Clovis people hunt these animals to extinction and then vanish themselves as their source of food disappeared? Or did the drier climate that came with the end of the Ice Age cause this **megafaunal extinction** (extinction of large animals)? Experts disagree, but what happened next was the creation of a much greater diversity of cultures as people adapted to this new situation in various ways. Hunters on the Great Plains continued to pursue bison, which largely avoided the fate of the mammoths. Others learned to live in the desert, taking advantage of seasonal plants and smaller animals, while those who lived near the sea, lakes, or streams drew on local fish and birds. Many peoples of the Americas retained their gathering and hunting way of life into modern times, while others became farmers and, in a few favored regions, later developed cities and large-scale states.

Into the Pacific

The last phase of the great human migration took place in the Pacific Ocean and was distinctive in many ways. It occurred quite recently, jumping off only about 3,500 years ago from the Bismarck and Solomon Islands near New Guinea as well as from the islands of the Philippines. It was everywhere a waterborne migration, making use of oceangoing canoes and remarkable navigational skills, and it happened very quickly and over a huge area of the planet. Speaking Austronesian languages that trace back to southern China, these oceanic voyagers had settled every habitable piece of land in the Pacific basin within about 2,500 years. Other Austronesians had sailed west from Indonesia across the Indian Ocean to settle the island of Madagascar off the coast of eastern Africa. These extraordinary **Austronesian migrations** made the Austronesian family of languages the most geographically widespread in the world and Austronesian trading networks, reaching some

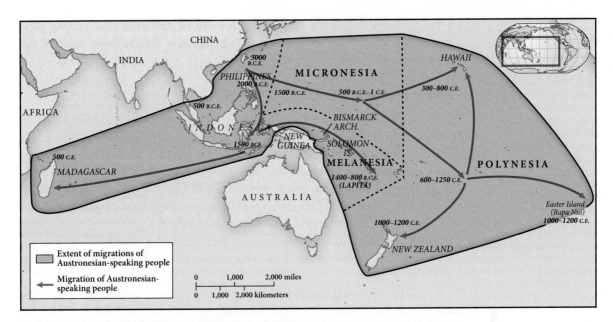

Map 1.2 Migration of Austronesian-Speaking Peoples
People speaking Austronesian languages completed the human settlement of the earth quite recently as they settled the islands of the vast Pacific and penetrated the Indian Ocean to Madagascar, off the coast of southeast Africa.

5,000 miles from western Indonesia to the mid-Pacific, the most extensive. With the occupation of Aotearoa (New Zealand) and Rapa Nui (Easter Island) around 1000 to 1200 C.E., the initial human settlement of the planet was finally complete (see Map 1.2).

In contrast with all of the other initial migrations, these Pacific voyages were undertaken by agricultural people who carried both domesticated plants and animals in their canoes. Both men and women made these journeys, suggesting a deliberate intention to colonize new lands. Virtually everywhere they went, two developments followed. One was the creation of highly stratified societies or chiefdoms, of which ancient Hawaiian society is a prime example. The other development was extensive deforestation and the quick extinction of many species of animals, especially large flightless birds such as the *moa* of New Zealand, which largely vanished within a century of this human intrusion into a pristine environment.

Paleolithic Lifeways

During their long journeys across the earth, Paleolithic people created a multitude of separate and distinct societies, each with its own history, culture, language, identity, stories, and rituals, but the limitations of a gathering and hunting technology using stone tools also imposed some commonalities on these ancient people. Based

Guided Reading Question
....
■ **COMPARISON**
How did Austronesian migrations differ from other early patterns of human movement?

on the archeological record and on observations of gathering and hunting peoples that still existed in recent centuries, scholars have sketched out some of the common features of these early societies.

The First Human Societies

Above all else, these Paleolithic societies were small, consisting of bands of twenty-five to fifty people, in which all relationships were intensely personal and normally understood in terms of kinship. The available technology permitted only a very low population density and ensured an extremely slow rate of population growth. Paleolithic bands were seasonally mobile or nomadic, moving frequently and in regular patterns to exploit the resources of wild plants and animals on which they depended. The low productivity of a gathering and hunting economy normally did not allow the production of much surplus, and because people were on the move so often, transporting an accumulation of goods was out of the question.

All of this resulted in highly egalitarian societies that lacked the many inequalities of wealth and power that came later with agricultural and urban life. With no formal chiefs, kings, bureaucrats, soldiers, nobles, or priests, Paleolithic men and women were perhaps freer of human tyranny and oppression than any later kind of human society, even if they were more constrained by the forces of nature. Without specialists, most people possessed the same set of skills, although male and female tasks often differed sharply. The male role as hunter, especially of big game, perhaps gave rise to one of the first criteria of masculine identity: success in killing large animals.

Contemporary Gathering and Hunting Peoples: The San of Southern Africa A very small number of gathering and hunting peoples have maintained their ancient way of life into the twenty-first century. Here two young men from the Jul'hoan !Kung San of southern Africa set a trap for small animals in 2009. (robertharding/Alamy)

Relationships between women and men usually were far more equal than in later societies. As the primary food gatherers, women provided the bulk of the family's sustenance. One study undertaken during the 1960s of the San people, a surviving gathering and hunting society in southern Africa, found that plants, normally gathered by women, provided 70 percent of the diet, while meat, hunted by men, accounted for just 30 percent. This division of labor underpinned what anthropologist Richard Lee called "relative equality between the sexes with no-one having the upper hand." Among the San, teenagers engaged quite freely in sex play, and the concept of female virginity was apparently unknown, as were rape, wife beating, and the sexual double standard. Although polygamy was permitted, most marriages were in fact monogamous because women strongly resisted sharing a husband with another wife. Frequent divorce among very young couples allowed women to leave unsatisfactory marriages easily. Lee found that longer-term marriages seemed to be generally fulfilling and stable. Both men and women expected a satisfying sexual relationship, and both occasionally took lovers, although discreetly.[9]

When the British navigator and explorer Captain James Cook first encountered the gathering and hunting peoples of Australia in 1770, he described them, perhaps a little enviously, in this way:

> They live in a Tranquillity which is not disturb'd by the Inequality of Conditions: The Earth and sea of their own accord furnishes them with all things necessary for life, they covet not Magnificent houses, Household-stuff. . . . In short they seem'd to set no value upon any thing we gave them. . . . They think themselves provided with all the necessarys of Life.[10]

The Europeans who settled permanently among such people some twenty years later, however, found a society in which physical competition among men was expressed in frequent one-on-one combat and in formalized but bloody battles. It also meant recurrent, public, and quite brutal beatings of wives by their husbands.[11] This evidence coincides with Richard Lee's observations about conflict and violence among the San of southern Africa, where frequent arguments about the distribution of meat or the laziness or stinginess of particular people generated serious disputes, as did rivalries among men over women. More generally, recent studies have found that in Paleolithic societies some 15 percent of deaths occurred through violence at the hands of other people, a rate far higher than in later civilizations, where violence was largely monopolized by the state.[12] Although sometimes romanticized by outsiders, the relative equality of Paleolithic societies did not always ensure a utopia of social harmony.

Like all other human cultures, Paleolithic societies had rules and structures. A gender-based division of labor usually cast men as hunters and women as gatherers. Values emphasizing reciprocal sharing of goods resulted in clearly defined rules about distributing the meat from an animal kill. Various rules about incest and adultery governed sexual behavior, while understandings about who could hunt or gather in particular territories regulated economic activity. Leaders arose as needed

Guided Reading Question

■ CHANGE

In what ways did a gathering and hunting economy shape other aspects of Paleolithic societies?

to organize a task such as a hunt, but permanent power was not conferred on individuals.

Economy and the Environment

For a long time, modern people viewed their gathering and hunting ancestors as primitive and impoverished, barely eking out a living from the land. In more recent decades, anthropologists studying contemporary Paleolithic societies—those that survived into the twentieth century—began to paint a different picture. They noted that gathering and hunting people frequently worked fewer hours to meet their material needs than did people in agricultural or industrial societies and so had more leisure time. One scholar referred to them as **"the original affluent society,"** not because they had so much but because they wanted or needed so little.[13] Nonetheless, life expectancy was low, probably little more than thirty-five years on average. Life in the wild was surely dangerous, and dependency on the vagaries of nature rendered it insecure as well.

But Paleolithic people also acted to alter the natural environment substantially. The use of deliberately set fires in the landscape to encourage the growth of particular plants certainly changed the environment and in Australia led to the proliferation of fire-resistant eucalyptus trees at the expense of other plant species. In many ecosystems, especially small ones like Pacific islands, the arrival of humans resulted in the rapid extinction of some native plants and animals. In Australia and North America the majority of large animals disappeared long before our ancestors learned to farm or fashion weapons from metal. Other hominid, or human-like, species (such as the Neanderthals in Europe or "Flores man," discovered in 2003 in Indonesia) also perished after living side by side with *Homo sapiens* for millennia. Whether their disappearance occurred through massacre, interbreeding, peaceful competition, or something unrelated to the human presence, ultimately they did not survive the rise of humankind. Thus the biological environment inhabited by gathering and hunting peoples was not wholly natural but was shaped in part by their own hands.

The Realm of the Spirit

The religious or spiritual dimension of Paleolithic culture has been hard to pin down, because bones and stones tell us little about what people thought, art is subject to many interpretations, and the experience of contemporary gathering and hunting peoples may not reflect the distant past. Clear evidence exists, however, for a rich and distinctive spiritual life. The presence of rock art deep inside caves and far from living spaces suggests a "ceremonial space" separate from ordinary life. The extended rituals of contemporary Australian Aboriginals, which sometimes last for weeks, confirm this impression, as do numerous and elaborate burial sites found throughout the world. No full-time religious specialists or priests led these ceremonies, but part-time **shamans** (people believed to be especially skilled at dealing with the spirit world) emerged as the need arose. Such people sometimes entered an altered state of consciousness or a trance while performing the ceremonies, often with the aid of psychoactive drugs.

Precisely how Paleolithic people understood the nonmaterial world is hard to reconstruct, and speculation abounds. Linguistic evidence from ancient Africa suggests a variety of understandings: some Paleolithic societies were apparently monotheistic; others saw several levels of supernatural beings, including a creator deity, various territorial spirits, and the spirits of dead ancestors; still others believed in an impersonal force suffused throughout the natural order that could be accessed by shamans during a trance dance.[14] The prevalence of Venus figurines and other symbols all across Europe has convinced some, but not all, scholars that Paleolithic religious thought had a strongly feminine dimension, embodied in a Great Goddess and concerned with the regeneration and renewal of life.[15] Many gathering and hunting peoples likely developed a cyclical view of time derived from recurring natural cycles: sunrise and sunset; changing seasons; the phases of the moon; patterns of female fertility—birth, menstruation, pregnancy, new birth—and, of course, life, death, and new life. These understandings of the cosmos, which saw endlessly repeated patterns of regeneration and disintegration, differed from later Western views, which saw time moving in a straight line toward some predetermined goal. Nor did Paleolithic people make sharp distinctions between the material and spiritual worlds, for they understood that animals, rocks, trees, mountains, and much more were animated by spirits or possessed souls of their own.

The Willendorf Venus Less than four and a half inches in height and dating to about 25,000 years ago, this female figure, which was found near the town of Willendorf in Austria, has become the most famous of the many Venus figurines. Certain features—the absence of both face and feet, the coils of hair around her head, the prominence of her breasts and sexual organs—have prompted much speculation among scholars about the significance of these intriguing carvings. (Naturhistorisches Museum, Vienna, Austria/ Ali Meyer/Bridgeman Images)

Settling Down: The Great Transition

Though glacially slow by contemporary standards, changes in Paleolithic cultures occurred over time as people moved into new environments, as populations grew, as climates altered, and as different human groups interacted with one another. For example, all over the Afro-Eurasian world after 25,000 years ago, a tendency toward the miniaturization of stone tools is evident, analogous perhaps to the miniaturization of electronic components in the twentieth century. Known as micro-blades, these smaller and more refined spear points, arrowheads, knives, and scrapers were carefully struck from larger cores and often mounted in antler, bone, or wooden handles. Another important change involved the collection of wild grains. This innovation originated in northeastern Africa around 16,000 years ago and represented a major addition to the food supply beyond the use of roots, berries, and nuts.

But the most striking and significant change in the lives of Paleolithic peoples occurred as the last Ice Age came to an end between 16,000 and 10,000 years ago. What followed was a general global warming, though one with periodic fluctuations and cold snaps. Unlike the contemporary global warming, generated by human activity and especially the burning of fossil fuels, this ancient warming phase was a wholly natural phenomenon, part of a long cycle of repeated heating and cooling characteristic of the earth's climatic history. Plants and animals that had

Guided Reading Question

■ **CHANGE**
Why did some Paleolithic peoples abandon earlier, more nomadic ways and begin to live a more settled life?

struggled in the Ice Age climate now flourished and increased their range, providing a much richer and more diverse environment for many human societies. Under these improved conditions, human populations grew, and some previously nomadic gathering and hunting communities, but not all of them, found it possible to settle down and live in more permanent settlements or villages. These societies were becoming both larger and more complex, and it was less possible to simply move away if trouble struck. Settlement also meant that households could store and accumulate goods to a greater degree than previously. Because some people were more energetic, more talented, or luckier than others, the thin edge of inequality gradually began to wear away the egalitarianism of Paleolithic communities.

Changes along these lines emerged in many places. Paleolithic societies in Japan, known as Jomon, settled down in villages by the sea, where they greatly expanded the number of animals, both land and marine, that they consumed. They also created some of the world's first pottery, along with dugout canoes, paddles, bows, bowls, and tool handles, all made from wood. A similar pattern of permanent settlement, a broader range of food sources, and specialized technologies is evident in parts of Scandinavia, Southeast Asia, North America, and the Middle East between 12,000 and 4,000 years ago. In Labrador, longhouses appear in the archeological record between 7,500 and 3,500 years ago, some of them accommodating 100 people. Far more elaborate burial sites in many places testify to the growing complexity of human communities and the kinship systems that bound them together. Separate cemeteries for dogs suggest that humankind's best friend was also our first domesticated animal friend. Some of the most stunning and unexpected achievements of such sedentary Paleolithic people come from the archeological complex of **Göbekli Tepe** (goh-BEHK-lee TEH-peh) in southeastern Turkey, described more fully in the Zooming In feature on page 25.

Studies of more recent gathering and hunting societies, which were able to settle permanently in particular resource-rich areas, show marked differences from their more nomadic counterparts. Among the Chumash of southern California, for example, early Spanish settlers found peoples who had developed substantial and permanent structures accommodating up to seventy persons; hereditary political elites; elements of a market economy, including the use of money and private ownership of some property; and the beginnings of class distinctions.

This **Paleolithic settling down**—and the changes that followed from it—marked a major turn in human history, away from countless millennia of nomadic journeys by very small communities. It also provided the setting within which the next great transition would occur. Growing numbers of men and women, living in settled communities, placed a much greater demand on the environment than did small bands of people on the move. Therefore, it is perhaps not surprising that among the innovations that emerged in some of these more complex gathering and hunting societies was yet another way for increasing the food supply—agriculture.

PRACTICING HISTORICAL THINKING

How do you understand the significance of the long Paleolithic era in the larger context of world history?

Göbekli Tepe: Monumental Construction before Agriculture

Perhaps the most stunning archeological discovery of recent decades comes from the site known as Göbekli Tepe, or "potbelly hill," in south-eastern Turkey, which has been under excavation since the mid-1990s. Dating to almost 12,000 years ago, this twenty-five-acre complex currently consists of about 200 massive limestone pillars, some as tall as eighteen feet and weighing as much as fifty tons. Carved in a T shape, perhaps to represent human beings with arms outstretched, they were arranged in a set of walled circles or rings. Five such circles have been unearthed so far, with another twenty or so awaiting excavation. Gracefully carved wild animals—gazelles, snakes, boars, foxes, lions, scorpions, vultures—decorate the pillars. Göbekli Tepe was probably a ceremonial or religious site, for little evidence of long-term human habitation has been found. Dubbed "the world's oldest temple," it likely attracted worshippers or pilgrims from many miles around and may well have served as a place of ritual burials, although no actual graves have yet been found.

The most amazing feature of Göbekli Tepe involves those who constructed it, for they were clearly gathering and hunting peoples, living at least part of the year in settled villages. No evidence of agriculture or domesticated animals has emerged. Rather, the tens of thousands of animal bone fragments found at the site suggest that those who built the complex dined on wild gazelles, pigs, sheep, deer, vultures, and ducks, as well as wild plants native to the area. Thus Göbekli Tepe represents a kind of monumental construction long associated only with agricultural societies and civilizations, forcing scholars to rethink their understanding of the late Paleolithic era.

Göbekli Tepe.

Carved Lion on a Stone Pillar at Göbekli Tepe.

How did such pre-agricultural peoples with only the simplest of stone tools carve, transport, and erect such enormous structures? What kind of social organization facilitated their remarkable achievement? What did this complex mean to those who created it? Since stones and bones tell us little about these matters, many mysteries remain.

Although Göbekli Tepe was the product of pre-agricultural peoples, the process of its construction may well have played a role in the breakthrough to farming in this region. Klaus Schmidt, the chief archeologist at the site for many years, argued that the need for food to supply those who built and maintained this massive religious complex may well have triggered the development of agriculture in the area. Certainly, some of the earliest domesticated wheat has been located just twenty miles away and at roughly the same date. If this connection holds, it suggests that the human impulse to worship collectively played a significant role in generating the epic transformation of the Agricultural Revolution.

Scholars have long believed that large-scale construction, settled village life, and institutional religion were generated by agricultural societies. The finds at Göbekli Tepe and elsewhere now suggest that these achievements may have figured in the creation of those farming communities. Perhaps they were precursors to agriculture rather than products of it.

QUESTIONS

In what ways has Göbekli Tepe forced historians to rethink earlier views? How does this archeological discovery affect your own understanding of the Paleolithic era?

photos: Vincent J. Musi/National Geographic Creative

Breakthroughs to Agriculture

The chief feature of the long Paleolithic era—and the first human process to operate on a global scale—was the initial settlement of the earth. Then, beginning around 12,000 years ago, a second global pattern began to unfold—agriculture. The terms "Neolithic (New Stone Age) Revolution" and "Agricultural Revolution" both refer to the deliberate cultivation of particular plants as well as the taming and breeding of particular animals. Thus a whole new way of life gradually replaced the earlier practices of gathering and hunting in most parts of the world. Although it took place over centuries and millennia, the coming of agriculture represented a genuinely revolutionary transformation of human life all across the planet and provided the foundation for almost everything that followed: growing populations, settled villages, animal-borne diseases, horse-drawn chariot warfare, cities, states, empires, civilizations, writing, literature, and much more.

Among the most revolutionary aspects of the age of agriculture was a new relationship between humankind and other living things, for now men and women were not simply using what they found in nature but actively changing nature as well. They were consciously "directing" the process of evolution. The actions of farmers in the Americas, for example, transformed corn from a plant with a cob of an inch or so to one measuring about six inches by 1500. Later efforts more than doubled that length. Farmers everywhere stamped the landscape with a human imprint in the form of fields with boundaries, terraced hillsides, irrigation ditches, and canals. Animals too were transformed, as selective breeding produced sheep that grew more wool, cows that gave more milk, and chickens that laid more eggs than their wild counterparts. This was "domestication"—the taming, and the changing, of nature for the benefit of humankind. In many agricultural communities, however, gathering, hunting, and fishing did not quickly disappear, but long continued to supplement agriculture and animal husbandry as food sources.

A further revolutionary aspect of the agricultural age is summed up in the term "intensification." It means getting more for less, in this case more food and resources—far more—from a much smaller area of land than was possible with a gathering and hunting technology. More food meant more people. Growing populations in turn required an even more intensive exploitation of the environment. Thus was launched the continuing human effort to "fill the earth and subdue it," as the biblical story in Genesis recorded God's command to Adam and Eve.

Common Patterns

Perhaps the most extraordinary feature of the Neolithic or Agricultural Revolution was that it occurred, separately and independently, in many widely scattered parts of the world: the Fertile Crescent of Southwest Asia, several places in sub-Saharan Africa, China, Southeast Asia, New Guinea, Mesoamerica, the Andes, and eastern North America (see Map 1.3). Even more remarkably, all of this took place at roughly the same time (at least as measured by the 250,000-year span of human history on the planet)—between 12,000 and 4,000 years ago. So why was the Agricultural Revolution so late in the history of humankind? What was unique about the period after 10,000 B.C.E. that may have triggered or facilitated this vast upheaval? In what different ways did the Agricultural Revolution take shape in its various locations? How did it spread from its several points of origin to the rest of the earth? And what impact did it have on the making of human societies?

It is surely no accident that the Agricultural Revolution coincided with the end of the last Ice Age, a process of global warming that began some 16,000 years ago. By about 11,000 years ago, the Ice Age was over, and climatic conditions similar to those of our own time generally prevailed. Ice ages had come and gone earlier in the earth's history, caused by minor periodic changes in the earth's orbit around the sun. The end of the last Ice Age, however, coincided with the migration of *Homo sapiens* across the planet and created new conditions that made agriculture more possible in some areas, even as rising sea levels inundated other regions (see Map 1.1). Combined perhaps with active hunting by human societies, climate change in some places helped to push into extinction various species of large mammals on which Paleolithic people had depended, thus adding to the pressure to find new food sources. The warmer, wetter, and more stable conditions, particularly in the tropical and temperate regions of the earth, also permitted the flourishing of more wild plants, especially cereal grasses, which were the ancestors of many domesticated crops. What climate change took away with one hand, it apparently gave back with the other.

Over their long history, gathering and hunting peoples had already developed a deep knowledge of the natural world and, in some cases, the ability to manage it actively. They had learned to make use of a large number of plants and to hunt and eat both small and large animals, creating what archeologists call a "broad-spectrum diet." In the Middle East, people had developed sickles for cutting newly available wild grain, baskets to carry it, mortars and pestles to remove the husk, and storage pits to preserve it. In hindsight, much of this looks like a kind of unintentional preparation for agriculture. Because women in particular had long been intimately associated with collecting wild plants, they were the likely innovators who led the way to deliberate farming, with men perhaps taking the lead in domesticating animals.

Using available technologies, and benefiting from the global warming at the end of the last Ice Age, gathering and hunting peoples in various resource-rich areas were able to settle down and establish more permanent villages, abandoning their nomadic ways and more intensively exploiting the local area. In settling down, however, they found themselves now required to support growing populations. Evidence for increasing human numbers around the world during this period of global warming has persuaded some scholars that agriculture was a response to the need for additional food, perhaps even a "food crisis." Such conditions surely motivated people to experiment and to innovate in an effort to increase the food supply. Clearly, many of the breakthroughs to agriculture occurred only *after* gathering and hunting peoples had already grown substantially in numbers and had established a sedentary way of life.

Guided Reading Question

■ **CHANGE**
What accounts for the emergence of agriculture after countless millennia of human life without it?

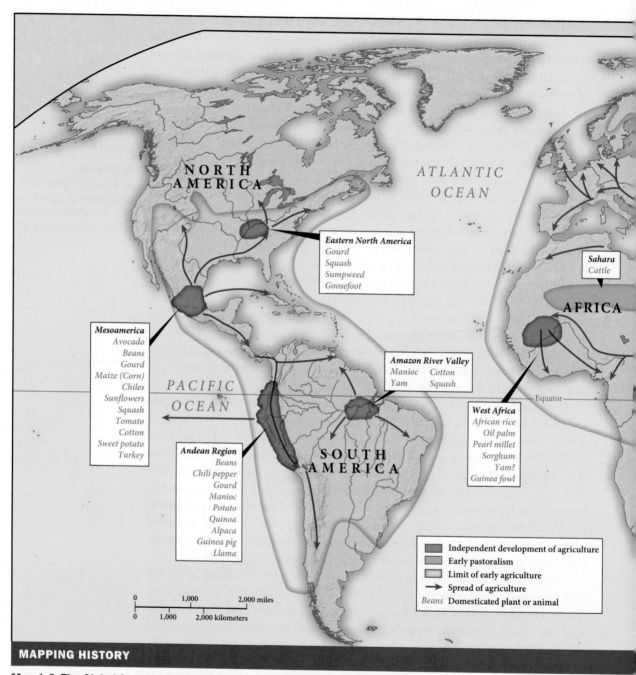

MAPPING HISTORY

Map 1.3 The Global Spread of Agriculture and Pastoralism

From ten or more separate points of origin, agriculture spread to adjacent areas, eventually encompassing almost all of the world's peoples.

READING THE MAP: On which continents did early pastoral societies develop? Which continents fostered no early pastoral societies?

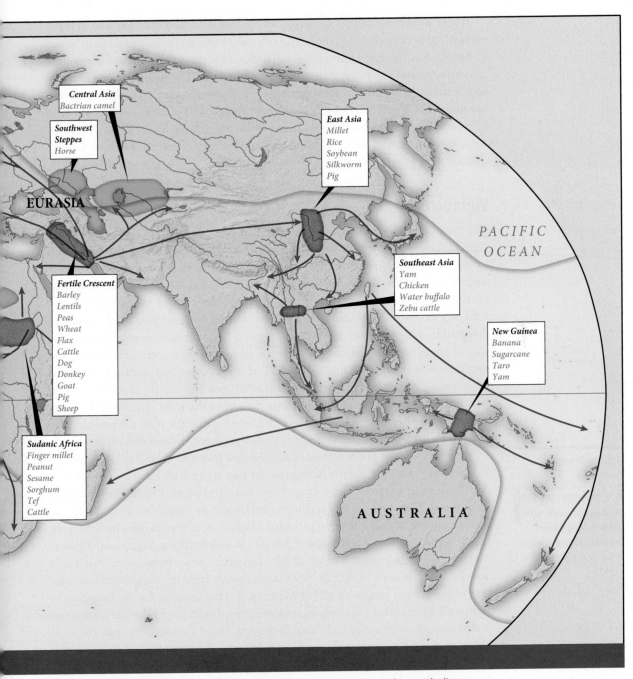

Central Asia
Bactrian camel

Southwest Steppes
Horse

East Asia
Millet
Rice
Soybean
Silkworm
Pig

EURASIA

PACIFIC OCEAN

Southeast Asia
Yam
Chicken
Water buffalo
Zebu cattle

Fertile Crescent
Barley
Lentils
Peas
Wheat
Flax
Cattle
Dog
Donkey
Goat
Pig
Sheep

New Guinea
Banana
Sugarcane
Taro
Yam

Sudanic Africa
Finger millet
Peanut
Sesame
Sorghum
Tef
Cattle

AUSTRALIA

INTERPRETING THE MAP: How might you describe the climatic regions where agriculture developed independently? Were they in equatorial tropical zones, arctic zones, and/or in regions in between called temperate zones? What factors might explain this distribution?

These were some of the common patterns that facilitated the Agricultural Revolution. New opportunities appeared with the changed climatic conditions at the end of the Ice Age. New knowledge and technology emerged as human communities explored and exploited that changed environment. The disappearance of many large mammals, growing populations, newly settled ways of life, and fluctuations in the process of global warming—all of these represented pressures or incentives to increase food production and thus to minimize the risks of life in a new era. From some combination of these opportunities and incentives emerged the profoundly transforming process of the Agricultural Revolution.

Variations

This new way of life initially operated everywhere with a simple technology—the digging stick or hoe. Plows were developed much later. But the several transitions to this hoe-based agriculture, commonly known as horticulture, varied considerably, depending on what plants and animals were available locally. For example, potatoes were found in the Andes region, but not in Africa or Asia; wheat and wild pigs existed in the Fertile Crescent, but not in the Americas. Furthermore, of the world's 200,000 plant species, only several hundred have been domesticated, and in more recent centuries just five of these—wheat, corn, rice, barley, and sorghum—have supplied more than half of the calories that sustain human life. Only fourteen species of large mammals have been successfully domesticated, of which sheep, pigs, goats, cattle, and horses have been the most important. Thus the kind of Agricultural Revolution that unfolded in particular places depended very much on what happened to be available locally; in short, it depended on sheer luck.

Guided Reading Question

■ **COMPARISON**

In what different ways did the Agricultural Revolution take shape in various parts of the world?

Among the most favored areas—and the first to experience a full Agricultural Revolution—was the **Fertile Crescent**, an area sometimes known as Southwest Asia, consisting of present-day Iraq, Syria, Israel/Palestine, Jordan, and southern Turkey (see Map 1.4). In this region, an extraordinary variety of wild plants and animals capable of domestication provided a rich array of species on which the now largely settled gathering and hunting people could draw. What triggered the transition to agriculture remains a much-debated question. Some have argued that a cold and dry spell between 11,000 and 9500 B.C.E., a very rapid but temporary interruption in the general process of global warming, was the stimulus for the transition to farming. Larger settled populations, now threatened with the loss of the wild plants and animals on which they had come to depend, found a solution in domestication, either during or soon after this cold and dry period passed. Figs were apparently the first cultivated crop, dating to about 9400 B.C.E. In the millennium or so that followed, wheat, barley, rye, peas, lentils, sheep, goats, pigs, and cattle all came under human control, providing the foundation for the world's first agricultural societies.

Archeological evidence suggests that the transition to a fully agricultural way of life in parts of this region took place quite quickly, within as few as 500 years. Signs of that transformation included large increases in the size of settlements, which now

Map 1.4 The Fertile Crescent
Located in what is now called the Middle East, the Fertile Crescent was the site of many
significant processes in early world history, including a major breakthrough to agriculture and
later the development of one of the First Civilizations.

housed as many as several thousand people. In these agricultural settings, archeologists have found major innovations: the use of sun-dried mud bricks; the appearance of monuments or shrine-like buildings; displays of cattle skulls; more elaborate
human burials, including the removal of the skull; and more sophisticated tools,
such as sickles, polished axes, and awls.

At roughly the same time, or perhaps a bit later, another process of domestication was unfolding on the African continent in the eastern part of what is now
the Sahara in present-day Sudan. Between 10,000 and 5,000 years ago, this region
received more rainfall than it currently does, had extensive grassland vegetation, and
was "relatively hospitable to human life."[16] During these millennia, domesticated
cattle appeared in the region, though whether they were tamed locally or were
introduced from the Fertile Crescent is still debated. Around 6,000 years ago, the
donkey was also domesticated in northeastern Africa near the Red Sea and spread
from there into Southwest Asia, even as the practice of raising sheep and goats
moved in the other direction.

In terms of farming, the African pattern again was somewhat different. Unlike
the Fertile Crescent, where a number of plants were domesticated in a small area,
sub-Saharan Africa witnessed the emergence of several widely scattered farming

practices. Sorghum, which grows well in arid conditions, was the first grain to be "tamed" in the eastern Sahara region. In the highlands of Ethiopia, teff, a tiny, highly nutritious grain, as well as enset, a relative of the banana, came under cultivation. In the forested region of West Africa, yams, oil palm trees, okra, and the kola nut (used as a flavoring for cola drinks) emerged as important crops. The scattered location of these domestications generated a less productive agriculture than in the more favored and compact Fertile Crescent, but a number of African domesticates—sorghum, castor beans, gourds, millet, the donkey—subsequently spread to enrich the agricultural practices of Eurasian peoples.

Yet another pattern of agricultural development took shape in the Americas. Like the Agricultural Revolution in Africa, the domestication of plants in the Americas occurred separately in a number of locations—in the coastal Andean regions of western South America, in Mesoamerica, in the Mississippi River valley, and perhaps in the Amazon basin. Surely the most distinctive common feature of these regions was the relative absence of animals that could be domesticated. Of the fourteen major species of large mammals that have been brought under human control, just two, the llama and alpaca, existed in the Western Hemisphere, and only in the Andes region, where they proved enormously useful for food, fiber, and transportation. Without goats, sheep, pigs, cattle, or horses, the peoples of the Americas lacked sources of protein, manure (for fertilizer), and power (to draw plows or pull carts, for example) that were widely available to societies in the Afro-Eurasian world. Because they could not depend on domesticated animals for meat, many agricultural peoples in the Americas relied more on hunting and fishing than did peoples in the Eastern Hemisphere. While the Americas lacked the cereal grains that were widely available in Afro-Eurasia, they had **maize** or corn, first domesticated in southern Mexico by 4000 to 3000 B.C.E. Unlike the cereal grains of the Fertile Crescent, which closely resemble their wild predecessors, the ancestor of corn was a mountain grass that looks nothing like what we now know as corn or maize. Thousands of years of selective adaptation were required to develop a sufficiently large cob and number of kernels to sustain a productive agriculture, an achievement that one geneticist has called "arguably man's first, and perhaps his greatest, feat of genetic engineering."[17] Thus while Middle Eastern societies quite rapidly replaced their gathering and hunting economy with agriculture, that process took several thousand years in Mesoamerica. Beyond maize, Native American farmers domesticated squash, beans, potatoes, sunflowers, quinoa, pigweed, and goosefoot, which were harvested on a large scale.

Another difference in the unfolding of the Agricultural Revolution lay in the north/south orientation of the Americas, which required agricultural practices to move through, and adapt to, quite distinct climatic and vegetation zones if they were to spread. The east/west axis of North Africa / Eurasia meant that agricultural innovations could spread more rapidly because they were entering roughly similar environments. Thus corn, beans, and squash, which were first domesticated in Mesoamerica, took several thousand years to travel the few hundred miles from their Mexican

The Statues of Ain Ghazal Among the largest of the early agricultural settlements investigated by archeologists is that of Ain Ghazal, located in the modern state of Jordan. Inhabited from about 7200 to 5000 B.C.E., in its prime it was home to some 3,000 people, who lived in multiroomed stone houses; cultivated barley, wheat, peas, beans, and lentils; and herded domesticated goats. These remarkable statues, around three feet tall and made of limestone plaster applied to a core of bundled reeds, were among the most startling finds at that site. Did they represent heroes, gods, goddesses, or ordinary people? No one really knows. (Courtesy, Department of Antiquities of Jordan [DoA]/Photo by John Tsantesi, Courtesy, Dr. Gary O. Rollefson)

homeland to the southwestern United States and another thousand years or more to arrive in eastern North America. The llama, guinea pig, quinoa, and potato, which were domesticated in the Andean highlands, never reached Mesoamerica.

The Globalization of Agriculture

From the various places where it originated, agriculture spread gradually to much of the rest of the earth, although for a long time it coexisted with gathering and hunting ways of life, even as it eroded and diminished those practices. Broadly speaking, this extension of farming occurred in two ways. The first, known as diffusion, refers to the gradual spread of agricultural techniques, and perhaps of the plants and animals themselves, but without the extensive movement of agricultural people. Neighboring groups exchanged ideas and products in a down-the-line pattern of communication. A second process involved the slow colonization or migration of agricultural peoples as growing populations pushed them outward.

Triumph and Resistance

Guided Reading Question

....

■ CONNECTION

In what ways did agriculture spread? Where and why was it sometimes resisted?

Some combination of diffusion and migration underpinned the spread of agriculture to new regions, and the adoption of farming practices was at times accompanied by the spread of languages as well. For instance, between 6500 and 4000 B.C.E. the agricultural package of Southwest Asia spread into Europe, Central Asia, Egypt, and North Africa. In the case of Europe, the adoption of agriculture was accompanied by the spread into the region of Indo-European languages, which had originated further east in Anatolia or, as some scholars suggest, in the area north of the Black and Caspian Seas. Within Africa, the development of agricultural societies in the southern half of the continent is associated with the **Bantu migration**, the movement of peoples speaking one or another of the some 400 Bantu languages. Beginning from what is now southern Nigeria or Cameroon around 3000 B.C.E., Bantu-speaking people moved east and south over the next several millennia, taking with them their agricultural, cattle-raising, and, later, ironworking skills, as well as their languages. They generally absorbed, killed, or drove away the indigenous Paleolithic peoples or exposed them to animal-borne diseases to which they had no immunities. A similar process brought agricultural Austronesian-speaking people, who originated in southern China, to the Philippine and Indonesian islands, with similar consequences for their earlier inhabitants (see Map 1.2, page 19).

Bantu Migration

The globalization of agriculture was a prolonged process, lasting 10,000 years or more after its first emergence in the Fertile Crescent, but it did not take hold everywhere. The Agricultural Revolution in highland New Guinea, for example, generated a number of domesticated plants including yams, taro, bananas, and sugarcane. But while these spread to parts of Island Southeast Asia, they did not pass to the nearby peoples of Australia, who remained steadfastly committed to gathering and hunting ways of life. The people of the west coast of North America, arctic regions, and southwestern Africa also maintained their gathering and hunting economies into the modern era.

Some of those who resisted the swelling tide of agriculture lived in areas unsuitable to farming, such as harsh desert or arctic environments; others lived in regions of particular natural abundance, so they felt little need for agriculture. Such societies found it easier to resist agriculture if they were not in the direct line of advancing, more powerful farming people. But many of the remaining gathering and hunting peoples knew about agricultural practices from nearby neighbors, suggesting that they quite deliberately chose to resist it in favor of the freer life of their Paleolithic ancestors. Nonetheless, by the beginning of the Common Era, the global spread of agriculture had reduced gathering and hunting peoples to a small and dwindling minority of humankind.

Guided Reading Question

....

■ CHANGE

What changes did the Agricultural Revolution bring in its wake?

The Culture of Agriculture

In many accounts, the Agricultural Revolution is presented as "progress"—a great leap forward—for humankind. If evolutionary success or an increase in numbers is a measure of progress, then the Agricultural Revolution certainly fits that description, for it led to a substantial increase in human population, as the greater productivity of agriculture was able to support many more people. By 8000 B.C.E. an early agricultural settlement uncovered near Jericho in present-day Israel probably had 2,000 to 3,000 people, a vast increase in the size of human communities compared to much smaller Paleolithic bands. On a global level, scholars estimate that the world's population was about 6 million around 10,000 years ago, before the Agricultural Revolution had a pervasive impact, and shot up to some 50 million by 5,000 years ago and 250 million by the beginning of the Common Era. Here was the real beginning of the human dominance over other forms of life on the planet.

That dominance was reflected in major environmental transformations. In a growing number of places, forests and grasslands became cultivated fields and grazing lands. Human selection modified the genetic composition of numerous plants and animals. In parts of the Middle East, within a thousand years after the beginning of settled agricultural life, some villages were abandoned when soil erosion and deforestation led to declining crop yields, which could not support mounting populations. Human life too changed dramatically in farming communities, for agriculture usually required a settled, village-based way of life. An example of such an early agricultural settlement, now called **Banpo**, has been uncovered in northern China, dating to around 6,000 years ago. Millet, pigs, and dogs had been domesticated, but diets were supplemented with wild plants, animals, and fish. Some forty-five houses covered with thatch laid over wooden beams provided homes to perhaps 500 people. More than 200 storage pits permitted the accumulation of grain, and six kilns and pottery wheels enabled the production of various pots, vases, and dishes, many decorated with geometric designs and human and animal images. A large central space suggests an area for public religious or political activity, and a trench surrounding the village indicates some common effort to defend the community.

But beyond growing populations, did such villages represent "progress," so often associated with the Agricultural Revolution? Farming involved hard work and more of it than in many earlier gathering and hunting societies. The remains of early agricultural people show some deterioration in health—more tooth decay, malnutrition, anemia, slipped disks, arthritis, and hernias; a shorter physical stature; and diminished life expectancy. Living close to animals subjected humans to new diseases—smallpox, flu, measles, chicken pox, malaria, tuberculosis, rabies—while living in larger communities generated epidemics for the first time in human history. Furthermore, since farming peoples often relied heavily on a single plant (rice, wheat, or potatoes), they were vulnerable to famine in case of crop failure, drought, or other catastrophes, while their foraging ancestors had drawn on a much wider range of food resources. The advent of agriculture bore costs as well as benefits.

Agricultural villages, however, also generated an explosion of technological innovation. Mobile Paleolithic peoples had little use for pots, but such vessels were essential for settled societies, and their creation and elaboration accompanied agriculture everywhere. So too did the weaving of textiles, made possible by collecting the fibers of domesticated plants (cotton and flax, for example) and raising animals such as sheep. Evidence for the invention of looms of several kinds dates back to 7,000 years ago, and textiles, some elaborately decorated, show up in Peru, Switzerland, China, and Egypt. Like agriculture itself, weaving was a technology in which women were probably the primary innovators, as it was a task compatible with their childbearing and child-rearing responsibilities. Another technology associated with the Agricultural Revolution was metallurgy. The working of gold and copper, then bronze, and, later, iron became part of the jewelry-, tool-, and weapon-making skill set of humankind. The long "stone age" of human technological history was coming to an end, and the age of metals was beginning.

A further set of technological changes, beginning around 4000 B.C.E., has been labeled the **secondary products revolution**.[18] These technological innovations involved new uses for domesticated animals, beyond their meat and hides. Agricultural people in parts of Europe, Asia, and Africa learned to milk their animals, to harvest their wool, and to enrich the soil with their manure. Even more important, they learned to ride horses and camels and to hitch various animals to plows and carts. Because these animals did not exist in the Americas, this revolutionary new source of power and transportation was available only in the Eastern Hemisphere.

Finally, the Agricultural Revolution presented to humankind the gift of wine and beer, often a blessing, sometimes a curse. As barley, wheat, rice, and grapes were domesticated, their potential for generating alcoholic beverages soon became apparent. The Chinese were making a rice-based wine combined with honey and fruit by about 7000 B.C.E., while grape wine was consumed in Iran by 5400 B.C.E., only 600 years after grapes were domesticated in nearby regions. The precise origins of beer are unclear, but its use was already quite widespread in the Middle East by 4000 B.C.E., when a pictogram on a seal from Mesopotamia showed two figures using straws to drink beer from a large pottery jar. Regarded as a gift from the gods, beer, like bread, was understood in Mesopotamia as something that could turn a savage into a fully human and civilized person.[19] In the Americas, an alcoholic beverage known as *chicha* had been produced from maize, manioc, honey, and various fruits from ancient times and was the drink of choice in the Inca court.

If the Agricultural Revolution meant "progress" in certain ways, it also claimed many victims. While the farming frontier expanded relentlessly,

Nok Culture The agricultural and iron-using Nok culture of northern Nigeria in West Africa generated a remarkable artistic tradition of terra-cotta, or fired-clay, figures depicting animals and, especially, people. This one dates to somewhere between 500 B.C.E. and 50 C.E. Some scholars have dubbed this and many similar Nok sculptures "thinkers." Does this notion reflect a present-day sensibility, or is it an insight into the mentality of the ancient artist who created the image? (Werner Forman Archive/ Bridgeman Images) gathering and hunting societies were almost everywhere eroded as foragers became farmers or married into farming communities; as diseases spread from agricultural neighbors; and as more powerful farming communities violently displaced Paleolithic peoples. The plaintive cry of Gudo Mahiya, recorded at the beginning of this chapter, was certainly an echo of many such laments over many centuries.

And what of the animals? Like their human counterparts, certain animals such as cattle, pigs, sheep, and chickens greatly increased their numbers as their habitats became global. But they lost, of course, the freedom of the wild as they lived under the constraint, and often the lash, of their human masters. Many suffered a much shortened life-span as they were slaughtered at a young age for human consumption. Others were required to pull carts and plows or to transport humans on their backs, while some were castrated or branded. Mothers and their offspring were frequently separated shortly after birth. No wonder one scholar has called the Agricultural Revolution a "terrible catastrophe" for the majority of domesticated animals. For humans and animals alike, reproductive success for the species often translated into great suffering for many individuals.[20]

Social Variation in the Age of Agriculture

The resources generated by the Agricultural Revolution opened up vast new possibilities for the construction of human societies, but they led to no single or common outcome. Differences in the natural environment, the encounter with strangers, and, sometimes, deliberate choices gave rise to several distinct kinds of societies early on in the age of agriculture, all of which have endured into modern times.

Pastoral Societies

One variation of great significance grew out of the difference between the domestication of plants and the domestication of animals. Many societies made use of both, but in regions where farming was difficult or impossible—arctic tundra, certain grasslands, and deserts—some people came to depend far more extensively on their animals, such as sheep, goats, cattle, horses, camels, or reindeer. Animal husbandry was a "distinct form of food-producing economy," relying on the products of animals.[21] Those animals could turn grass or waste products into meat, fiber, hides, and milk; they were useful for transport and warfare; and they could walk to market. Known as herders, pastoralists, or nomads, peoples largely dependent on their domesticated animals emerged most prominently in Central Asia, the Arabian Peninsula, the Sahara, and parts of eastern and southern Africa. What they had in common was mobility, for they moved seasonally as they followed the changing patterns of the vegetation necessary as pasture for their animals. Some lived a nomadic existence of constant seasonal movement, but for others it was possible to combine permanent settlements in lowland areas and the movement of animals to more mountainous pasturelands in the summer.

Guided Reading Question

■ **COMPARISON**
What different kinds of societies emerged out of the Agricultural Revolution?

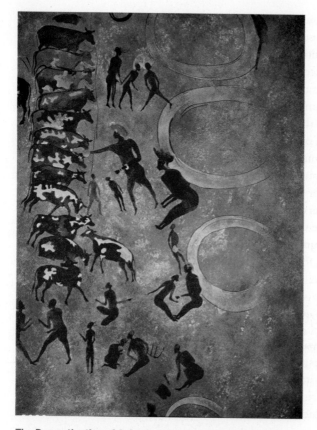

The Domestication of Animals Although farming often gets top billing in discussions of the Agricultural Revolution, the raising of animals was equally important, for they provided meat, pulling power, transportation (in the case of horses and camels), and manure. Animal husbandry also made possible pastoral societies, which were largely dependent on their domesticated animals. This rock art painting from the Sahara (now southeastern Algeria) dates to somewhere around 4000 B.C.E. and depicts an early pastoral community. The white ovals represent a group of huts. (Musée de l'Homme, Paris, France/Erich Lessing/ Art Resource, NY)

The particular animals central to pastoral economies differed from region to region. The domestication of horses by 4000 B.C.E. and the mastery of horseback-riding skills several thousand years later enabled the growth of pastoral peoples all across the steppes of Central Asia by the first millennium B.C.E. Although organized primarily in kinship-based clans or tribes, these nomads periodically created powerful military confederations, which played a major role in the history of Eurasia for thousands of years. In the Inner Asian, Arabian, and Saharan deserts, domesticated camels made possible the human occupation of forbidding environments. (See Zooming In: The Arabian Camel, Chapter 7, page 296.) The grasslands south of the Sahara and in parts of eastern Africa supported cattle-raising pastoralists. In the Americas, llamas and alpacas were tremendously important in the economy of Andean civilizations, but only in a few pockets in the Andes did human communities rely as heavily on their domesticated animals as did the pastoral peoples of the Afro-Eurasian world.

The relationship between nomadic herders and their farming neighbors has been one of the enduring themes of Afro-Eurasian history. Frequently, it was a relationship of conflict, as pastoral peoples, unable to produce their own agricultural products, were attracted to the wealth and sophistication of agrarian societies and sought access to their richer grazing lands as well as their food crops and manufactured products. The biblical story of the deadly rivalry between two brothers—Cain, a "tiller of the ground," and Abel, a "keeper of sheep"—reflects this ancient conflict, which persisted well into modern times. But not all was conflict between pastoral and agricultural peoples. The more peaceful exchange of technologies, ideas, products, and people across the ecological frontier of pastoral and agricultural societies also served to enrich and to change both sides.

Within **pastoral societies**, the relative equality of men and women, characteristic of most Paleolithic societies, persisted, perhaps because women's work was so essential. Women were centrally involved in milking animals, in processing that milk, and in producing textiles such as felt, which was widely used in Central Asia for tents, beds, rugs, and clothing. Among the Saka pastoralists in what is now Azerbaijan, women rode horses and participated in battles along with men.

A number of archeological sites around the Black Sea have revealed high-status women buried with armor, swords, daggers, and arrows. In the Xinjiang region of western China, still other women were buried with the apparatus of healers and shamans, strongly suggesting an important female role in religious life.

Agricultural Village Societies

For thousands of years, people practiced agriculture using digging sticks or hoes, rather than plows, and even after plows came into use, many societies continued with hoe-based or horticultural farming. Most such hoe-based agricultural peoples lived in settled villages such as Banpo or Jericho, but to varying degrees they continued to augment their agricultural livelihood with gathering, hunting, and fishing. They also retained much of the social and gender equality of gathering and hunting communities, as they continued to do without kings, chiefs, bureaucrats, or aristocracies.

An example of this type of social order can be found at **Çatalhüyük** (cha-TAHL-hoo-YOOK), a very early agricultural village in southern Turkey, which flourished between 7400 and 6000 B.C.E. A careful excavation of the site revealed a population of several thousand people who buried their dead under their houses and then filled the houses with dirt and built new ones on top, layer upon layer. No streets divided the houses, which were constructed adjacent to one another. People moved about the village on adjoining rooftops, from which they entered their homes. Despite the presence of many specialized crafts, few signs of inherited social inequality have surfaced. Nor is there any indication of male or female dominance, although men were more closely associated with hunting wild animals and women with plants and agriculture. "Both men and women," concludes one scholar, "could carry out a series of roles and enjoy a range of positions, from making tools to grinding grain and baking to heading a household."[22]

In many horticultural villages, women's critical role as farmers as well as their work in the spinning and weaving of textiles no doubt contributed to a social position of relative equality with men. Some such societies traced their descent through the female line and practiced marriage patterns in which men left their homes to live with their wives' families. Archeologist Marija Gimbutas has highlighted the prevalence of female imagery in the art of early agricultural societies in Europe and Anatolia, which has suggested to her a widespread cult of the Goddess, focused on "the mystery of birth, death and the renewal of life."[23] But early agriculture did not produce identical gender systems everywhere. Some societies practiced patrilineal descent and required a woman to live in the household of her husband. Grave sites in early Eastern European farming communities reveal fewer adult females than males, indicating perhaps the practice of female infanticide. Some early written evidence from China suggests a long-term preference for male children. These variations in practice suggest that gender roles were likely determined more by cultural preference than by any biological need for a sexual division of labor and power.

In all of their diversity, many village-based agricultural societies flourished well into the modern era, usually organizing themselves in terms of kinship groups or lineages, which incorporated large numbers of people well beyond the immediate or extended family. Such a system provided the framework within which large numbers of people could make and enforce rules, maintain order, and settle disputes without going to war. In short, the lineage system performed the functions of government, but without the formal apparatus of government, and thus did not require kings or queens, chiefs, or permanent officials associated with a state organization. Despite their democratic qualities and the absence of centralized authority, village-based lineage societies sometimes developed modest social and economic inequalities. Elders could exploit the labor of junior members of the community and sought particularly to control women's reproductive powers, which were essential for the growth of the lineage. People with special knowledge, skills, or experience could achieve higher status and greater influence. Among the Igbo of southern Nigeria well into the twentieth century, "title societies" enabled men and women of wealth and character to earn a series of increasingly prestigious "titles" that set them apart from other members of their community, although these honors could not be inherited. Lineages also sought to expand their numbers, and hence their prestige and power, by incorporating war captives or migrants in subordinate positions, sometimes as slaves.

Given the frequent oppressiveness of organized political power in human history, agricultural village societies represent an intriguing alternative to the states, kingdoms, and empires so often highlighted in the historical record. They pioneered the human settlement of vast areas; adapted to a variety of environments; maintained a substantial degree of social and gender equality; created numerous cultural, artistic, and religious traditions; and interacted continuously with their neighbors.

Chiefdoms

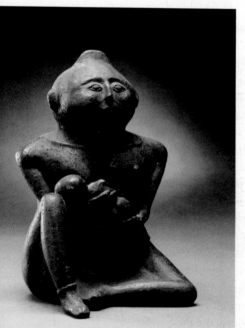

Cahokia: A Nursing Mother Effigy Bottle Among the artifacts uncovered in the North American chiefdom of Cahokia is this effigy bottle in the shape of a nursing mother, dating from 1200 to 1400 C.E. (Photo © The Detroit Institute of Arts/St. Louis Museum of Science & Natural History, Missouri, USA/Bridgeman Images)

In other places, agricultural village societies came to be organized politically as **chiefdoms**, in which inherited positions of power and privilege introduced a more distinct element of inequality, but unlike later kings, chiefs could seldom use force to compel the obedience of their subjects. Instead, chiefs relied on their generosity or gift giving, their ritual status, or their personal charisma to persuade their followers. The earliest such chiefdoms seem to have emerged in the Tigris-Euphrates river valley called Mesopotamia (present-day Iraq), sometime after 6000 B.C.E., when temple priests may have organized irrigation systems and controlled trade with nearby societies.

Many chiefdoms followed in all parts of the world, and the more recent ones have been much studied by anthropologists. For example, chiefdoms emerged everywhere in the Pacific islands, which had been colonized by agricultural Polynesian peoples. Chiefs usually derived from a senior lineage, tracing their descent to the first son of an imagined ancestor. With both religious and secular functions, chiefs led important rituals and ceremonies, organized the community for warfare, directed its economic life, and sought to resolve internal conflicts. They collected tribute from commoners in the form of food, manufactured goods, and raw materials. These items in turn were redistributed to warriors, craftsmen, religious specialists, and other subordinates, while chiefs kept enough to maintain their prestigious positions and imposing lifestyle. In North America as well, a remarkable series of chiefdoms emerged in the eastern woodlands, where an extensive array of large earthen mounds testify to the organizational capacity of these early societies. The largest of them, known as Cahokia, flourished around 1100 C.E. (See "North America: Ancestral Pueblo and Mound Builders" in Chapter 6.)

Thus the Agricultural Revolution radically transformed both the trajectory of the human journey and the evolution of life on the planet. This epic process granted to one species, *Homo sapiens*, a growing power over many other species of plants and animals and made possible an increase in human numbers far beyond what a gathering and hunting economy could support.

But if agriculture provided humankind with the power to dominate nature, it also, increasingly, enabled some people to dominate others. This was not immediately apparent, and for several thousand years, and much longer in some places, agricultural villages and pastoral communities retained elements of the social equality that had characterized Paleolithic life. Slowly, though, many of the resources released by the Agricultural Revolution accumulated in the hands of a few. Rich and poor, chiefs and commoners, landowners and dependent peasants, rulers and subjects, dominant men and subordinate women, slaves and free people—these distinctions, so common in the record of world history, took shape most extensively in highly productive agricultural settings, which generated a substantial economic surplus. There the endless elaboration of such differences, for better or worse, became a major feature of those distinctive agricultural societies known to us as "civilizations."

> **PRACTICING HISTORICAL THINKING**
>
> What was revolutionary about the Agricultural Revolution?

REFLECTIONS

The Uses of the Paleolithic

Even when it is about the distant past, history is also about those who tell it in the present. We search the past, always, for our own purposes. For example, modern people were long inclined to view their Paleolithic or gathering and hunting ancestors as primitive or superstitious, unable to exercise control over nature, and ignorant of its workings. Such a view was, of course, a kind of self-congratulation, designed to highlight the "progress" of modern humankind. It was a way of saying, "Look how far we have come."

In more recent decades, however, growing numbers of people, disillusioned with modernity, have looked to the Paleolithic era for material with which to criticize, rather than celebrate, contemporary life. Feminists have found in gathering and hunting peoples a much more gender-equal society and religious thinking that featured the divine feminine, qualities that encouragingly suggested that patriarchy was neither inevitable nor eternal. Environmentalists have sometimes identified peoples in the distant past who were uniquely in tune with the natural environment rather than seeking to dominate it. Some nutritionists have advocated a "Paleolithic diet" of wild plants and animals as well suited to our physiology. Critics of modern materialism and competitive capitalism have been delighted to discover societies in which values of sharing and equality predominated over those of accumulation and hierarchy. Still others have asked, in light of the long Paleolithic era, whether the explosive population and economic growth of recent centuries should be considered normal or natural. Perhaps they are better seen as extraordinary, possibly even pathological. All of these uses of the Paleolithic have been a way of asking, "What have we lost in the mad rush to modernity, and how can we recover it?"

Both those who look with disdain on Paleolithic "backwardness" and those who praise, often quite romantically, its simplicity and equality seek to use these ancient people for their own purposes. None of us can be entirely detached when we view the past, but this is not necessarily a matter for regret. What we may lose in objectivity, we gain in passionate involvement with the historical record and with the many men and women who have inhabited it. Despite its remoteness from us in time and manner of living, the Paleolithic era resonates still in the twenty-first century, reminding us of our kinship with these distant people and the significance of that kinship to finding our own way in a very different world.

Second Thoughts

What's the Significance?

Neolithic Revolution, 10

Paleolithic era, 10

Venus figurines, 16

Dreamtime, 17

Clovis culture, 18

megafaunal extinction, 18

Austronesian migrations, 18

"the original affluent society," 22

shamans, 22

Göbekli Tepe, 24

Paleolithic settling down, 24

Fertile Crescent, 30

maize, 32

Bantu migration, 34

Banpo, 35

secondary products revolution, 36

pastoral societies, 38

Çatalhüyük, 39

chiefdoms, 40

Big Picture Questions

1. In what ways did various Paleolithic societies differ from one another, and how did they change over time?
2. The Agricultural Revolution marked a decisive and progressive turning point in human history. What evidence might you offer to support this claim, and how might you argue against it?
3. How did early agricultural societies differ from those of the Paleolithic era?
4. Was the Agricultural Revolution inevitable? Why did it occur so late in the story of humankind?
5. In what different ways did human beings relate to the natural world during the early and long phases of our history explored in the chapter?

Next Steps: For Further Study

Elizabeth Wayland Barber, *Women's Work: The First 20,000 Years* (1994). Explores the role of women in early technological development, particularly textile making.

David Christian, *This Fleeting World: A Short History of Humanity* (2008). A lovely essay by a leading world historian, which condenses parts of his earlier *Maps of Time* (2004).

Jean Clottes, *What Is Paleolithic Art?*, 2016. A personal and contemplative examination of Paleolithic art and its relationship to shamanism by a prominent French archeologist.

Steven Mithen, *After the Ice: A Global Human History, 20,000–5000 B.C.* (2004). An imaginative tour of world archeological sites during the Agricultural Revolution.

Lauren Ristvet, *In the Beginning* (2007). A brief account of human evolution, Paleolithic life, the origins of agriculture, and the First Civilizations, informed by recent archeological discoveries.

Fred Spier, *Big History and the Future of Humanity* (2011). An effort to place human history in the context of cosmic, geological, and biological history with a focus on the growth of complexity.

James Suzman, *Affluence without Abundance: The Disappearing World of the Bushmen* (2017). A thoughtful and readable account of the Bushmen, a gathering and hunting society in southern Africa, and their encounter with the modern world.

Mark B. Tauger, *Agriculture in World History* (2011). An overview of the origins and significance of farming on a global scale.

"The Agricultural Revolution," http://www.youtube.com/watch?v=Yocja_N5s1I. An eleven-minute animated survey from John Green's *Crash Course World History* series.

The Bradshaw Foundation, "The Cave Paintings of the Lascaux Cave," http://www.bradshawfoundation.com/lascaux/index.php. Text, images, and videos introduce the Paleolithic paintings from the Lascaux Cave in France.

The Australian Dreamtime

The Aboriginal, or native, peoples of Australia have inhabited their continent for tens of thousands of years, living in hundreds of distinct social and linguistic groups. Until the arrival of Europeans in the late eighteenth century, they practiced a gathering and hunting way of life. These peoples have persisted into the twenty-first century as a small minority in modern Australia, and a dwindling few of them still practice their ancient culture. Over an enormously long period of time, they developed an elaborate cosmology, or understanding of the world. Known collectively as the Dreamtime, this cosmology found expression in an evolving body of orally transmitted traditions or stories and in numerous rock art paintings scattered across Australia and frequently retouched or painted over. These stories and images linked the landscape and its human and animal inhabitants to distant events and ancient ancestors.

A contemporary Aboriginal artist, Semon Deeb, explains:

> Around the beginning the Ancestral Beings rose from the folds of the earth and stretching up to the scorching sun they called, "I am!" As each Ancestor sang out their name, "I am Snake," "I am Honey Ant," they created the most sacred of their songs. Slowly they began to move across the barren land naming all things and thus bringing them into being. Their words forming verses as the Ancestors walked about, they sang mountains, rivers and deserts into existence. Wherever they went, their songs remained, creating a web of Songlines over the Country. As they traveled, the Ancestors hunted, ate, made love, sang and danced leaving a trail of Dreaming along the songlines. Finally at the end of their journey the Ancestral Beings sang "back into" the earth where they can be seen as land formations, sleeping.[24]

Over the past two centuries, many Dreamtime stories have been collected and set down in writing, even as new versions have emerged. And the prolific rock art of ancient Aboriginal peoples, which also expressed the Dreamtime outlook, has attracted the attention of many scholars. The tales and images presented here illustrate these Aboriginal efforts to give meaning and shape to their experience.

SOURCE 1.1 Understanding Creation

People everywhere have sought to understand the beginnings of things and in doing so to frame human life in some larger and more meaningful context. In this and other stories from Australia, creation occurred in the Dreamtime, or the "time before time," when ancient ancestral beings brought into existence the latent possibilities of a world that was frozen or asleep. Then they disappeared when their work was finished. But they remained present in the sun, moon, and stars, in the features of the landscape, in the animals of the world, and in paintings on the surface of large rock formations.

■ How might you compare this story to creation accounts in other societies?

■ What is the relationship between Yhi and Baiame in creating and sustaining the world? Do they play equal roles, or is one superior to the other?

■ In what ways are human beings and other living creatures made aware of their connection to the spirit world?

Yhi Brings Life to the World | Oral tradition recorded in 20th century

In the beginning the world lay quiet, in utter darkness. There was no vegetation, no living or moving thing on the bare bones of the mountains. No wind blew across the peaks. There was no sound to break the silence.

The world was not dead. It was asleep, waiting for the soft touch of life and light. . . . Somewhere in the immensity of space Yhi [a sun goddess of light and creation] stirred in her sleep, waiting for the whisper of Baiame, the Great Spirit [a creator deity, Sky Father], to come to her.

Then the whisper came, the whisper that woke the world. . . . Yhi floated down to earth and began a pilgrimage that took her far to the west, to the east, to north, and south. Where her feet rested on the ground, there the earth leaped in ecstasy. Grass, shrubs, trees, and flowers sprang from it, lifting themselves towards the radiant source of light. Yhi's tracks crossed and recrossed until the whole earth was clothed with vegetation.

Her first joyous task completed, Yhi, the sun goddess, rested on the Nullarbor Plain. . . .

"The work of creation is well begun," Baiame said, "but it has only begun. . . . Take your light into the caverns of earth and see what will happen."

Yhi rose and made her way into the gloomy spaces beneath the surface. There were no seeds there to spring to life at her touch. Harsh shadows lurked behind the light. . . . "Sleep, sleep, sleep," the evil spirits wailed, but the shapes had been waiting for the caressing warmth of the sun goddess. Filmy wings opened, bodies raised themselves on long legs. . . . Soon Yhi was surrounded by myriads of insects, creeping, flying, swarming from every dark corner. . . . They followed her out into the world, into the sunshine, into the embrace of the waiting grass and leaves and flowers. . . . [Now] Yhi sped up the hill slopes. . . . She disappeared into the caverns, chilled by the black ice that hung from the roofs and walls. . . . Birds and animals gathered round her, singing in their own voices, racing down the slopes, choosing homes for themselves, drinking in a new world of light, colour, sound, and movement.

"It is good. My world is alive," Baiame said.

Yhi took his hand and called in a golden voice to all the things she had brought to life. "This is the land of Baiame. It is yours forever, to enjoy. Baiame is the Great Spirit. He will guard you and listen to your requests. I have nearly finished my work, so you must listen to my words."

"I shall send you the seasons of summer and winter—summer with warmth which ripens fruit ready for eating, winter for sleeping while the cold winds sweep through the world and blow away the refuse of summer. These are changes that I shall send you . . . , the creatures of my love. Soon I shall leave you and live far above in the sky. When you die your bodies will remain here, but your spirits will come to live with me."

One by one the birds and animals woke up, as they have done every morning since the first dawn. After the first shock of darkness they knew that day would succeed night, that there would always be a new sunrise and sunset, giving hours of daylight for work and play, and night for sleeping. . . .

One last deed remained to be done, because the dark hours of night were frightening for some of the creatures. Yhi sent the Morning Star to herald her coming each day. Then, feeling sorry for the star in her loneliness, she gave her Bahloo, the Moon, for her husband. A sigh of satisfaction arose from the earth when the white moon sailed majestically across the sky, giving birth to myriads of stars, making a new glory in the heavens.

Source: "Yhi Brings Life to the World," in A. W. Reed, *Aboriginal Stories of Australia* (Chatsworth, New South Wales: New Holland, 1980), 11–14.

■ ■ ■

SOURCE 1.2 **The Rainbow Serpent**

A common theme of many Dreamtime stories involved the Rainbow Serpent, which was usually associated with creation, fertility, or social harmony. Images of the Rainbow Serpent in the rock art of Australia date back many thousands of years. (See an image of the Rainbow Serpent on page 17.)

■ What does this version of the Rainbow Serpent story seek to explain?

■ In what ways does the story relate to social problems of Aboriginal peoples?

The Rainbow Serpent Awakens | Oral tradition recorded in 20th century

---

In the Dreamtime all earth lay sleeping. Nothing moved. Nothing grew. One day the Rainbow Serpent awoke from her slumber and came out from under the ground. She travelled far and wide and eventually grew tired and curled up and slept. She left marks of her sleeping body and her winding tracks. Then she returned to the place where she had first appeared, and called to the frogs, "Come out!"

The frogs came out slow because their bellies were heavy with water, which they had stored in their sleep. The Rainbow Serpent tickled their stomachs and when the frogs laughed, water ran all over the earth to fill the tracks of the Rainbow Serpents' wanderings. This is how lakes and rivers were formed.

With water, grass and trees sprang up. Also all animals awoke and followed the Rainbow Serpent across the land. They were happy on earth and each lived and gathered food with his own tribe. Some animals live in rocks, others on the plains and others in trees and in the air.

The Rainbow Serpent made laws that they all were to obey, but some became quarrelsome and made trouble. The Rainbow Serpent said, "Those who keep my laws will be rewarded; I shall give them human form. Those who break my laws will be punished and turned to stone, never to walk the earth again."

The lawbreakers became stone and turned to mountains and hills, but those who kept the laws were turned into human form. The Rainbow Serpent gave each of them their own totem of the animal, bird or reptile from whence they came. The tribes knew themselves by their totems. Kangaroo, emu, carpet snake, and many, many more. So no one would starve, the Rainbow Serpent ruled that no man should eat of his totem, but only of other totems. This way there was food for everyone.

The tribes lived together on the land given to them by the Rainbow Serpent or Mother of Life and knew the land would always be theirs, and no one should ever take it from them.

Source: http://www.expedition360.com/australia_lessons_literacy/2001/09/dreamtime_stories_the_rainbow.html

■ ■ ■

SOURCE 1.3 **Explaining the World in Aboriginal Rock Art** ▶

The Dreamtime found expression, not only in orally transmitted stories, but also in the rock art of the Aboriginal peoples all across Australia. Created in the unrecorded past by unknown artists, some of these paintings date to 20,000 or more years ago, and many have been repainted or touched up repeatedly over the centuries. Aboriginal peoples have understood these images, not as the work of human artists, but as the actual ancestral beings themselves, able to convey their spiritual energy to their descendants. By engaging with these paintings, Aboriginal peoples "explain and map the landscape. . . . Rock-art is a tangible expression of the continuing presence of Ancestral Beings who moulded and humanized the landscape."[25]

In Source 1.3, painted on a rock face in northern Australia's Kakudu National Park, the largest and main figure at the top is Namondjok, a Creation Ancestor, who according to some accounts can be seen in the sky at night as a dark spot in the Milky Way galaxy. To the right is Namarrgon, or Lightning Man, who generates the tremendous lightning storms that occur during the rainy season. The arc around his body represents the lightning, while the axes on his head, elbow, and feet are used to split the dark clouds, creating thunder and lightning. The female figure beneath Namondjok is Barrginj, the wife of Lightning Man, while below her is a group of elaborately dressed people.

■ What might an Aboriginal viewer learn about nature from this painting?

■ What might he or she understand about the cosmic hierarchy and the position of human beings within it?

■ Why do you think the artist positioned ordinary people at the bottom of the picture? What might they be doing? Could the positioning of Barrginj have meaning as well?

■ Notice the distinctive X-ray style, which depicts the internal bones and organs of the figures while also showing their outward appearance. What intentions might lie behind such a style?

Namondjok and the Lightning Man

Kakadu National Park, Northern Territory, Australia/
Werner Forman Archive/Bridgeman Images

■ ■ ■

SOURCE 1.4 Understanding Death

Death marks the end of a life, but an awareness of death shapes much of the living of our lives. And so humans everywhere have sought to understand death, with an eye perhaps to avoiding or delaying it. In the Australian Dreamtime, the immortal ancestor Purukapali was responsible for the introduction of death into the world. The story that follows is one version of this event.

■ How does this story account for the entry of death into human life?

■ What responses to death are suggested in the story?

■ Does such a story carry any meaning to people today?

How Death Came: The Purukapali Myth │ Oral tradition recorded in 20th century

In the pleasant land of the Tiwi people, Purukapali lived with his wife, Bima, and their infant son, Djinini. This was in the earliest days when spirits became men and death had not yet come to the earth. In their camp also lived Purukapali's younger brother, Tjapara, strong and handsome. Many times the brothers stalked wallaby together, but most often it was Purukapali who carried game into the camp and received the women's praise.

Tjapara had no wife and he hungered for Bima. One morning after the brothers had returned from the hunt, Bima rose and placed the sleeping Djinini beside her husband, who was skinning a slain wallaby.

"I go find yams," she said. "Guard the child. He will sleep now and will have my milk when I return."

She picked up a net bag and walked off into the bush. Tjapara watched her swinging hips and said, "I saw shellfish at the shore. I will go gather them," and he strode off toward the beach, leaving Puru-kapali with the sleeping child.

As soon as he was well out of sight, Tjapara quickly circled back through the bush and came upon Bima as she bent over her digging stick. Softly he crept upon her and clasped her from behind. "Lie with me," he urged.

[*And so she did, spending the entire day with Tjapara. Meanwhile, her young child died for lack of his mother's milk. When she finally returned to her home*], she found Djinini on the grass, cold and still. Death had come to him in the early darkness. . . . Now Purukapali turned on his wife. "He was hungry. He cried for you and you did not come. Now he is gone from us and will not return," said the father. . . . Bima began to moan and beat her breast. "I am a bad woman, for I let my son die," she cried. . . .

Bima lashed out at Tjapara in despair. "You killed him!" she accused, "for you would not let me go." Now did Purukapali understand. . . . He picked up a forked fighting stick and attacked. "You, too, shall die!" he screamed at his brother. . . . Tjapara fled to a tall tree and frantically began to climb. When he reached the top limb, he let out a great shout and leaped into the sky, rising higher and higher until he reached the moon.

Purukapali returned to camp and took Djinini's body in his arms. "I shall die with my son," he announced to the Tiwi people. "And all who now live also shall die." Then he danced the first ceremony of death and sang of the events that led to it. "This shall be your pukamani [funeral] ceremony," he decreed, "and you shall dance it to remember those who die." Purukapali wrapped his son in paperbark, walked backward into the sea, and disappeared. As he sank beneath the surface, a whirlpool formed which marks the spot to this day.

Bima lived on, but grief soon made her haggard and old. She too wandered about the camp, complaining in a shrill voice until she too died. Her spirit lived on as the curlew bird, which still flits and cries mournfully about the beaches.

Tjapara became the Moon Man. He can be seen in the night sky, his face marked by the bruises and wounds that Purukapali inflicted. He still feels Purukapali at his heels, for he never ceases his restless journey. Hungry from his travels, he gorges on crabmeat, growing rounder and fatter each day until he has feasted so much he falls sick. His wasting body is the waning moon. Each month he dies, but after three days he comes back to life and begins his journey once again. His loneliness is over, for he has found many wives, the planets, who accompany him on his journey across the sky.

So death comes to the people of earth, the Tiwi say, but always life returns.

Source: Louis A. Allen, *Time before Morning* (New York: Thomas Y. Crowell, 1975), 215–19.

■ ■ ■

SOURCE 1.5 Hunting in Aboriginal Rock Art ▶

This painting depicts a hunting scene, featuring either ordinary people or the thin Mimi spirits, said to inhabit the nooks and crannies of the area's rock formations and credited with teaching humans how to paint, hunt, and cook kangaroo meat. Notice the spears that the hunters carry. Various kinds of spears and spear-throwing devices had earlier replaced or supplemented the boomerang. The painting is located at the Ubirr art site in Australia's Kakadu National Park, where rock art dates to many thousands of years ago.

■ If the painting depicts real people or hunters, what purposes might it serve?

■ What different understandings might emerge if the painting is seen as portraying Mimi spirits?

■ How do Sources 1.3 and 1.5 reflect the outlook of the Dreamtime stories?

Aboriginal Hunters

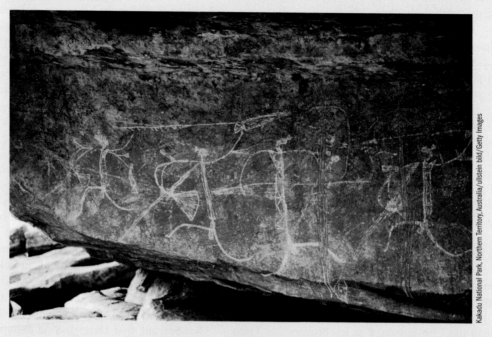

Kakadu National Park, Northern Territory, Australia/ullstein bild/Getty Images

DOING HISTORY

1. **Considering human commonality and diversity:** The study of world history highlights both the common humanity of people from all times and places and the vast differences that have separated particular cultures from one another. How might these sources illustrate both of these perspectives?

2. **Linking sources and text narrative:** How do these sources support or amplify the narrative account of the Paleolithic era in Chapter 1? How might they challenge or contradict that narrative?

3. **Considering the relationship of technology and culture:** How might the gathering and hunting technology of these Australian peoples have shaped their cultural understandings as expressed in these stories and paintings? Does it make sense to evaluate technology as more or less "advanced"? Should culture be assessed in the same way?

4. **Pondering relevance:** How might these sources from a very different time and place speak to us in the modern world of the twenty-first century? Or are they only of historical interest?

5. **Thinking about sources:** These stories were only committed to writing over the past two centuries and the paintings may have been redone many times; how does this affect their usefulness as historical sources for the distant past?

Australian Aboriginal Culture

Since written sources are absent, stories and art are often ambiguous, and the dating of events is uncertain, scholars interested in ancient Aboriginal culture have relied heavily on observations and accounts from more recent times. What follows are two such descriptions of ancient Aboriginal life. Voice 1.1, focusing on economic and social life, comes from a historian, Dale Kerwin, who is himself an Aboriginal Australian. Voice 1.2, from an anthropologist, Barbara West, examines the Dreamtime cosmology of Aboriginal peoples.

■ To what extent do these selections emphasize broad similarities between Aboriginal and more modern societies, and in what ways do they stress the differences?

■ What conception of "time" is conveyed in Voice 1.2 and its notion of "the everywhen"? In what ways does this Aboriginal understanding compare with how modern historians approach time?

■ How do these selections complement or challenge the narrative description of Paleolithic life in Chapter 1?

■ **Integrating Primary and Secondary Sources:** How might evidence from the Dreamtime stories and rock art support or challenge the ideas contained in these selections?

VOICE 1.1

Dale Kerwin on the Economic and Social Life of Aboriginal Australians | 2012

Aboriginal people mastered the environment and because of this had ample spare time to pursue other activities such as the arts and political gatherings. Not all people were engaged in food gathering activities; some were engaged in ceremonial activities and trade. . . . [S]ome Aboriginal people choose to travel long distances to trade nuts, stories, and material goods. . . . There is much evidence that Aboriginal society was, and is, dynamic with the sharing of ceremonies and songs with each other and the adoption of various creator spirits. . . . The dynamic nature of Aboriginal society can also be seen in the development of technologies that master the environment. The spearthrower

is a multipurpose tool, which when used as a launcher would extend the throwing range of a spear. It would also be used for carrying tools, so that it became a toolbox. The spearthrower was also used as digging tool and a bowl for food and the stone adze attached to one end would be used as a knife. . . . Aboriginal societies had some members who toiled and collected sufficient food to sustain people in specialized positions such as religious practitioners, specialized craft practitioners, . . . or merchants.

Source: Dale Kerwin, *Aboriginal Dreaming Paths and Trading Routes* (Eastbourne: Sussex Academic Press, 2012), 8, 9, 14.

VOICE 1.2

Barbara West on Aboriginal Dreamtime Cosmology | 2010

Dreaming stories form the basis of Australian Aboriginal religion. They provide explanations for why the world is the way it is. They usually relate to the actions of ancestors, who created the world. The world depicted in these stories is much more complex than that of most westerners for whom the natural and supernatural, past and present, sacred and profane are separate. For Aboriginal Australians, these planes of existence are intertwined. Ancient ancestors created the world and everything in it including rocks, lakes, animals, humans, the wind, and rain, but are also active in the present. Their past actions cannot be separated from present actions especially in ritual which remakes the world each time it is undertaken. The songlines or footprints of these ancient ancestors continue to cross the Australian continent and carry information back and forth from one community to another. Sacred spaces along these lines coexist with everyday or profane spaces, often materialize in rocks, rivers, and other geological features. . . . Anthropologists sometimes use "the everywhen" to refer to the context of the Dreaming stories in order to indicate their timelessness.

Source: Barbara A. West and Francis Murphy, *A Brief History of Australia* (New York: Facts on File, 2010), 27.

First Civilizations

Cities, States, and Unequal Societies

3500 B.C.E.–600 B.C.E.

Something New: The Emergence of Civilizations
Introducing the First Civilizations
The Question of Origins
An Urban Revolution

The Erosion of Equality
Hierarchies of Class
Hierarchies of Gender
Patriarchy in Practice

The Rise of the State
Coercion and Consent
Writing and Accounting
The Grandeur of Kings

Comparing Mesopotamia and Egypt
Environment and Culture
Cities and States
Interaction and Exchange

Reflections: "Civilization": What's in a Word?

"Sometimes the weight of civilization can be overwhelming. The fast pace . . . the burdens of relationships . . . the political strife . . . the technological complexity — it's enough to make you dream of escaping to a simpler life more in touch with nature."[1] Found on the website of an organization called Mother Nature Network, this expression of discontent with modernity, written in 2010, reflects the perspectives of the back-to-the-land movement that began in the mid-1960s as an alternative to the pervasive materialism of modern life. Growing numbers of urban dwellers, perhaps as many as a million in North America, exchanged their busy city lives for a few acres of rural land and a very different way of living.

This urge to "escape from civilization" has long been a central feature in modern life. It found expression in Henry David Thoreau's musings on his sojourn at Walden Pond. It is a large part of the "cowboy" image in American culture, and it permeates environmentalist efforts to protect the remaining wilderness areas of the country. Nor has this impulse been limited to modern societies and the Western world. The ancient Chinese teachers of Daoism likewise urged their followers to abandon the structured and demanding world of urban and civilized life and to immerse themselves in the eternal patterns of the natural order. It is a strange paradox that we count the creation of civilizations among the major achievements of humankind and yet people within them have often sought to escape the constraints, artificiality, hierarchies, and other discontents of civilized living. ■

« **Raherka and Mersankh** Writing was among the defining features of civilizations almost everywhere. In ancient Egyptian civilization, the scribes who possessed this skill enjoyed both social prestige and political influence. This famous statue shows Raherka, an "inspector of the scribes" during Egypt's Fifth Dynasty (ca. 2350 B.C.E.), in an affectionate pose with his wife, Mersankh.

So what exactly are these civilizations that have generated such ambivalent responses among their inhabitants? When, where, and how did they first arise in human history? What changes did they bring to the people who lived within them? Why might some people criticize or seek to escape from them?

As historians commonly use the term, "civilization" represents a new and particular type of human society, made possible by the immense productivity of the Agricultural Revolution. Such societies encompassed far larger populations than any earlier form of human community and for the first time concentrated some of those people in sizable cities. Both within and beyond these cities, people were organized and controlled by states whose leaders could use force to compel obedience. Profound differences in economic function, skill, wealth, and status sharply divided the people of civilizations, making them far less equal and subject to much greater oppression than had been the case in earlier Paleolithic communities, agricultural villages, pastoral societies, or chiefdoms. Pyramids, temples, palaces, elaborate sculptures, written literature, and complex calendars, as well as more elaborate class and gender hierarchies, slavery, and large-scale warfare—all of these have been among the cultural products of civilization.

SEEKING THE MAIN POINT

What distinguished "civilizations" from earlier Paleolithic and Neolithic societies? And in what ways did these "civilizations" differ from one another?

Something New: The Emergence of Civilizations

Like agriculture, civilization was a global phenomenon, showing up independently in seven major locations scattered around the world during the several millennia after 3500 B.C.E. and in a number of other smaller expressions as well (see Map 2.1). In the long run of human history, these civilizations—small breakthroughs to new city- and state-based societies—gradually absorbed, overran, or displaced people practicing other ways of living. Over the next 5,000 years, civilization, as a unique kind of human community, gradually encompassed ever-larger numbers of people and extended over ever-larger territories, even as particular civilizations rose, fell, revived, and changed.

Introducing the First Civilizations

Guided Reading Question

■ **CHANGE**
When and where did the First Civilizations emerge?

The earliest of these civilizations emerged around 3500 B.C.E. to 3000 B.C.E. in three places. One was the "cradle" of Middle Eastern civilization, expressed in the many and competing city-states of **Sumer**. Sumer was located in the southern reaches of Mesopotamia, a term referring to the region between the Tigris and Euphrates rivers, mostly in present-day Iraq. Much studied by archeologists and historians, Sumerian civilization likely gave rise to the world's earliest written language, which was used initially by officials to record the goods received by various temples. Later, Sumerian cities were absorbed into the larger empires of Akkad, Babylon, and Assyria, which encompassed much of Mesopotamia. Almost simultaneously, the Nile River valley in northeastern Africa witnessed the emergence

Landmarks for Chapter 2*

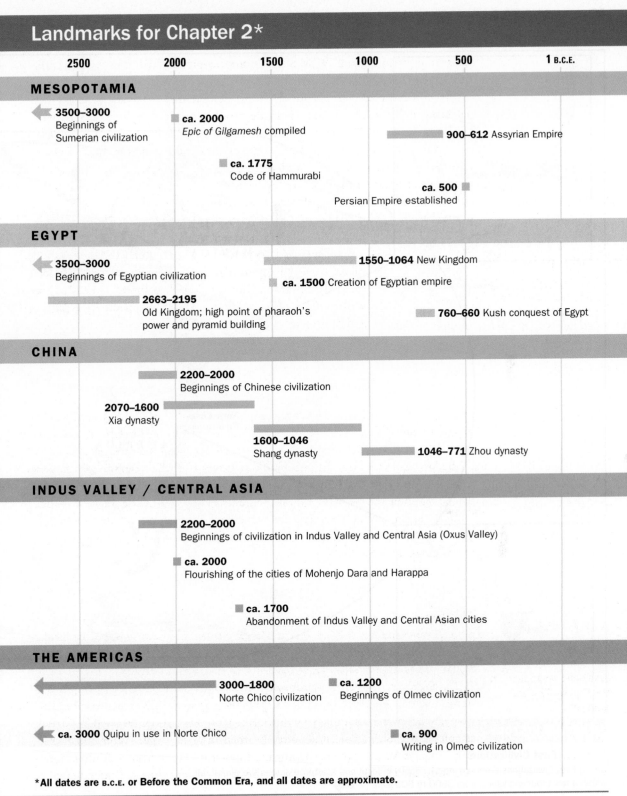

| | 2500 | 2000 | 1500 | 1000 | 500 | 1 B.C.E. |

MESOPOTAMIA

3500–3000
Beginnings of
Sumerian civilization

ca. 2000
Epic of Gilgamesh compiled

900–612 Assyrian Empire

ca. 1775
Code of Hammurabi

ca. 500
Persian Empire established

EGYPT

3500–3000
Beginnings of Egyptian civilization

1550–1064 New Kingdom

ca. 1500 Creation of Egyptian empire

2663–2195
Old Kingdom; high point of pharaoh's
power and pyramid building

760–660 Kush conquest of Egypt

CHINA

2200–2000
Beginnings of Chinese civilization

2070–1600
Xia dynasty

1600–1046
Shang dynasty

1046–771 Zhou dynasty

INDUS VALLEY / CENTRAL ASIA

2200–2000
Beginnings of civilization in Indus Valley and Central Asia (Oxus Valley)

ca. 2000
Flourishing of the cities of Mohenjo Dara and Harappa

ca. 1700
Abandonment of Indus Valley and Central Asian cities

THE AMERICAS

3000–1800
Norte Chico civilization

ca. 1200
Beginnings of Olmec civilization

ca. 3000 Quipu in use in Norte Chico

ca. 900
Writing in Olmec civilization

*All dates are B.C.E. or Before the Common Era, and all dates are approximate.

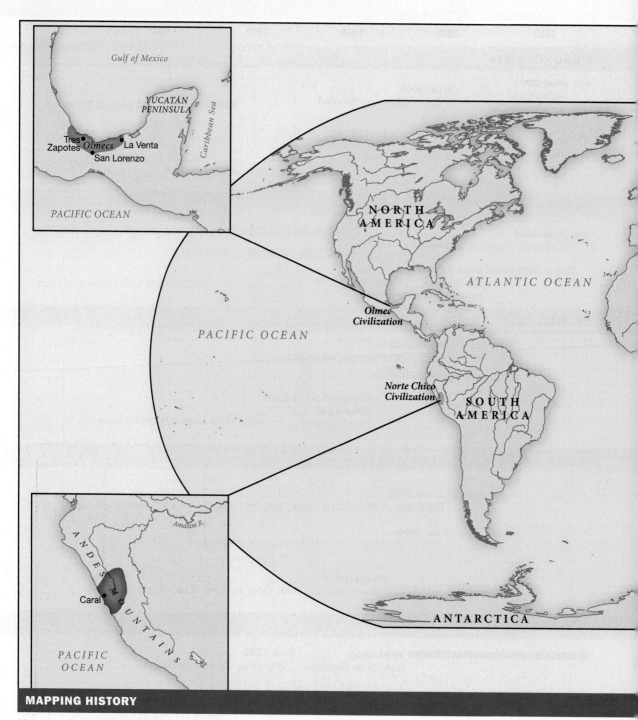

Map 2.1 First Civilizations

Seven First Civilizations emerged independently in locations scattered across the planet, all within a few thousand years, from 3500 to 600 B.C.E.

READING THE MAP: Which First Civilizations both emerged along major river valleys and built major urban centers along those rivers?

MAKING CONNECTIONS: Compare this map with Map 1.3, which shows areas where agriculture emerged independently. To what extent did First Civilizations take shape in the same regions where agriculture also emerged?

Caral, a City of Norte Chico

In early 2001, published reports of archeological excavations at a site called Caral set off a firestorm of amazed commentary in both academic circles and the popular media. And no wonder! Archeologists had uncovered, about fourteen miles inland from the coast of Peru, an urban center dating to the time of the Egyptian pyramids, around 2600 B.C.E., far earlier than any previously known urban settlements in the Americas. Thus Egyptian and Mesopotamian claims to the status of "First Civilizations" were now joined by those of Peru.

Stonework at Caral.

Most obviously impressive about Caral was its elaborate and monumental architecture. One of its six pyramids stood sixty feet tall and occupied an area the size of four football fields. Circular sunken plazas, temples, an amphitheater, stairways, and many residential spaces, including apartment-style complexes, likewise emerged from the excavations. An intricate irrigation system funneled water from the nearby Supe River to agricultural fields.

Smaller finds at the site convey something about ordinary life in Caral. A clay figure with long hair, a colorful costume, and a decorative necklace suggested a shaman, who served as an intermediary between the gods and humans at Caral. The skeleton of a baby, wrapped in layers of fine cloth, had been carefully buried with a necklace of stone beads. Dozens of beautifully carved flutes and cornets made of condor, pelican, deer, and llama bones revealed an instrumental musical tradition. A *quipu*, consisting of knotted cords and later widely used by the Incas for accounting purposes, pointed to an element of cultural continuity in the Andes region that spanned over 4,000 years.

Archeologists also discovered remains of plants that enhanced sexual performance, as well as hallucinogenic drugs, long used in the Andes and elsewhere in religious

photo: Richard Hirano/El Comercio de Peru/Newscom

of the civilization of **Egypt**, famous for its pharaohs and pyramids, as well as a separate civilization known as **Nubia**, farther south along the Nile. Unlike the city-states of Sumer, Egyptian civilization took shape as a unified territorial state in which cities were rather less prominent. Later in this chapter, we will compare these two First Civilizations in greater detail.

Less well known and only recently investigated by scholars was a third early civilization that was developing along the central coast of Peru from roughly 3000 B.C.E. to 1800 B.C.E., at about the same time as the civilizations of Egypt and Sumer. This desert region received very little rainfall, but it was punctuated by dozens of rivers that brought the snowmelt of the adjacent Andes Mountains to the Pacific Ocean. Along a thirty-mile stretch of that coast and in the nearby interior, a series of some twenty-five urban centers emerged in an area known as **Norte Chico**, the largest of which was **Caral**, in the Supe River valley. (See Zooming In: Caral, a City of Norte Chico, above.)

Norte Chico was a distinctive civilization in many ways. Its cities were smaller than those of Sumer and show less evidence of economic specialization.

ceremonies. A possible hint about Caral's religious outlook derives from a drawing etched on a gourd, which shows a sharp-toothed figure wearing a hat and holding long sticks or rods in each hand. It clearly resembles the Staff God prevalent in later Andean civilizations. And the remains of a young man found in a ceremonial place suggest the possibility of human sacrifice.

Nor was Caral an isolated instance of urban living. More than twenty other related sites in the river valleys of the area make up what scholars are now calling the Norte Chico civilization. Caral and other inland cities had close relationships with coastal communities, exchanging their agricultural products such as cotton, beans, squash, and sweet potatoes for sardines and anchovies, whose bones have been found in abundance in Caral. Goods from as far away as present-day Ecuador, the high Andes, and the rain forests that lay to the east suggest a network of wider relationships.

But what was missing from Caral has proved equally intriguing. Grain-based agriculture, pottery, metallurgy,

The bone flutes found at Caral.

and writing—all features of urban life in Egypt and Mesopotamia—were noticeably absent in Caral. Do we therefore need to revisit the criteria for defining a "First Civilization"? Warfare too apparently played little role in Caral, as no walls, fortresses, weapons, or signs of violent destruction have appeared in the archeological record. Does this mean that Caral uniquely enjoyed "a thousand years of peace," as one of the lead excavators suggested? Was trade rather than warfare the stimulus to creating a complex society? Perhaps so, but it is early in the study of this distinctive civilization.

QUESTIONS

In what ways do recent discoveries at Caral invite reconsideration of Andean civilization and of the history of the earliest civilizations generally? What do you find most surprising about Caral?

The economy was based to an unusual degree on an extremely rich fishing industry in anchovies and sardines along the coast. These items apparently were exchanged for cotton, essential for fishing nets, as well as food crops such as squash, beans, and guava, all of which were grown by inland people in the river valleys using irrigation agriculture. Unlike Egyptian and Sumerian societies, this Peruvian civilization did not rest on grain-based farming; its people did not develop pottery or writing; and few sculptures, carvings, or drawings have been uncovered so far. Furthermore, the cities of Norte Chico lacked defensive walls, and archeologists have discovered little evidence of warfare, such as burned buildings and mutilated corpses. Norte Chico apparently "lighted a cultural fire" in the Andes and established a pattern for the many Andean civilizations that followed—Chavín, Moche, Wari, Tiwanaku, and Inca.[2]

Somewhat later, at least four additional First Civilizations made their appearance. In the Indus and Saraswati river valleys of what is now Pakistan, a remarkable civilization arose during the third millennium B.C.E. By 2000 B.C.E., it embraced a far larger area than Sumer, Egypt, or coastal Peru and was expressed primarily in its elaborately planned cities. All across this huge area, common patterns prevailed: standardized weights, measures, architectural styles, even the size of bricks. As elsewhere, irrigated agriculture provided the economic foundation for the civilization, and a written language, thus far undeciphered, provides evidence of a literate culture for the few.

Unlike its Middle Eastern counterparts, the **Indus Valley civilization** apparently generated no palaces, temples, elaborate graves, kings, or warrior classes. In short, the archeological evidence provides little indication of a political hierarchy or centralized state. This absence of evidence has sent scholars scrambling to provide an explanation for the obvious specialization, coordination, and complexity that the Indus Valley civilization exhibited. A series of small republics, rule by priests, an early form of the caste system—all of these have been suggested as alternative mechanisms of integration in this first South Asian civilization. Although no one knows for sure, the possibility that the Indus Valley may have housed a sophisticated civilization without a corresponding state has excited the imagination of scholars. (See Working with Evidence: Indus Valley Civilization, page 84.)

Whatever its organization, the local environmental impact of the Indus Valley civilization, as of many others, was heavy and eventually undermined its ecological foundations. Repeated irrigation increased the amount of salt in the soil and lowered crop yields. The making of mud bricks, dried in ovens, required an enormous amount of wood for fuel, generating large-scale deforestation and soil erosion. Thus environmental degradation contributed significantly to the abandonment of these magnificent cities by about 1700 B.C.E. Nonetheless, many features of this early civilization—ceremonial bathing, burning of incense, ritual fire altars, yoga positions, bulls and elephants as religious symbols, styles of clothing and jewelry—continued to nourish the later civilization of the Indian subcontinent.[3]

The early Chinese civilization, dating to perhaps 2200 B.C.E., was very different from that of the Indus Valley. The ideal—if not always the reality—of a centralized state was evident from the days of the Xia (shyah) dynasty (2070–1600 B.C.E.), whose legendary monarch Wu organized flood control projects that "mastered the waters and made them to flow in great channels." Subsequent dynasties—the Shang (1600–1046 B.C.E.) and the Zhou (JOH) (1046–771 B.C.E.)—substantially enlarged the Chinese state, erected lavish tombs for their rulers, and buried thousands of

Shang Dynasty Bronze This bronze tiger, created around 1100 B.C.E., illustrates Chinese skill in working with bronze and the mythological or religious significance of the tiger as a messenger between heaven and the human world. (© Martha Avery/Getty Images)

human sacrificial victims to accompany them in the next world. By the Zhou dynasty, a distinctive Chinese political ideology had emerged, featuring a ruler, known as the Son of Heaven. This monarch served as an intermediary between Heaven and Earth and ruled by the Mandate of Heaven only so long as he governed with benevolence and maintained social harmony among his people. This civilization also had writing; an early form of written Chinese has been discovered on numerous oracle bones, which were intended to predict the future and to assist China's rulers in the task of governing. Like Egypt, China has experienced an impressive continuity of identity as a distinct civilization from its earliest expression into modern times.

Central Asia was the site of yet another First Civilization. In the Oxus or Amu Darya River valley and nearby desert oases (what is now northern Afghanistan and southern Turkmenistan), a quite distinctive and separate civilization took shape very quickly after 2200 B.C.E.

An Oxus Valley Axe Head Dating to around 2000 B.C.E., this exquisitely wrought axe head derives from the Oxus Valley civilization. It features in the center a heroic human figure with a bird's head and talons fighting with a wild boar on the upper right and a winged dragon on the lower left. (The Metropolitan Museum of Art, New York, NY, USA/Purchase, Harris Brisbane Dick Fund and James N. Spear and Schimmel Foundation Inc. Gifts, 1982/agefotostock Art Collection/AGE Fotostock)

Within two centuries, a number of substantial fortified centers had emerged, containing residential compounds, artisan workshops, and temples, all surrounded by impressive walls and gates. Economically based on irrigation agriculture and stock raising, this **Central Asian** or **Oxus civilization** had a distinctive cultural style, expressed in its architecture, ceramics, burial techniques, seals, and more, though it did not develop a literate culture. Evidence for an aristocratic social hierarchy comes from depictions of gods and men in widely differing dress performing various functions, from eating at a banquet to driving chariots to carrying heavy burdens. Visitors to this civilization would have found occasional goods from China, India, and Mesopotamia, as well as products from pastoral nomads of the steppe land and the forest dwellers of Siberia. According to a leading historian, this Central Asian civilization was the focal point of a "Eurasian-wide system of intellectual and commercial exchange."[4] Compared to Egyptian and Mesopotamian civilizations, however, it had a relatively brief history, for by 1700 B.C.E., it had faded away as a civilization, at about the same time as a similar fate befell its Indus Valley counterpart. Its cities were abandoned and apparently forgotten until their resurrection by archeologists in the twentieth century. And yet its influence persisted, as elements of this civilization's cultural style show up much later in Iran, India, and the eastern Mediterranean world.

A final First Civilization, known as the Olmec, took shape around 1200 B.C.E. along the coast of the Gulf of Mexico near present-day Veracruz in southern Mexico. Based on an agricultural economy of maize, beans, and squash, Olmec cities arose from a series of competing chiefdoms and became ceremonial centers filled with elaborately decorated temples, altars, pyramids, and tombs of rulers. The most famous artistic legacy of the Olmecs lay in some seventeen colossal basalt heads, weighing twenty tons or more (see the "Olmec Head" image, page 73). Recent discoveries suggest that the Olmecs may well have created the first written language in the Americas by about 900 B.C.E. Sometimes regarded as the "mother civilization" of Mesoamerica, **Olmec civilization** generated cultural patterns—mound building, artistic styles, urban planning, a game played with a rubber ball, ritual sacrifice, and bloodletting by rulers—that spread widely throughout the region and influenced subsequent civilizations, such as the Maya and Teotihuacán.

Beyond these seven First Civilizations, other smaller civilizations also flourished. Lying south of Egypt in the Nile Valley, an early Nubian civilization (3400–3200 B.C.E.) known as Ta-Seti was clearly distinctive and independent of its northern neighbor, although Nubia was later involved in a long and often contentious relationship with Egypt. Likewise in China, a large city known as Sanxingdui, rich in bronze sculptures and much else, arose separately but at the same time as the more well-known Shang dynasty. As a new form of human society, civilization was beginning its long march toward encompassing almost all of humankind by the twentieth century. At the time, however, these breakthroughs to new forms of culture and society were small islands of innovation in a sea of people living in much older ways.

The Question of Origins

Scholars of all kinds—archeologists, anthropologists, sociologists, and historians—have been arguing about the origins of civilization for a very long time, with no end in sight. Amid all the controversy, one thing seems reasonably clear: civilizations had their roots in the Agricultural Revolution. That is the reason they appeared so late in the human story, for only an agricultural technology permitted human communities to produce sufficient surplus to support large populations and the specialized or elite minorities who did not themselves produce food. But not all agricultural societies or chiefdoms developed into civilizations, so something else must have been involved. It is the search for this "something else" that has provoked such great debate among scholars.

The need to organize large-scale irrigation projects, growing populations, the desire to protect favored groups, the stimulus of trade, the demands of warfare—all of these have figured in the debate about the origins of civilization. Geography surely played a role as well, for civilizations often took shape in biologically rich and productive environments such as wetlands, estuaries, and river basins. Anthropologist Robert

Guided Reading Question
....
■ **CHANGE**
What accounts for the initial breakthroughs to civilization?

Carneiro combined several of these factors in a thoughtful approach to the question. He argued that a growing density of population, producing more congested and competitive societies, was a fundamental motor of change, especially in areas where rich agricultural land was limited, either by geography (oceans, deserts, mountains) or by powerful neighboring societies. Such settings provided incentives for innovations, such as irrigation or plows that could produce more food, because opportunities for territorial expansion were not readily available. But circumscribed environments with dense populations also generated intense competition among rival groups, which led to repeated warfare. A strong and highly organized state was a decided advantage in such competition. Because losers could not easily flee to new lands, they were absorbed into the winner's society as a lower class. Successful leaders of the winning side emerged as elites with an enlarged base of land, a class of subordinated workers, and a powerful state at their disposal—in short, a civilization.[5]

Although such a process was relatively rapid by world history standards, it took many generations, centuries, or perhaps millennia to evolve. It was, of course, an unconscious undertaking in which the participants had little sense of the long-term outcome as they coped with the practical problems of life on a day-to-day basis. What is surprising, though, is the rough similarity of the outcome in many widely separated places from about 3500 B.C.E. to the beginning of the Common Era.

However they got started (and much about this is still guesswork), the First Civilizations, once established, represented a very different kind of human society than anything that came before. All of them were based on highly productive agricultural economies. Various forms of irrigation, drainage, terracing, and flood control enabled these early civilizations to tap the food-producing potential of their regions more intensively. All across the Afro-Eurasian hemisphere, though not in the Americas, animal-drawn plows and metalworking greatly enhanced the productivity of farming. Ritual sacrifice, sometimes including people, accompanied the growth of civilization, and the new rulers normally served as high priests, their right to rule legitimated by association with the sacred.

An Urban Revolution

It was the resources from agriculture that made possible one of the most distinctive features of the First Civilizations—cities. What would an agricultural villager have made of **Uruk**, ancient Mesopotamia's largest city? Uruk had walls more than twenty feet tall and a population around 50,000 in the third millennium B.C.E. At the city's center, visible for miles around, was a stepped pyramid, or ziggurat, topped with a temple (see the photo of a ziggurat on page 71). Inside the city, this village visitor would have found other temples as well, serving as centers of ritual performance and as places for the redistribution of stored food. Numerous craftspeople labored as masons, copper workers, and weavers and in many other specialties, while bureaucrats helped administer the city. It was, surely, a "vibrant, noisy, smelly, sometimes bewildering and dangerous, but also exciting place."[6] Here is how the

Epic of Gilgamesh, Mesopotamia's ancient epic poem dating to around 2000 B.C.E., describes the city:

> Come then, Enkidu, to ramparted Uruk, / Where fellows are resplendent in
>   holiday clothing,
> Where every day is set for celebration, / Where harps and drums are played.
> And the harlots too, they are fairest of form, / Rich in beauty, full of delights,
> Even the great gods are kept from sleeping at night.[7]

**Guided Reading
Question**

■ **CHANGE**
What was the role
of cities in the early
civilizations?

Equally impressive to a village visitor would have been the city of **Mohenjo Daro** (moe-hen-joe DAHR-oh), which flourished along the banks of the Indus River around 2000 B.C.E. With a population of perhaps 40,000, Mohenjo Daro and its sister city of **Harappa** featured large, richly built houses of two or three stories, complete with indoor plumbing, luxurious bathrooms, and private wells. Streets were laid out in a grid-like pattern, and beneath the streets ran a complex sewage system. Workers lived in row upon row of standardized two-room houses. Grand public buildings, including what seems to be a huge public bath, graced the city, while an enormous citadel was surrounded by a brick wall some forty-five feet high.

Even larger, though considerably later, was the Mesoamerican city of Teoti-huacán (tay-uh-tee-wah-KAHN), located in the central valley of Mexico. It housed perhaps 150,000 people in the middle of the first millennium C.E. Broad avenues, dozens of temples, two huge pyramids, endless stone carvings and many bright frescoes, small apartments for the ordinary, palatial homes for the wealthy—all of this must have seemed another world for a new visitor from a distant village. In shopping for obsidian blades, how was she to decide among the 350 workshops in the city? In seeking relatives, how could she find her way among many different compounds, each surrounded by a wall and housing a different lineage? And what would she make of a neighborhood composed entirely of Maya merchants from the distant coastal lowlands?

Cities, then, were central to most of the First Civilizations, though to varying degrees. They were political/administrative capitals; they functioned as centers for the production of culture, including art, architecture, literature, ritual, and ceremony; they served as marketplaces for both local and long-distance exchange; and they housed most manufacturing activity. Everywhere they generated a unique kind of society, compared to earlier agricultural villages or Paleolithic camps. Urban society was impersonal, for it was no

A Mask from Teotihuacán This mask illustrates the kind of facial adornment—a nose pendant and ear spools—often worn by members of the nobility in Teotihuacán. (Museo Nacional de Antropología, Mexico City, Mexico/Bridgeman Images)

longer possible to know everyone. Relationships of class and occupation emerged alongside those of kinship and village loyalty. Most notably, the degree of specialization and inequality far surpassed that of all preceding human communities.

The Erosion of Equality

Among the most novel features of early urban life, at least to our imaginary village visitor, was the amazing specialization of work outside of agriculture—scholars, officials, merchants, priests, and artisans of all kinds. In ancient Sumer, even scribes were subdivided into many categories: junior and senior scribes, temple scribes and royal scribes, scribes for particular administrative or official functions. None of these people, of course, grew their own food; they were supported by the highly productive agriculture of farmers.

Hierarchies of Class

Alongside the occupational specialization of the First Civilizations lay their vast inequalities—in wealth, status, and power. As ingenuity and technology created more productive economies, the greater wealth now available was everywhere piled up rather than spread out. Early signs of this erosion of equality were evident in the more settled and complex gathering and hunting societies and in agricultural chiefdoms, but the advent of urban-based civilizations multiplied and magnified these inequalities many times over, as the more egalitarian values of earlier cultures were everywhere displaced. This transition represents one of the major turning points in the social history of humankind.

As the First Civilizations took shape, inequality and hierarchy soon came to be regarded as normal and natural. Upper classes everywhere enjoyed great wealth in land or salaries, were able to avoid physical labor, had the finest of everything, and occupied the top positions in political, military, and religious life. Frequently, they were distinguished by the clothing they wore, the houses they lived in, and the manner of their burial. Early Chinese monarchs bestowed special robes, banners, chariots, weapons, and ornaments on their regional officials, and all of these items were graded according to the officials' precise location in the hierarchy. In the Babylonian Empire the punishments prescribed in the famous **Code of Hammurabi** (hahm-moo-RAH-bee) (ca. 1775 B.C.E.) depended on social status. A free-born commoner who struck a person of equal rank had to pay a small fine, but if he struck "a man who is his superior, he [would] receive 60 strokes with an oxtail whip in public." Clearly, class had consequences.

In all of the First Civilizations, free commoners represented the vast majority of the population and included artisans of all kinds, lower-level officials, soldiers and police, servants, and, most numerous of all, farmers. It was their surplus production—appropriated through a variety of taxes, rents, required labor, and tribute payments—that supported the upper classes. At least some of these people were aware of, and resented, these forced extractions and their position in the social hierarchy.

Guided Reading Question

■ **CHANGE**
In what ways was social inequality expressed in early civilizations?

Most Chinese peasants, for example, owned little land of their own and worked on plots granted to them by royal or aristocratic landowners. An ancient poem compared the exploiting landlords to rats and expressed the farmers' vision of a better life:

> Large rats! Large rats! / Do not eat our spring grain!
> Three years have we had to do with you. / And you have not been willing to
>   think of our toil.
> We will leave you, / And go to those happy borders.
> Happy borders, happy borders! / Who will there make us always to groan?[8]

At the bottom of social hierarchies everywhere were slaves. Evidence for slavery dates to well before the emergence of civilization and was clearly present in some gathering and hunting societies and early agricultural communities. But the practice of "people owning people" flourished on a larger scale in urban- and state-based civilizations. Female slaves, captured in the many wars among rival Mesopotamian cities, were put to work in large-scale semi-industrial weaving enterprises, while males helped to maintain irrigation canals and construct ziggurats. Others worked as domestic servants in the households of their owners. In all of the First Civilizations, slaves—derived from prisoners of war, criminals, and debtors—were available for sale; for work in the fields, mines, homes, and shops of their owners; or on occasion for sacrifice. From the days of the earliest civilizations until the nineteenth century, slavery was everywhere an enduring feature of these more complex societies.

Its practice in ancient times, however, varied considerably from place to place. Egypt and the Indus Valley civilizations initially had far fewer slaves than did Mesopotamia, which was highly militarized. Later, the Greeks of Athens and the Romans employed slaves far more extensively than did the Chinese or Indians (see "The Making of Roman Slavery" in Chapter 5). Furthermore, most ancient slavery differed from the type of slavery practiced in the Americas during recent centuries: in the early civilizations, slaves were not a primary agricultural labor force; many children of slaves could become free people; and slavery was not associated primarily with "blackness" or with Africa.

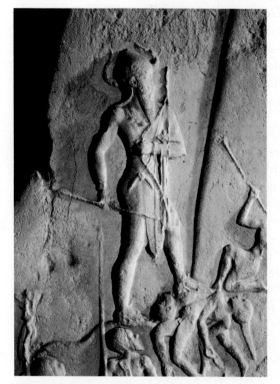

War and Slavery This Mesopotamian victory monument, dating to about 2200 B.C.E., shows the Akkadian ruler Naram-Sin crushing his enemies. Prisoners taken in such wars were a major source of slaves in the ancient world. (Musée du Louvre, Paris, France/Bridgeman Images)

Hierarchies of Gender

No divisions of human society have held greater significance for the lives of individuals than those of sex and gender. Sex describes the obvious biological differences between males and females. More important to historians, however, has been gender, which refers to the many and varied ways that cultures have assigned meaning to those sexual differences. To be gendered as masculine or feminine defines the roles and behavior considered appropriate for men and women in every human community. At least since the emergence of the First Civilizations, and in some cases even earlier, gender systems have supported **patriarchy**, which refers to a social system in which women have been made markedly subordinate to men in the family and in society generally. The inequalities of gender, like those of class, decisively shaped the character of the First Civilizations and of those that followed.

The patriarchal ideal regarded men as superior to women and sons preferable to daughters. Men had legal and property rights unknown to most women. Public life in general was associated with masculinity, which defined men as rulers, warriors, scholars, and heads of households. Women's roles—both productive and reproductive—took place in the home, mostly within a heterosexual family, where women were defined largely by their relationship to a man: as a daughter, wife, mother, or widow. Frequently men could marry more than one woman and claim the right to regulate the social and sexual lives of the wives, daughters, and sisters in their families. Widely seen as weak but feared as potentially disruptive, women required both the protection and control of men.

For men and women alike, gender and class intersected to shape the lives of individuals. Most men, of course, were far from prominent and exercised little power, except perhaps over the women and children of their own families. Upper-class women often experienced a privileged but highly restricted life, for they were largely limited to the home and the management of servants or slaves. By contrast, the vast majority of women always had to be out in public, working in the fields, tending livestock, buying and selling in the streets, or serving in the homes of their social superiors. A few women also operated in roles defined as masculine, acting as rulers, priests, and scholars, while others pushed against the limits and restrictions assigned to women. But most women no doubt accepted their assigned roles, unable to imagine anything approaching gender equality, even as most men genuinely believed that they were protecting and providing for their women.

The big question for historians lies in trying to explain the origins of this kind of pervasive patriarchy. Clearly it was neither natural nor of long standing. For millennia beyond measure, gathering and hunting societies had developed gender systems without the sharp restrictions and vast inequalities that characterized civilizations. Early farming societies, those using a hoe or digging stick for cultivation, continued the relative gender equality that had characterized Paleolithic peoples. What was it, then, about civilization that seemed to generate a more explicit and restrictive patriarchy?

One approach to answering this question highlights the role of a new and more intensive form of agriculture, involving the use of animal-drawn plows and the keeping and milking of large herds of animals. Unlike earlier farming practices that relied on a hoe or digging stick, plow-based agriculture meant heavier work, which men were better able to perform. Taking place at a distance from the village, this

Guided Reading Question

■ **CHANGE**
In what ways have historians tried to explain the origins of patriarchy?

new form of agriculture was perhaps less compatible with women's primary responsibility for child rearing and food preparation. Furthermore, the growing population of civilizations meant that women were more often pregnant and thus more deeply involved in child care than before. Hence, in plow-based communities, men took over most of the farming work, and the status of women declined correspondingly, even though their other productive activities—weaving and food preparation, for example—continued. "As women were increasingly relegated to secondary tasks," writes archeologist Margaret Ehrenberg, "they had fewer personal resources with which to assert their status."[9] But in much of Africa, all of the agricultural areas of the Americas, and parts of Southeast Asia, hoe-based farming persisted and with it, arguably, less restrictive lives for women.

Women have long been identified not only with the home but also with nature, for they are central to the primordial natural process of reproduction. But civilization seemed to highlight culture, or the human mastery of nature, through agriculture, monumental art and architecture, and creation of large-scale cities and states. Did this mean, as some scholars have suggested, that women were now associated with an inferior dimension of human life (nature), while men assumed responsibility for the higher order of culture?[10]

Warfare and professionally led armies, central to many of the First Civilizations, surely contributed to patriarchy. With military service largely restricted to men, its growing prominence in the affairs of civilizations enhanced the values, power, and prestige of a male warrior class and cemented the association of masculinity with organized violence and with the protection of society, especially its women.

Private property and commerce, also prominent among the First Civilizations, may have helped to shape early patriarchies. Without sharp restrictions on women's sexual activity, how could a father be certain that family property would be inherited by his offspring? In addition, the buying and selling associated with commerce were soon applied to male rights over women, as female slaves, concubines, and wives were exchanged among men.

Patriarchy in Practice

Whatever the precise origins of patriarchy, women's subordination permeated the First Civilizations, marking a gradual change from the more equal relationships of men and women within agricultural villages or Paleolithic bands. By the second millennium B.C.E. in Mesopotamia, various written laws codified and sought to enforce a patriarchal family life that offered women a measure of paternalistic protection while insisting on their submission to the unquestioned authority of men. Central to these laws was the regulation of female sexuality. A wife caught sleeping with another man might be drowned at her husband's discretion, whereas he was permitted to enjoy sexual relations with his female servants, though not with another man's wife. Divorce was far easier for the husband than for the wife. Rape was a serious offense, but the injured party was primarily the father or the husband of the victim, rather than the violated woman herself. While wealthy women might own and operate their own businesses or act on behalf of their powerful husbands, they too saw themselves as dependent. "Let all be well with [my husband]," prayed one such wife, "that I may prosper under his protection."[11]

Furthermore, women in Mesopotamian civilization were sometimes divided into two sharply distinguished categories. Under an Assyrian law code that was in effect between the fifteenth and eleventh centuries B.C.E., respectable women, those under the protection and sexual control of one man, were required to be veiled when outside the home, whereas nonrespectable women, such as slaves and prostitutes, were forbidden to wear veils and were subject to severe punishment if they presumed to cover their heads.

Guided Reading Question

■ **COMPARISON**
How did Mesopotamian and Egyptian patriarchy differ from each other?

Finally, in some places, the powerful goddesses of earlier times were gradually relegated to the home and hearth. They were replaced in the public arena by dominant male deities, who now were credited with the power of creation and fertility and viewed as the patrons of wisdom and learning. This "demotion of the goddess," argued historian Gerda Lerner, found expression in the Hebrew Scriptures, in which a single male deity, Yahweh (YAH-way), alone undertakes the act of creation without any participation of a female counterpart. Yet this demotion did not occur always or everywhere; in Mesopotamia, for example, the prominent goddess Inanna, or Ishtar, long held her own against male gods and was regarded as a goddess of love and sexuality as well as a war deity.

Thus expressions of patriarchy varied among the First Civilizations. Egypt, while clearly patriarchal, afforded its women greater opportunities than did most other First Civilizations. In Egypt, women were recognized as legal equals to men, able to own property and slaves, to administer and sell land, to make their own wills, to sign their own marriage contracts, and to initiate divorce. Moreover, married women in Egypt were not veiled as they were at times in Mesopotamia. Royal women occasionally exercised significant political power, acting as regents for their young sons or, more rarely, as queens in their own right. Clearly, though, this was seen as abnormal, for Egypt's most famous queen, Hatshepsut (r. 1472–1457 B.C.E.), was sometimes portrayed in statues as a man, dressed in male clothing and sporting the traditional false beard of the pharaoh.

The Rise of the State

What, we might reasonably ask, held ancient civilizations together despite the many tensions and complexities of urban living and the vast inequalities of civilized societies? The answer, in large part, lay in yet another distinctive feature of the First Civilizations—states. Organized around particular cities or larger territories, early states were headed almost everywhere by kings, who employed a variety of ranked officials, exercised a measure of control over society, and defended against external enemies. The state is a quite recent invention in human history, replacing, or at least supplementing, kinship as the basic organizing principle of society and exercising far greater power than earlier chiefdoms. But the power of central states in the First Civilizations was limited and certainly not "totalitarian" in the modern sense of that term. The temple and the private economy rivaled and checked the power of rulers, and most authority was local rather than directed from the capital.

Coercion and Consent

Early states in Mesopotamia, Egypt, China, Mesoamerica, and elsewhere drew their power from various sources, all of which helped to integrate their societies. One basis of authority lay in the recognition that the complexity of life in cities or densely populated territories required some authority to coordinate and regulate the community. Someone had to organize the irrigation systems of river valley civilizations. Someone had to direct efforts to defend the city or territory against aggressive outsiders. Someone had to adjudicate conflicts among the many different peoples, unrelated to one another, who rubbed elbows in the streets of early cities. The state, in short, solved certain widely shared problems and therefore had a measure of voluntary support among the population. For many people, it was surely useful.

Guided Reading Question

....

■ **CHANGE**
What were the sources of state authority in the First Civilizations?

The state, however, was more useful for some people than for others, for it also served to protect the privileges of the upper classes, to require farmers to give up a portion of their product to support city-dwellers, and to demand work on large public projects such as pyramids and fortifications. If necessary, state authorities had the ability, and the willingness, to use force to compel obedience. As recorded in the Jewish scriptures of the Old Testament, the prophet Samuel warned the ancient people of Israel about the "ways of the king":

> He will take your sons and make them serve with his chariots and horses. . . .
> Some he will assign to be commanders . . . and others to plow his ground and
> reap his harvest, and still others to make weapons of war and equipment for his
> chariots. He will take your daughters to be perfumers and cooks and bakers. He
> will take the best of your fields and vineyards and olive groves and give them to
> his attendants. He will take a tenth of your grain and of your vintage and give
> it to his officials and attendants. Your male and female servants and the best of
> your cattle and donkeys he will take for his own use. He will take a tenth of
> your flocks, and you yourselves will become his slaves.[12]

Such was the power of the state, as rulers accumulated the resources to pay for officials, soldiers, police, and attendants. This capacity for violence and coercion marked off the states of the First Civilizations from earlier chiefdoms, whose leaders had only persuasion, prestige, and gifts to back up their authority. But as states increasingly monopolized the legitimate right to use violence, rates of death from interpersonal violence declined as compared to earlier nonstate communities.[13]

Force, however, was not always necessary, for the First Civilizations soon generated ideas suggesting that state authority as well as class and gender inequalities were normal, natural, and ordained by the gods. Rulers in many places were thought to be morally responsible for the care of their subjects, especially in times of crisis or catastrophe. Kingship everywhere was associated with the sacred. Ancient Chinese kings were known as the Son of Heaven, and only they or their authorized priests could perform the rituals and sacrifices necessary to keep the cosmos in balance, thus preventing war, pestilence, and natural disaster. Egyptians, most of all, invested their pharaohs with divine qualities. Rulers claimed to embody all the major gods of Egypt, and their supernatural power ensured the regular flooding of the Nile and the defeat of the country's enemies.

But if religion served most often to justify unequal power and privilege, it might also on occasion be used to restrain, or even undermine, the established order. Hammurabi claimed that his law code was inspired by Marduk, the chief god of Babylon, and was intended to "bring about the rule of righteousness in the land, to destroy the wicked and the evil-doers; so that the strong should not harm

A Mesopotamian Ziggurat This massive ziggurat/temple to the Mesopotamian moon god Nanna was built around 2100 B.C.E. in the city of Ur. The solitary figure standing atop the staircase illustrates the size of this huge structure. (© Richard Ashworth/Robert Harding)

the weak."[14] Another Mesopotamian monarch, Urukagina from the city of Lagash, claimed authority from the city's patron god for reforms aimed at ending the corruption and tyranny of a previous ruler. In China during the Western Zhou dynasty (1046–771 B.C.E.), emperors ruled by the Mandate of Heaven, but their bad behavior could result in the removal of that mandate and their overthrow.

Writing and Accounting

A further support for state authority lay in the remarkable invention of writing. It was a powerful and transforming innovation, regarded almost everywhere as a gift from the gods, while people without writing often saw it as something magical or supernatural. Distinctive forms of writing emerged in most of the First Civilizations (see Snapshot, page 72), sustaining them and their successors in many ways. Literacy defined elite status and conveyed enormous prestige to those who possessed it. For Egyptians, a scribe earned a kind of immortality through his writing, for it persisted long after his death. Because it can be learned, writing also provided a means for some commoners to join the charmed circle of the literate. Writing as propaganda, celebrating the great deeds of the kings, was prominent, especially among the Egyptians

SNAPSHOT Writing in Ancient Civilizations

Most of the early writing systems were logophonetic, using symbols to designate both whole words and particular sounds or syllables. Chinese characters, which indicated only words, were an exception. None of the early writing systems employed alphabets.

Location	Type	Initial Use	Example	Comment
Sumer	Cuneiform: wedge-shaped symbols on clay tablets representing objects, abstract ideas, sounds, and syllables	Records of economic transactions, such as temple payments and taxes	bird	Regarded as the world's first written language; other languages such as Babylonian and Assyrian were written with Sumerian script
Egypt	Hieroglyphs ("sacred carvings"): a series of signs that denote words and consonants (but not vowels or syllables)	Business and administrative purposes; later used for religious inscriptions, stories, poetry, hymns, and mathematics	rain, dew, storm	For everyday use, less formal systems of cursive writing (known as hieratic and demotic) were developed
Andes	Quipu: a complex system of knotted cords in which the color, length, type, and location of knots conveyed mostly numerical meaning	Various accounting functions; perhaps also used to express words	numerical data (possibly in codes), words, and ideas	Widely used in the Inca Empire; recent discoveries place quipus in Caral some 4,600 years ago
Indus River Valley	Some 400 pictographic symbols representing sounds and words, probably expressing a Dravidian language currently spoken in southern India	Found on thousands of clay seals and pottery; probably used to mark merchandise	6 fish	As yet undeciphered
China	Oracle bone script: pictographs (stylized drawings) with no phonetic meaning	Inscribed on turtle shells or animal bones; used for divination (predicting the future) in the royal court of Shang dynasty rulers	horse	Direct ancestor of contemporary Chinese characters
Olmec	Signs that represent sounds (syllables) and words; numbering system using bars and dots	Used to record the names and deeds of rulers and shamans, as well as battles and astronomical data	jaguar	Structurally similar to later Mayan script; Olmec calendars were highly accurate and the basis for later Mesoamerican calendars

and later among the Maya. A hymn to the pharaoh, dating to about 1850 B.C.E., extravagantly praised the Egyptian ruler:

> He has come unto us . . . and has given peace to the two Riverbanks and has made Egypt to live; he hath banished its suffering; he has caused the throat of the subjects to breathe and has trodden down foreign countries; he has delivered them that were robbed; he has come unto us, that we may [nurture up?] our children and bury our aged ones.[15]

In Mesopotamia and elsewhere, writing served an accounting function, recording who had paid their taxes, who owed what to the temple, and how much workers had earned. Thus it immensely strengthened bureaucracy. Complex calendars indicated precisely when certain rituals should be performed. Writing also gave weight and specificity to orders, regulations, and laws. Hammurabi's famous law code, while correcting certain abuses, made crystal clear that fundamental distinctions divided men and women and separated slaves, commoners, and people of higher rank.

Once it had been developed, writing, like religion, proved hard to control and operated as a wild card in human affairs. It gave rise to literature and philosophy, to astronomy and mathematics, and, in some places, to history, often recording what had long been oral traditions. On occasion, the written word proved threatening, rather than supportive, to rulers. China's so-called First Emperor, Qin Shihuangdi (r. 221–210 B.C.E.), allegedly buried alive some 460 scholars and burned their books when they challenged his brutal efforts to unify China's many warring states, or so his later critics claimed (see "China: From Warring States to Empire," Chapter 3). Thus writing became a major arena for social and political conflict, and rulers have always sought to control it.

The Grandeur of Kings

Yet another source of state authority derived from the lavish lifestyle of elites, the impressive rituals they arranged, and the imposing structures they created. Everywhere, kings, high officials, and their families lived in luxurious palaces or homes, dressed in splendid clothing, bedecked themselves with the loveliest jewelry, and were attended by endless servants. Their deaths triggered elaborate burials, of which the pyramids of the Egyptian pharaohs were perhaps the most ostentatious. Monumental palaces, temples, ziggurats, pyramids, and statues conveyed the imposing power of the state

Olmec Head This colossal statue, some eight feet high and weighing twenty-four tons, is one of seventeen such carvings, dating to the first millennium B.C.E., that were discovered in the territory of the ancient Olmec civilization. Thought to represent individual rulers, each of the statues has a distinct and realistically portrayed face. (© Danny Lehman/Corbis/VCG/Getty Images)

PRACTICING HISTORICAL THINKING

In what ways might the advent of "civilization" have marked a revolutionary change in the human condition? And in what ways did it carry on earlier patterns from the past?

and its elite rulers. The Olmec civilization of Mesoamerica (1200–400 B.C.E.) erected enormous human heads, some more than ten feet tall and weighing at least twenty tons, carved from blocks of basalt and probably representing particular rulers. Somewhat later, the Maya Temple of the Great Jaguar, 154 feet tall, was the most impressive among many temples, pyramids, and palaces that graced the city of Tikal. All of this must have seemed overwhelming to common people in the cities and villages of the First Civilizations.

Comparing Mesopotamia and Egypt

A productive agricultural technology, city living, distinct class and gender inequalities, the emerging power of states—all of these were common features of First Civilizations across the world and also of those that followed. Still, these civilizations were not everywhere the same, for differences in political organization, religious beliefs and practices, the role of women, and much more gave rise to distinctive traditions. Nor were they static. Like all human communities, they changed over the centuries. Finally, these civilizations did not exist in complete isolation, for they participated in networks of interactions with near and sometimes more distant neighbors. In looking more closely at two of these First Civilizations—Mesopotamia and Egypt—we can catch a glimpse of the differences, changes, and connections that characterized early civilizations.

Environment and Culture

Guided Reading Question

■ **COMPARISON**
In what ways did Mesopotamian and Egyptian civilizations differ from each other?

The civilizations of both Mesopotamia and Egypt grew up in river valleys and depended on their rivers to sustain a productive agriculture in otherwise-arid lands. Those rivers, however, were radically different. At the heart of Egyptian life was the Nile, "that green gash of teeming life," which rose predictably every year to bring the soil and water that nurtured a rich Egyptian agriculture. The Tigris and Euphrates rivers, which gave life to Mesopotamian civilization, also rose annually, but "unpredictably and fitfully, breaking man's dikes and submerging his crops"[16] (see Map 2.2). Furthermore, an open environment without serious obstacles to travel made Mesopotamia far more vulnerable to invasion than the much more protected space of Egypt, which was surrounded by deserts, mountains, seas, and to its south by unnavigable stretches of the Nile. For long periods of its history, Egypt enjoyed a kind of "free security" from external attack that Mesopotamians clearly lacked.

But does the physical environment shape the human cultures that develop within it? Most historians are reluctant to endorse a "geography is destiny" outlook, but in the case of Mesopotamia and Egypt, it is hard to deny some relationship between the physical setting and culture. Mesopotamia's location within a precarious, unpredictable, and often-violent environment arguably contributed to an

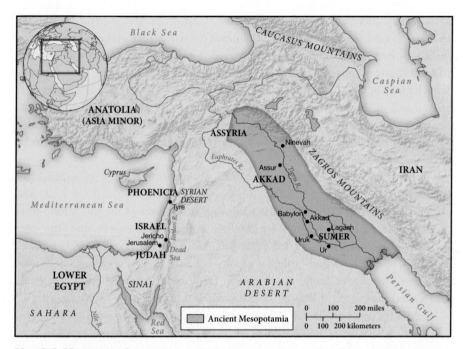

Map 2.2 Mesopotamia

After about 1,000 years of independent and competitive existence, the city-states of Sumer were incorporated into a number of larger imperial states based in Akkad, Babylon, and then Assyria.

outlook suggesting that humankind was caught in an inherently disorderly world, was subject to the whims of capricious and quarreling gods, and had to face death without much hope of a blessed life beyond. A Mesopotamian poet complained: "I have prayed to the gods and sacrificed, but who can understand the gods in heaven? Who knows what they plan for us? Who has ever been able to understand a god's conduct?"[17]

By contrast, elite literate culture in Egypt, developing in a more stable, predictable, and beneficent environment, produced a rather more cheerful and hopeful outlook on the world. The rebirth of the sun every day and of the river every year seemed to assure Egyptians that life would prevail over death. The amazing pyramids, constructed during Egypt's Old Kingdom (2663–2195 B.C.E.), reflected the firm belief that at least the pharaohs and other high-ranking people could successfully make the journey to eternal life in the Land of the West. Incantations for the dead describe an afterlife of abundance and tranquillity that Gilgamesh could only have envied. Over time, larger groups of people, beyond the pharaoh and his entourage, came to believe that they too could gain access to the afterlife if they followed proper procedures and lived a morally upright life. Thus Egyptian civilization not only affirmed the possibility of eternal life but also expanded access to it.

If the different environments of Mesopotamia and Egypt shaped their societies and cultures, those civilizations, with their mounting populations and growing demand for resources, likewise had an impact on the environment.[18] The *Epic of Gilgamesh* inscribed in mythology the deforestation of Mesopotamia. When the ruler Gilgamesh sought to make for himself "a name that endures" by building walls, ramparts, and temples, he required much timber. But to acquire it, he had first to kill Humbaba, appointed by the gods to guard the forests. The epic describes what happened next: "Then there followed confusion. . . . Now the mountains were moved and all the hills, for the guardian of the forest was killed. They attacked the cedars. . . . So they pressed on into the forest . . . and while Gilgamesh felled the first of the trees of the forest, Enkidu [the friend of Gilgamesh] cleared their roots as far as the banks of Euphrates."[19]

In Sumer (southern Mesopotamia), such deforestation and the soil erosion that followed from it sharply decreased crop yields between 2400 and 1700 B.C.E. Also contributing to this disaster was the increasing salinization of the soil, a long-term outcome of intensive irrigation. By 2000 B.C.E., there were reports that "the earth turned white" as salt accumulated in the soil. As a result, wheat was largely replaced by barley, which is far more tolerant of salty conditions. This ecological deterioration clearly weakened Sumerian city-states, facilitated their conquest by foreigners, and shifted the center of Mesopotamian civilization permanently to the north.

Egypt, by contrast, created a more sustainable agricultural system, which lasted for thousands of years and contributed to the remarkable continuity of its civilization. Whereas Sumerian irrigation involved a complex and artificial network of canals and dikes that led to the salinization of the soil, its Egyptian counterpart was much less intrusive, simply regulating the natural flow of the Nile. Such a system avoided the problem of salty soils, allowing Egyptian agriculture to emphasize wheat production, but it depended on the general regularity and relative gentleness of the Nile's annual flooding. On occasion, that pattern was interrupted, with serious consequences for Egyptian society. An extended period of low floods between 2250 and 1950 B.C.E. led to sharply reduced agricultural output, large-scale starvation, the loss of livestock, and, consequently, social upheaval and political disruption. Nonetheless, Egypt's ability to work *with* its more favorable natural environment enabled a degree of stability and continuity that proved impossible in Sumer, where human action intruded more heavily into a less benevolent natural setting.

Cities and States

Politically as well as culturally and environmentally, Mesopotamian and Egyptian civilizations differed sharply. For its first thousand years (3200–2350 B.C.E.), Mesopotamian civilization, located in the southern Tigris-Euphrates region known as Sumer, was organized in a dozen or more separate and independent city-states. Each city-state was ruled by a king, who claimed to represent the city's patron deity and who controlled the affairs of the walled city and surrounding rural area. Quite remarkably, some 80 percent of the population of Sumer lived in one or another of these city-states, making Mesopotamia the most thoroughly urbanized society of ancient times. The chief reason for this massive urbanization, however, lay in the great flaw of this system, for frequent warfare among these Sumerian city-states caused people living in rural areas to flee to the walled cities for protection. With no overarching authority, rivalry over land and water often led to violent conflict.

These conflicts, together with environmental devastation, eventually left Sumerian cities vulnerable to outside forces, and after about 2350 B.C.E., stronger peoples from northern Mesopotamia conquered Sumer's warring cities, bringing an end to the Sumerian phase of Mesopotamian civilization. First the Akkadians (2350–2000 B.C.E.), and later the Babylonians (1900–1500 B.C.E.) and the Assyrians (900–612 B.C.E.), created larger territorial states or bureaucratic empires that encompassed all or most of Mesopotamia. Periods of political unity now descended upon this First Civilization, but it was unity imposed from outside.

Egyptian civilization, by contrast, began its history around 3100 B.C.E., with the merger of several earlier states or chiefdoms into a unified territory that stretched some 1,000 miles along the Nile. For an amazing 3,000 years, the Egypt of the pharaohs maintained its unity and independence, though with occasional interruptions. A combination of wind patterns that made it easy to sail south along the Nile and a current flowing north facilitated communication, exchange, unity, and stability within the Nile Valley. Here was a record of political longevity and continuity that the Mesopotamians and many other ancient peoples could not replicate. An Egyptian territorial state and cultural identity persist still in northeastern Africa.

Cities in Egypt were less important than in Mesopotamia, although political capitals, market centers, and major burial sites gave Egypt an urban presence as well. Most people lived in agricultural villages along the river rather than in urban centers, perhaps because Egypt's greater security made it less necessary for people to gather in fortified towns. The focus of the Egyptian state resided in the pharaoh, believed to be a god in human form. He alone ensured the daily rising of the sun and the annual flooding of the Nile. All of the country's many officials served at his pleasure, and access to the afterlife lay in proximity to him and burial in or near his towering pyramids.

This image of the pharaoh and his role as an enduring symbol of a unified Egyptian civilization persisted over the course of three millennia, but the realities of Egyptian political life did not always match these ideals. By 2400 B.C.E., the power of the pharaoh had diminished, as local officials and nobles assumed greater authority. Having been been awarded their own land, they were able to pass their positions on to their sons. When changes in the weather resulted in the Nile's repeated failure to flood properly around 2200 B.C.E., the authority of the pharaoh was severely discredited, and Egypt dissolved for several centuries into a series of local principalities.

Even when centralized rule was restored around 2000 B.C.E., the pharaohs never regained their old power and prestige. Kings were now warned that they too would have to account for their actions at the Day of Judgment. Nobles no longer sought to be buried near the pharaoh's pyramid but instead created their own more modest tombs in their own areas. Osiris, the god of the dead, became increasingly prominent, and all worthy men, not only those who had been close to the pharaoh in life, could aspire to immortality in his realm.

Interaction and Exchange

Although Mesopotamia and Egypt represented separate and distinct civilizations, they interacted frequently with each other and with both near and more distant neighbors. Even in these ancient times, the First Civilizations were embedded in larger networks of commerce, culture, and power. None of them stood alone.

Guided Reading Question

....

■ **CONNECTION**
In what ways were Mesopotamian and Egyptian civilizations shaped by their interactions with near and distant neighbors?

Egypt's early agriculture, for example, drew upon wheat and barley, which likely reached Egypt from Mesopotamia, as well as gourds, watermelon, domesticated donkeys, and cattle, which came from the Sudan to the south. The practice of "divine kingship" probably derived from the central or eastern Sudan, where small-scale agricultural communities had long viewed their rulers as sacred and buried them with various servants and officials. From this complex of influences, the Egyptians created something distinct and unique, but that civilization had roots in both Africa and Southwest Asia.

Furthermore, once they were established, both Mesopotamia and Egypt carried on long-distance trade, mostly in luxury goods destined for the elite. Sumerian merchants had established seaborne contact with the Indus Valley civilization as early as 2300 B.C.E., while Indus Valley traders and their interpreters had taken up residence in Mesopotamia. Other trade routes connected Mesopotamia to Anatolia (present-day Turkey), Egypt, Iran, and Afghanistan. During Akkadian rule over Mesopotamia, a Sumerian poet described its capital of Agade:

> In those days the dwellings of Agade were filled with gold, / its bright-shining houses were filled with silver,
> into its granaries were brought copper, tin, slabs of lapis lazuli [a blue gemstone],
> its silos bulged at the sides . . . / its quay where the boats docked were all bustle.[20]

All of this and more came from far away.

Egyptian trade likewise extended far afield. In addition to being involved with the Mediterranean and the Middle East, Egyptian trading journeys extended deep into Africa, including Nubia, south of Egypt in the Nile Valley, and Punt, along the East African coast of Ethiopia and Somalia. One Egyptian official described his return from an expedition to Nubia: "I came down with three hundred donkeys laden with incense, ebony, . . . panther skins, elephant tusks, throw sticks, and all sorts of good products."[21]

Along with trade goods went cultural influence from the civilizations of Mesopotamia and Egypt. Among the smaller societies of the region to feel this influence were the Hebrews. Their sacred writings, recorded in the Old Testament, showed the influence of Mesopotamia in the "eye for an eye" principle of their legal system and in the story of a flood that destroyed the world. The Phoenicians, who were commercially active in the Mediterranean basin from their homeland in present-day Lebanon, also were influenced by Mesopotamian civilization. They venerated Astarte, a local form of the Mesopotamian fertility goddess Ishtar. They also adapted the Sumerian cuneiform method of writing to a much easier alphabetic system, which later became the basis for Greek and Latin writing. Various Indo-European peoples, dispersing probably from north-central Anatolia (the site of contemporary Turkey), also incorporated Sumerian deities into their own religions as well as bronze metallurgy and the wheel into their economies. When their widespread migrations carried them across much of Eurasia, they took these Sumerian cultural artifacts with them.

Egyptian cultural influence likewise spread in several directions. Nubia, located to the south of Egypt in the Nile Valley, not only traded with its more powerful neighbor but also was subject to periodic military intervention and political control from Egypt. Skilled Nubian archers were actively recruited for service as mercenaries in Egyptian armies. They often married Egyptian women and were buried in Egyptian style. All of this led to the diffusion of Egyptian culture in Nubia, expressed in building Egyptian-style pyramids, worshipping Egyptian gods and goddesses, and making use of Egyptian hieroglyphic writing. Despite this cultural borrowing, Nubia remained a distinct civilization, developing its own alphabetic script, retaining many of its own gods, developing a major ironworking industry by 500 B.C.E., and asserting its political independence whenever possible. The Nubian kingdom of Kush, in fact, invaded Egypt in 760 B.C.E. and ruled it for about 100 years.

In the Mediterranean basin, clear Egyptian influence is visible in the art of the Minoan civilization, which emerged on the island of Crete about 2500 B.C.E. More controversial has been the claim by some scholars that ancient Greek culture—its

Egypt and Nubia This wall painting from the tomb of an Egyptian court official, dating to the fifteenth century B.C.E., shows Nubians bringing animals as tribute to Egyptian authorities. (James Morris/AKG Images)

MAPPING HISTORY

Map 2.3 An Egyptian Empire

During the New Kingdom period after 1550 B.C.E., Egypt became for several centuries an empire, extending its political control southward into Nubia and northward into Palestine and Syria.

READING THE MAP: What geographical features and political realities influenced the extent and shape of the Egyptian New Kingdom empire?

INTERPRETING THE MAP: What geographic factors might have made it difficult for Egyptian pharaohs to expand their empire farther or even maintain its New Kingdom borders?

art, religion, philosophy, and language—drew heavily upon Egyptian as well as Mesopotamian precedents. Influence was not a one-way street, however, as Egypt and Mesopotamia likewise felt the impact of neighboring peoples. Pastoral peoples, speaking Indo-European languages and living in what is now southern Russia, had domesticated the horse by perhaps 4000 B.C.E. and later learned to tie that powerful animal to wheeled carts and chariots. This new technology provided a fearsome military potential that enabled various chariot-driving peoples, such as the Hittites, to threaten ancient civilizations. Based in Anatolia, the Hittites sacked the city of Babylon in 1595 B.C.E. Several centuries later, conflict between the Hittites and Egypt over control of Syria resulted in the world's first written peace treaty. But chariot technology was portable, and soon both the Egyptians and the Mesopotamians incorporated it into their own military forces. In fact, this powerful military innovation, together with the knowledge of bronze metallurgy, spread quickly and widely, reaching China by 1200 B.C.E. There it enabled the creation of a strong Chinese state ruled by the Shang dynasty. All of these developments provide evidence of at least indirect connections across parts of the Afro-Eurasian landmass in ancient times. Even then, no civilization was wholly isolated from larger patterns of interaction.

In Egypt, the centuries following 1650 B.C.E. witnessed the migration of foreigners from surrounding regions and conflict with neighboring peoples, shaking the sense of security that this Nile Valley civilization had long enjoyed. It also stimulated the normally complacent Egyptians to adopt a number of technologies pioneered earlier in Asia, including the horse-drawn chariot; new kinds of armor, bows, daggers, and swords; improved methods of spinning and weaving; new musical instruments; and olive and pomegranate trees. Absorbing these foreign innovations, Egyptians went on to create their own empire, both in Nubia and in the eastern Mediterranean regions of Syria and Palestine. By 1500 B.C.E., the previously self-contained Egypt became for several centuries an imperial state bridging Africa and Asia, ruling over substantial numbers of non-Egyptian peoples (see Map 2.3). It also became part of an international political system that included the Babylonian and later Assyrian empires of Mesopotamia as well as many other peoples of the region. Egyptian and Babylonian rulers engaged in regular diplomatic correspondence, referred to one another as "brother," exchanged gifts, and married their daughters into one another's families. Or at least they tried to. While Babylonian rulers were willing to send their daughters to Egypt, the Egyptians were exceedingly reluctant to return the favor, claiming that "from ancient times the daughter of the king of Egypt has not been given to anyone." To this rebuff, the disappointed Babylonian monarch replied:"You are a king and you can do as pleases you....Send me [any] beautiful woman as if she were your daughter. Who is to say this woman is not the daughter of the king?"[22]

REFLECTIONS

"Civilization": What's in a Word?

In examining the First Civilizations, we are worlds away from life in agricultural villages or Paleolithic camps. Strangely enough, historians have been somewhat uncertain as to how to refer to these new forms of human community. Following common practice, we have called them "civilizations," but scholars have reservations about the term for two reasons. The first is its implication of superiority. In popular usage, "civilization" suggests refined behavior, a "higher" form of society, something unreservedly positive. The opposite of "civilized"—"barbarian,""savage," or "uncivilized"—is normally understood as an insult implying inferiority. That, of course, is precisely how the inhabitants of many civilizations have viewed outsiders, particularly those neighboring peoples living without the alleged benefit of cities and states.

Modern assessments of the First Civilizations reveal a profound ambiguity about these new, larger, and more complex societies. On the one hand, these civilizations have given us inspiring art, profound reflections on the meaning of life, more productive technologies, increased control over nature, and the art of writing—all of which have been cause for celebration. On the other hand, as anthropologist Marvin Harris noted, "human beings learned for the first time how to bow, grovel, kneel, and kowtow."[23] Massive inequalities, state oppression, slavery, large-scale warfare, the subordination of women, and epidemic disease also accompanied the rise of civilization, generating discontent, rebellion, and sometimes the urge to escape. This ambiguity about the character of civilizations has led some historians to avoid the word, referring to early Egypt, Mesopotamia, and other regions instead as complex societies, urban-based societies, or state-organized societies.

A second reservation about using the term "civilization" derives from its implication of solidity—the idea that civilizations represent distinct and widely shared identities with clear boundaries that mark them off from other such units. It is unlikely, however, that many people living in Mesopotamia, Norte Chico, or ancient China felt themselves part of a shared culture. Local identities defined by occupation, clan affiliation, village, city, or region were surely more important for most people than those of some larger civilization. At best, members of an educated upper class who shared a common literary tradition may have felt themselves part of some more inclusive civilization, but that left out most of the population. Moreover, unlike modern nations, none of the earlier civilizations had definite borders. Any identification with that civilization surely faded as distance from its core region increased. Finally, the line between civilizations and other kinds of societies is not always clear. Just when does a village or town become a city? At what point does a chiefdom become a state?

Despite these reservations, this book continues to use the term "civilization," both because it is so deeply embedded in our way of thinking about the world and because no alternative concept has achieved widespread acceptance. For historians, however, "civilization" is a purely descriptive term, referring to a distinctive type of human society—one with cities and states—without implying any judgment or assessment, any sense of superiority or inferiority. Furthermore "civilization" serves to define broad cultural patterns in particular geographic regions—Mesopotamia, the Peruvian coast, or China, for example—even though many people living in those regions may have been more aware of differences and conflicts than of those commonalities.

Second Thoughts

What's the Significance?

Sumer, 54

Egypt, 58

Nubia, 58

Norte Chico, 58

Caral, 58

Indus Valley civilization, 60

Central Asian/Oxus civilization, 61

Olmec civilization, 62

Uruk, 63

Epic of Gilgamesh, 64

Mohenjo Daro/Harappa, 64

Code of Hammurabi, 65

patriarchy, 67

Big Picture Questions

1. How does historians' use of the term "civilization" differ from popular usage? How do you use it?
2. "Civilizations were held together largely by force." Do you agree with this assessment, or were there other mechanisms of integration as well?
3. How did the various First Civilizations differ from one another?
4. **Looking Back:** To what extent did civilizations represent "progress" in comparison with earlier Paleolithic and Neolithic societies? And in what ways did they constitute a setback for humankind?

Next Steps: For Further Study

Cyril Aldred, *The Egyptians* (1998). A brief account from a widely recognized expert.

Jonathan M. Kenoyer, *Ancient Cities of the Indus Valley Civilization* (1998). A thorough and beautifully illustrated study by a leading archeologist of the area.

Samuel Noah Kramer, *History Begins at Sumer* (1981). A classic account of Sumerian civilization, filled with wonderful stories and anecdotes.

David B. O'Connor, *Ancient Nubia: Egypt's Rival in Africa* (1994). An overview of this ancient African civilization, with lovely illustrations based on a museum exhibit.

Christopher A. Pool, *Olmec Archeology and Early Mesoamerica* (2007). A scholarly and up-to-date account of the earliest civilization in Mesoamerica.

James C. Scott, *Against the Grain: The Deep History of the Earliest States* (2017). An up-to-date review of the scholarship on the origins of agrarian state-based civilizations with an emphasis on the many negative consequences of that landmark development.

Robert Thorp, *China in the Early Bronze Age: Shang Civilization* (2006). An accessible and scholarly account of early Chinese civilization informed by recent archeological discoveries.

"The Ancient Indus Valley Civilization 3500–1700 B.C.E.," http://www.harappa.com. Everything you want to know about the Indus Valley civilization in hundreds of vivid pictures, videos, essays, books, and articles.

The British Museum, "Ancient Egypt," http://www.ancientegypt.co.uk/menu.html. An interactive exploration of Egyptian civilization from the British Museum.

Indus Valley Civilization

In most accounts of the First Civilizations, Egypt and Mesopotamia hold center stage. And yet the civilization of the Indus River valley was much larger, and its archeological treasures have been equally impressive, though clearly distinctive. This civilization flourished around 2000 B.C.E., about a thousand years later than its better-known counterparts in the Middle East and Northeast Africa. By 1700 B.C.E., Indus Valley civilization was in decline, as the center of Indian or South Asian civilization shifted gradually eastward to the plains of the Ganges River. In the process, all distinct memory of the earlier Indus Valley civilization vanished, to be rediscovered only in the early twentieth century as archeologists uncovered its remarkable remains. Here is yet another contrast with Egypt and Mesopotamia, where conscious memory of earlier achievements persisted long after those civilizations had passed into history. The images that follow are drawn from archeological investigations of the Indus Valley civilization and offer us a glimpse of its achievements and unique features. Since its written language was limited in extent and has not yet been deciphered, scholars have been highly dependent on its physical remains for understanding this First Civilization.

SOURCE 2.1 Cityscape of Mohenjo Daro ▶

Among the most distinctive elements of the Indus Valley civilization were its cities, of which Mohenjo Daro and Harappa were the largest and are the most thoroughly investigated. Laid out systematically on a grid pattern and clearly planned, they were surrounded by substantial walls made from mud bricks of a standardized size and interrupted by imposing gateways. Inside the walls, public buildings, market areas, large and small houses, and craft workshops stood in each of the cities' various neighborhoods. Many houses had indoor latrines, while wide main streets and narrow side lanes had drains to carry away polluted water and sewage. Source 2.1 is a modern drawing of ancient Mohenjo Daro.

■ Based on this image, how would you describe Mohenjo Daro to someone who had never seen it?

■ How useful are such modern reconstructions in understanding ancient civilizations?

Wall Painting of Mohenjo Daro Reconstruction | **20th century**

Mohenjo-Daro Archeological Museum, Sindh Province, Pakistan/Roland and Sabrina Michaud/akg-images

■ ■ ■

SOURCE 2.2 A Seal from the Indus Valley ▶

In many ancient and more recent societies, seals have been used for imprinting an image on a document or a product. Archeologists have frequently found such seals in Indus Valley cities. They often incorporate the image of an animal—a bull, an elephant, a crocodile, a buffalo, or even a mythic creature such as a unicorn—and a title or inscription in a still-undeciphered script. Thus the seals were accessible to an illiterate worker loading goods on a boat as well as to literate merchants or officials. Particular seals may well have represented a specific clan, a high official, a particular business, or a prominent individual. Unicorn seals have been the most numerous finds and were often used to make impressions on clay tags attached to bundled goods, suggesting that their owners were involved in trade or commerce. Because bull seals, such as the one shown in Source 2.2, were rarer, their owners may have been high-ranking officials or members of a particularly powerful clan. The bull, speculates archeologist Jonathan Kenoyer, "may symbolize the leader of the herd, whose strength and virility protects the herd and ensures the procreation of the species, or it may stand for a sacrificial animal."[24] Indus Valley seals, as well as pottery, have been found in Mesopotamia, indicating an established trade between these two First Civilizations.

■ How might a prominent landowner, a leading official, a clan head, or a merchant make use of such a seal?

■ What meaning might you attach to the use of animals as totems or symbols of a particular group or individual?

■ Notice the five characters of the Indus Valley script at the top of the seal. Do a little research on the script with an eye to understanding why it has proved so difficult to decipher.

A Humped Cattle Seal from Mohenjo Daro | **19th century** B.C.E.

National Museum of Pakistan, Karachi, Pakistan/De Agostini Picture Library/A. Dagli Orti/Bridgeman Images

■ ■ ■

SOURCE 2.3 **Man from Mohenjo Daro** ▶

The most intriguing features of the Indus Valley civilization involve what is miss-ing, at least in comparison with ancient Egypt and Mesopotamia. Archeologists have found no grand temples or palaces; no elite burial places filled with great wealth; no images of warfare, conquest, or the seizing of captives; no monuments to celebrate powerful rulers. These absences have left scholars guessing about the social and political organization of this civilization. Nonetheless, the archeology reveals a social hierarchy that included some elite groups. Source 2.3, a statue seven inches tall and found in Mohenjo Daro, likely depicts one of these elite men.

■ What specific features of the statue can you point out?

■ What possible indication of elite status can you identify?

■ What overall impression does the statue convey?

■ In the past some scholars have argued that this statue depicts a "priest king." Do you see any evidence that he is either a priest or a king? To what extent is such speculation helpful? In what ways might it be problematic?

Statue of an Elite Man | 3rd millennium B.C.E.

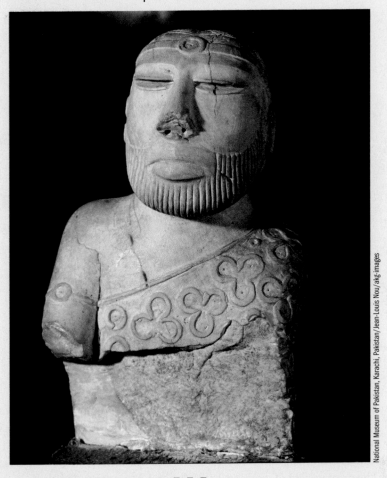

National Museum of Pakistan, Karachi, Pakistan/Jean-Louis Nou/akg-images

■ ■ ■

SOURCE 2.4 **Cart and Oxen from Mohenjo Daro** ▶

Indus Valley statuary can also provide insight into the everyday lives of commoners. Made over 3,500 years ago, this simple stone model of a cart being pulled by two oxen depicts what must have been a common sight in both major cities and the countryside. Such carvings may have served as children's toys, reminding us that some aspects of life, like the need to amuse and distract children, are shared by parents in all times and places.

■ What might an archeologist learn by carefully examining a statue like this? The driver of this cart appears to be female. If so, what does this cart suggest about gender roles in the Indus Valley civilization?

■ What do you think might be the purpose of such a toy beyond simple amusement?

Stone Model of a Cart Pulled by Two Oxen | ca. **2400** B.C.E.

National Museum of Pakistan, Karachi, Pakistan/Universal Images Group/Art Resource, NY

• • •

SOURCE 2.5 Dancing Girl ▶

Limited archeological evidence suggests that some urban women played important social and religious roles in Indus Valley civilization. Figurines of women or goddesses are more common than those of men. Women, apparently, were buried near their mothers and grandmothers, while men were not interred with their male relatives. The great variety of clothing, hairstyles, and decorations displayed on female figurines indicates considerable class, ethnic, and perhaps individual variation.

Among the most delightful discoveries in the Indus Valley cities is the evocative statue shown in Source 2.5. It is about four inches tall and dates to around 2500 B.C.E. This young female nude is known generally as the "dancing girl." Cast in bronze using a sophisticated "lost wax" method, this statue provides evidence for a well-developed copper/bronze industry. The figure herself was portrayed in a dancer's pose, her hair gathered in a bun and her left arm covered with bangles and holding a small bowl. Both her arms and legs seem disproportionately long. She has been described variously as a queen, a high-status woman, a sacred temple dancer, and a tribal girl. Although no one really knows her precise identity, she has evoked wide admiration and appreciation. Mortimer Wheeler, a famous British archeologist, described her as "a girl perfectly, for the moment, perfectly confident of herself and the world." American archeologist Gregory Possehl, also active in the archeology of the Indus Valley civilization, commented, "We may not be certain that she was a dancer, but she was good at what she did and she knew it."[25]

■ What features of this statue may have provoked such observations?

■ How do you react to this statue? What qualities does the figure evoke?

■ What does Source 2.5 suggest about views of women, images of female beauty, and attitudes about sexuality and the body?

An Indus Valley Girl | ca. 2500 B.C.E.

National Museum of India, New Delhi, India/Bridgeman Images

DOING HISTORY

1. **Using art as evidence:** What can we learn about the Indus Valley civilization from these visual sources? How does our level of understanding of this civilization differ from that of Egypt and Mesopotamia, where plentiful written records are available?

2. **Considering accessibility:** Do you think that the art of civilizations, such as that of the Indus Valley, resonates more with modern people than artistic products of earlier eras? Is it possible to speak of artistic "progress" or "development," or should we be content with simply noticing differences?

3. **Comparing representations of people:** Notice the various ways that human figures were portrayed in the images shown in Chapters 1 and 2, both those in the chapter narrative and in the Working with Evidence features. How might you define those differences? Can you identify changes from the Paleolithic to the Neolithic eras and then to the age of First Civilizations? How are gender differences represented in these images?

4. **Seeking further evidence:** What additional kinds of archeological discoveries would further our understanding of the Indus Valley civilization?

The State . . . or Its Absence . . . in the Indus Valley

These two selections explore what we can learn about Indus Valley political life and the types of evidence that support these conclusions. In Voice 2.1 the archeologist Gregory Possehl discusses the Indus Valley in the context of other ancient civilizations. Voice 2.2, from the anthropologist and archeologist Jonathan Mark Kenoyer, examines what can be surmised about the political structure of Indus Valley civilization.

■ What specific features of other First Civilizations are missing in the Indus Valley historical record?

■ What types of sources do scholars use to piece together Indus political culture?

■ Which arguments do you find convincing, and which ideas are more speculative?

■ **Integrating Primary and Secondary Sources:** How might Source 2.3 support or counter the claims made by these scholars?

VOICE 2.1

Gregory Possehl on Indus Valley Civilization in Context | 2002

The Indus Civilization is something of a faceless socio-cultural system. Individuals, even prominent ones, do not readily emerge from the archaeological record, as they do in Mesopotamia and Dynastic Egypt, for example. There are no clear signs of kingship in the form of sculpture or palaces. There is no evidence for a state bureaucracy or the other trappings of "stateness." Nor is there evidence for a state religion in the form of large temples or other monumental public works.

It is clear that the Indus Civilization is . . . just as complex in its own way as the archaic civilizations of Mesopotamia and Dynastic Egypt or the Maya and Inca of the New World. But the Indus Civilization was not organized as a state, if by *state* we adhere to the criteria previously outlined [royal sculptures/palaces and state bureaucracies/religions].

It is its marked deviance from the norm of ancient sociocultural complexity that makes the Indus civilization fascinating. . . . To my knowledge, there is, for example, no close parallel to it in either the archeological or ethnographic record. In that sense, the Indus

Civilization comes across as a kind of counterintuitive civilization, possibly "strange" because there are no existing examples that we can point to as comparative.

Source: Gregory L. Possehl, *The Indus Civilization: A Contemporary Perspective* (New York: AltaMira, 2002), 6.

VOICE 2.2

Jonathan Kenoyer on Political Life in the Indus Valley | 1998

The political organization of these cities was probably not a hereditary monarchy, where one would expect to see palaces and royal storehouses. On the contrary numerous large buildings and public spaces in the lower town at Mohenjo-daro and on Mound F at Harappa support the interpretation that several distinct elite groups were living in the [major] cities. . . .

Due to the long distances between the four major cities [400 miles between Harappa and Mohenjo Daro], it is highly unlikely that a single ruler ever dominated the entire Indus Valley. Each of the largest cities may have been organized as an independent city-state, with different communities competing for control. At times a single charismatic leader may have ruled the city, but most of the time it was probably controlled by a small group of elites, comprised of merchants, landowners and ritual specialists. . . .

The famous stone sculptures found at Mohenjo-daro may represent the rise and fall of one such community of the ruling elite. These stone sculptures were found on the surface of the site or in the topmost levels, buried under the fallen walls of the latest Indus structures. Because all of these sculptures were broken, many scholars feel that they were intentionally vandalized. However, they were made from relatively soft stone, and some may have been damaged [through natural weathering or building collapses]. . . .

If the distribution of the sculptures can be taken to indicate residence localities, then these communities were living on the citadel mound as well as in different neighborhoods of the lower city. . . . It is likely that the individuals depicted in these sculptures were influential citizens or even rulers at Mohenjo-daro.

Source: Jonathan Mark Kenoyer, *Ancient Cities of the Indus Valley Civilization* (Oxford: Oxford University Press, 1998), 100 and 102.

PART 2

Continuity and Change in the Second-Wave Era

600 B.C.E.–600 C.E.

Chapter 3 State and Empire in Eurasia / North Africa, 600 B.C.E.–600 C.E.

Chapter 4 Culture and Religion in Eurasia / North Africa, 600 B.C.E.–600 C.E.

Chapter 5 Society and Inequality in Eurasia / North Africa, 600 B.C.E.–600 C.E.

Chapter 6 Commonalities and Variations: Africa, the Americas, and Pacific Oceania, 600 B.C.E.–1200 C.E.

THE BIG PICTURE

The Globalization of Civilization

Studying world history has much in common with using the zoom lens of a camera. Sometimes, we pull the lens back to get a picture of the global panorama. At other times, we zoom in a bit for a middle-range shot of a particular region or civilization, or even farther for a close-up of some specific individual, event, or place. As we bid farewell to the First Civilizations, we look broadly, and briefly, at the entire age of agricultural civilizations, a period from about 3500 B.C.E., when the earliest of the First Civilizations arose, to about 1750 C.E., when the first Industrial Revolution launched a new and distinctively modern phase of world history. During these more than 5,000 years, the most prominent large-scale trend was the globalization of civilization as this new form of human community increasingly spread across the planet, encompassing more people and larger territories.

The first wave of that process, addressed in Chapter 2, was already global in scope, with expressions in Asia, Africa, and the Americas. But those First Civilizations, impressive as they were, also proved fragile. By the middle of the first millennium B.C.E., all of them had collapsed, fragmented, or been absorbed into new and larger empires. But there was no going back, for "civilization" as a form of social organization proved resilient as well. Thus, in the 1,200 years between 600 B.C.E. and 600 C.E., new or enlarged urban-centered and state-based societies emerged to replace the First Civilizations in the Mediterranean basin, the Middle East, India, China, Mesoamerica, and the Andes. In short, the development of civilization was becoming a global process.

Many of these second-wave civilizations likewise perished, as the collapse of the Roman Empire, Han dynasty China, and the Maya cities reminds us. They were followed by yet a third wave of civilizations, from roughly 600 to 1500 C.E., including those of China, Western Europe, West Africa, Russia, and the Islamic World (see Part 3). Furthermore, smaller expressions of civilization began to take shape elsewhere—in Ethiopia and West Africa, in Japan, Korea, Indonesia, Vietnam, and Cambodia. Thus the globalization of civilization continued apace. So too did the interaction of civilizations with one another and with the gathering and hunting peoples, agricultural village societies, and pastoral communities who were their neighbors.

But how did these second and third waves of civilization differ from the first ones? From a panoramic perspective, the answer is "not much." States and empires rose, expanded, and collapsed. But little fundamental change occurred amid these fluctuations. Monarchs continued to rule most of the new civilizations; women remained subordinate to men in all of them; a sharp divide between the elite and everyone else persisted almost everywhere, as did the practice of slavery. Furthermore, no technological or economic breakthrough occurred to create new kinds of human societies as the Agricultural Revolution had done earlier or as the Industrial Revolution would do much later.

But if we zoom in a bit more closely, significant changes emerge, even if they did not result in a thorough transformation of human life. Global population, for example, grew more rapidly, though with important fluctuations, as the Snapshot illustrates. This rate of growth, though rapid in comparison with Paleolithic times, was quite slow if measured against the explosive expansion of the past century. Another change lies in the growing size of the states or empires that structured civilizations. The Roman, Persian, Indian, and Chinese empires of second-wave civilizations, as well as the Arab, Mongol, and Inca empires of the third wave, all dwarfed the city-states of Mesopotamia and the Egypt of the pharaohs.

Second- and third-wave civilizations also generated important innovations in many spheres. Those in the cultural realm have been perhaps the most widespread and enduring.

SNAPSHOT World Population during the Age of Agricultural Civilization

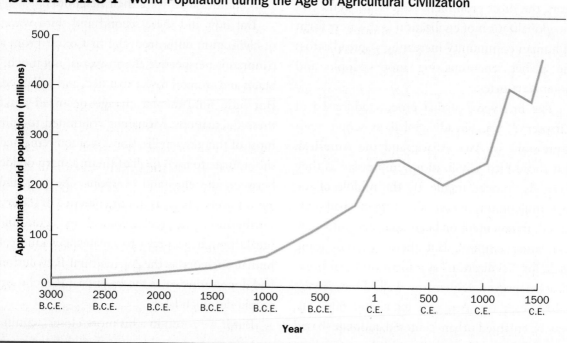

Data from Stephen K. Sanderson, *Social Transformation* (Oxford: Blackwell, 1995), 103.

The philosophical/religious systems of Confucianism and Daoism in China; Hinduism and Buddhism in India; Greek rationalism in the Mediterranean; and Judaism, Zoroastrianism, Christianity, and Islam in the Middle East—these traditions have provided the moral and spiritual framework within which most of the world's peoples have sought to order their lives.

Furthermore, technological innovations considerably enhanced human potential for manipulating the environment. "Chinese inventions and discoveries," wrote one prominent historian, "passed in a continuous flood from East to West for twenty centuries before the scientific revolution."[1] They included silk-handling machinery, the wheelbarrow, a better harness for draft animals, the crossbow, iron casting, gunpowder and firearms, the magnetic compass, paper, printing, porcelain, and more. India pioneered the crystallization of sugar and techniques for the manufacture of cotton textiles. Roman technological achievements were particularly apparent in construction and civil engineering—the building of roads, bridges, aqueducts, and fortifications—and in the art of glassblowing.

Nor were social hierarchies immune to change and challenge. India's caste system grew far more elaborate over time. Roman slaves and Chinese peasants on occasion rose in rebellion. Some Buddhist and Christian women found a measure of autonomy and opportunities for leadership and learning in the monastic communities of their respective traditions. Gender systems, too, fluctuated in the intensity with which women were subordinated to men.

A further process of change following the end of the First Civilizations lay in the emergence of far more elaborate, widespread, and dense networks of communication and exchange that connected many of the world's peoples to one another. Technologies diffused widely across large areas, as did religions and diseases, often borne by long-distance trade routes, such as the Silk Roads, that traversed Eurasia. In all of these ways, the world became quite different from what it had been in the age of the First Civilizations, even though economic and social patterns had not fundamentally changed.

The first three chapters of Part 2 focus in a thematic fashion on the Eurasian/North African civilizations of the second-wave era (600 B.C.E.–600 C.E.), which hosted the vast majority of the world's population, some 80 percent or more. Chapter 3 introduces them by examining and comparing their political frameworks and especially the empires that took shape in most of them. Far more enduring than their empires were the cultural or religious traditions that second-wave civilizations generated. These are examined, also comparatively, in Chapter 4. The social life of these civilizations, expressed in class, caste, slavery, and gender relationships, also varied considerably, as Chapter 5 spells out. In Chapter 6, the historical spotlight turns to inner Africa, the Americas, and Pacific Oceania, asking whether their histories paralleled Eurasian patterns or explored alternative possibilities.

In recalling this second-wave phase of the human journey, we will have occasion to compare the experiences of its various peoples, to note their remarkable achievements, to lament the tragedies that befell them and the suffering to which they gave rise, and to ponder their continuing power to fascinate us still.

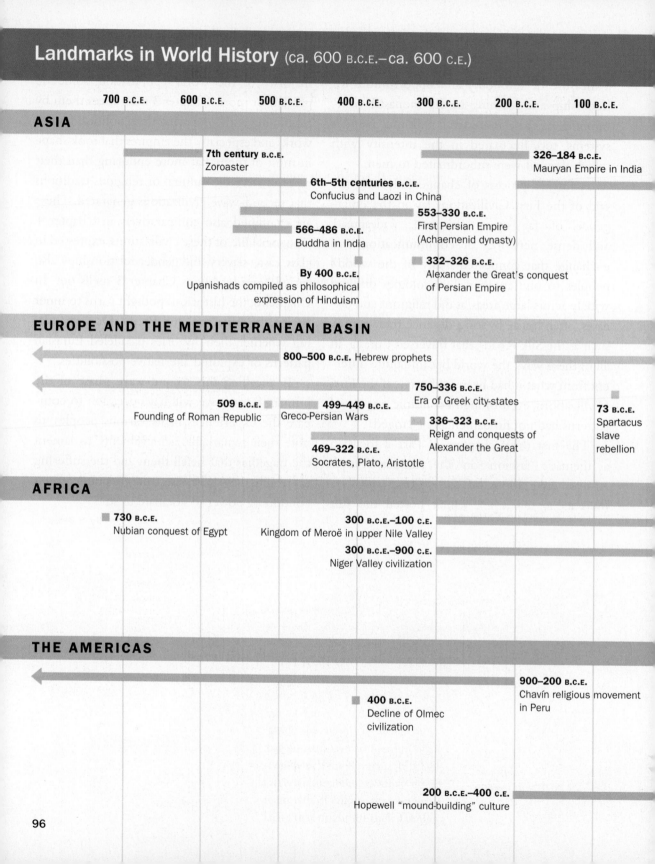

Landmarks in World History (ca. 600 B.C.E.–ca. 600 C.E.)

| | 700 B.C.E. | 600 B.C.E. | 500 B.C.E. | 400 B.C.E. | 300 B.C.E. | 200 B.C.E. | 100 B.C.E. |

ASIA

7th century B.C.E.
Zoroaster

6th–5th centuries B.C.E.
Confucius and Laozi in China

553–330 B.C.E.
First Persian Empire
(Achaemenid dynasty)

566–486 B.C.E.
Buddha in India

By 400 B.C.E.
Upanishads compiled as philosophical
expression of Hinduism

332–326 B.C.E.
Alexander the Great's conquest
of Persian Empire

326–184 B.C.E.
Mauryan Empire in India

EUROPE AND THE MEDITERRANEAN BASIN

800–500 B.C.E. Hebrew prophets

750–336 B.C.E.
Era of Greek city-states

509 B.C.E.
Founding of Roman Republic

499–449 B.C.E.
Greco-Persian Wars

336–323 B.C.E.
Reign and conquests of
Alexander the Great

469–322 B.C.E.
Socrates, Plato, Aristotle

73 B.C.E.
Spartacus
slave
rebellion

AFRICA

730 B.C.E.
Nubian conquest of Egypt

300 B.C.E.–100 C.E.
Kingdom of Meroë in upper Nile Valley

300 B.C.E.–900 C.E.
Niger Valley civilization

THE AMERICAS

900–200 B.C.E.
Chavín religious movement
in Peru

400 B.C.E.
Decline of Olmec
civilization

200 B.C.E.–400 C.E.
Hopewell "mound-building" culture

200 B.C.E.–200 C.E.
Flourishing of Chinese empire:
Qin and Han dynasties

184 C.E.
Yellow Turban Rebellion
in China

300–800 C.E.
Spread of Buddhism in China

320–550 C.E.
Gupta dynasty in India

200 B.C.E.–200 C.E. High point of Roman Empire

1st century C.E.
Life of Jesus and Paul

4th century C.E.
Christianity becomes official
state religion in Roman Empire

476 C.E.
Collapse of western
Roman Empire

400 C.E.
Bantu cultures/peoples reach South Africa

50 C.E. Rise of Axum

300 C.E. Beginnings of trans-Saharan trade

4th century C.E.
Introduction of Christianity
to Axum

500 C.E.
Arrival of banana in
eastern Africa

100–800 C.E.
Moche civilization

250–900 C.E.
Maya civilization

300–600 C.E.
Teotihuacán

400–1000 C.E.
Wari and Tiwanaku

Museum of Qin Figures, Lintong, Xi'an, Shaanxi, China/Laurent Lecat/akg-images

CHAPTER 3

State and Empire in Eurasia / North Africa

600 B.C.E.–600 C.E.

Empires and Civilizations in Collision: The Persians and the Greeks
The Persian Empire
The Greeks
Collision: The Greco-Persian Wars
Collision: Alexander and the Hellenistic Era

Comparing Empires: Roman and Chinese
Rome: From City-State to Empire
China: From Warring States to Empire
Consolidating the Roman and Chinese Empires
The Collapse of Empires

Intermittent Empire: The Case of India

Reflections: Enduring Legacies of Second-Wave Empires

Are We Rome? It was the title of a thoughtful book, published in 2007, asking what had become a familiar question in the early twenty-first century: "Is the United States the new Roman Empire?"[1] With the collapse of the Soviet Union by 1991 and the subsequent U.S. invasions of Afghanistan and Iraq, some commentators began to make the comparison. The United States' enormous multicultural society, its technological achievements, its economically draining and overstretched armed forces, its sense of itself as unique and endowed with a global mission, its concern about foreigners penetrating its borders, its apparent determination to maintain military superiority—all of this invited comparison with the Roman Empire.

Supporters of a dominant role for the United States argued that Americans must face up to their responsibilities as "the undisputed master of the world" as the Romans did in their time. Critics warned that the Roman Empire became overextended abroad and corrupt and dictatorial at home and then collapsed, suggesting that a similar fate may await the American empire. Either way, the point of reference was an empire that had passed into history some 1,500 years earlier, a continuing reminder of the significance of the distant past for our contemporary world. In fact, for at least several centuries, that empire has been a source of metaphors and "lessons" about personal morality, corruption, political life, military expansion, and much more.

Even in a world largely critical of empires, they still excite the imagination of historians and readers of history alike. The earliest empires show up in the era of the First Civilizations when Akkadian, Babylonian, and Assyrian empires encompassed the city-states of Mesopotamia and established an enduring imperial tradition in the Middle East. Egypt became an imperial state when it temporarily ruled Nubia and the lands of

« Terra-Cotta Warrior Part of the immense funerary complex of terra-cotta warriors constructed for the Chinese ruler Qin Shihuangdi, this crossbow marksman represents the military power that reunified a divided China under the Qin dynasty in 221 B.C.E.

the eastern Mediterranean. Following in their wake were many more empires, whose rise and fall have been central features of world history for the past 4,000 years. ■

But what exactly is an empire? At one level, empires are simply states, political systems that exercise coercive power. The term, however, is normally reserved for larger and more aggressive states, those that conquer, rule, and extract resources from other states and peoples. Thus empires have generally encompassed a considerable variety of peoples and cultures within a single political system, and they have often been associated with political or cultural oppression. Frequently, empires have given political expression to a civilization or culture, as in the Chinese and Persian empires. But civilizations have also flourished without a single all-encompassing state or empire, as in the competing city-states of Mesopotamia, Greece, and Mesoamerica or the many rival states of post-Roman Europe. In such cases, civilizations were expressed in elements of a common culture rather than in a unified political system.

The major Eurasian empires of the second-wave era—those of Persia, Greece under Alexander the Great, Rome, China during the Qin (chihn) and Han dynasties, and India during the Mauryan (MORE-yuhn) and Gupta dynasties—shared a set of common problems. Would they seek to impose the culture of the imperial heartland on their varied subjects? Would they rule conquered people directly or through established local authorities? How could they extract the wealth of empire in the form of taxes, tribute, and labor while maintaining order in conquered territories? And they also shared a common destiny, as they vanished into history.

Why have these and other empires been of such lasting fascination to both ancient and modern people? Perhaps part of the reason is that they were so big, creating a looming presence in their respective regions. Their armies and their tax collectors were hard to avoid. Perhaps they fascinate also because they were so bloody. The violence of conquest easily grabs our attention, and certainly all of these empires were founded and sustained at a great cost in human life. Many people have found the collapse of these once-powerful states likewise intriguing. But empires have also commanded attention simply because they were influential. Probably the majority of humankind before the twentieth century lived out their lives in empires, where they were often governed by rulers culturally different from themselves. These imperial states brought together people of quite different traditions and religions and so stimulated the exchange of ideas, cultures, and values. Despite their violence, exploitation, and oppression, empires also imposed substantial periods of peace and security, which fostered economic and artistic development, commercial exchange, and cultural mixing. In many places, empire also played an important role in defining masculinity, as conquest generated a warrior culture that gave particular prominence to the men who created and ruled those imperial states.

SEEKING THE MAIN POINT

How might you assess—both positively and negatively—the role of empires in the history of the second-wave era?

Landmarks for Chapter 3

600 B.C.E.	400 B.C.E.	200 B.C.E.	1 C.E.	200 C.E.	400 C.E.	600 C.E.

THE PERSIAN WORLD

550–330 B.C.E.
Persian Empire

522–486 B.C.E.
Reign of Darius

331 B.C.E. Defeat at the hands of Alexander

490 and 480 B.C.E.
Greeks defeat Persia in major battles

THE MEDITERRANEAN WORLD

750–336 B.C.E.
Era of the Greek city-states

509 B.C.E.
Founding of Rome

200 B.C.E.–200 C.E.
High point of Roman Empire

499–449 B.C.E.
Greco-Persian Wars

334–323 B.C.E.
Conquests of Alexander the
Great/beginning of Hellenistic era

ca. 476 C.E.
Collapse of western Roman Empire

431–404 B.C.E.
Peloponnesian War

THE CHINESE WORLD

500–221 B.C.E.
Age of warring states

221–210 B.C.E.
Reign of Qin Shihuangdi

581–618 C.E.
Reunification of China under Sui dynasty

THE SOUTH ASIAN WORLD

ca. 600 B.C.E.
Crystallization of a northern Indian civilization

326–184 B.C.E.
Mauryan dynasty empire

320–550 C.E.
Gupta dynasty empire

268–232 B.C.E.
Reign of Ashoka

Empires and Civilizations in Collision: The Persians and the Greeks

The centuries between 600 B.C.E. and 600 C.E. witnessed the flowering of second-wave civilizations in the Mediterranean world, the Middle East, India, and China. For the most part, these distant civilizations did not directly encounter one another, as each established its own political system, cultural values, and ways of organizing society. A great exception to that rule lay in the Mediterranean world and in the Middle East, where the emerging Persian Empire and Greek civilization, physically adjacent to each other, experienced a centuries-long interaction and clash. It was one of the most consequential cultural encounters of the ancient world.

The Persian Empire

By the mid-sixth century B.C.E., the largest and most impressive of the world's empires was that of the Persians, an Indo-European people whose homeland lay on the Iranian plateau just north of the Persian Gulf. Living on the margins of the earlier Mesopotamian civilization, the Persians under the Achaemenid (ah-KEE-muh-nid) dynasty (550–330 B.C.E.) constructed an imperial system that drew on previous examples, such as the Babylonian and Assyrian empires, but far surpassed them all in both size and splendor. Under the leadership of the famous monarchs Cyrus (r. 559–530 B.C.E.) and Darius (r. 522–486 B.C.E.), Persian conquests quickly reached from Egypt to India, encompassing in a single state some 35 to 50 million people, an immensely diverse realm containing dozens of peoples, states, languages, and cultural traditions (see Map 3.1).

Guided Reading Question

■ **COMPARISON**
How did Persian and Greek civilizations differ in their political organization and values?

The **Persian Empire** centered on an elaborate cult of kingship in which the monarch, secluded in royal magnificence, could be approached only through an elaborate ritual. When the king died, sacred fires all across the land were extinguished, Persians were expected to shave their hair in mourning, and the manes of horses were cut short. Ruling by the will of the great Persian god Ahura Mazda (uh-HOORE-uh MAHZ-duh), kings were absolute monarchs, more than willing to crush rebellious regions or officials. Interrupted on one occasion while engaged with his wife, Darius ordered the offender, a high-ranking nobleman, killed, along with his entire clan. In the eyes of many, Persian monarchs fully deserved their effusive title—"Great king, King of kings, King of countries containing all kinds of men, King in this great earth far and wide." Darius himself best expressed the authority of the Persian ruler when he observed, "What was said to them by me, night and day, it was done."[2]

But more than conquest and royal decree sustained the empire. An effective administrative system placed Persian governors, called *satraps* (SAY-traps), in each of the empire's twenty-three provinces, while lower-level officials were drawn from local authorities. A system of imperial spies, known as the "eyes and ears of the King," represented a further imperial presence in the far reaches of the empire.

Map 3.1 The Persian Empire

At its height, the Persian Empire was the largest in the world. It dominated the lands of the First Civilizations in the Middle East and was commercially connected to neighboring regions.

A general policy of respect for the empire's many non-Persian cultural traditions also cemented the state's authority. Cyrus won the gratitude of the Jews when in 539 B.C.E. he allowed those exiled in Babylon to return to their homeland and rebuild their temple in Jerusalem (see "Judaism" in Chapter 4). In Egypt and Babylon, Persian kings took care to uphold local religious cults in an effort to gain the support of their followers and officials. The Greek historian Herodotus commented that "there is no nation which so readily adopts foreign customs. They have taken the dress of the Medes and in war they wear the Egyptian breastplate. As soon as they hear of any luxury, they instantly make it their own."[3] (See more on Herodotus's perceptions of Persia in Working with Evidence, Source 3.1, page 130.) For the next 1,000 years or more, Persian imperial bureaucracy and court life, replete with administrators, tax collectors, record keepers, and translators, provided a model for all subsequent regimes in the region, including, later, those of the Islamic world.

The infrastructure of empire included a system of standardized coinage, predictable taxes levied on each province, and a newly dug canal linking the Nile

Persepolis The largest palace in Persepolis, the Persian Empire's ancient capital, was the Audience Hall. The emperor officially greeted visiting dignitaries at this palace, which was constructed around 500 B.C.E. This relief, which shows a lion attacking a bull and Persian guards at attention, adorns a staircase leading to the Audience Hall. (Bridgeman Images)

with the Red Sea, which greatly expanded commerce and enriched Egypt. A "royal road," some 1,700 miles in length, facilitated communication and commerce across this vast empire. Caravans of merchants could traverse this highway in three months, but agents of the imperial courier service, using a fresh supply of horses every twenty-five to thirty miles, could carry a message from one end of the road to another in a week or two. Herodotus was impressed. "Neither snow, nor rain, nor heat, nor darkness of night," he wrote, "prevents them from accomplishing the task proposed to them with utmost speed." And an elaborate underground irrigation system sustained a rich agricultural economy in the semi-arid conditions of the Iranian plateau and spread from there throughout the Middle East and beyond.

Elaborate imperial centers, particularly Susa and Persepolis (per-SEP-uh-lis), reflected the immense wealth and power of the Persian Empire. Palaces, audience halls, quarters for the harem, monuments, and carvings made these cities into powerful symbols of imperial authority. Materials and workers alike were drawn from all corners of the empire and beyond. Inscribed in the foundation of Persepolis was Darius's commentary on what he had set in motion: "And Ahura Mazda was of such a mind, together with all the other gods, that this fortress [should] be built. And [so] I built it. And I built it secure and beautiful and adequate, just as I was intending to."[4]

The Greeks

It would be hard to imagine a sharper contrast than that between the huge and centralized Persian Empire, governed by an absolute and almost unapproachable monarch, and the small competing city-states of classical Greece, which allowed varying degrees of popular participation in political life. Like the Persians, the Greeks were an Indo-European people whose early history drew on the legacy of the First Civilizations, especially Egypt. The classical Greece of historical fame emerged around 750 B.C.E. as a new civilization and flourished for about 400 years before it was incorporated into a succession of foreign empires. During that relatively short period, the civilization of Athens and Sparta, of Plato and Socrates, of Zeus and Apollo took shape and collided with its giant neighbor to the east.

Map 3.2 Classical Greece and Its Colonies

The classical civilization of Greece was centered on a small peninsula of southeastern Europe, but Greek settlers planted elements of that civilization along the coasts of the Mediterranean and Black seas.

Calling themselves Hellenes, the Greeks created a distinctive civilization, particularly in comparison with that of the Persians. The total population of Greece and the Aegean basin was just 2 million to 3 million, a fraction of that of the Persian Empire. Furthermore, Greek civilization took shape on a small peninsula, deeply divided by steep mountains and valleys. Its geography certainly contributed to its political organization, which found expression, not in a Persian-style empire, but in hundreds of city-states or small settlements (see Map 3.2). Most were quite modest in size, with between 500 and 5,000 male citizens or free men. But Greek civilization, like its counterparts elsewhere, also left a decisive environmental mark on the lands it encompassed. Smelting metals such as silver, lead, copper, bronze, and iron required enormous supplies of wood, leading to deforestation and soil erosion. Plato declared that the area around Athens had become "a mere relic of the original country. . . . All the rich soil has melted away, leaving a country of skin and bone."[5]

Each of these city-states was fiercely independent and in frequent conflict with its neighbors, yet they had much in common, speaking the same language and worshipping the same gods. Every four years they temporarily suspended their continual conflicts to participate together in the Olympic Games, which began in 776 B.C.E. But this emerging sense of Greek cultural identity did little to overcome the endemic political rivalries of the larger city-states, including Athens, Sparta, Thebes, and Corinth, among many others.

Like the Persians, the Greeks were an expansive people, but their expansion took the form of settlement in distant places rather than conquest and empire. Pushed by a growing population, Greek traders in search of iron and impoverished Greek farmers in search of land undertook a remarkable emigration. Between 750 and 500 B.C.E., the Greeks established settlements all around the Mediterranean basin and the rim of the Black Sea. Settlers brought Greek culture, language, and building styles to these new lands, even as they fought, traded, and intermarried with their non-Greek neighbors.

The most distinctive feature of Greek civilization, and the greatest contrast with Persia, lay in the extent of popular participation in political life that occurred within at least some of the city-states. It was the idea of "citizenship," of free people managing the affairs of state and of equality for all citizens before the law, that was so unique. A foreign king, observing the operation of the public assembly in Athens, was amazed that male citizens as a whole actually voted on matters of policy: "I find it astonishing," he noted, "that here wise men speak on public affairs, while fools decide them."[6] Compared to the rigid hierarchies, inequalities, and absolute monarchies of Persia and other ancient civilizations, the Athenian experiment was remarkable. This is how one modern scholar defined it:

> Among the Greeks the question of who should reign arose in a new way.
> Previously the most that had been asked was whether one man or another
> should govern and whether one alone or several together. But now the
> question was whether all the citizens, including the poor, might govern and
> whether it would be possible for them to govern as citizens, without
> specializing in politics. In other words, should the governed themselves
> actively participate in politics on a regular basis?[7]

The extent of participation and the role of "citizens" varied considerably, both over time and from city to city. Early in Greek history, only wealthy and well-born men had the rights of full citizenship, such as speaking and voting in the assembly, holding public office, and fighting in the army. Gradually, men of the lower classes, mostly small-scale farmers, also obtained these rights as they gained the means to

Guided Reading Question

■ CHANGE

How did semidemocratic governments emerge in some of the Greek city-states?

purchase the armor and weapons that would allow them to serve as hoplites, or infantrymen, in the armies of the city-states. In many places, strong but benevolent rulers known as tyrants emerged for a time, usually with the support of the poorer classes, to challenge the prerogatives of the wealthy. Sparta developed a distinctive political and social system, famous for its extreme military discipline and its large population of helots, conquered people who lived in slave-like conditions. Most political authority was vested in its Council of Elders, composed of twenty-eight men over the age of sixty, who came from the wealthier and more influential segment of society and served for life.

It was in Athens that the Greek experiment in political participation achieved its most distinctive expression. Early steps in this direction were the product of intense class conflict, leading almost to civil war. A reforming leader named Solon emerged in 594 B.C.E. to push Athenian politics in a more democratic direction, breaking the hold of a small group of aristocratic families. Debt slavery was abolished, access to public office was opened to a wider group of men, and all citizens were allowed to take part in the Assembly. Later reformers such as Cleisthenes (KLEYE-sthuh-nees) and Pericles extended the rights of citizens even further. By 450 B.C.E., all holders of public office were chosen by lot and were paid, so that even the poorest could serve. The Assembly, where all citizens could participate, became the center of political life.

Athenian democracy was direct rather than representative, and it was distinctly limited. Women, slaves, and foreigners, who together constituted far more than half of the population, were wholly excluded from political participation. Nonetheless, political life in Athens was a world away from that of the Persian Empire and even from that of many other Greek cities.

Collision: The Greco-Persian Wars

In recent centuries, many writers and scholars have claimed classical Greece as the foundation of Western or European civilization. But the ancient Greeks themselves looked primarily to the East—to Egypt and the Persian Empire. In Egypt, Greek scholars found impressive mathematical and astronomical traditions on which they built. And Persia represented both an immense threat and later, under Alexander the Great, an opportunity for Greek empire building.

If ever there was an unequal conflict between civilizations, surely it was the collision of the Greeks and the Persians during a half century of intermittent military conflict known to us as the **Greco-Persian Wars** (499–449 B.C.E.). The confrontation between the small and divided Greek cities and Persia, the world's largest empire, grew out of their respective patterns of expansion. A number of Greek settlements on the Anatolian seacoast, known to the Greeks as Ionia, came under Persian control as that empire extended its domination to the west. In 499 B.C.E., some of these Ionian Greek cities revolted against Persian domination and found support from Athens on the Greek mainland. Outraged by this assault from the

Guided Reading Question
....
■ **CONNECTION**
What were the consequences for both sides of the encounter between the Persians and the Greeks?

remote and upstart Greeks, the Persians, twice in ten years (490 and 480 B.C.E.), launched major military expeditions to punish the Greeks in general and Athens in particular. Against all odds and all expectations, the Greeks held them off, defeating the Persians on both land and sea.

Though no doubt embarrassing, their defeat on the far western fringes of the empire had little effect on the Persians. However, it had a profound impact on Greece and especially on Athens, whose forces had led the way to victory. Beating the Persians in battle was a source of enormous pride for Greeks. In their view, this victory was the product of Greek freedoms, which had motivated men to fight with extraordinary courage for what they valued so highly. It contributed to a European construction of the world as sharply divided between East and West in which Persia represented Asia and despotism, and Greece signified Europe and freedom. The Greek victory also radicalized Athenian democracy, for it had been men of the poorer classes who had rowed their ships to victory and who were now in a position to insist on full citizenship. The fifty years or so after the Greco-Persian Wars were not only the high point of Athenian democracy but also the Golden Age of Greek culture. During this period, the Parthenon, that marvelous temple to the Greek goddess Athena, was built; Greek theater was born from the work of Aeschylus, Sophocles, and Euripides; and Socrates was beginning his career as a philosopher and an irritant in Athens.

But Athens's Golden Age was also an era of incipient empire. In the Greco-Persian Wars, Athens had led a coalition of more than thirty Greek city-states on the basis of its naval power, but Athenian leadership in the struggle against Persian aggression had spawned an imperialism of its own. After the war, Athens's efforts to solidify its dominant position among the allies led to intense resentment and finally to a bitter civil war (431–404 B.C.E.), with Sparta taking the lead in defending the traditional independence of Greek city-states. In this bloody conflict, known as the **Peloponnesian War**, Athens was defeated, and the Greeks exhausted themselves and magnified their distrust of one another. Thus the way was open to their eventual takeover by the growing forces of Macedonia, a frontier kingdom on the northern fringes of the Greek world. The glory days of the Greek experiment were over, but the spread of Greek culture was just beginning.

Collision: Alexander and the Hellenistic Era

By 338 B.C.E. Philip II, king of Macedonia, had politically unified Greece under his rule — something the Greeks themselves had been unable to achieve — but this unification came at the cost of the prized independence of its various city-states. It also set in motion a second round in the collision of Greece and Persia as Philip's son, known later as **Alexander the Great**, prepared to lead a massive Greek expedition against the Persian Empire. Such a project appealed to those who sought vengeance for the earlier Persian assault on Greece, but it also served to unify the fractious Greeks in a war against their common enemy.

The story of this ten-year expedition (334–323 B.C.E.), accomplished while Alexander was still in his twenties, has become the stuff of legend (see Map 3.3). Surely it was among the greatest military feats of the ancient world in that it created a Greek empire from Egypt and Anatolia in the west to Afghanistan and India in the east. In the process, the great Persian Empire was thoroughly defeated; its capital, Persepolis, was looted and burned; and Alexander was hailed as the "king of Asia." In Egypt, Alexander, then just twenty-four years old, was celebrated as a liberator from Persian domination, was anointed as pharaoh, and

Guided Reading Question

■ **CONNECTION**
What changes did Alexander's conquests bring in their wake?

MAPPING HISTORY

Map 3.3 Alexander's Empire and Successor States

Alexander's conquests, though enormous, did not long remain within a single empire, for his generals divided those lands into three successor states shortly after Alexander's death. This was the Hellenistic world within which Greek culture spread.

READING THE MAP: During which stage of Alexander's empire-building enterprise did he establish the most new cities?

MAKING CONNECTIONS: Compare this map with Map 3.2, which shows an earlier period of Greek political and cultural expansion. How would you describe the differences between the two processes of expansion? Are they similar in any way?

was declared by Egyptian priests to be the "son of the gods." Arrian, a later Greek historian, described Alexander in this way:

> His passion was for glory only, and in that he was insatiable. . . . Noble indeed was his power of inspiring his men, of filling them with confidence, and in the moment of danger, of sweeping away their fear by the spectacle of his own fearlessness.[8]

Alexander died in 323 B.C.E., without returning to Greece, and his empire was soon divided into three kingdoms, ruled by leading Macedonian generals.

From the viewpoint of world history, the chief significance of Alexander's amazing conquests lay in the widespread dissemination of Greek culture during what historians call the **Hellenistic era** (323–30 B.C.E.). Elements of that culture, generated in a small and remote Mediterranean peninsula, now penetrated the lands of the First Civilizations—Egypt, Mesopotamia, and India—resulting in one of the great cultural encounters of the ancient world.

The major avenue for the spread of Greek culture lay in the many cities that Alexander and later Hellenistic rulers established throughout the empire. Complete with Greek monuments, sculptures, theaters, markets, councils, and assemblies, these cities attracted many thousands of Greek settlers serving as state officials, soldiers, or traders. **Alexandria** in Egypt—the largest of these cities, with half a million people—was an enormous cosmopolitan center where Egyptians, Greeks, Jews, Babylonians, Syrians, Persians, and many others rubbed elbows. A harbor with space for 1,200 ships facilitated long-distance commerce. Greek learning flourished thanks to a library of some 700,000 volumes and the Museum, which sponsored scholars and writers of all kinds.

From cities such as these, Greek culture spread. From the Mediterranean to India, Greek became the language of power and elite culture. The Indian monarch Ashoka published some of his decrees in Greek, while an independent Greek state was established in Bactria in what is now northern Afghanistan. The attraction of many young Jews to Greek culture prompted the Pharisees to develop their own school system, as this highly conservative Jewish sect feared for the very survival of Judaism.

Cities such as Alexandria were very different from the original city-states of Greece, both in their cultural diversity and in the absence of the

Alexander the Great This mosaic of Alexander on horseback comes from the Roman city of Pompeii. It depicts the Battle of Issus (333 B.C.E.), in which Greek forces, although considerably outnumbered, defeated the Persian army, led personally by Emperor Darius III.
(ullstein bild via Getty Images)

independence so valued by Athens and Sparta. Now they were part of large conquest states ruled by Greeks: the Ptolemaic (TOL-uh-MAY-ik) empire in Egypt and the Seleucid empire in Persia. These were imperial states, which, in their determination to preserve order, raise taxes, and maintain the authority of the monarch, resembled the much older empires of Mesopotamia, Egypt, Assyria, and Persia. Macedonians and Greeks, representing perhaps 10 percent of the population in these Hellenistic kingdoms, were clearly the elite and sought to keep themselves separate from non-Greeks.

In Egypt, for example, different legal systems for Greeks and native Egyptians maintained this separation. An Egyptian agricultural worker complained that because he was an Egyptian, his supervisors despised him and refused to pay him.[9] Periodic rebellions expressed resentment at Greek arrogance, condescension, and exploitation. But the separation between the Greeks and native populations was by no means complete, and a fair amount of cultural interaction and blending occurred. Alexander himself had taken several Persian princesses as his wives and actively encouraged intermarriage between his troops and Asian women. In both Egypt and Mesopotamia, Greek rulers patronized the building of temples to local gods and actively supported their priests. A growing number of native peoples were able to become Greek citizens by obtaining a Greek education, speaking the language, dressing appropriately, and assuming Greek names. In India, Greeks were assimilated into the hierarchy of the caste system as members of the Kshatriya (warrior) caste, while in Bactria a substantial number of Greeks converted to Buddhism, including one of the Bactrian kings, Menander. A school of Buddhist art that emerged in the early centuries of the Common Era depicted the Buddha in human form for the first time, but in Greek-like garb with a face resembling the god Apollo. Clearly, not all was conflict between the Greeks and the peoples of the East.

In the long run, much of this Greek cultural influence faded as the Hellenistic kingdoms that had promoted it weakened and vanished by the first century B.C.E. While it lasted, however, it represented a remarkable cultural encounter, born of the collision of two empires and two second-wave civilizations. In the western part of that Hellenistic world, Greek rule was replaced by that of the Romans, whose empire, like Alexander's, also served as a vehicle for the continued spread of Greek culture and ideas.

Comparing Empires: Roman and Chinese

While the adjacent civilizations of the Greeks and the Persians collided, two other empires were taking shape—the Roman Empire on the far western side of Eurasia and China's imperial state on the far eastern end. They flourished at roughly the same time (200 B.C.E.–200 C.E.); they occupied a similar area (about 1.5 million square miles); and they encompassed populations of a similar size (50 to 60 million). They were the giant empires of their time, shaping the lives of close to half of the world's population. Unlike the Greeks and the Persians, the

Romans and the Chinese were only dimly aware of each other and had almost no direct contact. Historians, however, have seen them as fascinating variations on an imperial theme and have long explored their similarities and differences.

Rome: From City-State to Empire

Like the Persian Empire, that of the Romans took shape initially on the margins of the civilized world and was an unlikely rags-to-riches story. Beginning as a small and impoverished city-state on the western side of central Italy in the eighth century B.C.E., Rome later became the center of an enormous imperial state that encompassed the Mediterranean basin and included parts of continental Europe, Britain, North Africa, and the Middle East.

Originally ruled by a king, around 509 B.C.E. Roman aristocrats threw off the monarchy and established a republic in which the men of a wealthy class, known as patricians, dominated. Executive authority was exercised by two consuls, who were advised by a patrician assembly, the Senate. Deepening conflict with the poorer classes, called plebeians (plih-BEE-uhns), led to important changes in Roman political life. A written code of law offered plebeians some protection from abuse; a system of public assemblies provided an opportunity for lower classes to shape public policy; and a new office of tribune, who represented plebeians, allowed them to block unfavorable legislation. Romans took great pride in this political system, believing that they enjoyed greater freedom than did many of their more autocratic neighbors. The values of the republic — rule of law, the rights of citizens, the absence of pretension, upright moral behavior, keeping one's word — were later idealized as "the way of the ancestors."

With this political system and these values, the Romans launched their empire-building enterprise, a prolonged process that took more than 500 years (see Map 3.4). That empire began in the 490s B.C.E. with the Romans gaining control first over their Latin neighbors in central Italy and then, during the next several hundred years, over most of the Italian peninsula. Between 264 and 146 B.C.E., victory in the Punic Wars with Carthage, a powerful empire with its capital in North Africa, extended Roman control over the western Mediterranean, including Spain, and made Rome a naval power. Subsequent expansion in the eastern Mediterranean brought the ancient civilizations of Greece, Egypt, and Mesopotamia under Roman domination. Rome also expanded into territories in Southern and Western Europe, including present-day France and Britain. By early in the second century C.E., the Roman Empire had reached its maximum extent.

No overall design or blueprint drove the building of empire, nor were there any precedents to guide the Romans. What they created was something wholly new — an empire that encompassed the entire Mediterranean basin and beyond. It was a piecemeal process, which the Romans invariably saw as defensive. Each addition of territory created new vulnerabilities, which could be relieved only by more conquests. For some, the growth of empire represented opportunity. Poor soldiers hoped for land, loot, or salaries that might lift their families out of poverty. The well-to-do

Guided Reading Question

■ CHANGE

How did Rome grow from a single city to the center of a huge empire?

MAPPING HISTORY

Map 3.4 The Roman Empire

At its height in the second century C.E., the Roman Empire incorporated the entire Mediterranean basin, including the lands of the Carthaginian Empire, the less developed region of Western Europe, the heartland of Greek civilization, and the ancient civilizations of Egypt and Mesopotamia.

READING THE MAP: Where were the imperial borders demarcated by geographical features like rivers, oceans, or deserts? Where were they not?

MAKING CONNECTIONS: Comparing Map 3.4 with Maps 3.3 and 3.1, which regions of the former Persian and Greek empires did the Roman Empire incorporate?

---

or well-connected gained great estates, earned promotions, and sometimes achieved public acclaim and high political office. The wealth of long-established societies in the eastern Mediterranean (Greece and Egypt, for example) beckoned, as did the resources and food supplies of the less developed regions, such as Western Europe. There was no shortage of motivation for the creation of the Roman Empire.

Although Rome's central location in the Mediterranean basin provided a convenient launching pad for empire, it was the army, "well-trained, well-fed, and well-rewarded," that built the empire.[10] Drawing on the growing population of Italy, that army was often brutal in war. Carthage, for example, was utterly destroyed; the city was razed to the ground, and its inhabitants were either killed or sold into slavery. Nonetheless, Roman authorities could be generous to former enemies. Some were granted Roman citizenship; others were treated as allies and allowed to maintain their local rulers. As the empire grew, so too did political forces in Rome that favored its continued expansion and were willing to commit the necessary manpower and resources.

Centuries of empire building and the warfare that made it possible had an impact on Roman society and values. That vast process, for example, shaped Roman understandings of gender and the appropriate roles of men and women. Rome was becoming a warrior society in which the masculinity of upper-class male citizens was defined in part by a man's role as a soldier and a property owner. In private life, this translated into absolute control over his wife, children, and slaves, including the theoretical right to kill them without interference from the state. This ability of a free man and a Roman citizen to act decisively in both public and private life lay at the heart of ideal male identity. A Roman woman could participate proudly in this warrior culture by bearing brave sons and inculcating these values in her offspring.

Queen Boudica This statue in London commemorates the resistance of the Celtic people of eastern Britain against Roman rule during a revolt in 60–61 c.E., led by Queen Boudica. A later Roman historian lamented that "all this ruin was brought upon the Romans by a woman, a fact which in itself caused them the greatest shame." (Daniel Boulet, photographer)

Strangely enough, by the early centuries of the Common Era the wealth of empire, the authority of the imperial state, and the breakdown of older Roman social patterns combined to offer women in the elite classes a less restricted life than they had known in the early centuries of the republic. Upper-class Roman women had never been as secluded in the home as were their Greek counterparts, and now the legal authority of their husbands was curtailed by the intrusion of the state into what had been private life. The head of household, or *pater familias*, lost his earlier power of life and death over his family. Furthermore, such women could now marry without transferring legal control to their husbands and were increasingly able to manage their own finances and take part in the growing commercial economy of the empire. According to one scholar, Roman women of the wealthier classes gained "almost complete liberty in matters of property and marriage."[11] At the other end of the social spectrum, Roman conquests brought many thousands of women as well as men into the empire as slaves, who were often brutally treated and subject to the whims of their masters (see "The Making of Roman Slavery" in Chapter 5).

The relentless expansion of empire raised yet another profound question for Rome: could republican government and values survive the acquisition of a huge empire? The wealth of empire enriched a few, enabling them to acquire large estates and many slaves, while pushing growing numbers of free farmers into the cities and poverty. Imperial riches also empowered a small group of military leaders—Marius, Sulla, Pompey, Julius Caesar—who recruited their troops directly from the ranks of the poor and whose fierce rivalries brought civil war to Rome during the first century B.C.E. Traditionalists lamented the apparent decline of republican values—simplicity, service, free farmers as the backbone of the army, the authority of the Senate—amid the self-seeking ambition of the newly rich and powerful. When the dust settled from the civil war, Rome was clearly changing, for authority was now vested primarily in an emperor, the first of whom was Octavian, later granted the title of **Augustus** (r. 27 B.C.E.–14 C.E.), which implied a divine status for the ruler. The republic was history; Rome had become an empire and its ruler an emperor.

But it was an empire with an uneasy conscience, for many felt that in acquiring an empire, Rome had betrayed and abandoned its republican origins. Augustus was careful to maintain the forms of the republic—the Senate, consuls, public assemblies—and referred to himself as "first man" rather than "king" or "emperor," even as he accumulated enormous personal power. And in a bow to republican values, he spoke of the empire's conquests as reflecting the "power of the Roman people" rather than of the Roman state. Despite this rhetoric, he was emperor in practice, if not in name, for he was able to exercise sole authority, backed up by his command of a professional army. Later emperors were less reluctant to flaunt their imperial prerogatives.

During the first two centuries C.E., this empire in disguise provided security, grandeur, and relative prosperity for the Mediterranean world. This was the *pax Romana*, the Roman peace, the era of imperial Rome's greatest extent and greatest authority.

China: From Warring States to Empire

About the same time, on the other side of Eurasia, another huge imperial state was in the making—China. Here, however, the task was understood differently. It was not a matter of creating something new, as in the case of the Roman Empire, but of restoring something old. As one of the First Civilizations, a Chinese state had emerged as early as 2200 B.C.E. and under the Xia, Shang, and Zhou dynasties had grown progressively larger. By 500 B.C.E., however, this Chinese state was in shambles. Any earlier unity vanished in an "age of warring states," featuring the endless rivalries of seven competing kingdoms.

Trung Trac: Resisting the Chinese Empire

Empires have long faced resistance from people they conquer, and never more fiercely than in Vietnam, which was incorporated into an expanding Chinese empire for over a thousand years (111 B.C.E.–939 C.E.). Among the earliest examples of Vietnamese resistance to this occupation was that led around 40 C.E. by Trung Trac and her younger sister Trung Nhi, daughters in an aristocratic, military family. Trung Trac married a prominent local lord, Thi Sach, who was a vocal opponent of offensive Chinese policies — high taxes, even on the right to fish in local rivers; required payoffs to Chinese officials; and the imposition of Chinese culture on the Vietnamese. In response to this opposition, the Chinese governor of the region ordered Thi Sach's execution.

This personal tragedy provoked Trung Trac to take up arms against the Chinese occupiers, and she quickly gained a substantial following among peasants and aristocrats alike. Famously addressing some 30,000 soldiers, while dressed in full military regalia rather than the expected mourning clothes, she declared to the assembled crowd:

Foremost I will avenge my country.
Second I will restore the Hung lineage.
Third I will avenge the death of my husband.
Lastly I vow that these goals will be accomplished.

Within months, her forces had captured sixty-five towns, and, for two years, they held the Chinese at bay, while Trung Trac and Trung Nhi ruled a briefly independent state as co-queens. Chinese sources referred to Trung Trac as a "ferocious warrior." During their rule, the sisters eliminated the hated tribute taxes imposed by the Chinese and sought to restore the authority of Vietnamese aristocrats. A large military force, said to number roughly 80,000, counted among its leaders thirty-six female "generals," including the Trung sisters' mother.

Soon, however, Chinese forces overwhelmed the rebellion, and Trung Trac's support faded. Later Vietnamese records explained the failure of the revolt as a consequence of its female leadership. In traditional Vietnamese accounts, the Trung sisters committed suicide, jumping into a nearby river, as did a number of their followers.

Trung Trac and Trung Nhi.

Although the revolt failed, it lived on in stories and legends to inspire later Vietnamese resistance to invaders — Chinese, French, Japanese, and American alike. Men were reminded that women had led this rebellion. "What a pity," wrote a thirteenth-century Vietnamese historian, "that for a thousand years after this, the men of our land bowed their heads, folded their arms, and served the northerners [Chinese]."[12] To this day, temples, streets, and neighborhoods bear the name of the Trung sisters, and a yearly celebration in their honor coincides with International Women's Day. Usually depicted riding on war elephants and wielding swords, these two women also represent the more fluid gender roles then available to some Vietnamese women in comparison to the stricter patriarchy prevalent in China.

QUESTION

How might you imagine the reactions to the Trung sisters' revolt from Chinese officials; Vietnamese aristocrats; Vietnamese peasants, both male and female; and later generations of Vietnamese men and women?

photo: CPA Media

To many Chinese, this was a wholly unnatural and unacceptable condition, and rulers in various states vied to reunify China. One of them, known to history as **Qin Shihuangdi** (chihn shee-HUANG-dee) (i.e., Shihuangdi from the state of Qin), succeeded brilliantly. The state of Qin had already developed an effective bureaucracy, subordinated its aristocracy, equipped its army with iron weapons, and enjoyed rapidly rising agricultural output and a growing population. It also had adopted a political philosophy called Legalism, which advocated clear rules and harsh punishments as a means of enforcing the authority of the state. With these resources, Shihuangdi (r. 221–210 B.C.E.) launched a military campaign to reunify China and in just ten years soundly defeated the other warring states. Believing that he had created a universal and eternal empire, he grandly named himself Shihuangdi, which means the "first emperor." Unlike Augustus, he showed little ambivalence about empire. Subsequent conquests extended China's boundaries far to the south into the northern part of Vietnam, to the northeast into Korea, and to the northwest, where the Chinese pushed back the nomadic pastoral people of the steppes. (See Zooming In: Trung Trac, page 116, for an example of resistance to Chinese expansion.) Although the boundaries fluctuated over time, Shihuangdi laid the foundations for a unified Chinese state, which has endured, with periodic interruptions, to the present (see Map 3.5).

Building on earlier precedents, the Chinese process of empire formation was far more compressed than the centuries-long Roman effort, but it was no less dependent on military force and no less brutal. Scholars who opposed Shihuangdi's policies were executed and their books burned. Aristocrats who resisted his centralizing policies were moved physically to the capital. Hundreds of thousands of laborers were recruited to construct the Great Wall of China, designed to keep out northern "barbarians," and to erect a monumental mausoleum as the emperor's final resting place. More positively, Shihuangdi imposed a uniform system of weights, measures, and currency and standardized the length of axles for carts and the written form of the Chinese language.

As in Rome, the creation of the Chinese empire had domestic repercussions, but they were brief and superficial compared to Rome's transition from republic to empire. The speed and brutality of Shihuangdi's policies ensured that his own Qin dynasty did not last long, and it collapsed unmourned in 206 B.C.E. The **Han dynasty** that followed (206 B.C.E.–220 C.E.) retained the centralized features of Shihuangdi's creation, although it moderated the harshness of his policies, adopting a milder and moralistic Confucianism in place of Legalism as the governing philosophy of the state. It was Han dynasty rulers who consolidated China's imperial state and established the political patterns that lasted into the twentieth century.

Guided Reading Question

■ **COMPARISON**

Why was the Chinese empire able to take shape so quickly, while that of the Romans took centuries?

Map 3.5 Classical China
The brief Qin dynasty brought unity to the heartland of Chinese civilization, and the much longer Han dynasty extended its territorial reach south toward Vietnam, east to Korea, and west into Central Asia. To the north lay the military confederacy of the nomadic Xiongnu.

Consolidating the Roman and Chinese Empires

Once established, these two huge imperial systems shared a number of common features. Both, for example, defined themselves in universal terms. The Roman writer Polybius spoke of bringing "almost the entire world" under the control of Rome, while the Chinese state was said to encompass "all under heaven." Both of them invested heavily in public works—roads, bridges, aqueducts, canals, protective walls—all designed to integrate their respective domains militarily and commercially.

Furthermore, Roman and Chinese authorities both invoked supernatural sanctions to support their rule. By the first century C.E., Romans began to regard their deceased emperors as gods and established a religious cult to bolster the authority of living rulers. It was the refusal of early Christians to take part in this cult that provoked their periodic persecution by Roman authorities.

In China, a much older tradition had long linked events on Earth with the invisible realm called "Heaven." Neither a place nor a supreme being, Heaven was an impersonal moral force that regulated the universe. Emperors were called the Son of Heaven and were said to govern by the Mandate of Heaven so long as they ruled morally and with benevolence. Peasant rebellions, "barbarian" invasions, or disastrous floods were viewed as signs that the emperor had ruled badly and had thus lost the Mandate of Heaven. Among the chief duties of the emperor was the performance of various rituals thought to maintain the appropriate relationship between Heaven and Earth.

Guided Reading Question

■ **EXPLANATION**
Why were the Roman and Chinese empires able to enjoy long periods of relative stability and prosperity?

Both of these second-wave civilizations also absorbed a foreign religious tradition—Christianity in the Roman world and Buddhism in China—although the process unfolded somewhat differently. In the case of Rome, Christianity was born as a small sect in a remote corner of the empire. Aided by the *pax Romana* and Roman roads, the new faith spread slowly for several centuries, particularly among the poor and lower classes. Women were prominent in the leadership of the early Church, as were a number of more well-to-do individuals from urban families. After suffering intermittent persecution, Christianity in the fourth century C.E. obtained state support from emperors who hoped to shore up a tottering empire with a common religion, and thereafter the religion spread quite rapidly. (See "Society and the Church" in Chapter 10.)

In the case of China, by contrast, Buddhism came from India, far beyond the Chinese world. It was introduced to China by Central Asian traders and received little support from Han dynasty rulers. In fact, the religion spread only modestly among Chinese until after the Han dynasty collapsed (220 C.E.), when it appealed to people who felt bewildered by the loss of a predictable and stable society. Not until the Sui (sway) dynasty emperor Wendi (r. 581–604 C.E.) reunified China did the new religion gain state support, and then only temporarily. Buddhism thus became one of several alternative cultural traditions in a complex Chinese mix, while Christianity, though divided internally, ultimately became the dominant religious tradition throughout Europe. (See "China and Buddhism" in Chapter 8.)

The Roman and Chinese empires also had a different relationship to the societies they governed. Rome's beginnings as a small city-state meant that Romans, and even Italians, were always a distinct minority within the empire. The Chinese empire, by contrast, grew out of a much larger cultural heartland, already ethnically Chinese. Furthermore, as the Chinese state expanded, especially to the south, it actively assimilated the non-Chinese, or "barbarian," people. In short, they became Chinese, culturally, linguistically, and through intermarriage in physical appearance as well. Many Chinese in modern times are in fact descended from people who at one point or another were not Chinese at all.

The Roman Empire offered a different kind of assimilation to its subject peoples. Gradually and somewhat reluctantly, the empire granted Roman citizenship to various individuals, families, or whole communities for their service to the empire or in recognition of their adoption of Roman culture. In 212 C.E., Roman

Roman Actors This mosaic from Pompeii, likely created during the first century C.E., depicts the staging of a theatrical production. (DEA Picture Library/A Dagli Orti/Getty Images)

citizenship was bestowed on almost all free men of the empire. Citizenship offered clear advantages—the right to hold public office, to serve in the Roman military units known as legions, to wear a toga, and more—but it conveyed a legal status, rather than cultural assimilation, and certainly did not erase other identities, such as being Greek, Egyptian, or a citizen of a particular city.

Various elements of Roman culture—its public buildings, its religious rituals, its Latin language, its style of city life—were attractive, especially in Western Europe, where urban civilization was something new. In the eastern half of the empire, however, things Greek retained tremendous prestige. Many elite Romans in fact regarded Greek culture—its literature, philosophy, and art—as superior to their own and proudly sent their sons to Athens for a Greek education. To some extent, the two blended into a mixed Greco-Roman tradition, which the empire disseminated throughout the realm. Other non-Roman cultural traditions—such as the cult of the Persian god Mithra or the compassionate Egyptian goddess Isis, and, most extensively, the Jewish-derived religion of Christianity—also spread throughout the empire. Nothing similar occurred in Han dynasty China, except for Buddhism, which established a modest presence, largely among foreigners. Chinese culture experienced little competition from older, venerated, or foreign traditions.

It was widely recognized across much of East Asia—in Japan, Korea, and Vietnam, for example—as the model to which others should conform.

Language served these two empires in important but contrasting ways. Latin, an alphabetic language depicting sounds, gave rise to various distinct languages—Spanish, Portuguese, French, Italian, Romanian—whereas Chinese did not. Chinese characters, which represented words or ideas more than sounds, were not easily transferable to other languages. Written Chinese, however, could be understood by all literate people, no matter which spoken dialect of the language they used. Thus Chinese, more than Latin, served as an instrument of elite assimilation. For all of these reasons, the various peoples of the Roman Empire were able to maintain their separate cultural identities far more than was the case in China.

Politically, both empires established effective centralized control over vast regions and huge populations, but the Chinese, far more than the Romans, developed an elaborate bureaucracy to hold the empire together. The Han emperor Wudi (r. 141–87 B.C.E.) established an imperial academy for training officials for an emerging bureaucracy with a curriculum based on the writings of Confucius. This was the beginning of a civil service system, complete with examinations and selection by merit, which did much to integrate the Chinese

A Chinese Musician This Chinese stone relief from the fifth century C.E. depicts a "celestial musician," a minor Buddhist deity, playing a *pipa,* a string instrument of Central Asian origin. (De Agostini Picture Library/G. Dagli Orti/Bridgeman Images)

empire and lasted into the early twentieth century. Roman administration was a somewhat ramshackle affair, relying more on regional aristocratic elites and the army to provide cohesion. Unlike the Chinese, however, the Romans developed an elaborate body of law, applicable equally to all people of the realm, that dealt with matters of justice, property, commerce, and family life. Chinese and Roman political development thus generated different answers to the question of what made for good government. For those who inherited the Roman tradition, it was good laws, whereas for those in the Chinese tradition, it was good men.

Finally, both Roman and Chinese civilizations had marked effects on the environment in various ways. The Roman poet Horace complained of the noise and smoke of the city and objected to the urban sprawl that extended into the adjacent fertile lands. Rome's mining operations, the smelting of metals, its large-scale agriculture, and its growing population—all of this led to extensive deforestation and consequent soil erosion. The shortage of wood in the heartland of the empire led to the relocation of some ceramic workshops to Gaul, where timber was more plentiful. Lead pollution, derived from the smelting of lead ores in open furnaces and from lead water pipes and cooking pots, shows up in the bones of Roman burials and as far away as Greenland, where studies of the ice cap indicate that lead in the atmosphere increased during Roman times. Here is perhaps the earliest example of international atmospheric pollution.

Large-scale Chinese ironworking during the Han dynasty likewise contributed to substantial urban air pollution, while a rapidly growing and dense population practicing intensive agriculture stripped the north China plain of its ancient forest cover, causing sufficient soil erosion to turn the Hwang-ho River its characteristic yellow-brown color. What had been known simply as "the River" now became the Yellow River, which frequently flooded with devastating results and over many centuries dramatically changed course. In addition, as China expanded north and west into the steppe lands of the pastoral peoples, military/agricultural colonies of Chinese farmers turned pasturelands into farmlands, plowing up long-established sod. When the Chinese state subsequently grew weaker or actually collapsed, such farms were abandoned, wind erosion took hold, and deserts emerged.

The Collapse of Empires

Empires rise, and then, with some apparent regularity, they fall, and in doing so, they provide historians with one of their most intriguing questions: what causes the collapse of these once-mighty structures? In China, the Han dynasty empire came to an end in 220 C.E.; the traditional date for the final disintegration of the Roman Empire is 476 C.E., although a process of decline had been under way for several centuries. In the Roman case, however, only the western half of the empire collapsed, while the eastern part, subsequently known as the Byzantine Empire, maintained the tradition of imperial Rome for another thousand years.

Despite these differences, a number of common factors have been associated with the end of these imperial states. At one level, they both simply got too big, too overextended, and too expensive to be sustained by the available resources, and no fundamental technological breakthrough was available to enlarge these resources. Furthermore, the growth of large landowning families with huge estates and political clout enabled them to avoid paying taxes, turned free peasants into impoverished tenant farmers, and diminished the authority of the central government. In China, such conditions led to a major peasant revolt, known as the Yellow Turban Rebellion, in 184 C.E. (see "Peasants" in Chapter 5).

Rivalry among elite factions created instability in both empires and eroded imperial authority. In China, persistent tension between castrated court officials (eunuchs) loyal to the emperor and Confucian-educated scholar-bureaucrats weakened the state. In the Roman Empire between 235 and 284 C.E., some twenty-six individuals claimed the title of Roman emperor, only one of whom died of natural causes. In addition, epidemic disease ravaged both societies, though more extensively in the Roman world. The population of the Roman Empire declined by 25 percent in the two centuries following 250 C.E., a demographic disaster that meant diminished production, less revenue for the state, and fewer men available to defend the empire's long frontiers.

Historians have often linked the collapse of empires with environmental factors as well, more often with reference to Rome than to Han dynasty China. Considerable fluctuations in the climate after about 250 C.E. led to drought in the third century, cold and wet conditions in the fourth, and increased rainfall and cooler temperatures in the fifth, all of which generated substantial soil erosion and declining agricultural productivity. The North African breadbasket of the empire suffered from serious salinization and increasingly desert-like conditions. The extent to which such factors contributed to the collapse of the Roman Empire remains a point of dispute among scholars.

To these mounting internal problems was added a growing threat from nomadic or semi-agricultural peoples occupying the frontier regions of both empires. The Chinese had long developed various ways of dealing with the Xiongnu and other nomadic people to the north—building the Great Wall to keep them out, offering them trading opportunities at border markets, buying them off with lavish gifts, contracting marriage alliances with nomadic leaders, and conducting periodic military campaigns against them. But as the Han dynasty weakened in the second and third centuries C.E., such peoples more easily breached the frontier defenses and set up a succession of "barbarian states" in north China. Culturally, however, many of these foreign rulers gradually became Chinese, encouraging intermarriage, adopting Chinese dress, and setting up their courts in Chinese fashion.

Guided Reading Question

■ **CHANGE**
What internal and external factors contributed to the collapse of the Roman and Chinese empires?

Anglo-Saxon Treasure This purse hinge recovered from the royal grave site at Sutton Hoo—one of the greatest hordes of Anglo-Saxon treasure ever found in England—is an exquisite piece of seventh-century barbarian art that combines intricate gold work inlaid with gemlike garnets and glass. The paired images in the center depict birds of prey hunting smaller birds—perhaps ducks. The outer pair comprise men standing between beasts. Above are three plaques decorated with elaborate geometric patterns, which are a hallmark of Germanic art from this period. (DEA Picture Library/Getty Images)

A weakening Roman Empire likewise faced serious problems from Germanic-speaking peoples living on its northern frontier. Growing numbers of these people began to enter the empire in the fourth century C.E.—some as mercenaries in Roman armies and others as refugees fleeing the invasions of the ferocious Huns, who were penetrating Europe from Central Asia. Once inside the declining empire, various Germanic groups established their own kingdoms, at first controlling Roman emperors and then displacing them altogether by 476 C.E. Unlike the nomadic groups in China, who largely assimilated Chinese culture, Germanic kingdoms in Western Europe developed their own ethnic identities—Visigoths, Franks, Anglo-Saxons, and others—even as they drew on Roman law and adopted Roman Christianity. Far more than in China, the fall of the western Roman Empire produced a new culture, blending Latin and Germanic elements, which provided the foundation for the hybrid civilization that would arise in Western Europe.

The collapse of empire meant more than the disappearance of centralized government and endemic conflict. In post-Han China and post-Roman Europe, it also meant the decline of urban life, a contracting population, less area under cultivation, diminishing international trade, and vast insecurity for ordinary people. It must have seemed that civilization itself was unraveling.

The most significant difference between the collapse of empire in China and that in the western Roman Empire lay in what happened next. In China, after about 350 years of disunion, disorder, frequent warfare, and political chaos, a Chinese imperial state, similar to that of the Han dynasty, was reassembled under the Sui (581–618 C.E.), Tang (618–907), and Song (960–1279) dynasties. Once again, a single emperor ruled; a bureaucracy selected by examinations governed; and the ideas of Confucius informed the political system. Such a Chinese empire persisted into the early twentieth century.

The story line of European history following the end of the western Roman Empire was very different indeed. No large-scale, centralized, imperial authority encompassing all of Western Europe has ever been successfully reestablished there for any length of time. The memory of Roman imperial unity certainly persisted, and many subsequently tried unsuccessfully to re-create it. But most of Western Europe dissolved into highly decentralized political systems involving nobles, knights and vassals, kings with little authority, various city-states in Italy, and small territories ruled by princes, bishops, or the pope. From this point on, Europe would be a civilization without an encompassing imperial state.

Why were Europeans unable to reconstruct something of the unity of their classical empire, while the Chinese clearly did? Surely the greater cultural homogeneity of Chinese civilization made that task easier than it was amid the vast ethnic and linguistic diversity of Europe. The absence in the Roman legacy of a strong bureaucratic tradition also contributed to European difficulties, whereas in China the bureaucracy provided some stability even as dynasties came and went. The Chinese also had in Confucianism a largely secular ideology that placed great value on political matters in the here and now. The Roman Catholic Church in

Europe, however, was frequently at odds with state authorities, and its "otherworldliness" did little to support the creation of large-scale empires. Finally, Chinese agriculture was much more productive than that of Europe, and for a long time its metallurgy was more advanced. These conditions gave Chinese state builders more resources to work with than were available to their European counterparts.

PRACTICING HISTORICAL THINKING

In comparing the Roman and Chinese empires, which do you find more striking—their similarities or their differences?

Intermittent Empire: The Case of India

Among the second-wave civilizations of Eurasia, empire loomed large in Persian, Mediterranean, and Chinese history, but it played a rather less prominent role in Indian history. The demise of the Indus Valley civilization by 1500 B.C.E. was followed over the next thousand years by the creation of a new civilization based farther east, along the Ganges River on India's northern plain.

By 600 B.C.E. what would become the second-wave civilization of South Asia had begun to take shape across northern India. Politically, that civilization emerged as a fragmented collection of towns and cities, some small republics governed by public assemblies, and a number of regional states ruled by kings. An astonishing range of ethnic, cultural, and linguistic diversity also characterized this civilization, as an endless variety of peoples migrated into India from Central Asia across the mountain passes in the northwest. These features of Indian civilization—political fragmentation and vast cultural diversity—have informed much of South Asian history throughout many centuries, offering a sharp contrast to the pattern of development in China. What gave Indian civilization a recognizable identity and character was neither an imperial tradition nor ethno-linguistic commonality, but rather a distinctive religious tradition,

Map 3.6 Empire in South Asia

Large-scale empires in the Indian subcontinent were less frequent and less enduring than those in China. Two of the largest efforts were those of the Mauryan and Gupta dynasties.

Guided Reading Question
....

■ **COMPARISON**
Why were centralized empires so much less prominent in India than in China?

known later to outsiders as Hinduism, and a unique social organization, the caste system. These features of Indian life are explored further in Chapters 4 and 5.

Nonetheless, empires and emperors were not entirely unknown in India's long history. Northwestern India had been briefly ruled by the Persian Empire and then conquered by Alexander the Great. These Persian and Greek influences helped stimulate the first and largest of India's short experiments with a large-scale political system, the **Mauryan Empire** (326–184 B.C.E.), which encompassed all but the southern tip of the subcontinent (see Map 3.6).

The Mauryan Empire was an impressive political structure, equivalent to the Persian, Chinese, and Roman empires, though not nearly as long-lasting. With a population of perhaps 50 million, the Mauryan Empire boasted a large military force, a civilian bureaucracy with various ministries, and a large contingent of spies to provide the rulers with local information. A famous treatise called the *Artha-shastra* (*The Science of Worldly Wealth*) articulated a pragmatic, even amoral, political philosophy for Mauryan rulers. It was, according to one scholar, "a book that frequently discloses to a king what calculating and sometimes brutal measures he must carry out to preserve the state and the common good."[13] The state also operated many industries—spinning, weaving, mining, shipbuilding, and armaments. This complex apparatus was financed by taxes on trade, on herds of animals, and especially on land, from which the monarch claimed a quarter or more of the crop.

Mauryan India is perhaps best known for one of its emperors, **Ashoka** (r. 268–232 B.C.E.), who left a record of his activities and his thinking in a series of edicts carved on rocks and pillars throughout the kingdom. Ashoka's conversion to Buddhism and his moralistic approach to governance gave his reign a different tone than that of China's Shihuangdi or Greece's Alexander the Great, who, according to legend, wept because he had no more worlds to conquer. Ashoka's legacy to modern India has been that of an enlightened ruler, who sought to govern in accord with the religious values and moral teachings of Hinduism and Buddhism.

Despite his good intentions, these policies did not long preserve the empire, which broke apart soon after Ashoka's death. About 600 years later, a second brief imperial experiment, known as the **Gupta Empire** (320–550 C.E.), took shape. Faxian, a Chinese Buddhist traveler in India at the time, noted a generally peaceful, tolerant, and prosperous land, commenting that the ruler "governs without decapitation or corporal punishment." Free hospitals, he reported, were available to "the destitute, crippled and diseased," but he also noticed "untouchables" carrying bells to warn upper-caste people of their polluting presence.[14] Culturally, the Gupta era witnessed a flourishing of art, literature, temple building, science, mathematics, and medicine, much of it patronized by rulers. Indian trade with China also thrived, and Indian commerce reached as far as the Roman world. When a Germanic leader named Alaric laid siege to Rome in 410 C.E., he demanded 3,000 pounds of Indian pepper to spare the city.

Thus India's political history resembled that of Western Europe after the collapse of the Roman Empire far more than that of China or Persia. Neither imperial

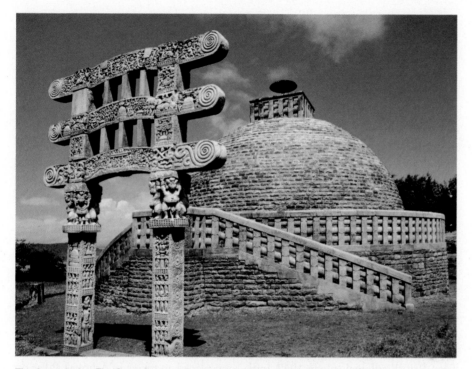

The Great Stupa The Great Stupa of Sanchi, the oldest stone building in India, was commissioned by Ashoka in the third century B.C.E. to house precious relics of the Buddha.
(© Luca Tettoni/Bridgeman Images)

nor regional states commanded the kind of loyalty or exercised the degree of influence that they did in other second-wave civilizations. India's unparalleled cultural diversity surely was one reason, as were invasions from Central Asia, which repeatedly smashed emerging states that might have provided the nucleus for an all-India empire. Finally, India's social structure, embodied in a caste system linked to occupational groups, made for intensely local loyalties at the expense of wider identities.

Nonetheless, a frequently vibrant economy fostered a lively internal commerce and made India the focal point of an extensive network of trade in the Indian Ocean basin. In particular, its cotton textile industry long supplied cloth throughout the Afro-Eurasian world. Strong guilds of merchants and artisans provided political leadership in major towns and cities, and their wealth supported lavish temples, public buildings, and religious festivals. Great creativity in religious matters generated Hindu and Buddhist traditions that later penetrated much of Asia. Indian mathematics and science, especially astronomy, were also impressive; Indian scientists plotted the movements of stars and planets and recognized quite early that the earth was round. Clearly, the absence of consistent imperial unity did not prevent the evolution of a lasting civilization.

REFLECTIONS

Enduring Legacies of Second-Wave Empires

These second-wave empires have long ago passed into history, but their descendants have kept them alive in memory, for they have proved useful, even in the twentieth and early twenty-first centuries. Such ancient empires have provided legitimacy for contemporary states, inspiration for new imperial ventures, and abundant warnings and cautions for those seeking to criticize more recent empires. For example, in bringing communism to China in the twentieth century, the Chinese leader Mao Zedong compared himself to Shihuangdi, the unifier of China and the brutal founder of its Qin dynasty. Reflecting on his campaign against intellectuals in general and Confucianism in particular, Mao declared to a Communist Party conference: "Emperor Qin Shihuang was not that outstanding. He only buried alive 460 Confucian scholars. We buried 460 thousand Confucian scholars. . . . To the charge of being like Emperor Qin, of being a dictator, we plead guilty."[15]

In contrast, modern-day Indians, who have sought to present their country as a model of cultural tolerance and nonviolence, have been quick to link themselves to Ashoka and his policies of inclusiveness. When the country became independent from British colonial rule in 1947, India soon placed an image of Ashoka's Pillar on the new nation's currency.

In the West, it has been the Roman Empire that has provided a template for thinking about political life. Many in Great Britain celebrated their own global empire as a modern version of the Roman Empire. If the British had been civilized by Roman rule, then surely Africans and Asians would benefit from falling under the control of the "more civilized" British. Likewise, to the Italian fascist dictator Benito Mussolini, his country's territorial expansion during the 1930s and World War II represented the creation of a new Roman Empire. Most recently, the United States' dominant role in the world has prompted the question, are the Americans the new Romans?

Historians frequently cringe as politicians and students use (and perhaps misuse) historical analogies to make their case for particular points of view in the present. But we have little else to go on except history in making our way through the complexities of contemporary life, and historians themselves seldom agree on the "lessons" of the past. Lively debate about the continuing relevance of these ancient empires shows that although the past may be gone, it surely is not dead.

Second Thoughts

What's the Significance?

Persian Empire, 102

Athenian democracy, 107

Greco-Persian Wars, 107

Peloponnesian War, 108

Alexander the Great, 108

Hellenistic era, 110

Alexandria, 110

Augustus, 115

pax Romana, 115

Qin Shihuangdi, 117

Han dynasty, 117

Mauryan Empire, 126

Ashoka, 126

Gupta Empire, 126

Big Picture Questions

1. What common features can you identify in the empires described in this chapter? In what ways did they differ from one another? What accounts for those differences?
2. Are you more impressed with the "greatness" of empires or with their destructive and oppressive features? Why?
3. Do you think that these second-wave empires hold "lessons" for the present, or are contemporary circumstances sufficiently unique as to render the distant past irrelevant?
4. **Looking Back:** How do these empires of the second-wave civilizations differ from the political systems of the First Civilizations?

Next Steps: For Further Study

Jane Burbank and Frederick Cooper, *Empires in World History* (2010). A fascinating account by two major scholars of the imperial theme across the world. Chapter 2 compares the Roman and Chinese empires.

Stanley Burstein, *The World from 1000 B.C.E. to 300 C.E.* (2017). An up-to-date account of Afro-Eurasian civilizations and their relationships by a prominent historian of the ancient world.

Arthur Cotterell, *The First Emperor of China* (1988). A biography of Shihuangdi.

Sarah Pomeroy et al., *Ancient Greece* (1999). A highly readable survey of Greek history by a team of distinguished scholars.

Walter Scheidel, ed., *Rome and China: Comparative Perspectives on Ancient World Empires* (2009). Places the historical trajectory and various themes of Roman and Han dynasty empires in a comparative context.

Romila Thapar, *Ashoka and the Decline of the Mauryas* (1961). A classic study of India's early empire builder.

Illustrated History of the Roman Empire, http://www.roman-empire.net. An interactive website with maps, pictures, and much information about the Roman Empire.

BBC, "The Immortal Emperor. Qin Shi Huang," presented by Tony Spawforth, 1996, https://www.youtube.com/watch?v=_6zcd68h-hs. A documentary film about China's "first emperor" and his enormous funerary complex of terra-cotta warriors.

Perceptions of Outsiders in the Ancient World

The peoples of ancient Eurasia did not live in splendid isolation from one another. Nor did they inhabit the kind of deeply interconnected and globalized world that the past century has created. But through war, commerce, the migration of peoples, the spread of religions, and sheer geographic proximity, some of those peoples became sharply aware of one another and developed mental images of life beyond the familiar confines of their own culture. What distortions arose as they pondered those outside their circle? How did the "other" provide opportunities to question or critique their own society? How and in what contexts were outsiders depicted in ancient art and in writing? The sources that follow provide five examples of this process from the ancient world.

SOURCE 3.1 A Greek Historian on Persia

Born to a wealthy Greek family in Asia Minor, Herodotus (ca. 485–425 B.C.E.) came of age when the wars between the Greeks and Persians were still recent memories. He devoted much of his life to recording the history of that great conflict in a series of books known as *The Histories*. In doing so, he pretty much invented for the Western world the craft of history as a systematic and connected narrative based on research. As a man of means, he was able to travel widely in the Persian Empire, Egypt, Syria, Babylon, Sicily, and Italy, making notes of what he saw and collecting stories, myths, and oral recollections along the way. The selection that follows contains some of his personal impressions of Persia.

- What cultural differences does Herodotus notice between Greek ways of living and those of Persia?

- What posture does Herodotus take toward these differences? He does refer to Persians as "barbarians," but at the time that term may have meant simply "non-Greek," without the implication of "savage" or "uncivilized" that it later acquired. Does he express a critical view of the Persians or a more positive understanding?

- What parts of this account might be helpful to historians seeking to describe life in ancient Persia? What might a historian learn about the Greeks' views of themselves from this description?

HERODOTUS | *The Histories* | **mid-5th century** B.C.E.

The customs that I know the Persians follow are these. They have no images of the gods and no temples or altars; they consider the use of them a sign of foolishness. This comes, I think, from their not believing the gods to have the same nature as human beings, as the Greeks imagine. The Persians' practice is to climb to the tops of the highest mountains to offer sacrifices to Zeus, the Greek name for the chief god of the universe. The Persians use this god's name to refer to the whole extent of the sky. They also sacrifice to the sun and moon, to the earth, to fire, to water, and to the winds. . . .

Of all the days in the year, the one they celebrate the most is their birthday. It is customary to serve much more food on that day than usual. The richer Persians have an ox, a horse, a camel, and an ass roasted whole for the meal; poorer people cook smaller kinds of cattle. They eat relatively few main courses but many extra courses, which they serve a few dishes at a time. For this reason, the Persians say that the Greeks leave a meal hungry because they have nothing worth mentioning served to them as an extra after the meats and that if the Greeks did have extra courses served, they would never stop eating. The Persians love wine and drink large amounts of it. . . .

When they meet another person in the street, you can tell if the people meeting are of equal status by the following indication: If they are, instead of speaking, they kiss each other on the lips. In the case where one is a little inferior to the other, the kiss is given on the cheek. Where the difference of rank is great, the inferior lies down on the ground in front of the superior. . . . The farther away other peoples live, the less the Persians respect them. The reason is that they regard themselves as very greatly superior in all respects to the rest of humanity, believing that other peoples' excellence is directly proportional to how close they live to Persia. . . .

No one so readily adopts foreign customs as the Persians. For this reason, they wear clothing like that of the Medes, considering it superior to their own. In war, they wear Egyptian armor to protect their chests. As soon as they hear of any luxury from any country, they instantly make it their own. In particular, they learned from the Greeks to have sex with adolescent boys. Each man has several wives and an even greater number of concubines.

In terms of manliness, manly courage on the battlefield is the greatest proof, with fathering many sons the second greatest. . . . They carefully educate their sons from the age of five to the age of twenty in only three subjects: riding horses, shooting arrows, and speaking the truth. Until boys are five, they are not allowed to come into the sight of their fathers, but instead spend their time with the women. They do this so that if the child dies young, the father will not be saddened at losing him.

I praise this custom and the following one too. The king does not put anyone to death for a single instance of wrong-doing, and no Persian inflicts an extreme penalty on a slave for a single instance of wrong-doing.

I can say all these things about the Persians with complete certainty, relying on my own personal knowledge.

Source: Herodotus, *The Histories*, 1:131–37, 140, in *Herodotus and Sima Qian: The First Great Historians of Greece and China*, edited by Thomas R. Martin (Boston: Bedford/St. Martin's, 2010), 46–49.

■ ■ ■

SOURCE 3.2 **A Greek Goldsmith Depicts the Scythians** ▶

Nomadic Scythian pastoralists who grazed their animals on the vast grasslands north of the Black Sea traded extensively with Greek colonies along the coast. Skilled craftsmen in these settlements regularly created luxury items for nomadic elites like this magnificent gold beaker dating from the fourth century B.C.E. The beaker depicts scenes from the everyday life of pastoralists, including the stringing of a bow, the bandaging of a wound, and, in the scene depicted here, the pulling of a tooth—a common if painful procedure in the ancient world. Found in a Scythian grave on the Crimean Peninsula, the lifelike figures reflect Greek artistic sensibilities, but the hairstyles and clothing are distinctly Scythian.

■ An elite Scythian most likely commissioned this beaker. How does this information shape how you think about this Greek depiction of the Scythians?

■ Does the beaker offer any evidence that the Greek craftsman who made it had directly encountered Scythians?

■ Both the beaker and Herodotus present Greek views of other cultures. What does the beaker add to the insights offered by Herodotus?

Scythian Cup, Crimea | **4th century B.C.E.**

State Hermitage Museum, St. Petersburg, Russia/Archives Charmet/Bridgeman Images

■ ■ ■

SOURCE 3.3 A Roman Historian on the Germans

Occupying much of Central Europe north of the Roman Empire, ancient Germanic-speaking peoples were never a single "nation" but rather a collection of tribes, clans, and chiefdoms. They were regarded by the Romans as barbarians, though admired and feared for their military skills. These Germanic peoples were famously described by Tacitus (56–117 C.E.), a Roman official and well-known historian. Tacitus himself had never visited the lands of the people he describes; rather, he relied on earlier written documents and interviews with merchants and soldiers who had traveled and lived in the region. Unlike Herodotus, he wrote about people who lived without the states and cities characteristic of civilizations.

- What can we learn from Tacitus's account about the economy, politics, society, and culture of the Germanic peoples of the first century C.E.?

- Which statements of Tacitus might you regard as reliable, and which are more suspect? Why?

- Modern scholars have argued that Tacitus used the Germanic peoples to criticize aspects of his own Roman culture. What evidence might support this point of view?

- What differences might you notice between Herodotus's description of Persian civilization and Tacitus's discussion of an agricultural village society?

TACITUS | *Germania* | **1st century** C.E.

The tribes of Germany are free from all taint of intermarriages with foreign nations, and they appear as a distinct, unmixed race, like none but themselves. . . . All have fierce blue eyes, red hair, huge frames, fit only for a sudden exertion. They are less able to bear laborious work. Heat and thirst they cannot in the least endure; to cold and hunger their climate and their soil inure them. . . .

They choose their kings by birth, their generals by merit. These kings have not unlimited or arbitrary power, and the generals do more by example than by authority. . . . And what most stimulates their courage is that their squadrons or battalions, instead of being formed by chance or by a fortuitous gathering, are composed of families and clans. Close by them, too, are those dearest to them, so that they hear the shrieks of women, the cries of infants. . . .

Tradition says that armies already wavering and giving way have been rallied by women who, with earnest entreaties and bosoms laid bare, have vividly represented the horrors of captivity, which the Germans fear with such extreme dread on behalf of their women. . . . They even believe that the female sex has a certain sanctity and prescience, and they do not despise their counsels, or make light of their answers. . . .

Mercury is the deity whom they chiefly worship, and on certain days they deem it right to sacrifice to him even with human victims. . . . Augury and divination by lot no people practice more diligently. . . .

When they go into battle, it is a disgrace for the chief to be surpassed in valor, a disgrace for his followers not to equal the valor of the chief. . . . Feasts and entertainments, which though inelegant, are plentifully furnished, are their only pay. The means of this bounty come from war or rapine. Nor are they as easily persuaded to plough the earth and to wait for the year's produce as to challenge an enemy and earn the honor of wounds. Nay, they actually think it tame and stupid to acquire by the sweat of toil what they might win by their blood.

Whenever they are not fighting, they pass much of their time in hunting, and still more in idleness, giving themselves up to sleep and to feasting, the bravest and the most warlike doing nothing, and surrendering the management of the household of the home, and of the land, to the women, the old men, and all the weakest members of the family. . . . It is the custom of the states to bestow by voluntary and individual contribution on the chief a present of cattle or of grain, which, while accepted as a compliment, supplies their wants. They are particularly delighted by gifts from neighboring tribes . . . such as choice steeds, heavy armor, trappings, and neckchains. We have now taught them to accept money also.

It is well known that the nations of Germany have no cities, and that they do not even tolerate closely contiguous dwellings. They live scattered and apart. . . . No use is made by them of stone or tile; they employ timber for all purposes, rude masses without ornament or attractiveness. . . .

Their marriage code, however, is strict, and indeed no part of their manners is more praiseworthy. Almost alone among barbarians they are content with one wife, except a very few among them. . . .

Very rare for so numerous a population is adultery, the punishment of which is prompt, and in the husband's power. Having cut off the hair of the adulteress and stripped her naked, he expels her from the house in the presence of her kinfolk, and then flogs her through the whole village. The loss of chastity meets with no indulgence; neither beauty, youth, nor wealth will procure the culprit a husband.

To limit the number of their children or to destroy any of their subsequent offspring is accounted infamous, and good habits are here more effectual than good laws elsewhere. . . .

It is the duty among them to adopt the feuds as well as the friendships of a father or a kinsman. These feuds are not implacable; even homicide is expiated by the payment of a certain number of cattle and of sheep, and the satisfaction is accepted by the entire family, greatly to the advantage of the state, since feuds are dangerous in proportion to a people's freedom. . . .

[S]laves are not employed after our manner with distinct domestic duties assigned to them, but each one has the management of a house and home of his own. The master requires from the slave a certain quantity of grain, of cattle, and of clothing, as he would from a tenant, and this is the limit of subjection.

Source: Alfred John Church and William Jackson Brodribb, *The Agricola and Germania of Tacitus* (London: Macmillan, 1877), 87ff.

■ ■ ■

SOURCE 3.4 A Roman Depiction of Sarmatians ▶

Germans were not the only people to periodically threaten the borders of the Roman Empire. Various groups of pastoralists from north of the Black Sea regularly migrated west, raiding and sometimes invading Roman territory, especially along the Danube River. The Romans respected the military prowess of these nomadic horsemen, whom they frequently fought and sometimes absorbed into their armies. Dating from the second century C.E., this bas-relief sculpture of pastoralist Sarmatians battling Roman forces was one scene among dozens carved onto a nearly one-hundred-foot-tall triumphal column in Rome celebrating the victories of Emperor Trajan. It depicts the distinctly heavily armored Sarmatian cavalry fleeing from advancing Romans. Some Sarmatians were taken as prisoners to Rome by Trajan in 104 C.E. to participate in victory celebrations, which may explain why they were incorporated into the column.

- Trajan's column was created to celebrate the emperor's victories. How might its purpose affect how you interpret and use this source?

- Notice the detailed depiction of Sarmatian weapons and their distinctive scale-like armor, which protected both rider and horse. What can these elements of the sculpture tell us about Roman knowledge of their enemies?

- What can the depiction of Scythians in Source 3.2 and Sarmatians here tell us about the pastoralists that lived on the northern fringes of the Greek and Roman civilizations?

Scene from Trajan's Column, Rome | **107–113** C.E.

Pictures from History/Bridgeman Images

■ ■ ■

SOURCE 3.5 A Chinese Historian on the Xiongnu

During the time of the Han dynasty, the Chinese historian and high official Sima Qian (ca. 145–86 B.C.E.), like his Roman counterpart Tacitus, had occasion to observe and describe neighboring "barbarian" peoples and their history. In Sima Qian's case, those people were the Xiongnu, pastoral nomads living to the north of China's Great Wall. China's relationship with these peoples fluctuated, involving war, trade, exchange of ambassadors, and periodic treaties (see "China and the

Northern Nomads" in Chapter 8). While the Chinese generally felt enormously superior to such "uncivilized" people, they were compelled on occasion to accommodate the military prowess of the Xiongnu. The following excerpts from Sima Qian's enormous history of ancient China illustrate his understanding of these people, who long represented a mirror through which the Chinese defined their image of themselves.

- Based on this document and what you know about Chinese life, what aspects of Xiongnu culture would likely appear most different or distasteful to Sima Qian?

- What can you infer about the relationship between China and the Xiongnu from the letter of Emperor Wen? How do you imagine he and Sima Qian felt about that letter?

- How might Sima Qian have reacted to the depictions of pastoralists in Sources 3.2 and 3.4?

SIMA QIAN | *Records of the Grand Historian* | ca. 100 B.C.E.

The ancestor of the Xiongnu descended from the ruler of the Xia dynasty, whose name was Qun Wei. From before the time of Emperors [of the third millennium B.C.E.], there have been barbarians . . . living in northern uncivilized areas and wandering around herding animals. They herd mainly horses, cattle, and sheep, but also some unusual animals, such as camels, donkeys, mules, and wild horses. . . . They move around looking for water and pasture and have no walled settlements or permanent housing. They do not farm, but they do divide their land into separate holdings under different leaders. They have no writing, and all contracts are verbal. When their children can ride a sheep, they begin to use bows and arrows to shoot birds and rodents. When they are older, they shoot foxes and rabbits for food. In this way, all the young men are easily able to become archers and serve as cavalry. It is their custom when times are easy to graze their animals and hunt with the bow for their living, but when hard times come, they take up weapons to plunder and raid. This is their innate nature. Their long-range weapons are bows and arrows; they use swords and spears in close combat. When they have the advantage in battle, they advance, but if not, they retreat, since there is no shame in running away. They are only concerned with self-interest, knowing nothing of proper behavior or justice.

Everyone, including the chiefs, eats the meat of their domesticated animals and wears clothing of hides and coats of fur. The men who are in their prime eat the fattiest and best food, while the elderly eat what is left over, since the Xiongnu treasure the strong and healthy but place little value on the weak and old. When his father dies, a son marries his stepmother, and when brothers die, the surviving brothers marry their widows. . . .

Following a battle . . . they are allowed to keep the plunder that they have seized. They make slaves of any prisoners of war. Therefore, when they make war, each warrior works for his own profit. They are very skilled at using decoy soldiers to trick opponents to their destruction. As soon as they see the enemy, they go after their booty like a flock of birds hungry for prey, but when they are defeated they disperse and evaporate. . . .

[*In describing the fluctuating relationship between the Chinese and the Xiongnu, Sima Qian quotes a letter written by the Chinese emperor Wen in 162 B.C.E. to the Xiongnu.*]

"The emperor respectfully asks about the health of the chief of the Xiongnu. Your ambassadors . . . have brought us two horses. We accept them with respect.

In accordance with what the previous emperor decreed the chief of the Xiongnu was to command the region north of the Great Wall where men shoot arrows from their bows, while we were to rule the region south of the wall, where the people live in houses and wear hats and sashes. Under this arrangement, the multitudes of inhabitants of these areas would get their food and clothing by farming, weaving, or hunting, fathers and sons would live side by side, rulers and officials would both be safe, and no one would act violently or rebel. We have heard, however, that a number of evil and deluded men, whose greed for wealth has overcome them, have forsaken justice and broken our peace treaty, paying no heed to what will happen to the multitudes of inhabitants and destroying the harmony that has been in place between the rulers of our two lands.

This, however, is now past history. You said in your [earlier] letter to me that, since our two nations have been brought together again in peace and our two rulers are again in agreement, you want to rest your army and let your horses graze, so that there may be prosperity and happiness for generation upon generation, and so that we can begin again to exist peacefully and harmoniously. We enthusiastically agree with what you said. . . . As long as we and the chief of the Xiongnu join together to walk this path . . . then no one in the entire world will fail to benefit. . . . Since the Xiongnu live in the north, where the country is cold and the severe frosts arrive early in the year, we have ordered our imperial officials to send annually to the chief of the Xiongnu a specified amount of grain, yeast, gold, silk cloth, thread, fiber stuffing for clothing, and other items.

The world currently is experiencing a secure peace, and our peoples are undisturbed. We and the chief of the Xiongnu must be like their parents. When we look back at the past, we recognize that the plans of our officials came to nothing as a result of minor things and insignificant causes. Nothing of this sort deserves to overturn the concord existing between brothers."

Source: Sima Qian, *The Records of the Historian*, chap. 110 in *Herodotus and Sima Qian: The First Great Historians of Greece and China*, edited by Thomas R. Martin (Boston: Bedford/St. Martin's, 2010), 129–30, 133, 136–37.

DOING HISTORY

1. **Making comparisons:** How might you compare the perceptions of outsiders in Sources 3.1, 3.3, and 3.5? Did the authors notice the same features of these societies? Did they focus more on what was exotic or different rather than on what may have been familiar? Did they adopt a similar posture toward the peoples they were describing? Were they simply reporting what they observed, or were they making judgments as well?

2. **Describing the "uncivilized":** Sources 3.2, 3.3, 3.4, and 3.5 all describe or depict peoples living beyond the boundaries of "civilization." To what extent did they describe or depict these peoples in a similar fashion? How do their descriptions differ?

3. **Relating encounters and observations:** How might the political or military relationships among different peoples affect perceptions of those peoples?

Early Sources on Foreign Cultures

Descriptions of ancient societies, particularly by eyewitness observers from other cultures, provide a rich but problematic source for modern historians. In the passages that follow, two such historians grapple with some of the potential difficulties with using descriptions of cultures written by outsiders. In Voice 3.1, Stephen Gosch and Peter Stearns examine some of the common problems with travelers' accounts and their implications for how historians use them. In Voice 3.2, Jerry Bentley explores the emergence of the concept of "barbarian" in Greek and Chinese thinking.

■ What key problems with travelers' accounts as historical sources do Gosch and Stearns identify?

■ Compare and contrast the emergence and meaning of "barbarian" in Greece and China. Which elements are similar? Which are distinctive?

■ **Integrating Primary and Secondary Sources:** From your reading of Herodotus's description of Persia (Source 3.1), do you agree with the argument in Voice 3.1 that Herodotus's account is only useful for understanding his own beliefs and the outlook of his audience, or do you think that his account also provides useful evidence about Persia?

■ **Integrating Primary and Secondary Sources:** What aspects of Tacitus's account of the Germans (Source 3.3) and Sima Qian's description of the Xiongnu (Source 3.5) support Bentley's description of barbarians in Greek and Chinese thinking? What aspects contradict or question his assertions?

VOICE 3.1

Stephen Gosch and Peter Stearns on Travelers' Accounts as Historical Sources | 2008

But can premodern travelers be believed? Are the narratives that they produced credible sources of evidence for modern scholars? Strabo, a Greek traveler in the first century CE, once wrote, "Everybody who tells the story of his own travels is a braggart." . . .

Premodern travelers not only frequently bragged about their experiences, they also depicted some of the peoples they encountered en route as strange and weird, as "others" quite different from, and often inferior to, themselves. An aspect of much travel writing before 1500, to which all students must remain alert, is the contrast, often implied rather than explicit, between "we" who are "normal" and "they" who are "bizarre." Some of the travelers . . . went even further spicing up their narratives with fantastic stories of monstrous beings, usually said to inhabit the outer edges of the earth. . . .

The bragging, the "othering" and the fantasies about strange creatures and monsters in premodern travel narratives, have led some researchers to reject much of this writing as of not real value to the historian. Some scholars, mostly in the field of literary studies, have argued that premodern travel is useful, but only for understanding the beliefs of the traveler and the expectations of his or her audience at home. One of the most interesting recent books about Herodotus . . . makes precisely this claim.

Source: Stephen S. Gosch and Peter N. Stearns, *Premodern Travel in World History* (New York: Routledge, 2008), 4.

VOICE 3.2

Jerry Bentley on the Idea of "Barbarian" | 1993

In Greek usage, the term *barbarian* originally was a linguistic rather than a social or cultural category: it referred to an individual who did not speak Greek. After Greeks became prominent in Mediterranean trade and began to develop an increasingly sophisticated civilization, about the eighth century B.C.E., the term *barbarian* took on strong connotations of cultural inferiority. The presence in Greek city-states of increasing numbers of foreign slaves—barbarians by definition—reinforced this semantic shift. Over time, the association of barbarism with inferiority encouraged settled, civilized peoples to adopt an aggressive and sometimes violent policy toward their nomadic or less urbanized neighbors. . . . By no means, though, was the notion of barbarism an exclusively western concept. Owen Lattimore has shown how early Chinese agriculturalists and steppe nomads progressively differentiated themselves, largely as a result of the almost inexorable enlargement by Chinese of the zone dedicated to agriculture. . . . As they enlarged the agricultural zone, they encountered mixed agriculturalists and herding peoples, whom they either absorbed into their own ranks or pushed into steppe regions beyond the point where settled agriculture was a practical activity. . . . Political, social, and cultural differentiation followed naturally from the radically different economic and environmental conditions of agricultural and steppe societies. Chinese soon came to regard nomadic steppe peoples as barbarians and to place relations with them under close supervision.

Source: Jerry H. Bentley, *Old World Encounters: Cross-Cultural Contacts and Exchanges in Pre-Modern Times* (New York: Oxford University Press, 1993), 23–24.

Culture and Religion in Eurasia / North Africa

600 B.C.E.–600 C.E.

China and the Search for Order
  The Legalist Answer
  The Confucian Answer
  The Daoist Answer
Cultural Traditions of Classical India
  South Asian Religion: From Ritual Sacrifice to Philosophical Speculation
  The Buddhist Challenge
  Hinduism as a Religion of Duty and Devotion
Toward Monotheism: The Search for God in the Middle East
  Zoroastrianism
  Judaism
The Cultural Tradition of Classical Greece: The Search for a Rational Order
  The Greek Way of Knowing
  The Greek Legacy
The Birth of Christianity . . . with Buddhist Comparisons
  The Lives of the Founders
  The Spread of New Religions
  Institutions, Controversies, and Divisions
Reflections: Religion and Historians

In September of 2009, Kong Dejun returned to China from her home in Great Britain. The occasion was a birthday celebration for her ancient ancestor Kong Fuzi, or Confucius, born 2,560 years earlier. Together with some 10,000 other people—descendants, scholars, government officials, and foreign representatives—Kong Dejun attended ceremonies at the Confucian Temple in Qufu, the hometown of China's famous sage. "I was touched to see my ancestor being revered by people from different countries and nations," she said.[1] What made this celebration remarkable was that it took place in a country still ruled by the Communist Party, which had long devoted enormous efforts to discrediting Confucius and his teachings. In the view of communist China's revolutionary leader, Mao Zedong, Confucianism was associated with class inequality, patriarchy, feudalism, superstition, and all things old and backward. But the country's ancient teacher and philosopher had apparently outlasted its revolutionary hero, for now the Communist Party has claimed Confucius as a national treasure and has established over 300 Confucian Institutes to study his writings. He appears in TV shows and movies, even as many anxious parents offer prayers at Confucian temples when their children are taking the national college entrance exams.

Buddhism and Daoism (DOW-i'zm) have also experienced something of a revival in China, as thousands of temples, destroyed during the heyday of communism, have been repaired and reopened. Christianity too has grown rapidly since the death of Mao in 1976. Here are reminders, in a Chinese context, of the continuing appeal of cultural traditions forged long ago. Those traditions are among the most enduring legacies that second-wave civilizations have bequeathed to the modern world. ∎

« **China's Cultural Traditions** In this idealized painting, attributed to the Chinese artist Wang Shugu (1649–1730), the Chinese teacher Confucius presents a baby Buddha to the Daoist master Laozi. The image illustrates the assimilation of a major Indian religion into China as well as the generally peaceful coexistence of these three traditions.

While the states and empires of Eurasia and North Africa transformed the political framework of the civilizations in these areas, the cultural and religious dimension of life in this huge region also changed dramatically. In China, it was the time of Confucius and Laozi (low-ZUH), whose teachings gave rise to Confucianism and Daoism, respectively. In India, a series of religious writings known as the Upanishads gave expression to the classical philosophy of what we know as Hinduism, while a religious reformer, Siddhartha Gautama (sih-DHAR-tuh GOW-tau-mah), set in motion a separate religion known later as Buddhism. In the Middle East, a distinctively monotheistic religious tradition appeared, expressed in Persian Zoroastrianism and in Judaism. Later, this Jewish religious outlook became the foundation for both Christianity and Islam. Finally, in Greece, a rational and humanistic tradition found expression in the writings of Socrates, Plato, Aristotle, and many others.

But alongside these larger and more extensive cultural systems, a multitude of locally embedded and orally transmitted religious traditions also flourished. Within the major civilizations, these "little traditions" interacted constantly with the emerging "great traditions." Thus ancient Greek gods persisted even as classical Greek philosophy took shape; older practices of Chinese ancestor veneration came to be incorporated in the emerging tradition of Confucianism; and Jews continued to be attracted to foreign deities despite the growing prominence of the one God, Yahweh. Furthermore, in societies that lay beyond the zone of civilization, such as those in Aboriginal Australia, local traditions linked living human beings to the land, to the vegetable and animal worlds, to their ancestors, and to the gods or spirits that inhabited everything. In this chapter, however, the spotlight falls on those larger cultural or religious traditions that emerged from the civilizations of the second-wave era and that have persisted into the twenty-first century.

SEEKING THE MAIN POINT

Fundamentally, the religions of the second-wave era were similar. Does the material of this chapter support or challenge this idea?

China and the Search for Order

By the eighth century B.C.E., the authority of China's Zhou dynasty had substantially weakened, and by 500 B.C.E. any unity that China had earlier enjoyed was long gone and violence grew in its wake. It was during these dreadful centuries of disorder and turmoil, known as the era of warring states (ca. 500–221 B.C.E.), that a number of Chinese thinkers began to consider how order might be restored, how the apparent tranquility of an earlier time could be realized again (see "China: From Warring States to Empire" in Chapter 3). From their reflections emerged classical cultural traditions of Chinese civilization.

The Legalist Answer

One answer to the problem of disorder—though not the first to emerge—was a hardheaded and practical philosophy known as **Legalism**. To Legalist thinkers,

Landmarks for Chapter 4

| 600 B.C.E. | 400 B.C.E. | 200 B.C.E. | 1 C.E. | 200 C.E. | 400 C.E. | 600 C.E. |

CHINA

ca. 551–479 B.C.E.
Life of Confucius

206 B.C.E.–220 C.E.
Confucianism prominent in Han dynasty

221–206 B.C.E.
Legalism prominent in Qin dynasty

184–204 C.E.
Yellow Turban Rebellion; informed by
Daoist beliefs

INDIA

ca. 800–400 B.C.E.
Upanishads compiled

ca. 300 C.E.
Bhagavad Gita compiled
in final form

ca. 566–486 B.C.E.
Life of Buddha

ca. 650 C.E.
Bhakti forms of Hinduism emerge

MIDDLE EAST

ca. 7th century B.C.E.(?)
Life of Zoroaster

4 B.C.E.–29 C.E.
Life of Jesus

ca. 45–65 C.E.
Paul's missionary journeys in eastern
Mediterranean region

586 B.C.E.
Jewish exile in Babylon

ca. 100–313 C.E.
Intermittent persecutions
of Christians in Roman Empire

310–380 C.E.
Christianity becomes state religion in
Armenia, Axum, and the Roman Empire

GREECE

ca. 600–300 B.C.E.
Greek rationalism

469–399 B.C.E.
Life of Socrates

429–348 B.C.E.
Life of Plato

384–322 B.C.E.
Life of Aristotle

143

the solution to China's problems lay in rules or laws, clearly spelled out and strictly enforced through a system of rewards and punishments. "If rewards are high," wrote Han Fei, one of the most prominent Legalist philosophers, "then what the ruler wants will be quickly effected; if punishments are heavy, what he does not want will be swiftly prevented."[2]

Legalists generally entertained a rather pessimistic view of human nature. Most people, they believed, were stupid and shortsighted. Only the state and its rulers could act in their long-term interests. Doing so meant promoting farmers and soldiers, the only two groups in society who performed essential functions, while suppressing merchants, aristocrats, scholars, and other classes regarded as useless.

Legalist thinking provided inspiration and methods for the harsh reunification of China under Shihuangdi and the Qin dynasty (221–206 B.C.E.), but the brutality of that short dynasty thoroughly discredited Legalism. Although its techniques and practices played a role in subsequent Chinese statecraft, few philosophers or rulers ever again openly advocated its ideas as the sole guide for Chinese political life. The Han dynasty (206 B.C.E.–220 C.E.) and all subsequent dynasties drew instead on the teachings of China's greatest sage — Confucius.

The Confucian Answer

Born to an aristocratic family in the state of Lu in northern China, Confucius (551–479 B.C.E.) was both learned and ambitious. Believing that he had found the key to solving China's problem of disorder, he spent much of his adult life seeking a political position from which he might put his ideas into action. But no such opportunity came his way. Perhaps it was just as well, for it was as a thinker and a teacher that Confucius left a profound imprint on Chinese history and culture and also on other East Asian societies, such as Korea and Japan. After his death, his students collected his teachings in a short book called the *Analects*, and later scholars elaborated and commented endlessly on his ideas, creating a body of thought known as **Confucianism**.

The Confucian answer to the problem of China's disorder was very different from that of the Legalists. Not laws and punishments, but the moral example of superiors was the Confucian key to a restored social harmony. For Confucius, human society consisted primarily of unequal relationships: the father was superior to the son; the husband to the wife; the older brother to the younger brother; and, of course, the ruler to the subject. If the superior party in each of these relationships behaved with sincerity, benevolence, and genuine concern for others, then the inferior party would be motivated to respond with deference and obedience. Harmony would then prevail. As Confucius put it, "The relation between superiors and inferiors is like that between the wind and the grass. The grass must bend when the wind blows across it." Thus, in both family life and in political life, the cultivation of *ren* — human-heartedness, benevolence, goodness — was the essential ingredient of a tranquil society.

Guided Reading Question

▪ COMPARISON
What different answers to the problem of disorder arose in classical China?

Guided Reading Question

▪ DESCRIPTION
Why has Confucianism been defined as a "humanistic philosophy" rather than a supernatural religion?

Filial Piety The long-enduring social order that Confucius advocated began at home with unquestioning obedience and the utmost respect for parents and other senior members of the family. This Qing dynasty woodcut illustrates the proper filial relationship between father and son in a variety of circumstances.
(Private Collection/Roland and Sabrina Michaud/akg-images)

But how were these humane virtues to be nurtured? Because people have a capacity for improvement, the key to moral progress was education, particularly an immersion in language, literature, history, philosophy, and ethics, all applied to the practical problems of government. Ritual and ceremonies were also important, for they conveyed the rules of appropriate behavior in the many and varying circumstances of life. For the "superior person," or "gentleman" in Confucian terms, serious personal reflection and a willingness to strive continuously to perfect his moral character were essential.

Such ideas had a pervasive influence in Chinese life as Confucianism became almost synonymous with Chinese culture. As China's bureaucracy took shape during and after the Han dynasty, Confucianism became the central element of the educational system, which prepared students for the examinations required to gain official positions. Thus generation after generation of China's male elite was steeped in the ideas and values of Confucianism.

In Confucian thinking, the family became a model for political life, a kind of miniature state. Filial piety, the honoring of one's ancestors and parents, was both valuable in itself and a training ground for the reverence due to the emperor and state officials. Such views of the family were rigidly patriarchal and set the tone for defining the lives of women and men alike. They were linked to a hierarchical and gendered understanding of the cosmos in which an inferior and receptive Earth, associated with the feminine, was in balance with the superior and creative principle of Heaven, associated with the masculine. Thus the subordinate and deferential position of women in relation to men was rooted in the structure of the cosmos itself. What this meant for women was spelled out by a somewhat later woman writer, **Ban Zhao** (bahn jow) (45–116 C.E.), in a famous work called *Lessons for Women*. "Let a woman modestly yield to others. . . . Always let her seem to tremble and to fear. . . . Then she may be said to humble herself before others."[3] Ban Zhao called for greater attention to education for young girls, not because they were equal to boys, but so that a young woman might be better prepared to serve her husband. Education for boys, on the other hand, enabled them to more effectively control their wives.

Corresponding Confucian virtues for ideal men were contained in the paired concepts of *wen* and *wu*, both limited largely to males. The superior principle of wen referred to the refined qualities of rationality, scholarship, and literary and artistic abilities, while wu focused attention on physical and martial achievements. Thus men alone, and superior men at that, were eligible for the civil service exams that led to political office and high prestige, while military men and merchants occupied a distinctly lower position in a male social hierarchy.[4]

Beyond defining gender expectations, Confucianism also placed great importance on history, for the ideal good society lay in the past. Confucian ideas were reform- ist, perhaps even revolutionary, but they were consistently presented as an effort to restore a past golden age. Those ideas also injected a certain democratic element into Chinese elite culture, for the great sage had emphasized that "superior men" and potential government officials were those of outstanding moral character and intellectual achievement, not simply those of aristocratic background. Usually only young men from wealthy families could afford the education necessary for passing examinations, but on occasion villagers could find the resources to sponsor one of their bright sons, potentially propelling him into the stratosphere of the Chinese elite while bringing honor and benefit to the village itself.

Confucian ideas were clearly used to legitimate the many inequalities of Chinese society, but they also established certain expectations for the superior parties in China's social hierarchy. Thus emperors should keep taxes low, administer justice, and provide for the material needs of the people. Those who failed to govern by these moral norms forfeited the Mandate of Heaven and invited upheaval and their replacement by another dynasty. Likewise, husbands should deal kindly with their wives and children, lest they invite conflict and disharmony in the family.

Finally, Confucianism marked Chinese elite culture by its secular, or nonreligious, character. Confucius did not deny the reality of gods and spirits. In fact, he advised people to participate in family and state rituals "as if the spirits were present," and he believed that the universe had a moral character with which human beings should align themselves. But the thrust of Confucian teaching was distinctly this- worldly and practical, concerned with human relationships, effective government, and social harmony. Members of the Chinese elite generally acknowledged that magic, the gods, and spirits were perhaps necessary for the lower orders of society, but educated people, they argued, would find them of little help in striving for moral improvement and in establishing a harmonious society.

The Daoist Answer

No civilization has ever painted its cultural outlook in a single color. As Confucian thinking became generally known in China, a quite different school of thought also took shape. Known as **Daoism**, it was associated with the legendary figure Laozi, who, according to tradition, was a sixth-century-B.C.E. archivist. He is said to have penned a short poetic volume, the *Daodejing* (DOW-DAY-JIHNG) (*The Way and Its Power*), before vanishing in the wilderness to the west of China on his water buffalo.

In many ways, Daoist thinking ran counter to that of Confucius, who had emphasized the importance of education and earnest striving for moral improvement and good government. The Daoists ridiculed such efforts as artificial and useless, claiming that they generally made things worse. In the face of China's disorder and chaos, Daoists urged withdrawal into the world of nature and encouraged behavior that was spontaneous, individualistic, and natural. Whereas Confucius focused on the world of human relationships, the Daoists turned the spotlight on the immense realm of nature and its mysterious unfolding patterns in which the "ten thousand things" appeared, changed, and vanished. "Confucius roams within society," the Chinese have often said. "Laozi wanders beyond."

The central concept of Daoist thinking is *dao*, an elusive notion that refers to the way of nature, the underlying and unchanging principle that governs all natural phenomena. The dao "moves around and around, but does not on this account suffer," wrote Laozi in the *Daodejing*. "All life comes from it. It wraps everything with its love as in a garment, and yet it claims no honor, for it does not demand to be lord. I do not know its name and so I call it the Dao, the Way, and I rejoice in its power."[5]

Amid the world of civilization, so highly valued by Confucius, the Daoists yearned for an earlier time, "an age of perfect virtue" that had been disrupted by Confucian striving for something better. Then, according to one Daoist master, "there were no paths and ramps on the mountains and no boats upon the bridges. . . . There were vast numbers of animals and grasses, and trees reached their natural growth. Wild animals could be taken for walks on leashes, and one could climb up to the nests of magpies and other birds." Such a vision of human harmony with nature contrasted sharply with the Confucian outlook, which urged "the development of a world of culture from a nature experienced as hostile." To Confucians, humankind "disposes over the world of [wild] things, tames wild animals, and brings cowed vermin under his control."[6] In contrast,

Guided Reading Question

■ **COMPARISON**
How did the Daoist outlook differ from that of Confucianism?

Chinese Landscape Painting
Focused largely on mountains and water, Chinese landscape paintings were much influenced by the Daoist search for harmony with nature. Thus human figures and buildings were usually eclipsed by towering peaks, waterfalls, clouds, mists, and trees. This thirteenth-century ink-on-silk painting illustrates that sensibility. The poem at the top reads: "Night rains cleansed the capital's suburban farms, / Morning sun brightens the emperor's city; / People work happily in a good year, / Dancing and singing they cross a path in the field." (Art Collection 2/Alamy)

individual Daoists often fled to the mountains, where they might experience the dao in union with nature. (See Sources 8.3 and 8.4 in Working with Evidence, Chapter 8, pages 350–353.)

Applied to human life, Daoism invited people to withdraw from the world of political and social activism, to disengage from the public life so important to Confucius, and to align themselves with the way of nature. It meant simplicity in living, small self-sufficient communities, limited government, and the abandonment of education and active efforts at self-improvement. "Give up learning," declares the *Daodejing*, "and put an end to your troubles." The flavor of the Daoist approach to life is evident in this passage from the *Daodejing*, describing a small and simple society:

> Though there were individuals with the abilities of ten or a hundred men,
> there should be no employment of them . . . ;
> Though they had boats and carriages, they should have no occasion to ride in
> them;
> There should be a neighbouring state within sight . . . ,
> but I would make the people . . . not have any intercourse with it.[7]

Like Confucianism, the Daoist perspective viewed family life as central to Chinese society, though the element of male/female hierarchy was downplayed in favor of complementarity and balance between the sexes.

The Yin Yang Symbol

Despite its various differences with the ideas of Confucianism, the Daoist perspective was widely regarded by elite Chinese as complementing rather than contradicting Confucian values (see the opening image in this chapter). Such an outlook was facilitated by the ancient Chinese concept of *yin* and *yang*, which expressed a belief in the unity of opposites (see figure). Thus a scholar-official might pursue the Confucian project of "government by goodness" during the day, but upon returning home in the evening or following his retirement, he might well behave in a more Daoist fashion — pursuing the simple life, reading Daoist philosophy, practicing meditation and breathing exercises in mountain settings, or enjoying painting, poetry, or calligraphy.

Daoism also shaped the culture of ordinary people as it entered popular religion. This kind of Daoism sought to tap the power of the dao for practical uses and came to include magic, fortune-telling, and the search for immortality. It also on occasion provided an ideology for peasant uprisings, such as the Yellow Turban Rebellion (184–204 C.E.), which imagined a utopian society without the oppression of governments and landlords. In its many and varied forms, Daoism, like Confucianism, became an enduring element of the Chinese cultural tradition.

Cultural Traditions of Classical India

The cultural development of Indian civilization was far different from that of China. Whereas Confucianism paid little attention to the gods, spirits, and speculation about religious matters, Indian elite culture embraced the Divine and all things spiritual with enthusiasm and generated elaborate philosophical visions about the nature of ultimate reality. But the Indian religious tradition—later called Hinduism—differed from other world religions as well. Unlike Buddhism, Christianity, or Islam, Hinduism had no historical founder; rather, it grew up over many centuries along with Indian civilization. Although it later spread into Southeast Asia, Hinduism was not a missionary religion seeking converts, but was, like Judaism, associated with a particular people and territory.

In fact, "Hinduism" was never a single tradition at all, and the term itself derived from outsiders—Greeks, Muslims, and later the British—who sought to reduce the infinite variety of Indian cultural patterns into a recognizable system. From the inside, however, Hinduism dissolved into a vast diversity of gods, spirits, beliefs, practices, rituals, and philosophies. This endlessly variegated Hinduism served to incorporate into Indian civilization the many diverse peoples who migrated into or invaded the South Asian peninsula over many centuries and several millennia. Its ability to accommodate this diversity gave India's cultural development a distinctive quality.

South Asian Religion: From Ritual Sacrifice to Philosophical Speculation

Despite the fragmentation and variety of Indian cultural and religious patterns, an evolving set of widely recognized sacred texts provided some commonality. The earliest of these texts, known as the **Vedas** (VAY-duhs), were collections of poems, hymns, prayers, and rituals. Compiled by priests called Brahmins, the Vedas were for centuries transmitted orally and were reduced to writing in Sanskrit around 600 B.C.E. In the Vedas, historians have caught fleeting glimpses of Indian civilization in its formative centuries (1500–600 B.C.E.). Those sacred writings tell of small competing chiefdoms or kingdoms, of sacred sounds and fires, of numerous gods, rising and falling in importance over the centuries. They also suggest a clearly patriarchal society, but one that afforded upper-class women somewhat greater opportunities than they later enjoyed. Vedic women participated in religious sacrifices, sometimes engaged in scholarship and religious debate, were allowed to wear the sacred thread that symbolized ritual purity in the higher castes, and could on occasion marry a man of their own choosing. The Vedas described as well the elaborate ritual sacrifices that Brahmin priests performed and for which they received substantial payments, enabling them to acquire enormous power and wealth, sometimes exceeding even that of kings and warriors.

As ritual became mechanical, formal, and expensive, criticism of Brahmins also grew. From this dissatisfaction arose another body of sacred texts, the **Upanishads** (oo-PAHN-ee-shahds). Composed by largely anonymous thinkers between 800 and 400 B.C.E., these were mystical and highly philosophical works that sought to probe the inner meaning of the rituals prescribed in the Vedas. In the Upanishads, external ritual gave way to introspective thinking, which expressed in many and varied formulations the central concepts of philosophical Hinduism that have persisted into

Guided Reading Question
....
■ **CHANGE**
In what ways did the religious traditions of South Asia change over the centuries?

modern times. Chief among them was the idea of Brahman, the World Soul, the final and ultimate reality. Beyond the multiplicity of material objects and individual persons and beyond even the various gods themselves lay this primal unitary energy or divine reality infusing all things, similar in some ways to the Chinese notion of the dao. This alone was real; the immense diversity of existence that human beings perceived with their senses was but an illusion.

The fundamental assertion of philosophical Hinduism was that the individual human soul, or *atman*, was in fact a part of Brahman. Beyond the quest for pleasure, wealth, power, and social position, all of which were perfectly normal and quite legitimate, lay the effort to achieve the final goal of humankind—union with Brahman, an end to our illusory perception of a separate existence. This was *moksha* (MOHK-shuh), or liberation, compared sometimes to a bubble in a glass of water breaking through the surface and becoming one with the surrounding atmosphere.

Hindu Ascetics Hinduism called for men in the final stage of life to leave ordinary ways of living and withdraw into the forests to seek spiritual liberation, or moksha. Here, in an illustration from an early thirteenth-century Indian manuscript, a holy man explores a text with three disciples in a secluded rural setting. (Musée des Arts Asiatiques-Guimet, Paris, France/© RMN–Grand Palais/Art Resource, NY)

Achieving this exalted state was held to involve many lifetimes, and the notion of *samsara*, or rebirth/reincarnation, became a central feature of Hindu thinking. Human souls migrated from body to body over many lifetimes, depending on the actions of individuals. This was the law of *karma*. Pure actions, appropriate to one's station in life, resulted in rebirth in a higher social position or caste. Thus the caste system of distinct and ranked groups, each with its own duties, became a register of spiritual progress.

If Hinduism underpinned caste, it also legitimated and expressed India's gender system. As South Asian civilization crystallized during the second-wave era, its patriarchal features tightened. Women were increasingly seen as "unclean below the navel," forbidden to learn the Vedas, and excluded from public religious rituals. The Laws of Manu, probably composed in the early centuries of the Common Era, advocated child marriage for girls to men far older than themselves and famously proclaimed: "In childhood a female must be subject to her father; in youth to her husband; when her lord [husband] is dead to her sons; a woman must never be independent."[8]

And yet some aspects of Hinduism served to empower women. Sexual pleasure was considered a legitimate goal for both men and women, and its many and varied techniques were detailed in the *Kamasutra*. Many Hindu deities were female, some life-giving and faithful and others, like Kali, fiercely destructive. Women were particularly prominent in the growing devotional cults dedicated to particular deities, where neither gender nor caste was an obstacle to spiritual fulfillment.

A further feature of Hindu religious thought lay in its provision of different paths to the ultimate goal of liberation, or moksha. Various ways to this final release, appropriate to people of different temperaments, were spelled out in Hindu teachings. Some might achieve moksha through knowledge or study; others by means of detached action in the world, doing one's ordinary work without regard to consequences; still others through passionate devotion to some deity or through extended meditation practice. Such ideas—carried by Brahmin priests and wandering ascetics or holy men, who had withdrawn from ordinary life to pursue their spiritual development—became widely known throughout India.

The Buddhist Challenge

About the same time as philosophical Hinduism was emerging, another movement took shape that soon became a distinct and separate religious tradition—Buddhism. Unlike Hinduism, this new faith had a historical founder, **Siddhartha Gautama** (ca. 566–ca. 486 B.C.E.), a prince from a small north Indian state. According to Buddhist tradition, the prince had enjoyed a sheltered and delightful youth until he encountered human suffering in the form of an old man, a sick person, and a corpse. Shattered by these revelations of aging, illness, and death, Siddhartha determined to find the cause of such sufferings and a remedy for them. And so, at the age of twenty-nine, the young prince left his luxurious life as well as his wife and child, shed his royal jewels, cut off his hair, and set off on a quest for enlightenment. This act of severing his ties to the attachments of ordinary life is known in Buddhist teaching as the Great Renunciation.

What followed were six years of spiritual experimentation that finally led Siddhartha to an ancient fig tree in northern India, now known as the Bodhi (enlightenment) tree. There, Buddhist sources tell us, he began a forty-nine-day period of intensive meditation that ended with an indescribable experience of spiritual realization. Now he was the **Buddha**, the man who had awakened. For the next forty years, he taught what he had learned, setting in motion the cultural tradition of Buddhism.

"I teach but one thing," the Buddha said, "suffering and the end of suffering." To the Buddha, suffering or sorrow—experiencing life as imperfect, impermanent, and unsatisfactory—was the central and universal feature of human life. This kind of suffering derived from desire

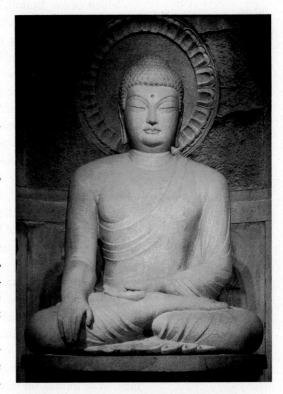

The Buddha's Enlightenment Dating from the late eighth century in Korea, this monumental and beautifully proportioned sculpture portrays the Buddha at the moment of his enlightenment, symbolized by his right hand touching the earth. Seated on a lotus pedestal, this image of the Buddha also shows the *ushnisha*, the round oval at the top of his head, which represents his spiritual attainment, and the dot in the center of his forehead indicating wisdom. This sculpture is located in the Seokguram Grotto or cave, where it is surrounded by numerous supernatural figures and by two Indian gods. It is widely considered a masterpiece of Buddhist art and is a Korean National Treasure. (Copyright © Cultural Heritage Administration of Korea, Courtesy of the Academy of Korean Studies, South Korea)

**Guided Reading
Question**

....

■ **COMPARISON**

In what ways did
Buddhism reflect Hindu
traditions, and in what
ways did it challenge
them?

or craving for individual fulfillment, from attachment to that which inevitably changes, particularly to the notion of a core self or ego that is uniquely and solidly "me." The cure for this "dis-ease" lay in living a modest and moral life combined with meditation practice. Those who followed the Buddhist path most fully could expect to achieve enlightenment, or *nirvana*, a virtually indescribable state in which individual identity would be "extinguished" along with all greed, hatred, and delusion. With the pain of unnecessary suffering finally ended, the enlightened person would experience an overwhelming serenity, even in the midst of difficulty, as well as an immense loving-kindness, or compassion, for all beings. It was a simple message, elaborated endlessly and in various forms by those who followed the Buddha.

Much of the Buddha's teaching reflected the Hindu traditions from which it sprang. The idea that ordinary life is an illusion, the concepts of karma and rebirth, the goal of overcoming the incessant demands of the ego, the practice of meditation, the hope for final release from the cycle of rebirth—all of these Hindu elements found their way into Buddhist teaching. In this respect, Buddhism was a simplified and more accessible version of Hinduism.

Other elements of Buddhist teaching, however, sharply challenged prevailing Hindu thinking. Rejecting the religious authority of the Brahmins, the Buddha ridiculed their rituals and sacrifices as irrelevant to the hard work of dealing with one's suffering. Nor was he much interested in abstract speculation about the creation of the world or the existence of God, for such questions, he declared, "are not useful in the quest for holiness; they do not lead to peace and to the direct knowledge of *nirvana*." Individuals had to take responsibility for their own spiritual development with no help from human authorities or supernatural beings. It was a path of intense self-effort, based on personal experience. The Buddha also challenged the inequalities of a Hindu-based caste system, arguing that neither caste position nor gender was a barrier to enlightenment. The possibility of "awakening" was available to all.

But when it came to establishing a formal organization of the Buddha's most devoted followers, the prevailing patriarchy of Indian society made itself felt. Only after considerable resistance did the Buddha reluctantly allow women to join a newly created order of monks, and they could do so only in a separate order of nuns, who were subjected to a series of rules that clearly subordinated them to men. Male monks, for example, could officially admonish the nuns, but the reverse was forbidden. Such policies reflected a particular strain of Buddhist thinking that viewed women as a distracting obstacle to male enlightenment.

Nonetheless, thousands of women flocked to join the Buddhist order of nuns, where they found a degree of independence unavailable elsewhere in Indian society. Buddhist nuns delighted in the relative freedom of their order, where they largely ran their own affairs, were forbidden to do household chores, and devoted themselves wholly to the search for "awakening," which many apparently achieved. A nun named Mutta declared: "I am free from the three crooked things: mortar, pestle, and my crooked husband. I am free from birth and death and all that dragged me back."[9]

Gradually, Buddhist teachings found an audience in India. Buddhism's egalitarian message appealed especially to lower-caste groups and to women. The availability of its teaching in the local language of Pali, rather than the classical Sanskrit, made it accessible. Establishing monasteries and stupas (commemorative monuments containing relics of the Buddha) on the site of neighborhood shrines to earth spirits or near a sacred tree linked the new religion to local traditions. The most dedicated followers joined monasteries, devoting their lives to religious practice and spreading the message among nearby people. State support during the reign of Ashoka (r. 268–232 B.C.E.) likewise helped the new religion gain a foothold in India as a distinct tradition separate from Hinduism.

As Buddhism spread, both within and beyond India, differences in understanding soon emerged, particularly as to how nirvana could be achieved or, in a common Buddhist metaphor, how to "cross the river" to the far shore of enlightenment. The Buddha had taught a rather austere doctrine of intense self-effort, undertaken most actively by monks and nuns who withdrew from society to devote themselves fully to the quest. This early version of the new religion, known as **Theravada** (Teaching of the Elders), portrayed the Buddha as an immensely wise teacher and model, but certainly not divine. It was more psychological than religious, a set of practices rather than a set of beliefs. The gods, though never completely denied, played little role in assisting believers in crossing the river. Each person had to row his or her own boat. Clearly, this was not for everyone.

As the message of the Buddha gained a mass following and spread across much of Asia, some of its early features—rigorous and time-consuming meditation practice, a focus on monks and nuns withdrawn from ordinary life, the absence of accessible supernatural figures able to provide help and comfort—proved difficult for many converts. And so the religion adapted. A new form of the faith, **Mahayana Buddhism**, developed in the early centuries of the Common Era and offered greater accessibility, a spiritual path available to a much wider range of people beyond the monks and ascetics, who were the core group in early Buddhism.

In most expressions of Mahayana Buddhism, enlightenment (or becoming a Buddha) was available to everyone; it was possible within the context of ordinary life, rather than a monastery; and it might occur within a single lifetime rather than over the course of many lives. While Buddhism had originally put a premium on spiritual wisdom or insight, Mahayana expressions of the faith emphasized compassion—the ability to feel the sorrows of other people as if they were one's own. This compassionate religious ideal found expression in the notion of bodhisattvas, fully enlightened beings who postponed their own final liberation in order to assist a suffering humanity. They were spiritual beings on their way to "Buddhahood." Furthermore, the historical Buddha himself became something of a god, and both earlier and future Buddhas were available to offer help. Elaborate descriptions and artistic representations of these supernatural beings, together with various levels of Heavens and Hells, transformed Buddhism into a popular religion of salvation.

Guided Reading Question

■ **COMPARISON**
What is the difference between the Theravada and Mahayana expressions of Buddhism?

Furthermore, religious merit, leading to salvation, might now be earned by acts of piety and devotion, such as contributing to the support of a monastery, and that merit might be transferred to others. This was the Great Vehicle, providing spiritual assistance and allowing far more people to make the voyage across the river. In many forms and variations, Mahayana Buddhism took root in China, Japan, Korea, Southeast Asia, and elsewhere. (See Working with Evidence: Representations of the Buddha, page 176, for the evolution of Buddhism reflected in images and stories.)

Hinduism as a Religion of Duty and Devotion

Strangely enough, Buddhism as a distinct religious practice ultimately died out in the land of its birth as it was reincorporated into a broader Hindu tradition, but it spread widely and flourished, particularly in its Mahayana form, in other parts of Asia. Buddhism declined in India perhaps in part because the mounting wealth of monasteries and the economic interests of their leading figures separated them from ordinary people. Competition from Islam after 1000 C.E. also played a role. But the most important reason for the waning of Buddhism in India was the growth during the first millennium C.E. of a new kind of popular Hinduism that was more accessible than the elaborate sacrifices of the Brahmins or the philosophical speculations of intellectuals. Expressed in the widely known epic poems called the *Mahabharata* (mah-hah-BAH-rah-tah) and the *Ramayana*, this revived Hinduism indicated more clearly that action in the world and the detached performance of caste duties (as a priest, farmer, merchant, or sweeper, for example) might also provide a path to liberation. It was perhaps a response to the challenge of Buddhism.

A much-beloved Hindu text known as the **Bhagavad Gita** (BUH-guh-vahd GEE-tuh) (compiled in its final form by 300 C.E.) conveyed the message that ordinary people, not just Brahmins, could also find spiritual fulfillment by selflessly performing the ordinary duties of their lives: "The man who, casting off all desires, lives free from attachments, who is free from egoism, and from the feeling that this or that is mine, obtains tranquility." Withdrawal from the world and asceticism were not the only ways to moksha.

Also becoming increasingly prominent was yet another religious path—the way of devotion to one or another of India's many gods and goddesses. Beginning in south India and moving northward between 600 and 1000 C.E., this *bhakti* (BAHK-tee) (worship) **movement** involved the intense adoration of and identification with a particular deity through songs, prayers, and rituals. By far the most popular deities were Vishnu, the protector and preserver of creation who was associated with mercy and goodness, and Shiva, a god representing the Divine in its destructive aspect, but many others also had their followers. This form of Hindu expression sometimes pushed against the rigid caste and gender hierarchies of Indian society by inviting all to an adoration of the Divine. Krishna, an incarnation of Vishnu as portrayed in the Bhagavad Gita, had declared that "those who take

Guided Reading Question

··

■ **CHANGE**
What new emphases characterized Hinduism as it responded to the challenge of Buddhism?

shelter in Me, though they be of lower birth—women, vaishyas [merchants] and shudras [workers]—can attain the supreme destination."

The proliferation of gods and goddesses, and of their bhakti cults, occasioned very little friction or serious religious conflict. "Hinduism," writes a leading scholar, "is essentially tolerant, and would rather assimilate than rigidly exclude."[10] This capacity for assimilation extended to an already-declining Buddhism, which for many people had become yet another cult worshipping yet another god. The Buddha in fact was incorporated into the Hindu pantheon as the ninth incarnation of Vishnu. By 1000 C.E., Buddhism had largely disappeared as a separate religious tradition within India.

Thus a constantly evolving and enormously varied South Asian religious tradition had been substantially transformed. An early emphasis on ritual sacrifice had given way to that of philosophical speculation, devotional worship, and detached action in the world. In the process, that tradition had generated Buddhism, which became the first of the great universal religions of world history, and then had absorbed that new faith back into the fold of an emerging popular Hinduism.

> ### PRACTICING HISTORICAL THINKING
>
> How did the evolution of cultural traditions in India and China differ during the era of second-wave civilizations?

Toward Monotheism: The Search for God in the Middle East

Paralleling the evolution of Chinese and Indian cultural traditions was the movement toward a distinctive monotheistic religious outlook in the Middle East, which found expression in Persian Zoroastrianism and in Judaism. Neither of these religions themselves spread very widely, but the monotheism that they nurtured became the basis for both Christianity and Islam, which have shaped so much of world history over the past 2,000 years. Amid the proliferation of gods and spirits that had long characterized religious life throughout the ancient world, monotheism—the idea of a single supreme deity, the sole source of all life and being—was a radical cultural innovation. That conception created the possibility of a universal religion, open to all of humankind, but it could also mean an exclusive and intolerant faith.

Zoroastrianism

During the glory years of the powerful Persian Empire, a new religion arose to challenge the polytheism of earlier times. Tradition dates its Persian prophet, Zarathustra (Zoroaster to the Greeks), to the sixth or seventh century B.C.E., although some scholars place him centuries earlier. Whenever he actually lived, his ideas took hold in Persia and received a degree of state support during the

The Zoroastrian Tradition in Persia Dating to around 500 B.C.E., this cylinder seal impression depicts the winged disk, symbolizing the Zoroastrian creator god Ahura Mazda, watching over the Persian emperor Darius during a lion hunt. Persian emperors were powerful patrons of the Zoroastrian faith, and Ahura Mazda was often depicted protecting or guiding their activities. (Werner Forman Archive/Bridgeman Images)

Achaemenid dynasty (550–330 B.C.E.). Appalled by the endemic violence of recurring cattle raids, Zarathustra recast the traditional Persian polytheism into a vision of a single unique god, Ahura Mazda, who ruled the world and was the source of all truth, light, and goodness. This benevolent deity was engaged in a cosmic struggle with the forces of evil, embodied in an equivalent supernatural figure, Angra Mainyu. Ultimately this struggle would be decided in favor of Ahura Mazda, aided by the arrival of a final savior who would restore the world to its earlier purity and peace. At a day of judgment, those who had aligned with Ahura Mazda would be granted new resurrected bodies and rewarded with eternal life in Paradise. Those who had sided with evil and the "Lie" (which found expression as greed, anger, and envy) were condemned to everlasting punishment. **Zoroastrianism** (zohr-oh-ASS-tree-ahn-i'zm) thus placed great emphasis on the free will of humankind and the necessity for each individual to choose between good and evil.

The Zoroastrian faith achieved widespread support within the Persian heartland, although it also found adherents in other parts of the empire, such as Egypt, Mesopotamia, and Anatolia. But it never became an active missionary religion and did not spread widely beyond the region. Alexander the Great's invasion of the Persian Empire and the subsequent Greek-ruled Seleucid dynasty (330–155 B.C.E.) were disastrous for Zoroastrianism, as temples were plundered, priests slaughtered,

Guided Reading Question

■ **CONNECTION**
What aspects of Zoroastrianism and Judaism later found a place in Christianity and Islam?

and sacred writings burned. But the new faith managed to survive this onslaught and flourished again during the Parthian (247 B.C.E.–224 C.E.) and Sassanid (224–651 C.E.) dynasties. It was the arrival of Islam and an Arab empire that occasioned the final decline of Zoroastrianism in Persia. Like Buddhism, the Zoroastrian faith vanished from its place of origin, but unlike Buddhism, it did not spread beyond Persia in a recognizable form. Some elements of the Zoroastrian belief system, however, did become incorporated into other religious traditions. The presence of many Jews in the Persian Empire meant that they surely became aware of Zoroastrian ideas. Many of those ideas—including the conflict of God and an evil counterpart (Satan); the notion of a last judgment and resurrected bodies; and a belief in the final defeat of evil, the arrival of a savior (Messiah), and the remaking of the world at the end of time—found a place in an evolving Judaism. Some of these teachings, especially the concepts of Heaven and Hell, later became prominent in those enormously influential successors to Judaism—Christianity and Islam. Thus the Persian tradition of Zoroastrianism continued to echo well beyond its disappearance in the land of its birth.

Judaism

While Zoroastrianism emerged in the greatest empire of its time, **Judaism**, the Middle East's other ancient monotheistic tradition, was born among one of the region's smaller and, at the time, less significant peoples—the Hebrews, also known as Jews. Their traditions, recorded in the Hebrew scriptures, tell of a dramatic history leading to the establishment around 1000 B.C.E. of a small state that soon split into two parts—a northern kingdom called Israel and a southern state called Judah.

In a region politically dominated by the large empires of Assyria, Babylon, and Persia, these tiny Hebrew communities lived a precarious existence. Israel was conquered by Assyria in 722 B.C.E., and many of its inhabitants were deported to distant regions, where they assimilated into the local culture. In 586 B.C.E., the kingdom of Judah likewise came under Babylonian control, and its elite class was shipped off to exile. "By the rivers of Babylon," wrote one of their poets, "there we sat down, yea, we wept, when we remembered Zion [Jerusalem]." In Babylonian exile these people, now calling themselves Jews, retained and renewed their cultural identity, and later a small number were able to return to their homeland. A large part of that identity lay in their unique religious ideas. It was in creating that religious tradition, rather than in building a powerful empire, that this small people cast a long shadow in world history.

From their unique historical memory of exodus from Egyptian slavery and exile in Babylon, the Hebrews evolved over many centuries a distinctive conception of God. Unlike the peoples of Mesopotamia, India, Greece, and elsewhere—all of whom populated the invisible realm with numerous gods and goddesses—Jews found in their God, whom they called Yahweh (YAH-way), a powerful and jealous

Guided Reading Question

■ **DESCRIPTION**
What was distinctive about the Jewish religious tradition?

Ancient Israel

deity, who demanded their exclusive loyalty. "Thou shalt have no other gods before me"—this was the first of the Ten Commandments. It was a difficult requirement, for as the Hebrews turned from a pastoral life to agriculture, many of them were attracted by the fertility gods of neighboring peoples. Their neighbors' goddesses were also attractive, offering a kind of spiritual support that the primarily masculine Yahweh could not. Foreign deities also entered Hebrew culture through royal treaty obligations with nearby states. Thus the emerging Hebrew conception of the Divine was not quite monotheism, for the repeated demands of the Hebrew prophets to turn away from other gods show that those deities remained real for many Jews. Over time, however, the priesthood that supported the one-god theory triumphed. The Jews came to understand their relationship to Yahweh as a contract or a covenant. In return for their sole devotion and obedience to God's laws, Yahweh would consider the Jews his chosen people, favoring them in battle, causing them to grow in numbers, and bringing them prosperity and blessing.

Unlike the bickering, arbitrary, polytheistic gods of Mesopotamia or ancient Greece, who were associated with the forces of nature and behaved in quite human fashion, Yahweh was increasingly seen as a lofty, transcendent deity of utter holiness and purity. But unlike the impersonal conceptions of ultimate reality found in Daoism and Hinduism, Yahweh was encountered as a divine person with whom people could actively communicate. He also acted within the historical process, bringing the Jews out of Egypt or using foreign empires to punish them for their disobedience.

Furthermore, for some, Yahweh was transformed from a god of war, who ordered his people to "utterly destroy" the original inhabitants of the Promised Land, to a god of social justice and compassion for the poor and the marginalized, especially in the passionate pronouncements of Jewish prophets. One of them, Isaiah, describes Yahweh as rejecting the empty rituals of his chosen but sinful people: "What to me is the multitude of your sacrifices, says the Lord. . . . Wash yourselves, make yourselves clean, . . . cease to do evil, learn to do good; seek justice; correct oppression; defend the fatherless; plead for the widow."[11]

Here was a distinctive conception of the Divine—singular, transcendent, personal, ruling over the natural order, engaged in history, and demanding social justice and moral righteousness above sacrifices and rituals. This set of ideas sustained a separate Jewish identity in both ancient and modern times, and it was this understanding of God that provided the foundation on which those later Abrahamic faiths of Christianity and Islam were built.

Jewish understanding of the natural world likewise informed all three religious traditions. The Jewish scriptures pronounced the world of nature as real and positively valued, not simply an illusion or a distraction from spiritual concerns, as in some versions of Hindu or Buddhist thinking. The first chapter of Genesis ends with God's review of his creation: "And God saw everything that he had made, and behold it was very good." Moreover, the material world disclosed or revealed something of the divine mystery. The writer of the Psalms affirmed that "the heavens declare the glory of God and the firmament shows his handiwork." Finally, Jewish tradition gave humankind a distinct role within God's creation. They were to "have dominion . . . over all the earth," even as Adam and Eve in the Garden of Eden were instructed "to till it and keep it." For some, this has meant permission to exploit the world's resources and its other creatures for human purposes, while for others it has been a mandate to preserve and protect the natural order.

The Cultural Tradition of Classical Greece: The Search for a Rational Order

Unlike the Jews, the Persians, or the civilization of India, Greek thinkers of the second-wave era generated no lasting religious tradition of world historical importance. The religion of these city-states brought together the unpredictable, quarreling, and lustful gods of Mount Olympus, secret fertility cults, oracles predicting the future, and the ecstatic worship of Dionysus, the god of wine. The distinctive feature of the classical Greek cultural tradition was the willingness of many Greek intellectuals to abandon this mythological framework, to affirm that the world was a physical reality governed by natural laws, and to assert that human rationality could both understand these laws and work out a system of moral and ethical life. In separating science and philosophy from conventional religion, the Greeks developed a way of thinking that bore some similarity to the secularism of Confucian thought in China.

The Greek Way of Knowing

The foundations of this **Greek rationalism** emerged in the three centuries between 600 and 300 B.C.E., coinciding with the flourishing of Greek city-states, especially Athens, and with the growth of its artistic, literary, and theatrical traditions. The enduring significance of Greek thinking lay not so much in the answers it provided to life's great issues, for the Greeks seldom agreed with one another, but rather in their way of asking questions. Their emphasis on argument, logic, and the relentless questioning of received wisdom; their confidence in human reason; their enthusiasm for puzzling out the world without much reference to the gods—these were the defining characteristics of the major Greek thinkers.

The great exemplar of this approach to knowledge was **Socrates** (469–399 B.C.E.), an Athenian philosopher who walked about the city engaging others in conversation about the good life. He wrote nothing, and his preferred manner of teaching was not the lecture or exposition of his own ideas but rather a constant questioning of the assumptions and logic of his students' thinking. Concerned always to puncture the pretentious, he challenged conventional ideas about the importance of wealth and power in living well, urging instead the pursuit of wisdom and virtue. He was

Guided Reading Question
....

■ **DESCRIPTION**
What were the distinctive features of the Greek intellectual tradition?

critical of Athenian democracy and on occasion had positive things to say about Sparta, the great enemy of his own city. Such behavior brought him into conflict with city authorities, who accused him of corrupting the youth of Athens and sentenced him to death. At his trial, he defended himself as the "gadfly" of Athens, stinging its citizens into awareness. "I shall question, and examine and cross-examine him," he declared, "and if I find that he does not possess virtue, but says he does, I shall rebuke him for scorning the things that are most important and caring more for what is of less worth."[12]

The earliest of the classical Greek thinkers, many of them living on the Ionian coast of Anatolia, applied this rational and questioning way of knowing to the world of nature. For example, Thales, drawing on Babylonian astronomy, predicted an eclipse of the sun and argued that the moon simply reflected the sun's light. He was also one of the first Greeks to ask about the fundamental nature of the universe and came up with the idea that water was the basic stuff from which all else derived, for it existed as solid, liquid, and gas. Others argued in favor of air or fire or some combination. Democritus suggested that atoms,

Plato in Conversation This first-century-B.C.E. Roman mosaic depicts Plato (second from left) seated among students and other philosophers in conversation. This image reflects the continued importance of Greek philosophy in the Roman world and illustrates the type of setting in which Plato taught. (World History Archive/Image Asset Management/AGE Fotostock)

tiny "uncuttable" particles, collided in various configurations to form visible matter. Pythagoras believed that beneath the chaos and complexity of the visible world lay a simple, unchanging mathematical order. What these thinkers had in common was a commitment to a rational and nonreligious explanation for the material world.

Such thinking also served to explain the functioning of the human body and its diseases. Hippocrates and his followers came to believe that the body was composed of four fluids, or "humors," that caused various ailments when out of proper balance. He also traced the origins of epilepsy, known to the Greeks as "the sacred disease," to simple heredity, arguing that it "has a natural cause . . . like other afflictions."[13] A similar approach informed Greek thinking about the ways of humankind. Herodotus, who wrote about the Greco-Persian Wars, explained his project as an effort to discover "the reason why they fought one another." This assumption that human reasons lay behind the conflict, not simply the whims of the gods, was what made Herodotus a historian in the modern sense of that word. Ethics and government also figured importantly in Greek thinking. **Plato** (429–348 B.C.E.) famously sketched out in *The Republic* a design for a good society. It would be ruled by a class of highly educated "guardians" led by a "philosopher-king." Such people would be able to penetrate the many illusions of the material world and to grasp the "world of forms," in which ideas such as goodness, beauty, and justice lived a real and unchanging existence. Only such people, he argued, were fit to rule.

Aristotle (384–322 B.C.E.), a student of Plato and a teacher of Alexander the Great, represents the most complete expression of the Greek way of knowing, for he wrote or commented on practically everything. With an emphasis on empirical observation, he cataloged the constitutions of 158 Greek city-states, identified hundreds of species of animals, and wrote about logic, physics, astronomy, the weather, and much else besides. Famous for his reflections on ethics, he argued that "virtue" was a product of rational training and cultivated habit and could be learned. As to government, he urged a mixed system, combining the principles of monarchy, aristocracy, and democracy. (See Controversies: Debating Religion and the Axial Age, page 162, for a discussion of controversial issues surrounding the emergence of Greek rationalism and other philosophical and religious traditions of this period.)

The Greek Legacy

The rationalism of the Greek tradition was clearly not the whole of Greek culture. The gods of Mount Olympus continued to be a reality for many people, and the ecstatic songs and dances that celebrated Dionysus, the god of wine, were anything but rational and reflective. The death of Socrates at the hands of an Athenian jury showed that philosophy could be a threat as well as an engaging pastime. Nonetheless, Greek rationalism, together with Greek art, literature, and theater, persisted long after the glory days of Athens were over. Alexander's empire and that of the Romans facilitated the spread of Greek culture within the Mediterranean basin and beyond, and many leading Roman figures sent their children to be educated in Athens at the Academy, which Plato had founded. An emerging Christian theology was expressed in terms of Greek philosophical concepts, especially those of Plato. Even after the western Roman Empire collapsed, classical Greek texts were preserved in the eastern half, known as the Byzantine Empire or Byzantium.

In the West, however, direct access to Greek texts was far more difficult in the chaotic conditions of post-Roman Europe, and for centuries Greek scholarship was neglected in favor of distinctly Christian writers. Much of that legacy was subsequently rediscovered after the twelfth century C.E. as European scholars

Debating Religion and the Axial Age

In 1947 a German philosopher, Karl Jaspers, coined a new term—the Axial Age. It referred to a time of particular creativity that gave rise to new cultural traditions all across Eurasia, but particularly in China, India, the Middle East, and the eastern Mediterranean region between 800 to 200 B.C.E. Here was an "axis," a pivot, or a major turning point in human cultural history, as Buddhism, Hinduism, Judaism, Confucianism, Daoism, and Greek rationalism began to take shape.[14]

It has been a controversial idea. Why, for example, did groups or individuals willing to challenge established traditions emerge during these centuries? Historians have noted disruptions to established patterns of life that may have opened the way to new thinking, but they do not always agree on which disruptions to emphasize.[15] Were economic factors the cause—an emerging iron-age technology, which generated more productive economies and more deadly warfare; greater prosperity in urban centers; or increased trade and the use of money? Or perhaps political disruptions were more important, such as the breakdown of political order during China's "age of warring states" or the endemic rivalries of Greek city-states. Social factors, such as a growing resentment against the pretensions and privileges of Brahmin priests, were likely part of the appeal of an emerging Buddhist faith. All of these disruptions, occurring in already literate societies, perhaps led thinkers to question older outlooks and to come up with new solutions to fundamental questions.

But how much did these Axial Age traditions have in common? The most enthusiastic advocates of the Axial Age idea believed they shared a great deal. All these traditions sought an alternative to an earlier polytheism, in which the activities of various gods and spirits explained what happened in this world. These gods and spirits had generally been seen as similar to human beings, though much more powerful. Through ritual and sacrifice, men and women might placate the gods or persuade them to do human bidding. In contrast, the new cultural traditions of the Axial Age sought to define a single source of order and meaning in the universe, some moral or religious realm that was sharply different from and higher than the sphere of human life.

Axial Age thinkers also shared a skepticism about the ability of human language to capture this Absolute or Ultimate Reality. Laozi in China famously declared that "the Dao that can be named is not the eternal Dao." The task of humankind, according to these new ways of thinking, was not so much about seeking intellectual clarity or beseeching the gods for favors as it was about transforming oneself morally or spiritually by aligning with that higher order. Living morally, controlling desire, taming the ego, and developing compassion—these were the goals of Axial Age traditions.

Those traditions also meant that people might more easily question and criticize their rulers or their societies, for now there was a higher point of reference from which to judge all of human life. Thus Jewish prophets strongly denounced the injustices of their society, and the Buddha challenged India's ancient caste system. Religion was becoming more clearly ethical. And at least implicitly, the Axial Age traditions suggested the possibility of a universal spiritual outlook available to everyone.

gained access to classical Greek texts. From that point on, the Greek legacy has been viewed as a central element of an emerging "Western" civilization. It played a role in formulating an updated Christian theology, in fostering Europe's seventeenth-century Scientific Revolution, and in providing a point of departure for much of European philosophy.

But despite these broad similarities, many historians and other scholars have been sharply critical or entirely dismissive of the Axial Age idea. Some critics have argued that the concept of an Axial Age greatly overestimated the uniqueness of what occurred during those few centuries in the first millennium B.C.E. After all, ancient Egyptian religion had long emphasized the moral behavior of individuals and judgment after death. In addition, the fourteenth-century-B.C.E. pharaoh Akhenaten directly challenged traditional Egyptian religion as he vigorously promoted a quasi-monotheistic faith focused on worship of the sun god Aten. Furthermore, the major religious breakthroughs of both Christianity and Islam, the most prominent religions of the past 2,000 years, occurred well after the Axial Age had supposedly ended. Was it not somewhat arrogant or condescending to think that religious creativity was limited to those few centuries? Was it appropriate for Karl Jaspers, who first articulated the Axial Age idea, to declare that pre-Axial religion was "in some measure unawakened"?[16]

Furthermore, while advocates of the Axial Age concept found broad similarities among those emerging traditions, their critics noticed differences. Chinese and Greek thinkers focused more on the affairs of this world and credited human rationality with the power to understand that reality. Indian and Jewish thinkers, by contrast, explored the unseen realm of the Divine and the relationship of God or the gods to human life. While Jewish prophets located the transcendent realm in the activities of a highly personal deity actively involved in the world, Laozi, Confucius, and the Buddha largely avoided much discussion of the supernatural. This emphasis on sharp differences among cultural traditions undermined the idea of an Axial Age of common understandings.

Finally, critics of the Axial Age concept charge its proponents with "presentism," or reading the past through the lens of current values and problems. Karl Jaspers originally proposed the term in 1947, while the world was still reeling from the horrors of World War II. He, and many world historians after him, wanted desperately to find something that all of humankind might share, "a base for the unity of mankind" that was not specifically Christian or Western. And they found it in the Axial Age traditions, which, they believed, provided a foundation for moving toward a more unified and peaceful world. Critics maintain that although this may seem wonderful, in adopting the Axial Age idea as a solution for current problems, Jaspers and others gave it a solidity and coherence that it does not deserve.[17] The needs of the present do not provide a sound basis for uncovering the realities of the past.

Or do they? Would we have women's history without the demands of feminist movements? Would we have environmental history without an emerging awareness of environmental problems? Would we have world history without a growing recognition of global interdependence? Current realities always shape our understanding of the past, or at least the questions we pose about the past. Perhaps we have no choice but to conduct our historical inquiries with one eye firmly fixed on the present while the other gazes thoughtfully at the past. Navigating that tension is among the central tasks of all historical study. Both the advocates of the Axial Age idea and its critics are engaged in that enduring balancing act.

QUESTIONS TO CONSIDER

1. How might you summarize the benefits and limitations of the Axial Age idea?
2. Can you think of other examples of "presentism" in historical thinking?

Long before this European rediscovery, the Greek legacy had also entered the Islamic world. Systematic translations of Greek works of science and philosophy into Arabic, together with Indian and Persian learning, stimulated Muslim thinkers and scientists, especially in the fields of medicine, astronomy, mathematics, geography, and chemistry. It was in fact largely from Arabic translations of Greek writers that Europeans became reacquainted with the legacy of classical Greece, especially during the twelfth and thirteenth centuries. Despite the many centuries that have passed since the flourishing of ancient Greek culture, that tradition has remained, especially in the West, an inspiration for those who celebrate the powers of the human mind to probe the mysteries of the universe and to explore the equally challenging domain of human life.

The Birth of Christianity . . . with Buddhist Comparisons

About 500 years after the time of Confucius, the Buddha, and Socrates, a young Jewish peasant/carpenter in the remote province of Judaea in the Roman Empire began a brief three-year career of teaching and miracle working before he got in trouble with local authorities and was executed. In one of history's most unlikely stories, the life and teachings of that obscure man, barely noted in the historical records of the time, became the basis of the world's second great universal religion. This man, **Jesus of Nazareth** (ca. 4 B.C.E.–29 C.E.), and the religion of Christianity that grew out of his brief career had a dramatic impact on world history, often compared with that of India's Siddhartha Gautama, the Buddha.

The Lives of the Founders

The family background of the two teachers could hardly have been more different. Gautama was born to royalty and luxury, whereas Jesus was a rural or small-town worker from a distinctly lower-class family. But both became spiritual seekers, mystics in their respective traditions, who claimed to have personally experienced another and unseen level of reality. Those powerful religious experiences provided the motivation for their life's work and the personal authenticity that attracted their growing band of followers.

Guided Reading Question

■ **COMPARISON**
How would you compare the lives and teachings of Jesus and the Buddha? In what different ways did the two religions evolve after the deaths of their founders?

Both were "wisdom teachers," challenging the conventional values of their time, urging the renunciation of wealth, and emphasizing the supreme importance of love or compassion as the basis for a moral life. The Buddha had instructed his followers in the practice of *metta*, or loving-kindness, "cultivating a boundless heart toward all beings." In a similar vein during his famous Sermon on the Mount, Jesus told his followers "to love your enemies and pray for those who persecute you." Both Jesus and the Buddha called for the personal transformation of their followers, through "letting go" of the grasping that causes suffering, in the Buddha's teaching, or "losing one's life in order to save it," in the language of Jesus.

Despite these similarities, there were also some differences in their teachings and their life stories. Jesus inherited from his Jewish tradition an intense devotion to a single personal deity with whom he was on intimate terms, referring to him as Abba ("papa"). And he gained a reputation as a miracle worker. The Buddha's original message, by contrast, largely ignored the supernatural, involved no miracles, and taught a path of intense self-effort aimed at ethical living and mindfulness as a means of ending suffering. Furthermore, Jesus' teachings had a sharper social and political edge than did those of the Buddha. Jesus spoke more clearly on behalf of the poor and the oppressed, directly criticized the hypocrisies of the powerful, and deliberately associated with lepers, adulterous women, and tax collectors, all of whom were regarded as "impure." These actions reflected his lower-class background, the Jewish tradition of social criticism, and the reality of Roman imperial rule over his people, none of which corresponded to the Buddha's experience. Finally, Jesus' public life was very brief, probably less than three years, compared to more than forty years for the Buddha. His teachings had so antagonized both Jewish and Roman authorities that he was crucified as a political rebel. The Buddha's message was apparently less threatening to the politically powerful, and he died a natural death at age eighty.

The Spread of New Religions

Neither Jesus nor the Buddha had any intention of founding a new religion; rather, they sought to revitalize the traditions from which they had come. Nonetheless, Christianity and Buddhism soon emerged as separate religions, distinct from Judaism and Hinduism, proclaiming their messages to a much wider and more inclusive audience. In the process, both teachers were transformed by their followers into gods. According to many scholars, Jesus never claimed divine status, seeing himself as a teacher or a prophet whose close relationship to God could be replicated by anyone. The Buddha likewise viewed himself as an enlightened but fully human person, an example of what was possible for all who followed the path. But in Mahayana Buddhism, the Buddha became a supernatural being who could be worshipped and prayed to and was spiritually available to his followers. Jesus also soon became divine in the eyes of his early followers, such as Saint Paul and Saint John. According to one of the first creeds of the Church, he was "the Son of God, Very God of Very God."

The transformation of Christianity from a small Jewish sect to a world religion began with **Saint Paul** (ca. 6–67 C.E.), an early convert whose missionary journeys in the eastern Roman Empire led to the founding of small Christian communities that included non-Jews. The Good News of Jesus, Paul argued, was for everyone, and Gentile (non-Jewish) converts need not follow Jewish laws or rituals such as circumcision. In one of his many letters to these new communities, later collected as part of the New Testament, Paul wrote, "There is neither Jew nor Greek . . . neither slave nor free . . . neither male nor female, for you are all one in Christ Jesus."[18] (See the Snapshot for Saint Paul's place in a long line of "wisdom teachers" during the second-wave era.)

Guided Reading Question

■ **CHANGE**
In what ways was Christianity transformed in the five centuries following the death of Jesus?

SNAPSHOT Thinkers and Philosophies of the Second-Wave Era

Person	Date	Location	Religion/Philosophy	Key Ideas
Zoroaster	7th century B.C.E.(?)	Persia (present-day Iran)	Zoroastrianism	Single High God; cosmic conflict of good and evil
Hebrew prophets (such as Isaiah, Amos, Jeremiah)	9th–6th centuries B.C.E.	Eastern Mediterranean/ Palestine/Israel	Judaism	Transcendent High God; covenant with chosen people; social justice
Anonymous writers of Upanishads	800–400 B.C.E.	India	Brahmanism/Hinduism	Brahman (the single impersonal divine reality); karma; rebirth; goal of liberation (moksha)
Confucius	6th–5th centuries B.C.E.	China	Confucianism	Social harmony through moral example; secular outlook; importance of education; family as model of the state
Mahavira	6th century B.C.E.	India	Jainism	All creatures have souls; purification through nonviolence; opposed to caste
Siddhartha Gautama	6th–5th centuries B.C.E.	India	Buddhism	Suffering caused by desire/ attachment; end of suffering through modest and moral living and meditation practice
Laozi, Zhuangzi	6th–3rd centuries B.C.E.	China	Daoism	Withdrawal from the world into contemplation of nature; simple living; end of striving
Socrates, Plato, Aristotle	5th–4th centuries B.C.E.	Greece	Greek rationalism	Style of persistent questioning; secular explanation of nature and human life
Jesus	Early 1st century C.E.	Palestine/Israel	Christianity	Supreme importance of love based on intimate relationship with God; at odds with established authorities
Saint Paul	1st century C.E.	Palestine/Israel/ eastern Roman Empire	Christianity	Christianity as a religion for all; salvation through faith in Jesus Christ

Despite Paul's egalitarian pronouncement, early Christianity, like Buddhism, offered a mix of opportunities and restrictions for women. Jesus himself had interacted easily with a wide range of women, and they had figured prominently among his followers. One of them, Mary Magdalene, was arguably a part of his inner circle. And women played leadership roles in the "house churches" of the first century C.E. Nonetheless, some New Testament writings counseled women to "be subject to your husbands" and declared that "it is shameful for a woman to speak in church." Men were identified with the role of Christ himself, for "the husband is head of the wife as Christ is head of the Church."[19] It was not long before male spokesmen for the faith had fully assimilated older and highly negative views of women. As daughters of Eve, they were responsible for the introduction of sin and evil into the world and were the source of temptation for men.

On the other hand, Jesus' mother, Mary, soon became the focus of a devotional cult, and women were among the martyrs of the early Church. Prominent among them was **Perpetua** (181–203 C.E.), a young North African woman of Roman background who wrote a famous account of trial and imprisonment before she was "condemned to the beasts" for her refusal to renounce her Christian faith (see Zooming In: Perpetua, Christian Martyr, page 168). Growing numbers of Christian women, like their Buddhist counterparts, found a more independent space in the monasteries, even as the official hierarchy of the Church became wholly male.

Nonetheless, the inclusive message of early Christianity was one of the attractions of the new faith as it spread very gradually within the Roman Empire during the several centuries after Jesus' death (see Map 4.1). The earliest converts were usually lower-stratum people — artisans, traders, and a considerable number of women — mostly from towns and cities, while a scattering of wealthier, more prominent, and better-educated people later joined their ranks. The spread of the faith was often accompanied by reports of miracles, healings, and the casting out of demons — all of which were impressive to people thoroughly accustomed to expecting supernatural intervention in the events of ordinary life. Christian communities also attracted converts by the way their members cared for one another. By 300 C.E., perhaps 10 percent of the Roman Empire's population (some 5 million people) identified themselves as Christians.

Although Christians in the West often think of their faith as a European-centered religion, during the first six centuries of the Christian era, most followers of Jesus lived in Southwest Asia and Africa. The first Christian communities formed along the eastern Mediterranean coast, mostly in the major towns of Syria and Anatolia. But the faith soon took root elsewhere as well. A distinctive **Church of the East** spread from Syria into Persia, where it developed a unique liturgy with strong Jewish influences and a musical tradition of chants and hymns, all in Syriac — a language closely related to the Aramaic that Jesus spoke. Its missionaries took Christianity even farther to the east. By the fourth century, and perhaps much earlier, a well-organized Church had taken root in southern India, which later gained tax privileges and special rights from local rulers. In the early seventh century, a Persian monk named Alopen initiated a small but remarkable Christian experiment in China (see "Asian Christianity" in Chapter 10). A modest Christian presence in Central Asia was also an outgrowth of this Church of the East. To the north on the slopes of the Caucasus Mountains, the Kingdom of Armenia around 310 C.E. became the first place where rulers adopted Christianity as a state religion, providing the environment for the flowering of an Armenian church. To the south, a number of Arabs had become Christian by the time of Muhammad's birth in 570, and one of them was among the first to affirm Muhammad as an authentic prophet.

Perpetua, Christian Martyr

"The blood of the martyrs," declared the Christian writer Tertullian, "is the seed of the church." Few of those martyrs, whose stories so inspired the persecuted converts of the early Christian centuries, could match that of Perpetua, a young woman whose prison diary provides a highly personal account of her arrest and trial.[20]

Born in 181 C.E. in the North African city of Carthage, Perpetua hailed from an upper-class Roman family and was quite well educated, literate in Latin and probably Greek, and acquainted with Roman philosophical writings. By the time she entered the historical record at age twenty-two, she had given birth to a son, had lost her husband to either death or abandonment, and had recently begun to study Christianity, becoming part of a small but growing group of educated people who were turning toward the new faith. Coinciding with her conversion was a wave of persecutions ordered by the Roman

Perpetua.

emperor Septimus Severus, also of North African descent and a devotee of the Egyptian cult of Isis and Osiris. Severus sought to forbid new conversions rather than punish long-established Christians. In line with this policy, in 203 C.E., the hard-line governor of the region ordered the arrest of Perpetua along with four others—two slaves, one of them a woman named Felicitas who was eight months pregnant, and two free men. Before she was taken to the prison, however, Perpetua decisively confirmed her commitment to Christianity by accepting baptism.

Once in the "dark hole" of the prison, Perpetua was terrified. It was crowded and stiflingly hot, and she was consumed with anxiety for her child. Several fellow Christians managed to bribe the prison guards to permit Perpetua to nurse her baby son. Reunited with her child,

photo: Archbishop's Palace, Ravenna, Italy/Scala/Art Resource, NY

In Africa, a particularly vibrant center of Christianity developed in Egypt, where priests soon translated the Bible into the Egyptian language known as Coptic, and Egyptian Christians pioneered various forms of monasticism. By 400 C.E., hundreds of monasteries, cells, and caves dotted the desert, inhabited by reclusive monks dedicated to their spiritual practices. Increasingly, the language, theology, and practice of Egyptian Christianity diverged from that of Rome and Constantinople, giving expression to Egyptian resistance against Roman or Byzantine oppression. To the west of Egypt, a Church of North Africa furnished a number of the intellectuals of the early Church, including Saint Augustine, as well as many Christian martyrs to Roman persecution. (See Zooming In: Perpetua, Christian Martyr, above.) Here and elsewhere, the coming of Christianity provoked not only hostility from Roman political authorities but also tensions within families. The North African Carthaginian writer Tertullian (160–220 C.E.), known as the "father of Latin Christianity," described the kind of difficulties that might arise between a Christian wife and her "pagan" husband:

she found that "my prison had suddenly become a palace, so that I wanted to be there rather than anywhere else."

A few days later, Perpetua's deeply distressed non-Christian father arrived for a visit, hoping to persuade his only daughter to recant her faith and save her life and the family's honor. It was a heartbreaking encounter. "Daughter," he said, "have pity on my grey head. . . . Do not abandon me to be the reproach of men. Think of your brothers, think of your mother and your aunt, think of your child, who will not be able to live once you are gone. Give up your pride! You will destroy all of us!" Firm in her faith, Perpetua refused his entreaties, and she reported that "he left me in great sorrow."

On the day of her trial, with her distraught father in attendance, the governor Hilarianus also begged Perpetua to consider her family and renounce her faith by offering a sacrifice to the emperor. Again she refused and together with her four companions was "condemned to the beasts," a humiliating form of execution normally reserved for the lower classes. Although she was now permanently separated from her child, she wrote, "We returned to the prison in high spirits." During her last days in the prison, Perpetua and the others were treated "more humanely" and were allowed to visit with family and friends, as the head of the jail was himself a Christian.

But then, on the birthday of the emperor, this small band of Christians was marched to the amphitheater, "joyfully as though they were going to heaven," according to an eyewitness account. After the prisoners strenuously and successfully resisted dressing in the robes of pagan priests, the three men were sent into the arena to contend with a boar, a bear, and a leopard. Then it was the turn of the women, Perpetua and the slave Felicitas, who had given birth only two days earlier. When a mad cow failed to kill them, a soldier was sent to finish the work. As he approached Perpetua, he apparently hesitated, but as an eyewitness account put it, "she took the trembling hand of the young gladiator and guided it to her throat." Appended to her diary was this comment from an unknown observer: "It was as though so great a woman, feared as she was by the unclean spirit, could not be dispatched unless she herself were willing."

QUESTIONS

How might you understand the actions and attitudes of Perpetua? Is her experience accessible to people living in a largely secular modern society?

She is engaged in a fast; her husband has arranged a banquet. It is her
Christian duty to visit the streets and the homes of the poor; her husband
insists on family business. She celebrates the Easter Vigil throughout the night;
her husband expects her in his bed. . . .[21]

Farther south in Africa, by 350 C.E. Christianity had become the state religion of Axum, an emerging kingdom in what is now Eritrea and Ethiopia (discussed further in Chapter 6). This occurred during the same century as both Armenia and the Roman Empire officially endorsed Christianity. In Axum, a distinctively African expression of Christianity took root, with open-air services, the use of drums and stringed instruments in worship, and colorful umbrellas covering priests and musicians from the elements. Linked theologically and organizationally to Coptic Christianity in Egypt, the Ethiopian Church used Ge'ez, a local Semitic language and script, for its liturgy and literature.

MAPPING HISTORY

Map 4.1 The Spread of Early Christianity and Buddhism
In the five centuries after the birth of Jesus, Christianity found converts from Spain to Northeast
Africa, the Middle East, Central Asia, and India. In the Roman Empire, Axum, and Armenia,
the new religion enjoyed state support as well. Subsequently, Christianity took root solidly in
Europe and after 1000 C.E. in Russia. Meanwhile, Buddhism was spreading from its South Asian
homeland to various parts of Asia, even as it was weakening in India itself.

READING THE MAP: From its start on the eastern shore of the Mediterranean Sea, in which
direction did Christianity spread the farthest?

MAKING CONNECTIONS: Compare this map with Map 7.1: The Silk Roads and Map 7.2:
The Sea Roads, and identify regions where Christianity and Buddhism spread along these long-
distance trade routes.

In the Roman world, the strangest and most offensive feature of the new faith
was its exclusive monotheism and its antagonism to all other supernatural powers,
particularly the cult of the emperors. Christians' denial of these other gods caused
them to be tagged as "atheists" and was one reason behind the empire's intermittent
persecution of Christians during the first three centuries of the Common Era. All
of that ended with Emperor Constantine's conversion in the early fourth century
C.E. and the proclamation of Christianity as the state religion in 380 C.E.

Roman rulers sought to use an increasingly popular Christianity as glue to hold
together a very diverse population in a weakening imperial state. Constantine and

his successors thus provided Christians with newfound security and opportunities. The emperor Theodosius (r. 379–395 C.E.) enforced a ban on all polytheistic ritual sacrifices and ordered the temples that practiced them closed. Christians, by contrast, received patronage for their buildings, official approval for their doctrines, suppression of their rivals, and prestige from imperial recognition. All of this set in motion a process by which the Roman Empire, and later all of Europe, became overwhelmingly Christian. At the time, however, Christianity was expanding at least as rapidly to the east and south as it was to the west. In 500, few observers could have predicted that the future of Christianity would lie primarily in Europe.

The spread of Buddhism in India was quite different from that of Christianity in the Roman Empire. Even though Ashoka's support gave Buddhism a considerable boost, it was never promoted to the exclusion of other faiths. Ashoka sought harmony among India's diverse population through religious tolerance rather than religious uniformity. The kind of monotheistic intolerance that Christianity exhibited in the Roman world was quite foreign to Indian religious practice. Whereas Buddhism later died out in India as it was absorbed into a reviving Hinduism, no renewal of Roman polytheism occurred in the West, and Christianity became an enduring element of European civilization. Nonetheless, Christianity did adopt some elements of religious practice from the Roman world,

The First Christian Emperor Constantine Following Constantine's conversion, artists used both Roman imperial and Christian symbols to present him as a Christian emperor. In this circa fourth-century carving from what is now Croatia, Constantine is portrayed sitting on an imperial throne holding a Christian cross while a man lies prostrate before him. (DEA/A. DAGLI ORTI/Getty Images)

including, perhaps, the cult of saints and the dating of the birth of Jesus to the winter solstice. Finally, both of these new religions spread widely beyond their places of origin. Buddhism provided a network of cultural connections across much of Asia, while Christianity during its early centuries established an Afro-Eurasian presence.

Institutions, Controversies, and Divisions

As Christianity spread within the Roman Empire and beyond, it developed a hierarchical organization, with patriarchs, bishops, and priests—all men—replacing the house churches of the early years, in which women played a more prominent part. At least in some places, however, women continued to exercise leadership and even priestly roles, prompting Pope Gelasius in 494 to speak out sharply against those who encouraged women "to officiate at the sacred altars, and to take part in all matters imputed to the offices of the male sex, to which they do not belong."[22]

In general, though, the exclusion of women from the priesthood established a male-dominated clergy and a patriarchal church, which has lasted into the twenty-first century.

The emerging Christian movement was, however, anything but unified. Its immense geographic reach, accompanied by inevitable differences in language, culture, and political regime, ensured that a single focus for Christian belief and practice was difficult to achieve. Doctrinal differences also tore at the unity of Christianity and embroiled church authorities in frequent controversy about the nature of Jesus (was he human, divine, or both?), his relationship to God (equal or inferior?), and the always-perplexing concept of the Trinity (God as Father, Son, and Holy Spirit). There was debate as well about what writings belonged in the official New Testament, as dozens of letters, gospels, poems, and songs circulated among the early Christian communities. A series of church councils—at Nicaea (325 C.E.), Chalcedon (451 C.E.), and Constantinople (553 C.E.), for example—sought to define an orthodox, or correct, position on these and other issues, declaring those who disagreed as *anathema* and expelling them from the Church. The Church of the East, for example, adopted Nestorianism, which emphasized the human side of Jesus' nature, an idea rejected by the Roman Catholic and Eastern Orthodox Churches.

Beyond these theological debates, political and cultural differences generated division even among the orthodox. The bishop of Rome gradually emerged as the dominant leader, or pope, of the Church in the western half of the empire, but his authority was sharply contested in the East. This division contributed to the later split between the Latin, or Roman Catholic, and the Greek, or Eastern Orthodox, branches of Christendom, a division that continues to the present. Thus the Christian world of 500 C.E. was not only geographically extensive but also politically and theologically very diverse and highly fragmented.

Buddhists too clashed over various interpretations of the Buddha's teachings, and a series of councils failed to prevent the division between Theravada, Mahayana, and other approaches. A considerable proliferation of different sects, practices, teachings, and meditation techniques subsequently emerged within the Buddhist world, but these divisions generally lacked the "clear-cut distinction between 'right' and 'wrong' ideas" that characterized conflicts within the Christian world.[23] Although Buddhist states and warrior classes (such as the famous samurai of Japan) sometimes engaged in warfare, religious differences among Buddhists seldom provided the basis for the bitterness and violence that often accompanied religious conflict within Christendom. Nor did Buddhists develop the kind of overall religious hierarchy that characterized Christianity, although communities of monks and nuns, organized in monasteries, created elaborate rules to govern their internal affairs.

PRACTICING HISTORICAL THINKING

How might you understand the appeal of Buddhism and Christianity as opposed to the more rationalist approaches of Greek and Confucian philosophy?

REFLECTIONS

Religion and Historians

To put it mildly, religion has always been a sensitive subject, and no less so for historians than for anyone else. Seeking to understand the religious dimension of human life has generated various tensions and misunderstandings between scholars and believers.

One of these tensions involves the question of change. Most religions present themselves as timeless revelations from the beyond, partaking of eternity or at least reflecting ancient practice. In the eyes of historians, however, the religious aspect of human life changes as much as any other. The Hindu tradition changed from a religion of ritual and sacrifice to one of devotion and worship. Buddhism became more conventionally religious, with an emphasis on the supernatural, as it evolved from Theravada to Mahayana forms. A male-dominated hierarchical Christian Church, with its pope, bishops, priests, and state support, was very different from the small house churches that suffered persecution by imperial authorities in the early Christian centuries. The implication—that religions are largely a human phenomenon—has been troublesome to some believers.

Historians, on the other hand, have sometimes been uncomfortable in the face of claims by believers that they have actually experienced a divine reality. Certainly, modern scholars are in no position to validate or refute the spiritual claims of religious leaders and their many followers, but we need to take them seriously. Although we will never know precisely what happened to the Buddha as he sat in meditation in northern India or what transpired when Jesus spent forty days in the wilderness, clearly those experiences changed the two men and motivated their subsequent actions. Millions of their followers have also acted on the basis of what they perceived to be a compelling encounter with an unseen realm. This interior dimension of human experience, though difficult to grasp with any precision and impossible to verify, has been a significant mover and shaper of the historical process.

Yet a third problem arises from debates within particular religious traditions about which group most accurately represents the "real" or authentic version of the faith. Historians usually refuse to take sides in such disputes. They simply notice with interest that most human cultural traditions generate conflicting views, some of which become the basis for serious conflict in societies.

Reconciling personal religious convictions with the perspectives of modern historical scholarship is no easy task. At the very least, all of us can appreciate the immense human effort that has gone into the making of religious traditions, and we can acknowledge their enormous significance in the unfolding of the human story. They have shaped the meanings that billions of people over thousands of years have attached to the world they inhabit. These religious traditions have justified the vast social inequalities and oppressive states of human civilizations, but they have also enabled human beings to endure the multiple sufferings that attend human life, and on occasion they have stimulated reform and rebellion. And the religions born in second-wave civilizations have guided much of humankind in its endless efforts to penetrate the mysteries of the world beyond and of the world within.

Second Thoughts

What's the Significance?

Legalism, 142	Zoroastrianism, 156
Confucianism, 144	Judaism, 157
Ban Zhao, 145	Greek rationalism, 159
Daoism, 147	Socrates, 159
Vedas, 149	Plato, 161
Upanishads, 149	Aristotle, 161
Siddhartha Gautama (the Buddha), 151	Jesus of Nazareth, 164
Theravada Buddhism, 153	Saint Paul, 165
Mahayana Buddhism, 153	Perpetua, 167
Bhagavad Gita, 154	Church of the East, 167
bhakti movement, 154	

Big Picture Questions

1. Is a secular outlook on the world an essentially modern phenomenon, or does it have precedents in the second-wave era?
2. "Religion is a double-edged sword, both supporting and undermining political authority and social elites." How would you support both sides of this statement?
3. How would you define the appeal of the religious/cultural traditions discussed in this chapter? To what groups were they attractive, and why?
4. Imagine that you were a Christian traveler in the Eurasian world of 500 C.E. writing home about your encounter with other religious traditions. What similarities and differences might you notice? What might you appreciate in those traditions? And what might you find distasteful or appalling?
5. **Looking Back:** What relationships can you see between the political dimensions of second-wave civilizations described in Chapter 3 and their cultural or religious aspects discussed in this chapter?

Next Steps: For Further Study

Karen Armstrong, *The Great Transformation* (2006). A comparative and historical study of the major religions by a well-known scholar.

Robert N. Bellah, *Religion in Human Evolution: From the Paleolithic to the Axial Age* (2011). An impressive but controversial account of the origins of religion in general and those of second-wave civilizations in particular.

Diarmaid MacCulloch, *Christianity: The First 3000 Years* (2009). A magisterial account of Jewish and Christian history.

Huston Smith, *An Illustrated World's Religions* (1994). A sympathetic account of major world religions, beautifully illustrated, by a prominent scholar of comparative religion.

Arthur Waley, *Three Ways of Thought in Ancient China* (1983). A classic work, first published more than half a century ago, about the major philosophies of old China.

Jonathan S. Walters, *Finding Buddhists in Global History* (1998). A brief account that situates Buddhism in a world history framework.

Annenberg Learner, "Early Belief Systems," http://www.learner.org/vod/vod_window .html?pid=2148. Explores the origins of the religious impulse and many of the traditions covered in this chapter.

Hinduism Today Videos, "The History of Hindu India, Part One: From Ancient Times,"-directed and produced by Sushma Khadepaun in collaboration with Professor Shiva Bajpai, https://www.youtube.com/watch?v=dBZRTzXARWM&vl=en. A thoughtful examination of the origins and development of the Hindu tradition.

Representations of the Buddha

Buddhism derived from a single individual, Siddhartha Gautama, born in northern India around the middle of the first millennium B.C.E. Over many centuries, the religion evolved as it spread within and beyond India, attracting growing numbers of followers and intersecting with various cultures throughout Asia, including those of China, Japan, Tibet, Korea, Thailand, Burma, and Vietnam. But the figure of the Buddha remained central to all versions and variations of the faith. Perceptions of the Buddha took on the flavor of the various cultures in which Buddhism took root. In China, for example, descriptions of the Buddha emphasized his "filial piety," citing the conversion of his father.

Understandings of the Buddha found expression in the titles and qualities attributed to him, such as "the teacher of gods and men," the Blessed One, the "great cosmic person," and many others. A proliferating body of written texts—sermons, biographies, stories, and myths—also featured various understandings of the Buddha. Over time, these descriptions increasingly emphasized the superhuman and transcendent elements of the Buddha, portrayed his actions as miraculous and magical, and invoked numerous past and future Buddhas. He was also represented artistically in sculptures and paintings. But for almost five centuries after his death, artists depicted the Buddha as an empty throne, a horse with no rider, a tree, a wheel, a set of footprints, or in some other symbolic way, while largely shunning any image of him in human form. All of these played a role in Buddhist worship, prayer, and meditation, allowing his followers to experience the Buddha as a living presence in their own lives.

SOURCE 4.1 A Greco-Indian Buddha ▶

By the first century C.E., the impulse to show the Buddha in human form had surfaced, with some of the earliest examples coming from the region of South Asia in what is now northern Pakistan and eastern Afghanistan (see Map 3.3, page 109). That area had been a part of the empire of Alexander the Great and his Hellenistic successors during the three centuries before the birth of Jesus and had developed commercial ties to the Roman Empire. These early images of the Buddha reflect this Greco-Roman influence, portraying him with a face similar to that of the Greek god Apollo, dressed in a Roman-style toga, and with curly hair characteristic of the Mediterranean region.

Greco-Roman influence is apparent in Source 4.1. Dating from the second or third century C.E., it comes from India and depicts a famous scene from the life of the Buddha—his temptation by the demon Mara and Mara's seductive daughters while he was meditating under the Bodhi tree.

■ How are Mara and his daughters, shown on the right, portrayed in this relief?

■ What attitude characterizes the Buddha, shown on the left and surrounded by attendants?

■ One scholar has recently argued that "statues of the Buddha started to appear only after the cult of Apollo became established [in the region]. Buddhists felt threatened by the success of the new religious practices and began to create their own visual images."[24] How might this possibility shape your understanding of Greco-Roman cultural influences on Buddhism? Can you imagine other possible explanations for the creation of the first physical representations of the Buddha?

■ Does the idea that competition from a Greek religious cult caused Buddhists to create early images of the Buddha affect your analysis of this image?

The Temptation of the Buddha

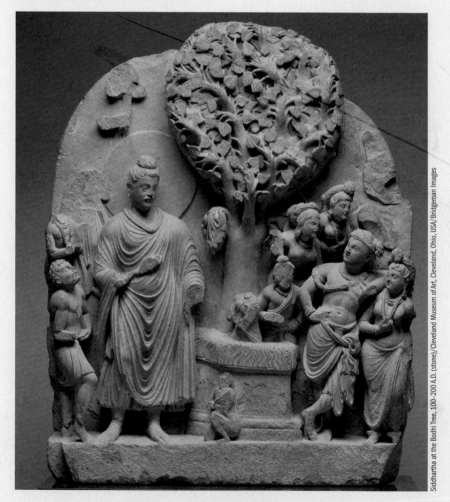

Siddhartha at the Bodhi Tree, 100–200 A.D. (stone)/Cleveland Museum of Art, Cleveland, Ohio, USA/Bridgeman Images

■ ■ ■

SOURCE 4.2 **A Classical Indian Buddha**

By the time of India's Gupta dynasty (320–550 C.E.), Greco-Roman influence in Buddhist art was fading, replaced by more completely Indian images of the Buddha. Such representations became the "classic" model illustrated in Source 4.2, which dates from the sixth century C.E. The Buddha's right hand with palm facing the viewer indicates reassurance, or "have no fear." The partially webbed fingers are among the *lakshanas*, or signs of a Buddha image, that denote the Buddha's unique status. So too is the hair knot on the top of his head, symbolizing enlightenment.

■ The elongated earlobes reflect the heavy, luxurious earrings that the Buddha wore earlier in his life before becoming the enlightened one. Why might the artist have included this detail in his depiction of the Buddha?

■ The creator of this statue intended to convey the Buddha's calm and detached posture toward the world. What features of the statue might illustrate this posture? What similarities and differences can you observe between this depiction of the Buddha and that in Source 4.1?

An Indian Buddha

The Metropolitan Museum of Art, New York, NY, USA/Purchase, Florance Waterbury Bequest, 1969 (69.222). Photo: Bruce White/Image copyright © The Metropolitan Museum of Art. Image source: Art Resource, NY

■ ■ ■

SOURCE 4.3 The Reputation of the Buddha in Ancient Buddhist Stories

Various perceptions of the Buddha found expression not only in artistic form, but also in the growing body of Buddhist texts, known as the Pali Canon, originally passed on orally and reduced to writing during the first century B.C.E. Source 4.3 recounts a conversation derived from one of these texts between the Buddha and a wandering holy man, Sakuludayin, about the qualities of various religious leaders in the area.

■ How might you summarize the perception of the Buddha reflected in this source?

■ To what extent are these qualities expressed in the artistic representations of the Buddha?

The Greater Discourse to Sakuludayin | ca. 1st century B.C.E.

[Sakuludayin reported:] And some said this: This recluse Gotama [the Buddha] is the head of an order, the head of a group, the teacher of a group, the well-known and famous founder of a sect regarded by many as a saint. He is honoured, respected, revered, and venerated by his disciples, and his disciples live in dependence on him. . . .

Once the recluse Gotama was teaching his Dhamma [truth, wisdom, teachings] to an assembly of several hundred followers and there a certain disciple of his cleared his throat. Thereupon one of his companions in the holy life nudged him with his knee. "Be quiet, venerable sir, make no noise; the Blessed One, the Teacher, is teaching us the Dhamma."

When the recluse Gotama is teaching the Dhamma to an assembly of several hundred followers, on that occasion there is no sound of his disciples' coughing or clearing their throats. For

then that large assembly is poised in expectancy . . . just as though a man were at a crossroads pressing out pure honey and a large group of people were poised in expectancy. . . .

"But, [asked the Buddha] how many qualities do you see in me because of which my disciples honour, respect, revere, and venerate me?" [Sakuludayin replied] "Venerable sir, I see five qualities in the Blessed One: . . . First, venerable sir, the Blessed One eats little. . . . Again, the Blessed One is content with any kind of robe. . . . Again, the Blessed One is content with any kind of resting place. . . . Again, venerable sir, the Blessed One is secluded and commends seclusion."

Source: Bhikkhu Nanamola and Bhikkhu Bodhi, trans., *The Middle Length Discourses of the Buddha* (Boston: Wisdom Publications, 1995), 631–32.

■ ■ ■

SOURCE 4.4 A Korean Bodhisattva of Compassion ▶

Across the world of Asian Mahayana Buddhism, a popular artistic representation of Buddhist values found expression in numerous images of bodhisattvas, those spiritually developed beings who delayed their own entry into nirvana to assist others on the path. The historical Buddha had on occasion described himself as a bodhisattva. In sculpture or painting, bodhisattvas became objects of worship and sources of comfort and assistance to many Buddhists. The most widely popular of the many bodhisattva figures was that of Avalokitesvara, known in China as Guan-yin and in Japan as Kannon. This Bodhisattva of Compassion, often portrayed as a woman or with distinctly feminine characteristics, was known as "the one who hears the cries of the world."

Among the most striking of the many representations of this bodhisattva are those that portray him or her with numerous heads, with which to hear the many cries of a suffering humanity, or with multiple arms to aid them. Source 4.4 provides an illustration of such a figure, a gilded wooden statue from Korea dating to the tenth or eleventh century C.E.

■ What elements of Buddhist imagery can you identify in this statue?

■ To whom might such an image appeal? And why?

■ How does this image differ from the classical Indian Buddha shown in Source 4.2?

A Bodhisattva of Compassion: Avalokitesvara with a Thousand Arms

■ ■ ■

SOURCE 4.5 **The Buddha and the Outcast**

According to Buddhist sacred texts, the Buddha himself both taught and practiced compassion. Among the most widely known of his teachings are those about
loving-kindness or compassion: "Like a caring mother holding and guarding the
life of her only child, so with a boundless heart of lovingkindness, hold yourself
and all beings as your beloved children." The story in Source 4.5, contained in the
Buddhist scriptures, conveys this sensibility in action from the perspective of an
untouchable cleaner named Sunita.

- How does this story convey the Buddhist ideal of compassion?

- In what ways was Sunita transformed by his encounter with the Buddha?

- How does the Buddha define a genuine Brahmin? How might Hindu Brahmins, with whom the Buddha was in frequent dispute, respond to this story?

Sunita the Outcast

In a lowly family I was born, poor, with next to no food. My work was degrading: I gathered the spoiled, the withered flowers from shrines and threw them away. People found me disgusting, despised me, disparaged me. Lowering my heart, I showed reverence to many.

Then I saw the One Self-awakened, arrayed with a squadron of monks, entering the city. . . . Throwing down my carrying pole, I approached him to do reverence. He—the supreme man—stood still out of sympathy just for me. After paying homage to the feet of the teacher [the Buddha], I stood to one side and requested the Going Forth [permission to enter the rank of monks] from him, supreme among all living beings. The compassionate Teacher, sympathetic to all the world, said: "Come, monk." That was my formal Acceptance.

Alone, I stayed in the wilds, untiring, I followed the Teacher's words, just as he, the Conqueror, had taught me. . . . Indra & Brahma [powerful Hindu/Buddhist deities] came to pay homage to me, hands palm-to-palm at their hearts: "Homage to you, O thoroughbred of men. . . . You, dear sir, are worthy of offerings."

Seeing me, arrayed with a squadron of devas [god-like spiritual beings], the Teacher smiled & said: "Through austerity, celibacy, restraint, and self-control: That's how one is a brahman. He is a brahman supreme."

Source: "Sunita the Outcaste" (Thag 12.2), translated from the Pali by Thanissaro Bhikkhu, *Access to Insight (BCBS Edition)*, November 30, 2013, http://www.accesstoinsight.org/tipitaka/kn/thag/thag.12.02.than.html.

■ ■ ■

SOURCE 4.6 A Chinese Buddha ▶

Mahayana Buddhism not only featured numerous bodhisattvas, but it also populated the spiritual universe with various Buddhas in addition to the historical Buddha. One of these is the Maitreya Buddha, or the Buddha of the Future, predicted to appear when the teachings of the historical Buddha have been lost or forgotten. In China, this Buddha of the future was sometimes portrayed as the "laughing Buddha," a fat, smiling, contented figure, said to be modeled on a tenth-century monk named Budai, who wandered the country merrily spreading happiness and good cheer while evoking contentment and abundance. Source 4.6 illustrates this Chinese Maitreya Buddha, together with some of his disciples, in a carving dating to the tenth through fourteenth centuries, in China's Feilai Feng caves.

- How does this Buddha image differ, both physically and in its religious implications, from the other Buddhas already discussed in this feature? Why might this image be appealing to some Buddhists, and why might others object to it?

- In what ways does this figure represent an adaptation of Buddhist imagery to Chinese culture? Consider what you know about Confucian and Daoist postures to the world.

The Chinese Maitreya Buddha

DOING HISTORY

1. **Tracing change:** What transformations in Buddhist belief and practice are disclosed in these sources?

2. **Identifying cultural adaptation:** What evidence do these sources provide about the blending of Buddhism into a variety of cultural settings?

3. **Understanding the growth of Buddhism:** What do these sources suggest about the appeal of Buddhism to growing numbers of people across Asia?

4. **Considering cultural boundaries:** To what extent are these sources meaningful to people outside the Buddhist tradition? In what ways might they speak to universal human needs or desires? What is specifically Buddhist or Asian about them?

On the Buddha

All of the preceding sources were the work of "insiders," reflecting the perceptions of the Buddha among those who operated within the Buddhist world at varying times and places in the distant past. Modern historians, particularly those from the Western world, are "outsiders," even if they are personally sympathetic with Buddhism. The following selections come to us from such historians, one American and the other British. Both John Strong (Voice 4.1) and Karen Armstrong (Voice 4.2) have written early-twenty-first-century biographies of the Buddha.

- What features of the Buddha's life does John Strong (Voice 4.1) emphasize? Why does he largely omit the supernatural and miraculous elements that so often accompany "insider" understandings of the Buddha?

- Why does Karen Armstrong in Voice 4.2 suggest that some Buddhists might be skeptical of any effort to create a modern biography of the Buddha? What aspects of the Buddha's life does she highlight?

- **Integrating Primary and Secondary Sources:** How do these modern scholarly reflections on the Buddha differ from the much earlier insider accounts and images? Which do you find more useful in understanding the life of Siddhartha Gautama?

VOICE 4.1

John Strong on the Context of the Buddha's Life | 2001

Historically speaking, we know very little for certain about the life of Siddhartha Gautama, the man who came to be known as the Buddha. Although no one today seriously questions his actual existence, debates still rage over the dates of his life . . . the contents of his teaching, and the nature of the religious community he is said to have founded. . . .

We know that the India of his day was caught up in a period of ferment and religious questioning spawned by the rise of new urban centers and the breakdown of old political systems. As two contemporary religious scholars put it: "The historical Buddha responded to

this kind of situation. . . . He was a renouncer and an ascetic . . . although it seems mild by Indian standards. He shared with other renunciants an ultimately somber view of life and its pleasures, and he practiced and recommended a mode of religious life in which individual participation in a specifically religious community was of primary importance. He experimented with the practices of . . . begging, wandering, celibacy, . . . self-restraint (yoga) and the like, and he organized a community in which discipline played a central role. Judging from the movement he inspired, he was not only an innovator but also a charismatic personality. Through the course of his ministry, he gathered around him a group of wandering mendicants and nuns as well as men and women who continued to live the life of householders."

Source: John S. Strong, *The Buddha: A Short Biography* (Oxford: Oneworld Publications, 2001), 1–2. Quotation from Frank E. Reynolds and Charles Hallisey, "Buddha," in *Encyclopedia of Religion* (New York: Macmillan, 1987), 2:321.

VOICE 4.2

Karen Armstrong on the Buddha and Biography | 2001

Some Buddhists might say that to write a biography of Sidhatta Gotama is a very un-Buddhist thing to do. In their view no authority should be revered, however august; Buddhists must rely on their own efforts and motivate themselves, not on a charismatic leader. One ninth century master . . . even went so far as to command his disciples: "If you meet the Buddha, kill the Buddha!" to emphasize the importance of maintaining this independence from authority figures. . . . Throughout his life, he [the Buddha] fought against the cult of personality and endlessly deflected the attention of his disciples from himself. It was not his life and personality, but his teaching that was important. He believed he had woken up to a truth that was inscribed in the deepest structure of existence. It was a *dhamma*, . . . a fundamental law of life for gods, humans, and animals alike. By discovering this truth, he had become enlightened and had experienced a profound inner transformation; he had won peace and immunity in the midst of life's sufferings. Gotama has thus become a Buddha, an Enlightened or Awakened One. Any one of his disciples could achieve the same enlightenment if he or she followed this method. But if people start to revere Gotama the man, they would distract themselves from their task and the cult could become a prop, causing an unworthy dependence that could only impede spiritual progress.

Source: Karen Armstrong, *Buddha* (New York: Penguin Books, 2001), xi–xii.

Society and Inequality in Eurasia / North Africa

600 B.C.E.–600 C.E.

Society and the State in China
An Elite of Officials
The Landlord Class
Peasants
Merchants

Class and Caste in India
Caste as Varna
Caste as Jati
The Functions of Caste

Slavery: The Case of the Roman Empire
Slavery and Civilization
The Making of Roman Slavery

Comparing Patriarchies
A Changing Patriarchy: The Case of China
Contrasting Patriarchies: Athens and Sparta

Reflections: What Changes? What Persists?

"Caste has no impact on life today," declared Chezi K. Ganesan in 2010.[1] Certainly, Mr. Ganesan's low-caste background as a Nadar, ranking just above the "untouchables," has had little impact on the career of this prosperous high-tech businessman, who shuttles between California's Silicon Valley and the city of Chennai in southern India. Yet his grandfather could not enter Hindu temples, and until the mid-nineteenth century, the women of his caste, as a sign of their low status, were forbidden to cover their breasts in the presence of Brahmin men. But if caste has proven no barrier to Mr. Ganesan, it remains significant for many others in contemporary India. Personal ads for those seeking a marriage partner in many online services often indicate an individual's caste as well as other personal data. Affirmative action programs benefiting low-caste Indians have provoked great controversy and resentment among some upper-caste groups. The brutal murder of an entire Dalit, or "untouchable," family in 2006 sparked much soul-searching in the Indian media. So while caste has changed in modern India, it has also persisted. ■

《 Mother and Child Mothers and their children have been at the core of social life everywhere and a prominent theme of many artistic traditions. This lovely statue comes from the Sunga dynasty, which flourished in northeastern India from about 185 to 73 B.C.E., after the collapse of the Mauryan Empire.

The past several centuries have called into question social patterns long assumed to be natural and permanent. The French, Russian, and Chinese revolutions challenged and destroyed ancient monarchies and class hierarchies; the abolitionist movement of the nineteenth century attacked slavery, largely unquestioned for millennia; the women's movement has confronted long and deeply held patriarchal assumptions about the proper relationship between the sexes; and during and after India's struggle for independence from Great Britain in the twentieth century, some have challenged their country's ancient caste system. Nevertheless, caste, class, patriarchy, and even slavery have certainly not vanished from human society, even now. During the era of second-wave civilizations in Eurasia, such patterns of inequality prevailed widely and generated social tensions that endured well beyond that era.

As Chapter 3 pointed out, millions of individual men and women inhabiting the civilizations of Eurasia and North Africa lived within a political framework of states or empires. They also occupied a world of ideas, religions, and values that derived both from local folkways and from the teaching of the great religious or cultural traditions born in the second-wave era, as described in Chapter 4. In this chapter, the focus turns to the social arrangements of these civilizations— relationships between rich and poor, powerful and powerless, slaves and free people, and men and women. Those relationships shaped the daily lives and the life chances of everyone and provided the foundation for political authority as well as challenges to it.

Like the First Civilizations, those of the second-wave era were sharply divided along class lines, and they too were patriarchal, with women clearly subordinated to men in most domains of life. In constructing their societies, however, these second-wave civilizations differed substantially from one another. Chinese, Indian, and Mediterranean civilizations provide numerous illustrations of the many and varied ways in which these peoples organized their social lives. The assumptions, tensions, and conflicts accompanying these social patterns provided much of the distinctive character and texture that distinguished these diverse civilizations from one another.

SEEKING THE MAIN POINT

To what extent were the massive inequalities of second-wave civilizations generally accepted, and in what ways were they resisted or challenged?

Society and the State in China

Chinese society was unique in the ancient world in the extent to which it was shaped by the actions of the state. Nowhere was this more apparent than in the political power and immense social prestige of Chinese state officials, all of them male. For more than 2,000 years, these officials, bureaucrats acting in the name of the emperor both in the capital and in the provinces, represented the cultural and social elite of Chinese civilization. This class had its origins in the efforts of early Chinese rulers to find administrators loyal to the central state rather than to their own families or regions. Philosophers such as Confucius had long advocated selecting such officials on the basis of merit and personal morality rather than birth or wealth. As the Han dynasty established its authority in China around 200 B.C.E., its rulers required each province to send men of promise to the capital, where they were examined and chosen for official positions based on their performance.

Landmarks for Chapter 5

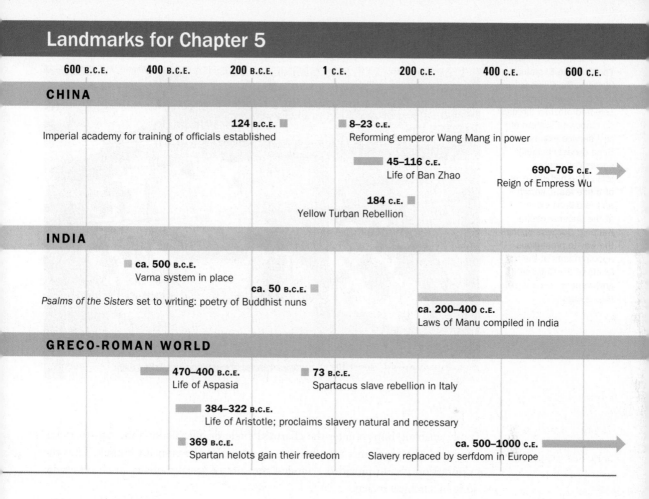

| 600 B.C.E. | 400 B.C.E. | 200 B.C.E. | 1 C.E. | 200 C.E. | 400 C.E. | 600 C.E. |

CHINA

124 B.C.E.
Imperial academy for training of officials established

8–23 C.E.
Reforming emperor Wang Mang in power

45–116 C.E.
Life of Ban Zhao

690–705 C.E.
Reign of Empress Wu

184 C.E.
Yellow Turban Rebellion

INDIA

ca. 500 B.C.E.
Varna system in place

ca. 50 B.C.E.
Psalms of the Sisters set to writing: poetry of Buddhist nuns

ca. 200–400 C.E.
Laws of Manu compiled in India

GRECO-ROMAN WORLD

470–400 B.C.E.
Life of Aspasia

73 B.C.E.
Spartacus slave rebellion in Italy

384–322 B.C.E.
Life of Aristotle; proclaims slavery natural and necessary

369 B.C.E.
Spartan helots gain their freedom

ca. 500–1000 C.E.
Slavery replaced by serfdom in Europe

An Elite of Officials

Over time, this system of selecting administrators evolved into the world's first professional civil service. In 124 B.C.E., Emperor Wudi established an imperial academy where potential officials were trained as scholars and immersed in texts dealing with history, literature, art, and mathematics, with an emphasis on Confucian teachings. By the end of the Han dynasty, it enrolled some 30,000 students, who were by then subjected to a series of written examinations to select officials of various grades. Private schools in the provinces funneled still more aspiring candidates into this examination system, which persisted until the early twentieth century. In theory open to all men, this system in practice favored those whose families were wealthy enough to provide the years of education required to pass even the lower-level exams. Proximity to the capital and family connections to the imperial court also helped in gaining a position in this highest of Chinese elites. Nonetheless, village communities or a local landowner might sponsor the education of a bright young man from a commoner

Guided Reading Question

■ **DESCRIPTION**
How would you characterize the social hierarchy of China during the second-wave era?

The Chinese Examination System The Chinese imperial government selected officials through an elaborate system of civil service exams. This Song dynasty painting shows candidates taking the highest level of these tests, known as the palace exams, at the imperial capital Kaifeng. Success opened the way to prestigious appointments at the top levels of the Chinese government. (Pictures from History/ Bridgeman Images)

family, enabling him to enter the charmed circle of officialdom. One rags-to-riches story told of a pig farmer who became an adviser to the emperor himself. Thus the examination system provided a modest measure of social mobility in an otherwise quite hierarchical society.

In later dynasties, that system grew even more elaborate and became an enduring and distinguishing feature of Chinese civilization. During the Tang dynasty, the famous poet and official Po Chu-I (772–846 C.E.) wrote a poem titled "After Passing the Examination," which shows something of the fame and fortune that awaited an accomplished student as well as the continuing loyalty to family and home that ideally marked those who succeeded:

> For ten years I never left my books, / I went up . . . and won unmerited praise.
> My high place I do not much prize; / The joy of my parents will first make me
>   proud.
> Fellow students, six or seven men, / See me off as I leave the City gate.
> My covered coach is ready to drive away . . . / On a Spring day the road that
>   leads to home.[2]

Those who made it into the bureaucracy entered a realm of high privilege and great prestige. Senior officials moved about in carriages and were bedecked with robes, ribbons, seals, and headdresses appropriate to their rank. Even lower officials who served in the provinces rather than the capital were distinguished by their polished speech, their cultural sophistication, and their urban manners as well as their political authority. Proud of their learning, they were the bearers, and often the makers, of Chinese culture. "Officials are the leaders of the populace," stated an imperial edict of 144 B.C.E., "and it is right and proper that the carriages they ride in and the robes that they wear should correspond to the degrees of their dignity."[3] Some of these men, particularly in times of political turmoil, experienced tension between their official duties and their personal inclination toward a more withdrawn life of reflective scholarship. (See Working with Evidence: China's Scholar-Officials in Chapter 8.)

The Landlord Class

Most officials came from wealthy families, and in China wealth meant land. When the Qin dynasty unified China by 210 B.C.E., most land was held by small-scale peasant farmers. But by the first century B.C.E., the pressures of population growth, taxation, and indebtedness had generated a class of large landowners as impoverished peasants found it necessary to sell their lands to more prosperous neighbors. This accumulation of land in sizable estates was a persistent theme in Chinese history and one that was frequently, though not very successfully, opposed by state authorities. Landlords of such large estates were often able to avoid paying taxes, thus decreasing state revenues and increasing the tax burden for the remaining peasants. In some cases, they could also raise their own military forces that might challenge the authority of the emperor.

One of the most dramatic state efforts to counteract the growing power of large landowners is associated with **Wang Mang**, a high court official of the Han dynasty who usurped the emperor's throne in 8 C.E. and immediately launched a series of startling reforms. A firm believer in Confucian good government, Wang Mang saw his reforms as re-creating a golden age of long ago in which small-scale peasant farmers represented the backbone of Chinese society. Accordingly, he ordered the great private estates to be nationalized and divided up among the landless. Government loans to peasant families, limits on the amount of land a family might own, and an end to private slavery were all part of his reform program, but these measures proved impossible to enforce. Opposition from wealthy landowners, nomadic invasions, poor harvests, floods, and famines led to the collapse of Wang Mang's reforms and his assassination in 23 C.E.

Large landowning families, therefore, remained a central feature of Chinese society, although the fate of individual families rose and fell as the wheel of fortune lifted them to great prominence or plunged them into poverty and disgrace. As a class, they benefited both from the wealth that their estates generated and from the power and prestige that accompanied their education and their membership in the official elite. The term "scholar-gentry" reflected their twin sources of privilege. With homes in both urban and rural areas, members of the scholar-gentry class lived luxuriously. Multi-storied houses, the finest of silk clothing, gleaming carriages, private orchestras, high-stakes gambling—all of this was part of the life of **China's scholar-gentry class**.

Peasants

Throughout the long course of China's civilization, the vast majority of its population consisted of peasants, living in small households representing two or three generations. Some owned enough land to support their families and perhaps even sell something on the local market. Many others could barely survive. Nature, the state, and landlords combined to make the life of most peasants extremely vulnerable. Famines, floods, droughts, hail, and pests could wreak havoc without warning. State authorities required the payment of taxes, demanded about a month's labor every year on various public projects, and conscripted young men for military service. During the Han dynasty, growing numbers of impoverished and desperate peasants had to sell out to large landlords and work as tenants or sharecroppers on their estates, where rents could run as high as one-half to two-thirds of the crop. Other peasants fled, taking to a life of begging or joining gangs of bandits in remote areas.

An eighth-century-C.E. Chinese poem by Li Shen reflects poignantly on the enduring hardships of peasant life:

Guided Reading
Question

■ CHANGE

What class conflicts disrupted Chinese society?

The cob of corn in springtime sown / In autumn yields a hundredfold.
No fields are seen that fallow lie: / And yet of hunger peasants die.
As at noontide they hoe their crops, / Sweat on the grain to earth down drops.
How many tears, how many a groan, / Each morsel on thy dish did mould![4]

Such conditions provoked periodic peasant rebellions, which have punctuated Chinese history for over 2,000 years. Toward the end of the second century C.E., wandering bands of peasants began to join together as floods along the Yellow River and resulting epidemics compounded the misery of landlessness and poverty. What emerged was a massive peasant uprising known as the **Yellow Turban Rebellion** because of the yellow scarves the peasants wore around their heads. That movement, which swelled to about 360,000 armed followers by 184 C.E., found leaders, organization, and a unifying ideology in a popular form of Daoism. Featuring supernatural healings, collective trances, and public confessions of sin, the Yellow Turban movement looked forward to the "Great Peace"—a golden age of equality, social harmony, and common ownership of property. Although the rebellion was suppressed by the military forces of the Han dynasty, the Yellow Turban and other peasant upheavals devastated the economy, weakened the state, and contributed to the overthrow of the dynasty a few decades later. Repeatedly in Chinese history, such peasant movements, often expressed in religious terms, registered the sharp class antagonisms of Chinese society and led to the collapse of more than one ruling dynasty.

The Yellow Turban Rebellion

Merchants

Peasants were oppressed in China and certainly exploited, but they were also honored and celebrated in the official ideology of the state. In the eyes of the scholar-gentry, peasants were the solid productive backbone of the country, and their hard work and endurance in the face of difficulties were worthy of praise. Merchants, however, did not enjoy such a favorable reputation in the eyes of China's cultural elite. They were widely viewed as unproductive, making a shameful profit from selling the work of others. Stereotyped as greedy, luxury loving, and materialistic, merchants stood in contrast to the presumed frugality, altruism, and cultured tastes of the scholar-gentry. They were also seen as a social threat, as their ill-gained wealth impoverished others, deprived the state of needed revenues, and fostered resentments.

Such views lay behind periodic efforts by state authorities to rein in merchant activity and to keep them under control. Early in the Han dynasty, merchants were forbidden to wear silk clothing, ride horses, or carry arms. Nor were they permitted to sit for civil service examinations or hold public office. State monopolies on profitable industries such as salt, iron, and alcohol limited merchant opportunities. Later dynasties sometimes forced merchants to loan large sums of money to the state. Despite this active discrimination, merchants frequently became quite wealthy. Some tried to achieve a more respectable elite status by purchasing landed estates or educating their sons for the civil service examinations. Many had backdoor relationships with state officials and landlords who found them useful and were not averse to profiting from business connections with merchants, despite their unsavory reputation.

Class and Caste in India

India's social organization shared certain broad features with that of China. In both civilizations, birth determined social status for most people; little social mobility was available for the vast majority; sharp distinctions and great inequalities characterized social life; and religious or cultural traditions defined these inequalities as natural, eternal, and ordained by the gods. Despite these similarities, the organization, flavor, and texture of ancient Indian society were distinctive compared to almost all other civilizations. These unique aspects of Indian society have long been embodied in what is now called the caste system, a term that comes from the Portuguese word *casta*, which means "race" or "purity of blood." That social organization emerged over thousands of years and in some respects has endured into modern times.

Caste as Varna

The origins of the caste system are at best hazy. Broadly speaking, however, the distinctive social system of India grew out of the interactions among South Asia's immensely varied cultures. Also contributing to the development of caste was the growth of economic and social differences among these peoples as the class inequalities common to "civilization" spread throughout the Ganges River valley and beyond.

Whatever the precise origins of the caste system, by around 500 B.C.E., the idea that society was forever divided into four ranked classes, or **varnas**, was deeply

Guided Reading Question

■ **DESCRIPTION**
What set of ideas was associated with India's caste-based society?

Caste in India This 1947 photograph from *Life* magazine illustrates the "purity and pollution" thinking that has long been central to the ideology of caste. It shows a high-caste landowner carefully dropping wages wrapped in a leaf into the outstretched hands of his low-caste workers. By avoiding direct physical contact with them, he escapes the ritual pollution that would otherwise ensue. (Margaret Bourke-White/The LIFE Picture Collection/Getty Images)

embedded in Indian thinking. Everyone was born into and remained within one of these classes for life. At the top of this hierarchical system were the Brahmins, priests whose rituals and sacrifices alone could ensure the proper functioning of the world. They were followed by the Kshatriya class, warriors and rulers charged with protecting and governing society. Next was the Vaisya class, originally commoners who cultivated the land. These three classes came to be regarded as possessing a distinctive nobility and purity, which was conveyed by the term "Aryan." They were also called the "twice-born," for they experienced not only a physical birth but also formal initiation into their respective varnas and status as people of prestigious Aryan descent. Far below these twice-born in the hierarchy of varna groups were the Sudras, native peoples incorporated into the margins of Aryan society in very subordinate positions. Regarded as servants of their social betters, they were not allowed to hear or repeat the Vedas, an early collection of religious texts, or to take part in Aryan rituals. So little were they valued that a Brahmin who killed a Sudra was penalized as if he had killed a cat or a dog.

According to varna theory, these four classes were formed from the body of the god Purusha and were therefore eternal and changeless. Although these divisions are widely recognized in India even today, historians have noted considerable social flux in ancient Indian history. Members of the Brahmin and Kshatriya groups, for example, were frequently in conflict over which ranked highest in the varna hierarchy, and only slowly did the Brahmins emerge clearly in the top position. Although theoretically purely Aryan, both groups absorbed various tribal peoples as Indian civilization expanded. Tribal medicine men or sorcerers found a place as Brahmins, while warrior groups entered the Kshatriya varna. The Vaisya varna, originally defined as cultivators, evolved into a business class with a prominent place for merchants, while the Sudra varna became the domain of peasant farmers. Finally a whole new category, ranking lower even than the Sudras, emerged in the "untouchables," men and women who did the work considered most unclean and polluting, such as cremating corpses, dealing with the skins of dead animals, and serving as executioners. (See Snapshot: Social Life and Duty in Classical India.")

SNAPSHOT   Social Life and Duty in Classical India

Much personal behavior in classical India, at least ideally, was regulated according to caste. Each caste was associated with a particular color, with a part of the body of the god Purusha, and with a set of duties.

Caste (Varna)	Color/Symbolism	Part of Purusha	Duties
Brahmin	white/spirituality	head	priests, teachers
Kshatriya	red/courage	shoulders	warriors, rulers
Vaisya	yellow/wealth	thighs	farmers, merchants, artisans
Sudra	black/ignorance	feet	labor
Untouchables (outside of the varna system; thus no color and not associated with Purusha)	—	—	polluted labor

Beyond caste, behavior was ideally defined in terms of four stages of life, at least for the first three varna groups. Each new stage was marked by a *samskara*, a ritual initiating the person into this new phase of life.

Stage of Life	Duties
Student	Boys live with a teacher (guru); learn Sanskrit, rituals, Vedas; practice obedience, respect, celibacy, nonviolence.
Householder	Marriage and family; men practice caste-based career/occupation; women serve as wives and mothers, perform household rituals and sacrifices, actively support children and elders.
Retirement	Both husband and wife withdraw to the forests following birth of grandchildren; diminished household duties; greater focus on spiritual practice; sex permitted once a month.
Wandering ascetic	Only for men (women return to household); total rejection of ordinary existence; life as wandering hermit without shelter or possessions; caste becomes irrelevant; focus on achieving moksha and avoiding future rebirth.

Caste as Jati

As the varna system took shape in India, another set of social distinctions also arose, based largely on occupations. In India as elsewhere, urban-based civilization gave rise to specialized occupations, many organized in guilds that regulated their own affairs in a particular region. Over time, these occupationally based groups, known as *jatis*, blended with the varna system to create India's unique caste-based society.

The many thousands of jatis became the primary cells of India's social life beyond the family or household, but each of them was associated with one of the great classes (varnas). Thus Brahmins were divided into many separate jatis, or sub-castes, as were each of the other varnas as well as the untouchables. In a particular region or village, each jati was ranked in a hierarchy known to all, from the highest of the Brahmins to the lowest of the untouchables. Marriage and eating together were permitted only within an individual's own jati. Each jati was associated with a particular set of duties, rules, and obligations that defined its members' unique and separate place in the larger society. Brahmins, for example, were forbidden to eat meat, while Kshatriyas were permitted to do so. Upper-caste women covered their breasts, while some lower-caste women were forbidden this privilege as a sign of their subordination. "It is better to do one's own duty badly than another's well"—this frequently quoted saying summed up the underlying idea of Indian society. With its many separate, distinct, and hierarchically ranked social groups, Indian society was quite different from that of China or the Greco-Roman world.

It was also unique in the set of ideas that explained and justified that social system. Foremost among them was the notion of **ritual purity and pollution** applied to caste groups. Brahmins or other high-caste people who came in contact with members of lower castes, especially those who cleaned latrines, handled corpses, or butchered and skinned dead animals, were in great danger of being polluted, or made ritually unclean. Thus untouchables were forbidden to use the same wells or to enter the temples designated for higher-caste people. Sometimes they were required to wear a wooden clapper to warn others of their approach. A great body of Indian religious writing defined various forms of impurity and the ritual means of purification.

A further support for this idea of inherent inequality and permanent difference derived from emerging Hindu notions of *karma*, *dharma*, and rebirth. Being born into a particular caste was generally regarded as reflecting the good or bad deeds (karma) of a previous life. Thus an individual's prior actions were responsible for his or her current status. Any hope for rebirth in a higher caste rested on the faithful and selfless performance of one's present caste duties (dharma) in this life. Doing so contributed to spiritual progress by subduing the relentless demands of the ego. Such teachings, like that of permanent impurity, provided powerful sanctions for the inequalities of Indian society. So too did the threat of social ostracism, because each jati had the authority to expel members who violated its rules.

Guided Reading Question

■ **COMPARISON**
What is the difference between varna and jati as expressions of caste?

No greater catastrophe could befall a person than this, for it meant the end of any recognized social life and the loss of all social support.

As caste restrictions tightened, it became increasingly difficult — virtually impossible — for individuals to raise their social status during their lifetimes. However, another kind of upward mobility enabled entire jatis, over several generations, to raise their standing in the local hierarchy of caste groups. By acquiring land or wealth, by adopting the behaviors of higher-caste groups, by finding some previously overlooked "ancestor" of a higher caste, a particular jati might slowly be redefined in a higher category. India's caste system was in practice rather more fluid and changing than the theory of caste might suggest.

India's social system thus differed from that of China in several ways. It gave priority to religious status and ritual purity (the Brahmins), whereas China elevated political officials to the highest of elite positions. The caste system divided Indian society into vast numbers of distinct social groups; China had fewer, but broader, categories of society — scholar-gentry, landlords, peasants, merchants. Finally, India's caste society defined these social groups far more rigidly than in China and provided even less opportunity for social mobility.

The Functions of Caste

This caste-based social structure shaped India's emerging civilization in various ways. Because caste (jati) was a very local phenomenon, rooted in particular regions or villages, it focused the loyalties of most people on a quite restricted territory and weakened the appeal or authority of larger all-Indian states. This localization is one reason that India, unlike China, seldom experienced an empire that encompassed the entire subcontinent (see "Intermittent Empire: The Case of India" in Chapter 3). Caste, together with the shared culture of a diverse Hinduism, provided a substitute for the state as an integrative mechanism for Indian civilization. It offered a distinct and socially recognized place for almost everyone. In looking after widows, orphans, and the destitute, jatis also provided a modest measure of social security and support. Even the lowest-ranking jatis had the right to certain payments from the social superiors whom they served.

Furthermore, caste represented a means of accommodating the many migrating or invading peoples who entered the subcontinent. The cellular, or honeycomb, structure of caste society allowed various peoples, cultures, and traditions to find a place within a larger Indian civilization while retaining something of their unique identity. The process of assimilation was quite different in China, where it meant becoming Chinese ethnically, linguistically, and culturally. Finally, India's caste system facilitated the exploitation of the poor by the wealthy and powerful. The multitude of separate groups into which it divided the impoverished and oppressed majority of the population made class consciousness and organized resistance across caste lines much more difficult to achieve.

PRACTICING HISTORICAL THINKING

How did India's caste system differ from China's class system?

Slavery: The Case of the Roman Empire

Beyond the inequalities of class and caste lay those of slavery, a social institution with deep roots in human history, extending into the Paleolithic era of gathering and hunting peoples, but expanding greatly in agricultural civilizations. Some have suggested that the early domestication of animals provided a model for enslaving people. Certainly, slave owners have everywhere compared their slaves to tamed animals. Aristotle, for example, observed that the ox is "the poor man's slave." War, patriarchy, and the notion of private property, all of which accompanied the First Civilizations, also contributed to the growth of slavery. Large-scale warfare generated numerous prisoners, and everywhere in the ancient world capture in war meant the possibility of enslavement. Early records suggest that women captives were the first slaves, usually raped and then enslaved as concubines, whereas male captives were killed. Patriarchal societies, in which men sharply controlled and perhaps even "owned" women, may have suggested the possibility of using other people, men as well as women, as slaves. The class inequalities of early civilizations, which were based on great differences in privately owned property, also made it possible to imagine people owning other people.

Slavery and Civilization

Whatever its precise origins, slavery generally meant ownership by a master, the possibility of being sold, working without pay, and the status of an "outsider" at the bottom of the social hierarchy. For most, it was a kind of "social death,"[5] for slaves usually lacked any rights or independent personal identity recognized by the larger society. By the time Hammurabi's law code casually referred to Mesopotamian slavery (ca. 1750 B.C.E.), it was already a long-established tradition in the region and in all the First Civilizations. Likewise, virtually all subsequent civilizations—in the Americas, Africa, and Eurasia—practiced some form of slavery.

Slave systems throughout history have varied considerably. In some times and places, such as ancient Greece and Rome, a fair number of slaves might be emancipated in their own lifetimes, through their owners' generosity or religious convictions or the desire to avoid caring for them in old age, and sometimes slaves were allowed to purchase their freedom with their own funds. In some societies, the children of slaves inherited the status of their parents, while in others, such as the Aztec Empire, they were considered free people. Slaves likewise varied considerably in the labor they were required to do, with some working for the state in high positions, others performing domestic duties in their owner's household, and still others toiling in fields or mines in large work gangs.

The second-wave civilizations of Eurasia differed considerably in the prominence and extent of slavery in their societies. In China, it was a minor element, amounting to perhaps 1 percent of the population. Among the earliest slaves in Han dynasty China were convicted criminals and their families, confiscated by the government

---

Guided Reading Question

■ **COMPARISON**
How did the inequalities of slavery differ from those of caste?

and sometimes sold to wealthy private individuals. In desperate circumstances, impoverished or indebted peasants might sell their children into slavery. In southern China, teenage boys of poor families could be purchased by the wealthy, for whom they served as status symbols. Chinese slavery, however, was never very widespread and did not become a major source of labor for agriculture or manufacturing.

In India as well, people could fall into slavery as criminals, debtors, or prisoners of war and served their masters largely in domestic settings, but religious writings and secular law offered, at least in theory, some protection for slaves. Owners were required to provide adequately for their slaves and were forbidden to abandon them in old age. According to one ancient text, "A man may go short himself or stint his wife and children, but never his slave who does his dirty work for him."[6] Slaves in India could inherit and own property and earn money in their spare time. A master who raped a slave woman was required to set her free and pay compensation. The law encouraged owners to free their slaves and allowed slaves to buy their freedom. All of this suggests that Indian slavery was more restrained than that of other ancient civilizations. Nor did Indian civilization depend economically on slavery, for most work was performed by lower-caste, though free, men and women.

The Making of Roman Slavery

In sharp contrast to other second-wave civilizations, slavery played an immense role in the Mediterranean, or Western, world. Although slavery was practiced in Chinese, Indian, and Persian civilizations, **Greco-Roman slavery** was far more central to social life. By a conservative estimate, classical Athens alone was home to perhaps 60,000 slaves, or about one-third of the total population. In Athens, ironically, the growth of democracy and citizenship was accompanied by the simultaneous growth of slavery on a mass scale. During the fourth century B.C.E., the greatest of the Greek philosophers, Aristotle (384–322 B.C.E.), developed the notion that some people were "slaves by nature" and should be enslaved for their own good and for that of the larger society.

"The ancient Greek attitude toward slavery was simple," writes one modern scholar. "It was a terrible thing to become a slave, but a good thing to own a slave."[7] Even poor households usually had at least one or two female slaves, who provided domestic work and sexual services for their owners. Although substantial numbers of Greek slaves were granted freedom by their owners, they did not usually become citizens or gain political rights. Nor could they own land or marry citizens, and particularly in Athens they had to pay a special tax. Their status remained "halfway between slavery and freedom."[8]

Practiced on an even larger scale, slavery was a defining element of Roman society. By the time of Christ, the Italian heartland of the Roman Empire had some 2 to 3 million slaves, representing 33 to 40 percent of the population. Not until the modern slave societies of the Caribbean, Brazil, and the southern United States was slavery practiced again on such an enormous scale. Wealthy Romans could own

Guided Reading Question

■ **COMPARISON**
How did Greco-Roman slavery differ from that of other classical civilizations?

many hundreds or even thousands of slaves. One woman in the fifth century C.E. freed 8,000 slaves when she withdrew into a life of Christian monastic practice. Even people of modest means frequently owned two or three slaves. In doing so, they confirmed their own position as free people, demonstrated their social status, and expressed their ability to exercise power. Slaves and former slaves also might be slave owners. One freedman during the reign of Augustus owned 4,116 slaves at the time of his death. (For more on Roman society, see Working with Evidence: Pompeii as a Window on the Roman World, page 215.)

As the Roman Empire grew, social disruption and new wealth set loose forces that transformed it into a society in which slaves played a large role in the economy. In the early republic, landowning freemen, who both tilled the soil and served in the army, provided the backbone of this agrarian society. But as the empire expanded through constant warfare, many ordinary Roman families found it difficult to maintain their small farms when the head of the household was away serving in the military. Meanwhile, conquest brought Rome unthinkable wealth in the form of plunder, slaves, and later taxes and tribute, which flowed especially to the most well connected in society. These elites bought the small holdings of impoverished Roman freemen to create large estates and staffed those estates with slave labor, freely available from recent conquests. Displaced freemen abandoned farming and congregated in the growing cities of the empire, becoming buyers of the foodstuffs produced by slave estates. Thus a combination of economic and political disruption caused by war and wealth, together with slave labor derived from conquest, propelled Rome down the road toward becoming a slave society.

Roman Slavery This Roman mosaic from the third century C.E. shows the slave Myro serving a drink to his master, Fructus. (Musée National du Bardo, Tunis, Tunisia/ G. Dagli Orti/De Agostini/REX/Shutterstock)

The vast majority of Roman slaves were prisoners captured in the many wars that accompanied the creation of the empire. In 146 B.C.E., following the destruction of the North African city of Carthage, some 55,000 people were enslaved en masse. From all over the Mediterranean basin, men and women were funneled into the major slave-owning regions of Italy and Sicily. Pirates also furnished slaves, kidnapping tens of thousands and selling them to Roman slave traders on the island of Delos. Roman merchants purchased still other slaves through networks of long-distance commerce extending to the Black Sea, the East African coast, and northwestern Europe. Slaves were also supplied through natural reproduction, as the children of slave mothers were regarded as slaves themselves. Such "home-born" slaves had a certain prestige and were thought to be less troublesome than those who had known freedom earlier in their lives. Finally, abandoned or exposed children could legally become the slave of anyone who rescued them.

Unlike American slavery of later times, Roman practice was not identified with a particular racial or ethnic group. Egyptians, Syrians, Jews, Greeks, Gauls, North Africans, and many other people found themselves enslaved. From within the empire and its adjacent regions, an enormous diversity of people were bought and sold at Roman slave markets.

Like slave owners everywhere, Romans regarded their slaves as "barbarians"— lazy, unreliable, immoral, prone to thieving—and came to think of certain peoples, such as Asiatic Greeks, Syrians, and Jews, as slaves by nature. Nor was there any serious criticism of slavery in principle, although on occasion owners were urged to treat their slaves in a more benevolent way. Even the triumph of Christianity within the Roman Empire did little to undermine slavery, for Christian teaching held that slaves should be "submissive to [their] masters with all fear, not only to the good and gentle, but also to the harsh."[9] In fact, the New Testament used the metaphor of slavery to describe the relationship of believers to God, styling them as "slaves of Christ," while Saint Augustine (354–430 C.E.) described slavery as God's punishment for sin. Thus slavery was deeply embedded in the religious thinking and social outlook of elite Romans.

Similarly, slavery was entrenched throughout the Roman economy. No occupation was off-limits to slaves except military service, and no distinction existed between jobs for slaves and those for free people. Frequently they labored side by side. In rural areas, slaves provided much of the labor force on the huge estates, or *latifundia*, that produced grain, olive oil, and wine, mostly for export, much like the later plantations in the Americas. There they often worked chained together. In the cities, slaves worked in their owners' households, but also as skilled artisans, teachers, doctors, business agents, entertainers, and actors. In the empire's many mines and quarries, slaves and criminals labored under brutal conditions. Slaves in the service of the emperor provided manpower for the state bureaucracy, maintained temples and shrines, and kept Rome's water supply system functioning. Trained in special schools, they also served as gladiators in the violent spectacles of Roman public life. Female slaves usually served as domestic servants but were also put to work in brothels, served as actresses and entertainers, and could be used sexually by their male owners. Thus slaves were represented among the highest and most prestigious occupations and in the lowest and most degraded.

Slave owners in the Roman Empire were supposed to provide the necessities of life to their slaves. When this occurred, slaves may have had a more secure life than was available to impoverished free people, who had to fend for themselves, but the price of this security was absolute subjection to the will of the master. Beatings, sexual abuse, and sale to another owner were constant possibilities. Lacking all rights in the law, slaves could not legally marry, although many contracted unofficial unions.

The Spartacus Slave Revolt

Despite the prominence of slavery in ancient civilizations, large-scale slave revolts were rare. One of the most impressive began in the Roman Empire during the summer of 73 B.C.E. when around seventy slaves escaped from a gladiator school at Capua, about 125 miles south of Rome. Grabbing knives and skewers from the kitchen on their way out, this small band of men, who had been trained to fight to the death for the entertainment of spectators, established

The death of Spartacus, 71 B.C.E.

a stronghold on nearby Mount Vesuvius and chose as their leader Spartacus, described by the historian Sallust as "a man of immense bodily strength and spirit."[10] The defeat of Roman forces sent to seize them encouraged other slaves and some free men to join the rebellion. Their numbers eventually swelled to as many as 120,000 men, women, and children at the height of the uprising, reflecting the large number of slaves employed on the great estates of southern Italy.

Roman authorities became increasingly concerned when Spartacus and his followers began to manufacture their own weapons and to organize into a more coherent military force, which defeated in turn several hurriedly assembled Roman armies and plundered the rich farming region of Campania. The fortunes of the rebels peaked in 72 B.C.E. when they briefly threatened Rome itself. Both sides treated their opponents brutally. The Greek historian Appian reported that Spartacus ordered the sacrifice of 300 Roman prisoners in honor of the slain rebel leader Crixus, while another historian claimed that Spartacus staged gladiatorial games using 400 captives. When the revolt was finally suppressed, captured rebel slaves received similarly brutal treatment from the Roman authorities.

Slaves often accumulated money or possessions, but such property legally belonged to their masters and could be seized at any time. If a slave murdered his master, Roman law demanded the lives of all of the victim's slaves. When one Roman official was killed by a slave in 61 C.E., every one of his 400 slaves was condemned to death. For an individual slave, the quality of life depended almost entirely on the character of the master. Brutal owners made life a living hell. Benevolent owners made life tolerable and might even grant favored slaves their freedom or permit them to buy that freedom. As in Greece, manumission of slaves was a widespread practice, but in the Roman Empire, unlike in Greece, freedom was accompanied by citizenship.

Roman slaves, like their counterparts in other societies, responded to enslavement in many ways. Most, no doubt, did what was necessary to survive, but there are recorded cases of Roman prisoners of war who chose to commit mass suicide rather than face the horrors of slavery. Others, once enslaved, resorted to the "weapons of the weak"—small-scale theft, sabotage, pretending illness, working poorly, and placing curses on their masters. Slaves fleeing to the anonymous crowds of the city or to remote rural areas prompted owners to post notices in public places,

Fearful for the safety of the capital, the Roman authorities acted decisively. They appointed Marcus Licinius Crassus, a rich and ambitious Roman aristocrat and military commander, to lead eight Roman legions, totaling perhaps 40,000 troops, against Spartacus and his rebels. Crassus cornered the slave army in the far south of Italy, and Spartacus soon realized that his followers faced a fight to the death. According to the historian Appian, he advertised their precarious situation to his troops by crucifying a Roman soldier "as a visual reminder to his own men of what would happen to them if they did not win."[11] Rather than be captured, Spartacus and the slaves with him chose to make a last stand.

The Greek historian Plutarch reports that Spartacus killed his horse in front of his troops to show that he had no intention of fleeing and led his forces in a final desperate engagement with Crassus's army. Even the most hostile of later historians recounted that Spartacus died bravely during the battle, though some claimed that his body was never found. For those who survived, a terrible vengeance followed as some 6,000 captured rebel slaves were nailed to crosses along the Appian Way, between Capua, where the rebellion began, and Rome. These crucified prisoners, spaced some thirty-five to forty yards apart for over a hundred miles, provided a clear warning to all others who contemplated rebellion.

Spartacus's revolt had little lasting effect on the society in which he lived. No further large-scale revolts took place in the Roman Empire, and Rome continued its economic system based on slave labor. Moreover, the rebellion occasioned little historical comment until the eighteenth century. However, over the past two and a half centuries, a number of groups have embraced Spartacus, casting him as an inspirational leader of the downtrodden who resisted injustice and subjugation. Marxists, socialists, and nationalists have all found something to admire in Spartacus and his rebellion. In the United States, Spartacus entered the popular imagination due in no small part to the success of the 1960 epic film *Spartacus*, starring Kirk Douglas as the rebel leader fighting against the odds to free the oppressed. While there is no historical evidence that Spartacus ever intended to abolish slavery or fundamentally reform Roman society, in modern times his heroic, if ultimately failed, quest for freedom has been recovered from the past, becoming for many an inspirational symbol of just resistance to oppression. In such ways, the past continues to resonate in the present.

QUESTIONS

What can Spartacus's revolt tell us about the nature of the slave system in the Roman Empire? How might you account for the renewed interest in Spartacus over the past several centuries?

asking for information about their runaways. Catching runaway slaves became an organized private business. Occasional murders of slave owners made masters conscious of the dangers they faced. "Every slave we own is an enemy we harbor" ran one Roman saying.[12]

On several notable occasions, the slaves themselves rose in rebellion. The most famous uprising occurred in 73 B.C.E. when a slave gladiator named **Spartacus** led seventy other slaves from a school for gladiators in a desperate bid for freedom that mushroomed into a huge uprising. (See Zooming In: The Spartacus Slave Revolt, page 202, for a more detailed account.) Nothing on the scale of Spartacus's rebellion occurred again in the Western world of slavery until the Haitian Revolution of the 1790s. But Haitian rebels sought the creation of a new society free of slavery altogether. None of the Roman slave rebellions, including that of Spartacus, had any such overall plan or goal. The rebels simply wanted to escape Roman slavery. Although rebellions created a perpetual fear in the minds of slave owners, slavery itself was hardly affected.

The Rebellion of Spartacus

Comparing Patriarchies

Social inequality was embedded not only in the structures of class, caste, and slavery, but also in the gender systems of second-wave civilizations, as patterns of male dominance practiced in the patriarchy of the First Civilizations were replicated and elaborated in those that followed. (See "Hierarchies of Gender" in Chapter 2.) The basic idea of patriarchy, involving the sharp subordination of women to men, found expression in the Laws of Manu, an Indian compilation of prescriptions for a good society that developed around 200 to 400 C.E. It tied a woman irrevocably to the men in her life—father, husband, and son—declaring that "a woman must never be independent." Such patriarchal attitudes have been so widespread and pervasive that historians have been slow to recognize that gender systems had a history, changing over time. New agricultural technologies, the rise or decline of powerful states, the incorporation of world religions, interaction with culturally different peoples—all of these developments and more generated significant change in understandings of what was appropriate masculine and feminine behavior. Most often, patriarchies were lighter and less restrictive for women in the early years of a civilization's development and during times of upheaval, when established ways of living were disrupted.

Furthermore, women were often active agents in the histories of their societies, even while largely accepting their overall subordination. As the central figures in family life, they served as repositories and transmitters of their peoples' culture. Some were able to occupy unorthodox and occasionally prominent positions outside the home as scholars, religious functionaries, managers of property and participants in commerce, and even as rulers or military leaders. In Britain, Egypt, and Vietnam, for example, women led efforts to resist their countries' incorporation into the Roman or Chinese empires. (In Chapter 3, see Zooming In: Trung Trac, page 116, and the statue of Boudica, page 114.) Both Buddhist and Christian nuns carved out small domains of relative freedom from male control. In India, Buddhist nuns composed hundreds of poems that were brought together in a collection known as the *Psalms of the Sisters*, probably during the first century B.C.E. Those writings became part of the officially recognized Buddhist scriptures and represent the only early text in any of the world's major religions that was written by and about women. But these changes or challenges to male dominance occurred within a patriarchal framework, and nowhere did they evolve out of or beyond that framework. Thus a kind of "patriarchal equilibrium" ensured the long-term persistence of women's subordination despite fluctuations and various efforts to redefine gender roles or push against gendered expectations.[13]

Nor was patriarchy everywhere the same. Restrictions on women were far sharper in urban-based civilizations than in those pastoral or agricultural societies that lay beyond the reach of cities and empires. The degree and expression of patriarchy also varied from one civilization to another, as the discussion of Mesopotamia and Egypt in Chapter 2 illustrated. And within particular civilizations, elite women both enjoyed privileges and suffered the restrictions of seclusion in the home to a much greater extent than their lower-class counterparts, whose economic circumstances required them to operate in the larger social arena. China provides a fascinating example of how patriarchy changed over time, while the contrasting patriarchies of Athens and Sparta illustrate clear variations even within the much smaller world of Greek civilization.

A Changing Patriarchy: The Case of China

As Chinese civilization took shape during the Han dynasty, elite thinking about gender issues became more explicitly patriarchal, more clearly defined, and linked to an emerging Confucian ideology. Long-established patterns of thinking in terms of pairs of opposites were now described in gendered and unequal terms. The superior principle of *yang* was viewed as masculine and related to Heaven, rulers, strength, rationality, and light, whereas *yin*, the lower feminine principle, was associated with the Earth, subjects, weakness, emotion, and darkness. Thus female inferiority was seen as permanent and embedded in the workings of the universe.

What this view meant more practically was spelled out repeatedly over the centuries in various Confucian texts. Two notions in particular summarized the ideal position of women, at least in the eyes of elite male writers. The adage "Men go out, women stay in" emphasized the public and political roles of men in contrast to the domestic and private domain of women. A second idea, known as the **"three obediences,"** emphasized a woman's subordination first to her father, then to her husband, and finally to her son. "Why is it," asked one text, "that according to the rites the man takes his wife, whereas the woman leaves her house [to join her husband's family]? It is because the *yin* is lowly, and should not have the initiative; it proceeds to the *yang* in order to be completed."[14]

The Chinese woman writer and court official Ban Zhao (45–116 C.E.) observed that the ancients had practiced three customs when a baby girl was born. She was placed below the bed to show that she was "lowly and weak," required always to "humble herself before others." Then she was given a piece of broken pottery to play with, signifying that "her primary duty [was] to be industrious." Finally, her birth was announced to the ancestors with an offering to indicate that she was responsible for "the continuation of [ancestor] worship in the home."[15]

Yet such notions of passivity, inferiority, and subordination were not the whole story of women's lives in ancient China. A few women, particularly the wives, concubines, or widows of emperors, were able on occasion to exercise considerable political authority. Several others led peasant rebellions. In doing so, they provoked much antifemale hostility on the part of male officials, who understood governance as a masculine task and often blamed the collapse of a dynasty or natural disasters on the "unnatural" and "disruptive" influence of women in political affairs. Others, however, praised women of virtue as wise counselors to their fathers, husbands, and rulers and depicted them positively as active agents.

Guided Reading Question

■ **CHANGE**
In what ways did the expression of Chinese patriarchy change over time, and why did it change?

Elite Chinese Women at Leisure This Ming dynasty (1368–1644) painting shows elite Chinese women at leisure in the imperial palace known as the Forbidden City. In the center of the painting two women play a board game called *weiqi*, while two others look on and a servant attends them with a fan. Elite Chinese women were largely confined in their living quarters, where they socialized among themselves. (Pictures from History/Bridgeman Images)

Within her husband's family, a young woman was clearly subordinate as a wife and daughter-in-law, but as a mother of sons, she was accorded considerable honor for her role in producing the next generation of male heirs to carry on her husband's lineage. When her sons married, she was able to exercise the significant authority of a mother-in-law. Furthermore, a woman, at least in the upper classes, often brought with her a considerable dowry, which was regarded as her own property and gave her some leverage within her marriage. Women's roles in the production of textiles, often used to pay taxes or to sell commercially, made a woman's labor quite valuable to the family economy. And a man's wife was sharply distinguished from his concubines, for she was legally mother to all her husband's children. Furthermore, peasant women could hardly follow the Confucian ideal of seclusion in the home, as their labor was required in the fields. Thus women's lives were more complex and varied than the prescriptions of Confucian orthodoxy might suggest.

Much changed in China following the collapse of the Han dynasty in the third century C.E. Centralized government vanished amid much political fragmentation and conflict. Confucianism, the main ideology of Han China, was discredited, while Daoism and Buddhism attracted a growing following. Pastoral and nomadic peoples invaded northern China and ruled a number of the small states that had replaced the Han government. These new conditions resulted in some loosening of the strict patriarchy of Han dynasty China over the next five or six centuries.

The cultural influence of nomadic peoples, whose women were far less restricted than those of China, was noticed, and criticized, by more Confucian-minded male observers. One of them lamented the sad deterioration of gender roles under the influence of nomadic peoples:

> In the north of the Yellow river it is usually the wife who runs the household. She will not dispense with good clothing or expensive jewelry. The husband has to settle for old horses and sickly servants. The traditional niceties between husband and wife are seldom observed, and from time to time he even has to put up with her insults.[16]

Ordinary Chinese Women at Work For a long time, the spinning and weaving of cloth were part of women's domestic work in China. In this detail from a Ming dynasty vase, women are shown weaving silk. (Detail from a vase [ceramic], Ming Dynasty [1368–1644]/Golestan Palace, Tehran, Iran/ Bridgeman Images)

Others criticized the adoption of nomadic styles of dress, makeup, and music. By the time of the Tang dynasty (618–907), writers and artists depicted elite women as capable of handling legal and business affairs on their own and on occasion riding horses and playing polo, bareheaded and wearing men's clothing. Tang legal codes even recognized a married daughter's right to inherit property from her family of birth. Such images of women were quite different from those of Han dynasty China.

A further sign of a weakening patriarchy and the cause of great distress to advocates of Confucian orthodoxy lay in the unusual reign of **Empress Wu** (r. 690–705 C.E.), a former high-ranking concubine in the imperial court who came to power amid much palace intrigue and was the only woman ever to rule China with the title of emperor. With the support of China's growing Buddhist establishment, Empress Wu governed despotically, but she also consolidated China's civil service examination system for the selection of public officials and actively patronized scholarship and the arts. Some of her actions seem deliberately designed to elevate the position of women. She commissioned the biographies of famous women, decreed that the mourning period for mothers be made equal to that for fathers, and ordered the creation of a Chinese character for "human being" that suggested the process of birth flowing from one woman without a prominent male role. Her reign was brief and unrepeated.

The growing popularity of Daoism provided new images of the feminine and new roles for women. Daoist texts referred to the *dao* as "mother" and urged the traditionally feminine virtues of yielding and passive acceptance rather than the male-oriented striving of Confucianism. Daoist sects often featured women as priests, nuns, or reclusive meditators, able to receive cosmic truth and to use it for the benefit of others. A variety of female deities from Daoist or Buddhist traditions found a place in Chinese village religion, while growing numbers of women found an alternative to family life in Buddhist monasteries. None of this meant an end to patriarchy, but it does suggest some change in the tone and expression of that patriarchy. However, during the Song dynasty that followed, a more restrictive patriarchy reemerged.

Contrasting Patriarchies: Athens and Sparta

The patriarchies of second-wave civilizations not only fluctuated over time but also varied considerably from place to place. Nowhere is this variation more apparent than in the contrasting cases of Athens and Sparta, two of the leading city-states of Greek civilization (see Map 3.2, page 105). Even within this small area, the opportunities available to women and the restrictions imposed on them differed substantially. Although Athens has been celebrated as a major expression of democracy and rationalism, its posture toward women was far more restrictive than that of the highly militaristic and much less democratic Sparta.

In the several centuries between about 700 and 400 B.C.E., as the free male citizens of Athens moved toward unprecedented participation in political life, the city's women experienced growing limitations. They had no role whatsoever in the Assembly, the councils, or the juries of Athens, which were increasingly the focus of life for free men. In legal matters, women had to be represented by a guardian, and court proceedings did not even refer to them by name, but only as someone's wife or mother.

Greek thinkers, especially Aristotle, provided a set of ideas that justified women's exclusion from public life and their general subordination to men. According to Aristotle, "A woman is, as it were, an infertile male. She is female in fact on account of a kind of inadequacy." That inadequacy lay in her inability to generate sperm, which contained the "form" or the "soul" of a new human being. Her role in the reproductive process was passive, providing a receptacle for the vital male contribution. Compared often to children or domesticated animals, women were associated with instinct and passion and lacked the rationality to take part in public life. "It is the best for all tame animals to be ruled by human beings," wrote Aristotle. "In the same way, the relationship between the male and the female is by nature such that the male is higher, the female lower, that the male rules and the female is ruled."[17]

As in China, elite Athenian women were expected to remain inside the home, except perhaps for religious festivals or funerals. Even within the home, women's space was quite separate from that of men. Although poorer women, courtesans, and prostitutes had to leave their homes to earn money, collect water, or shop, ideal behavior for upper-class women meant assigning these tasks to slaves or to men and

---

Guided Reading Question

■ **COMPARISON**

How did the patriarchies of Athens and Sparta differ from each other?

involved a radical segregation of male and female space. "What causes women a bad reputation," declared Andromache, a female character in the Greek playwright Euripides' *The Trojan Women*, "is not remaining inside."

Within the domestic realm, Athenian women were generally married in their midteens to men ten to fifteen years older than themselves. Their main function was the management of domestic affairs and the production of sons who would become active citizens. These sons were expected to acquire a literate education, while their sisters were normally limited to learning spinning, weaving, and other household tasks. The Greek writer Menander exclaimed: "Teaching a woman to read and write? What a terrible thing to do! Like feeding a vile snake on more poison." Nor did women have much economic power. Although they could own personal property obtained through dowry, gifts, or inheritance, land was usually passed through male heirs. By law, women were forbidden to buy or sell land and could negotiate contracts only if the sum involved was valued at less than a bushel of barley.

There were exceptions, although rare, to the restricted lives of upper-class Athenian women, the most notable of which was **Aspasia** (ca. 470–400 B.C.E.). She was born in the Greek city of Miletus, on the western coast of Anatolia, to a wealthy family that believed in educating its daughters. As a young woman, Aspasia found her way to Athens,

A Woman of Athens This grave stele from about 400 B.C.E. marked the final resting place of Hegeso, a wealthy Athenian woman, shown in the women's quarter of a Greek home examining her jewelry, perhaps for the last time, while attended by her slave. The domestic setting of this grave marker contrasts with that common for men, which usually showed them as warriors in a public space. (Grave stele of Hegeso/National Archeological Museum, Athens, Greece/Marie Mauzy/Art Resource, NY)

where her foreign birth gave her somewhat more freedom than was normally available to the women of that city. She soon attracted the attention of Pericles, Athens's leading political figure. The two lived together as husband and wife until Pericles' death in 429 B.C.E., although they were not officially married. Treated as an equal partner by Pericles, Aspasia proved to be a learned and witty conversationalist who moved freely in the cultured circles of Athens. Her foreign birth and her apparent influence on Pericles provoked critics to suggest that she was a *hetaera*, a professional, educated, high-class entertainer and sexual companion, similar to a Japanese geisha. Although little is known about Aspasia, a number of major Athenian writers commented about her, both positively and negatively. She was, by all accounts, a rare and remarkable woman in a city that offered little opportunity for individuality or achievement to its female population.

A Girl of Sparta This figurine portrays a young female Spartan athlete or runner. Compare her clothing with that worn by Hegeso in the photo "A Woman of Athens." (The British Museum, London, UK/Bridgeman Images)

The evolution of Sparta differed in many ways from that of Athens. Early on, Sparta solved the problem of feeding a growing population not by creating overseas colonies as did many Greek city-states, but by conquering its immediate neighbors and reducing them to a status of permanent servitude, not far removed from slavery. Called **helots**, these dependents far outnumbered the free citizens of Sparta and represented a permanent threat of rebellion. Solving this problem shaped Spartan society decisively. Sparta's answer was a militaristic regime, constantly ready for war to keep the helots in their place. To maintain such a system, all boys were removed from their families at the age of seven to be trained by the state in military camps, where they learned the ways of war. There they remained until the age of thirty. The ideal Spartan male was a warrior, skilled in battle, able to endure hardship, and willing to die for his city. Mothers are said to have told their sons departing for battle to "come back with your shield . . . or on it." Although economic equality for men was the ideal, it was never completely realized in practice. And unlike Athens, political power was exercised primarily by a small group of wealthy men.

This militaristic and far-from-democratic system had implications for women that, strangely enough, offered them greater freedoms and fewer restrictions. As in many warrior societies, their central task was reproduction—bearing warrior sons for Sparta. To strengthen their bodies for childbearing, girls were encouraged to take part in sporting events—running, wrestling, throwing the discus and javelin, even driving chariots. At times, women and men alike competed in the nude before mixed audiences. Their education, like that of boys, was prescribed by the state, which also insisted that newly married women cut their hair short, unlike adult Greek women elsewhere. Thus Spartan women were not secluded or segregated, as were their Athenian counterparts.

Furthermore, Spartan young women, unlike those of Athens, usually married men of their own age, about eighteen years old, thus putting the new couple on a more equal basis. Marriage often began with a trial period to make sure the new couple could produce children, with divorce and remarriage readily available if they could not. Because men were so often away at war or preparing for it, women exercised much more authority in the household than was the case in Athens and actively managed family estates, some of which they controlled as their inheritance. Despite the intentions of the government, these busy women limited their fertility, sometimes through the use of various birth control practices. Over time they produced too few children to maintain the Spartan population, leading to a demographic crisis. According to the Roman orator Cicero, they preferred the active life to "barbarous fertility," a development experienced in many other societies where women have secured greater control over their lives and activities.[18]

It is little wonder that the freedom of Spartan women appalled other Greeks, who believed that it undermined good order and state authority. Aristotle complained that the more egalitarian inheritance practices of Spartans led to their women controlling some 40 percent of landed estates. In Sparta, he declared, women "live in every sort of intemperance and luxury" and "the [male] rulers are ruled by women." Plutarch, a Greek writer during the heyday of the Roman Empire, observed critically that "the men of Sparta always obeyed their wives." Moreover, the clothing worn by Spartan women to give them greater freedom of movement seemed immodest to other Greeks. However, the freedoms of Sparta's women did not endure. After the helots permanently overthrew Spartan rule in 369 B.C.E., it seems that the Spartan government increasingly restricted the rights and status of women, bringing Sparta's gender practices more in line with those of its neighbors. Thus freedom for the helots gradually brought restrictions for Spartan women.

Sparta clearly was a patriarchy, with women serving as breeding machines for its military system and lacking any formal role in public life, but it was a less restrictive patriarchy than that of Athens. The joint efforts of men and women seemed necessary to maintain a huge class of helots in permanent subjugation at least until 369 B.C.E. Death in childbirth was considered the equivalent of death in battle, for both contributed to the defense of Sparta, and both were honored alike. In Athens, on the other hand, growing freedom and democracy were associated with the strengthening of the male-dominated, property-owning household, and within that household, the cornerstone of Athenian society, men were expected to exercise authority. Doing so required increasingly severe limitations and restrictions on the lives of women. Together, the cases of Athens and Sparta illustrate how the historical record appears in a different light when viewed through the lens of gender. Athens, so celebrated for its democracy and philosophical rationalism, offered little to its women, whereas Sparta, often condemned for its militarism and virtual enslavement of the helots, provided a somewhat wider scope for the free women of the city-state.

If Athenian and Spartan patriarchies differed substantially in the opportunities they offered to women, they were more similar in their posture toward homo-erotic relationships than other second-wave civilizations. Ancient Greeks generally approved of such relationships, and they were fairly common for both men and women, although this did not prevent their participants from entering heterosexual marriages as well. In Athens, the ideal homosexual relationship—between an older man and a young adolescent boy—was viewed as limited in time, for it was supposed to end when the boy's beard began to grow. Spartans possessed much the same attitudes, even if their homosexual relationships were shaped by a warrior society. Plato wrote that homosexual encounters in Sparta were the result of nudity in gymnasia and the custom of men dining together, while several historians refer to specific homosexual relationships between Spartan soldiers. One modern scholar noted that "records of Sparta from the classical period seem to refer to homosexual boyfriends at least as often as to wives."[19] Unlike contemporary Western societies, where sexuality is largely seen as an identity, in ancient Greece sexual choice was viewed more casually and as a matter of taste.

REFLECTIONS

What Changes? What Persists?

So what is more impressive in human history—the innovations and changes or the enduring patterns and lasting features? Our perception of change or continuity surely depends on when we are living. During the long Paleolithic and Neolithic eras, few people were aware of major changes in the larger patterns of life. Of course, change happened: nomadic peoples settled down in villages; agriculture developed; cities arose; states and empires took shape; class structures evolved; patriarchy emerged more sharply defined. But few of these changes occurred quickly enough to be noticeable in a single lifetime. It is among the great contributions of world history to call attention to transformations of which we might otherwise be unaware. In the modern era, and certainly in our own time, the pace of change has dramatically accelerated. We have come to value, celebrate, expect, and promote change in ways that many of our distant—and not so distant—ancestors would find unimaginable.

What might we say about the balance of change and persistence in the era of second-wave civilizations? Clearly, there was much that was new, even if those innovations had roots in earlier times. The Greek conquest of the Persian Empire under the leadership of Alexander the Great was both novel and unexpected. The Roman Empire encompassed the entire Mediterranean basin in a single political system for the first time. Buddhism and Christianity emerged as new, distinct, and universal religious traditions, although both bore the marks of their origin in Hindu and Jewish religious thinking, respectively. The collapse of dynasties, empires, and civilizations long thought to be solidly entrenched—the Chinese and Roman, for example—must surely have seemed to people of the time to be something fearfully new.

But much that was created in the second-wave era—particularly its social and cultural patterns—has demonstrated an impressive continuity throughout many centuries, even if it also changed in particular ways over time. China's scholar-gentry class retained its prominence throughout the ups and downs of changing dynasties into the twentieth century. India's caste-based social structure still endures as a way of thinking and behaving for hundreds of millions of men and women on the South Asian peninsula. Although slavery gave way to serfdom in post-Roman Europe (500–1000 C.E.), it was widely practiced in the Islamic world and massively extended in Europe's American colonies after 1500. Slavery remained an important and largely unquestioned feature of all civilizations until the nineteenth century, and in various forms it still exists. Patriarchy, with its assumptions of male superiority and dominance, has surely been the most fundamental, long-lasting, and taken-for-granted feature of all civilizations. Not until recent centuries have those assumptions effectively been challenged, and even so, patriarchy has continued to shape the lives and the thinking of the vast majority of humankind. And many hundreds of millions of people in the twenty-first century still honor or practice religious and cultural traditions begun during the second-wave era.

Persistence and change alike have long provided the inextricable warp and woof of both individual experience and historical study. Each of us no doubt ponders the tension between them in our own lives. Untangling their elusive relationship has figured prominently in the task of historians and has contributed much to the enduring fascination of historical study.

Second Thoughts

What's the Significance?

Wang Mang, 191

China's scholar-gentry class, 191

Yellow Turban Rebellion, 192

varnas,193

jatis, 196

ritual purity and pollution, 196

Greco-Roman slavery, 199

Spartacus, 203

"three obediences," 205

Empress Wu, 207

Aspasia, 209

helots, 210

Big Picture Questions

1. What might an observant Chinese traveler from the Han dynasty era find surprising or offensive in India or the Greco-Roman world? What similarities might he or she notice?
2. Why do you think slavery was so much more prominent in Greco-Roman civilization than in India or China?
3. What philosophical, religious, or cultural ideas served to legitimate the class and gender inequalities of second-wave civilizations?
4. What changes in the patterns of social life in second-wave civilizations can you identify? What accounts for these changes?
5. **Looking Back:** The cultural and social patterns of civilizations seem to endure longer than the political framework of states and empires. What evidence from Chapters 3, 4, and 5 might support this statement? How might you account for this phenomenon? Is there evidence that could support a contrary position?

Next Steps: For Further Study

Jeannine Auboyer, *Daily Life in Ancient India* (2002). A social history of ancient India, with a focus on caste, ritual, religion, and art.

Sue Blundell, *Women in Ancient Greece* (1999). A well-written academic study, with occasional humorous stories and anecdotes.

Sandra R. Joshel, *Slavery in the Roman World* (2010). An overview of slave life in the Roman Empire by an established scholar in the field.

Michael Lowe, *Everyday Life in Early Imperial China* (1968). A vivid description of social life during the Han dynasty.

Peter Stearns, *Gender in World History* (2015). A prominent world historian explores the relationship between changing gender roles and cross-cultural interactions.

Merry Wiesner-Hanks, *Gender in History* (2011). A thoughtful overview by a leading scholar in both women's history and world history.

BBC, "The Indian Caste System: An Introduction," part of the series "The Story of India," written and presented by Michael Wood, 2009, www.youtube.com/watch?v=Oh_xvKLhZHg. An excerpt from a BBC documentary dealing with the beginnings of caste in India.

Roy Rosenzweig Center for History and New Media, George Mason University, "Women in World History," http://chnm.gmu.edu/wwh/. Documents, reviews, and lesson plans for learning and teaching about women's history in a global context.

Pompeii as a Window on the Roman World

> You could hear the shrieks of women, the wailing of infants, and the shouting of men; some were calling their parents, others their children or their wives, trying to recognize them by their voices. People bewailed their own fate or that of their relatives, and there were some who prayed for death in their terror of dying. Many besought the aid of the gods, but still more imagined there were no gods left, and that the universe was plunged into eternal darkness for evermore.[20]

Written by a prominent Roman known as Pliny the Younger, this eyewitness account details reactions to the volcanic eruption of Mount Vesuvius, located on the southwestern side of the Italian peninsula, on August 24, 79 C.E. That eruption buried the nearby city of Pompeii and the smaller town of Herculaneum, located about 150 miles south of Rome, but it also preserved those cities, frozen in time, until archeologists began to uncover them in the mid-eighteenth century (see Map 3.4, page 113). Now substantially excavated, Pompeii is an archeological and historical treasure, offering a unique window into the life of a Roman city during the first century C.E.

As this city of some 12,000 to 15,000 people emerged from layers of ash, it stood revealed as a small but prosperous center of commerce and agriculture, serving as a point of entry for goods coming to southern Italy by sea. Pompeii also hosted numerous vineyards, production facilities for wine and olive oil, and a fisheries industry. Laid out in a grid pattern with straight streets, the city hosted numerous public facilities, including a central bathing/swimming pool, some twenty-five street fountains, various public bathhouses, and a large food market as well as many bars and small restaurants. More than thirty brothels, often featuring explicit erotic art, offered sexual services at relatively inexpensive prices. An inscription, apparently aimed at the many tourists visiting Pompeii, declared: "If anyone is looking for some tender love in this town, keep in mind that here all the girls are very friendly."

The houses of the wealthy were elegant structures, often built around a central courtyard, and were decorated with lovely murals displaying still-life images, landscapes, and scenes from Greek and Roman mythology. Carved on the threshold of one house was an expression of the entrepreneurial spirit of the town: "Gain is pure joy."

SOURCE 5.1 **Terentius Neo and His Wife**

The preserved art of Pompeii provides a glimpse into the city's social life, especially that of the more prosperous classes. Source 5.1 shows a portrait of Terentius Neo, a prominent businessman and magistrate (an elected public official), and his unnamed wife. He is wearing a toga and holding a papyrus scroll, while she wears a tunic and is holding a stylus, used for writing on the wax-covered wooden tablet that she carries. Her hair is styled in a fashion popular in the mid-first century.

■ What significance do you attribute to the lack of a name for the woman?

■ What is conveyed by highlighting the literacy of this couple?

■ How do you view these two people and their relationship to one another?

An Elite Couple of Pompeii | **1st century** C.E.

Museo Archeologico Nazionale, Naples, Italy/De Agostini Picture Library/Bridgeman Images

■ ■ ■

SOURCE 5.2 **A Pompeii Banquet**

Terentius Neo and his wife were no doubt served by slaves in their home, as slave owning was common in the Roman world, particularly among the upper classes. A wealthy household in Pompeii might own five to seven slaves. In the streets and homes of urban areas, slaves and free people mingled quite openly. Roman slavery was not distinguished by race, and the outward signs of urban slavery were few, especially for those practicing professions. Terentius Neo and his wife no doubt gave and attended banquets similar to the one depicted in Source 5.2, where well-to-do guests reclined on padded couches while slaves served them food and drink. Dancers, acrobats, and singers often provided entertainment at such events, which offered an occasion for elites to impress others with their lavish display of wealth and generosity.

- What signs of social status are evident in this painting? What conclusion might you draw from the gender balance at the banquet?

- How might you imagine the conversation at this event?

- What differences among the four slaves, shown in the foreground and second from the right at top, can you identify? Notice also the performing acrobat at the bottom right. What might these differences indicate about Roman slavery?

A Dinner with Friends | 1st century C.E.

Museo Archeologico Nazionale, Naples, Italy/Roger-Viollet, Paris/Bridgeman Images

■ ■ ■

SOURCE 5.3 From a Pompeii Tavern

The lives of the less exalted appear infrequently in the art of Pompeii, but the images in Source 5.3 provide some entrée into their world. These frescoes, a style of mural painting, were found on the wall of a *caupona*, an inn or tavern catering to the lower classes. The first image shows Myrtale, a prostitute, kissing a man, while the caption above reads: "I don't want to, with Myrtale." In the second image, a female barmaid serves two customers with a large jug and a cup, while they compete for her attention. In the third image, two men playing dice are arguing.

■ Why do you think a tavern owner might have such paintings in his place of business?

■ What might we learn about tavern life from these images?

■ What roles did women play in the tavern?

■ What differences do you notice between these paintings and those depicting the lives of the upper classes?

An Evening Out at a Pompeii Bar | **1st century C.E.**

Museo Archeologico Nazionale, Naples, Italy/
Photos: Fotografia Foglia/Scala/Art Resource, NY

SOURCE 5.4 **The Graffiti of Pompeii**

The ordinary life of Pompeii is also revealed in some 11,000 inscriptions written, painted, or incised on the walls all over the city. They include public notices, advertisements, political endorsements, poetic reflections, . . . and graffiti galore. Even locals were impressed at the proliferation of these inscriptions. One of them wrote: "Oh walls, you have held up so much tedious graffiti that I am amazed that you have not already collapsed in ruin."

■ What might historians learn about everyday life in Pompeii from these inscriptions?

■ Do you recognize some similarity to modern life in these inscriptions, or do they seem to derive from a wholly different time and place?

The Graffiti of Pompeii | **1st century C.E.**

Politics and Advertising

• If modesty in life should be considered worth anything at all, then Lucretius Fronto is worthy of the office.

• The late night drinkers unanimously support Marcus Cerrinius Vatia for aedile [a city official].

• May all who refuse to vote for Quintius be turned into a donkey.

• Thirty pairs of gladiators . . . will fight at Pompeii on April 8th–13th. There will be a beast hunt and awnings [to provide shade]. Aemilius Celer wrote this alone by the light of the moon.

Commerce and Business

• What a lot of tricks you use to deceive, innkeeper. You sell water but privately drink unmixed wine.

• A copper pot went missing from my shop. Anyone who returns it to me will receive 65 bronze coins. Twenty more will be given for information leading to the capture of the thief.

• We have wet the bed, innkeeper. I confess we have done wrong. If you want to know why, there was no chamber pot in the room.

• The city block of Arrii Pollii . . . is available for rent from July 1. There are shops on the first floor, upper stories, high class rooms and a house. A person interested in renting this property should contact Primus, the slave of Gnaeus Alleius Nigidus Maius.

Love and Lovers

• Adimetus got me pregnant.

• Sarra, you are not being very nice, leaving me all alone like this.

• If anyone does not believe in Venus, they should gaze at my girlfriend.

• Successus, a weaver, loves the innkeeper's slave girl named Iris. She, however, does not love him. Still he begs her to have pity on him. His rival wrote this. Goodbye.

• Love dictates to me as I write and Cupid shows me the way, but may I die if I should prefer to be god without you.

Miscellaneous

- Anyone who wants to defecate in this place is advised to move along. If you act contrary to this warning, you will have to pay a penalty. Children must pay [?] silver coins. Slaves will be beaten on their behinds.

- Once you are dead, you are nothing.

- Chie, I hope your hemorrhoids hurt so much that they burn worse than they ever have before.

- Hey, Lucius Istacidius, I consider a man a barbarian who does not invite me to dinner at his house.

- Pyrrhus says hello to his friend Chius. I have a heavy heart because I heard that you died. And so, my friend, I bid you goodbye.

Source: Brian Harvey, *Daily Life in Ancient Rome: A Sourcebook* (Indianapolis: Hackett, 2016), 145–49, 292, 311–12. All translations of these inscriptions are by Professor Brian Harvey of Kent State University.

■ ■ ■

SOURCE 5.5 Household Religion in Pompeii ▶

The excavated ruins of Pompeii disclose the religious as well as the social life of the Roman world in the first century C.E., before Christianity had spread widely. Based on ritual observance rather than doctrine or theology, Roman religious practice sought to obtain the favor of the gods as a way of promoting success, prosperity, and good fortune. A core expression of the diverse and eclectic world of Roman religion was the imperial cult. In Pompeii, a number of temples were dedicated to one or another of the deified emperors, employing together a large cadre of priests and priestesses. Linked to the imperial cult were temples devoted to the traditional Greco-Roman gods such as Apollo, Venus, and Jupiter.

Probably more important to ordinary people were their *lararia* (household shrines), often a niche in the wall that housed paintings or sculptures of *lares* (guardian spirits or deities believed to provide protection within the home). Families offered gifts of fruit, cakes, and wine to these spirits, and the lararia were the focal point for various sacrifices and rituals associated with birth, marriage, and death. Source 5.5 shows one of these shrines, uncovered in the home of a well-to-do freedman (former slave) named Vetti. In the center was the *genius*, the spirit of the male head of household. Dressed in a toga and offering a sacrifice, this spirit embodied the character of the man, especially his procreative powers, and so guaranteed many children for the household. Protecting the family from external danger were two lares, standing on either side of the genius and holding their drinking horns. The snake at the bottom represented still other benevolent guardian spirits of the family.

■ Why might such a shrine and the spirits it accommodated be more meaningful for many people than the state-approved cults?

■ What significance might you find in the temple-like shape of the lararium?

A Household Shrine from Pompeii │ **1st century** c.e.

House of the Vettii, Pompeii, Italy/Werner Forman Archive/Bridgeman Images

■ ■ ■

SOURCE 5.6 Mystery Religion in Pompeii ▶

In addition to the official cults and the veneration of household gods, by the first century C.E. a number of newer traditions, often called "mystery religions," were spreading widely in the Roman Empire. Deriving from the eastern realm of the empire and beyond (including Greece, Egypt, and Persia), they offered an alternative to the official cults, for they were more personal, emotional, and intimate, usually featuring a ritual initiation into sacred mysteries, codes of moral behavior, and the promise of an afterlife. Among the most popular of these mystery cults in Pompeii was that of Isis, an Egyptian goddess who restored her husband/brother, Osiris, to life and was worshipped as a compassionate protector of the downtrodden.

Another mystery cult, this one of Greek origin, was associated with Dionysus, a god of wine, ecstasy, and poetic inspiration, who was especially popular with women. Often associated with drunkenness, trance states, wild dancing, and unrestrained sexuality, the cult of Dionysus encouraged at least the temporary abandonment of conventional inhibitions and social restrictions as initiates sought union with Dionysus. A series of wall paintings on a Pompeii building known as the Villa of Mysteries depicts the process of initiation into the cult of Dionysus, perhaps in preparation for marriage.

Source 5.6 shows a particularly dramatic phase of that initiation in which a woman is ritually whipped, while a naked devotee dances ecstatically with a pair of cymbals above her head and a companion holds a rod of phallic symbolism sacred to Dionysus. In any such process of religious initiation, the initiate undergoes a series of trials or purifications in which he or she "dies" symbolically, achieves mystical union with the god, and is "reborn" into the new community of the cult.

- ■ How might you interpret the significance of the various aspects of the initiation process displayed here? Consider the role of whipping, the naked dancer, and the relationship of the initiate and the woman on whose lap she is resting her head.

- ■ Why might sexual union, symbolized by the rod, be significant in the initiation?

- ■ Why do you think Roman authorities took action against these mystery religions, even as they did against Christianity?

- ■ What did the mystery cults of Isis or Dionysus provide that neither the state cults nor household gods might offer?

An Initiation Ritual │ **1st century** c.e.

Villa of the Mysteries, Pompeii, Italy/Werner Forman Archive/Bridgeman Images

DOING HISTORY

1. **Characterizing Pompeii:** What does the art and graffiti of Pompeii, as reflected in these sources, tell us about the social and religious life of this small Roman city in the first century c.e.?

2. **Analyzing class differences:** What class or social distinctions are apparent in these sources?

3. **Identifying gender roles:** What do these sources suggest about the varied lives and social roles of women and men in Pompeii?

On Pompeii

Historians have long delighted in the opportunities that an uncovered Pompeii has offered them and have argued vigorously about the meaning of what they found there. In Voice 5.1, Mary Beard, a prominent British classics scholar, muses on the unique insights that Pompeii presents to students of the ancient world. Voice 5.2, from a recent book on the economy of Pompeii by Andrew Wilson and Miko Flohr, uses evidence from Pompeii to challenge older views of Roman life that emphasized mass poverty, the absence of economic growth, and very limited entrepreneurial activity.

- What is it about the archeological evidence from Pompeii that so enchants Mary Beard in Voice 5.1?

- How would you summarize the view of Pompeii's economy presented in Voice 5.2? What kind of evidence supports this view?

- **Integrating Primary and Secondary Sources:** To what extent does the evidence in the visual and documentary sources presented here support or challenge the conclusions of these contemporary historians?

- **Integrating Primary and Secondary Sources:** Taking all of these sources together, which do you find more impressive—the similarities of life in Pompeii to that of the contemporary world or the notion that Pompeii was a "world apart" compared to modern life?

VOICE 5.1

Mary Beard on the Artifacts of Pompeii | 2017

[I]t is the sheer ordinariness of [Pompeii and Herculaneum] that makes them so *extraordinary* for us . . . , from a touching child's cradle to lavish jewellery. . . . It is not just the simple fact of the cities' preservation—though . . . hopping across an ancient street on the real ancient stepping stones gives most visitors a thrill, as does a peek into the very seedy brothel down one of the city's back alleys. It is also the fact that in Pompeii and Herculaneum we come face to face, not with the rich, larger-than-life Romans who fill the history books, but with the average men, women and children, both slaves and free—the ones who are otherwise largely *hidden* from history.

. . . [O]ccasional glimpses of luxury are enticing. But . . . even more fascinating [are] . . . the places where the ordinary city folk lived, worked, ate, drank, bathed, or simply hung out. . . . In one set of baths in Pompeii a store of 500 pottery lamps was found, showing that they did try to do something about the gloom. . . . Or take the little shops that lined the streets [of both cities]. . . .

Some of these remains of everyday Roman life seem reassuringly familiar. The mosaic "Beware of the Dog" sign . . . would look at home on the gate of any modern dog-owning household. . . . But other features seem bafflingly alien. No one, for example, has ever quite worked out how to explain the presence of so many phalluses all over the city, carved into the road surface, hanging over ovens, on jewellery around the necks of children, or made into novelty lamps.

Source: Mary Beard, "Pompeii Exhibition," *The Telegraph*, April 10, 2017, http://www.telegraph.co.uk/history/pompeii/9848596/Pompeii-exhibition-Mary-Beard-on-life-in-Pompeii-and-Herculaneum.html.

VOICE 5.2

Andrew Wilson and Miko Flohr on the Economy of Pompeii | 2017

To sum up, Pompeiians consumed a rather varied diet, lived reasonably long and healthy lives, and had relatively easy access to consumer goods and art. The city's economy was highly monetized. . . . Continuous investment in commercial facilities like shops and workshops testifies [to] the vibrant and stable character of the Pompeian economy. . . . Pompeii was performing rather well. . . .

This book does not offer a lot of support for the more pessimistic readings of Roman economic performance. . . . Pompeii and its surrounding countryside were connected, directly or indirectly, to the Mediterranean trade system. . . . Without these networks, Pompeii would have been a different, and probably a smaller and less wealthy, city. . . . Pompeii . . . and Herculaneum were able not only to support the consumption of luxuries by a small group of elite households but also by large parts of the rest of the population. . . . This means that, under the right circumstances, Roman urban economies were able to provide opportunities for non-poor, non-elite households to accumulate wealth.

In the end, Pompeii was far more prosperous and this prosperity did reach down to much lower strata than . . . once thought.

Source: Andrew Wilson and Miko Flohr, eds., *The Economy of Pompeii* (Oxford: Oxford University Press, 2017), 15, 425.

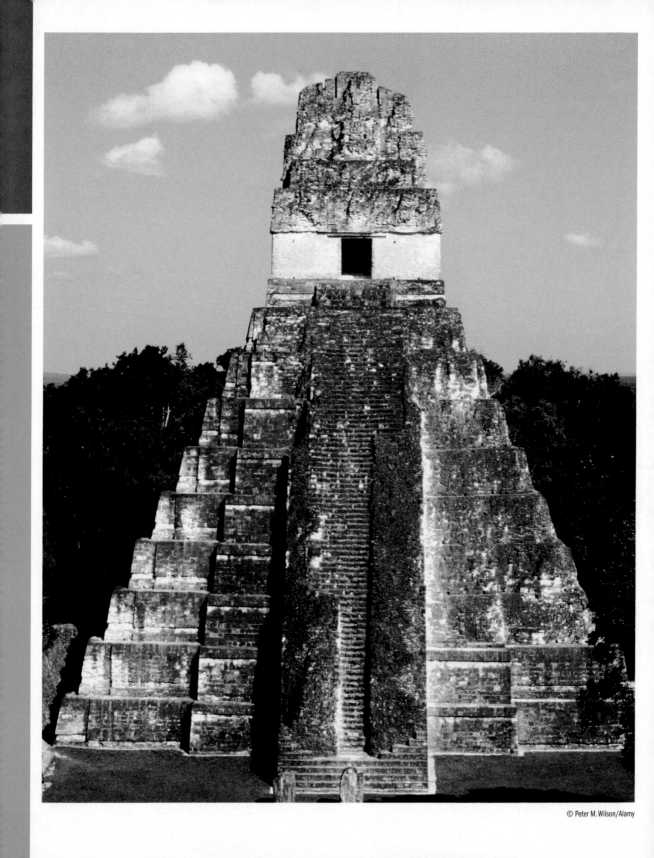

CHAPTER

6

Commonalities and Variations

Africa, the Americas, and Pacific Oceania

600 B.C.E.–1200 C.E.

Continental Comparisons

Civilizations of Africa
- Meroë: Continuing a Nile Valley Civilization
- Axum: The Making of a Christian Kingdom
- Along the Niger River: Cities without States

Civilizations of Mesoamerica
- The Maya: Writing and Warfare
- Teotihuacán: The Americas' Greatest City

Civilizations of the Andes
- Chavín: A Pan-Andean Religious Movement
- Moche: A Civilization of the Coast
- Wari and Tiwanaku: Empires of the Interior

Alternatives to Civilization
- Bantu Africa: Cultural Encounters and Social Variation
- North America: Ancestral Pueblo and Mound Builders
- Pacific Oceania: Peoples of the Sea

Reflections: Deciding What's Important: Balance in the Writing of World History

« **The Maya Temple of the Great Jaguar in Tikal** Located in the Maya city of Tikal in present-day Guatemala, this temple was constructed in the eighth century C.E. and excavated by archeologists in the late nineteenth century. It served as the tomb of the Tikal ruler Jasaw Chan K'awiil I (682–734). Some 144 feet tall, it was topped by a three-room temple complex and a huge roofcomb showing the ruler on his throne.

In early 2010, Bolivian president Evo Morales was inaugurated for his second term in office, the only Native American ever elected to that post. Before his official inauguration, Morales traveled to Tiwanaku (tee-wah-NAH-coo), the center of an impressive empire that had flourished in the Andean highlands between 400 and 1000 C.E., long before either the Incas or the Spanish ruled the area. There he sought to link himself and his administration to this ancient culture, a symbol of Bolivian nationalism and indigenous pride. On his arrival, Morales was ritually cleansed, offerings were made to traditional deities, and he was invested with symbols of both kingship and spiritual leadership, thus joining political and religious sources of authority.[1] Thus memories of this American second-wave civilization remained alive and were available for mobilizing political support and legitimating political authority in the very different circumstances of the early twenty-first century. ■

For many people, the second-wave era evokes most vividly the civilizations of Eurasia—the Greeks and the Romans, the Persians and the Chinese, and the Indians of South Asia—yet civilization also flourished elsewhere, both in the Americas and in sub-Saharan Africa. Furthermore, those peoples who did not organize themselves around cities or states likewise had histories of note and alternative ways of constructing their societies, although they are often neglected in favor of civilizations. This chapter explores the histories of the varied peoples of Africa, the Americas, and Pacific Oceania during

227

SEEKING THE MAIN POINT

To what extent did the histories of Africa, Oceania, and the Americas parallel those of Eurasia? In what ways did they forge new or different paths?

this phase of world history. On occasion, those histories will extend some centuries beyond the chronological boundaries of the second-wave era in Eurasia because patterns of historical development around the world did not always coincide precisely.

Continental Comparisons

At the broadest level, human cultures evolved in quite similar fashion around the world. All were part of that grand process of human migration that initially peopled the planet. Almost everywhere, gathering, hunting, and fishing long remained the sole basis for sustaining life and society. Then, in various parts of the three supercontinents—Eurasia, Africa, and the Americas—the momentous turn of the Agricultural Revolution took place independently, as noted in Chapter 1, and subsequently generated in all three regions those more complex societies that we know as civilizations, featuring cities, states, monumental architecture, and great social inequality, as described in Chapter 2. In these ways, the historical trajectory of the human journey has a certain unity and similarity across quite distinct continental regions. These commonalities provide the foundation for a genuinely global history of humankind.

Guided Reading Question
....
■ **COMPARISON**
What similarities and differences are noticeable in the historical development of the three major continents?

The world's human population was then distributed very unevenly across the three giant continents, as the Snapshot of population on page 230 indicates. Eurasia was then home to more than 85 percent of the world's people, Africa about 10 percent, the Americas around 5 percent, and Oceania less than 1 percent. That unevenness in population distribution, a pattern that has persisted to the present, is part of the reason that world historians focus more attention on Eurasia than on these other regions.

Another continental difference involved the absence in the Americas of most animals capable of domestication. This meant that few pastoral societies developed in the Western Hemisphere, and only in pockets of the Andes Mountains based on the herding of llamas and alpacas. No animals were available in the Americas to pull plows or carts or to be ridden into combat. Metallurgy in the Americas was likewise far less developed than in Eurasia and Africa, where iron tools and weapons played such an important role in economic and military life. In the Americas, writing was limited to the Mesoamerican region and was most highly developed among the Maya, whereas in Africa it was confined to the northern and northeastern parts of the continent. In Eurasia, by contrast, writing emerged elaborately in many regions. Furthermore, civilizations in Africa and the Americas were fewer in number and generally smaller than those of Eurasia, and larger numbers of people in those two continents lived outside the confines of any civilization in communities that did not feature cities and states.

A final continental comparison distinguishes the history of Africa from that of the Americas and Pacific Oceania. Geography placed Africa adjacent to Eurasia, while it separated the Americas and Oceania from both Africa and Eurasia. So parts of Africa were joined with Europe and Asia in a larger zone of Afro-Eurasian

Landmarks for Chapter 6

| 1200 B.C.E. | 800 B.C.E. | 400 B.C.E. | 1 C.E. | 400 C.E. | 800 C.E. | 1200 C.E. |

AFRICA

730 B.C.E.
Nubian conquest of Egypt

300 B.C.E.–100 C.E.
Kingdom of Meroë in upper Nile Valley

300 B.C.E.–900 C.E.
Niger Valley civilization in West Africa

4th century C.E.
Introduction of Christianity to Axum

ca. 400 C.E. Bantu-speaking peoples
established in southern Africa

NORTH AMERICA

200 B.C.E.–400 C.E.
Hopewell mound-building culture

ca. 860–1130 C.E.
Chaco Phenomenon

ca. 900–1250 C.E.
Cahokia

ca. 1200–1400 C.E.
Southeast Ceremonial Complex

CENTRAL AND SOUTH AMERICA

900–200 B.C.E.
Chavin movement

100–800 C.E.
Moche civilization in Peru

250–900 C.E.
Maya civilization

300–600 C.E.
Teotihuacán

400–1000 C.E.
Wari and Tiwanaku in the Andes

OCEANIA

1400–800 B.C.E.
Lapita culture

1100–1600 C.E.
Saudeleur dynasty on Pohnpei

ca. 1000 C.E.
Tongan trading network

1200 C.E.
Initial settlement of New Zealand

SNAPSHOT Continental Population in the Second-Wave Era and Beyond

(Note: Population figures for such early times are merely estimates and are often controversial among scholars. Percentages do not always total 100 percent due to rounding.)

	Eurasia	Africa	North America	Central/South America	Australia/ Oceania	Total World
Area (in square miles and as percentage of world total)						
	21,049,000 (41%)	11,608,000 (22%)	9,365,000 (18%)	6,880,000 (13%)	2,968,000 (6%)	51,870,000
Population (in millions and as percentage of world total)						
400 B.C.E.	127 (83%)	17 (11%)	1 (0.7%)	7 (5%)	1 (0.7%)	153
10 C.E.	213 (85%)	26 (10%)	2 (0.8%)	10 (4%)	1 (0.4%)	252
200 C.E.	215 (84%)	30 (12%)	2 (0.8%)	9 (4%)	1 (0.4%)	257
600 C.E.	167 (80%)	24 (12%)	2 (1%)	14 (7%)	1 (0.5%)	208
1000 C.E.	195 (77%)	39 (15%)	2 (0.8%)	16 (6%)	1 (0.4%)	253
1500	329 (69%)	113 (24%)	4.5 (0.9%)	53 (11%)	3 (0.6%)	477
1750	646 (83%)	104 (13%)	3 (0.4%)	15 (1.9%)	3 (0.4%)	771
2017	5,246 (69.5%)	1,256 (16.6%)	361 (4.8%)	646 (8.6%)	40 (0.5%)	7,549

Source: Population figures through 1750 are taken from Paul Adams et al., *Experiencing World History* (New York: New York University Press, 2000), 334; 2017 figures derive from "World Population by Region," Worldometers, http://www.worldometers.info/world-population/#region. Accessed December 8, 2017.

interaction. Early Christianity, for example, spread widely across North and Northeast Africa. Camels, probably originating in Arabia, enabled a trans-Saharan commerce that linked interior West Africa to the world of Mediterranean civilization. Bananas brought from Southeast Asia by Austronesian voyagers greatly enriched the diets of many African peoples. The Americas and Oceania, by contrast, developed almost wholly apart from this Afro-Eurasian network until that separation was breeched by the voyages of Columbus and later European explorers from 1492 on.

This chapter examines first the civilizations that emerged in sub-Saharan Africa and the Americas. Then our historical spotlight turns to those regions on both continents and Pacific Oceania that remained outside the zone of civilization. They remind us that the histories of many peoples unfolded without the cities, states, and empires that were so prominent within that zone.

Civilizations of Africa

When historians refer to Africa in premodern times, they are speaking generally of a geographic concept, a continental landmass, and not a cultural identity. Certainly few, if any, people living on the continent during the second-wave era thought of themselves as Africans. Like Eurasia or the Americas, Africa hosted numerous separate societies, cultures, and civilizations with vast differences among them as well as some interaction between them.

Many of these differences grew out of the continent's environmental variations. Small regions of Mediterranean climate in the northern and southern extremes, large deserts (the Sahara and the Kalahari), even larger regions of savanna grasslands, tropical rain forest in the continent's center, highlands and mountains in eastern Africa—all of these features, combined with the continent's enormous size, ensured endless variation among Africa's many peoples. Africa did, however, have one distinctive environmental feature: bisected by the equator, it was the most tropical of the world's three supercontinents. While some regions, such as highland Ethiopia, sustained very productive agriculture, elsewhere lower crop yields and diminished soil fertility prevailed, owing to heavy but sometimes erratic rainfall, long dry seasons, and the leaching of nutrients from ancient soils. Climatic conditions also spawned numerous disease-carrying insects and parasites that have long created serious health problems in many parts of the continent. It was within these environmental constraints that African peoples made their histories. In several distinct regions of the continent—the upper Nile Valley, northern Ethiopia/Eritrea, and the Niger River valley—small civilizations flourished during the second-wave era, while others followed later. A further African civilization falling partly within this time period grew up along the East African coast in conjunction with Indian Ocean commerce. Known as Swahili civilization, it is treated in greater detail in Chapter 7.

Meroë: Continuing a Nile Valley Civilization

In the Nile Valley south of Egypt lay the lands of Nubian civilization, almost as old as Egypt itself. Over many centuries, Nubians both traded and fought with Egypt, and on one occasion, in 730 B.C.E., the Nubian Kingdom of Kush conquered Egypt and ruled it for a century. While borrowing heavily from Egypt, Nubia remained a distinct and separate civilization. As Egypt fell increasingly under foreign control, Nubian civilization came to center on the southern city of **Meroë** (MER-oh-ee), where it flourished between 300 B.C.E. and 100 C.E. (see Map 6.1).

Politically, the Kingdom of Meroë was governed by an all-powerful and sacred monarch, a position held on at least ten occasions by women, governing alone or as co-rulers. Unlike the female pharaoh Hatshepsut in Egypt, who was portrayed in male clothing, Meroë queens appeared in sculptures as women and with a prominence and power equivalent to their male counterparts. In accordance with ancient traditions, such rulers were buried along with a number of human sacrificial victims.

Guided Reading Question

■ **CONNECTION**

How did the history of Meroë and Axum reflect interaction with neighboring civilizations?

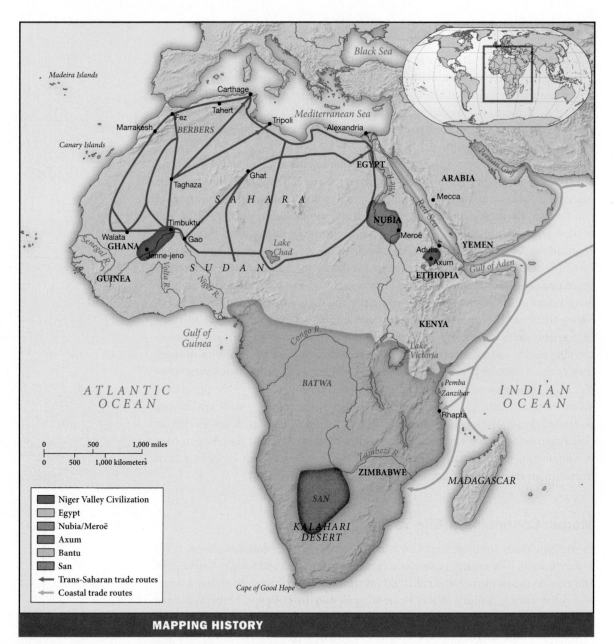

MAPPING HISTORY

Map 6.1 Africa in the Second-Wave Era

During the second-wave era, older African civilizations such as Egypt and Nubia persisted and changed, while new civilizations emerged in Axum and the Niger River valley. South of the equator, the process of Bantu expansion created many new societies and identities.

READING THE MAP: What major pathways can you identify that linked regions of Africa south of the Sahara Desert with North Africa and Eurasia?

INTERPRETING THE MAP: Does this map support the idea that major cities in the Sahara Desert and sub-Saharan West Africa were located primarily along trade routes?

The city of Meroë and other urban centers housed a wide variety of economic specialties — merchants, weavers, potters, and masons, as well as servants, laborers, and slaves. The smelting of iron and the manufacture of iron tools and weapons were especially prominent industries. The rural areas surrounding Meroë were populated by peoples who practiced some combination of herding and farming and paid periodic tribute to the ruler. Rainfall-based agriculture was possible in Meroë, and consequently farmers were less dependent on irrigation. This meant that the rural population did not need to concentrate so heavily near the Nile as was the case in Egypt.

The wealth and military power of Meroë derived in part from extensive long-distance trading connections, to the north via the Nile and to the east and west by means of camel caravans. Its iron weapons and cotton cloth, as well as its access to gold, ivory, tortoiseshells, and ostrich feathers, gave Meroë a reputation for great riches in the world of northeastern Africa and the Mediterranean. The discovery in Meroë of a statue of the Roman emperor Augustus, probably seized during a raid on Roman Egypt, testifies to contact with the Mediterranean world. Culturally, Meroë seemed to move away from the heavy Egyptian influence of earlier times. A local lion god, Apedemek, grew more prominent than Egyptian deities such as Isis and Osiris, while the use of Egyptian-style writing declined as a new and still-undeciphered Meroitic script took its place.

In the centuries following 100 C.E., the Kingdom of Meroë declined, in part because of deforestation caused by the need for wood to make charcoal for smelting iron. Furthermore, as Egyptian trade with the African interior switched from the Nile Valley route to the Red Sea, the resources available to Meroë's rulers diminished and the state weakened. The effective end of the Meroë phase of Nubian civilization came with the kingdom's conquest in the 340s C.E. by the neighboring and rising state of Axum. In the centuries that followed, three separate Nubian states emerged, and Coptic (Egyptian) Christianity penetrated the region. For almost a thousand years, Nubia was a Christian civilization, using Greek as a liturgical language and constructing churches in Coptic or Byzantine fashion. After 1300 or so, political division, Arab immigration, and the penetration of Islam eroded this Christian civilization, and Nubia became part of the growing world of Islam.

A Bracelet from Meroë This gold bracelet, dating to about 100 B.C.E., illustrates the skill of Meroë's craftsmen as well as the kingdom's reputation as one of the wealthiest states of the ancient world. The bracelet's depiction of a seated Hathor, a popular Egyptian goddess, shows the influence of Egyptian culture in Nubia. (Bracelet with image of Hathor, Nubian, Meroitic Period, 250–100 B.C. Findspot: Pyramid 8, Gebel Barkal, Nubia, Sudan. Gold and enamel. Overall: 1.8 x 5.7 x 5.1 cm. [$^{11}/_{16}$ x 2¼ x 2 in.]/ Photograph © 2018 Museum of Fine Arts, Boston/MFA Images/Harvard University–Boston Museum of Fine Arts Expedition, 20.333)

Axum: The Making of a Christian Kingdom

If Meroë represented the continuation of an old African/Nubian civilization, **Axum** marked the emergence of a new one. (For various accounts about or from Axum, see Working with Evidence: Axum and the World, page 260.) Axum lay in the Horn of Africa, in what is now Eritrea and northern Ethiopia (see Map 6.1). Its economic foundation was a highly productive agriculture that used a plow-based farming system, unlike most of the rest of Africa, which relied on the hoe or digging stick. Axum's agriculture generated substantial amounts of wheat, barley, millet, and teff, a highly nutritious grain unique to that region. By 50 C.E. or so, a substantial state had emerged, stimulated by its participation in the rapidly increasing Red Sea and Indian Ocean commerce, which was itself a product of growing Roman demand for Indian products, especially pepper. At Adulis, then the largest port on the East African coast, a wide range of merchants sought the products of the African interior—animal hides, rhinoceros horn, ivory, obsidian, tortoiseshells, and slaves. Taxes on this trade provided a major source of revenue for the Axumite state and the complex society that grew up within it. Thus the decline of Meroë and the rise of Axum were both connected to changing patterns of long-distance commerce.

The interior capital city, also known as Axum, was a center of monumental building and royal patronage for the arts. The most famous structures were huge stone obelisks, which most likely marked royal graves. Some of them were more than 100 feet tall and at the time were the largest structures in the world hewn from a single piece of rock. (See Source 6.2 in "Working with Evidence," page 261.) The language used at court, in the towns, and for commerce was Ge'ez, written in a script derived from South Arabia. The Axumite state exercised a measure of control over the mostly Agaw-speaking people of the country through a loose administrative structure focusing on the collection of tribute payments. To the Romans, Axum was the third major empire within the world they knew, following their own and the Persian Empire.

Through its connections to Red Sea trade and the Roman world, particularly Egypt, Axum was introduced to Christianity in the fourth century C.E. Its monarch at the time, King Ezana, adopted the new religion about the same time as Constantine did in the Roman Empire. Early in his reign, the kingdom's coins featured images of gods derived from southern Arabia, while by the end, they were inscribed with the Christian cross. Supported by royal authority, Christianity took root in Axum, linking that kingdom religiously to Egypt, where a distinctive Christian Church known as Coptic was already well established. Although Egypt later became largely Islamic, reducing its Christian community to a small minority, Christianity maintained a dominant position in the mountainous terrain of highland Ethiopia and in the early twenty-first century still represents the faith of perhaps 60 percent of the country's population.

During the fourth through the sixth centuries C.E., Axum mounted a campaign of imperial expansion that took its forces into the Kingdom of Meroë and across the Red Sea into Yemen in South Arabia. By 571, the traditional date for the birth of Muhammad, an Axumite army, including a number of African war elephants, had reached the gates of Mecca, but it was a fairly short-lived imperial venture.

The next several centuries were ones of decline for the Axumite state, owing partly to environmental changes, such as soil exhaustion, erosion, and deforestation, brought about by intensive farming. Equally important was the rise of Islam, which altered trade routes and diminished the revenue available to the Axumite state. Its last coins were struck in the early seventh century. When the state revived several centuries later, it was centered farther south on the Ethiopian plateau. In this new location, there emerged the Christian Church and the state that present-day Ethiopia has inherited, but the link to ancient Axum was long remembered and revered.

With their long-distance trading connections, urban centers, centralized states, complex societies, monumental architecture, written languages, and imperial ambitions, both Meroë and Axum paralleled on a smaller scale the major features of the second-wave civilizations of Eurasia. Furthermore, both were in direct contact with the world of Mediterranean civilizations. Across the continent in West Africa, a rather different civilization took shape.

Along the Niger River: Cities without States

The middle stretches of the Niger River in West Africa witnessed the emergence of a remarkable urbanization (see Map 6.1, page 232). A prolonged dry period during the five centuries after 500 B.C.E. brought growing numbers of people

The Legacy of Axumite Christianity While the Axumite kingdom faded away, its assimilation of Christianity proved an enduring legacy for Ethiopia, as illustrated by this late-fourteenth- or early-fifteenth-century depiction of the ascension of Jesus, with his disciples pointing upwards. (The Metropolitan Museum of Art, New York, NY, USA/Rogers Fund, 1998 [1998.66]/ Image copyright © The Metropolitan Museum of Art/Image source: Art Resource, NY)

from the southern Sahara into the fertile floodplain of the middle Niger in search of more reliable access to water. Accompanying them were their domesticated cattle, sheep, and goats; their agricultural skills; and their ironworking technology. Over many centuries (roughly 300 B.C.E.–900 C.E.), the peoples of this region created a distinctive city-based civilization. The most fully studied of the urban clusters that grew up along the middle Niger was the city of Jenne-jeno (jihn-AY jihn-OH), which at its high point probably housed more than 40,000 people.

Among the most distinctive features of the **Niger Valley civilization** was the apparent absence of a corresponding state structure. Unlike the cities of Egypt, China, the Roman Empire, or Axum, these middle Niger urban centers were not

Guided Reading Question

■ **DESCRIPTION**
How does the experience of the Niger Valley challenge conventional notions of "civilization"?

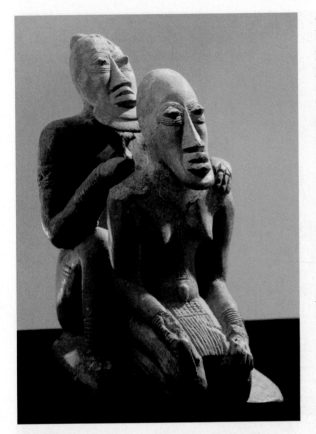

Terra-Cotta Statue from Jenne-jeno The artistic tradition of Niger Valley civilization includes a number of terra-cotta couples, reflecting perhaps the emphasis on the separate but complementary roles of men and women in much of African thought. This statue and others like it date to sometime after the twelfth century and may express the resistance of an indigenous tradition to the growing penetration of Islam. (Entwistle Gallery, London, UK/Werner Forman/Art Resource, NY)

encompassed within some larger imperial system. Nor were they like the city-states of ancient Mesopotamia, in which each city had its own centralized political structure, embodied in a monarch and his accompanying bureaucracy. According to a leading historian of the region, they were "cities without citadels," complex urban centers that apparently operated without the coercive authority of a state, for archeologists have found in their remains few signs of despotic power, widespread warfare, or deep social inequalities.[2] In this respect, these urban centers resemble the early cities of Norte Chico or the Indus Valley civilization, where likewise little archeological evidence of centralized state structures has been found.

In place of such hierarchical organization, Jenne-jeno and other cities of the region emerged as clusters of economically specialized settlements surrounding a larger central town. The earliest and most prestigious of these specialized occupations was iron smithing. Working with fire and earth (ore) to produce this highly useful metal, the smiths of the Niger Valley were both feared and revered. Archeologist Roderick McIntosh, a leading figure in the excavation of Jenne-jeno, argued that "their knowledge of the transforming arts—earth to metal, insubstantial fire to the mass of iron—was the key to a secret, occult realm of immense power and immense danger."[3]

Other specializations followed. Villages of cotton weavers, potters, leather workers, and griots (praise-singers who preserved and recited the oral traditions of their societies) grew up around the central towns. Gradually these urban artisan communities became occupational castes, whose members passed their jobs and skills to their children and could marry only within their own group. In the surrounding rural areas, as in all urban-based civilizations, farmers tilled the soil and raised their animals, but specialization also occurred in food production as various ethnic groups focused on fishing, rice cultivation, or some other agricultural pursuit. At least for a time, these middle Niger cities represented an African alternative to an oppressive state, which in many parts of the world accompanied an increasingly complex urban economy and society. A series of distinct and specialized economic groups shared authority and voluntarily used the services of one another, while maintaining their own identities through physical separation.

Accompanying this unique urbanization, and no doubt stimulating it, was a growing network of indigenous West African commerce. The middle Niger floodplain supported a rich agriculture and contained clay for pottery, but it lacked stone, iron ore, salt, and fuel. This scarcity of resources was the basis for a long-distance commerce that operated by boat along the Niger River and overland by donkey to the north and south. Jenne-jeno itself was an important transshipment point in this commerce, in which goods were transferred from boat to donkey or vice versa. By the 500s C.E., there is evidence of an even wider commerce, and at least indirect contact, from Mauritania in the west to present-day Mali and Burkina Faso in the east.

In the second millennium C.E., new historical patterns developed in West Africa (see "Gold, Salt, and Slaves" in Chapter 7). A number of large-scale states or empires emerged in the region—Ghana, Mali, and Songhay, among the most well known. At least partially responsible for this development was the flourishing of a camel-borne trans-Saharan commerce, previously but a trickle across the great desert. As West Africa became more firmly connected to North Africa and the Mediterranean, Islam penetrated the region, marking a gradual but major cultural transformation. All of this awaited West Africa in later centuries, submerging, but not completely eliminating, the decentralized city life of the Niger Valley.

Civilizations of Mesoamerica

Westward across the Atlantic Ocean lay an altogether separate world, later known as the Americas, which housed two major centers of civilization—Mesoamerica and the Andes. Together, they were home to the vast majority of the population of the Americas. But unlike the Egyptians and Mesopotamians or the Persians and the Greeks, these civilizations had little if any direct contact with each other. They shared, however, a rugged mountainous terrain with an enormous range of microclimates as well as great ecological and biological diversity. Arid coastal environments, steamy lowland rain forests, cold and windy highland plateaus cut by numerous mountains and valleys—all of this was often encompassed in a relatively small area. Such conditions contributed to substantial linguistic and ethnic diversity and to the development of many distinct and competing cities, chiefdoms, and states. It also meant that states, and sometimes individual families, sought "**vertical integration**," an effort to control a variety of ecological zones where a number of different crops and animals could flourish. The remarkable achievements of these early American civilizations occurred without the many large domesticated animals or ironworking technologies that were so important throughout the Eastern Hemisphere. In the Andes, an important exception to this generalization involved the domestication of the llama and alpaca, which offered food, fiber, and transport for the civilizations of that region and in a few places provided for a time the basis for largely pastoral communities.

Mesoamerican civilizations stretched from central Mexico to northern Central America. Despite its environmental and ethnic diversity, Mesoamerica was also a distinct region, bound together by elements of a common culture. Its many peoples shared an intensive agricultural technology devoted to raising maize, beans, chili peppers, and squash and based their economies on market exchange. They practiced religions featuring a similar pantheon of male and female deities, understood time as a cosmic cycle

Map 6.2 Civilizations of Mesoamerica
During the second-wave era, Maya civilization and the large city of Teotihuacán represented the most prominent features of Mesoamerican civilization.

Guided Reading Question

••••••••••••••••••••••••••••••••••••

■ **COMPARISON**
With what Eurasian civilizations might the Maya be compared?

of creation and destruction, practiced human sacrifice, and constructed monumental ceremonial centers. Furthermore, they employed a common ritual calendar of 260 days and hieroglyphic writing. During the first millennium B.C.E., the various small states and chiefdoms of the region, particularly the Olmec, exchanged various luxury goods used to display social status and for ritual purposes—jade, obsidian tools, ceramic pottery, shell ornaments, stingray spines, and turtle shells. As a result, aspects of Olmec culture, such as artistic styles, temple pyramids, the calendar system, and rituals involving human sacrifice, spread widely throughout Mesoamerica and influenced many of the civilizations that followed.

The Maya: Writing and Warfare

Among Mesoamerican civilizations, none has attracted more attention than that of the Maya. Scholars have traced the beginnings of the Maya people to ceremonial centers constructed as early as 2000 B.C.E. in present-day Guatemala and the Yucatán region of Mexico (see Map 6.2). During the first millennium B.C.E., a number of substantial urban centers with concentrated populations and monumental architecture had emerged in the region. But it was during a later phase of **Maya civilization**, between 250 and 900 C.E., that their most well-known cultural achievements emerged. Intellectuals, probably priests, developed a mathematical system that included the concept of zero and place notation and was capable of complex calculations. They combined this mathematical ability with careful observation of the night skies to plot the cycles of planets, to predict eclipses of the sun and the moon, to construct elaborate calendars, and to calculate accurately the length of the solar year. The distinctive art of the Maya elite was likewise impressive to later observers.

Accompanying these intellectual and artistic achievements was the creation of the most elaborate writing system in the Americas, which used both pictographs and phonetic or syllabic elements. Carved on stone and written on bark paper or deerskin books, Mayan writing recorded historical events, masses of astronomical data, and religious or mythological texts. Temples, pyramids, palaces, and public plazas abounded, graced with painted murals and endless stone carving.

The economic foundations for these cultural achievements were embedded in an "almost totally engineered landscape."[4] The Maya drained swamps, terraced hillsides, flattened ridgetops, and constructed an elaborate water-management system. Much of this underpinned a flourishing agriculture, which supported a very rapidly growing and dense population by 750 C.E. This agriculture sustained substantial elite classes of nobles, priests, merchants, architects, and sculptors, as well as specialized artisans producing pottery, tools, and cotton textiles. And it was sufficiently productive to free a large labor force for work on the many public structures that continue to amaze contemporary visitors.

Early scholars viewed Maya civilization somewhat romantically as a peaceful society led by gentle stargazing priest-kings devoted to temple building and intellectual pursuits. This view of Maya civilization changed as scholars realized that its many achievements took place within a highly fragmented political system of city-states, local lords, and regional kingdoms with no central authority, with frequent warfare, and with the extensive capture and sacrifice of prisoners. The larger political units of Maya civilization were densely populated urban and ceremonial centers, ruled by powerful kings and on a few occasions queens. They were divine rulers or "state shamans" able to mediate between humankind and the supernatural.

One of these cities, Tikal (tee-KAHL), contained perhaps 50,000 people, with another 50,000 or so in the surrounding countryside, by 750 C.E. (See this chapter's opening photo, of a temple from Tikal.) Some of these city-states had imperial ambitions, but none succeeded in creating a unified Maya empire. Various centers of Maya civilization rose and fell; fluctuating alliances among them alternated with periods of sporadic warfare; ruling families intermarried; the elite classes sought luxury goods from far away to bolster their authority and status. In its political dimensions, Maya civilization more closely resembled the competing city-states of ancient Mesopotamia or classical Greece than the imperial structures of Rome, Persia, or China.

But large parts of that imposing civilization collapsed with a completeness and finality rare in world history. Clearly, this was not a single or uniform phenomenon, as flourishing centers of Maya civilization persisted in the northern Yucatán, and many Maya survived to fight the Spanish in the sixteenth century. But in the southern regions where the collapse was most complete, its outcomes were devastating. In less than a century following the onset of a long-term drought in 840, the population of the low-lying southern heartland of the Maya dropped by 85 percent or more as famine, epidemics, and fratricidal warfare reaped a horrific toll. It was a catastrophe from which there was no recovery. Elements of Maya culture survived in scattered settlements, but the great cities were deserted, and large-scale construction and artistic work ceased. The last date inscribed in stone corresponds to 909–910 C.E. As a complex civilization, the Maya had passed into history.

Explaining this remarkable demise has long kept scholars guessing, with recent accounts focusing on ecological and political factors. Rapid population growth after 600 C.E. pushed total Maya numbers to perhaps 5 million or more and soon outstripped available resources, resulting in deforestation and the erosion of hillsides. Under such conditions, climate change in the form of prolonged droughts in the 800s may well have placed unbearable pressures on Maya society. Political disunity and endemic rivalries, long a prominent feature of Maya civilization, prevented a coordinated and effective response to the emerging catastrophe. Warfare in fact became more frequent as competition for increasingly scarce land for cultivation became sharper. Rulers dependent on ritual splendor for their legitimacy competed to mount ever more elaborate temples, palaces, and pageants, requiring more labor and taxes from their subjects and tribute from their enemies. Whatever the precise explanation, the Maya collapse, like that of the Romans and others, illustrates the fragility of civilizations, whether they are embodied in large empires or organized in a more decentralized fashion.

Teotihuacán: The Americas' Greatest City

At roughly the same time as the Maya flourished in the southern regions of Meso-america, the giant city of **Teotihuacán** (tay-uh-tee-wah-KAHN) was also emerging further north in the Valley of Mexico, where its control over important sources of green obsidian made it an increasingly important trading power in the region. Begun around 150 B.C.E. and apparently built to a plan rather than evolving haphazardly, the city by 550 C.E. had a population estimated at between 125,000 and 150,000. It was by far the largest urban complex in the Americas at the time and one of the six largest in the world. Physically, the city was enormously impressive, replete with broad avenues, spacious plazas, huge marketplaces, temples, palaces, apartment complexes, slums, waterways, reservoirs, drainage systems, and colorful murals. Along the main north/south boulevard, now known as the Avenue of the Dead, were the grand homes of the elite, the headquarters of state authorities, many temples, and two giant pyramids. At the Temple of the Feathered Serpent, archeologists have found the remains of some 200 people, their hands and arms tied behind them; they were the apparently unwilling sacrificial victims meant to accompany the high-ranking persons buried there into the afterlife.

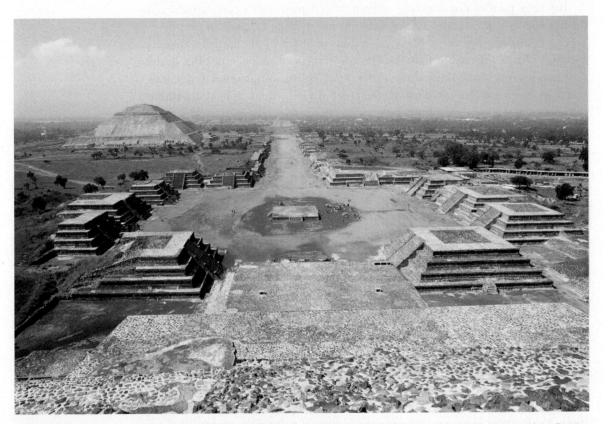

Teotihuacán Taken from the summit of the Pyramid of the Moon, this photograph looks down the famous Avenue of the Dead to the Pyramid of the Sun in the upper left. (Alison Wright/Science Source)

Off the main avenues of Teotihuacán in a grid-like pattern of streets lay thousands of residential apartment compounds, home to the city's commoners. In these compounds, perhaps in groups of related families or lineages, lived many of the farmers who tilled the lands outside the city, as well as thousands of Maya specialists — masons, leather workers, potters, construction laborers, merchants, and civil servants. Here also lived skilled makers of obsidian blades, who plied their trade in hundreds of separate workshops, generating products that were in great demand throughout Mesoamerica. At least two small sections of the city were reserved exclusively for foreigners.

Guided Reading Questions

■ **CONNECTION**
In what ways did Teotihuacán shape the history of Mesoamerica?

Buildings, both public and private, were decorated with mural paintings, sculptures, and carvings. Many of these works of art display abstract geometric and stylized images. Others depict gods and goddesses, arrayed in various forms — feathered serpents, starfish, jaguars, flowers, and warriors. One set of murals shows happy people cavorting in a paradise of irrigated fields, playing games, singing, and chasing butterflies, which were thought to represent the souls of the dead. Another, however, portrays dancing warriors carrying elaborate curved knives, to which were attached bleeding human hearts.

The art of Teotihuacán, unlike that of the Maya, has revealed few images of self-glorifying rulers or individuals. Nor did the city have a tradition of written public inscriptions as the Maya did, although a number of glyphs or characters indicate at least a limited form of writing. Nonetheless, Teotihuacán cast a huge shadow over Mesoamerica, particularly from 300 to 600 C.E. A core region of perhaps 10,000 square miles was administered directly from the city itself, while tribute was no doubt exacted from other areas within its broader sphere of influence. At a greater distance, the power of Teotihuacán's armies gave it a presence in the Maya heartland more than 600 miles to the east. At least one Maya city, Kaminaljuyú in the southern highlands, was completely taken over by the Teotihuacán military and organized as a colony. In the year 378 C.E., agents of Teotihuacán apparently engineered a coup in the lowland Maya city of Tikal that placed a collaborator on the throne and turned the city for a time into an ally or a satellite. Elsewhere — in the Zapotec capital of Monte Albán, for example — murals show unarmed persons from Teotihuacán engaged in what seem to be more equal diplomatic relationships.

At least some of this political and military activity was no doubt designed to obtain, either by trade or by tribute, valued commodities from afar — food products, cacao beans, tropical bird feathers, honey, salt, and medicinal herbs. The presence in Teotihuacán of foreigners, perhaps merchants, from the Gulf Coast and Maya lowlands, as well as much pottery from those regions, provides further evidence of long-distance trade. Moreover, the sheer size and prestige of Teotihuacán surely persuaded many, all across Mesoamerica, to imitate the architectural and artistic styles of the city. Thus, according to a leading scholar, "Teotihuacán meant something of surpassing importance far beyond its core area."[5] Almost a thousand years after its still-mysterious collapse around 650 C.E., the great metropolis was dubbed Teotihuacán, the "city of the gods," by the peoples of the Aztec Empire.

Map 6.3 Civilizations of the Andes

No single civilization dominated the Andes region during the second-wave era. Rather, a number of religious movements, states, and empires rose and fell before the entire region was encompassed by the Inca Empire in the fifteenth century.

Civilizations of the Andes

Yet another and quite separate center of civilization in the Americas lay in the dramatic landscape of the Andes. Bleak deserts along the coast supported human habitation only because they were cut by dozens of rivers flowing down from the mountains, offering the possibility of irrigation and cultivation. The offshore waters of the Pacific Ocean also provided an enormously rich marine environment with an endless supply of seabirds and fish. The Andes themselves, a towering mountain chain with many highland valleys, afforded numerous distinct ecological niches, depending on altitude. Andean societies generally sought access to the resources of these various environments through colonization, conquest, or trade—seafood from the coastal regions; maize and cotton from lower-altitude valleys; potatoes, quinoa, and pastureland for their llamas in the high plains; tropical fruits and coca leaves from the moist eastern slope of the Andes and the arid western slope as well (see Map 6.3).

The most well known of the civilizations to take shape in this environment was that of the Incas, which encompassed practically the entire region, some 2,500 miles in length, in the fifteenth century. Yet the Incas represented only the most recent and the largest in a long history of civilizations in the area. The coastal region of central Peru had in fact generated one of the world's First Civilizations, known as Norte Chico, dating back to around 3000 B.C.E. (see "Introducing the First Civilizations" in Chapter 2). During the two millennia between roughly 1000 B.C.E. and 1000 C.E., a number of Andean civilizations rose and passed away. Because none of them had developed writing, historians are largely dependent on archeology for an understanding of these civilizations.

Chavín: A Pan-Andean Religious Movement

In both the coastal and highland regions of Peru, archeologists have uncovered numerous local ceremonial centers or temple complexes, dating between 2000 and 1000 B.C.E. Then around 900 B.C.E., one such center, situated in the Andean highlands at a village called **Chavín** (cha-BEEN) de Huántar, became the focus of a religious movement that soon swept through both coastal and highland Peru, aided by its strategic location on trade routes to both the coastal region to the west and the Amazon rain forest to the east.

By perhaps 750 B.C.E., this small center had become a town of 2,000 to 3,000 people, with clear distinctions between an elite class, who lived in stone houses,

---

Guided Reading
Question

....

■ **CONNECTION**

What kind of influence did Chavín exert in the Andes region?

and ordinary people, with adobe dwellings. An elaborate temple complex included numerous galleries, hidden passageways, staircases, ventilation shafts, drainage canals, and distinctive carvings. Chavín artwork suggests influences from both the desert coastal region and the rain forests. Major deities were represented as jaguars, crocodiles, and snakes, all of them native to the Amazon basin. Shamans or priests likely made use of the San Pedro cactus, native to the Andes Mountains, employing its hallucinogenic properties to penetrate the supernatural world. Some of the fantastic artwork of this civilization — its jaguar-human images, for example — may well reflect the visions of these religious leaders.

Over the next several centuries, this blended religious movement proved attractive across much of Peru and beyond, as Chavín-style temple architecture, sculpture, pottery, religious images, and painted textiles were widely imitated within the region. Chavín itself became a pilgrimage site and perhaps a training center for initiates. Although some evidence suggests violence and warfare, no Chavín "empire" emerged. Instead, a widespread religious cult, erected on the back of a trading network, provided for the first time and for several centuries a measure of economic and cultural integration to much of the Peruvian Andes.

Moche: A Civilization of the Coast

By 200 B.C.E., the pan-Andes Chavín cult had faded, replaced by a number of regional civilizations. Among them, **Moche** (MOH-chee) civilization clearly stands out. Dominating a 250-mile stretch of Peru's northern coast and incorporating thirteen river valleys, the Moche people flourished between about 100 and 800 C.E. Their economy was rooted in a complex irrigation system, requiring constant maintenance, that funneled runoff from the Andes into fields of maize, beans, squash, and acres of cotton, all fertilized by rich bird droppings called guano. Moche fishermen also harvested millions of anchovies from the bountiful Pacific.

Politically, Moche was governed by warrior-priests, some of whom lived atop huge pyramids, the largest of which was constructed from 143 million sun-dried bricks. There shaman-rulers, often under the influence of hallucinogenic drugs, conducted ancient rituals that mediated between the world of humankind and that of the gods. They also presided over the ritual sacrifice of human victims, drawn from their many prisoners of war, which became central to the politico-religious life of the Moche. Images on Moche pottery show a ruler attired in a magnificent feather headdress and seated on a pyramid, while a parade of naked prisoners marches past him. Other scenes of decapitation and dismemberment indicate the fate that awaited those destined for sacrifice. For these rulers, the Moche world was apparently one of war, ceremony, and diplomacy.

The immense wealth of this warrior-priest elite and the exquisite artistry of Moche craftsmen are reflected in the elaborate burials accorded the rulers. (See Zooming In: The Lord of Sipan and the Lady of Cao, page 244.) In the absence of written texts, these artistic products are the most accessible aspect of Moche life, and much of what scholars know about the Moche world derives from the superb

Guided Reading Questions

■ **DESCRIPTION**
What features of Moche life characterize it as a civilization?

The Lord of Sipan and the Lady of Cao

In the mid- to late third century C.E., a prominent man of Moche society died in what is now Peru. We do not know his name, for a written language was not a part of Moche life. But since archeologists uncovered his final resting place in 1987, scholars have learned a great deal about him and about his culture. He was five feet four inches in height, relatively tall for his time and place, and was somewhere around forty years of age. The condition of his teeth and bones suggests that he ate a well-balanced diet and probably performed little physical labor during his life. The cause of his death is unclear, but scholars think that he may well have died of an epidemic disease during a severe famine.

Much more obvious is his high social status, for which he has been dubbed the Lord of Sipan, named for the town in Peru where the archeological site is located. Laid to rest in the official and ceremonial finery he likely donned in life, the Lord of Sipan was bedecked in gold. He wore a huge gold crescent headdress, a gold face mask, two necklaces with gold and silver beads in the shape of oversized

The Moche ruler in the center of the grave, dating to about 250 C.E., was about forty years old when he died and, at five feet four inches, was quite tall for the time.

peanuts, and gold earspools exquisitely inlaid with turquoise; he had a gold warrior's shield on his back and a golden scepter in his hand. Hundreds of pots contained food and drink, while 451 ceremonial objects also accompanied the burial. Guarding the entrance to his tomb was the skeleton of a man with his feet cut off, presumably to prevent him from leaving his post. Buried with the Lord of Sipan were six other individuals: a young child (perhaps his own?); two robust men (perhaps ritually sacrificed warriors?); and three young women (perhaps his wives?). A dog, claimed by local traditions to guide the dead into the afterworld, and two llamas also attended the lord in death. In its archeological significance and its material splendor, this burial site (see the photo above) has been compared to that of Tutankhamen, the young pharaoh of Egypt.

Clearly, the Lord of Sipan was a very high-ranking member of Moche's highly stratified society. Such lords received food from their subjects, some of which they passed on to

skill of its craftspeople, such as metalworkers, potters, weavers, and painters. Face masks, figures of animals, small earrings, and other jewelry items, many plated in gold, display amazing technical abilities and a striking artistic sensibility. Decorating Moche ceramic pottery are naturalistic portraits of noble lords and rulers and images from the life of common people, including the blind and the sick. Battle scenes show warriors confronting their enemies with raised clubs. Erotic encounters between men and women and gods making love to humans likewise represent common themes, as do grotesque images of the many Moche gods and goddesses. Much of this, of course, reflects the culture of the Moche elite. We know much less about the daily life of the farmers, fishermen, weavers, traders, construction workers, and servants whose labor made that elite culture possible.

These cultural achievements, however, rested on fragile environmental foundations, for the region was subject to drought, earthquakes, and occasional torrential lesser lords, and they had access to the rare and prestigious objects created for them by Moche's immensely skillful artisans. Various objects in the tomb correspond closely to images on Moche pottery and temple walls of prisoners being slaughtered and a warrior-priest collecting and drinking their blood. Perhaps the Lord of Sipan was one such warrior-priest.

Object found in the tomb of the Lady of Cao.

At the time the Lord of Sipan came to light, it was widely assumed that the ruling elite of Moche society was all male. Then in 2005, another remarkable burial site was uncovered, containing the intact body of a young woman who had died in childbirth around 450 C.E. while still in her twenties. Now known as the Lady of Cao, she had been carefully wrapped in hundreds of yards of cotton strips, wore long braided hair, and bore numerous tattoos of snakes, crabs, and spiders on her arms and legs. Accompanying her was a huge collection of elaborate grave goods indicating great wealth: fifteen elaborate necklaces, gold sewing needles, weaving tools, beautiful jewelry, and a vessel depicting a nursing mother. But beyond these feminine objects were more surprising signs of real power. Her nose rings featured designs of men wielding war clubs and heads being pecked by condors. Two copper and wood staffs, symbols of authority, were entombed with her, as well as many weapons,

including two massive war clubs and twenty-three spear throwers. "The war clubs are clear symbols not only of combat but of power," declared one member of the archeological team.[6]

So was the Lady of Cao a local ruler in her own right or simply a woman from an elite family? The case for her political and religious role has been strengthened by the subsequent discovery of eight more burials of prominent Moche women. One of them contained a tall silver goblet, very similar to those depicted in Moche artistic scenes of ritual sacrifice and the consumption of blood. Some scholars suggest that Moche society was highly decentralized, with men in positions of authority in some communities and women in others. Thus the Lord of Sipan and the Lady of Cao, though living several hundred years apart, may have played equivalent roles in Moche society.

QUESTIONS

What do we learn about Moche society from these two figures? If you could interview these individuals, what would you want to ask them? What might be inferred from these burials about Moche understandings of the afterlife?

rains associated with El Niño episodes (dramatic changes in weather patterns caused by periodic warming of Pacific Ocean currents). During the sixth century C.E., some combination of these forces caused extended ecological disruption, which seriously undermined Moche civilization. In these circumstances, the Moche were vulnerable to aggressive neighbors and possibly to internal social tensions as well. By the end of the eighth century C.E., that civilization had passed into history.

Wari and Tiwanaku: Empires of the Interior

Far more than the Moche and other coastal civilizations, the interior empires of **Wari** (wah-ree) and **Tiwanaku** provided a measure of political integration and cultural commonality for the entire Andean region. Growing out of ancient settlements, these two states flourished between 400 and 1000 C.E., Wari in the northern highlands and Tiwanaku to the south. Both were centered in large urban capitals, marked by monumental architecture and stratified populations numbering in the tens of thousands. Both governments collected surplus food in warehouses as an insurance against times of drought and famine.

Guided Reading Question

....

■ **DESCRIPTION**

What was the significance of Wari and Tiwanaku in the history of Andean civilization?

But neither state controlled a continuous band of territory. Adapting to their vertical environment, both empires established colonies at lower elevations on the eastern and western slopes of the Andes as well as throughout the highlands, seeking access to resources such as seafood, maize, chili peppers, cocoa, hallucinogenic plants, obsidian, and feathers from tropical birds. Caravans of llamas linked distant centers, allowing the exchange and redistribution of goods, while the religious prestige and ceremonial power of the capital city provided further integration. Cultural influences from the center, such as styles of pottery and textiles, spread well beyond the regions of direct political control. Similar religious symbols and images prevailed in both places, including the ancient Andean Staff God, a deity portrayed with a staff in each hand. Versions of this image have been found in Norte Chico, Chavín, and Moche sites as well, suggesting a long-term continuity in the religious culture of the Andean region.

But Wari and Tiwanaku were hardly carbon copies of each other. Wari's agriculture employed an elaborate system of hillside terracing and irrigation, using snowmelt from the Andes. Tiwanaku's highly productive farming economy, by contrast, utilized a "raised field" system in which artificially elevated planting surfaces in swampy areas were separated by small irrigation canals. Tiwanaku, furthermore, has become famous for its elaborately fitted stone walls and buildings, while Wari's tombs and temples were built of fieldstone set in mud mortar and covered with smooth plaster. Cities in the Wari region seemed built to a common plan and linked to the capital by a network of highways, which suggests a political system more tightly controlled from the center than in Tiwanaku.[7]

Despite these differences and a 300-mile common border, little overt conflict or warfare occurred between Wari and Tiwanaku. In areas where the two peoples lived near one another, they apparently did not mingle much. They each spoke their own language, wore different clothing, furnished their homes with distinctive goods, and looked to their respective capital cities for inspiration.

In the several centuries following 1000 C.E., both civilizations collapsed, their impressive cities permanently abandoned. What followed was a series of smaller kingdoms, one of which evolved into the Inca Empire that gave to Andean civilization a final and spectacular expression before all of the Americas was swallowed up in European empires from across the sea. The Incas themselves clearly drew on the legacy of Wari and Tiwanaku, adopting aspects of their imperial models and systems of statecraft, building on the Wari highway system, and utilizing similar styles of dress and artistic expression. Such was the prestige of Tiwanaku centuries after its collapse that the Incas claimed it as their place of origin.

PRACTICING HISTORICAL THINKING

What features common to all civilizations can you identify in the civilizations of Africa and the Americas? What distinguishing features give each of them a distinctive identity?

Alternatives to Civilization

Since historians are frequently preoccupied with civilizations, it is useful to remind ourselves that other ways of organizing human communities evolved alongside civilizations, and they too made history. Two such regions were Africa south of the equator and North America. They shared environments that featured plenty of land and relatively few people compared to the greater population densities and pressure on the land that characterized many civilizations. And a third region was Pacific Oceania, where small numbers of people navigated a sea covering about one-third of the world's surface, settled the mostly tiny specks of land that rose above the surface of that ocean, and created there a remarkable range of human communities.

Bantu Africa: Cultural Encounters and Social Variation

In the vast region of Africa south of the equator, the most significant development during the second-wave era involved the accelerating movement of Bantu-speaking peoples, cultures, and technologies into the enormous subcontinent. That process had begun many centuries earlier, probably around 3000 B.C.E., from a homeland region in what are now southeastern Nigeria and the Cameroons. Over the long run, some 400 distinct but closely related languages emerged, known collectively as Bantu. By the first century C.E., agricultural peoples speaking Bantu languages and now bearing an ironworking technology had largely occupied the forest regions of equatorial Africa, and at least a few of them had probably reached the East African coast. In the several centuries that followed, they established themselves quite rapidly in most of eastern and southern Africa (see Map 6.1, page 232), introducing immense economic and cultural changes to a huge region of the continent.

Bantu migration was not a conquest or invasion such as that of Alexander the Great; nor was it a massive and self-conscious migration like that of Europeans to the Americas in more recent times. Rather, it was a slow movement of peoples, perhaps a few extended families at a time. And sometimes Bantu expansion was less a movement of people than the diffusion of new patterns of living involving language, root crops, grains, sheep and cattle, pottery styles, and ironworking technology. In this way, already established communities could "become Bantu" without the wholesale migration of outsiders. Taken as a whole, these processes brought to Africa south of the equator a measure of cultural and linguistic commonality, marking it as a distinct region of the continent.

That movement of individuals and cultural patterns also generated numerous interactions among culturally distinct peoples. Among those encounters, none was more significant than that between the agricultural Bantu and the gathering and hunting peoples who earlier occupied this region of Africa. Their interaction was part of a long-term global phenomenon in which farmers largely replaced foragers as the dominant people on the planet.

Guided Reading Question

■ **CONNECTION**

In what ways did the process of Bantu expansion stimulate cross-cultural interaction?

In these encounters, Bantu-speaking farmers had various advantages. One was numerical, as agriculture generated a more productive economy and larger populations. A second advantage was a greater immunity to animal-borne disease, acquired by prolonged exposure to both parasitic and infectious illnesses common to farming and herding societies. Foraging peoples lacked that immunity, and many quickly succumbed when they encountered the agricultural newcomers. A third advantage was iron, so useful for tools and weapons when interacting with peoples still operating with stone-age technology. Thus gathering and hunting peoples were displaced, absorbed, or largely eliminated in most parts of Africa south of the equator—but not everywhere.

In the rain forest region of Central Africa, the foraging Batwa (Pygmy) people, at least some of them, became "forest specialists" who produced honey, wild game, elephant products, animal skins, and medicinal barks and plants, all of which entered regional trading networks in exchange for the agricultural products of their Bantu neighbors. Some also adopted Bantu languages, thus becoming Bantu linguistically, while maintaining a gathering and hunting lifestyle and a separate identity.

Bantu-speaking peoples themselves also changed as they encountered different environments and peoples. In the drier climate of East Africa, the yam-based agriculture of the West African Bantu homeland was unable to support their growing numbers, so Bantu farmers increasingly adopted grains as well as domesticated sheep and cattle from the already established people of the region. They also enriched their agriculture by acquiring a variety of food crops from Southeast Asia—coconuts, sugarcane, and especially bananas—which were brought to East Africa by Indonesian Malay sailors and immigrants early in the first millennium C.E. This agricultural package and its associated ironworking technology then spread throughout the vast area of eastern and southern Africa, probably reaching present-day South Africa by 400 C.E. Some newly "Bantuized" areas incorporated musical traditions, linguistic patterns, and kinship systems derived from the earlier inhabitants. From these interactions a common set of cultural and social practices diffused widely across Bantu Africa. One prominent historian described these practices:

> [They encompassed] in religion, the centrality of ancestor observances; in philosophy, the problem of evil understood as the consequence of individual malice or of the failure to honor one's ancestors; in music, an emphasis on polyrhythmic performance with drums as the key instrument; in dance, a new form of expression in which a variety of prescribed body movements took preference over footwork; and in agriculture, the pre-eminence of women as the workers and innovators.[8]

All of this became part of the common culture of Bantu-speaking Africa.

As Bantu-derived patterns of living became established in Africa south of the equator during the thousand or so years between 500 and 1500 C.E., a wide variety of quite distinct societies and cultures took shape. Some societies—in present-day Kenya, for example—organized themselves without any formal political specialists at all. Instead, they made decisions, resolved conflicts, and maintained order by using kinship structures or lineage principles supplemented by age grades, which joined men of a particular generation together across various lineages. Elsewhere, lineage heads who acquired a measure of personal wealth, or who proved skillful at mediating between the local spirits and the people, might evolve into chiefs with a modest political authority. In several areas, such as the region around Lake Victoria or present-day Zimbabwe, larger and more substantial kingdoms evolved. Along the East African coast after 1000 C.E., dozens of rival city-states linked the African interior with the commerce of the Indian Ocean basin (see "Sea Roads as a Catalyst for Change," in Chapter 7).

Many societies in the Bantu-speaking world developed gender systems that were markedly less patriarchal than those of established urban-based civilizations. Male ironworkers in the Congo River basin, for example, sought to appropriate the power and prestige of female reproductive capacity by decorating their furnaces with clay breasts and speaking of their bellows as impregnating the furnaces. Among the Luba people of Central Africa, male rulers operated in alliance with powerful women, particularly spirit mediums, who were thought to contain the spirit of the king. Only a woman's body was considered sufficiently strong to acquire this potent and dangerous presence. Luba art represented female ancestors as "keepers of secret royal knowledge." And across a wide area of south-central Africa, a system of "gender parallelism" associated female roles with village life (child care, farming, food preparation, making pots, baskets, and mats), while masculine identity revolved around hunting and forest life (fishing, trapping, collecting building materials and medicinal plants). It was a complementary or "separate but equal" definition of gender roles.[9]

In terms of religion, Bantu practice in general placed less emphasis on a High or Creator God, who was viewed as remote and largely uninvolved in ordinary life, and focused instead on ancestral or nature spirits. The power of dead ancestors might be accessed through rituals of sacrifice, especially of cattle. Supernatural power deriving from ancient heroes, ancestors, or nature spirits also resided in charms, which could be activated by proper rituals and used to control the rains, defend the village, achieve success in hunting, or identify witches. Belief in witches was widespread, reflecting the idea that evil or misfortune was the work of malicious people. Diviners, skilled in penetrating the unseen world, used dreams, visions, charms, or trances to identify the source of misfortune and to prescribe remedies. Was a particular illness the product of broken taboos, a dishonored ancestor, an unhappy nature spirit, or a witch? Was a remedy to be found

A Female Luba Ancestral Statue Representations of powerful women, often ancestral figures, were frequent in the wood carvings of the Bantu-speaking Luba people of Central Africa. Many of them showed women touching their breasts, a gesture signifying devotion, respect, and the holding of secret knowledge. (© Musée du Quai Branly – Jacques Chirac, Paris, France/Dist. RMN-Grand-Palais/Art Resource, NY)

Map 6.4 North America in the Second-Wave Era
A sparsely populated North America hosted a number of semi-sedentary agricultural societies as well as various gathering and hunting peoples rather than the "civilizations" characteristic of Mesoamerica and the Andes.

in a cleansing ceremony, a sacrifice to an ancestor, the activation of a charm, or the elimination of a witch?[10]

Unlike the major monotheistic religions, with their "once and for all" revelations from God through the Christian Bible or the Muslim Quran, Bantu religious practice was predicated on the notion of "continuous revelation"—the possibility of constantly receiving new messages from the world beyond through dreams, visions, or trance states. Moreover, unlike Buddhism, Christianity, or Islam, Bantu religions were geographically confined, intended to explain, predict, and control local affairs, with little missionary impulse or inclination toward universality.

North America: Ancestral Pueblo and Mound Builders

If the Americas hosted civilizations, cities, and empires in Mesoamerica and the Andes, they also housed various alternative forms of human community during the second-wave era and beyond. Arctic and subarctic cultures, the bison hunters of the Great Plains, the complex and settled communities of the Pacific coast of North America, nomadic bands living in the arid regions of southern South America—all of these represent the persistence of gathering and hunting ways of living.

Even more widespread—in the eastern woodlands of the United States, Central America, the Amazon basin, the Caribbean islands—were societies sustained by village-based agriculture. Owing to environmental or technological limitations, it was a less intensive and productive agriculture than in Mesoamerica or the Andes and supported usually much smaller populations (see Map 6.4 and Map 12.5, page 515). These peoples too made their own histories, changing in response to their unique environments, their interactions with outsiders, and their own visions of the world. The Anasazi of the southwestern United States, now called the Ancestral Pueblo, and the mound-building cultures of the eastern woodlands provide two illustrations from North America.

The southwestern region of North America, an arid land cut by mountain ranges and large basins, first acquired maize from its place of origin in Mesoamerica during the second millennium B.C.E., but it took roughly 2,000 years for that crop, later supplemented by beans and squash, to become the basis of a settled agricultural way of living. As maize was adapted to the local environment, permanent village life gradually took hold, with people initially living in pit houses below ground level. By 900 C.E., many of these villages also included kivas, much larger pit structures used for ceremonial purposes, which symbolized the widespread belief

Guided Reading Question

■ **COMPARISON**

How do the histories of these North American societies compare to that of African Bantu-speaking peoples?

that humankind emerged into this world from another world below. Individual settlements were linked to one another in local trading networks and sometimes in wider webs of exchange that brought them buffalo hides, copper, turquoise, seashells, macaw feathers, and coiled baskets from quite distant locations.

These processes of change—growing dependence on agriculture, increasing population, more intensive patterns of exchange—gave rise to larger settlements and adjacent aboveground structures known as pueblos. The most spectacular of these took shape in Chaco canyon in what is now northwestern New Mexico. There, between 860 and 1130 C.E., five major pueblos emerged. This **Chaco Phenomenon** encompassed 25,000 square miles and linked some seventy outlying settlements to the main centers. The largest of these towns, or "great houses," Pueblo Bonito, stood five stories high and contained more than 600 rooms and many kivas. Hundreds of miles of roads, up to forty feet wide, radiated out from Chaco, prompting much debate among scholars. Without wheeled carts or large domesticated animals, such an elaborate road system seems unnecessary for ordinary trade or travel. Did the roads represent, as some scholars speculate, a ceremonial or sacred landscape leading perhaps to an entrance to the underworld?

Among the Chaco elite were highly skilled astronomers who constructed an arrangement of three large rock slabs situated so as to throw a beam of light during the summer solstice across a spiral rock carving located behind this observatory. By the eleventh century, Chaco also had become a dominant center for the production of turquoise ornaments, which became a major item of regional commerce, extending as far south as Mesoamerica. Not all was sweetness and light, however. Warfare, internal conflict, and occasional cannibalism (a matter of much controversy among scholars) apparently increased in frequency as an extended period of drought in the half century following 1130 brought this flourishing culture to a rather abrupt end. By 1200, the great houses had been abandoned and their inhabitants scattered in small communities that later became the Pueblo peoples of more recent times.

Unlike the Chaco region in the southwest, the eastern woodlands of North America and especially the Mississippi River valley generated an independent Agricultural Revolution. By 2000 B.C.E., many of its peoples had domesticated local plant species, including sumpweed, goosefoot, some gourds and squashes, and a form of artichoke. Sunflowers, originally domesticated in Mesoamerica, also found a place in diets of eastern woodland peoples. These few plants, however, were not sufficient to support a fully settled agricultural village life; rather, they supplemented diets derived from gathering and hunting without fundamentally changing that ancient way of life. Such peoples created societies distinguished by arrays of large earthen mounds, found all over the United States east of the Mississippi, prompting archeologists to dub them the **Mound Builders**. The earliest of these mounds date to around 4000 B.C.E., but the most elaborate and widespread took shape between 200 B.C.E. and 400 C.E. The builders of these mounds created what is commonly called the **Hopewell culture**, after an archeological site in Ohio.

Several features of the Hopewell culture have intrigued archeologists. Particularly significant are the striking burial mounds and geometric earthworks, sometimes covering areas equivalent to several city blocks, and the wide variety of artifacts found within them—smoking pipes, human figurines, mica mirrors, flint blades, fabrics, and jewelry of all kinds. The mounds themselves were no doubt the focus of elaborate burial rituals, but some of them were aligned with the moon with such precision as to mark lunar eclipses. Developed most elaborately in the Ohio River valley, Hopewell-style earthworks, artifacts, and ceremonial pottery have also been found throughout the eastern woodlands region of North America. Hopewell centers in Ohio contained mica from the Appalachian Mountains, volcanic glass from Yellowstone, conch shells and a few sharks' teeth from the Gulf of Mexico, and copper from the Great Lakes. All of this suggests a large "Hopewell Interaction Sphere" linking this entire region in a loose network of exchange, as well as a measure of cultural borrowing of religious ideas and practices.[11]

The next and most spectacular phase in the history of these mound-building peoples took shape as corn-based agriculture, derived ultimately but indirectly from Mexico, gained ground in the Mississippi valley after 800 C.E., allowing larger populations and more complex societies to emerge. The dominant center was **Cahokia**, near present-day St. Louis, Missouri, which flourished from about 900 to 1250 C.E. Its central mound, a terraced pyramid of four levels, measured 1,000 feet long by 700 feet wide, rose more than 100 feet above the ground, and occupied fifteen acres. It was the largest structure north of Mexico, the focal point of a community numbering 10,000 or more people, and the center of a widespread trading network.

Evidence from burials and from later Spanish observers suggests that Cahokia and other centers of this Mississippi culture were stratified societies with a clear elite and with rulers able to mobilize the labor required to build such enormous structures. One high-status male was buried on a platform of 20,000 shell beads, accompanied by 800 arrowheads, sheets of copper and mica, and a number of sacrificed men and women nearby.[12] Well after Cahokia had declined and was abandoned, sixteenth-century Spanish and French explorers encountered another such chiefdom among the Natchez people, located in southwestern Mississippi. Paramount chiefs, known as Great Suns, dressed in knee-length fur coats and lived luxuriously in deerskin-covered homes. An elite class of "principal men" or "honored peoples" clearly occupied a different status from commoners, sometimes referred to as "stinkards." These sharp class distinctions were blunted by the requirement that upper-class people, including the Great Suns, had to marry "stinkards."

The military capacity of these Mississippi chiefdoms greatly impressed European observers, as this Spanish account indicates:

> The next day the cacique [paramount chief] arrived with 200 canoes filled with men, having weapons, . . . the warriors standing erect from bow to stern, holding bows and arrows. . . . [F]rom under the canopy where the chief man was, the course was directed and orders issued to the rest. . . . [W]hat with the awnings, the plumes, the shields, the pennons, and the number of people in the fleet, it appeared like a famous armada of galleys.[13]

Here then, in the eastern woodlands of North America, were peoples who independently generated a modest Agricultural Revolution, assimilated corn and beans from distant sources, developed increasingly complex chiefdoms, and created monumental structures, new technologies, and artistic traditions. Beyond the separate societies that emerged within this large area, scholars have noticed some similarities in artifacts, symbols, ceremonies, mythologies, and artistic styles, many of which seem related to marking the status of elites. A horned serpent, sometimes depicted with wings, and various animal-god representations were widely shared symbols, though the meaning of these symbols no doubt changed as they entered new cultural environments. Dubbed the Southeast Ceremonial Complex, the loose networks of connection that generated these similarities grew outward from Cahokia for several centuries after 1200 or so, continuing earlier patterns of interaction associated with the Hopewell cultural region. While no linguistic, cultural, or political unity emerged from these relationships, they testify to a measure of exchange, borrowing, and cultural adaptation across an enormous region of North America.

Pacific Oceania: Peoples of the Sea

The peoples of Pacific Oceania, like those of Bantu Africa and North America, created enduring human communities without the large cities, states, and empires so prominent in civilizations. But the ecological setting for these historical journeys was distinctive, for they took place on the islands of the immense Pacific: a few larger territories, such as New Guinea and New Zealand, as well as thousands of much smaller islands, many of them specks in the sea (see Map 6.5). New Guinea had been settled for perhaps 50,000 years, initially at a time when it was connected to Australia by a land bridge. But the rest of Oceania was the last part of the world to receive human settlers, who began arriving from Island Southeast Asia only about 3,500 years ago (see "Into the Pacific" in Chapter 1). By 1200 C.E., they had achieved a presence on every habitable piece of land throughout this enormous region. It was, as one historian summarized the process, "the greatest maritime expansion known to history."[14]

The settlers' arrival, however, produced an enormous and sometimes devastating environmental impact as humans entered and disrupted bountiful but fragile ecosystems, especially as their populations grew. Referring to some of the early settlers in Melanesia during the first millennium B.C.E., Pacific historian Ian Campbell wrote: "They hunted, gathered, and fished profligately, and burnt large tracts of previously undisturbed forests."[15] In New Zealand, initially settled much later, around 1200 C.E., human hunting largely eliminated the huge flightless *moa* bird within a century. Archeologists have discovered the remains of some 90,000 moa at a single butchery. A similar impact occurred in Hawaii and elsewhere as smaller birds fell victim to the rats, pigs, and dogs introduced by the settlers. Resource depletion, deforestation, and soil erosion followed, no doubt contributing to the abandonment of at least several dozen islands, as their inhabitants found themselves forced to flee or perish. Rapa Nui (Easter Island) in easternmost Polynesia had come almost to the point of

Guided Reading Question

■ **CHANGE**
What changes marked the history of Pacific Oceania?

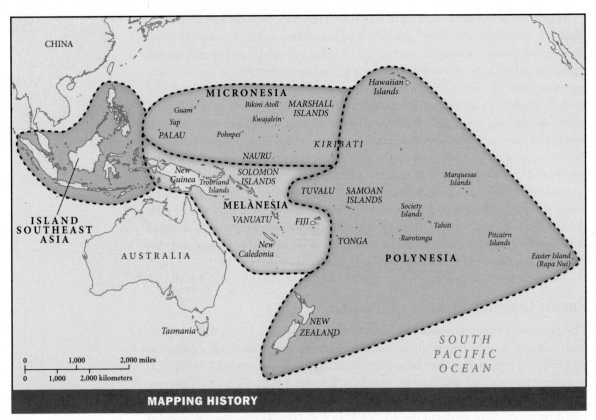

MAPPING HISTORY

Map 6.5 Pacific Oceania

Covering about one-third of the world's surface, the Pacific Ocean encompasses thousands of islands, which were home to many distinct societies but also constituted a cultural region that shared numerous commonalities and connections.

READING THE MAP: About how far is New Guinea from Easter Island (Rapa Nui)? Plot a course from New Guinea to Easter Island (Rapa Nui) using other islands as stopping-off points. How does an island-by-island approach change your impression of the journey?

MAKING CONNECTIONS: While reading "Pacific Oceania: Peoples of the Sea," trace on the map the chronological order in which the islands of the Pacific Ocean were settled. What patterns do you see? Which islands were settled last, and why?

ecological collapse by the time Europeans arrived in the eighteenth century, as much of its tree cover had vanished and many bird species had likewise disappeared. Human activity had surely contributed to this outcome with overhunting, overfishing, and the cutting down of forests. But Polynesian rats, whether introduced accidentally or intentionally by the original settlers to the island, were at least equally responsible, as their numbers exploded and they devoured the seeds of the palm trees.[16]

Growing populations also resulted in increased social complexity on some of the most densely populated islands. One example comes from the Micronesian island of **Pohnpei**, where an urban complex, constructed from stone and coral, served as the ceremonial, administrative, and burial center of a powerful

Saudeleur dynasty that governed the island for several centuries after 1100 C.E. This impressive urban center, later dubbed by Europeans the "Venice of the Pacific," contained numerous seawalls and canals, over ninety small artificial islands, marketplaces, and a large tomb and funerary complex. However, local legends tell of increasingly despotic rulers whose oppressive policies triggered a revolt by lower-ranking chiefs.

The Polynesian **Tonga Islands** witnessed yet another example of growing social complexity. By the fourteenth century, powerful rulers, known as Tu'i Tonga, stood at the head of a royal court that included many wives and concubines, various relatives, ceremonial attendants, prisoners of war, and specialized craftsmen such as carvers, navigators, and fishermen. The court collected and redistributed food and various gifts to lesser chiefs, who then did the same for their followers. The widespread military and commercial influence of Tonga in the central Pacific has led some scholars to regard it as an incipient empire, while others view it as a tributary network or a system of economic interdependence.

Given the vast distances separating these island societies, considerable diversity among them is hardly surprising. And yet they also participated in the making of a single cultural region with numerous commonalities and connections. Many of their cultural and dietary similarities derive from their common origin in Island Southeast Asia and ultimately from southern China as well as from a common Pacific environment. Variations developed from the adaptation of this shared heritage to the distinctive environment of particular islands—large or small, tropical or semi-tropical, sea-level coastal terrain or mountainous interior, uninhabited or containing established societies as in New Guinea. The relative isolation of these societies, as well as periodic contact with near and more distant neighboring islands, also shaped their histories.

Linguistically, the peoples of Oceania, despite their small numbers, have spoken hundreds of different languages, over 100 on the small island chain of Melanesian Vanuatu alone. But almost all of them are members of the Austronesian family of languages, whose speakers also include those of Malaysia, Indonesia, and Madagascar. New Guinea, however, is a different story, with well over 1,000 languages, most of which are part of the Papuan language family, derived from its much earlier settlement. Similarly, Pacific islanders everywhere practiced the art of body decoration called *tatau* (which became "tattoo" in English), but particularly in Polynesia each archipelago developed distinctive designs, reflecting its unique identity.

This pattern of diversity and unity found other expression as well, both among the three major regions of Melanesia, Micronesia, and Polynesia and within them. In economic life, for example, these people of the sea drew heavily on the ocean as a major source of food, while its shells were used as currency and tools. But they were also farmers, raising pigs, dogs, and fowl, while everywhere cultivating taro, a starchy root vegetable. Other crops—yams, sweet potatoes, breadfruit, coconut palms—were also cultivated as availability and conditions allowed.

In political and social life, Oceanic societies were generally organized as chiefdoms, but with considerable variation. On small islands, chiefs and priests could hardly be distinguished from anyone else, while village councils, operating by consensus, made decisions. In parts of Melanesia, so-called "big men," or locally influential individuals, exercised authority through ceremony, feasts, and gift giving. Elsewhere, societies were more stratified and authority more centralized. In New Zealand, the Maori people distinguished among chiefly families, commoners, and slaves derived from prisoners of war. Frequent warfare among its chiefdoms prevented greater political unity. In Hawaii and Tonga, by contrast, elaborate social hierarchies emerged with powerful rulers who had hundreds or even thousands of warriors at their disposal.

Women everywhere in ancient Oceania were considered dangerous and polluting, especially during menstruation and childbirth, and were isolated at those times. However, gender roles differed substantially from place to place. In Melanesia, women were more actively involved in food production, but in Polynesia their labor was directed more toward the making of mats and cloth. Throughout Polynesia, women were accorded high status, and women of chiefly families could exercise considerable power through their male relatives. Melanesian women, by contrast, were more sharply subordinated to men than their counterparts in other regions of Oceania.

The Moai of Rapa Nui The most iconic artistic representations of Polynesian culture are these huge stone figures called *moai*. Carved from volcanic rock on the island of Rapa Nui sometime between 1200 and 1600, they are thought to depict sacred ancestors or clan chiefs. Around 1,000 of them were quarried and carved, and hundreds were somehow transported up to eight miles to stand on stone platforms near the coast. The largest were some thirty-three feet tall and weighed over eighty tons. (© Ken Welsh/Bridgeman Images)

Religious life in Oceania was pragmatic, designed to protect against harm and to manipulate the spirits or gods in one's favor. It found expression in two pervasive concepts: *mana* and *tapu*. Mana was a spiritual energy or power, associated especially with chiefs and demonstrated by remarkable actions or great success. To maintain the purity of mana, ritual restriction or prohibitions known as tapu (which came into English as "taboo") served to make someone or something sacred or elevated far above the ordinary. Throughout Polynesia, only a particular official could handle the chief's food or his possessions. A Maori chief in New Zealand could not allow even his shadow to fall on food, for doing so made it forbidden to all others. Hawaiians prostrated themselves on the ground before their major chiefs. Since violating a tapu could result in death, religion provided supernatural sanctions for political authorities and social elites, as it has in so many other societies.

While much of this was common across all of Pacific Oceania, the gods, ghosts, ancestors, and spirits differed considerably, as did the role of priests or shamans as well as the associated rituals and artistic expression of religious life.

Despite the distances between these island societies, they were not wholly isolated from one another. Networks of exchange and communication—both regional and at a greater distance—allowed for some interaction among the various peoples of Oceania. Between roughly 1400 and 800 B.C.E., the spread of a distinctive pottery style known as Lapita throughout Melanesia and as far as Tonga and Samoa suggests a widespread pattern of exchange involving both commercial and ceremonial elements. During this time, obsidian from the island of New Britain off the northeastern coast of New Guinea had a distribution that extended over 4,000 miles from Borneo in Island Southeast Asia to Fiji in eastern Melanesia.

In western Micronesia, another system of exchange arose in the Caroline Island chain, with a particular focus on the island of **Yap**. It involved trade in commodities such as sea turtles, coconuts, and breadfruit; permission to fish near neighboring islands; and promises of refuge and shelter in times of famine. But it was also a set of tributary relationships in which the high-ranking island of Yap periodically received payments such as woven cloth, various coconut products, mats, and shells from islands of lesser rank up to 1,200 miles farther east. In return, the subordinates received gifts from Yap that exceeded the value of their tribute: wood for canoes, flint stone, food, and powdered turmeric, used as a skin paste and in coming-of-age rituals. Cast in terms of a parent-child relationship between Yap and the other islands, the whole system was supported by fears of powerful Yapese sorcery capable of generating great storms, should the required tribute not be forthcoming. Such trading circuits often contained an elaborate ceremonial element in which the exchange of noneconomic items—bracelets, necklaces, feathers, or shells—served to display status, to cement bonds of mutual assistance across great distances, and to confirm relationships of dominance and submission. Small island societies were invariably vulnerable and limited in resources; such networks of exchange provided insurance for their survival.

Polynesian networks of exchange also flourished in the centuries after 1000 C.E., with Tonga at the center of a system linked by trade with Samoa and Fiji. Finely woven Samoan mats were highly valued for displaying prestige, and large logs from Fiji were prized for the huge canoes that could be carved from them for Tonga's impressive warships. From the far eastern edge of Polynesia, sailors had apparently reached the coast of South America, from which they returned with sweet potatoes and bottle gourds. Taking hold in Rapa Nui, those domesticates from the Americas then entered Polynesian voyaging networks and found their way to Hawaii, New Zealand, and elsewhere, becoming a major food source.

Linked to Asia by their distant origins and to the Americas by the slender thread of the sweet potato, the peoples of Pacific Oceania lived largely, but not entirely, in a world apart from the rest of humankind.

REFLECTIONS

Deciding What's Important: Balance in the Writing of World History

Among the perennial problems that teachers and writers of world history confront is sorting through the vast record of times past and choosing what to include and what to leave out. A related issue involves the extent to which particular peoples or civilizations will be treated. Should the Persians get as much space as the Greeks? Does Africa merit equal treatment with Eurasia? Where do the Americas fit in the larger human story? What, in short, are the criteria for deciding what is important in recalling the history of the human venture?

One standard might be duration. Should ways of living that have endured for longer periods of time receive greater attention than those of lesser length? If historians followed only this criterion, then the Paleolithic era of gathering, hunting, and fishing societies should occupy 90 percent or more of any world history text. On the other hand, perhaps change is more important than continuity. If so, then something new merits more space than something old. Thus we pay attention to both agriculture and civilizations because they represent significant turning points in human experience.

Population provides yet another principle for determining inclusion. That, of course, is the reason that Eurasia / North Africa, with over 80 percent of the world's population, is addressed in three chapters of this section, whereas inner Africa, the Americas, and Pacific Oceania together receive just one chapter.

There is also the related issue of range of influence. Buddhism, Christianity, and Islam spread more widely and shaped the lives of more people than did the religions of the Maya or the Bantu-speaking peoples of Africa. Do they therefore deserve more extended treatment? Still another factor involves the availability of evidence. In this respect, Eurasia generated far more written records than either Africa or the Americas did, and therefore its history has been investigated far more thoroughly.

A final possible criterion involves the location of the historian and his or her audience. Those who have recently developed world history as a field of study have vigorously sought to counteract a Eurocentric telling of the human story. Still, is there anything inherently wrong with an account of world history that is centered on one's own people? Ethiopian high schools in the 1960s operated within an Afrocentric history curriculum, which focused first on Ethiopian history, then on Africa as a whole, and finally on the larger world. Might a world historian from the Middle East, for example, legitimately strike a somewhat different balance in the treatment of various civilizations than someone writing for a largely Western audience or for Chinese readers?

Any account of the world's past will mix and match these criteria in various and contested ways. Among historians, there exists neither a consensus about this question nor any formula to ensure a "proper" balance. You may want to consider whether the choices made in this chapter, and the book as a whole, are appropriate. What other choices might be possible?

Second Thoughts

What's the Significance?

Meroë, 231

Axum, 234

Niger Valley civilization, 235

vertical integration, 237

Maya civilization, 238

Teotihuacán, 240

Chavín, 242

Moche, 243

Wari and Tiwanaku, 245

Bantu migration, 247

Chaco Phenomenon, 251

Mound Builders, 251

Hopewell culture, 251

Cahokia, 252

Pohnpei, 254

Tonga Islands, 255

mana and *tapu*, 256

Yap, 257

Big Picture Questions

1. "The particular cultures and societies of Africa, the Americas, and Pacific Oceania discussed in this chapter developed largely in isolation." What evidence would support this statement, and what might challenge it?

2. How do you understand areas of the world, such as Bantu Africa, North America, and Pacific Oceania, that did not generate "civilizations"? Do you see them as "backward," as moving slowly toward civilization, or as simply different?

3. How did Africa's proximity to Eurasia shape its history? And how did America's separation from the Eastern Hemisphere affect its development?

4. **Looking Back:** "The histories of Africa and the Americas during the second-wave era largely resemble those of Eurasia." Do you agree with this statement? Explain why or why not.

Next Steps: For Further Study

Christopher Ehret, *The Civilizations of Africa* (2002). An overview of African history before 1800 by a prominent scholar.

Brian M. Fagan, *Ancient North America* (2005). A prominent archeologist's account of North American history.

Steven R. Fischer, *A History of the Pacific Islands* (2013). A recent account of the history of Pacific Oceania from ancient times to the present.

Eric Gilbert and Jonathan T. Reynolds, *Africa in World History* (2011). An accessible account of African history set in a global context.

Guy Gugliotta, "The Maya: Glory and Ruin," *National Geographic* (August 2007). A beautifully illustrated account of the rise and fall of Maya civilization.

Charles C. Mann, *1491: New Revelations of the Americas before Columbus* (2005). A journalist's thoughtful account, delightfully written, of the controversies surrounding the history of the Americas before 1492.

Annenberg Media, "Human Migration," 2004, https://www.learner.org/vod/vod_window.html?pid=2146. A video that demonstrates how historians trace migration patterns, including those of Bantu-speaking peoples in Africa.

National Geographic, "Lost Kingdom of the Maya," 1997, https://www.youtube.com/watch?v=bSd2POguPFk. A lovely documentary on classical Maya civilization and its collapse.

Axum and the World

In the world of ancient African history, Axum has occupied a unique position in several ways (see Map 6.1 and "Axum: The Making of a Christian Kingdom" in this chapter). It is one of the few places in Africa, outside of Egypt, for which considerable documentary evidence exists. Some of the written sources—royal inscriptions and coins, for example—derive from within Axum itself, while others come from Greco-Roman and Christian visitors. Furthermore, after the rise of Islam, Axum—and its Ethiopian successor state—was the major surviving outpost of a Christian tradition that had earlier spread widely across northern and northeastern Africa. Finally, Axum has demonstrated an impressive cultural and religious continuity. Even after the decline of the Axumite Empire by the eighth century C.E., the city of Axum remained a major pilgrimage site for Christians, while Ethiopian kings into the twentieth century were crowned there. The sources that follow offer a series of windows into this African kingdom.

SOURCE 6.1 The Making of an Axumite Empire

At its high point in the mid-fourth century C.E., Axum ruled an empire stretching from Meroë in the upper Nile Valley, across much of what is now Eritrea and Ethiopia, and incorporating parts of southern Arabia on the opposite side of the Red Sea. Source 6.1 comes from an Axumite inscription written in Greek on a stone throne adorned with figures of the Greek gods Hercules and Mercury. Commissioned by an unknown Axumite monarch, the inscription dates probably from the second or third century C.E. It was copied and then published in the sixth century by Cosmas, a Greek merchant born in Alexandria, Egypt, who had become a monk. This text describes some of the conquests that generated the Axumite Empire.

■ What evidence from the document itself dates it prior to Axum's acceptance of Christianity?

■ How would you describe the point of view from which the document was written?

■ What techniques of imperial control does the document reveal?

■ How would you describe the religious or ideological underpinnings of this empire? Why might the Axumite ruler who commissioned this inscription single out Ares, Zeus, and Poseidon for special attention?

Inscription on a Stone Throne | **2nd or 3rd century** C.E.

Having after this with a strong hand compelled the nations bordering on my kingdom to live in peace, I made war upon the following nations, and by force of arms reduced them to subjection. I warred first with the nation of Gaze [Axum, probably in an internal struggle for power], then with Agame and Sigye, and having conquered them, I exacted the half of all that they possessed.... [There follows a long list of other peoples that this ruler conquered.]

All these nations, protected though they were by mountains all but impregnable, I conquered, after engagements in which I was myself present. Upon their submission I restored their territories to them, subject to the payment of tribute. Many other tribes besides these submitted of their own accord, and became likewise tributary. And I sent a fleet and land forces against the Arabitae and Cinaedocolpitae who dwelt on the other side of the Red Sea [southern Arabia], and having reduced the sovereigns of both,

I imposed on them a land tribute and charged them to make traveling safe both by sea and by land....

I first and alone of the kings of my race made these conquests. For this success I now offer my thanks to my mighty god, Ares [the Greek god of warfare and slaughter], who begat me, and by whose aid I reduced all the nations bordering on my own country.... Having thus brought all the world under my authority to peace, I came down to Adulis and offered sacrifice to Zeus [chief god of the Greek pantheon], and to Ares, and to Poseidon [Greek god of the sea], whom I entreated to befriend all who go down to the sea in ships. Here also I reunited all my forces, and setting down this Chair [throne] in this place, I consecrated it to Ares in the twenty-seventh year of my reign.

Source: J. W. McCrindle, trans. and ed., *The Christian Topography of Cosmas, an Egyptian Monk* (London: Hakluyt Society, 1897), 59, 63–66.

■ ■ ■

SOURCE 6.2 The Columns of Axum ▶

Dating from around 300 C.E. and standing 79 feet tall, this column was one of the largest raised on an artificial terrace in Axum's capital. Carved to depict a building, it includes two false doors on the ground level and window frame designs on nine upper stories. While no inscriptions accompany any of the monuments, they likely marked the tombs of royalty. Made from single blocks of stone, the largest, at nearly 100 feet, still lies where it fell. According to one authority, it "is probably the largest—but not the longest—single block of stone that people anywhere have ever attempted to set on end."[17] The conversion of the Axum kings to Christianity brought an abrupt end to the practice of erecting royal funeral columns.

■ Why do you think these columns were carved to resemble multistory houses? Archeologists note that few if any houses in Axum would have been taller than three stories, so what might this ten-story structure convey?

■ Why might conversion to Christianity have led rulers to stop constructing columns to commemorate their burials?

An Axumite Monument | **late 3rd or early 4th century c.e.**

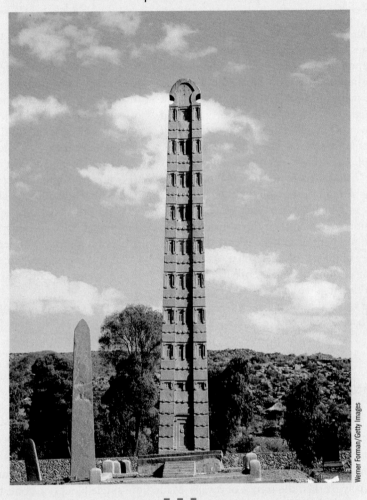

Werner Forman/Getty Images

■ ■ ■

SOURCE 6.3 The Coming of Christianity to Axum

The introduction of Christianity in the mid-fourth century C.E. represented a major change in the cultural history of Axum. It meant that Axum would be more closely aligned to Christian Egypt and Byzantium than to South Arabia, from which many of its earlier cultural traditions had derived. Source 6.3 relates the story of the coming of Christianity to Axum. It was written by Rufinus (345–410 C.E.), a Christian monk and writer who was born in Italy but spent much of his life in Jerusalem, where he heard this story from those who had taken part in it. Note that Greco-Roman writers of this time used "India" to refer vaguely to East Africa and southern Arabia as well as the South Asian peninsula.

- According to this document, by what means was Christianity introduced to Axum? What do you think was the relative importance of Frumentius and Aedesius, as opposed to Roman merchants living in Axum?

- Why do you think the Axumite royal family was so receptive to this foreign religion? How might the story differ if told from the ruling family's perspective?

- How does the fact that this document was written by outsiders shape the emphasis of the story?

RUFINUS | *On the Evangelization of Abyssinia* | late 4th century C.E.

Meropius, a philosopher from Tyre [a Roman-controlled city in what is now Lebanon], . . . decided to go to India [to study their world and investigate their regions]. Two little boys went with him. He had been educating them in the liberal arts because they were his relatives. The younger boy was named Aedesius, the older Frumentius.

During the journey the things Meropius studied and learned nourished his mind. Then, while headed home, the philosopher's ship had to land because the travelers needed water or some other necessities. Where they landed the barbarians had a custom of cutting the throats of all Romans they found among them whenever neighboring nations announced that their treaties with the Romans were broken. The barbarians attacked the philosopher's ship. They killed him and all with him likewise. But the little boys they found studying and doing their reading under a tree. The barbarians spared the boys out of pity and led them to their king [the ruler of Axum].

The king made Aedesius his cup bearer. But he trusted Frumentius to be his accountant and scribe because he understood that the boy had a sharp mind and wisdom. From then on the king honored and loved them both. When the king died, he left as his successor his wife, who had a little son. He granted the boys, now young men, free opportunity to do whatever they wanted. And the queen, as if she trusted no one in the kingdom more,

humbly asked them to share in taking care of the kingdom with her until her son was a young man. She especially wanted Frumentius to help because he had enough wisdom to direct a kingdom. . . .

[D]uring the time Frumentius directed the government of the kingdom, he carefully began to inquire—for God moved his mind and spirit—whether there were any Christians among the Roman merchants. And he gave the greatest power to these Christians and advised them to make meeting places in every part of the country so that they could congregate in them for prayer in the Roman manner. Moreover, he himself did the same to a much greater degree, and so encouraged others, motivated them with favor and benefits, offered whatever might be useful, supplied land for buildings and other necessities, and acted in every way to grow the Christian seed in the kingdom.

When the royal child for whom Aedesius and Frumentius were taking care of the kingdom became a young man, their task was fulfilled and they faithfully handed over everything to him. Then they returned again to our world [the Roman Empire], even though the queen and her son delayed their journey and asked them to remain.

Source: *The Church History of Rufinus of Aquileia,* book 10, sections 9 and 10. Translation from Latin by Edward M. Gutting, Missouri State University.

■ ■ ■

SOURCE 6.4 **Axum and the Gold Trade**

The foundations of the Axumite state lay not only in its military conquests and its adoption of a new religion but also in its economic ties to the larger world. Among these ties was its reputation as a major source of gold for the Roman Empire. Source 6.4 describes the distinctive fashion in which Axumite traders obtained the gold from the African peoples living on the margins of the Axumite state. The author, Cosmas (see Source 6.1), was involved in this trade.

■ How would you define the pattern of exchange described in this document? Was it state-directed trade, private enterprise, or both? To what problems of cross-cultural interaction was it a response?

■ Who, if anyone, had the upper hand in this trade? Was it conducted between politically equal parties?

■ What purposes did this trade serve for the people who mined and "sold" the gold?

COSMAS | *The Gold Trade of Axum* | **6th century C.E.**

The country known as that of Sasu is itself near the ocean . . . in which there are many gold mines. The King of the Axumites accordingly, every other year, through the governor of Agau, sends thither special agents to bargain for the gold, and these are accompanied by many other traders—upwards, say, of five hundred—bound on the same errand as themselves. They take along with them to the mining district oxen, lumps of salt, and iron, and when they reach its neighborhood, they make a halt at a certain spot and form an encampment, which they fence round with a great hedge of thorns. Within this they live, and having slaughtered the oxen, cut them in pieces, and lay the pieces on the top of the thorns, along with the lumps of salt and the iron. Then come the natives bringing gold in nuggets like peas, and lay one or two or more of these upon what pleases them—the pieces of flesh or the salt or the iron, and then they retire to some distance off. Then the owner of the meat approaches, and if he is satisfied he takes the gold away, and upon seeing this, its owner comes and takes the flesh or the salt or the iron. If, however, he is not satisfied, he leaves the gold, when the native, seeing that he has not taken it, comes and either puts down more gold, or takes up what he had laid down, and goes away. Such is the mode in which business is transacted with the people of that country, because their language is different and interpreters are hardly to be found.

The time they stay in that country is five days more or less, according as the natives, more or less readily coming forward, buy up all their wares. On the journey homeward they all agree to travel well-armed, since some of the tribes through whose country they must pass might threaten to attack them from a desire to rob them of their gold. The space of six months is taken up with this trading expedition, including both the going and the returning.

Source: J. W. McCrindle, trans. and ed., *The Christian Topography of Cosmas, an Egyptian Monk* (London: Hakluyt Society, 1897), 52–53.

■ ■ ■

SOURCE 6.5 **Axum Gold Coin**

Axum was the only kingdom in sub-Saharan Africa to mint coins in ancient times. This example from the first half of the fifth century depicts King Eon wearing his royal crown flanked by two grain stalks symbolizing abundance. Around the edge, his name and what may be his clan affiliation is inscribed in Greek, punctuated by four crosses advertising his Christian faith. Eon's predecessor and first Christian ruler of Axum, King Ezana (ca. 330–356), started this tradition and may have been the first ruler anywhere to mint coins with Christian crosses. Before Ezana, rulers had instead used a disk and crescent symbol representing sun and moon gods.

- The only surviving evidence for many Axumite kings is their coins. What can we learn about individual kings from their coinage?

- Some scholars have argued that Axumite coins may have been primarily intended to circulate beyond the borders of the kingdom. As evidence, they note that coins like this one used the same weight standards as Roman coins. What else about this coin supports the theory that it was intended to circulate outside of Axum? If true, what impression might King Eon have hoped to make on foreigners who came across his coin?

A "Christian Coin" from Axum

■ ■ ■

DOING HISTORY

1. **Assessing sources:** How does each of the written sources reflect the distinctive perspective of its author?

2. **Considering external influences:** Based on these sources, how would you describe Axum's various relationships with the world beyond its borders? How did its geographic location shape those relationships? (See Map 6.1, page 232.) In what ways did those external connections influence Axum's historical development?

3. **Explaining the rise and significance of Axum:** Based on these sources, how might you account for the flourishing of Axum? What was the economic, religious, and military significance of Axum within the region?

4. **Comparing civilizations:** In what ways might Axum be viewed as a smaller-scale version of the second-wave civilizations of Eurasia? In what ways was it different?

Christian Axum

The coming of Christianity to Axum was just one manifestation of a broader set of cross-cultural contacts and exchanges that tied Northeast Africa with Southwest Asia and the Mediterranean. In Voice 6.1, Erik Gilbert and Jonathan Reynolds, both specialists in African history, explore the transregional nature of early Christianity and the relationships between Axum, Egypt, and the eastern Mediterreanean that the new faith fostered. In Voice 6.2, Christopher Ehret, one of the leading scholars working in early African history, examines the role of trade in the gradual assimilation of Christianity into Axum society.

- Drawing on these two passages, describe the forces that brought Christianity to Axum. What do the two accounts agree on, and what distinct contributions does each make to your own conclusions?

- Beyond religious rewards, can you discern in these accounts any other benefits that a king of Axum might have hoped to secure through conversion to a religion that originated in the Roman world?

- **Integrating Primary and Secondary Sources:** In what ways might the primary sources in this feature support or challenge the conclusions about the emergence of Christianity made by Gilbert/ Reynolds and Ehert?

VOICE 6.1

Erik Gilbert and Jonathan Reynolds on the Transregional Nature of Early Christianity | 2004

It is notable that Ezana's conversion came very shortly after the conversion of the Roman Emperor Constantine. This fact represents a parallel example of Christianity's growing acceptance by political elites at the time. King Ezana's conversion not only fostered the spread of Christianity in the region of the upper Nile, but also helped forge trading links between Aksum and Christian communities of the Eastern Mediterranean. So deeply did Christianity become entrenched in the region that in the sixth century

[the Axumite ruler] King Kaleb invaded Yemen (in the southern Arabian Peninsula). The action was allegedly taken at the behest of the Byzantine Emperor Justinian and was ostensibly to protect Christian communities in Yemen from repression at the hands of the region's non-Christian population. Some scholars, however, discount the religious motivation of the two monarchs and stress that perhaps their goal was to weaken the Persian Empire and gain greater control over the lucrative trade that flowed through Arabia. Either way, the cooperation of Byzantine and Aksum monarchs says much about the transregional nature of early Christianity.

Source: Erik Gilbert and Jonathan Reynolds, *Africa in World History* (Boston: Pearson, 2004), 75.

VOICE 6.2

Christopher Ehret on the Role of Trade in the Coming of Christianity to Axum | 2002

Aksumite intellectual history in the fourth to sixth centuries illustrates a recurrent influence of trade on world history: trade routes are not only the conduit of goods from one part of the world to another but also the conduit of ideas. In particular the Levantine merchants who plied their commerce at Aksum's port city of Adulis included a number of Christians in the fourth century, and through these contacts Christianity was adopted by the fourth-century Aksumite king Ezana. At first a religion of limited outreach beyond the towns, Christianity in the late fifth and early sixth centuries began to be widely proselytized about the countryside by a number of Syrian monks. During this period . . . large numbers of Agaw [the native peoples of Axum] became Christian, and in many rural areas different dialects of Ge'ez, the written language of government and the towns, gradually became the first language of country folk too.

Source: Christopher Ehret, *The Civilizations of Africa* (Charlottesville: University of Virginia Press, 2002), 291.

PART 3

Civilizations and Encounters during the Third-Wave Era

600–1450

Chapter 7 Commerce and Culture, 600–1450

Chapter 8 China and the World: East Asian Connections, 600–1300

Chapter 9 The Worlds of Islam: Afro-Eurasian Connections, 600–1450

Chapter 10 The Worlds of Christendom: Contraction, Expansion, and Division, 600–1450

Chapter 11 Pastoral Peoples on the Global Stage: The Mongol Moment, 1200–1450

Chapter 12 The Worlds of the Fifteenth Century

THE BIG PICTURE

Patterns and Processes of the Third-Wave Era

In world history, the dates that define major periods of time are normally used symbolically rather than for denoting actual events. They point toward processes that mark major global transformations. In Part 3, the date 600 C.E. evokes the disruption, decline, or collapse of many second-wave states and civilizations between 200 and 800 C.E., including Han dynasty China, the western Roman Empire, Gupta India, Axum, Maya cities, Teotihuacán, and others. And 1450 highlights the start of European overseas expansion, which began to link the world's peoples together in new ways.

Third-Wave Civilizations

In the centuries between 600 and 1450, two large-scale processes occupied center stage in the unfolding drama of world history. First, a new phase in the continuing history of civilization took shape during these centuries. In some areas, wholly new civilizations arose where none had existed before: in Swahili city-states along the East African coast; in the West African kingdoms of Ghana, Mali, and Songhay; in Kievan Rus, located in what is now Ukraine and western Russia; in Japan, Korea, and Vietnam; in Srivijaya on the Indonesian island of Sumatra; and in the Angkor kingdom centered in present-day Cambodia. All of these represent a continuation of a long-established pattern in world history—the globalization of civilization. These newcomers to the growing number of civilizations borrowed heavily from larger or more established centers. So too did the new civilization that took shape in Western Europe following the collapse of the Roman Empire, combining Greco-Roman and Germanic elements in a distinctive blending.

The largest, most expansive, and most widely influential of the new third-wave civilizations was surely that of Islam. It began in Arabia in the seventh century C.E., projecting the Arab peoples into a prominent role as builders of an enormous empire while offering a new, vigorous, and attractive religion. As a new civilization defined by its religion, the world of Islam came to encompass many other centers of civilization, including Egypt, Mesopotamia, Persia, India, and Byzantium.

The persistence or reconstruction of already established civilizations represented yet another historical pattern during this third-wave era. The Byzantine Empire, embracing the eastern half of the old Roman Empire, continued the patterns of Mediterranean Christian civilization and persisted until 1453, when it was overrun by the Ottoman Turks. In China, following almost four centuries of fragmentation, the Sui, Tang, and Song dynasties (581–1279) restored China's imperial unity and reasserted its Confucian tradition. Indian civilization retained its ancient patterns of caste and religion amid vast cultural diversity, even as parts of India fell under the control of Muslim rulers.

Variations on this theme of continuing or renewing older traditions took shape in the Western Hemisphere. In Mesoamerica, the Mexica or Aztec people created a powerful and impressive state in the fifteenth century, drawing on earlier patterns of civilized life in that region. About the same time, on the western rim of South America, a Quechua-speaking people, now known as the Incas, incorporated various centers of Andean civilization into a huge bureaucratic empire. Both the Aztecs and the Incas gave a new expression to much older patterns of civilized life.

The Ties That Bind: Transregional Interaction in the Third-Wave Era

A second global pattern in the third-wave era involves heightened interaction among the world's various regions, cultures, and peoples. More than before, change in human societies was the product of contact with strangers, or at least with their ideas, armies, goods, or diseases. One vehicle for the interaction of culturally different peoples was long-distance trade, which grew considerably during the third-wave era: along the Silk Roads of Eurasia, within the Indian Ocean basin, across the Sahara, and along the Mississippi and other rivers. Everywhere it acted as an agent of change for all its participants. In places where such commerce was practiced extensively, it required that more people devote their energies to producing for a distant market rather than for consumption by their own communities. Those who controlled this kind of trade often became extremely wealthy, exciting envy or outrage among those less fortunate. Such exchange among distant lands also had political consequences, as many new states or empires were constructed on the basis of resources derived from long-distance commerce.

Yet another mechanism of cross-cultural interaction lay in large empires. Not only did they incorporate many distinct cultures within a single political system, but their size and stability also provided the security that encouraged travelers and traders to journey long distances from their homelands. Empires, of course, were nothing new in world history, but those of the third-wave era were larger. The Arab Empire, which accompanied the initial spread of Islam, stretched from Spain to India. Even more extensive was the Mongol Empire of the thirteenth and fourteenth centuries. In the Western Hemisphere, the Inca Empire encompassed dozens of distinct peoples in a huge state that ran some 2,500 miles along the spine of the Andes Mountains. Furthermore,

the largest of these empires were the creation of nomadic or pastoral peoples, while earlier empires in the Mediterranean basin, China, India, and Persia had been the work of settled farming societies.

Together, large-scale empires and long-distance trade gave rise to cosmopolitan urban centers such as Baghdad in what is now Iraq, Dunhuang in western China, Timbuktu in West Africa, and Malacca in Southeast Asia, where people of various backgrounds mixed and mingled. Conquest and commerce likewise facilitated the spread of ideas, technologies, food crops, and disease far beyond their points of origin. Thus Islam became an Afro-Eurasian phenomenon with an enormous reach. Chinese silk-making technology became available in Korea, Japan, the Middle East, and later in Europe. Corn gradually diffused from Mesoamerica to North America, where it stimulated population growth and the development of more complex societies. The plague, or Black Death, decimated many parts of Eurasia and North Africa as it made its deadly way from east to west in the fourteenth century.

Much of the readily visible "action" in the third-wave era, as in all earlier civilizations, featured male actors. The vast majority of rulers, traders, soldiers, religious officials, and long-distance travelers were men, as were most heads of households and families. The building of states and empires, so prominent in the third-wave era, meant war and conquest, fostering distinctly masculine warrior values and reinforcing the dominant position of men. Much of what follows in Part 3 is, frankly, men's history.

But behind all of this lay a vast realm of women's activity, long invisible to historians or simply assumed. Women sustained the family life that was the foundation of all human community; they were the repositories of language, religious ritual, group knowledge, and local history; their labor generated many of the products that entered long-distance trade routes as well as those that fed and clothed their communities. The changing roles and relationships of men and women and their understandings of gender also figure in the chapters that follow.

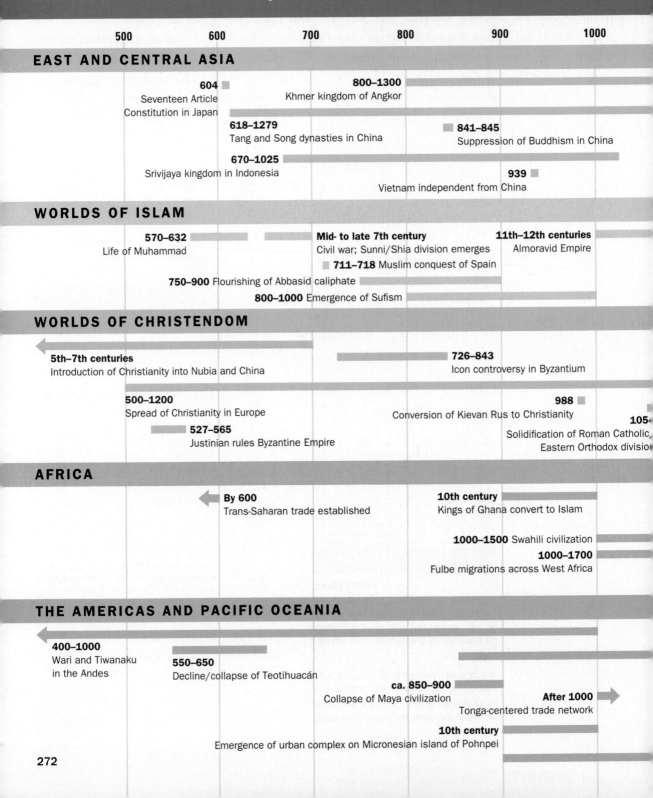

1100   1200   1300   1400   1500

1370–1405
Timur's conquests

1405–1433
Ming dynasty maritime
expeditions in Indian Ocean

1162–1227
Life of Chinggis Khan; beginning
of Mongol conquests

1207–1368
Mongol conquest/rule in China

1099
Crusaders seize
Jerusalem

1206
Delhi sultanate established in India

1258 Mongols sack Baghdad

1453
Ottoman Empire
conquers Constantinople

1095–ca. 1300
Crusades to the Holy Land

12th century
Christian Ethiopia constructs
monolithic churches at Lalibela

1453
Ottoman Turks take Constantinople;
end of Byzantine Empire

1204
Crusaders sack
Constantinople

1237–1480 Mongol rule in Russia

1347–1350
Black Death in Europe

1492
Columbus crosses the Atlantic;
Christian reconquest of Muslim Spain completed

12th century
Construction of rock-hewn churches
in Lalibela, Ethiopia

1324–1325
High point of Kingdom of Mali; Mansa Musa
pilgrimage to Mecca

1250–1350 Kingdom of Zimbabwe

15th century
African contact with Portuguese and Chinese maritime voyages

1200
Human occupation of New Zealand; extinction of large flightless birds

860–1130
Chaco culture among the Ancestral Pueblo

15th century
Flourishing of Aztec and Inca empires

900–1250 Flourishing of Cahokia chiefdom

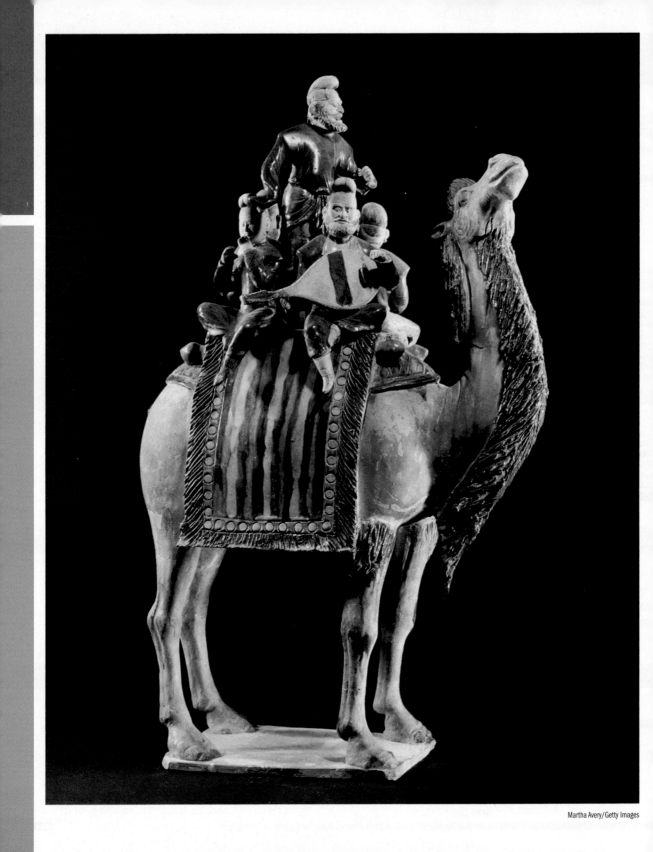

CHAPTER

7

Commerce and Culture

600–1450

Silk Roads: Exchange across Eurasia
 The Growth of the Silk Roads
 Goods in Transit
 Cultures in Transit
 Disease in Transit

Sea Roads: Exchange across the Indian Ocean
 Weaving the Web of an Indian Ocean World
 Sea Roads as a Catalyst for Change: Southeast Asia
 Sea Roads as a Catalyst for Change: East Africa

Sand Roads: Exchange across the Sahara
 Commercial Beginnings in West Africa
 Gold, Salt, and Slaves: Trade and Empire in West Africa

An American Network: Commerce and Connection in the Western Hemisphere

Reflections: Economic Globalization—Ancient and Modern

"In the spring of 2004, I was looking for an appropriate college graduation present for my son Ateesh and decided on an Apple iPod music player. . . . I placed my order online. . . . I was astonished by what followed. I received a confirmation e-mail within minutes . . . [and learned that] the product was being shipped . . . from Shanghai, China. . . . Ateesh's personalized iPod landed on our New Haven [Connecticut] doorstep barely 40 hours after I had clicked 'Buy.'"[1] To Nayan Chanda, a fifty-eight-year-old journalist, born and educated in India and at the time working at Yale University, this was an astonishing transaction. Probably it was less surprising to his son. But both of them, no doubt, understood this kind of commercial exchange as something quite recent in human history.

And in the speed of the transaction, it surely was. But from the perspective of world history, exchange among distant peoples is not altogether new, and the roots of economic globalization lie deep in the past. In fact, just three years after purchasing his son's iPod, Nayan Chanda wrote a well-received book titled *Bound Together*, describing how traders, preachers, adventurers, and warriors had long created links among peoples living in widely separated cultures and civilizations. Those early transregional interactions and their capacity for transforming human societies, for better and for worse, played an increasingly significant role in this era of third-wave civilizations. ■

《 Travels on the Silk Roads This Chinese ceramic figurine from the Tang dynasty (618–907 c.e.) shows a group of musicians riding on a camel along the famous Silk Road commercial network that long linked the civilizations of western and eastern Eurasia. The bearded figures represent Central Asian merchants, while the others depict Chinese.

The exchange of goods among communities occupying different ecological zones has long been a prominent feature of human history. Coastlands and

275

highlands, steppes and farmlands, islands and mainlands, valleys and mountains, deserts and forests—each generates different products. Furthermore, some societies have been able to monopolize, at least temporarily, the production of particular goods—such as silk in China, certain spices in Southeast Asia, and incense in southern Arabia—that others have found valuable. This uneven distribution of goods and resources has long motivated exchange, not only within particular civilizations or regions but among them as well. In the world of 600 to 1450, long-distance trade became more important than ever before in linking and shaping distant societies and peoples. For the most part, it was indirect, a chain of separate transactions in which goods traveled farther than individual merchants. Nonetheless, a network of exchange and communication extending all across the Afro-Eurasian world, and separately in parts of the Americas as well, slowly came into being.

Such commerce shaped the daily life of many millions. It altered habits of consumption; for example, West Africans imported scarce salt, so necessary for seasoning and preserving food, from distant mines in the Sahara in exchange for the gold of their region. Incense grown in southern Arabia found eager consumers all across the ancient Eurasian world, where it was used for medicinal purposes, for religious ceremonies, and as an antidote to the odors of unsanitary cities. Incense also bore the "aroma of eros." "I have perfumed my bed with myrrh, aloes, and cinnamon," declared a harlot featured in the Old Testament book of Proverbs. "Come, let us take our fill of love till morning."[2]

Trade also affected the working lives of many people, encouraging them to specialize in producing particular products for sale in distant markets rather than for use in their own communities. Merchants often became a distinct social group, viewed with suspicion by others because of their impulse to accumulate wealth without actually producing anything themselves. In some societies, trade became a means of social mobility, as Chinese merchants, for example, were able to purchase landed estates and establish themselves within the gentry class. Long-distance trade also enabled elite groups in society to distinguish themselves from commoners by acquiring prestigious goods from a distance—silk, tortoiseshell, jade, rhinoceros horn, or particular feathers. Trade also had the capacity to transform political life. The wealth available from controlling and taxing trade motivated the creation of states in various parts of the world and sustained those states once they had been constructed. Furthermore, commerce posed a set of problems to governments everywhere. Should trade be left in private hands, as in the Aztec Empire, or should it be controlled by the state, as in the Inca Empire? How should state authorities deal with men of commerce, who were both economically useful and potentially disruptive?

Moreover, the saddlebags of camel caravans or the cargo holds of merchant vessels carried more than goods. Trade became a vehicle for the spread of religious ideas, technological innovations, disease-bearing germs, and plants and animals to regions far from their places of origin. In this fashion, Buddhism made its way from India

Landmarks for Chapter 7

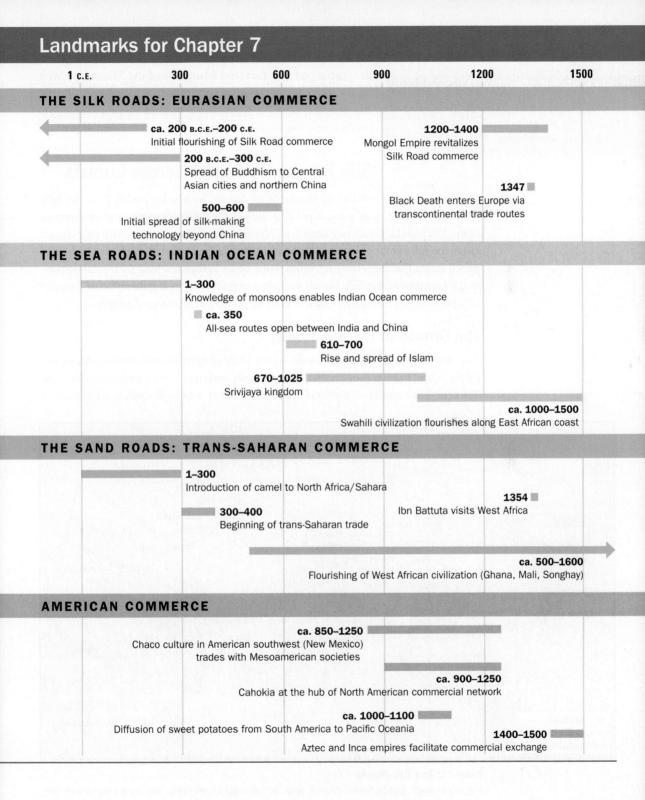

1 C.E.　300　600　900　1200　1500

THE SILK ROADS: EURASIAN COMMERCE

ca. 200 B.C.E.–200 C.E.
Initial flourishing of Silk Road commerce

1200–1400
Mongol Empire revitalizes
Silk Road commerce

200 B.C.E.–300 C.E.
Spread of Buddhism to Central
Asian cities and northern China

1347
Black Death enters Europe via
transcontinental trade routes

500–600
Initial spread of silk-making
technology beyond China

THE SEA ROADS: INDIAN OCEAN COMMERCE

1–300
Knowledge of monsoons enables Indian Ocean commerce

ca. 350
All-sea routes open between India and China

610–700
Rise and spread of Islam

670–1025
Srivijaya kingdom

ca. 1000–1500
Swahili civilization flourishes along East African coast

THE SAND ROADS: TRANS-SAHARAN COMMERCE

1–300
Introduction of camel to North Africa/Sahara

1354
Ibn Battuta visits West Africa

300–400
Beginning of trans-Saharan trade

ca. 500–1600
Flourishing of West African civilization (Ghana, Mali, Songhay)

AMERICAN COMMERCE

ca. 850–1250
Chaco culture in American southwest (New Mexico)
trades with Mesoamerican societies

ca. 900–1250
Cahokia at the hub of North American commercial network

ca. 1000–1100
Diffusion of sweet potatoes from South America to Pacific Oceania

1400–1500
Aztec and Inca empires facilitate commercial exchange

to Central and East Asia, and Islam crossed the Sahara into West
Africa. The pathogens that devastated much of Eurasia during the
Black Death, as well as technologies of gunpowder, printing, and
much more, also traversed the trade routes of the third-wave era.

Silk Roads: Exchange across Eurasia

The most famous of those networks of exchange, widely known now as the **Silk
Roads** after their most famous product, linked the various peoples and civilizations
of the Eurasian landmass (see Map 7.1). None of this network's numerous participants
knew the full extent of its reach, for it was largely a "relay trade" in which goods were
passed down the line, changing hands many times before reaching their final destination. Nonetheless, the Silk Roads provide a certain unity and coherence to Eurasian
history alongside the distinct stories of its separate civilizations and peoples.

The Growth of the Silk Roads

The beginnings of the Silk Roads lay in both geography and history. As a geographic unit, Eurasia is often divided into inner and outer zones that represent quite
different environments. Outer Eurasia consists of relatively warm, well-watered

Map 7.1 The Silk Roads
For 2,000 years, goods, ideas, technologies, and diseases made their way across Eurasia on the
several routes of the Silk Roads.

areas, suitable for agriculture, which provided the setting for the great civilizations of China, India, the Middle East, and the Mediterranean. Inner Eurasia—the lands of eastern Russia and Central Asia—lies farther north and has a harsher and drier climate, much of it not conducive to agriculture. Herding their animals from horseback, the pastoral people of this region had for centuries traded with and raided their agricultural neighbors to the south. Products of the forest and of semi-arid northern grasslands known as the steppes—such as hides, furs, livestock, wool, and amber—were exchanged for the agricultural products and manufactured goods of adjacent civilizations. The movement of pastoral peoples for thousands of years also served to diffuse Indo-European languages, bronze metallurgy, horse-based technologies, and more all across Eurasia.

The construction of the second-wave civilizations and their imperial states during the last five centuries B.C.E. clearly enhanced these ancient patterns of exchange. From the south, the Persian Empire invaded the territory of pastoral peoples in present-day Turkmenistan and Uzbekistan. From the west, Alexander the Great's empire stretched well into Central Asia. From the east, China's Han dynasty extended its authority westward, seeking to control the nomadic Xiongnu and to gain access to their horses, a distinctive Central Asian breed known to the Chinese as "heavenly horses" that had become important to Chinese military forces. By the early centuries of the Common Era, indirect trading connections, often brokered by pastoral peoples, linked these Eurasian civilizations in a network of transcontinental commerce.

Silk Road trading networks prospered most when large and powerful states provided relative security for merchants and travelers across long distances. Such conditions prevailed during the second-wave era when the Roman and Chinese empires anchored long-distance commerce at the western and eastern ends of Eurasia. Silk Road trade flourished again during the seventh and eighth centuries C.E. as the Byzantine Empire, the Muslim Abbasid (ah-BAH-sihd) dynasty, and Tang dynasty China created an almost continuous belt of strong states across Eurasia. In the thirteenth and fourteenth centuries, the Mongol Empire briefly encompassed almost the entire route of the Silk Roads in a single state, giving a renewed vitality to long-distance trade. Over many centuries, various technological innovations, such as yokes, saddles, and stirrups, made the use of camels, horses, and oxen more effective means of transportation across the vast distances of the Silk Roads.

Goods in Transit

During prosperous times especially, a vast array of goods (detailed in the Snapshot on page 280) made its way across the Silk Roads, often carried in large camel caravans that traversed the harsh and dangerous steppes, deserts, and oases of Central Asia. Most of these goods were luxury products destined for an elite and wealthy market, rather than staple goods, for only readily moved commodities of great value could compensate for the high costs of transportation across such long and forbidding distances.

Guided Reading Question

■ **CHANGE**
What lay behind the emergence of Silk Road commerce, and what kept it going for so many centuries?

SNAPSHOT Economic Exchange Along the Silk Roads

Region	Products Contributed to Silk Road Commerce
China	silk, bamboo, mirrors, gunpowder, paper, rhubarb, ginger, lacquerware, chrysanthemums
Forest lands of Siberia and grasslands of Central Asia	furs, walrus tusks, amber, livestock, horses, falcons, hides, copper vessels, tents, saddles, slaves
India	cotton textiles, herbal medicine, precious stones, spices, pepper, pearls, ebony
Middle East	dates, nuts, dried fruit, dyes, lapis lazuli, swords
Mediterranean basin	gold coins, glassware, glazes, grapevines, jewelry, artworks, perfume, wool and linen textiles, olive oil

It was silk that came to symbolize this Eurasian network of exchange. From the time of silk's origin in China, by 3000 B.C.E. or earlier, that civilization long held a monopoly on its production. After 300 B.C.E. or so, the precious fabric increasingly found a growing market all across the linked commercial network of the Afro-Eurasian world. Although the silk trade itself was largely in the hands of men, women figured hugely in the process in terms of both supply and demand. For many centuries, Chinese women, mostly in rural areas, were responsible for every step of the ingenious and laborious enterprise of silk production. They tended the mulberry trees on whose leaves silkworms fed; they unwound the cocoons in very hot water to extract the long silk fibers; they turned these fibers into thread and wove them into textiles. Thus Chinese homes became the primary site of textile production, with rural women as its main labor force. By the time of the Tang dynasty (618–907 C.E.), women were making a large contribution to the household economy, to technological innovation in the silk industry, and to the state, which depended heavily on peasant taxes, often paid in cloth. Nonetheless, many rural families persisted in poverty, as the thirteenth-century writer Wen-hsiang indicated:

> The silkworms have finished their third sleep and are famished. The family is poor, without cash to buy the mulberry leaves to feed them. What can they do? Hungry silkworms do not produce silk. . . . The daughter is twenty but does not have wedding clothes. Those the government sends to collect taxes are like tigers. If they have no clothes to dress their daughter, they can put the [wedding] off. If they have no silk to turn over to the government, they will go bankrupt.[3]

Guided Reading Question

■ **SIGNIFICANCE**
What made silk such a highly desired commodity across Eurasia?

Elite Chinese women, and their men as well, also furnished part of the demand for these luxurious fabrics, which marked their high status. So too did Chinese officials, who required huge quantities of silk to exchange for much-needed horses and to buy off "barbarian" invaders from the north. Beyond China, women in many cultures ardently sought Chinese silk for its comfort and its value as a fashion statement. The demand for silk, as well as for cotton textiles from India, was so great in the Roman Empire that various Roman writers were appalled at the drain of resources that it represented. They also were outraged at the moral impact of wearing revealing silk garments. "I can see clothes of silk," lamented Seneca the Younger in the first century C.E., "if materials that do not hide the body, nor even one's decency, can be called clothes. . . . Wretched flocks of maids labour so that the adulteress may be visible through her thin dress, so that her husband has no more acquaintance than any outsider or foreigner with his wife's body."[4]

By the sixth century C.E., the knowledge and technology for producing raw silk had spread beyond China. An old Chinese story attributes it to a Chinese princess who smuggled out silkworms in her turban when she was married off to a Central Asian ruler. However it happened, artisans in Korea, Japan, India, Persia, and the Byzantine Empire likewise learned how to produce this precious fabric.

As the supply of silk increased, its many varieties circulated even more extensively across Afro-Eurasian trade routes. In Central Asia, silk was used as currency and as a means of accumulating wealth. In both China and the Byzantine Empire, silk became a symbol of high status, and governments passed laws that restricted silk clothing to members of the elite. Furthermore, silk became associated with the sacred in the expanding world religions of Buddhism and Christianity. Chinese Buddhist pilgrims who made their way to India seeking religious texts and relics took with them large quantities of silk as gifts to the monasteries they visited. Buddhist monks in China received purple silk robes from Tang dynasty emperors as a sign of high honor. In the world of Christendom, silk wall hangings, altar covers, and vestments became highly prestigious signs of devotion and piety. Because no independent silk industry developed in Western Europe until the twelfth century C.E., a considerable market developed for silks imported from the Islamic world. Ironically, the splendor of Christian churches depended in part on Islamic trading networks and on silks manufactured in the Muslim world. Some of those silks were even inscribed with passages in Arabic from the Quran, unbeknownst to their European buyers.[5] By the twelfth century, the West African king of Ghana was wearing silk, and that fabric circulated in Egypt, Ethiopia, and along the East African coast as well.

A Muslim Silk Hanging in a Christian Cathedral This thirteenth-century silk hanging, created in the Islamic world, found a home in the Christian cathedral of Barcelona in Spain, illustrating that this precious fabric moved between civilizations. Around the seated figures is the text of the essential Muslim affirmation: "There is no God but God." (Werner Forman/Getty Images)

Guided Reading
Question
....
■ **CONNECTION**
What were the major
economic, social, and
cultural consequences
of Silk Road commerce?

Compared to contemporary global commerce, the volume of trade on the Silk Roads was modest, and its focus on luxury goods limited its direct impact on most people. Nonetheless, it had important economic and social consequences. Peasants in the Yangzi River delta of southern China sometimes gave up the cultivation of food crops, choosing to focus instead on producing silk, paper, porcelain, lacquerware, or iron tools, many of which were destined for the markets of the Silk Roads. In this way, the impact of long-distance trade trickled down to affect the lives of ordinary farmers. Furthermore, merchants could benefit immensely from their involvement in long-distance trade. One such individual, a twelfth-century Persian trader named Ramisht whose ships traversed the Indian Ocean and Red Sea, made a personal fortune with which he commissioned an enormously expensive covering made of Chinese silk for the Kaaba, the central shrine of Islam in Mecca.

Cultures in Transit

More important even than the economic impact of the Silk Roads was their role as a conduit of culture. Buddhism in particular, a cultural product of Indian civilization, spread widely throughout Central and East Asia, owing much to the activities of merchants along the Silk Roads. From its beginnings in India during the sixth century B.C.E., Buddhism had appealed to merchants, who preferred its universal message to that of a Brahmin-dominated Hinduism that privileged the higher castes. Indian traders and Buddhist monks, sometimes supported by rulers such as Ashoka, brought the new religion to the trans-Eurasian trade routes. To the west, Persian Zoroastrianism largely blocked the spread of Buddhism, but in the oasis cities of Central Asia, such as Merv, Samarkand, Khotan, and Dunhuang, Buddhism quickly took hold. By the first century B.C.E., many of the inhabitants of these towns had converted to Buddhism, and foreign merchant communities soon introduced it to northern China as well.

Guided Reading
Question
....
■ **CHANGE**
What accounted for the
spread of Buddhism
along the Silk Roads?

Particularly important in this process were the Sogdians, a Central Asian people whose merchants established an enduring network of exchange with China. Two such Sogdians living in China during the second century C.E. were instrumental in translating Sanskrit Buddhist texts into Chinese. Sogdians dominated Silk Road trade for much of the first millennium C.E., and their language became a medium of communication all along that commercial network.

Conversion to Buddhism in the oasis cities was a voluntary process, without the pressure of conquest or foreign rule. Dependent on long-distance trade, the inhabitants and rulers of those sophisticated and prosperous cities found in Buddhism a link to the larger, wealthy, and prestigious civilization of India. Well-to-do Buddhist merchants could earn religious merit by building monasteries and supporting monks. The monasteries in turn provided convenient and culturally familiar places of rest and resupply for merchants making the long and arduous trek across Central Asia. Many of these cities became cosmopolitan centers of learning and commerce.

Dunhuang Located in western China at a critical junction of the Silk Road trading network, Dunhuang was also a center of Buddhist learning, painting, and sculpture as that religion made its way from India to China and beyond. In some 492 caves, carved out of the rock between about 400 and 1400 C.E., a remarkable gallery of Buddhist art has been preserved. In this image the Buddha is surrounded by other enlightened beings or bodhisattvas. (Steve Vidler/Prisma by Dukas Presseagentur GmbH/Alamy)

Thousands of Buddhist texts, together with hundreds of cave temples lavishly decorated with murals and statues, have been discovered in the city of Dunhuang, where several branches of the Silk Roads joined to enter western China.

Outside of the oasis communities, Buddhism progressed only slowly among pastoral peoples of Central Asia. The absence of a written language was an obstacle to the penetration of a highly literate religion, and pastoralists' nomadic ways made the founding of monasteries, so important to Buddhism, quite difficult. But as pastoralists became involved in long-distance trade or came to rule settled agricultural peoples, Buddhism seemed more attractive. The nomadic Jie people, who controlled much of northern China after the collapse of the Han dynasty, are a case in point. Their ruler in the early fourth century C.E., Shi Le, became acquainted with a Central Asian Buddhist monk called Fotudeng who had traveled widely on the Silk Roads. The monk's reputation as a miracle worker, a rainmaker, and a fortune-teller and his skills as a military strategist cemented a personal relationship with Shi Le and led to the conversions of thousands and the construction of hundreds of Buddhist temples. In China itself, Buddhism remained for many centuries a religion of foreign merchants or foreign rulers. Only slowly did it become popular among the Chinese themselves, a process examined more closely in Chapter 8.

As Buddhism spread across the Silk Roads from India to Central Asia, China, and beyond, it also changed. The original faith had shunned the material world, but Buddhist monasteries in the rich oasis towns of the Silk Roads found themselves very much involved in secular affairs. Some of them became quite prosperous, receiving gifts from well-to-do merchants, artisans, and local rulers. The begging bowls of the monks became a symbol rather than a daily activity. Sculptures and murals in the monasteries depicted musicians and acrobats, women applying makeup, and even drinking parties, all of which suggested a more wealthy and worldly style of living, far removed from traditions of Buddhist asceticism.

Doctrines changed as well. It was the more devotional Mahayana form of Buddhism (see Chapter 4)—featuring the Buddha as a deity, numerous bodhisattvas, an emphasis on compassion, and the possibility of earning merit—that flourished on the Silk Roads, rather than the more austere psychological teachings of the historical Buddha. Moreover, Buddhism picked up elements of other cultures while in transit on the Silk Roads. In the Sogdian city of Samarkand, the use of Zoroastrian fire rituals apparently became a part of Buddhist practice. And in the area northwest of India that had been influenced by the invasions of Alexander the Great, statues of the Buddha reveal distinctly Greek and Roman influences in dress and physical features. In a similar way, the gods of many peoples along the Silk Roads were incorporated into Buddhist practice as bodhisattvas.

Disease in Transit

Beyond goods and cultures, diseases too traveled the trade routes of Eurasia, and with devastating consequences. Each of the major population centers of the Afro-Eurasian world had developed characteristic disease patterns, mechanisms for dealing with them, and in some cases immunity to them. But when contact among previously isolated human communities occurred, people were exposed to unfamiliar diseases for which they had little immunity or few effective methods of coping. The epidemics that followed often brought suffering and death on an enormous scale to rich and poor alike. An early example involved the Greek city-state of Athens, which in 430–429 B.C.E. was suddenly afflicted by a new and still-unidentified infectious disease that had entered Greece via seaborne trade from Egypt, killing perhaps 25 percent of its army and permanently weakening the city-state.

Even more widespread diseases affected the Roman Empire and Han dynasty China as the Silk Roads promoted contact all across Eurasia, particularly from the second century C.E. on. Smallpox, measles, various forms of plague, and perhaps malaria devastated the populations of both empires, contributing to their political collapse. Paradoxically, such disasters may well have strengthened the appeal of Christianity in Europe and Buddhism in China, for both of them offered compassion in the face of immense suffering.

Again in the period between 534 and 750 C.E., intermittent outbreaks of bubonic plague ravaged the coastal areas of the Mediterranean Sea. One leading theory suggests

Guided Reading Question

■ **CONNECTION**

What was the impact of disease along the Silk Roads?

that black rats and the infected fleas they bore carried the disease via the seaborne trade with India, Ethiopia, and Egypt. What followed was catastrophic. Constantinople, the capital city of the Byzantine Empire, lost thousands of people per day during a forty-day period in 534 C.E., according to a contemporary historian. The repeated recurrence of the disease over the next several centuries also weakened the ability of Christendom to resist Muslim armies from Arabia in the seventh century C.E.

The most well-known dissemination of disease was associated with the Mongol Empire, which briefly unified much of the Eurasian landmass during the thirteenth and fourteenth centuries C.E. (see "The Plague: An Afro-Eurasian Pandemic" in Chapter 11). That era of intensified interaction facilitated the spread of the **Black Death** — identified variously with the bubonic plague, anthrax, or a package of epidemic diseases — from China to Europe. Its consequences were enormous. Between 1346 and 1348, up to half of the population of Europe perished from the plague. "A dead man," wrote the Italian writer Boccaccio, "was then of no more account than a dead goat."[6] A similar death toll afflicted China and parts of the Islamic world. The Central Asian steppes, home to many nomadic peoples, including the Mongols, also suffered terribly, undermining Mongol rule and permanently altering the balance between pastoral and agricultural peoples to the advantage of settled farmers. In these and many other ways, disease carried by long-distance trade shaped the lives of millions and altered the historical development of entire civilizations.

In the long run of world history, the exchange of diseases gave Europeans a certain advantage when they confronted the peoples of the Western Hemisphere after 1500. Exposure over time had provided them with some degree of immunity to Eurasian diseases. In the Americas, however, the absence of domesticated animals, the less intense interaction among major centers of population, and isolation from the Eastern Hemisphere ensured that native peoples had little defense against the diseases of Europe and Africa. Thus, when their societies were suddenly confronted by Europeans and Africans from across the Atlantic, they perished in appalling numbers. Such was the long-term outcome of the very different histories of the two hemispheres.

Sea Roads: Exchange across the Indian Ocean

If the Silk Roads linked Eurasian societies by land, sea-based trade routes likewise connected distant peoples all across the Eastern Hemisphere. Since the days of the Phoenicians, Greeks, and Romans, the Mediterranean Sea had been an avenue of maritime commerce throughout the region, a pattern that continued during the third-wave era. The Italian city of Venice emerged by 1000 C.E. as a major center of that commercial network, with its ships and merchants active in the Mediterranean and Black seas as well as on the Atlantic coast. Much of its wealth derived from control of expensive and profitable imported goods from Asia, many of which came up the Red Sea through the Egyptian port of Alexandria. There Venetian merchants picked up those goods and resold them throughout the Mediterranean basin. This type of transregional exchange linked the maritime commerce of the

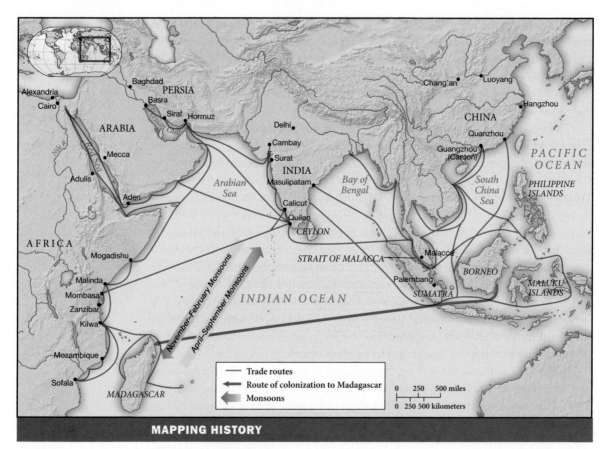

MAPPING HISTORY

Map 7.2 The Sea Roads

Paralleling the Silk Road trading network, a sea-based commerce in the Indian Ocean basin connected the many peoples between China and East Africa.

READING THE MAP: If a captain wanted to sail from Malindi on the east coast of Africa to Calicut in southern India, what months in the monsoon season would give favorable winds?

MAKING CONNECTIONS: Compare this map with Map 7.1: The Silk Roads. Where do the Silk and Sea Roads intersect? What different geographical obstacles might travelers or traders confront on these two routes?

Mediterranean Sea to the much larger and more extensive network of seaborne trade in the Indian Ocean basin.

Until the creation of a genuinely global oceanic system of trade after 1500, the Indian Ocean represented the world's largest sea-based system of communication and exchange, stretching from southern China to eastern Africa (see Map 7.2). Like the Silk Roads, these transoceanic trade routes — the **Sea Roads** — grew out of the vast environmental and cultural diversities of the region. The desire for various goods not available at home — such as porcelain from China, spices from the islands of Southeast Asia (present-day Indonesia), cotton goods and pepper from India, ivory and gold from the East African coast, incense from southern

Arabia—provided incentives for Indian Ocean commerce. Transportation costs were lower on the Sea Roads than on the Silk Roads because ships could accommodate larger and heavier cargoes than camels. Thus the Sea Roads could eventually carry more bulk goods and products destined for a mass market—textiles, pepper, timber, rice, sugar, wheat—whereas the Silk Roads were limited largely to luxury goods for the few.

What made Indian Ocean commerce possible were the monsoons, alternating wind currents that blew predictably northeast during the summer months and southwest during the winter (see Map 7.2). An understanding of monsoons and a gradually accumulating technology of shipbuilding and oceanic navigation drew on the ingenuity of many peoples—Chinese, Malays, Indians, Arabs, Swahilis, and others. Collectively they made "an interlocked human world joined by the common highway of the Indian Ocean."[7]

But this world of Indian Ocean commerce did not involve exchanges between entire regions and certainly not between "countries," even though historians sometimes write about India, Indonesia, Southeast Asia, or East Africa as a matter of convenience. It operated rather across a network of towns and cities whose merchants often had more in common with one another than with the people of their own hinterlands.[8] These urban centers, strung out around the entire Indian Ocean basin, provided the nodes of this widespread commercial network.

Weaving the Web of an Indian Ocean World

The world of Indian Ocean commerce was long in the making, dating back to the time of the First Civilizations. Archeological finds in both Mesopotamia and India have disclosed seaborne trade via the Persian Gulf between ancient Mesopotamia and the Indus Valley civilization. The ancient Egyptians, and later the Phoenicians, likewise traded down the Red Sea, exchanging their manufactured goods for gold, ivory, frankincense, and slaves from the coasts of Ethiopia, Somalia, and southern Arabia. These ventures mostly hugged the coast and took place over short distances. Malay sailors, however, jumped off from the islands of present-day Indonesia during the first millennium B.C.E. and made their way in double-outrigger canoes across thousands of miles of open ocean to the East African island of Madagascar. There they introduced their Austronesian language and their crops—bananas, coconuts, and taro—which soon spread to the mainland, where they greatly enriched the diets of African peoples.

An Arab Dhow Painted by the thirteenth-century Arab artist Al-Wasiti, this image shows an oceangoing vessel of Indian or Arab origin known as a *dhow*, which was central to the commerce of the Sea Roads. In use in the Red Sea and Indian Ocean since at least the early centuries of the Common Era, dhows used triangular sails and were constructed by sewing or stitching the boards of the hull together with fibers, cords, or thongs without nails. (Miniature from the "Maqam" or "Assembly" illustrated by Yahya ibn Mahmud al-Wasiti, 1237/Pictures from History/Bridgeman Images)

SNAPSHOT Economic Exchange in the Indian Ocean Basin

Region	Products Contributed to Indian Ocean Commerce
Mediterranean basin	ceramics, glassware, wine, gold, olive oil
East Africa	ivory, gold, iron goods, slaves, tortoiseshells, quartz, leopard skins
Arabia	frankincense, myrrh, perfumes
India	grain, ivory, precious stones, cotton textiles, spices, timber, tortoiseshells
Southeast Asia	tin, sandalwood, cloves, nutmeg, mace
China	silks, porcelain, tea

The tempo of Indian Ocean commerce picked up during the early centuries of the Common Era, as mariners learned how to ride the monsoons. Various technological innovations also facilitated Indian Ocean trade — improvements in sails, new kinds of ships such as Chinese *junks* and Indian or Arab *dhows*, new means of calculating latitude such as the astrolabe, and evolving versions of the magnetic needle or compass. Merchants from the Roman world, mostly Greeks, Syrians, and Jews, established settlements in southern India and along the East African coast. The introduction of Christianity into both Axum and Kerala (in southern India) testifies to the long-term cultural impact of that trade. In the eastern Indian Ocean and the South China Sea, Chinese and Southeast Asian merchants likewise generated a growing commerce, and by 100 C.E. Chinese traders had reached India.

The fulcrum of this growing commercial network lay in India itself. Its ports bulged with goods from both west and east, as illustrated in the Snapshot above. Its merchants were in touch with Southeast Asia by the first century C.E., and settled communities of Indian traders appeared throughout the Indian Ocean basin and as far away as Alexandria in Egypt. Indian cultural practices such as Hinduism and Buddhism, as well as South Asian political ideas, began to take root in Southeast Asia.

Guided Reading Question

■ CHANGE
What lay behind the flourishing of Indian Ocean commerce in the postclassical millennium?

In the era of third-wave civilizations between 600 and 1450, two major processes changed the landscape of the Afro-Eurasian world and wove the web of Indian Ocean exchange even more densely than before. One was the economic and political revival of China, some four centuries after the collapse of the Han dynasty (see Chapter 8). Especially during the Tang and Song dynasties (618–1279), China reestablished an effective and unified state, which actively encouraged maritime trade. China's population shifted southward along with many of the most productive parts of the commercial economy, which grew impressively during this period. This geographic shift led to the expansion of Chinese maritime trade as Chinese products poured out of southern port towns into the circuits of Indian Ocean commerce, even as the thriving Chinese economy attracted goods from India and

Southeast Asia. Chinese technological innovations, such as larger ships and the magnetic compass, likewise added to the momentum of commercial growth.

A second transformation in the world of Indian Ocean commerce involved the sudden rise of Islam in the seventh century C.E. and its subsequent spread across much of the Afro-Eurasian world (see Chapter 9). Unlike Confucian culture, which was quite suspicious of merchants, Islam was friendly to commercial life; the Prophet Muhammad himself had been a trader. The creation of an Arab Empire, stretching from the Atlantic Ocean through the Mediterranean basin and all the way to India, brought together in a single political system an immense range of economies and cultural traditions and provided a vast arena for the energies of Muslim traders.

Those energies greatly intensified commercial activity in the Indian Ocean basin. Middle Eastern gold and silver flowed into southern India to purchase pepper, pearls, textiles, and gemstones. Muslim merchants and sailors, as well as Jews and Christians living within the Islamic world, established communities of traders from East Africa to the south China coast. Efforts to reclaim wasteland in Mesopotamia to produce sugar and dates for export stimulated a slave trade from East Africa, which landed thousands of Africans in southern Iraq to work on plantations and in salt mines under horrendous conditions. A massive fifteen-year revolt (868–883) among these slaves badly disrupted the Islamic Abbasid Empire before that rebellion was brutally crushed.

Beyond these specific outcomes, the expansion of Islam gave rise to an international maritime culture by 1000, shared by individuals living in the widely separated port cities around the Indian Ocean. The immense prestige, power, and prosperity of the Islamic world stimulated widespread conversion, which in turn facilitated commercial transactions. Even those who did not convert to Islam, such as Buddhist rulers in Burma, nonetheless regarded it as commercially useful to assume Muslim names. Thus was created "a maritime Silk Road . . . a commercial and informational network of unparalleled proportions."[9] After 1000, the culture of this network was increasingly Islamic.

Sea Roads as a Catalyst for Change: Southeast Asia

Oceanic commerce transformed all of its participants in one way or another, but nowhere more so than in Southeast Asia and East Africa, at opposite ends of the Indian Ocean network. In both regions, trade stimulated political change as ambitious or aspiring rulers used the wealth derived from commerce to construct larger and more centrally governed states or cities. Both areas likewise experienced cultural change as local people were attracted to foreign religious ideas from Confucian, Hindu, Buddhist, or Islamic sources. As on the Silk Roads, trade was a conduit for culture.

Located between the major civilizations of China and India, Southeast Asia was situated by geography to play an important role in the evolving world of Indian Ocean commerce. During the third-wave era, a series of cities and states or kingdoms

Guided Reading Question

■ **CONNECTION**

In what ways did Indian influence register in Southeast Asia?

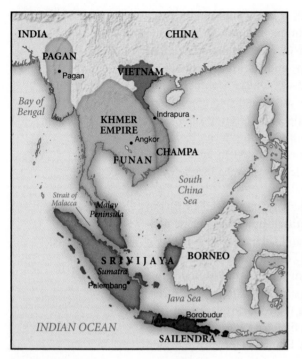

Map 7.3 Southeast Asia, ca. 1200 C.E.
Both mainland and island Southeast Asia were centrally involved in the commerce of the Indian Ocean basin, and both were transformed by that experience.

emerged on both the islands and mainland of Southeast Asia that represented new civilizations in this vast region (see Map 7.3). That process paralleled a similar development of new civilizations in East and West Africa, Japan, Russia, and Western Europe in what was an Afro-Eurasian phenomenon. In Southeast Asia, many of those new societies were stimulated and decisively shaped by their interaction with the sea-based trade of the Indian Ocean.[10]

The case of **Srivijaya** (SREE-vih-juh-yuh) illustrates the connection between commerce and state building. When Malay sailors, long active in the waters around Southeast Asia, opened an all-sea route between India and China through the Straits of Malacca around 350 C.E., the many small ports along the Malay Peninsula and the coast of Sumatra began to compete intensely to attract the growing number of traders and travelers making their way through the straits. From this competition emerged the Malay kingdom of Srivijaya, which dominated this critical choke point of Indian Ocean trade from 670 to 1025. A number of factors—Srivijaya's plentiful supply of gold; its access to the source of highly sought-after spices, such as cloves, nutmeg, and mace; and the taxes levied on passing ships—provided resources to attract supporters, to fund an embryonic bureaucracy, and to create the military and naval forces that brought some security to the area.

The inland states on the mainland of Southeast Asia, whose economies were based more on domestically produced rice than on international trade, nonetheless participated in the commerce of the region. The state of Funan, which flourished during the first six centuries of the Common Era in what is now southern Vietnam and eastern Cambodia, hosted merchants from both India and China. Archeologists have found Roman coins as well as trade goods from Persia, Central Asia, and Arabia in the ruins of its ancient cities. The Khmer kingdom of Angkor (flourished 800–1300) exported exotic forest products, receiving in return Chinese and Indian handicrafts, while welcoming a considerable community of Chinese merchants. Traders from Champa in what is now central and southern Vietnam operated in China, Java, and elsewhere, practicing piracy when trade dried up.

Beyond the exchange of goods, commercial connections served to spread elements of Indian culture across much of Southeast Asia, even as Vietnam was incorporated into the Chinese sphere of influence. (See "Vietnam and China" in Chapter 8.) Indian alphabets such as Sanskrit and Pallava were used to write a number of Southeast Asian languages. Indian artistic forms provided models for Southeast Asian sculpture and architecture, while the Indian epic *Ramayana* became widely popular across the region.

Borobudur This huge Buddhist monument in Java, constructed probably in the ninth century c.e., was later abandoned and covered with layers of volcanic ash and vegetation as Java came under Islamic influence. It was rediscovered by British colonial authorities in the early nineteenth century and has undergone several restorations over the past two centuries. Although Indonesia is a largely Muslim country, its small Buddhist minority still celebrates the Buddha's birthday at Borobudur. (Luca Tettoni/robertharding/Alamy)

Politically, Southeast Asian rulers and elites found attractive the Indian belief that leaders were god-kings, perhaps reincarnations of a Buddha or the Hindu deity Shiva. Srivijayan monarchs, for example, employed Indians as advisers, clerks, or officials and assigned Sanskrit titles to their subordinates. The capital city of Palembang was a cosmopolitan place, where even the parrots were said to speak four languages. While these rulers drew on indigenous beliefs that chiefs possessed magical powers and were responsible for the prosperity of their people, they also made use of imported Indian political ideas and Buddhist religious concepts, which provided a "higher level of magic" for rulers as well as the prestige of association with Indian civilization.[11] They also sponsored the creation of images of the Buddha and various bodhisattvas whose faces resembled those of deceased kings and were inscribed with traditional curses against anyone who would destroy them. Srivijaya grew into a major center of Buddhist observance and teaching, attracting thousands of monks and students from throughout the Buddhist world. The seventh-century Chinese monk Yi Jing was so impressed that he advised Buddhist monks headed for India to study first in Srivijaya for several years.

Elsewhere as well, elements of Indian culture took hold in Southeast Asia. The Sailendra kingdom in central Java, an agriculturally rich region closely allied with Srivijaya, mounted a massive building program between the eighth and tenth

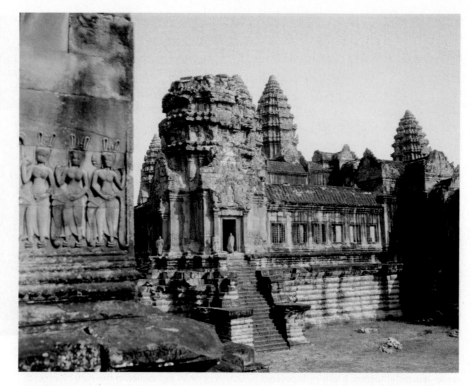

Angkor Wat Constructed in the early twelfth century, the Angkor Wat complex was designed as a state temple dedicated to the Hindu god Vishnu and was lavishly decorated with carved bas-reliefs depicting scenes from Hindu mythology. By the late thirteenth century, it was in use by Buddhists, as it is to this day. This photo shows a small section of the temple and three Buddhist monks in their saffron robes. (Jose Fuste Raga/ Getty Images)

centuries featuring Hindu temples and Buddhist monuments. The most famous, known as Borobudur, is an enormous mountain-shaped structure of ten levels, with a three-mile walkway and elaborate carvings illustrating the spiritual journey from ignorance and illusion to full enlightenment. The largest Buddhist monument any-where in the world, it is nonetheless a distinctly Javanese creation, whose carved figures have Javanese features and whose scenes are clearly set in Java, not India. Its shape resonated with an ancient Southeast Asian veneration of mountains as sacred places and the abode of ancestral spirits. Borobudur represents the process of Buddhism becoming culturally grounded in a new place.

Hinduism too, though not an explicitly missionary religion, found a place in Southeast Asia. It was well established in the Champa kingdom, for example, where Shiva was worshipped, cows were honored, and phallic imagery was prominent. But the prosperous and powerful Angkor kingdom of the twelfth century C.E. hosted the most stunning architectural expression of Hinduism in the temple complex known as **Angkor Wat**. The largest religious structure in the premodern world, it sought to express a Hindu understanding of the cosmos centered on a myth-ical Mount Meru, the home of the gods. Later, it was used by Buddhists as well, with little sense of contradiction. To the west of Angkor, the state of Pagan like-wise devoted enormous resources to shrines, temples, and libraries inspired by both Hindu and Buddhist faiths.

This extensive Indian influence in Southeast Asia has led some scholars to speak of the "Indianization" of the region, similar perhaps to the earlier spread of Greek culture within the empires of Alexander the Great and Rome. In the case of Southeast Asia, however, no imperial control accompanied Indian cultural influence. It was a matter of voluntary borrowing by independent societies that found Indian traditions and practices useful and were free to adapt those ideas to their own needs and cultures. Traditional religious practices mixed with the imported faiths or existed alongside them with little conflict. And much that was distinctively Southeast Asian persisted despite influences from afar. In family life, for example, most Southeast Asian societies traced an individual's ancestry from both the mother's and father's line, in contrast to India and China, where patrilineal descent was practiced. Furthermore, Southeast Asian women had fewer restrictions and a greater role in public life than women in the more patriarchal civilizations of China and India. They were generally able to own property together with their husbands and to initiate divorce. A Chinese visitor to Angkor observed, "It is the women who are concerned with commerce." Women in Angkor also served as gladiators, warriors, and members of the palace staff, and as poets, artists, and religious teachers. Almost 1,800 realistically carved images of women decorate the temple complex of Angkor Wat. In neighboring Pagan, a thirteenth-century queen, Pwa Saw, exercised extensive political and religious influence for some forty years amid internal intrigue and external threats, while donating some of her lands and property to a Buddhist temple. Somewhat later, but also via Indian Ocean commerce, Islam too began to penetrate Southeast Asia as the world of seaborne trade brought yet another cultural tradition to the region.

Sea Roads as a Catalyst for Change: East Africa

On the other side of the Indian Ocean, the transformative processes of long-distance trade were likewise at work, giving rise to **Swahili civilization**. Emerging in the eighth century C.E., this civilization took shape as a set of commercial city-states stretching all along the East African coast, from present-day Somalia to Mozambique.

The earlier ancestors of the Swahili lived in small farming and fishing communities, spoke Bantu languages, and traded with the Arabian, Greek, and Roman merchants who occasionally visited the coast during the second-wave era. But what stimulated the growth of Swahili cities was the far more extensive commercial life of the western Indian Ocean following the rise of Islam. As in Southeast Asia, local people and aspiring rulers found opportunity for wealth and power in the growing demand for East African products associated with an expanding Indian Ocean commerce. Gold, ivory, quartz, leopard skins, and sometimes slaves acquired from interior societies, as well as iron and processed timber manufactured along the coast, found a ready market in Arabia, Persia, India, and beyond. At least one East African giraffe found its way to Bengal in northeastern India, and from there was sent on

Guided Reading Question
....
■ **CONNECTION**
What was the role of Swahili civilization in the world of Indian Ocean commerce?

to China. In response to such commercial opportunities, an African merchant class developed, villages turned into sizable towns, and clan chiefs became kings. A new civilization was in the making.

Between 1000 and 1500, that civilization flourished along the coast, and it was a very different kind of society from the farming and pastoral cultures of the East African interior. It was thoroughly urban, centered in cities of 15,000 to 18,000 people, such as Lamu, Mombasa, Kilwa, Sofala, and many others. Like the city-states of ancient Greece, each Swahili city was politically independent, was generally governed by its own king, and was in sharp competition with other cities. No imperial system or larger territorial states unified the world of Swahili civilization. Nor did any of these city-states control a critical choke point of trade, as Srivijaya did for the Straits of Malacca. Swahili cities were commercial centers that accumulated goods from the interior and exchanged them for the products of distant civilizations, such as Chinese porcelain and silk, Persian rugs, and Indian cottons. While the transoceanic journeys occurred largely in Arab vessels, Swahili craft navigated the coastal waterways, concentrating goods for shipment abroad. This long-distance trade generated class-stratified urban societies with sharp distinctions between a mercantile elite and commoners.

Culturally as well as economically, Swahili civilization participated in the larger Indian Ocean world. Arab, Indian, and Persian merchants were welcome visitors, and some settled permanently. Many ruling families of Swahili cities claimed Arab or Persian origins as a way of bolstering their prestige, even while they dined from Chinese porcelain and dressed in Indian cottons. The Swahili language, widely spoken in East Africa today, was grammatically an African tongue within the larger Bantu family of languages, but it was written in Arabic script and contained a number of Arabic loan words. A small bronze lion found in the Swahili city of Shanga and dating to about 1100 illustrates the distinctly cosmopolitan character of Swahili culture. It depicted a clearly African lion, but it was created in a distinctly Indian artistic style and was made from melted-down Chinese copper coins.[12]

Furthermore, Swahili civilization rapidly became Islamic. Introduced by Arab traders, Islam was voluntarily and widely adopted within the Swahili world. Like Buddhism in Southeast Asia, Islam linked Swahili cities to the larger Indian Ocean world, and these East African cities were soon dotted with substantial mosques. When Ibn Battuta (IH-buhn ba-TOO-tuh), a widely traveled Arab scholar, merchant, and public official, visited the Swahili coast in the early fourteenth century, he found altogether Muslim societies in which religious leaders often spoke Arabic, and all were eager to welcome a learned Islamic visitor. But these were African Muslims, not colonies of transplanted Arabs. A prominent historian of Ibn Battuta's travels commented on Swahili society: "The rulers, scholars, officials, and big merchants as well as the port workers, farmers, craftsmen, and slaves, were dark-skinned people speaking African tongues in everyday life."[13]

The Swahili Coast of East Africa

Islam sharply divided the Swahili cities from their African neighbors to the west, for neither the new religion nor Swahili culture penetrated much beyond the coast until the nineteenth century. Economically, however, the coastal cities acted as intermediaries between the interior producers of valued goods and the Arab merchants who carried them to distant markets. Particularly in the southern reaches of the Swahili world, this relationship extended the impact of Indian Ocean trade well into the African interior. Hundreds of miles inland, between the Zambezi and Limpopo rivers, lay rich sources of gold, much in demand on the Swahili coast. The emergence of a powerful state, known as **Great Zimbabwe**, seems clearly connected to the growing trade in gold to the coast as well as to the wealth embodied in its large herds of cattle. At its peak between 1250 and 1350, Great Zimbabwe had the resources and the labor power to construct huge stone enclosures entirely without mortar, with walls sixteen feet thick and thirty-two feet tall. "[It] must have been an astonishing sight," writes a recent historian, "for the subordinate chiefs and kings who would have come there to seek favors at court."[14] Here in the interior of southeastern Africa lay yet another example of the reach and transforming power of Indian Ocean commerce.

> **PRACTICING HISTORICAL THINKING**
>
> To what extent did the Silk Roads and the Sea Roads operate in a similar fashion? How did they differ?

Sand Roads: Exchange across the Sahara

In addition to the Silk Roads and the Sea Roads, another important pattern of long-distance trade—this one across the vast reaches of the Sahara in a series of **Sand Roads**—linked North Africa and the Mediterranean world with the land and peoples of interior West Africa. Like the others, these Sand Road commercial networks had a transforming impact, stimulating and enriching West African civilization and connecting it to larger patterns of world history during the third-wave era.

Commercial Beginnings in West Africa

Trans-African trade, like the commerce of the Silk Roads and the Sea Roads, was rooted in environmental variation. The North African coastal regions, long part of Roman or later Arab empires, generated cloth, glassware, weapons, books, and other manufactured goods. The great Sahara held deposits of copper and especially salt, and its oases produced sweet and nutritious dates. While the sparse populations of the desert were largely pastoral and nomadic, farther south lived agricultural peoples who grew a variety of crops, produced their own textiles and metal products, and mined a considerable amount of gold. These agricultural regions of sub-Saharan Africa are normally divided into two ecological zones: the savanna grasslands immediately south of the Sahara, which produced grain crops such as millet and sorghum, and the forest areas farther south, where root and tree crops such as yams and kola nuts predominated. These quite varied environments provided the economic incentive for the exchange of goods.

The Arabian Camel

Animals have their own histories, and they have long played a large role in human history as well. Consider the single-humped Arabian camel, for thousands of years an important means of transport and a beast of burden on the Silk and Sand Roads. Even today, the Arabian camel is a common sight across northern Africa and the Middle East. But it took millennia for this breed of camel to spread beyond its native Arabian Peninsula, where it had been domesticated by 3000 B.C.E. Camels were initially valued by Arab tribesmen for their milk; however, over time their endurance and ability to carry heavy loads resulted in their adoption as pack animals along the caravan routes between the frankincense- and myrrh-producing regions of southern Arabia and cities on the northern edges of the peninsula.

Part of a camel caravan.

photo: BnF, Dist. RMN–Grand Palais/Art Resource, NY

This trade slowly introduced Arabian camels to the rest of the Middle East, where they were well established by 500 B.C.E. But the invention of a new saddle that allowed each animal to carry a heavier load transformed the camel into the most versatile and efficient form of transport in the region by 100 B.C.E. Ultimately the camel displaced the ox and cart, which for millennia had been a mainstay for moving goods. The advantages of the camel were significant. Camels ate desert plants that thrived on lands unsuitable to agriculture, while oxen required fodder grown on arable land. Moreover, camels carried loads on their backs rather than pulling carts made of wood, a scarce resource in the Middle East. In many parts of the region, the camel's triumph was complete. By 500 C.E., wheeled vehicles had

The earliest long-distance trade within this huge region was not across the Sahara at all, but largely among the agricultural peoples themselves in the area later known to Arabs as the Sudan, or "the land of black people." On the basis of this trade, a number of independent urban clusters emerged by the early centuries of the Common Era, giving rise to the Niger Valley civilization, described in Chapter 6.

Gold, Salt, and Slaves: Trade and Empire in West Africa

A major turning point in African commercial life occurred with the introduction of the **Arabian camel** to North Africa and the Sahara in the early centuries of the Common Era. (See Zooming In: The Arabian Camel, above.) This remarkable animal, which could go for ten days without water, finally made possible the long trek across the Sahara. It was camel-owning dwellers of desert oases who initiated regular trans-Saharan commerce by 300 to 400 C.E. Several centuries later, North African Arabs, now bearing the new religion of Islam, also organized caravans across the desert.

What these Arab merchants sought, above all else, was gold, which was found in some abundance in the border areas straddling the grasslands and the forests of disappeared entirely from most of the Middle East, and the camel maintained its dominance for fifteen hundred years. In the 1780s, a French traveler in Syria commented, "It is noteworthy that in all of Syria no wagon or cart is seen."[15] Only with the emergence of the automobile in the twentieth century did the camel decisively lose its advantage over wheeled vehicles. From the Middle East, Arabian camels and related hybrid species moved along the Silk Roads, becoming a major means of transport as far away as modern Afghanistan. Only the cold climatic conditions of Central Asia halted their spread. In the frigid Gobi Desert, it was the Arabian camel's cousin—the two-humped Bactrian camel—that traders relied upon to carry their loads.

The Arabian camel had perhaps an even more profound impact on long-distance trade across the Sahara. Before the arrival of the camel, the western Sahara proved an imposing barrier to trade. Just a trickle of goods flowed across the vast arid region, often through indirect exchange. The first camels most likely filtered into western Africa from the Middle East along the southern borders of the Sahara around 200 B.C.E., and they probably arrived after 100 C.E. in Roman North Africa, where they were used for a variety of purposes, including the plowing of fields. From the time of their arrival, camels stimulated trade and contact across the Sahara, but these exchanges really took off when the Arab conquerors of North Africa brought their expertise in camel caravan trading to the region in the sixth century C.E. At their height, caravans of up to 5,000 camels regularly crossed the Sahara on several established routes, traveling mostly at night because of the heat. Covering 15 to 25 miles per day, it could take seventy days to traverse the desert, but profits from trade in gold, ivory, salt, and slaves made the journey worthwhile. These trade routes facilitated the emergence of empires in West Africa and the spread of Islam into the region. The Arabian camel remained the chief source of transport between sub-Saharan West Africa and the Mediterranean for over a thousand years, until European ships sailing along the Atlantic coast challenged their dominance in the fifteenth century.

QUESTIONS

Was the disappearance of the wheel an advance in terms of transport in the Middle East? What impact did the Arabian camel have on long-distance trade in Eurasia and Africa? How might reliance on the camel rather than the wheel affect human settlements?

West Africa. From its source, it was transported by donkey to transshipment points on the southern edge of the Sahara and then transferred to camels for the long journey north across the desert. African ivory, kola nuts, and slaves were likewise in considerable demand in the desert, the Mediterranean basin, and beyond. In return, the peoples of the Sudan received horses, cloth, dates, various manufactured goods, and especially salt from the rich deposits in the Sahara.

Thus the Sahara was no longer simply a barrier to commerce and cross-cultural interaction; for a thousand years, it was a major international trade route that fostered new relationships among distant peoples. As in Southeast Asia and East Africa, this trans-Saharan trade provided both incentives and resources for the construction of new and larger political structures. The West African peoples living in the savannah grasslands between the forests and the desert were in the best position to take advantage of these new opportunities. Between roughly 500 and 1600, a new **West African civilization** took shape in the region, stretching from the Atlantic coast to Lake Chad. It included the states of Ghana, Mali, Songhay, and Kanem, as well as numerous towns and cities such as Kumbi Saleh, Jenne, Timbuktu, Gao, Gobir, Kano, and others (see Map 7.4).

Guided Reading Question
....
■ **CONNECTION**
What changes did trans-Saharan trade bring to West Africa?

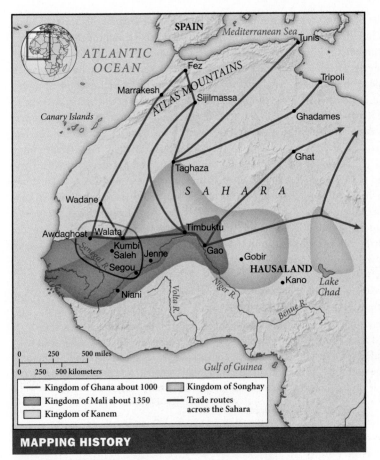

MAPPING HISTORY

Map 7.4 The Sand Roads

For a thousand years or more, the Sahara was an ocean of sand that linked the interior of West Africa with the world of North Africa and the Mediterranean but separated them as well.

READING THE MAP: Which cities were built at points where the Sand Roads trade routes arrived at the Niger River?

INTERPRETING THE MAP: The Kingdom of Mali was much larger than the earlier Kingdom of Ghana. What might you infer from the map about the motives for Mali's westward expansion?

All of these states were monarchies with elaborate court life and varying degrees of administrative complexity and military forces at their disposal. All drew on the wealth of trans-Saharan trade, taxing the merchants who conducted it. In the wider world, these states soon acquired a reputation for great riches. An Arab traveler in the tenth century c.e. described the ruler of **Ghana** as "the wealthiest king on the face of the earth because of his treasures and stocks of gold."[16] At its high point in the fourteenth century, the rulers of **Mali** monopolized the import of strategic goods such as horses and metals; levied duties on salt, copper, and other merchandise; and reserved large nuggets of gold for themselves while permitting the free export of gold dust. (See Working with Evidence, Source 7.4, for an early sixteenth-century account of this West African civilization.)

This growing integration with the world of international commerce generated the social complexity and hierarchy characteristic of all civilizations. Royal families and elite classes, mercantile and artisan groups, military and religious officials, free peasants and slaves—all of these were represented in this emerging West African civilization. So too were gender hierarchies, although without the rigidity of more established Eurasian civilizations. Rulers, merchants, and public officials were almost always male, and by 1200 earlier matrilineal descent patterns had been largely replaced by those tracing descent through the male line. Male bards, the repositories for their communities' history, often viewed powerful women as dangerous, not to be trusted, and a seductive distraction for men. But ordinary women were central to agricultural production and weaving; royal women played important political roles in many places; and oral traditions and mythologies frequently portrayed a complementary rather than hierarchal relationship between the sexes. According to a recent scholar:

> Men [in West African civilization] derive[d] their power and authority by releasing and accumulating *nyama* [a pervasive vital power] through acts of transforming one thing into another—making a living animal dead in hunting, making a lump of metal into a fine bracelet at the smithy. Women derive[d] their power from similar acts of transformation—turning clay into pots or turning the bodily fluids of sex into a baby.[17]

Certainly, the famous Muslim traveler Ibn Battuta, visiting Mali in the mid-fourteenth century, was surprised, and appalled, at the casual intimacy of unmarried men and women, despite their evident commitment to Islam.

As in all civilizations, slavery found a place in West Africa. Early on, most slaves had been women, working as domestic servants and concubines. As West African civilization crystallized, however, male slaves were put to work as state officials, porters, craftsmen, miners harvesting salt from desert deposits, and especially agricultural laborers producing for the royal granaries on large estates or plantations. Most came from non-Islamic and stateless societies farther south, which were raided during the dry season by cavalry-based forces of West African states. A song in honor of one eleventh-century ruler of Kanem boasted of his slave-raiding achievements:

> The best you took (and sent home) as the first fruits of battle. The children crying on their mothers you snatched away from their mothers. You took the slave wife from a slave, and set them in lands far removed from one another.[18]

Most of these slaves were used within this emerging West African civilization, but a **trans-Saharan slave trade** also developed. Between 1100 and 1400, perhaps 5,500 slaves per year made the perilous trek across the desert, where most were put to work in the homes of the wealthy in Islamic North Africa.

The states of this West African civilization developed substantial urban and commercial centers—such as Kumbi Saleh, Jenne, Timbuktu, Gao, Gobir, and Kano—where traders congregated and goods were exchanged. Some of these cities also became centers of manufacturing, creating finely wrought beads, iron tools, or cotton textiles, some of which entered the circuits of commerce. Visitors described them as cosmopolitan places where court officials, artisans, scholars, students, and local and

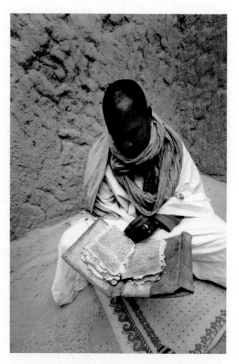

Manuscripts of Timbuktu The West African city of Timbuktu, a terminus of the Sand Road commercial network, became an intellectual center of Islamic learning—both scientific and religious. Its libraries were stocked with books and manuscripts, often transported across the Sahara from the heartland of Islam. Many of these have been preserved and are now being studied once again. (Alex Dissanayake/Getty Images)

foreign merchants all rubbed elbows. As in East Africa, Islam accompanied trade and became an important element in the urban culture of West Africa. Thus the growth of long-distance trade had stimulated the development of a West African civilization, which was linked to the wider networks of exchange in the Eastern Hemisphere.

An American Network: Commerce and Connection in the Western Hemisphere

Before the voyages of Columbus, the world of the Americas developed quite separately from that of Afro-Eurasia. But if the Silk, Sea, and Sand Roads linked the diverse peoples of the Eastern Hemisphere, did a similar network of interaction join and transform the various societies of the Western Hemisphere?

Clearly, direct connections among the various civilizations and cultures of the Americas were less densely woven than in the Afro-Eurasian region. The llama and the potato, both domesticated in the Andes, never reached Mesoamerica; nor did the writing system of the Maya diffuse to Andean civilizations. The Aztecs and the Incas, contemporary civilizations in the fifteenth century, had little if any direct contact with each other. The limits of these interactions owed something to the absence of horses, donkeys, camels, wheeled vehicles, and large oceangoing vessels, all of which facilitated long-distance trade and travel in Afro-Eurasia.

Geographic or environmental differences added further obstacles. The narrow bottleneck of Panama, largely covered by dense rain forests, surely inhibited contact between South and North America. Furthermore, the north/south orientation of the Americas—which required agricultural practices to move through, and adapt to, quite distinct climatic and vegetation zones—slowed the spread of agricultural products. By contrast, the east/west axis of Eurasia meant that agricultural innovations could diffuse more rapidly because they were entering roughly similar environments. Thus nothing equivalent to the long-distance trade of the Silk, Sea, or Sand Roads of the Eastern Hemisphere arose in the Americas, even though local and regional commerce flourished in many places. Nor did distinct cultural traditions spread widely to integrate distant peoples, as Buddhism, Christianity, and Islam did in the Afro-Eurasian world.

Nonetheless, scholars have discerned "a loosely interactive web stretching from the North American Great Lakes and upper Mississippi south to the Andes."[19] (See Map 7.5.) Partly, it was a matter of slowly spreading cultural elements, such as the gradual diffusion of maize from its Mesoamerican place of origin to the southwestern United States and then on to eastern North America as well as to much of South America in the other direction. A game played with rubber balls on an outdoor court has left traces in the Caribbean, Mexico, and northern South America. The spread of particular pottery styles and architectural conventions likewise suggests at least indirect contact over wide distances.

Commerce too played an important role in the making of this "**American web**." A major North American chiefdom at Cahokia, near present-day St. Louis, lay at the center of a widespread trading network. Those linkages brought to Cahokia shells from the Atlantic coast, copper from the Lake Superior region, buffalo hides from the Great Plains, obsidian from the Rocky Mountains, and mica from the southern Appalachian Mountains. Sturdy dugout canoes plied the rivers of the eastern woodlands, loosely connecting their diverse societies.

Early European explorers and travelers along the Amazon and Orinoco rivers of South America reported active networks of exchange that may well have operated for many centuries among densely populated settlements of agricultural peoples. Caribbean peoples using large oceangoing canoes had long conducted an inter-island trade, and the Chincha people of southern coastal Peru undertook a privately organized ocean-based exchange in copper, beads, and shells along the Pacific coasts of Peru and Ecuador in large seagoing rafts. Another regional commercial network, centered in Mesoamerica, extended north to what is now the southwestern United States

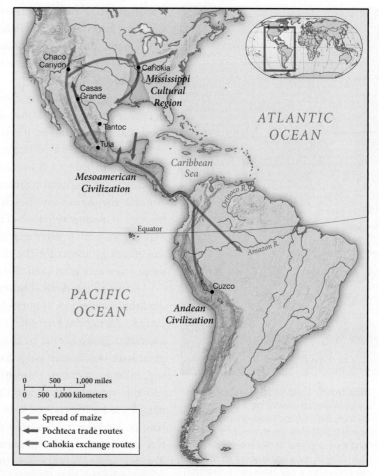

Map 7.5 The American Web

Transcontinental interactions within the American web were more modest than those of the Afro-Eurasian hemisphere. The most intense areas of exchange and communication occurred within the Mississippi valley, Mesoamerican, and Andean regions.

and south to Ecuador and Colombia. Many items from Mesoamerica—copper bells, macaw feathers, tons of shells—have been found in the Chaco region of New Mexico. Residents of Chaco also drank liquid chocolate, using jars of Maya origin and cacao beans imported from Mesoamerica, where the practice began. Turquoise, mined and worked by the people of Chaco (see "North America: Ancestral Pueblo and Mound Builders" in Chapter 6), flowed in the other direction.

But the most active and dense networks of communication and exchange in the Americas lay within, rather than between, the regions that housed the two great civilizations of the Western Hemisphere—Mesoamerica and the Andes. During the flourishing of Mesoamerican civilization (200–900 C.E.), both the Maya cities in the Yucatán area of Mexico and Guatemala and the huge city-state of

Inca Roads Used for transporting goods by pack animal or sending messages by foot, the Inca road network included some 2,000 inns where travelers might find food and shelter. Messengers, operating in relay, could cover as many as 150 miles a day. Here contemporary hikers still make use of an old Inca trail road. (William H. Mullins/Science Source)

Teotihuacán in central Mexico maintained commercial relationships with one another and throughout the region. In addition to this land-based trade, the Maya conducted a seaborne commerce, using large dugout canoes holding forty to fifty people, along both the Atlantic and Pacific coasts.

Although most of this trade was in luxury goods rather than basic necessities, it was critical to upholding the position and privileges of royal and noble families. Items such as cotton clothing, precious jewels, and feathers from particular birds marked the status of elite groups and served to attract followers. Controlling access to such high-prestige goods was an important motive for war among Mesoamerican states. Among the Aztecs of the fifteenth century, professional merchants known as *pochteca* (pohch-TEH-cah) undertook large-scale trading expeditions both within and well beyond the borders of their empire, sometimes as agents for the state or for members of the nobility, but more often acting on their own as private businessmen.

Unlike in the Aztec Empire, in which private traders largely handled the distribution of goods, economic exchange in the Andean Inca Empire during the fifteenth century was a state-run operation, and no merchant group similar to the Aztec pochteca emerged there. Instead, great state storehouses bulged with immense quantities of food, clothing, military supplies, blankets, construction materials, and more, all carefully recorded on *quipus* (knotted cords used to record numerical data) by a highly trained class of accountants. From these state centers, goods were transported as needed by caravans of human porters and llamas across the numerous roads and bridges of the empire. Totaling some 20,000 miles, Inca roads traversed the coastal plain and the high Andes in a north/south direction, while lateral roads linked these diverse environments and extended into the eastern rain forests and plains as well. Despite the general absence of private trade, local exchange took place at highland fairs and along the borders of the empire with groups outside the Inca state.

REFLECTIONS

Economic Globalization—Ancient and Modern

The densely connected world of the modern era, linked by ties of commerce and culture around the planet, has paralleled much earlier patterns. Particularly in the era of third-wave civilizations, the Silk, Sea, and Sand Roads of the Afro-Eurasian world and the looser networks of the American web linked distant peoples both economically and culturally, prompted the emergence of new states, and sustained elite privileges in many ancient civilizations. In those ways, they resembled the globalized world of modern times.

In other respects, though, the networks and webs of the premodern millennium differed sharply from those of more recent centuries. Most people still produced primarily for their own consumption rather than for the market, and a much smaller range of goods was exchanged in the marketplaces of the world. Far fewer people then were required to sell their own labor for wages, an almost universal practice in modern economies. Because of transportation costs and technological limitations, most trade was in luxury goods rather than in necessities. In addition, the circuits of commerce were rather more limited than the truly global patterns of exchange that emerged after 1500.

Furthermore, the world economy of the modern era increasingly had a single center—industrialized Western European countries—which came to dominate much of the world both economically and politically during the nineteenth century. Though never completely equal, the economic relationships of earlier times occurred among much more equivalent units. For example, no one region dominated the complex pattern of Indian Ocean exchange, although India and China generally offered manufactured goods, while Southeast Asia and East Africa mostly contributed agricultural products or raw materials. And with the exception of the brief Mongol control of the Silk Roads and the Inca domination of the Andes for a century, no single power exercised political control over the major networks of world commerce.

Economic relationships among third-wave civilizations, in short, were more balanced and multicentered than those of the modern era. Although massive inequalities occurred within particular regions or societies, interaction among the major civilizations operated on a rather more equal basis than in the globalized world of the past several centuries. With the rise of China, India, Turkey, and Brazil as major players in the world economy of the twenty-first century, are we perhaps witnessing a return to that earlier pattern?

Second Thoughts

What's the Significance?

Silk Roads, 278

Black Death, 285

Sea Roads, 286

Srivijaya, 290

Angkor Wat, 292

Swahili civilization, 293

Great Zimbabwe, 295

Sand Roads, 295

Arabian camel, 296

West African civilization, 297

Ghana, 298

Mali, 298

trans-Saharan slave trade, 299

American web, 301

pochteca, 302

Big Picture Questions

1. What motivated and sustained the long-distance commerce of the Silk Roads, Sea Roads, and Sand Roads?
2. Why did the peoples of the Eastern Hemisphere develop long-distance trade more extensively than did those of the Western Hemisphere?
3. "Cultural change often derived from commercial exchange in the third-wave era." What evidence from this chapter supports this observation?
4. In what ways was Afro-Eurasia a single interacting zone, and in what respects was it a vast region of separate cultures and civilizations?
5. **Looking Back:** Compared to the cross-cultural interactions of earlier times, what was different about those of the third-wave era?

Next Steps: For Further Study

Jerry Bentley, *Old World Encounters* (1993). A wonderfully succinct and engaging history of cross-cultural interaction all across Afro-Eurasia before 1500.

William J. Bernstein, *A Splendid Exchange* (2008). A global account of "how trade shaped the world."

E. W. Bovill, *The Golden Trade of the Moors* (1970). A classic account of the trans-Saharan trade.

K. N. Chaudhuri, *Trade and Civilization in the Indian Ocean* (1985). A well-regarded study that treats the Indian Ocean basin as a single region linked by both commerce and culture during the third-wave era.

Barry Cunliffe, *By Steppe, Desert, and Ocean: The Birth of Eurasia* (2015). Examines all of Eurasia over 10,000 years, with special focus on the Silk and Sea Roads that bound it together.

Philip Curtin, *Cross-Cultural Trade in World History* (1984). Explores long-distance trade as a generator of social change on a global level.

Xinru Liu, *The Silk Road in World History* (2010). A brief, accessible, and up-to-date account by a leading scholar.

J. R. McNeill and William H. McNeill, *The Human Web* (2003). A highly regarded survey of the evolving networks of human interaction by two leading world historians.

Marion Mayer-Hohdahl, "The Last Salt Caravan," Journeyman.tv, 2013, http://www.youtube.com/watch?v=yNwQeLFk74o. A ten-minute trailer for a documentary showing an early twenty-first-century camel caravan crossing the Sahara, reminiscent of much earlier caravans of the Sand Roads network.

Daniel Waugh, University of Washington, "Silk Road Seattle," 2007, http://depts.washington.edu/silkroad/. A wonderful website about the Silk Roads with many artistic images, primary sources, and maps as well as extensive narrative descriptions of that vast network of exchange.

Travelers' Tales and Observations

During the third-wave era, as long-distance trade flourished and large transregional empires grew, opportunities increased for individuals to travel far beyond their homelands. Their accounts have provided historians with invaluable information about particular regions and cultures, as well as about interactions among disparate peoples. The authors of these accounts, perhaps inadvertently, also reveal much about themselves and about the perceptions and misperceptions generated by cross-cultural encounters. The sources that follow offer examples of how intrepid long-distance travelers described distant lands and how artists and mapmakers depicted faraway regions for those who stayed at home.

SOURCE 7.1 A Chinese Buddhist in India

In 629, Xuanzang (SCHWEN-ZAHNG) (600–664 C.E.), a highly educated Buddhist monk from China, made a long and difficult journey to India through some of the world's most daunting deserts and mountain ranges, returning home in 645 C.E. after sixteen years abroad. His motives, like those of many other Buddhist travelers to India, were essentially religious. He wrote, "I regretted that the teachings of [Buddhism] were not complete and the scriptures deficient in my own country. . . . That was why I decided to travel to the West."[20] In India, the homeland of Buddhism, he hoped to find the teachers and the sacred texts that would answer his questions and resolve the many disputes that had created serious divisions within the Buddhist community of his own country.

During a ten-year stay in India, Xuanzang visited many of the holy sites associated with the Buddha's life and studied with leading Buddhist teachers, particularly those at Nalanda, a huge monastic complex dedicated to Buddhist scholarship (see Map 7.1, page 278). He traveled widely within India and established a personal relationship with Harsha, the ruler of the state that then encompassed much of northern India. On his return journey to China, he carried hundreds of manuscripts, at least seven statues of the Buddha, and even some relics. Warmly greeted by the Chinese emperor, Xuanzang spent the last two decades of his life translating the texts he had collected into Chinese. He also wrote an account of his travels, known as the *Record of the Western Regions,* from which this selection is drawn. It conveys something of Xuanzang's impressions of Indian civilization in the seventh century C.E.

- What surprised or impressed Xuanzang on his visit to India? What features of Indian life might seem most strange to a Chinese visitor?

- How might this selection illustrate or contradict the descriptions of Indian civilization found in Chapters 3–5?

- What can this document contribute to our understanding of Buddhist practice in India?

XUANZANG | *Record of the Western Regions* | 7th century C.E.

On Towns and Villages

The towns and villages have inner gates; the walls are wide and high; the streets and lanes are tortuous, and the roads winding. The thoroughfares are dirty and the stalls arranged on both sides of the road with appropriate signs. Butchers, fishers, dancers, executioners, and scavengers, and so on [untouch-ables], have their abodes without [outside] the city. In coming and going these persons are bound to keep on the left side of the road till they arrive at their homes. Their houses are surrounded by low walls and form the suburbs. . . .

On Buddhist Studies

The different schools are constantly at variance, and their contending utterances rise like the angry waves of the sea. The different sects have their separate masters. . . . There are eighteen schools, each claiming pre-eminence. . . . According to their fraternity, they are governed by distinctive rules and regulations. . . . When a man's renown has reached to a high distinction, then at different times he convokes an assembly for discussion. He judges of the superior or inferior talent of those who take part in it; he distinguishes their good or bad points; he praises the clever and reproves the faulty; if one of the assembly distinguishes himself by refined language, subtle investigation, deep penetration, and severe logic, then he is mounted on an elephant covered with precious ornaments, and conducted by a numerous suite to the gates of the convent.

If, on the contrary, one of the members breaks down in his argument, or uses poor and inelegant phrases, or if he violates a rule in logic and adapts his words accordingly, they proceed to disfigure his face with red and white, and cover his body with dirt and dust, and then carry him off to some deserted spot or leave him in a ditch. Thus they distinguish between the meritorious and the worthless, between the wise and the foolish.

On Caste and Marriage

With respect to the division of families, there are four classifications. The first is called the Brâhman, men of pure conduct. They guard themselves in religion, live purely, and observe the most correct principles. The second is called Kshattriya, the royal caste. For ages they have been the governing class: they apply themselves to virtue and kindness. The third is called Vaiśyas, the merchant class: they engage in commercial exchange, and they follow profit at home and abroad. The fourth is called Sûdra, the agricultural class: they labor in plowing and tillage. In these four classes purity or impurity of caste assigns to every one his place. When they marry they rise or fall in position according to their new relationship. They do not allow promiscuous marriages between relations. A woman once married can never take another husband. Besides these there are other classes of many kinds that intermarry according to their several callings.

On Manners and Justice

With respect to the ordinary people, although they are naturally light-minded, yet they are upright and honorable. In money matters they are without craft, and in administering justice they are considerate. They dread the retribution of another state of existence, and make light of the things of the present world. They are not deceitful or treacherous in their conduct, and are faithful to their oaths and promises. In their rules of government there is remarkable rectitude, whilst in their behavior there is much gentleness and sweetness. With respect to criminals or rebels, these are few in number, and only occasionally troublesome. When the laws are broken or the power of the ruler violated, then the matter is clearly sifted and the offenders imprisoned. There is no infliction of corporal punishment; they are simply left to live or die, and are not counted among men. When the rules of propriety or justice are violated, or when a man fails in fidelity or filial piety, then they cut his nose or his ears off, or his hands and feet, or expel him from the country or drive him out into the desert wilds. For other faults, except these, a small payment of money will redeem the punishment. In the investigation of criminal cases

there is no use of rod or staff to obtain proofs (*of guilt*).

Source: Samuel Beal, trans., *Su-Yu-Ki: Buddhist Records of the Western World* (London: K. Paul, Trench, Trubner, 1906), vol. 1, bk. 2, 73–74, 80–84.

■ ■ ■

SOURCE 7.2 A European Christian in China

Of all the travelers along the Silk Road network, the best known and most celebrated, at least in the West, was Marco Polo (1254–1324). Born and raised in the prosperous commercial city-state of Venice in northern Italy, he was a member of a family engaged in the long-distance trade of the Mediterranean and Black Sea regions. At the age of seventeen, Marco accompanied his father and an uncle on an epic journey across Eurasia that, by 1275, brought the Polos to China, recently conquered by the Mongols. It was, in fact, the relative peace that the Mongols had created in their huge transcontinental empire that facilitated the Polos' journey (see Map 11.1, page 458). For the next seventeen years, they lived in China, where they were employed in minor administrative positions by Khubilai Khan, the country's Mongol ruler. During these years, Marco Polo apparently traveled widely within China, where he gathered material for a book about his travels, which he dictated to a friend after returning home in 1295. The selection that follows conveys Marco Polo's description of Hangzhou—one of the largest cities in the world at the time—which he refers to as Kinsay. Polo tells his reader that he constructed this description from both his visit to Hangzhou and a written account of the city sent to the Mongol khan in the hopes of sparing the city from destruction following its conquest.

■ How would you describe Marco Polo's impressions of the city? What did he notice? What surprised him?

■ Why did Marco Polo describe the city as "the finest and the noblest in the world"?

■ What marks his account of the city as that of a foreigner and a Christian?

■ What evidence of China's engagement with a wider world does this account offer?

MARCO POLO | *The Travels of Marco Polo* | **1299**

The city is beyond dispute the finest and the noblest in the world. . . . First and foremost, then, the document stated the city of Kinsay to be so great that it hath an hundred miles of compass. And there are in it 12,000 bridges of stone. . . . [Most scholars consider these figures a considerable exaggeration.]

[T]here were in this city twelve guilds of the different crafts, and that each guild had 12,000 houses in the occupation of its workmen. Each of these houses contains at least twelve men, whilst some contain twenty and some forty. . . . And yet all these craftsmen had full occupation, for many other cities of the kingdom are supplied from this city with what they require.

[T]he number and wealth of the merchants, and the amount of goods that passed through their hands, were so enormous that no man could form a just estimate thereof. . . [T]hose masters of the different crafts . . . neither they nor their wives ever touch a piece of work with their own hands, but live as nicely and delicately as if they were kings and queens. . . .

Inside the city there is a Lake . . . and all round it are erected beautiful palaces and mansions, of the richest and most exquisite structure that you can imagine, belonging to the nobles of the city. There are also on its shores many abbeys and churches of the Idolaters [Buddhists]. In the middle of the Lake are two Islands, on each of which stands a rich, beautiful, and spacious edifice, furnished in such style as to seem fit for the palace of an Emperor. And when any one of the citizens desired to hold a marriage feast, or to give any other entertainment, it used to be done at one of these palaces. And everything would be found there ready to order, such as silver plate, trenchers, and dishes, napkins and table-cloths, and whatever else was needful. . . .

Both men and women are fair and comely, and for the most part clothe themselves in silk, so vast is the supply of that material, both from the whole district of Kinsay, and from the imports by traders from other provinces. And you must know they eat every kind of flesh, even that of dogs and other unclean beasts, which nothing would induce a Christian to eat. . . .

You must know also that the city of Kinsay has some 3,000 baths, the water of which is supplied by springs. They are hot baths, and the people take great delight in them, frequenting them several times a month, for they are very cleanly in their persons. They are the finest and largest baths in the world. . . .

And the Ocean Sea comes within twenty-five miles of the city at a place called Ganfu, where there is a town and an excellent haven, with a vast amount of shipping which is engaged in the traffic to and from India and other foreign parts, exporting and importing many kinds of wares, by which the city benefits. . . .

I repeat that everything appertaining to this city is on so vast a scale, and the Great [Khan's] yearly revenues therefrom are so immense, that it is not easy even to put it in writing. . . .

In this part are the ten principal markets, though besides these there are a vast number of others in the different parts of the town. . . . [T]oward the [market] squares are built great houses of stone, in which the merchants from India and other foreign parts store their wares, to be handy for the markets. In each of the squares is held a market three days in the week, frequented by 40,000 or 50,000 persons, who bring thither for sale every possible necessary of life, so that there is always an ample supply of every kind of meat and game. . . .

Other streets are occupied by the Physicians, and by the Astrologers, who are also teachers of reading and writing; and an infinity of other professions have their places round about those squares. In each of the squares there are two great palaces facing one another, in which are established the officers appointed by the King to decide differences arising between merchants, or other inhabitants of the quarter. . . .

The natives of the city are men of peaceful character, both from education and from the example of their kings, whose disposition was the same. They know nothing of handling arms, and keep none in their houses. You hear of no feuds or noisy quarrels or dissensions of any kind among them. Both in their commercial dealings and in their manufactures they are thoroughly honest and truthful, and there is such a degree of good will and neighborly attachment among both men and women that you would take the people who live in the same street to be all one family.

Source: *The Book of Ser Marco Polo, the Venetian, Concerning the Kingdoms and Marvels of the East*, translated and edited by Henry Yule (London: John Murray, 1871), 2:145–50, 158, 160–61.

■ ■ ■

SOURCE 7.3 **A European Artist Depicts Asia**

While Marco Polo's account is largely devoid of the wondrous monsters and races of humans that peopled many earlier European accounts of the East, his book did not immediately overturn these more fanciful ideas about distant lands. Source 7.3, an image that was created to illustrate an elaborate manuscript copy of Polo's book, provides a revealing window into the persistence of older ideas. Drawn around 1400, it depicts three mythical creatures—a blemmyae or headless man, a sciopod or single-footed man, and a cyclops or one-eyed monster—none of which are mentioned in Polo's text.

- What about the three figures and the landscape in which they are placed might evoke ideas of wilderness or barbarity in the viewer?

- Why might an artist commissioned to decorate Polo's book of travels choose to incorporate these mythical creatures despite their absence in the accompanying text?

- What does this source add to our understanding of how Europeans viewed East Asia in the early fifteenth century?

The Marvelous Races of the East | ca. 1410

From the "Livre des Merveilles du Monde," ca. 1410–1412 (tempera on vellum)/Boucicaut Master (fl. 1390-1430) (and workshop)/Bibliothèque Nationale de France, Paris, France/Bridgeman Images

■ ■ ■

SOURCE 7.4 **A Moroccan Diplomat in West Africa**

Known to the world by his European-derived nickname of Leo Africanus, this widely traveled Arabic-speaking Muslim was actually born as al-Hassan Ibn Muhammad al Wazzan in Granada, Spain, during the late fifteenth century, just as Islam was being pushed out of that country. His family moved to Fez in Morocco, where he was educated in Islamic law. Later, he served the sultan of Morocco as a diplomat and commercial agent, traveling widely in North Africa, the Middle East, Italy, and West Africa. On one of these journeys, he was captured by pirates and wound up in Rome, where he came to the attention of Pope Leo X. There he apparently converted to Christianity, at least for a time, though he later chose to live in Muslim North Africa and likely returned to his original Muslim faith. It was during his stay in Italy that he completed in 1526 the book for which he is most clearly remembered, *The History and Description of Africa*, based on observations and knowledge picked up during his travels. Later published in many languages, it became a major source of European knowledge of the African Islamic world, much as Marco Polo's writings introduced Europeans to China. In the following excerpts from that book, Leo Africanus describes several of the major kingdoms and cities of West African civilization.

- Based on these accounts, how does Leo Africanus characterize West African civilization? What can you infer about his own attitude toward this civilization?

- What connections between West Africa and a wider world are evident in these passages?

- What can you learn about the role of slavery in West Africa at a time before the Atlantic slave trade had become big business?

- Why do you think these passages say so little about the practice of Islam, focusing instead on political and economic matters? (Keep in mind that the book was first published in Italy and in Italian.) Despite this omission, what can you infer about variations in Islamic observance in West African civilization at this time?

LEO AFRICANUS | *The History and Description of Africa* | 1526

The City of Timbuktu

All its houses are . . . cottages, built of mud and covered with thatch. However, there is a most stately mosque to be seen, whose walls are made of stone and lime, and a princely palace also constructed by the highly skilled craftsmen of Granada. Here there are many shops of artisans and merchants, especially of those who weave linen and cotton, and here Barbary [Muslim North African] merchants bring European cloth. The inhabitants, and especially resident aliens, are exceedingly rich, since the present king married both of his daughters to rich merchants. Here are many wells, containing sweet water. Whenever the Niger River overflows, they carry the water into town by means of sluices. This region yields great quantities of grain, cattle, milk, and butter, but salt is very scarce here, for it is brought here by land from Tegaza, which is five hundred miles away.

The rich king of Timbuktu has many plates and scepters of gold, some of which weigh 1,300 pounds, and he keeps a magnificent and well-furnished court. When he travels anywhere, he rides upon a camel, which is led by some of his noblemen. He does so likewise when going to war, and all his soldiers ride upon horses. Whoever wishes to speak to this king must first of all fall down before his feet and then taking up earth must sprinkle it on his own head and shoulders. . . . [The king] always has under arms 3,000 horsemen and a great number of foot soldiers who shoot poisoned arrows. They often skirmish with those who refuse to pay tribute and whomever they capture they sell to the merchants of Timbuktu. Here very few horses are bred. . . . Their best horses are brought out of North Africa. As soon as the king learns that any merchants have come to the town with horses, he commands that a certain number be brought before him. Choosing the best horse for himself, he pays a most liberal price for it. . . .

Here are great numbers of [Islamic] religious teachers, judges, scholars and other learned persons, who are bountifully maintained at the king's expense. Here too are brought various [Arabic] manuscripts or written books from Barbary, which are sold for more money than any other merchandise.

The coin of Timbuktu is gold, without any stamp or inscription, but in matters of small value they use certain shells from the kingdom of Persia.

The inhabitants are gentle and cheerful and spend a great part of the night in singing and dancing throughout the city streets. They keep large numbers of male and female slaves, and their town is greatly vulnerable to fire. At the time of my second visit, almost half the town burned down in the space of five hours.

The Kingdom of Borno

They embrace no religion at all, being neither Christian, Muhametans [Muslims], nor Jews, nor any other profession, but living after a brutish manner, having wives and children in common. . . . They have a most powerful prince. . . . He has in readiness as many as three thousand horsemen and a huge number of foot soldiers; for all his subjects are so serviceable and obedient to him, that whenever he commands them, they will arm themselves and will follow him wherever he leads them. They pay him no tribute except tithes on their grain; neither does the king have any revenues to support his state except the spoils he gets from his enemies by frequent invasions and assaults. He is in a state of perpetual hostility with a certain people who live beyond the desert of Seu, who in times past marching with a huge army of footsoldiers over the said desert, devastated a great part of the Kingdom of Borno. Whereupon the king sent for the merchants of Barbary and ordered them to bring him a great store of horses: for in this country they exchange horses for slaves, and sometimes give fifteen or twenty slaves for a horse. And by this means there were a great many horses bought although the merchants were forced to stay for their slaves until the king returned home as a conqueror with a great number of captives, and satisfied his creditors for his horses. Frequently it happens that the merchants must stay three months before the king returned from the wars. . . . Sometimes he does not bring home enough slaves to satisfy the merchants and sometimes they are forced to wait a whole year. . . . And yet the king seems marvelously rich, because his spurs, bridles, platters, dishes, pots, and other vessels are made of gold. The king is extremely covetous and would rather pay his debts in slaves rather than gold.

Source: Leo Africanus, *The History and Description of Africa*, edited by Robert Brown (London: The Hakluyt Society, 1896), 3:824–25, 833–34.

■ ■ ■

SOURCE 7.5 **A Korean World Map** ▶

Created in Korea in 1402, the Kangnido map by the Confucian scholar Kwŏn Kŭn is the oldest world map from East Asia of which copies survive. It provides an East Asian perspective on the world in the early fifteenth century, a period immediately following the collapse of the Mongol Empire, which had put distant regions of the Afro-Eurasia world into more sustained contact than ever before. The Kangnido map drew upon earlier maps from China, Korea, Japan, and the Islamic world. While Korea features prominently, appearing larger than Africa, China is understood as the center of the world, as Kwŏn Kŭn makes clear in the preface: "The world is very wide. We do not know how many tens of thousands of *li* there are from China in the center to the four seas in the outer limits." (A *li* is a Chinese unit of distance, about a third of a mile.) The map includes hundreds of place names for even the most remote regions of Eurasia. Most of those for North Africa and Europe incorporate Arabic or Persian roots, revealing the influence of Islamic maps and mapmakers brought to East Asia by the Mongols. Regional labels not original to the map have been added to help you orient yourself. Note that the Mediterranean Sea is clearly outlined between Africa and Europe but is not colored in. Also note that much of the center of Africa is shaded in, indicating either a large body of water or perhaps the Sahara Desert.

■ Compare this map with a modern map of Africa and Eurasia. Which regions does the map depict most accurately? Which are least accurate? Why might this be the case?

■ What can a map like this tell us about East Asian knowledge of Eurasia and Africa around 1400?

■ How does this map reflect a China-centered view of the world?

■ What types of questions might this map help historians to answer?

The Honkōji Copy of the Kangnido Map, Korea | **15th century**

Pictures from History/Bridgeman Images

DOING HISTORY

1. **Describing a foreign culture:** All of these sources were created by outsiders to the peoples or societies they described. What different postures toward these foreign cultures are evident in the sources? How did the travelers' various religions shape their perception of the places they visited?

2. **Defining the self-perception of authors:** What can we learn from Sources 7.1, 7.2, and 7.4 about the men who wrote them? What motivated them to travel so far from home? How did they define themselves in relationship to the societies they observed?

3. **Assessing the credibility of sources:** What information in these sources would be most valuable for historians? What about these sources might be viewed with the most skepticism? You will want to consider the creators' purposes and their intended audiences.

4. **Considering outsiders' accounts:** What are the advantages and limitations for historians in drawing on the observations of foreign observers?

On Travel Writers

Travel accounts provide rich and often unique sources for historians, but they must be handled with care. The two selections that follow consider issues that historians confront when studying travelers' accounts. In Voice 7.1, John Larner, an expert on Marco Polo, examines the suspicion put forward by some that Polo never traveled to China. In Voice 7.2, Natalie Zemon Davis, a prominent historian of the early modern period, explores the audiences for which Leo Africanus wrote his book.

■ Why have scholars questioned whether Marco Polo actually traveled to China?

■ How might Leo Africanus have altered his account for a North African rather than Italian audience?

■ **Integrating Primary and Secondary Sources:** How do these two voices influence your reading of the Polo and Africanus selections in the source feature?

VOICE 7.1

John Larner on Whether Polo Really Traveled to China │ 1999

From the eighteenth century, as a result above all of Marco's silence about many things in the China of his own time, the suspicion has been aroused in some readers that we are faced here with a fiction, the nagging doubt that the whole of Marco's story of having been to China is untrue. Why does he never mention the Great Wall? Why is there nothing about what, in the fourteenth century, Odoric da Pordenone [another traveler] was to notice: fishing with cormorants, or the binding up of young girls' feet? Why nothing on printing, Chinese script, acupuncture, tea or tea-houses? Why no mention of Confucianism or Taoism? Had he actually *seen* China . . . ? It is not too difficult to offer answers to most of these points. The myth of the Great Wall, for instance, obscures . . . the fact that much of it had fallen down by the thirteenth century. Almost everything the tourist is normally shown today was built in the sixteenth century. Referred to as the "sensi" or "sensin," Taoist monks are in fact briefly mentioned in

chapter LXXV. Foot binding was at this period limited to upper class ladies who were confined to their houses, and would be rarely observed by anyone outside their family. Tea-culture at that time had not reached North and Central China where Marco mostly resided. . . . [I]t can also easily be thought that Marco identified himself so strongly with Mongol rulers that he was indifferent to the mass of the population over whom they rule.

Source: John Larner, *Marco Polo and the Discovery of the World* (New Haven, CT: Yale University Press, 1999), 59.

VOICE 7.2

Natalie Zemon Davis on Leo Africanus's Audiences │ 2006

He [Leo Africanus] was keeping notes throughout his travels and consulting manuscripts whenever he could; he may have had an initial plan for a book and partial drafts of some sections in Arabic on his person when he was kidnapped. However that may be, it was in Italy that he became an author, and the final version [of his book] bears the stamp of his stay there. . . .

In a sense, though, [Leo Africanus] wrote his book with two audiences in mind. His primary audience was in Italy. For his Italian readers he searched for equivalents in weights, measures, coinages, foods, and material objects. For them, he sought Italian translations for words with no perfect equivalent. . . . For them, he struggled valiantly to transcribe Arabic words, names, and place names. . . . For Italian readers, too, he included only those animals "not found in Europe or that were in some ways different from those in Europe."

Yet [he] also had African or at least North African readers and listeners in part of his mind as he composed. He must have imagined at least a few of them as possible readers of this Italian manuscript, and many of them as potential readers of a much revised Arabic version.

Source: Natalie Zemon Davis, *Trickster Travels: A Sixteenth-Century Muslim between Worlds* (New York: Hill and Wang, 2006), 105–7.

CHAPTER 8

China and the World

East Asian Connections

600–1300

Together Again: The Reemergence of a Unified China
A "Golden Age" of Chinese Achievement
Women in the Song Dynasty

China and the Northern Nomads: A Chinese World Order in the Making
The Tribute System in Theory
The Tribute System in Practice
Cultural Influence across an Ecological Frontier

Coping with China: Comparing Korea, Vietnam, and Japan
Korea and China
Vietnam and China
Japan and China

China and the Eurasian World Economy
Spillovers: China's Impact on Eurasia
On the Receiving End: China as Economic Beneficiary

China and Buddhism
Making Buddhism Chinese
Losing State Support: The Crisis of Chinese Buddhism

Reflections: Why Do Things Change?

《 Chinese Astronomy The impressive achievements of Chinese astronomy included the observation of sunspots, supernovae, and solar and lunar eclipses as well as the construction of elaborate star maps and astronomical devices such as those shown here. The print itself is of Japanese origin and depicts a figure wearing the dragon robes of a Chinese official. It illustrates the immense cultural influence of China on its smaller Japanese neighbor.

"There is only one Earth in the universe and we mankind have only one homeland," observed the Chinese president Xi Jinping during his address before the United Nations in January 2017. "The Paris agreement is a milestone in the history of climate governance. We must ensure that this endeavor is not derailed."[1] With these words, the leader of China signaled his country's willingness to take a global leadership role in limiting climate change even as the United States was poised to withdraw from the Paris Accords under its new president Donald Trump. China's remarkable economic development since the 1980s had transformed it by the early twenty-first century into a major global power and one of the largest consumers of fossil fuels on the planet. Its decision to embrace the Paris Accords mattered to peoples and nations around the globe.

From the viewpoint of world history, China's recent prominence on the world stage was hardly something new, and its nineteenth- and twentieth-century position as a "backward," weak, or "developing" country was distinctly at odds with its long history. Its leadership on climate change provided another example of China resuming in recent years a much older and more powerful role in world affairs. ■

n the world of third-wave civilizations, even more than in earlier times, China cast a long shadow. Its massive and powerful civilization, widely imitated by adjacent peoples, gave rise to a China-centered set of relationships encompassing Tibet, Korea, Japan, and Vietnam. China extended its borders deep into Central Asia, while its wealthy and cosmopolitan culture attracted visitors from all over Eurasia. Far beyond its near neighbors, China's

317

booming economy and many technological innovations had ripple effects all across the Afro-Eurasian world.

Even as China so often influenced the world, it too was changed by its many interactions with non-Chinese peoples. Northern nomads—"barbarians" to the Chinese—frequently posed a military threat and on occasion even conquered and ruled parts of China. The country's growing involvement in international trade stimulated important social, cultural, and economic changes within China itself. Buddhism, a religion of Indian origin, took root in China, and, to a much lesser extent, so did Christianity and Islam. In short, China's engagement with the wider world became a very significant element in the global interactions of the third-wave era.

> **SEEKING THE MAIN POINT**
>
> Chinese history has often been viewed in the West as impressive perhaps, but largely static or changeless and self-contained or isolated. In what ways might the material in this chapter counteract such impressions?

Together Again: The Reemergence of a Unified China

The collapse of the Han dynasty around 220 C.E. ushered in more than three centuries of political fragmentation in China and signaled the rise of powerful and locally entrenched aristocratic families. It also meant the incursion of northern nomads, many of whom learned Chinese, dressed like Chinese, married into Chinese families, and governed northern regions of the country in a Chinese fashion. Such conditions of disunity, unnatural in the eyes of many thoughtful Chinese, discredited Confucianism and opened the door to a greater acceptance of Buddhism and Daoism among the elite. Those centuries also witnessed substantial Chinese migration southward toward the Yangzi River valley, a movement of people that gave southern China some 60 percent of the country's population by 1000. That movement of Chinese people, accompanied by their intensive agriculture, set in motion a vast environmental transformation marked by the destruction of the old-growth forests that once covered much of the country and the retreat of the elephants that had inhabited those lands. Around 800 C.E., the Chinese official and writer Liu Zongyuan lamented what was happening:

> A tumbled confusion of lumber as flames on the hillside crackle
> Not even the last remaining shrubs are safeguarded from destruction
> Where once mountain torrents leapt—nothing but rutted gullies.[2]

A "Golden Age" of Chinese Achievement

While the collapse of the western Roman Empire led to permanent political fragmentation, the fall of China's Han dynasty did not, for China regained its earlier political unity under the **Sui dynasty** (581–618). Its emperors solidified that unity by vastly extending the country's canal system, which stretched some 1,200 miles

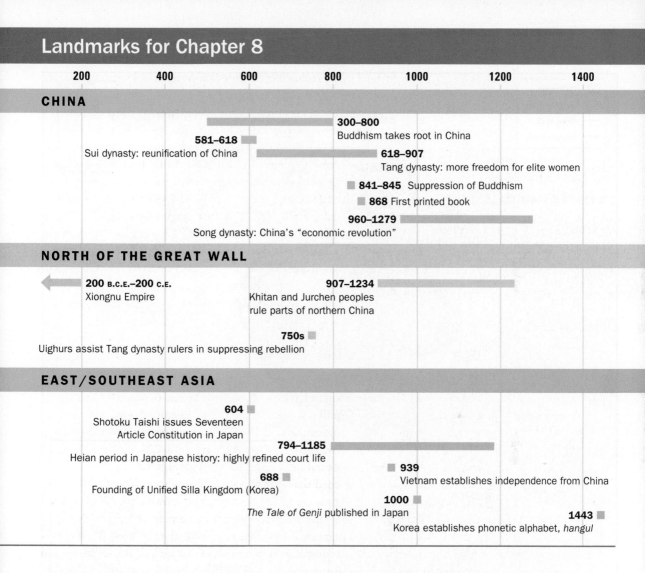

Landmarks for Chapter 8

	200	400	600	800	1000	1200	1400

CHINA

300–800
Buddhism takes root in China

581–618
Sui dynasty: reunification of China

618–907
Tang dynasty: more freedom for elite women

841–845 Suppression of Buddhism

868 First printed book

960–1279
Song dynasty: China's "economic revolution"

NORTH OF THE GREAT WALL

200 B.C.E.–200 C.E.
Xiongnu Empire

907–1234
Khitan and Jurchen peoples
rule parts of northern China

750s
Uighurs assist Tang dynasty rulers in suppressing rebellion

EAST/SOUTHEAST ASIA

604
Shotoku Taishi issues Seventeen
Article Constitution in Japan

794–1185
Heian period in Japanese history: highly refined court life

939
Vietnam establishes independence from China

688
Founding of Unified Silla Kingdom (Korea)

1000
The Tale of Genji published in Japan

1443
Korea establishes phonetic alphabet, *hangul*

---

in length and is described by one scholar as "an engineering feat without parallel in the world of its time."[3] Those canals linked northern and southern China economically and contributed much to the prosperity that followed. But the ruthlessness of Sui emperors and a futile military campaign to conquer Korea exhausted the state's resources, alienated many people, and prompted the overthrow of the dynasty.

This dynastic collapse, however, witnessed no prolonged disintegration of the Chinese state. The two dynasties that followed—the **Tang dynasty** (618–907) and the **Song dynasty** (960–1279)—built on the Sui foundations of renewed unity (see Map 8.1). Together they established patterns of Chinese life that endured into the twentieth century. Culturally, this era has long been regarded as a "golden age" of arts and literature, setting standards of excellence in poetry, landscape painting, and ceramics. Particularly during the Song dynasty, an explosion of scholarship gave rise to Neo-Confucianism, an effort to revive Confucian thinking while incorporating some of the insights of Buddhism and Daoism.

Guided Reading Question

....

■ **CHANGE**

Why are the centuries of the Tang and Song dynasties in China sometimes referred to as a "golden age"?

MAPPING HISTORY

Map 8.1 Tang and Song Dynasty China

During the third-wave era, China interacted extensively with its neighbors. The Tang dynasty extended Chinese control deep into Central Asia. Under the Song dynasty, nomadic Jurchen peoples conquered much of northern China, creating two states—the Song in the south and the Jin in the north. Both claimed to be the heirs to the Tang dynasty and thus the true emperors of China.

READING THE MAP: Compare the extent of Tang dynasty China to that of Southern Song dynasty China. Which major regions did the Tang control that the Southern Song did not?

MAPPING COMPARISONS: Compare the extent of Song dynasty China on Map 8.1 with that of Han dynasty China on Map 3.5. What differences are apparent in the relationship between China and the northern "barbarians"?

Politically, the Tang and Song dynasties built a state structure that endured for a thousand years. Six major ministries—personnel, finance, rites, army, justice, and public works—were accompanied by the Censorate, an agency that exercised surveillance over the rest of the government, checking on the character and competence of public officials. To staff this bureaucracy, the examination system was revived and made more elaborate, facilitated by the ability to print books for the first time in world history. Schools and colleges proliferated to prepare candidates for the rigorous exams, which became a central feature of upper-class life. A leading world historian has described Tang dynasty China as "the best ordered state in the world."[4]

Selecting officials on the basis of merit represented a challenge to established aristocratic families' hold on public office. Still, a substantial percentage of official positions went to the sons of the privileged, even if they had not passed the exams. Moreover, because education and the examination system grew far more rapidly than the number of official positions, many who passed lower-level exams could not be accommodated with a bureaucratic appointment. Often, however, they were able to combine landowning and success in the examination system to maintain an immense cultural prestige and prominence in their local areas. (See Working with Evidence: China's Scholar-Officials, page 348, for more on the life of the "scholar-official" class.)

Underlying these cultural and political achievements was **China's economic revolution**, which made Song dynasty China "by far the richest, most skilled, and most populous country on earth."[5] The most obvious sign of China's prosperity was its rapid growth in population, which jumped from about 50 million or 60 million during the Tang dynasty to 120 million by 1200. Behind this doubling of the population were remarkable achievements in agricultural production, particularly the adoption of a fast-ripening and drought-resistant strain of rice from Vietnam.

Many people found their way to the cities, making China the most urbanized country in the world. Dozens of Chinese cities numbered over 100,000, while the Song dynasty capital of **Hangzhou** was home to more than a million people. A Chinese observer in 1235 provided a vivid description of that city.[6] Specialized markets abounded for meat, herbs, vegetables, books, rice, and much more, with troupes of actors performing for the crowds. Restaurants advertised their unique offerings, including pickled dates, juicy lungs, and pigs' feet. "Luxuriant inns," marked by red lanterns, featured prostitutes and "wine chambers equipped with beds." Specialized agencies managed elaborate dinner parties for the wealthy, complete with a Perfume and Medicine Office to "help sober up the guests." Schools for musicians offered thirteen different courses. Numerous clubs provided companionship for poets, fishermen, Buddhists, physical fitness enthusiasts, antiques collectors, horse lovers, and many other groups. No wonder the Italian visitor Marco Polo described Hangzhou later in the thirteenth century as "beyond dispute the finest and noblest [city] in the world."[7] (See Working with Evidence: Travelers' Tales and Observations, Source 7.2, page 307, for a fuller description of Marco Polo's impressions of Hangzhou.)

Gunpowder

The Chinese Tang and Song dynasties (618–1279) witnessed a golden age of technological innovation in China. Both woodblock and movable type generated the world's first printed books, while Chinese innovations in navigational and shipbuilding technologies led the world. Among these many developments, the invention of gunpowder stands out because it spawned a permanent revolution in military affairs that had global dimensions. But gunpowder, a mixture of saltpeter, sulfur, and charcoal, was not originally developed for use in war. Instead, it was an accidental byproduct of the search by Daoist alchemists for an elixir of immortality. Indeed, the first reference to gunpowder appeared in a mid-ninth-century

A tenth-century Chinese Buddhist painting depicting demons armed with a fire lance and grenade.

Daoist text that warns alchemists not to mix together its component parts because "smoke and flames result, so that [the alchemists'] hands and faces have been burnt, and even the whole house where they were working burned down."[8] This association with alchemy may explain why the Chinese referred to gunpowder as *huo yao*, or "fire

photo: akg-images/Pictures from History

drug." The same properties that made gunpowder so dangerous in an alchemist's lab attracted the interest of those seeking to entertain and amaze audiences through fireworks and pyrotechnic displays, especially at the Chinese imperial court.

Military authorities also noticed its potential as a weapon, and its uses in war developed rapidly during the Song dynasty. At first, military engineers drew on the incendiary rather than the explosive possibilities of gunpowder. In 1044, an imperial official wrote a tract for the emperor on military technologies that included two recipes for gunpowder, both for weapons designed to set fire to their targets. Decades later, Song engineers borrowed techniques from fireworks makers to produce "Thunderclap Bombs" designed to scare and disorient opposing troops through noise and light. While these bombs were not yet powerful

Industrial production likewise soared. In both large-scale enterprises employing hundreds of workers and in smaller backyard furnaces, China's iron industry increased its output dramatically. By the eleventh century, it was providing the government with 32,000 suits of armor and 16 million iron arrowheads annually, in addition to supplying metal for coins, tools, construction, and bells in Buddhist monasteries. This industrial growth was fueled almost entirely by coal, which also came to provide most of the energy for heating homes and cooking and no doubt generated considerable air pollution. Technological innovation in other fields also flourished. Inventions in printing, both woodblock and movable type, generated the world's first printed books, and by 1000 relatively cheap books on religious, agricultural, mathematical, and medical topics became widely available in China. Its navigational and shipbuilding technologies led the world. The Chinese invention enough to kill large numbers of the enemy, a chronicler of a siege of the Song capital in 1127 described them as "hitting the lines of the enemy well and throwing them into great confusion."

Through the twelfth and early thirteenth centuries, both the Song dynasty, which controlled southern China, and the Jin, which controlled much of the north, continued to develop ever more powerful gunpowder weapons. Engineers experimented with gunpowder blends that included larger quantities of saltpeter, the nitrate-rich substance that gives gunpowder its explosiveness. When the Mongols invaded northern China in 1231, the defenders of the capital, Kaifeng, were able to deploy what they called the "Heaven-Shaking Thunder Crash Bomb" against Mongol forces. An eyewitness recorded that "the attacking soldiers were blown to bits, not even a trace being left behind."

The Mongols recognized the effectiveness of gunpowder, and following their conquest of China, encouraged engineers to continue to develop new weapons. During the thirteenth and fourteenth centuries, powerful bombs were produced with such names as "Match for Ten Thousand Enemies Bomb" and the "Bone-Burning and Bruising Fire Oil Magic Bomb." At the same time, Chinese technicians developed the first rockets, which were employed in battle from the middle of the thirteenth century. These experiments with more powerful forms of gunpowder culminated in the emergence of weapons designed to fire projectiles. The first of these evolved from earlier fire lances, bamboo or metal tubes filled with gunpowder that spewed flames and sparks. However, unlike the fire lance, which used the incendiary properties of gunpowder to attack the enemy, these new guns used its explosive power as a propellant to fire projectiles. Handheld guns were in regular use by the second half of the thirteenth century; cannons were common on the battlefield by 1350.

Gunpowder and gunpowder-based weapons spread rapidly across Eurasia from the thirteenth century on, changing the nature of warfare wherever they were adopted. While there is some debate as to exactly when gunpowder arrived in India, the Middle East, and Europe, it is clear that the Mongols' use of gunpowder weapons in their conquests spurred its spread and use. Its rapid adoption ensured that by the sixteenth century the "fire drug" developed by Daoist alchemists in search of immortality had sparked what scholars have labeled the gunpowder revolution in warfare, transforming military conflict across the globe. Gunpowder remained the dominant explosive used in war until the advent of nitroglycerin in the mid-nineteenth century.

It is more than a little ironic that a substance originally derived from a search for happiness and immortality would result in unimaginable human suffering and an untold number of deaths. Such are the unintended outcomes of human effort.

QUESTION

What can the development of gunpowder-based weapons tell us about technological innovation in China?

---

of **gunpowder** created within a few centuries a revolution in military affairs that had global dimensions. (See Zooming In: Gunpowder, page 322.) But China's remarkable industrial revolution stalled, perhaps because the country was repeatedly invaded and devastated by nomadic peoples from the north, culminating in the Mongol conquests of the thirteenth century.

These innovations occurred within the world's most highly commercialized society, in which producing for the market, rather than for local consumption, became a very widespread phenomenon. An immense network of internal waterways stretching perhaps 30,000 miles—canals, rivers, and lakes—facilitated the cheap movement of goods, allowing peasants to grow specialized crops for sale while they purchased rice or other staples on the market. In addition, government demands for taxes paid in cash rather than in kind required peasants to sell

Kaifeng This detail comes from a huge watercolor scroll, titled *Upper River during Qing Ming Festival*, originally painted during the Song dynasty. It illustrates the urban sophistication of Kaifeng and other Chinese cities at that time and has been frequently imitated and copied since then. (© VIEW STOCK RF/age-fotostock)

something—their products or their labor—in order to meet their obligations. The growing use of paper money, as well as financial instruments such as letters of credit and promissory notes, further contributed to the commercialization of Chinese society. Two prominent scholars have described the outcome: "Output increased, population grew, skills multiplied, and a burst of inventiveness made Song China far wealthier than ever before—or than any of its contemporaries."[9] (See Snapshot, page 339.)

Women in the Song Dynasty

The "golden age" of Song dynasty China was perhaps less than "golden" for many of its women, for that era marked yet another turning point in the history of Chinese patriarchy. Under the influence of steppe nomads, whose women led less restricted lives, elite Chinese women of the Tang dynasty era, at least in the north, had participated in social life with greater freedom than in earlier times. Paintings and statues show aristocratic women riding horses, while the Queen Mother of the West, a Daoist deity, was widely worshipped by female Daoist priests and practitioners. By the Song dynasty, however, a reviving Confucianism and rapid economic growth seemed to tighten patriarchal restrictions on women and to restore some of the earlier Han dynasty notions of female submission and passivity.

Once again, Confucian writers emphasized the subordination of women to men and the need to keep males and females separate in every domain of life. The Song dynasty historian and scholar Sima Guang (1019–1086) summed up the prevailing view: "The boy leads the girl, the girl follows the boy; the duty of husbands to be resolute and wives to be docile begins with this."[10] For men, masculinity came to be defined less in terms of horseback riding, athleticism, and the warrior values of northern nomads and more in terms of the refined pursuits of calligraphy, scholarship, painting, and poetry. Corresponding views of feminine qualities emphasized women's weakness, reticence, and delicacy. Women were also frequently viewed as a distraction to men's pursuit of a contemplative and introspective life. The remarriage of widows, though legally permissible, was increasingly condemned, for "to walk through two courtyards is a source of shame for a woman."[11]

Guided Reading Question

■ **CHANGE**
In what ways did women's lives change during the Tang and Song dynasties?

The most compelling expression of a tightening patriarchy lay in **foot binding**. Apparently beginning among dancers and courtesans in the tenth or eleventh century C.E., this practice involved the tight wrapping of young girls' feet, usually breaking the bones of the foot and causing intense pain. During and after the Song dynasty, foot binding found general acceptance among elite families and later became even more widespread in Chinese society. It was associated with new images of female beauty and eroticism that emphasized small size, frailty, and deference and served to keep women restricted to the "inner quarters," where Confucian tradition asserted that they belonged. Many mothers imposed this painful procedure on their daughters, perhaps to enhance their marriage prospects and to assist them in competing with concubines for the attention of their husbands.[12] For many women, it became a rite of passage, and their tiny feet and the beautiful slippers that encased them became a source of some pride, even a topic of poetry for some literate women. Foot binding also served to distinguish Chinese women from their "barbarian" counterparts and elite women from commoners and peasants.

Furthermore, a rapidly commercializing economy undermined the position of women in the textile industry. Urban workshops and state factories, run by men, increasingly took over the skilled tasks of weaving textiles, especially silk, which had previously been the work of rural women in their homes. Although these women continued to tend silkworms and spin silk thread, they had lost the more lucrative income-generating work of weaving silk fabrics. But as their economic role in textile production declined, other opportunities beckoned in an increasingly prosperous Song China. In the cities, women operated restaurants, sold fish and vegetables, and worked as maids, cooks, and dressmakers. The growing prosperity of elite families funneled increasing numbers of women into roles as concubines, entertainers, courtesans, and prostitutes. Their ready availability surely reduced the

Foot Binding While the practice of foot binding painfully deformed the feet of young girls and women, it was also associated aesthetically with feminine beauty, particularly in the delicate and elaborately decorated shoes that encased their bound feet. (foot: Jodi Cobb/National Geographic Creative; shoe: ClassicStock/Masterfile)

ability of wives to negotiate as equals with their husbands, setting women against one another and creating endless household jealousies.

In other ways, the Song dynasty witnessed more positive trends in the lives of women. Their property rights expanded, allowing women to control their own dowries and to inherit property from their families. "Neither in earlier nor in later periods," writes one scholar, "did as much property pass through women's hands" as during the Song dynasty.[13] Furthermore, lower-ranking but ambitious officials strongly urged the education of women, so that they might more effectively raise their sons and increase the family's fortune. Song dynasty China, in short, offered a mixture of tightening restrictions and new opportunities to its women.

China and the Northern Nomads: A Chinese World Order in the Making

Among China's various interactions with a larger Eurasian world, the most endur-ing and intense involved the many nomadic pastoral or semi-agricultural peoples of the steppes north of the Great Wall. Living in areas unable to sustain Chinese-style farming, these northern nomads had long focused their economies around the rais-ing of livestock (sheep, cattle, goats) and the mastery of horse riding. Organized locally in small, mobile, kinship-based groups, these peoples also periodically created much larger and powerful states or confederations that could draw on the impressive horsemanship and military skills of virtually the entire male population of their societies. Such specialized pastoral societies needed grain and other agricultural products from China, and their leaders developed a taste for Chinese manufactured and luxury goods—wine and silk, for example—with which they could attract and reward followers. Thus the nomads were drawn like a magnet toward China, trading, raiding, and extorting to obtain the resources so vital to their way of life. For 2,000 years or more, pressure from the steppes and the intrusion of nomadic peoples were constant factors in China's historical development.

From the nomads' point of view, the threat often came from the Chinese, who periodically directed their own military forces deep into the steppes, built the Great Wall to keep the nomads out, and often proved unwilling to allow pastoral peoples easy access to trading opportunities within China. And yet the Chinese needed the nomads and especially their horses, which were essential for the Chinese military. Other products of the steppes and the forests beyond, such as skins, furs, hides, and amber, were also of value in China. Furthermore, pastoral nomads controlled much of the Silk Road trading network, which funneled goods from the West into China. The continuing interaction between China and the northern nomads brought together peoples occupying different environments, practicing different economies, governing themselves with different institutions, and thinking about the world in quite different ways.

Guided Reading Question

■ **CONNECTION**
How did the Chinese and their nomadic neighbors to the north view each other?

The Tribute System in Theory

An enduring outcome of this cross-cultural encounter was a particular view the Chinese held of themselves and of their neighbors, fully articulated by the time of the Han dynasty (ca. 200 B.C.E.–200 C.E.) and lasting for more than two millennia. That understanding cast China as the "middle kingdom," the center of the world, infinitely superior to the "barbarian" peoples beyond its borders. With its long history, great cities, refined tastes, sophisticated intellectual and artistic achievements, bureaucratic state, literate elite, and prosperous economy, China represented "civilization." All of this, in Chinese thinking, was in sharp contrast to the rude cultures and primitive life of the northern nomads, who continually moved about "like beasts and birds," lived in tents, ate mostly meat and milk, and practically lived on their horses, while making war on everyone within reach. Educated Chinese saw their own society as self-sufficient, requiring little from the outside world, while barbarians, quite understandably, sought access to China's wealth and wisdom. Furthermore, China was willing to permit that access under controlled conditions, for its sense of superiority did not preclude the possibility that barbarians could become civilized Chinese. China was a "radiating civilization," graciously shedding its light most fully to nearby barbarians and with diminished intensity to those farther away.

The Tribute System This eighteenth-century Korean painting depicts a Korean diplomatic mission to Qing China approaching the city of Sanhaegwan on its way to offer tribute to the emperor in Beijing, 190 miles away. Such tribute missions offered opportunities for the Korean delegation to see something of China. According to diaries of Korean envoys, they categorized sites along the route to Beijing under such titles as historical, curiosity, or spectacle. (© Copyright The Korean Christian Museum at Soongsil University, Courtesy of the Academy of Korean Studies, South Korea)

Guided Reading Question

■ **CONNECTION**
What assumptions underlay the tribute system?

That worldview also took shape as a practical system for managing China's relationship with these people. Known as the **tribute system**, it was a set of practices that required non-Chinese authorities to acknowledge Chinese superiority and their own subordinate place in a Chinese-centered world order. Foreigners seeking access to China had to send a delegation to the Chinese court, where they would perform the kowtow, a series of ritual bowings and prostrations, and present their tribute—products of value from their countries—to the Chinese emperor. In return for these expressions of submission, he would grant permission for foreigners to trade in China's rich markets and would provide them with gifts or "bestowals," often worth far more than the tribute they had offered. This was the mechanism by which successive Chinese dynasties attempted to regulate their relationships with northern nomads; with neighboring states such as Korea, Vietnam, Tibet, and Japan; and, after 1500, with those European barbarians from across the sea.

Often, this system seemed to work. Over the centuries, countless foreign delegations proved willing to present their tribute, say the required words, and perform the rituals necessary for gaining access to the material goods of China. Aspiring non-Chinese rulers also gained prestige as they basked in the reflected glory of even this subordinate association with the great Chinese civilization. The official titles, seals of office, and ceremonial robes they received from China proved useful in their local struggles for power.

The Tribute System in Practice

But the tribute system also disguised some realities that contradicted its assumptions. On occasion, China was confronting not separate and small-scale barbarian societies, but large and powerful nomadic empires able to deal with China on at least equal terms. An early nomadic confederacy was the **Xiongnu Empire**, established about the same time as the Han dynasty (ca. 200 B.C.E.) and eventually reaching from Manchuria to Central Asia (see Map 3.5, page 118). Devastating Xiongnu raids into northern China persuaded the Chinese emperor to negotiate an arrangement that recognized the nomadic state as a political equal, promised its leader a princess in marriage, and, most important, agreed to supply him annually with large quantities of grain, wine, and silk. In return for these goods, so critical for the functioning of the nomadic state, the Xiongnu agreed to refrain from military incursions into China. The basic realities of the situation were summed up in this warning to the Han dynasty in the first century B.C.E.:

> Just make sure that the silks and grain stuffs you bring the Xiongnu are the right measure and quality, that's all. What's the need for talking? If the goods you deliver are up to measure and good quality, all right. But if there is any deficiency or the quality is no good, then when the autumn harvest comes, we will take our horses and trample all over your crops.[14]

Something similar occurred during the Tang dynasty as a series of Turkic empires arose in Mongolia. Like the Xiongnu, they too extorted large "gifts" from the Chinese. One of these peoples, the Uighurs, actually rescued the Tang dynasty from a serious internal revolt in the 750s. In return, the Uighur leader gained one of the Chinese emperor's daughters as a wife and arranged a highly favorable exchange of poor-quality horses for high-quality silk, which brought half a million rolls of the precious fabric annually into the Uighur lands. Despite the rhetoric of the tribute system, the Chinese were not always able to dictate the terms of their relationship with the northern nomads.

Steppe nomads were generally not much interested in actually conquering and ruling China. It was easier and more profitable to extort goods from a functioning Chinese state. On occasion, however, that state broke down and various nomadic groups moved in to "pick up the pieces," conquering and governing parts of China. Such a process took place following the fall of the Han dynasty and again after the collapse of the Tang dynasty, when the Khitan (kee-THAN) (907–1125) and then the Jin, or Jurchen (JER-chihn) (1115–1234), peoples established states that encompassed parts of China as well as major areas of the steppes to the north. Both of them required the Chinese Song dynasty, located farther south, to deliver annually huge quantities of silk, silver, and tea, some of which found its way into the Silk Road trading network. The practice of "bestowing gifts on barbarians," long a part of the tribute system, allowed the proud Chinese to imagine that they were still in control of the situation even as they were paying heavily for protection from nomadic incursion. Those gifts, in turn, provided vital economic resources to nomadic states.

Cultural Influence across an Ecological Frontier

When nomadic peoples actually ruled parts of China, some of them adopted Chinese ways, employing Chinese advisers, governing according to Chinese practice, and, at least for the elite, immersing themselves in Chinese culture and learning. This process of "becoming Chinese" went furthest among the Jurchen, many of whom lived in northern China and learned to speak Chinese, wore Chinese clothing, married Chinese husbands and wives, and practiced Buddhism or Daoism.

On the whole, however, Chinese culture had only a modest impact on the nomadic people of the northern steppes. Unlike the native peoples of southern China, who were gradually absorbed into Chinese culture, the pastoral societies north of the Great Wall generally retained their own cultural patterns. Few of them were incorporated, at least not for long, within a Chinese state, and most lived in areas where Chinese-style agriculture was simply impossible. Under these conditions, there were few incentives for adopting Chinese culture wholesale. But various modes of interaction—peaceful trade, military conflict, political negotiations, economic extortion, some cultural influence—continued across the ecological frontier that divided two quite distinct and separate ways of life. Each was necessary for the other.

**Guided Reading
Question**

■ **CONNECTION**
In what ways did China and the nomads influence each other?

On the Chinese side, elements of steppe culture had some influence in those parts of northern China that were periodically conquered and ruled by nomadic peoples. The founders of the Sui and Tang dynasties were in fact of mixed nomad and Chinese ancestry and came from the borderland region where a blended Chinese/Turkic culture had evolved. High-ranking members of the imperial family personally led their troops in battle in the style of Turkic warriors. Furthermore, Tang dynasty China was awash with foreign visitors from all over Asia—delegations bearing tribute, merchants carrying exotic goods, and bands of clerics or religious pilgrims bringing new religions such as Christianity, Islam, Buddhism, and Manichaeism. For a time in the Tang dynasty, almost anything associated with "Western barbarians"—Central Asians, Persians, Indians, Arabs—had great appeal among northern Chinese elites. Their music, dancing, clothing, foods, games, and artistic styles found favor among the upper classes. The more traditional southern Chinese, feeling themselves heir to the legacy of the Han dynasty, were sharply critical of their northern counterparts for allowing women too much freedom, for drinking yogurt rather than tea, and for listening to "Western" music, all of which they attributed to barbarian influence. Around 800 C.E., the poet Yuan Chen gave voice to a growing backlash against this too-easy acceptance of things "Western":

> Ever since the Western horsemen began raising smut and dust,
> Fur and fleece, rank and rancid, have filled Hsien and Lo [two Chinese cities].
> Women make themselves Western matrons by the study of Western makeup.
> Entertainers present Western tunes, in their devotion to Western music.[15]

Coping with China: Comparing Korea, Vietnam, and Japan

Also involved in tributary relationships with China were the newly emerging states and civilizations of Korea, Vietnam, and Japan. Unlike the northern nomads, these societies were thoroughly agricultural and sedentary. During the first millennium C.E., they were part of a larger process—the globalization of civilization—that produced new city- and state-based societies in various parts of the world. Proximity to their giant Chinese neighbor decisively shaped the histories of these new East Asian civilizations, for all of them borrowed major elements of Chinese culture. But unlike the native peoples of southern China, who largely became Chinese, the peoples of Korea, Vietnam, and Japan did not. They retained distinctive identities, which have lasted into modern times. While resisting Chinese political domination, they also appreciated Chinese culture and sought the source of Chinese wealth and power. Korea, Vietnam, and Japan, however, encountered China and responded to it in quite different ways.

Korea and China

Immediately adjacent to northeastern China, the Korean peninsula and its people have long lived in the shadow of their imposing neighbor (see Map 8.2). Temporary Chinese conquest of northern Korea during the Han dynasty and some colonization by Chinese settlers provided an initial channel for Chinese cultural influence, particularly in the form of Buddhism. Emerging in the first century B.C.E. and reaching their most powerful and sophisticated forms between the fourth and seventh century C.E., early Korean states all referred to their rulers with the Chinese term *wang* (king). Bitter rivals with one another, they also strenuously resisted Chinese political control, except when they found it advantageous to join with China against a local enemy. In the seventh century, one of these states—the **Silla** (SHEE-lah) **kingdom**—allied with Tang dynasty China to bring some political unity to the peninsula for the first time, founding what is known as the Unified Silla Kingdom. But Chinese efforts to set up puppet regimes and to assimilate Koreans to Chinese culture provoked sharp military resistance, persuading the Chinese to withdraw their military forces in 688 and to establish a tributary relationship with a largely independent Korea.

Under a succession of dynasties—the Unified Silla (688–900), Koryo (918–1392), and Joseon (1392–1910)—Korea generally maintained its political independence while participating in China's tribute system. Its leaders actively embraced the connection with China and, especially during the Silla dynasty, sought to turn their small state into a miniature version of Tang China.

Tribute missions to China provided legitimacy for Korean rulers and models of court life and administrative techniques, which they sought to replicate back home. A new capital city of Kumsong was modeled directly on the Chinese capital

Guided Reading Question

■ **CONNECTION**
In what ways did China have an influence in Korea, Vietnam, and Japan? In what ways was that influence resisted?

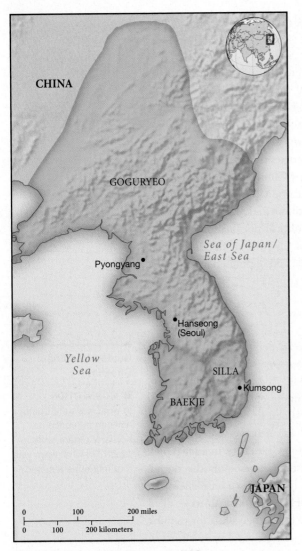

Map 8.2 Korean Kingdoms, ca. 500 C.E.
The three early kingdoms of Korea were brought together by the seventh century in a unified state, which was later governed by a series of dynastic regimes.

of Chang'an (chahng-ahn). Tribute missions also enabled both official and private trade, mostly in luxury goods such as ceremonial clothing, silks, fancy teas, Confucian and Buddhist texts, and artwork. All of this enriched the lives of a Korean aristocracy that was becoming increasingly Chinese in culture. Thousands of Korean students were sent to China, where they studied primarily Confucianism but also the sciences and the arts. Buddhist monks visited centers of learning and pilgrimage in China and brought back popular forms of Chinese Buddhism, which quickly took root in Korea. Schools for the study of Confucianism, using texts in the Chinese language, were established in Korea. In these ways, Korea became a part of the expanding world of Chinese culture, and refugees from the peninsula's many wars carried Chinese culture to Japan as well.

These efforts to plant Confucian values and Chinese culture in Korea had what one scholar has called an "overwhelmingly negative" impact on Korean women, particularly after 1300.[16] Early Chinese observers noticed, and strongly disapproved of, free-choice marriages in Korea as well as the practice of women singing and dancing together late at night. With the support of the Korean court, Chinese models of family life and female behavior, especially among the elite, gradually replaced the more flexible Korean patterns. Earlier, a Korean woman had generally given birth and raised her young children in her parents' home, where she was often joined by her husband. This was now strongly discouraged, for Confucian orthodoxy demanded that a married woman belonged to her husband's family. Other Korean customs—funeral rites in which a husband was buried in the sacred plot of his wife's family, the remarriage of widowed or divorced women, and female inheritance of property—also eroded under the pressure of Confucian orthodoxy. So too did the practice of plural marriages for men. In 1413, a legal distinction between primary and secondary wives required men to identify one of their wives as primary. Because she and her children now had special privileges and status, sharp new tensions emerged within families. Korean restrictions on elite women, especially widows, came to exceed even those in China itself.

Still, Korea remained Korean. After 688, the country's political independence, though periodically threatened, was largely intact. Chinese cultural influence, except for Buddhism, had little impact beyond the aristocracy and certainly did not penetrate the lives of Korea's serf-like peasants. Nor did it register among Korea's many slaves, amounting to about one-third of the country's population by 1100. In fact, Korean Buddhist monasteries used slaves to cultivate their lands. A Chinese-style examination system to recruit government officials, though encouraged by some Korean rulers, never assumed the prominence that it gained in Tang and Song dynasty China. Korea's aristocratic class was able to maintain an even stronger monopoly on bureaucratic office than its Chinese counterpart did. And in the mid-1400s, Korea moved toward greater cultural independence by developing a phonetic alphabet, known as *hangul* (HAHN-gool), for writing the Korean language. Although resisted by conservative male elites, who were long accustomed to using the more prestigious Chinese characters to write Korean, this new form of writing gradually took hold, especially in private correspondence, in popular fiction, and among women. Clearly part of the Chinese world order, Korea nonetheless retained a distinctive culture as well as a separate political existence.

Vietnam and China

At the southern fringe of the Chinese cultural world, the people who eventually came to be called Vietnamese had a broadly similar historical encounter with China (see Map 8.3). As in Korea, the elite culture of Vietnam borrowed heavily from China—adopting Confucianism, Daoism, Buddhism, administrative techniques, the examination system, and artistic and literary styles—even as its popular culture remained distinctive. And, like Korea, Vietnam achieved political independence while participating fully in the tribute system as a vassal state.

Unlike Korea, however, the cultural heartland of Vietnam in the Red River valley was fully incorporated into the Chinese state for more than a thousand years (111 B.C.E.–939 C.E.). Regarded by the Chinese as "southern barbarians," the Vietnamese were ruled by Chinese officials who expected to fully assimilate this rich rice-growing region into China culturally as well as politically. To these officials, it was simply a further

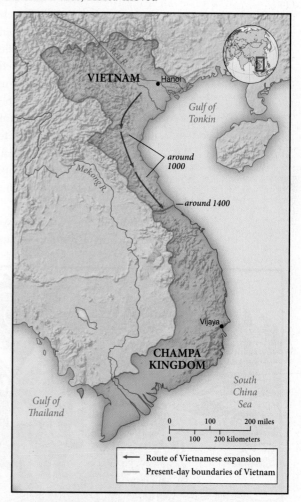

Map 8.3 Vietnam

As Vietnam threw off Chinese control, it also expanded to the south, while remaining wary of its larger Chinese neighbor to the north.

extension of the southward movement of Chinese civilization. Thus Chinese-style irrigated agriculture was introduced; Vietnamese elites were brought into the local bureaucracy and educated in Confucian-based schools; Chinese replaced the local language in official business; Chinese clothing and hairstyles became mandatory; and large numbers of Chinese, some fleeing internal conflicts at home, flooded into the relative security of what they referred to as "the pacified south," while often despising the local people. The heavy pressure of the Chinese presence generated not only a Vietnamese elite thoroughly schooled in Chinese culture but also periodic rebellions, on several occasions led by women. (See Zooming In: Trung Trac, Chapter 3, page 116.)

The weakening of the Tang dynasty in the early tenth century C.E. finally enabled a particularly large rebellion to establish Vietnam as a separate state, though one that carefully maintained its tributary role, sending repeated missions to do homage at the Chinese court. Nonetheless, successive Vietnamese dynasties found the Chinese approach to government useful, styling their rulers as emperors, claiming the Mandate of Heaven, and making use of Chinese court rituals, while expanding their state steadily southward. More so than in Korea, a Chinese-based examination system in Vietnam functioned to undermine an established aristocracy, to provide some measure of social mobility for commoners, and to create a merit-based scholar-gentry class to staff the bureaucracy. Furthermore, members of the Vietnamese elite class remained deeply committed to Chinese culture, viewing their own country less as a separate nation than as a southern extension of a universal civilization, the only one they knew.

Beyond the elite, however, there remained much that was uniquely Vietnamese, such as a distinctive language, a fondness for cockfighting, and the habit of chewing betel nuts. More importantly, Vietnam long retained a greater role for women in social and economic life, despite heavy Chinese influence. In the third century C.E., a woman leader of an anti-Chinese resistance movement declared: "I want to drive away the enemy to save our people. I will not resign myself to the usual lot of women who bow their heads and become concubines." Female nature deities and a "female Buddha" continued to be part of Vietnamese popular religion, even as Confucian-based ideas took root among the elite. In the centuries following independence from China, as Vietnam expanded to the south, northern officials tried in vain to impose more orthodox Confucian

Independence for Vietnam In 938, Vietnamese forces under the leadership of General Ngo Quyen defeated the Chinese in the Battle of Bach Dang River, thus ending a thousand years of direct Chinese rule. This image is one of many that celebrate that victory. (Pictures from History/CPA Media)

gender practices in place of local customs that allowed women to choose their own husbands and married men to live in the households of their wives. So persistent were these practices that a seventeenth-century Chinese visitor opined, with disgust, that Vietnamese preferred the birth of a girl to that of a boy. These features of Vietnamese life reflected larger patterns of Southeast Asian culture that distinguished it from China. And like Koreans, the Vietnamese developed a variation of Chinese writing called *chu nom* ("southern script"), which provided the basis for an independent national literature and a vehicle for the writing of most educated women.

Japan and China

Unlike Korea and Vietnam, the Japanese islands were physically separated from China by 100 miles or more of ocean and were never successfully invaded or conquered by their giant mainland neighbor (see Map 8.4). Thus Japan's very extensive borrowing from Chinese civilization was wholly voluntary, rather than occurring under conditions of direct military threat or outright occupation. The high point of that borrowing took place during the seventh to the ninth centuries C.E., as the first more or less unified Japanese state began to emerge from dozens of small clan-based aristocratic chiefdoms. That state found much that was useful in Tang dynasty China and set out, deliberately and systematically, to transform Japan into a centralized bureaucratic state on the Chinese model.

The initial leader of this effort was **Shotoku Taishi** (572–622), a prominent aristocrat from one of the major clans. He launched a series of large-scale missions to China that took hundreds of Japanese monks, scholars, artists, and students to the mainland. In 604 C.E. Shotoku issued the Seventeen Article Constitution, proclaiming the Japanese ruler a Chinese-style emperor and encouraging both Buddhism and Confucianism. In good Confucian fashion, that document emphasized the moral quality of rulers as a foundation for social harmony. In the decades that followed, Japanese authorities adopted Chinese-style court rituals as well as the Chinese calendar. Later, they likewise established Chinese-based taxation systems, law codes, government ministries, and a provincial administration, at least on paper. Two capital cities, first Nara and then Heian-kyo (Kyoto), were both modeled on the Chinese capital of Chang'an.

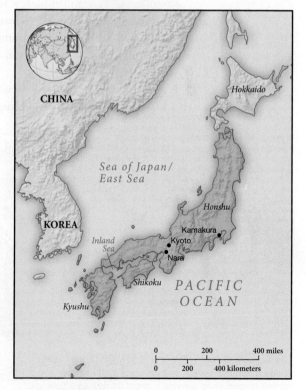

Map 8.4 Japan
Japan's distance from China enabled it to maintain its political independence and to draw selectively from Chinese culture.

Chinese culture, no less than its political practices, also found favor in Japan. Various schools of Chinese Buddhism took root, first among the educated and literate classes and later more broadly in Japanese society. Buddhism deeply affected Japanese art, architecture, education, medicine, views of the afterlife, and attitudes toward suffering and the impermanence of life. The Chinese writing system—and with it an interest in historical writing, calligraphy, and poetry—likewise proved attractive among the elite.

The absence of any compelling threat from China made it possible for the Japanese to be selective in their borrowing. By the tenth century, deliberate efforts to absorb additional elements of Chinese culture diminished, and formal tribute missions to China stopped, although private traders and Buddhist monks continued to make the difficult journey to the mainland. Over many centuries, the Japanese combined what they had assimilated from China with elements of their own tradition into a distinctive Japanese civilization.

In the political realm, for example, the Japanese never succeeded in creating an effective centralized and bureaucratic state to match that of China. Although the court and the emperor retained an important ceremonial and cultural role, their real political authority over the country gradually diminished in favor of competing aristocratic families, both at court and in the provinces. As political power became increasingly decentralized, local authorities developed their own military forces, the famous *samurai* warrior class of Japanese society. Bearing their exquisite curved swords, the samurai developed a distinctive set of values featuring bravery, loyalty, endurance, honor, great skill in martial arts, and a preference for death over surrender. This was **bushido** (boo-shee-doh), the way of the warrior. Japan's celebration of the samurai and of military virtues contrasted sharply with China's emphasis on intellectual achievements and political office holding, which were accorded higher prestige than bearing arms. "The educated men of the land," wrote a Chinese minister in the eleventh century, "regard the carrying of arms as a disgrace."[17] The Japanese, clearly, did not agree.

Religiously as well, Japan remained distinctive. Although Buddhism in many forms took hold in the country, it never completely replaced the native

The Samurai of Japan This late nineteenth-century image shows a samurai warrior on horseback clad in armor and a horned helmet while carrying a sword as well as a bow and arrows. The prominence of martial values in Japanese culture was one of the ways in which Japan differed from its Chinese neighbor, despite much borrowing. (Library of Congress, Prints and Photographs Division, LC-DIG-jpd-01046)

beliefs and practices, which focused attention on numerous *kami*, sacred spirits associated with human ancestors and various natural phenomena. Much later referred to as Shinto, this tradition provided legitimacy to the imperial family, based on claims of descent from the sun goddess. Because veneration of the kami lacked an elaborate philosophy or ritual, it conflicted very little with Buddhism. In fact, numerous kami were assimilated into Japanese Buddhism as local expressions of Buddhist deities or principles.

Japanese literary and artistic culture likewise evolved in distinctive ways, despite much borrowing from China. As in Korea and Vietnam, there emerged a unique writing system that combined Chinese characters with a series of phonetic symbols. A highly stylized Japanese poetic form, known as tanka, developed early and has remained a favored means of expression ever since. Particularly during the Heian period of Japanese history (794–1185), a highly refined aesthetic culture found expression at the imperial court, even as the court's real political authority melted away. Court aristocrats and their ladies lived in splendor, composed poems, arranged flowers, and conducted their love affairs. "What counted," wrote one scholar, "was the proper costume, the right ceremonial act, the successful turn of phrase in a poem, and the appropriate expression of refined taste."[18] Much of our knowledge of this courtly culture comes from the work of women writers, who composed their diaries and novels in the vernacular Japanese script rather than in the classical Chinese used by elite men. *The Tale of Genji*, a Japanese novel written by the woman author Murasaki Shikibu around 1000, provides an intimate picture of the intrigues and romances of court life.

At this level of society, Japan's women, unlike those in Korea, largely escaped the more oppressive features of Chinese Confucian culture, such as the prohibition of remarriage for widows and seclusion within the home. Perhaps this is because the most powerful Chinese influence on Japan occurred during the Tang dynasty, when Chinese elite women enjoyed considerable freedom. Japanese women continued to inherit property; Japanese married couples often lived apart or with the wife's family; and marriages were made and broken easily. None of this corresponded to Confucian values. When Japanese women did begin to lose status in the twelfth century and later, it had less to do with Confucian pressures than with the rise of a warrior culture. As the personal relationships of samurai warriors to their lords replaced marriage alliances as a political strategy, the influence of women in political life was reduced, but this was an internal Japanese phenomenon, not a reflection of Chinese influence.

Guided Reading Question

■ **COMPARISON**
In what different ways did Japanese and Korean women experience the pressures of Confucian orthodoxy?

Lady Murasaki Shikibu Lady Murasaki Shikibu drew on her experience as a lady-in-waiting at the imperial court to craft her famous novel, *The Tale of Genji*. She allegedly began to write the novel in 1004 at the Buddhist temple of Ishiyama-dera under the inspiration of a full moon, as depicted in this eighteenth-century woodblock print. (Ukiyo-e [Japanese woodblock print] by Harunobu Suzuki, ca. 1767/Pictures from History/Bridgeman Images)

PRACTICING HISTORICAL THINKING

In what different ways did Korea, Vietnam, Japan, and northern nomads experience and respond to Chinese influence?

Japan's ability to borrow extensively from China while developing its own distinctive civilization perhaps provided a model for its encounter with the West in the nineteenth century. Then, as before, Japan borrowed selectively from a foreign culture without losing either its political independence or its cultural uniqueness.

China and the Eurasian World Economy

Beyond China's central role in East Asia was its economic interaction with the wider world of Eurasia generally. On the one hand, China's remarkable economic growth, taking place during the Tang and Song dynasties, could hardly be contained within China's borders and clearly had a major impact throughout Eurasia. On the other hand, China was recipient as well as donor in the economic interactions of the third-wave era, and its own economic achievements owed something to the stimulus of contact with the larger world.

Spillovers: China's Impact on Eurasia

One of the outcomes of China's economic revolution lay in the diffusion of its many technological innovations to peoples and places far from East Asia. (See Snapshot, page 339, for a wider view of Chinese technological achievements.) Paper-making, known in China since the Han dynasty, spread to Korea and Vietnam by the fourth century C.E., to Japan and India by the seventh, to the Islamic world by the eighth, to Muslim Spain by 1150, to France and Germany in the 1300s, and to England in the 1490s. Printing, likewise a Chinese invention, rapidly reached Korea, where movable type became a highly developed technique, and Japan as well. Both technologies were heavily influenced by Buddhism, which accorded religious merit to the reproduction of sacred texts. The Islamic world, however, highly valued handwritten calligraphy and generally resisted printing as impious until the nineteenth century. The adoption of printing in Europe was likewise delayed because of the absence of paper until the twelfth century. Then movable type was reinvented by Johannes Gutenberg in the fifteenth century, although it is unclear whether he was aware of Chinese and Korean precedents. With implications for mass literacy, bureaucracy, scholarship, the spread of religion, and the exchange of information, papermaking and printing were Chinese innovations of revolutionary and global dimensions.

Chinese technologies were seldom simply transferred from one place to another. More often, a particular Chinese technique or product stimulated innovations in more distant lands in accordance with local needs.[19] For example, as the Chinese formula for gunpowder, invented in the ninth century, became available in Europe, together with some early and simple firearms, these innovations triggered the development of cannons in the early fourteenth century. Soon cannons appeared in the Islamic world, and by the 1350s they were in common use in China itself,

Guided Reading Question

■ **CONNECTION**
In what ways did China participate in the world of Eurasian commerce and exchange, and with what outcomes?

SNAPSHOT Chinese Technological Achievements

Before the technological explosion of the European Industrial Revolution during the eighteenth and nineteenth centuries, China had long been the major center of global technological innovation. Many of those inventions spread to other civilizations, where they stimulated imitation or modification. Since Europe was located at the opposite end of the Eurasian continent from China, it often took considerable time for those innovations to give rise to something similar in the West. That lag is also a measure of the relative technological development of the two civilizations in premodern times.

Innovation	First Used in China (approximate)	Adoption/Recognition in the West: Time Lag in Years (approximate)
Iron plow	6th–4th century B.C.E.	2,000+
Cast iron	4th century B.C.E.	1,000–1,200
Efficient horse collar	3rd–1st century B.C.E.	1,000
Paper	2nd century B.C.E.	1,000
Wheelbarrow	1st century B.C.E.	900–1,000
Rudder for steering ships	1st century C.E.	1,100
Iron chain suspension bridge	1st century C.E.	1,000–1,300
Porcelain	3rd century C.E.	1,500
Magnetic compass for navigation	9th–11th century C.E.	400
Gunpowder	9th century C.E.	400
Chain drive for transmission of power	976 C.E.	800
Movable type printing	1045 C.E.	400

Source: Compiled from Joseph Needham, *Science and Civilization in China* (Cambridge: Cambridge University Press, 1965), 1:242; and Robert Temple, *The Genius of China* (New York: Simon and Schuster, 1986).

which first used cast iron rather than bronze in their construction. But the highly competitive European state system drove the "gunpowder revolution" much further and more rapidly than in China's imperial state. Chinese textile, metallurgical, and naval technologies such as the magnetic compass likewise stimulated imitation and innovation all across Eurasia.

In addition to its technological influence, China's prosperity during the Song dynasty greatly stimulated commercial life and market-based behavior all across the Afro-Eurasian trading world. China's products—silk, porcelain, lacquerware—found eager buyers from Japan to East Africa, and everywhere in between. The immense size and wealth of China's domestic economy also provided a ready market for hundreds of commodities from afar. For example, the lives of many thousands of people in the spice-producing islands of what is now Indonesia were transformed as they came to depend on Chinese consumers' demand for their products. "[O]ne hundred million [Chinese] people," wrote historian William McNeill, "increasingly caught up within a commercial network, buying and selling to supplement every day's livelihood, made a significant difference to the way other human beings made their livings throughout a large part of the civilized world."[20] Such was the ripple effect of China's economic revolution.

On the Receiving End: China as Economic Beneficiary

But Chinese interaction with the wider world was not a one-way street, for China too was changed by its engagement with other parts of Eurasia. During the third-wave era, for example, China had learned about the cultivation and processing of both cotton and sugar from India. From Vietnam, around 1000, China gained access to the new, fast-ripening, and drought-resistant strains of rice that made a highly productive rice-based agriculture possible in the drier and more rugged regions of southern China. This marked a major turning point in Chinese history, as the frontier region south of the Yangzi River grew rapidly in population, overtaking the traditional centers of Chinese civilization in the north. In the process, the many non-Chinese peoples of the area were painfully overwhelmed by Chinese military forces and by the migration of at least a million Han Chinese farmers by 1400.

Technologically as well, China's extraordinary burst of creativity owed something to the stimulus of cross-cultural contact. Awareness of Persian windmills, for example, spurred the development of a distinct but related device in China. Printing arose from China's growing involvement with the world of Buddhism, which put a spiritual premium on the reproduction of the Buddha's image and of short religious texts that were carried as charms. It was in Buddhist monasteries during the Tang dynasty that the long-established practice of printing with seals was elaborated by Chinese monks into woodblock printing. The first printed book, in 868 C.E., was a famous Buddhist text, the *Diamond Sutra*.

A further transforming impact of China's involvement with a wider world derived from its growing participation in Indian Ocean trade. By the Tang dynasty, thousands of ships annually visited the ports of southern China, and settled communities of foreign merchants—Arabs, Persians, Indians, Southeast Asians—turned some of these cities into cosmopolitan centers. Buddhist temples, Muslim mosques and cemeteries, and Hindu phallic sculptures graced the skyline of Quanzhou, a coastal city in southern China. Occasionally the

The *Diamond Sutra* The world's earliest dated printed book was produced in China in 868. It was a scroll of the *Diamond Sutra*, a classical text of Mahayana Buddhism measuring fifteen feet in length and printed from carved woodblocks. This image shows the frontispiece of that text, depicting the Buddha teaching while surrounded by a collection of monks and bodhisattvas. This copy of the *Diamond Sutra* dates to the first half of the tenth century. (Frontispiece to "The Diamond Sutra" painted in ink and colors on paper, ca. 901-950/© The Trustees of the British Museum/Art Resource, NY)

tensions of cultural diversity erupted in violence, such as the massacre of tens of thousands of foreigners in Canton during the 870s when Chinese rebel forces sacked the city. Indian Ocean commerce also contributed much to the transformation of southern China from a subsistence economy to one more heavily based on producing for export. In the process, merchants achieved a degree of social acceptance not known before, including their frequent appointment to high-ranking bureaucratic positions. Finally, much-beloved stories of the monkey god, widely popular even in contemporary China, derived from Indian sources transmitted by Indian Ocean commerce.

China and Buddhism

By far the most important gift that China received from India was neither cotton nor sugar, but a religion, Buddhism. Until the adoption of Marxism in the twentieth century, Buddhism was the only large-scale cultural borrowing in Chinese history. It also made China into a launching pad for Buddhism's dispersion to Korea and from there to Japan as well (see Map 8.5).

Making Buddhism Chinese

Buddhism initially entered China via the Silk Road trading network during the first and second centuries C.E. The stability and prosperity of the Han dynasty, then at its height, ensured that the new "barbarian" religion held little appeal for native Chinese. Furthermore, the Indian culture from which Buddhism sprang was at odds with Chinese understandings of the world in many ways. Buddhism's commitment to a secluded and monastic life for monks and nuns seemed to dishonor Chinese family values, and its concern for individual salvation or enlightenment appeared selfish, contradicting the social orientation of Confucian thinking. Furthermore, the Buddhist concept of infinite eons of time, endlessly repeating themselves, was quite a stretch for the Chinese, who normally thought in terms of finite family generations or dynastic cycles. No wonder that for the first several centuries C.E., Buddhism was largely the preserve of foreign merchants and monks living in China.

In the half millennium between roughly 300 and 800 C.E., however, Buddhism took solid root in China within both elite and popular culture, becoming a permanent, though fluctuating, presence in Chinese life. It began, arguably, with the collapse of the Han dynasty around 200 C.E. The chaotic, violent, and politically fragmented centuries that followed seriously discredited Confucianism and opened the door to alternative understandings of the world. Nomadic rulers, now governing much of northern China, found Buddhism useful in part because it was foreign. "We were born out of the marches [beyond the realm of Chinese culture]," declared one of them, "and though we are unworthy, we have complied with our appointed destiny and govern the Chinese as their prince. . . . Buddha being a barbarian god is the very one we should worship."[21] Rulers and elite families provided

Guided Reading Question

■ **CHANGE**
What facilitated the rooting of Buddhism within China?

MAPPING HISTORY

Map 8.5 The World of Asian Buddhism

Originating in India, Buddhism later spread widely throughout much of Asia to provide a measure of cultural or religious commonality across this vast region.

READING THE MAP: Trace the routes and speed with which Buddhism spread from its heartland along the Ganges River. How quickly did it reach China, Korea, Japan, and Tibet? Why might it have taken longer to become established in Korea, Japan, and Tibet?

MAKING CONNECTIONS: Comparing Map 8.5 with Map 7.1: The Silk Roads, identify regions where Buddhism spread along this long-distance trade route. How quickly did Buddhism establish itself along the Silk Roads?

patronage for Buddhist monasteries, temples, and works of art. In southern China, where many northern aristocrats had fled following the disastrous decline of the Han dynasty, Buddhism provided some comfort in the face of a collapsing society. Its emphasis on ritual, morality, and contemplation represented an intellectually and aesthetically satisfying response to times that were so clearly out of joint.

Meanwhile, Buddhist monasteries increasingly provided an array of services for ordinary people. In them, travelers found accommodation; those fleeing from China's many upheavals discovered a place of refuge; desperate people received charity; farmers borrowed seed for the next planting; the sick were treated; and children learned to read. And for many, Buddhism was associated with access to magical powers as reports of miracles abounded. Battles were won, rain descended on drought-ridden areas, diseases were cured, and guilt was relieved—all through the magical ministrations of charismatic monks.

Accompanying all of this was a serious effort by monks, scholars, and translators to present this Indian religion in terms that Chinese could more readily grasp. Thus the Buddhist term *dharma*, referring to the Buddha's teaching, was translated as *dao*, or "the way," a notion long familiar in both Daoist and Confucian thinking. The Buddhist notion of "morality" was rendered with the Confucian term that referred to "filial submission and obedience." Some Indian concepts were modified in the process of translation. For example, the idea that "husband supports wife," which reflected a considerable respect for women and mothers in early Indian Buddhism, became in translation "husband controls wife."[22]

As Buddhism took hold in China, it was primarily in its broader Mahayana form—complete with numerous deities, the veneration of relics, many heavens and hells, and bodhisattvas to aid the believer—rather than its more psychological and individualistic Theravada form (see "The Buddhist Challenge" in Chapter 4). One of the most popular expressions of Buddhism in China was the Pure Land School, in which faithfully repeating the name of an earlier Buddha, the Amitabha, was sufficient to ensure rebirth in a beautifully described heavenly realm, the Pure Land. In its emphasis on salvation by faith, without arduous study or intensive meditation, Pure Land Buddhism became a highly popular and authentically Chinese version of the Indian faith.

China's reunification under the Sui and early Tang dynasties witnessed growing state support for Buddhism. The Sui emperor Wendi (r. 581–604 C.E.) had monasteries constructed at the base of China's five sacred mountains, further identifying the imported religion with traditional Chinese culture. He even used Buddhism to justify his military campaigns. "With a hundred victories in a hundred battles," he declared, "we promote the practice of the ten Buddhist virtues."[23] By 600 C.E., some 4,000 monasteries had been established. With state support and growing popular acceptance, they became centers of great wealth. They were largely exempt from taxation and owned large estates; ran businesses such as oil presses, water mills, and pawn shops; collected gems, gold, and lavish works of art; and employed millions of slaves, serfs, and other unfree and dependent workers. But Buddhism never achieved the independence from state authorities that the Christian Church acquired in Europe. The examinations for becoming a monk were supervised by the state, and education in the monasteries included the required study of the Confucian classics. In the mid-ninth century, the state showed quite dramatically just how much control it could exercise over the Buddhist establishment.

Losing State Support: The Crisis of Chinese Buddhism

The impressive growth of **Chinese Buddhism** was accompanied by a persistent undercurrent of resistance and criticism. Some saw the Buddhist establishment, at least potentially, as a "state within a state" and a challenge to imperial authority. More important was a deepening resentment of its enormous wealth. One fifth-century critic, referring to monks, put the issue squarely: "Why is it that their ideals are noble and far-reaching and their activities still are base and common? [They] become merchants and engage in barter, wrangling with the masses for profit."[24] Nor did the environmental impact of Buddhist monasteries escape the notice of state officials. In 707 C.E., one such official wrote: "Extensive construction of monasteries are undertaken and large mansions are built. Even though for such works trees are felled to the point of stripping the mountains, it does not suffice.... Though earth is moved to the point of obstructing roads, it does not suffice."[25] When state treasuries were short of funds, government officials cast a covetous eye on these wealthy and tax-exempt monasteries. Furthermore, Buddhism was clearly of foreign origin and offensive for that reason to some Confucian and Daoist thinkers. The celibacy of the monks and their withdrawal from society, the critics argued, undermined the Confucian-based family system of Chinese tradition.

Such criticisms took on new meaning in the changed environment of China after about 800 C.E. Following centuries of considerable foreign influence in China, a growing resentment against foreign culture, particularly among the literate classes, increasingly took hold. The turning point may well have been the An Lushan rebellion (755–763), in which a general of foreign origin led a major revolt against the Tang dynasty. Whatever its origin, an increasingly xenophobic reaction set in among the upper classes, reflected in a desire to return to an imagined "purity" of earlier times. In this setting, the old criticisms of Buddhism became more sharply focused. In 819, Han Yu, a leading figure in the Confucian counterattack on Buddhism, wrote a scathing memorial to the emperor criticizing his willingness to honor a relic of the Buddha's finger.

> Now the Buddha was of barbarian origin. His language differed from Chinese speech; his clothes were of a different cut; his mouth did not pronounce the prescribed words of the Former Kings.... He did not recognize the relationship between prince and subject, nor the sentiments of father and son.... I pray that Your Majesty will turn this bone over to the officials that it may be cast into water or fire.[26]

Guided Reading Question

■ **CHANGE**
What were the major sources of opposition to Buddhism within China?

Several decades later, the Chinese state took direct action against the Buddhist establishment as well as against other foreign religions. A series of imperial decrees between 841 and 845 ordered some 260,000 monks and nuns to return to normal life as tax-paying citizens. Thousands of monasteries, temples, and shrines were either destroyed or turned to public use, while the state confiscated the lands, money, metals, and serfs belonging to monasteries. Buddhists were now forbidden to use gold, silver, copper, iron, and gems in constructing their images. These actions dealt a serious blow to Chinese Buddhism. Its scholars and monks were scattered, its creativity was diminished, and its institutions came even more firmly under state control.

Despite this persecution, Buddhism did not vanish from China. At the level of elite culture, its philosophical ideas played a role in the reformulation of Confucian thinking that took place during the Song dynasty. At the village level, Buddhism became one element of Chinese popular religion, which also included the veneration of ancestors, the honoring of Confucius, and Daoist shrines and rituals. Temples frequently included statues of Confucius, Laozi, and the Buddha, with little sense of any incompatibility among them. "Every black-haired son of Han," the Chinese have long said, "wears a Confucian thinking cap, a Daoist robe, and Buddhist sandals." (See the opening photo for Chapter 4.) Unlike in Europe, where an immigrant religion triumphed over and excluded all other faiths, Buddhism in China became assimilated into Chinese culture alongside its other traditions.

REFLECTIONS

Why Do Things Change?

Explaining how and why human societies change is perhaps the central issue that historians confront, no matter which societies or periods of time they study. Those who specialize in the history of some particular culture or civilization often emphasize sources of change operating within those societies, although there is intense disagreement as to which are most significant. The ideas of great thinkers, the policies of leaders, struggles for power, the conflict of classes, the invention of new technologies, the growth or decline in population, variations in climate or weather—all of these and more have their advocates as the primary motor of historical transformation.

Of course, it is not necessary to choose among them. The history of China illustrates the range of internal factors that have driven change in that civilization. The political conflicts of the "era of warring states" provided the setting and the motivation for the emergence of Confucianism and Daoism, which in turn have certainly shaped the character and texture of Chinese civilization over many centuries.

The personal qualities and brutal policies of China's "first emperor" Shihuangdi surely played a role in China's unification and in the brief duration of the Qin dynasty. The subsequent creation of a widespread network of canals and waterways, as well as the country's technological achievements, maintained that unity over very long periods of time. But the massive inequalities of Chinese society generated the peasant upheavals that periodically shattered that unity and led to new ruling dynasties. Sometimes natural events, such as droughts and floods, triggered those rebellions.

World historians, more than those who study particular civilizations or nations, have been inclined to find the primary source of change in contact with strangers, in external connections and interactions, whether direct or indirect. The history of China and East Asia provides plenty of examples for this point of view. Conceptions of China as the "middle kingdom," infinitely superior to all surrounding societies, grew out of centuries of involvement with its "barbarian" neighbors. Some of those neighbors became Chinese as China's imperial reach grew, especially to the south. Even those that did not, such as Koreans, Vietnamese, and Japanese, were decisively transformed by proximity to the "radiating civilization" of China. China's own cuisine, so distinctive in recent centuries, may well be a quite recent invention, drawing heavily on Indian and Southeast Asian cooking. Buddhism, of course, is an obvious borrowing from abroad, although its incorporation into Chinese civilization and its ups and downs within China owed much to internal cultural and political realities.

In the end, clear distinctions between internal and external sources of change in China's history—or that of any other society—are perhaps misleading. The boundary between "inside" and "outside" is itself a constantly changing line. Should the borderlands of northern China, where Chinese and Turkic peoples met and mingled, be regarded as internal or external to China itself? And, as the histories of Chinese Buddhism and of Japanese culture so clearly indicate, what comes from beyond is always transformed by what it encounters within.

Second Thoughts

What's the Significance?

Sui dynasty, 318

Tang dynasty, 319

Song dynasty, 319

China's economic revolution, 321

Hangzhou, 321

gunpowder, 323

foot binding, 325

tribute system, 328

Xiongnu Empire, 329

Silla kingdom, 331

hangul, 333

chu nom, 335

Shotoku Taishi, 335

bushido, 336

Chinese Buddhism, 344

Big Picture Questions

1. How can you explain the changing reception of Buddhism in China?
2. How did China influence the world of the third-wave era? How was China itself transformed by its encounters with the wider world?
3. How might China's position in the world during the Tang and Song dynasty era compare to its emerging role in global affairs in the twenty-first century?
4. **Looking Back:** In what ways did Tang and Song dynasty China resemble the earlier Han dynasty period, and in what ways had China changed?

Next Steps: For Further Study

Samuel Adshead, *Tang China: The Rise of the East in World History* (2004). Explores the role of China within the larger world.

Patricia Buckley Ebrey, *The Inner Quarters* (1993). A balanced account of the gains and losses experienced by Chinese women during the changes of the Song dynasty.

Mark Elvin, *The Retreat of the Elephants: An Environmental History of China* (2004). Explores the environmental cost of civilization in a Chinese setting.

James L. Huffman, *Japan in World History* (2010). The first three chapters of this recent work place Japan's early history in the framework of world history.

Paul S. Ropp, *China in World History* (2010). An up-to-date telling of China's historical development, cast in a global context.

Arthur F. Wright, *Buddhism in Chinese History* (1959). An older account filled with wonderful stories and anecdotes.

Ben Hedges and Christy Sammett (producers), "Discovering China: The Song Dynasty," NTD Television, https://www.youtube.com/watch?v=QO7NHZJ-eE4. A brief documentary with lovely visuals that highlights the achievements of Song dynasty China.

Karin Yuen, "Early Heian Period: Japanese Art History," Little Art Talks, 2015, https://www.youtube.com/watch?v=5WEvKtaj0cQ. A short documentary on the cultural history of Japan during the early centuries of the Heian period (794–1185), when Chinese influence was at its height.

China's Scholar-Officials

China's elite class—those men who had passed the highest-level examinations and held important offices in the state bureaucracy—represented only a tiny fraction of their country's huge population, but they established the tone and set the standards of elite behavior for Chinese civilization (see "An Elite of Officials" in Chapter 5). Active in political affairs and social life, they also honored leisure, contemplation, poetry, painting, and calligraphy. In the images and documents that follow, we catch a glimpse of how these scholar-officials lived and what they valued.

SOURCE 8.1 Scholar-Officials and the Emperor ▶

The close association of China's scholar class with the country's political life is reflected in Source 8.1, which shows a group of scholar-officials drinking tea and wine together with the emperor, who is presiding at the left. The painting is usually attributed to the emperor Huizong (1082–1135), who was himself a noted painter, poet, calligrapher, and collector. This emperor's great attention to the arts rather than to affairs of state gained him a reputation as a negligent and dissolute ruler. His reign ended in disgrace as China suffered a humiliating defeat at the hands of the northern nomadic Jin people, who took the emperor captive.

- How would you describe this event to someone who had not attended it?
- What might you say about the relationship of the emperor and the scholar-officials?
- How might you imagine the conversation around this table?
- In painting this picture, what do you think the emperor was trying to convey?

Scholars Gathering in a Bamboo Garden | **12th century**

Ink and color on silk, 15th century/Private Collection/Photo © Christie's Images/Bridgeman Images

■ ■ ■

SOURCE 8.2 **A Gathering of Scholars** ▶

Confucian cultural ideals gave great prominence to literature, poetry, and scholarly pursuits as activities appropriate for "gentlemen." Confucius himself had declared that "gentlemen make friends through literature, and through friendship increase their benevolence." For some, a more reclusive life devoted to study, painting, poetry, and conversation with friends represented an honorable alternative to government service. Thus literary gatherings of scholars and officials were common themes in Tang and Song dynasty paintings. Source 8.2 provides an illustration of such an event. It portrays the eighth-century poet-official Wang Changling, shown in his red scholar-official's robe seated by the table, talking with three friends.

■ What marks these figures as cultivated men of literary or scholarly inclination?

■ Notice the various gazes of the four figures. What do they suggest about the character of this gathering and the relationships among its participants?

■ Do you think the artist was seeking to convey an idealized image of what a gathering of "gentlemen" ought to be or a realistic portrayal of an actual event? What elements of the painting support your answer?

Scholars of the Liuli Hall | late 13th century

© age-fotostock/Art Collection/age-fotostock

■ ■ ■

SOURCE 8.3 **A Solitary Scholar** ▶

Chinese scholar-officials are often shown as solitary contemplatives, immersing themselves in nature. The famous Song dynasty painter Ma Yuan (1160–1225) depicted such an image in his masterpiece entitled *On a Mountain Path in Spring*, showing a scholar walking in the countryside watching several birds, while his servant trails behind carrying his master's *qin* (lute). A short poem in the upper right, composed by the reigning emperor Ningzong, reads: "The wild flowers dance when brushed by my sleeves. Reclusive birds make no sound as they shun the presence of people."[27]

■ How would you define the mood of this painting? What posture toward the natural environment does it suggest? What techniques did Ma Yuan use to convey this mood or posture?

■ How might this painting reflect the perspectives of Daoism (see "The Daoist Answer" in Chapter 4)? In what respects does it differ from the more Confucian tone of Source 8.2?

■ During Ma Yuan's lifetime, the northern part of China was coming under the control of the feared Mongols. How might an awareness of this situation affect our understanding of this painting?

MA YUAN | *On a Mountain Path in Spring* | early 13th century

Paul Fearn/Alamy

• • •

SOURCE 8.4 Tang Dynasty Poetry

The sensibility evoked in Ma Yuan's painting also found expression in much of Chinese poetry, which was a central feature in the lives of almost everyone in the educated classes, scholar-officials and emperors alike. They studied poetry, wrote poetry, and shared their creations with one another both privately and on social occasions. At first poems were hand-copied on calligraphic scrolls, but after printing became widely available during the ninth century C.E., they appeared in printed books as well. Friendship, wine, war, loss and parting, aging and death, social criticism—all of these found a place in classical Chinese poetry. But it was nature—rivers, fields, gardens, clouds, seasons, and, above all, mountains—that most fundamentally animated the classical poetry of China. "Artist-intellectuals found their spiritual home in mountains,"[28] wrote David Hinton, a prominent

American translator of Chinese poetry. The poems that follow offer a brief glimpse into the intellectual and spiritual life of Chinese scholar-officials, through the writings of three of the greatest Tang dynasty poets: Li Po, Wang Wei, and Du Fu. Each of them served in official positions or aspired to do so, while yearning for immersion in the wilderness and in their poetry.

- How might you characterize the sensibility reflected in these poems?

- What relationship between poet and nature can you discern? Is the poet a detached observer, an interested witness, or an active participant in the natural order? To what relationship with nature do the poets aspire?

- What elements of Daoist or Buddhist feeling can you identify in these poems? Notice the reference to "the Way" in Selection C.

SOURCE 8.4A

LI PO │ *The Mountain and Me* │ 8th century

The birds have vanished into the sky
And now the last cloud drains away.
We sit together, the mountain and me
    until only the mountain remains.

Source: "Zazen on Ching-t'ing Mountain" in *Crossing the Yellow River: Three Hundred Poems from the Chinese,* trans. Sam Hamill (Buffalo, NY: Tiger Bark Press, 2000).

SOURCE 8.4B

LI PO │ *Drinking Alone with the Moon* │ 8th century

From a pot of wine among the flowers
I drank alone. There was no one with me—
Till, raising my cup, I asked the bright
    moon
To bring me my shadow and make us three.
Alas, the moon was unable to drink
And my shadow tagged me vacantly;
But still for a while I had these friends
To cheer me through the end of spring. . . .
I sang. The moon encouraged me.
I danced. My shadow tumbled after.

As long as I knew, we were boon companions.
And then I was drunk, and we lost one
    another. . . .
Shall goodwill ever be secure?
I watch the long road of the River of Stars
    [the Milky Way].

Source: *Tang Shi— 300 Tang Poems,* translated by Witter Bynner, 1929, http://wengu.tartarie.com/wg/wengu.php?l=Tangshi&no=6. Also in Witter Bynner, *The Jade Mountain: A Chinese Anthology* (New York: Alfred A. Knopf, 1929).

SOURCE 8.4C

WANG WEI │ *My Retreat at Mount Zhongnan* │ 8th century

My heart in middle age found the Way.
And I came to dwell at the foot of this
    mountain.

When the spirit moves, I wander alone
Amid beauty that is all for me. . . .
I will walk till the water checks my path,

Then sit and watch the rising clouds —
And some day meet an old wood-cutter
And talk and laugh and never return.

Source: *Tang Shi — 300 Tang Poems*, translated by Witter Bynner, 1929, http://wengu.tartarie.com/wg/wengu.php?l=Tangshi&no=123. Also in Witter Bynner, *The Jade Mountain: A Chinese Anthology* (New York: Alfred A. Knopf, 1929).

SOURCE 8.4D
DU FU | *A View of Taishan* | 8th century

What shall I say of the Great Peak? —
The ancient dukedoms are everywhere green,
Inspired and stirred by the breath of creation,
With the Twin Forces balancing day and
   night. . . .
I bare my breast toward opening clouds,
I strain my sight after birds flying home.
When shall I reach the top and hold
All mountains in a single glance?

Source: *Tang Shi — 300 Tang Poems*, translated by Witter Bynner, 1929, http://wengu.tartarie.com/wg/wengu.php?l=Tangshi&no=8. Also in Witter Bynner, *The Jade Mountain: A Chinese Anthology* (New York: Alfred A. Knopf, 1929).

■ ■ ■

SOURCE 8.5 Scholar-Officials at Play ▶

Not all was poetry and contemplation of nature in the lives of China's scholar-officials. Nor were men and women always so strictly segregated as the preceding sources may suggest. Source 8.5 illustrates another side of Chinese elite life. These images are part of a long tenth-century scroll painting titled *The Night Revels of Han Xizai*. Apparently, the Tang dynasty emperor Li Yu became concerned that one of his ministers, Han Xizai, was overindulging in suspicious nightlong parties in his own home. He therefore commissioned the artist Gu Hongzhong to attend these parties secretly and to record the events in a painting, which he hoped would shame his wayward but talented official into more appropriate and dignified behavior. The entire scroll shows men and women together, sometimes in flirtatious situations, while open sleeping areas suggest sexual activity.

■ What kinds of entertainment were featured at this gathering?

■ What aspects of these parties shown in the scroll paintings might have caused the emperor some concern? In what respects might these kinds of gatherings run counter to Confucian values?

■ How are women portrayed in this image? In what ways are they relating to the men in the paintings?

GU HONGZHONG | *The Night Revels of Han Xizai* | **10th century**

Beijing Eastphoto Stockimages, Co., Ltd./Alamy

DOING HISTORY

1. **Describing elite society:** Based on these sources, write a brief description of the activities and outlook of China's scholar-officials during the Tang and Song dynasties.

2. **Defining the self-image of scholar-officials:** What do these sources suggest about how members of this elite class ideally viewed themselves?

3. **Identifying cultural influences:** In what ways did Confucian, Daoist, or Buddhist teachings shape the lives and values of the scholar-official class?

4. **Seeking additional sources:** What other kinds of sources might provide further insight into the lives of Chinese elites?

Assessing China's Scholar-Officials

Contemporary scholars have both criticized and celebrated China's official elite, as the following sources indicate. Voice 8.1 is that of Jacques Garnet, a prominent French historian of China, while Voice 8.2 comes from David Hinton, who is the premier American translator of Chinese philosophical and poetic texts.

- How do these two selections differ in their assessment of China's scholar-official class? On what might they agree?

- With which of these sources do you feel more sympathetic?

- **Integrating Primary and Secondary Sources:** In what ways might the images and documents above support or challenge the conclusions of these two accounts?

VOICE 8.1

Jacques Garnet on the "Learned Culture" of Song Dynasty China | 1996

. . . [T]he governing class of the eleventh to thirteenth centuries, consisting of rich, educated families usually living in an urban environment on the income from their estates, despised physical effort and wished to stand aloof from traditions of the steppe and from popular amusements. The profession of arms . . . had lost its prestige ever since the armies had consisted of mercenaries recruited from the dregs of society. The intellectual, contemplative, learned . . . aspects of the arts and letters among the Chinese upper classes asserted itself in the Sung period and was to remain dominant under the Ming and Ch'ing dynasties. . . . Henceforth, the lettered Chinese . . . was to be a pure intellectual who thought that games of skill and athletic competitions were things

for the lower classes. This deeply rooted contempt in the governing classes for physical effort and aptitude was to persist down to our own day. . . . [O]nly learned literature, calligraphy, the collection of books and works of art, and the designing of gardens found favor with the educated classes.

Source: Jacques Garnet, *A History of Chinese Civilization* (Cambridge: Cambridge University Press, 1996), 331.

VOICE 8.2

David Hinton on "Public Service" and "Mountain Seclusion" | 2005

The deep commitment felt by intellectuals in ancient China to both the Confucian realm of social responsibility and the Taoist realm of spiritual self-cultivation gave rise to a recluse ideal that answered both of these commitments. In the most mythic version of this ideal, a sage recluse living contentedly in the mountains recognizes that the nation is in crisis and needs his wisdom—so he reluctantly joins the government; resolves the crisis; and then, having no interest in the wealth and renown associated with that life, returns to cultivate his simple life of spiritual depth in the mountains. This ideal was enacted by countless intellectuals in ancient China, though in a bit more realistic form. They devoted themselves to public service, always watching for a chance to spend time in mountain seclusion (often at monasteries) and at some point retired permanently from government service to live as recluses.

Source: David Hinton, *Mountain Home: The Wilderness Poetry of Ancient China* (New York: New Directions Books, 2005), 210.

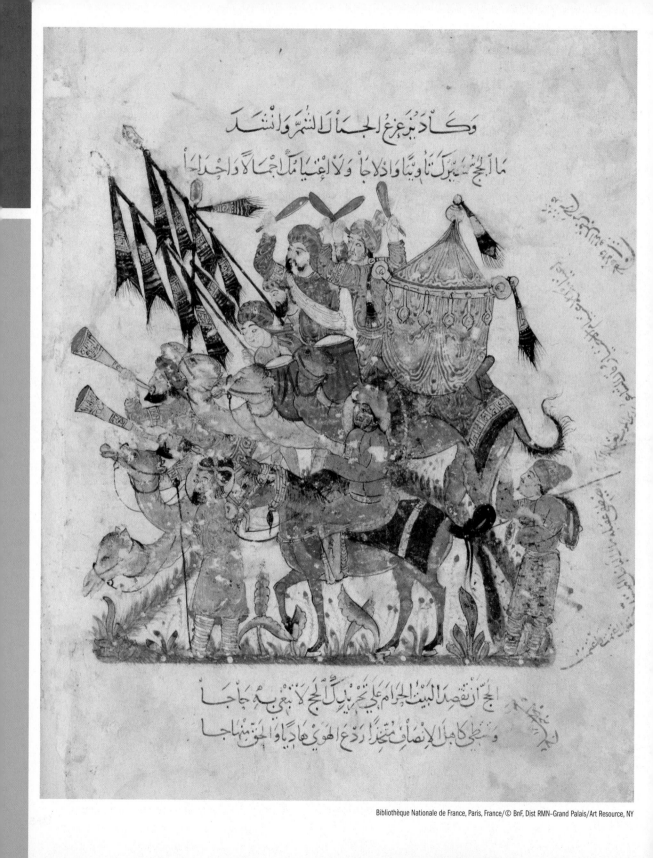

The Worlds of Islam

Afro-Eurasian Connections

600–1450

The Birth of a New Religion
  The Homeland of Islam
  The Messenger and the Message
  The Transformation of Arabia

The Making of an Arab Empire
  War, Conquest, and Tolerance
  Conversion
  Divisions and Controversies
  Women and Men in Early Islam

Islam and Cultural Encounter:
  A Four-Way Comparison
  The Case of India
  The Case of Anatolia
  The Case of West Africa
  The Case of Spain

The World of Islam as a New
  Civilization
  Networks of Faith
  Networks of Exchange

Reflections: Past and Present:
  Choosing Our History

Hassan Kargbo, a citizen of the small West African country of Sierra Leone, is a "ChrisMus," which in local parlance is a person who identifies with both Christianity and Islam. "I see it as the same religion," he stated. Interviewed in early 2014, he acknowledged going to church every Sunday, wearing a Jesus bracelet, and praying at a mosque every day. Kelfala Conteh, the caretaker of an ancient mosque in Sierra Leone's capital of Freetown, reported, "Of course [Christians] come here. We have both Christians and Muslims praying side by side." Wurie Bah, another Muslim from Freetown, said, "We all believe in God. If my friends invite me to church, of course I will go." On one of the colorfully decorated minibuses that carry passengers around the city is the declaration that "God loves Allah."[1]

In the world of the early twenty-first century, where headlines often highlight bitter struggles among Muslims and violent conflict with Christians, Jews, or Hindus, it is perhaps useful to recall places such as Sierra Leone where religious tolerance is both practiced and celebrated. Nor is it alone. Indonesia, the most heavily populated Muslim country in the world, has inscribed freedom of religion in its constitution; has officially recognized Christian, Hindu, and Buddhist holidays as well as those of Islam; and has generally maintained peace among its various religious communities. And millions of ordinary Muslims all around the world have long lived in peaceful proximity to neighbors belonging to different religious communities.

The vast diversity of contemporary Islam echoes the earlier history of this newest of humankind's major religions. During the first Muslim millennium (600–1600), the Islamic world found expression in various forms—Sunni, Shia, Sufi, Arab, Persian, Turkic, West African—some displaying a

« The Hajj The pilgrimage to Mecca, known as the *hajj*, has long been a central religious ritual in Islamic practice. It also embodies the cosmopolitan character of Islam as pilgrims from all over the vast Islamic realm assemble in the city where the faith was born. This painting, dating to 1237, shows a group of joyful pilgrims, led by a band, on their way to Mecca.

broad acceptance of diversity and others engaged in serious and at times violent conflict with those of a different religious outlook.

Furthermore, both then and now, the world of Islam occupied a central position in the larger global arena. During its first millennium, peoples claiming allegiance to Islam represented a highly successful, prosperous, and expansive civilization encompassing parts of Africa, Europe, the Middle East, and Asia. In our own times, the relationship of the Islamic world to the wider world has been shaped by the many, varying, and continuing efforts of Muslim societies to overcome several centuries of humiliating European intrusion and to find their place in modern international life. ■

The significance of a burgeoning Islamic world during the third-wave era was enormous. It thrust the previously marginal and largely nomadic Arabs into a central role in world history, for it was among them and in their language that the newest of the world's major religions was born. The sudden emergence and rapid spread of that religion in the seventh century C.E. was accompanied by the creation of a huge empire that stretched from Spain to India. Both within that empire and beyond it, a new and innovative civilization took shape, drawing on Arab, Persian, Turkic, Greco-Roman, South Asian, and African cultures. It was clearly the largest and most influential of the new third-wave civilizations. Finally, the broad reach of Islam generated many of the great cultural encounters of this era as Islamic civilization challenged and provoked Christendom, penetrated and was transformed by African cultures, and also took root in India, Central Asia, and Southeast Asia.

> **SEEKING THE MAIN POINT**
>
> In what ways did the civilization of Islam draw on other civilizations in the Afro-Eurasian world? And in what respects did it shape or transform those civilizations?

The Birth of a New Religion

Most of the major religious or cultural traditions of the second-wave era had emerged from the core of established civilizations—Confucianism and Daoism from China, Hinduism and Buddhism from India, and Zoroastrianism from Persia. Christianity and Islam, by contrast, emerged more from the margins of Mediterranean and Middle Eastern civilizations. Christianity appeared among a small Middle Eastern people, the Jews, in a remote province of the Roman Empire, while Islam took hold in the cities and deserts of the Arabian Peninsula.

The Homeland of Islam

The central region of the Arabian Peninsula had long been inhabited by nomadic Arabs, known as Bedouins, who herded their sheep and camels in seasonal migrations. These peoples lived in fiercely independent clans and tribes that often engaged

Landmarks for Chapter 9

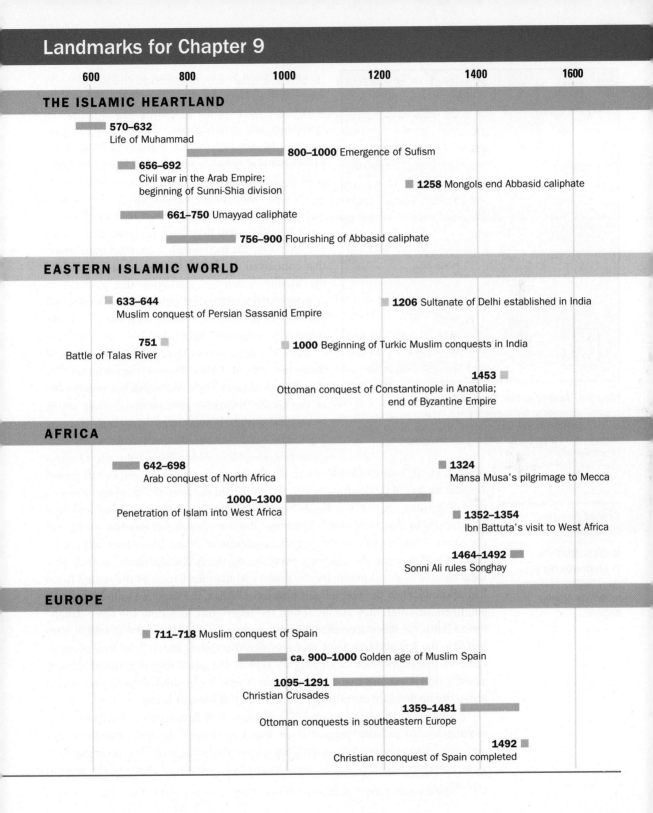

	600	800	1000	1200	1400	1600

THE ISLAMIC HEARTLAND

570–632
Life of Muhammad

800–1000 Emergence of Sufism

656–692
Civil war in the Arab Empire;
beginning of Sunni-Shia division

1258 Mongols end Abbasid caliphate

661–750 Umayyad caliphate

756–900 Flourishing of Abbasid caliphate

EASTERN ISLAMIC WORLD

633–644
Muslim conquest of Persian Sassanid Empire

1206 Sultanate of Delhi established in India

751
Battle of Talas River

1000 Beginning of Turkic Muslim conquests in India

1453
Ottoman conquest of Constantinople in Anatolia;
end of Byzantine Empire

AFRICA

642–698
Arab conquest of North Africa

1324
Mansa Musa's pilgrimage to Mecca

1000–1300
Penetration of Islam into West Africa

1352–1354
Ibn Battuta's visit to West Africa

1464–1492
Sonni Ali rules Songhay

EUROPE

711–718 Muslim conquest of Spain

ca. 900–1000 Golden age of Muslim Spain

1095–1291
Christian Crusades

1359–1481
Ottoman conquests in southeastern Europe

1492
Christian reconquest of Spain completed

Map 9.1 Arabia at the Time of Muhammad
Located adjacent to the Byzantine and Persian empires, the
eastern coast of Arabia was the site of a major trade route
between the Indian Ocean and the Mediterranean Sea.

**Guided Reading
Question**

....

■ **DESCRIPTION**

In what ways did the
early history of Islam
reflect its Arabian
origins?

---

in bitter blood feuds with one another. They recognized a variety of gods, ancestors, and nature
spirits; valued personal bravery, group loyalty, and
hospitality; and greatly treasured their highly expres-
sive oral poetry. But there was more to Arabia than
camel-herding nomads. In scattered oases, the highlands of Yemen, and interior mountain communities,
sedentary village-based agriculture was practiced,
and in the northern and southern regions of Arabia,
small kingdoms had flourished in earlier times. Arabia also sat astride increasingly important trade routes
that connected the Indian Ocean world with that of
the Mediterranean Sea, a location that gave rise to
cosmopolitan commercial cities, whose values and
practices were often in conflict with those of traditional Arab tribes (see Map 9.1).

One of those cities, Mecca, came to occupy a
distinctive role in Arabia. Though somewhat off the
major long-distance trade routes, Mecca was the site
of the Kaaba, the most prominent religious shrine
in Arabia, which housed representations of some
360 deities and was the destination for many religious pilgrims. Mecca's dominant tribe, the Quraysh
(koor-EYE'SH), controlled access to the Kaaba, and its leading families had grown
wealthy by taxing the local trade that accompanied the annual pilgrimage season.

Furthermore, Arabia was located on the periphery of two established and rival
civilizations of that time—the Byzantine Empire, heir to the Roman world, and
the Sassanid Empire, heir to the imperial traditions of Persia. Many Jews and Christians, as well as some Zoroastrians, lived among the Arabs, and their monotheistic
ideas became widely known. By the time of Muhammad, most of the settled Arabs
had acknowledged the preeminent position of Allah, the supreme god of the Arab
pantheon, although they usually found the lesser gods, including the three daughters of Allah, far more accessible. Moreover, they increasingly identified Allah with
Yahweh, the Jewish High God, and regarded themselves too as "children of Abraham." A few Arabs were beginning to explore the possibility that Allah/Yahweh
was the only God and that the many others residing in the Kaaba and in shrines
across the peninsula were nothing more than "helpless and harmless idols."[2]

To an outside observer around 600, it might well have seemed that Arabs were
moving toward Judaism religiously or that Christianity, the most rapidly growing religion in western Asia, would encompass Arabia as well. Any such expectations, however, were thoroughly confounded by the dramatic events of the seventh
century.

The Messenger and the Message

The catalyst for those events and for the birth of this new religion was a single individual, **Muhammad** Ibn Abdullah (570–632 C.E.), who was born in Mecca to a Quraysh family. As a young boy, Muhammad lost his parents, came under the care of an uncle, and worked as a shepherd to pay his keep. Later he became a trader and traveled as far north as Syria. At the age of twenty-five, he married a wealthy widow, Khadija, herself a prosperous merchant, with whom he fathered six children. A highly reflective man deeply troubled by the religious corruption and social inequalities of Mecca, he often undertook periods of withdrawal and meditation in the arid mountains outside the city. There, like the Buddha and Jesus, Muhammad had a powerful, overwhelming religious experience that left him convinced, albeit reluctantly, that he was Allah's messenger to the Arabs, commissioned to bring to them a scripture in their own language. (See Working with Evidence, Sources 9.1 to 9.3, pages 391–396, for three images from the life of Muhammad.)

According to Muslim tradition, the revelations began in 610 and continued periodically over the next twenty-two years. Those revelations, recorded in the **Quran**, became the sacred scriptures of Islam, which to this day most Muslims regard as the very words of God and the core of their faith. Intended to be recited rather than simply read for information, the Quran, Muslims claim, when heard in its original Arabic, conveys nothing less than the very presence of the Divine. Its unmatched poetic beauty, miraculous to Arabic-speaking Muslims, convinced many that it was indeed a revelation from God. One of the earliest converts testified to its power: "When I heard the Quran, my heart was softened and I wept and Islam entered into me."[3]

In its Arabian setting, the Quran's message, delivered through Muhammad, was revolutionary. Religiously, it was radically monotheistic, presenting Allah as the only God, the all-powerful Creator, the "Lord sustainer of the worlds, the Compassionate, the Caring, master of the day of reckoning" and known to human beings "on the farthest horizon and within their own selves."[4] Here was an exalted conception of Deity that drew heavily on traditions of Jewish and Christian monotheism. As "the Messenger of God," Muhammad presented himself in the line of earlier prophets—Abraham, Moses, Jesus, and many others. He was the last, "the seal of the prophets," bearing God's final revelation to humankind. It was not so much a call to a new faith as an invitation to return to the old and pure religion of Abraham from which Jews, Christians, and Arabs alike had deviated. Jews had wrongly conceived of themselves as a uniquely "chosen people"; Christians had made their prophet into a god; and Arabs had become wildly polytheistic. To all of this, the message of the Quran was a corrective.

Submission to Allah ("Muslim" means "one who submits") was the primary obligation of believers and the means of achieving a God-conscious life in this world and a place in Paradise after death. According to the Quran, however, submission

Guided Reading Question

■ **DESCRIPTION**
What did the Quran expect from those who followed its teachings?

Muslims, Jews, and Christians The close relationship of three Middle Eastern monotheistic traditions is illustrated in this fifteenth-century Persian painting, which portrays Muhammad leading Moses, Abraham, Jesus, and other prophets in prayer. The fire surrounding the Prophet's head represents his religious fervor. The painting reflects the Islamic belief that the revelations granted to Muhammad built on and completed those given earlier to Jews and Christians. (Bibliothèque Nationale de France, Paris, France/© BnF, Dist. RMN-Grand Palais/Art Resource, NY)

was not merely an individual or a spiritual act, for it involved the creation of a whole new society. Over and again, the Quran denounced the prevailing social practices of an increasingly prosperous Mecca: the hoarding of wealth, the exploitation of the poor, the charging of high rates of interest on loans, corrupt business deals, the abuse of women, and the neglect of widows and orphans. Like the Jewish prophets of the Old Testament, the Quran demanded social justice and laid out a prescription for its implementation. It sought a return to the older values of Arab tribal life — solidarity, equality, concern for the poor — which had been undermined, particularly in Mecca, by growing wealth and commercialism.

The message of the Quran challenged not only the ancient polytheism of Arab religion and the social injustices of Mecca but also the entire tribal and clan structure of Arab society, which was so prone to war, feuding, and violence. The just and moral society of Islam was the ***umma*** (OOM-mah), the community of all believers, replacing tribal, ethnic, or racial identities. In this community, women too had an honored and spiritually equal place. "The believers, men and women, are protectors of one another," declared the Quran.[5] The umma, then, was to be a new and just community, bound by common belief rather than by territory, language, or tribe.

The core message of the Quran — the remembrance of God — was effectively summarized as a set of five requirements for believers known as the **Pillars of Islam**. The first pillar expressed the heart of the Islamic message: "There is no god but God, and Muhammad is the messenger of God." The second pillar was ritual prayer, performed five times a day, which reminded believers that they were living in the presence of God. The third pillar, almsgiving, reflected the Quran's repeated demands for social justice by requiring believers to give generously to support the poor and needy of the community. The fourth pillar established a month of fasting during Ramadan, which meant abstaining from food, drink, and sexual relations from the first light of dawn to sundown. It provided an occasion for self-purification and a reminder of the needs of the hungry. The fifth pillar encouraged a pilgrimage to Mecca, known as the *hajj* (HAHJ), during which believers from all over the Islamic world assembled once a year and put on identical simple white clothing as they rehearsed key events in Islamic history. For at least the few days of the hajj, the many worlds of Islam must surely have seemed a single realm.

A further requirement for believers, sometimes called the sixth pillar, was "struggle," or *jihad* in Arabic. Its more general meaning, which Muhammad referred to as the "greater jihad," was an interior personal effort of each believer against greed and selfishness, a spiritual striving toward living a God-conscious life. In its "lesser" form, the "jihad of the sword," the Quran authorized armed struggle against the forces of unbelief and evil as a means of establishing Muslim rule and of defending the umma from the threats of infidel aggressors. The understanding and use of the jihad concept have varied widely over the many centuries of Islamic history and remain a matter of much controversy among Muslims in the twenty-first century.

The Transformation of Arabia

As the revelations granted to Muhammad became known in Mecca, they attracted a small following of some close relatives, a few prominent Meccan leaders, and an assortment of lower-class dependents, freed slaves, and members of poorer clans. Those teachings also soon attracted the vociferous opposition of Mecca's elite families, particularly those of Muhammad's own tribe, the Quraysh. Muhammad's claim to be a "messenger of Allah," his unyielding monotheism, his call for social reform, his condemnation of Mecca's business practices, and his apparent disloyalty to his own tribe enraged the wealthy and ruling families of Mecca. So great had this opposition become that in 622 Muhammad and his small band of followers emigrated to the more welcoming town of Yathrib, soon to be called Medina, the city of the Prophet. This agricultural settlement of mixed Arab and Jewish population had invited Muhammad to serve as an arbitrator of their intractable conflicts. The emigration to Yathrib, known in Arabic as the *hijra* (HIJJ-ruh) ("the journey"), was a momentous turning point in the early history of Islam and thereafter marked the beginning of a new Islamic calendar.

The new community, or umma, that took shape in Medina was a kind of "supertribe," but very different from the traditional tribes of Arab society. Membership was a matter of belief rather than birth, allowing the community to expand rapidly. Furthermore, all authority, both political and religious, was concentrated in the hands of Muhammad, who proceeded to introduce radical changes. Charging interest on loans was outlawed as exploitative, tax-free marketplaces were established, and a mandatory payment to support the poor was imposed.

In Medina, Muhammad not only began to create a new society but also declared his movement's independence from its earlier affiliation with Judaism. In the early years, he had anticipated a warm response from Jews and Christians, based on a common monotheism and prophetic tradition, and had directed his followers to pray facing Jerusalem. But when some Jewish groups allied with his enemies, Muhammad acted harshly to suppress them, exiling some and enslaving or killing others. This was not, however, a general suppression of Jews, since others among them remained loyal to Muhammad's new state. But the Prophet now redirected his followers' prayer toward Mecca, essentially declaring Islam an Arab religion, though one with a universal message.

Guided Reading Question

■ **CHANGE**
How was Arabia transformed by the rise of Islam?

Islamic Scholars at Work As the umma—the community of all believers—grew and developed, mosques and their libraries became a focus for the faithful's study of Islam. In this twelfth-century miniature, scholars are listening intently to the figure reading from a book, while numerous texts lie stacked on shelves in the background. With a written text as the core of their religion, Muslims were a "people of the book." (Arabic miniature, 12th Century/De Agostini Picture Library/Bridgeman Images)

From its base in Medina, the Islamic community rapidly extended its reach throughout Arabia. Early military successes against Muhammad's Meccan opponents convinced other Arab tribes that the Muslims and their God were on the rise, and they sought to negotiate alliances with the new power. The religious appeal of the new faith, the end of incessant warfare among feuding tribes, periodic military actions skillfully led by Muhammad, and the Prophet's willingness to enter into marriage alliances with leading tribes—all of this contributed to the consolidation of Islamic control throughout Arabia. In 630, Muhammad triumphantly and peacefully entered Mecca itself, purging the Kaaba of its idols and declaring it a shrine to the one God, Allah. By the time Muhammad died in 632, most of Arabia had come under the control of this new Islamic state, and many had embraced the new faith.

Thus the birth of Islam differed sharply from that of Christianity. Jesus' teaching about "giving to Caesar what is Caesar's and to God what is God's" reflected the minority and subordinate status of the Jews within the Roman Empire. Early Christians found themselves periodically persecuted by Roman authorities for more than three centuries, requiring them to work out some means of dealing with an often-hostile state. The answer lay in the development of a separate church hierarchy and the concept of two coexisting authorities, one religious and one political, an arrangement that persisted even after the state became Christian.

The young Islamic community, by contrast, constituted a state, and soon a huge empire, at the very beginning of its history. Muhammad was not only a religious figure but also, unlike Jesus or the Buddha, a political and military leader able to implement his vision of an ideal Islamic society. Nor did Islam give rise to a separate religious organization. No professional clergy mediating between God and humankind emerged within Islam. Teachers, religious scholars, prayer leaders, and judges within an Islamic legal system did not have the religious role that priests held in the Christian world. No distinction between religious law and civil law, so important within Christendom, existed within the realm of Islam. One law, known as the *sharia* (shah-REE-ah), regulated, at least in theory, political, economic, social, and religious life. The sharia (literally, "a path to water," which is the source of life) evolved over the several centuries following the birth of this new religion and found expression in a number of separate schools of Islamic legal practice.

In little more than twenty years (610–632), a profound transformation had occurred in the Arabian Peninsula. What would subsequently become a new religion had been born, though it was one with roots in earlier Jewish, Christian, and Zoroastrian traditions. A new and vigorous state had emerged, bringing peace to the warring tribes of Arabia. Within that state, a distinctive society had begun to take shape, one that served ever after as a model for Islamic communities everywhere. In his farewell sermon, Muhammad described the outlines of this community:

> All mankind is from Adam and Eve, an Arab has no superiority over a non-Arab nor a non-Arab has any superiority over an Arab; also a white has no superiority over a black nor a black has any superiority over a white — except by piety and good action. Learn that every Muslim is a brother to every Muslim and that the Muslims constitute one brotherhood.[6]

The Making of an Arab Empire

In the centuries that followed the Prophet's death, the energies born of those vast changes in Arabia profoundly transformed much of the Afro-Eurasian world. The new Arab state became a huge empire, encompassing all or part of Egyptian, Roman/Byzantine, Persian, Mesopotamian, and Indian civilizations. The Islamic faith spread widely within and outside that empire. So too did the culture and language of Arabia, as many Arabs migrated far beyond their original homeland and many others found it advantageous to learn Arabic. From the mixing and blending of these many peoples emerged the new and distinctive third-wave civilization of Islam, bound by the ties of a common faith but divided by differences of culture, class, politics, gender, and religious understanding. These enormously consequential processes — the making of a new religion, a new empire, and a new civilization — were central to world history during the third-wave era.

War, Conquest, and Tolerance

Within a few years of Muhammad's death in 632, Arab armies engaged the Byzantine and Persian Sassanid empires, the great powers of the region, and within a century an Arab empire stretched from Spain to India (see Map 9.2). Weakened by periodic bouts of plague and their endemic rivalries, the Persian Sassanid Empire had been defeated by Arab forces by 644, while Byzantium, the remaining eastern regions of the old Roman Empire, soon lost the southern half of its territories. Beyond these victories, Muslim forces, operating on both land and sea, swept westward across North Africa (642–698), conquered Spain in the early 700s, and attacked southern France. To the east, Arab armies reached the Indus River and seized some of the major oasis towns of Central Asia. In 751, they inflicted a crushing defeat on Chinese forces in the Battle of Talas River, which checked the further expansion of China to the west and made possible the conversion to Islam of Central Asia's Turkic-speaking people. Most of the violence of conquest involved imperial armies, though on occasion civilians too were caught up in the fighting

MAPPING HISTORY

Map 9.2 The Arab Empire and the Initial Expansion of Islam, 622–900 c.e.
Far more so than with Buddhism or Christianity, the initial spread of Islam was both rapid and extensive. And unlike the other two world religions, Islam quickly gave rise to a huge empire, ruled by Muslim Arabs, that encompassed many of the older civilizations of the region.

READING THE MAP: During what period of time did the Arab Empire expand most rapidly?

MAKING CONNECTIONS: By comparing Map 9.2 with Maps 7.1 and 7.2, answer the following: At what places might the Abbasid caliphate have been able to control the flow of goods along the Silk and Sea roads between Western Europe and China/India around 800 c.e.?

and suffered terribly. (See Working with Evidence, Source 9.5A, page 398, for an eyewitness account of the conquest in Palestine.)

The motives driving the creation of the Arab Empire were broadly similar to those of other empires. The merchant leaders of the new Islamic community wanted to capture profitable trade routes and wealthy agricultural regions. Individual Arabs found in military expansion a route to wealth and social promotion. The need to harness the immense energies of the Arabian transformation was also important. The fragile unity of the umma threatened to come apart after Muhammad's death, and external expansion provided a common task for the community.

Guided Reading Question

....

■ **CHANGE**

Why were Arabs able to construct such a huge empire so quickly?

While many among the new conquerors viewed the mission of empire in terms of jihad, bringing righteous government to the peoples they conquered, this did not mean imposing a new religion. In fact, for the better part of a century after Muhammad's death, his followers usually referred to themselves as "believers," a term that appears in the Quran far more often than "Muslims" and one that included pious Jews and Christians as well as newly monotheistic Arabs. Such a posture eased the acceptance of the new political order, for many people recently incorporated in the emerging Arab Empire were already monotheists and familiar with the core ideas and practices of the "believers' movement"—prayer, fasting, pilgrimage, revelation, and prophets. Furthermore, the new rulers were remarkably tolerant of established Jewish and Christian faiths. The first governor of Arab-ruled Jerusalem was a Jew. Many old Christian churches continued to operate and new ones were constructed. A Christian patriarch in Iraq wrote to one of his bishops around 647 C.E., observing that the new rulers "not only do not fight Christianity, they even commend our religion, show honor to the priests and monasteries and saints of the Lord, and make gifts to the monasteries and churches."[7] Formal agreements or treaties recognized Jews, Christians, and Zoroastrians as "people of the book," giving them the status of *dhimmis* (dihm-mees), protected but second-class subjects. Such people were permitted to freely practice their own religion, so long as they paid a special tax known as the *jizya*. (See Working with Evidence, Source 9.5B, page 398, for an agreement between invading Arab forces and the Christian people of Tiflis in the Caucasus region.) Theoretically the tax was a substitute for military service, supposedly forbidden to non-Muslims. In practice, many dhimmis served in the highest offices within Muslim kingdoms and in their armies as well.

In other ways too, the Arab rulers of an expanding empire sought to limit the disruptive impact of conquest. To prevent indiscriminate destruction and exploitation of conquered peoples, occupying Arab armies were restricted to garrison towns, segregated from the native population. Local elites and bureaucratic structures were incorporated into the new Arab Empire. Nonetheless, the empire worked many changes on its subjects, the most enduring of which was the mass conversion of Middle Eastern peoples to what became by the eighth century the new and separate religion of Islam.

Conversion

For some people, no doubt, converting to Islam was or subsequently became a matter of profound spiritual or psychological transformation, but far more often, at least initially, it was "social conversion," motivated more by convenience than conviction.[8] It happened at various rates and in different ways, but in the four centuries or so after the death of Muhammad, millions of individuals and many whole societies within the Arab Empire found their cultural identity bound up with a belief in Allah and the message of his prophet. They had become Muslims.

In some ways, perhaps, the change was not so dramatic, as major elements of Islam—monotheism; ritual prayer and cleansing ceremonies; fasting; divine revelation;

Guided Reading Question

■ **EXPLANATION**
What accounts for the widespread conversion to Islam?

the ideas of Heaven, Hell, and final judgment—were quite familiar to Jews, Christians, and Zoroastrians. Furthermore, Islam was from the beginning associated with the sponsorship of a powerful state, quite unlike the experience of early Buddhism or Christianity. Conquest called into question the power of old gods, while the growing prestige of the Arab Empire attracted many to Islam. Although deliberately forced conversion was rare and explicitly forbidden in the Quran, living in an Islamic-governed state provided a variety of incentives for claiming Muslim identity. Slaves and prisoners of war were among the early converts, particularly in Persia. Converts could also avoid the jizya, the tax imposed on non-Muslims. People aspiring to official positions found conversion to Islam an aid to social mobility. In Islam, merchants found a religion friendly to commerce. The Prophet himself had been a trader, acting as a commercial agent for his wife Khadija. As Islamic law developed over several centuries, it defined what merchants might expect from one another and so reduced the uncertainty of long-distance commerce. And in the expansive Arab Empire, merchants enjoyed a huge and secure arena for trade.

Conversion was not an automatic or easy process. Vigorous resistance delayed conversion for centuries among the Berbers of North Africa; a small group of zealous Spanish Christians in the ninth century provoked their own martyrdom by publicly insulting the Prophet; and some Persian Zoroastrians fled to avoid Muslim rule. More generally, though, a remarkable and lasting religious transformation occurred throughout the Arab Empire.

In Persia, for example, between 750 and 900, about 80 percent of the population made the transition to a Muslim religious identity. But they did so in a manner quite distinct from the people of Iraq, Syria, Egypt, and North Africa. In these regions, converts to Islam gradually abandoned their native languages, adopted Arabic, and came to see themselves as Arabs. In Iran or Persia, by contrast, Arab conquest did not involve cultural Arabization, despite some initial efforts to impose the Arabic language. By the tenth century, the vast majority of Persians had become Muslims, but the Persian language (called Farsi in Iran) flourished, enriched now by a number of Arabic loan words and written in an Arabic script. In 1010, that language received its classic literary expression when the Persian poet Ferdowsi completed his epic work, the *Shahnama* (*The Book of Kings*). A huge text of some 60,000 rhyming couplets, it recorded the mythical and pre-Islamic history of Iran and gave an enduring expression to a distinctly Persian cultural identity. Thus, in places where large-scale Arab migration had occurred, such as Egypt, North Africa, and Iraq, Arabic culture and language, as well as the religion of Islam, took hold. Such areas are today both Muslim and Arab, while the peoples of Iran, Turkey, Pakistan, Indonesia, and West Africa, for example, have "Islamized" without "Arabizing."

The preservation of Persian language and culture had enormous implications for the world of Islam. In Iran, Central Asia, India, and later in the Ottoman Empire, Islam was accompanied by pervasive Persian influences. Persian administrative and bureaucratic techniques; Persian court practices with their palaces, gardens, and splendid garments; Persian architecture, poetry, music, and painting—all of this decisively shaped the high culture of these eastern Islamic lands. One of the Abbasid caliphs, himself an Arab, observed: "The Persians ruled for a thousand years and did not need us Arabs even for a day. We have been ruling them for one or two centuries and cannot do without them for an hour."[9]

Divisions and Controversies

The ideal of a unified believer's community, so important to Muhammad, proved difficult to realize as conquest and conversion vastly enlarged the Islamic umma. A central problem involved leadership and authority in the absence of Muhammad's towering presence. Who should hold the role of caliph (KAY-lihf), the successor to Muhammad as the political leader of the umma, the protector and defender of the faith? That issue crystallized a variety of emerging conflicts within the Islamic world—between early and later converts, among various Arab tribes and factions, between Arabs and non-Arabs, and between privileged and wealthy rulers and their far less fortunate subjects. Many of these political and social conflicts found expression in religious terms as various understandings of the Quran and of Muhammad's life and teachings took shape within the growing Islamic community.

The first four caliphs, known among most Muslims as the Rightly Guided Caliphs (632–661), were close "companions of the Prophet," selected by the Muslim elders of Medina. Division surfaced almost immediately as a series of Arab tribal rebellions and new "prophets" persuaded the first caliph, Abu Bakr, to suppress them forcibly. The third and fourth caliphs, Uthman and Ali, were both assassinated, and from 656 to 661, less than twenty-five years after Muhammad's death, civil war pitted Muslim against Muslim. A second civil war (680–692) continued that bitter and often savage family feud among the leaders of the "believers movement."

Out of that conflict emerged one of the deepest and most enduring rifts within the Islamic world. On one side were the Sunni (SOON-nee) Muslims, who held that the caliphs were rightful political and military leaders, selected by the Islamic community. On the other side of this sharp divide was the Shia (SHEE-ah) (an Arabic word meaning "party" or "faction") branch of Islam. Its adherents felt strongly that leadership in the Islamic world should derive from the line of Ali and his son Husayn, blood relatives of Muhammad, both of whom died at the hands of their political or religious enemies. If the caliph was the idealized communal leader for Sunnis, *imams* (leaders) served this purpose for most of the Shia Muslims. They were widely thought to have some special charisma based on descent from the Prophet, giving them a religious authority that the caliphs lacked and allowing them to infallibly interpret divine revelation and law.

Thus what began as a purely political conflict acquired over time a deeper significance. For much of early Islamic history, Shia Muslims saw themselves as the minority opposition within Islam. They felt that history had taken a wrong turn and that they were "the defenders of the oppressed, the critics and opponents of privilege and power," while the Sunnis were the advocates of the established

Guided Reading Question

■ COMPARISON

What is the difference between Sunni and Shia Islam?

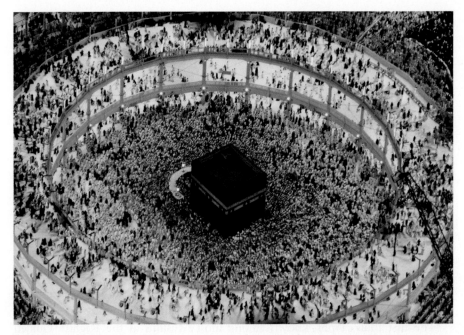

The Kaaba Located in Mecca, this stone structure, covered with a black cloth and known as the Kaaba, was originally home to the numerous deities of pre-Islamic Arabia. Cleansed by Muhammad, it became the sacred shrine of Islam and the destination of countless pilgrims undertaking the hajj. This photograph from 2015 shows worshippers praying around the Kaaba at the end of Ramadan, the holy month devoted to fasting. (AFP/Getty Images)

order.[10] Various armed revolts by Shias over the centuries, most of which failed, led to a distinctive conception of martyrdom and to the expectation that their defeated leaders were merely in hiding and not really dead and that they would return in the fullness of time. Thus a messianic element entered Shia Islam. The Sunni/Shia schism became a lasting division in the Islamic world, reflected in conflicts among various Islamic states, and was exacerbated by further splits among the Shia. Those divisions echo still in the twenty-first century.

As the Arab Empire grew, its caliphs were transformed from modest Arab chiefs into absolute monarchs, "the shadow of God on earth," of the Byzantine or Persian variety, complete with elaborate court rituals, a complex bureaucracy, a standing army, and centralized systems of taxation and coinage. They were also subject to the dynastic rivalries and succession disputes common to other empires. The first dynasty, following the era of the Rightly Guided Caliphs, came from the Umayyad (oo-MEYE-ahd) family (r. 661–750). Under the leadership of the **Umayyad caliphate**, the Arab Empire expanded greatly, caliphs became hereditary rulers, and the capital moved from Medina to the cosmopolitan Roman/Byzantine city of Damascus in Syria. Its ruling class was an Arab military aristocracy, drawn from various tribes. But Umayyad rule provoked growing criticism and unrest. The emerging Shia faction viewed the Umayyad caliphs as illegitimate usurpers, and non-Arab

Muslims resented their second-class citizenship in the empire. Many Arabs protested the luxurious living and impiety of their rulers. The Umayyads, they charged, "made God's servants slaves, God's property something to be taken by turns among the rich, and God's religion a cause of corruption."[11]

Such grievances lay behind the overthrow of the Umayyads in 750 and their replacement by a new Arab dynasty, the Abbasids. With a splendid new capital in Baghdad, the **Abbasid caliphate** presided over a flourishing and prosperous Islamic civilization in which non-Arabs, especially Persians, now played a prominent role. But the political unity of the Abbasid Empire did not last long. Beginning in the mid-ninth century, many local governors or military commanders effectively asserted the autonomy of their regions, while still giving formal allegiance to the caliph in Baghdad. Long before Mongol conquest put an official end to the Abbasid Empire in 1258, the Islamic world had fractured politically into a series of "sultanates," many ruled by Persian or Turkish military dynasties.

Guided Reading Question
....
■ **COMPARISON**
In what ways were Sufi Muslims critical of mainstream Islam?

A further tension within the world of Islam, though one that seldom produced violent conflict, lay in different answers to one central question: what does it mean to be a Muslim, to submit wholly to Allah? One answer lay in the development of the sharia, the body of Islamic law developed primarily in the eighth and ninth centuries by religious scholars, Sunni and Shia alike, who were known as the *ulama*. Based on the Quran, the life and teachings of Muhammad, deductive reasoning, and the consensus of scholars, the emerging sharia addressed in great detail practically every aspect of life. It was a blueprint for an authentic Islamic society, providing meticulous guidance for prayer and ritual cleansing; marriage, divorce, and inheritance; business and commercial relationships; the treatment of slaves; political life; personal hygiene; dietary requirements; and much more. Debates among the ulama led to the creation of four schools of law among Sunni Muslims and still others in the lands of Shia Islam. To the ulama and their followers, living as a Muslim meant following the sharia and thus participating in the creation of an Islamic society.

A second and quite different understanding of the faith emerged between 800 and 1000 C.E. among those who saw the worldly success of Islamic civilization as a distraction and deviation from the purer spirituality of Muhammad's time. Known as Sufis (SOO-fees), they represented Islam's mystical dimension, in that they sought a direct and personal experience of the Divine. Through renunciation of the material world, meditation on the words of the Quran, the chanting of the names of God, the use of music and dance, and the veneration of

Sufis and Worldly Power This early seventeenth-century painting from India illustrates the tension between Sufis and worldly authorities. Here the Muslim Mughal emperor Jahangir, seated on an hourglass throne, gives his attention to the white-bearded Sufi holy man rather than to the prominent men, including a European figure, shown in the bottom left. (bpk Bildagentur/Museum für Islamische Kunst, Staatliche Museen, Berlin, Germany/Photo: Georg Niedermeiser/Art Resource, NY)

Mullah Nasruddin, the Wise Fool of Islam

In the Islamic world, a mullah was a man of some learning, often a local cleric or leader of a village mosque. Far and away the most famous and beloved of mullahs is Nasruddin, considered both a wise man and a fool, both a sage and a simpleton. Stories about him have circulated for centuries and were well known long before the earliest written references to him appeared in the thirteenth century. Many peoples have claimed him, some have sought to find a historical figure on which he is based, and in the Turkish city of Aksehir there is even a tomb and an annual Nasruddin festival, where people dress in costumes to reenact his jokes and stories.

In fact, Mullah Nasruddin has long been an imaginary folk character within the world of Islam and especially among Sufis, gently expressing a skeptical attitude toward the rational mind, sanctimonious posturing, human vanity, and the many faces of the ego. His tales usually take place in a village setting and highlight the limitations of the intellect; the role of humor and intuition in spiritual life; the importance of generosity,

Mullah Nasruddin.

tolerance, and humility; and the many mysteries of existence. The only way to get acquainted with Mullah Nasruddin is to reflect on some of his tales. Here are just a few of the thousands:[12]

- The Mullah was in Mecca for the pilgrimage and had fallen asleep with his feet pointing toward the Kaaba, the large black cube that is the central shrine of Islam. He was awakened and rebuked by some pious Muslims, who told him it was offensive to have his dirty feet pointing at the Kaaba, where God himself resided. The Mullah apologized profusely and then added, "Perhaps you could move my feet to some place where God is *not* present."

- Mullah Nasruddin was invited to a formal reception and upon entering took the seat of greatest honor. Approached by the chief of the guard, he was asked if he was a diplomat, a minister of the king, or perhaps

Muhammad and various "saints," adherents of **Sufism** pursued an interior life, seeking to tame the ego and achieve spiritual union with Allah. To describe that inexpressible experience, they often resorted to metaphors of drunkenness or the embrace of lovers. "Stain your prayer rug with wine," urged the famous Sufi poet Hafiz, referring to the intoxication of the believer with the Divine Presence. (See the Zooming In feature on Mullah Nasruddin, above, for an expression of popular or folk Sufism.)

This mystical tendency in Islamic practice, which became widely popular by the ninth and tenth centuries, was at times sharply critical of the more scholarly and legalistic practitioners of the sharia. To Sufis, establishment teachings about the law and correct behavior, while useful for daily living, did little to bring the believer into the presence of God. Furthermore, Sufis felt that many of the ulama had been compromised by their association with worldly and corrupt governments. Sufis therefore the king himself in disguise. To each of these queries, he replied, "No, I am more than that." "Then who are you?" demanded the guard. His answer: "I am nobody."

- A villager rushed to tell the Mullah about visions of God he had been having. He asked if this meant he had become enlightened. The Mullah replied by asking him about his goats and servants. The man was enraged at this apparent dismissal of his visions. Then the Mullah explained, "If you are becoming more tender and kind toward your goats and servants, then you are on the way to enlightenment. If not, your visions are an illusion of your ego."

- Mullah Nasruddin was asked to present a lecture on "the nature of Allah" in the local mosque together with many highly learned scholars. When the scholars had finished their eloquent and wise expositions, the humble Mullah arose and hesitantly began his talk by declaring "Allah is an eggplant," while holding one of the vegetables aloft. An uproar followed at this blasphemy. When he was finally given a chance to explain himself, the Mullah declared, "Everyone before me has spoken of what they do not know or have never seen. But we can all see this eggplant. Can anyone deny that Allah is manifest in all things?" When no one was willing to dispute the point, the Mullah concluded, "Well, then Allah is an eggplant."

- One evening, after spending many hours in the local tavern, a thoroughly intoxicated Mullah was stumbling along the streets. A local police official approached him and asked, "Who are you? Where did you come from? Where are you going? Why are you out so late?" The Mullah replied, "If I had answers to all those questions, I'd be home already." [Note: To Sufis, taverns and drunkenness often symbolized spiritual insight or mystical "intoxication" with the Divine.]

- When some neighbors told Nasruddin that his donkey was lost, the Mullah exclaimed, "Thank goodness I was not on the donkey or I'd be lost as well." [Note: In Sufi circles, the donkey has long symbolized the unruly human ego.]

The Mullah's tales have been understood on several levels. Most obviously, they are jokes. But they also convey moral teachings about individual behavior as well as social commentary. And especially for Sufis, they have become a spiritual resource, gradually dissolving limited and culturally conditioned thinking, while opening the way to more fully realizing humanity's divine potential.

QUESTIONS

Pick several of these tales and explain in your own words the lessons they might convey for Muslims. In what ways might these tales be considered subversive of established authorities? Might they strike a chord with contemporary sensibilities of our own time?

often charted their own course to God, implicitly challenging the religious authority of the ulama. For these orthodox religious scholars, Sufi ideas and practice sometimes verged on heresy, as Sufis on occasion claimed unity with God, received new revelations, or incorporated novel religious practices from outside the Islamic world.

Despite their differences, adherents of the legalistic emphasis of the sharia and practitioners of Sufi spirituality coexisted, mostly peacefully, mixing and mingling, collaborating and disagreeing, in various combinations. For many centuries, roughly 1100 to 1800, Sufism was central to mainstream Islam, and many, perhaps most, Muslims affiliated with one or another Sufi organization, making use of its spiritual practices. Nonetheless, differences in emphasis about the essential meaning of Islam remained an element of tension and sometimes discord within the Muslim world.

Women and Men in Early Islam

What did the rise of Islam and the making of the Arab Empire mean for the daily lives of women and their relationship with men? Virtually every aspect of this question has been and remains highly controversial. The debates begin with the Quran itself. Did its teachings release women from earlier restrictions, or did they impose new limitations? At the level of spiritual life, the Quran was quite clear and explicit: men and women were equal. Numerous passages in the Quran use gender-inclusive language, referring to "believers, both men and women."

Guided Reading Question

■ **CHANGE**

How did the rise of Islam change the lives of women?

But in social terms, and especially within marriage, the Quran, like the written texts of almost all civilizations, viewed women as inferior and subordinate: "Men have authority over women because Allah has made the one superior to the other, and because they spend their wealth to maintain them. Good women are obedient."[13] More specifically, the Quran provided a mix of rights, restrictions, and protections for women. Female infanticide, for example, widely practiced in many cultures as a means of gender selection, was now forbidden for Muslims. Women were given control over their own property, particularly their dowries, and were granted rights of inheritance, but at half the rate of their male counterparts. Marriage was considered a contract between consenting parties, thus making marriage by capture illegitimate. Divorce was possible for both parties, although it was far more readily available for men. The practice of taking multiple husbands, which operated in some pre-Islamic Arab tribes, was prohibited, while polygyny (the practice of having multiple wives) was permitted, though more clearly regulated than before. Men were limited to four wives and required to treat each of them equally. (The difficulty of doing so has been interpreted by some as virtually requiring monogamy.) Men were, however, permitted to have sexual relations with female slaves, but any children born of those unions were free, as was the mother once her owner died. Furthermore, men were strongly encouraged to marry orphans, widows, and slaves.

Such Quranic prescriptions were but one factor shaping the lives of women and men. At least as important were the long-established practices of the societies into which Islam spread and the growing sophistication, prosperity, and urbanization of Islamic civilization. As had been the case in Athens and China during their "golden ages," Muslim women, particularly in the upper classes, experienced growing restrictions as Islamic civilization flourished culturally and economically in the Abbasid era. In early Islamic times, a number of women played visible public roles, particularly Muhammad's youngest wife, Aisha. Women prayed in the mosques, although separately, standing beside the men. Nor were women generally veiled or secluded. As the Arab Empire grew in size and splendor, however, the position of women became more restricted. The second caliph, Umar, asked women to offer prayers at home. Now veiling and the seclusion of women became standard practice among the upper and ruling classes, removing them from public life. Separate quarters within the homes of the wealthy were the domain of women, from which they could emerge only completely veiled. The caliph Mansur (r. 754–775) carried this separation of the sexes even further when he ordered a separate bridge for women to be built over the

Euphrates River in the new capital of Baghdad. Such seclusion was less possible for lower-class women, who lacked the servants of the rich and had to leave the home for shopping or work.

Such practices derived far more from established traditions of Middle Eastern cultures than from the Quran itself, but they soon gained an Islamic rationale in the writings of Muslim thinkers. The famous philosopher and religious scholar al-Ghazali clearly saw a relationship between Muslim piety and the separation of the sexes:

> It is not permissible for a stranger to hear the sound of a pestle being pounded by a woman he does not know. If he knocks at the door, it is not proper for the woman to answer him softly and easily because men's hearts can be drawn to [women] for the most trifling [reason]. . . . However, if the woman has to answer the knock, she should stick her finger in her mouth so that her voice sounds like that of an old woman.[14]

Women and Worship This thirteenth-century painting by the well-known Arab artist/illustrator al-Wasiti, born in southern Iraq, depicts women sitting separately on an upstairs balcony of a mosque while listening to a sermon. The Quran defined both male and female believers as equal before God, but long-established social customs in many Muslim societies prescribed the separation of men and women in public and especially during times of worship. (Miniature from the "Maqam" or "Assembly" of Yahya ibn Mahmud al-Wasiti, 1237/Pictures from History/Bridgeman Images)

Other signs of a tightening patriarchy—such as "honor killing" of women by their male relatives for violating sexual taboos and, in some places, clitoridectomy (female genital cutting)—likewise derived from local cultures, with no sanction in the Quran or Islamic law. Where they were practiced, such customs often came to be seen as Islamic, but they were certainly not limited to the Islamic world. In many cultures, concern with family honor linked to women's sexuality dictated harsh punishments for women who violated sexual taboos. Negative views of women, presenting them variously as weak, deficient, and a sexually charged threat to men and social stability, emerged in the *hadiths* (hah-DEETHS), traditions about the sayings or actions of Muhammad that became an important source of Islamic law.

Even as women faced growing restrictions in society generally, Islam, like Buddhism and Christianity, also offered new outlets for them in religious life. While Sunni Islam prohibited women from studying in madrassas (religious schools or colleges), it did allow them to become transmitters of the hadiths by studying with prominent scholars. Aisha, a fourteenth-century woman from Damascus, attracted students of her own after studying under some of the most renowned teachers of her generation and gained such a reputation for her learning that a seventeenth-century historian described her as her generation's most reliable transmitter of the hadith. Within the world of Shia Islam, women teachers of the faith were called mullahs, the same as their male counterparts. Islamic education, either in the home or in Quranic schools, allowed some to become literate and a few to achieve higher levels of learning. Visits to the tombs of major Islamic figures, as well as the ritual of the public bath, likewise provided some opportunity for women to interact with other women beyond their own family circle.

Sufi mystical practice allowed a greater role for women than did mainstream Islam, for the spiritual equality that the Quran accorded to male and female alike allowed women also to aspire to union with God. Among the earliest of well-known Sufi practitioners was Rabia, an eighth-century woman from Basra in southern Iraq who renounced numerous proposals of marriage and engaged, apparently successfully, in repeated religious debates with men. But for some male Sufi scholars, such as the twelfth-century mystical poet Attar, Rabia's spiritual attainments meant that "she is a man and one cannot any more call her a woman."[15]

Islam and Cultural Encounter: A Four-Way Comparison

In its earliest centuries, the rapid spread of Islam had been accompanied by the creation of an immense Arab Empire, very much in the tradition of earlier Mediterranean and Middle Eastern empires. By the tenth century, however, little political unity remained, and in 1258 even the powerless symbol of that earlier unity vanished as Mongol forces sacked Baghdad and killed the last Abbasid caliph. But even as the empire disintegrated, the civilization that was born within it grew and flourished. Perhaps the most significant sign of a flourishing Islamic civilization was the continued spread of the religion both within and beyond the boundaries of a vanishing Arab Empire (see Map 9.3), although that process differed considerably from place to place. The examples of India, Anatolia, West Africa, and Spain illustrate the various ways that Islam penetrated these societies as well as the rather different outcomes of these epic cultural encounters.

The Case of India

In South Asia, Islam found a permanent place in a long-established civilization when invasions by Turkic-speaking warrior groups from Central Asia, recently converted to Islam, brought the faith to northern India. Thus Turkic peoples became the third major carrier of Islam, after the Arabs and Persians, as their conquests initiated an enduring encounter between Islam and a Hindu-based Indian civilization. Beginning around 1000, those conquests gave rise to a series of Turkic and Muslim regimes that governed much of India until the British takeover in the eighteenth and nineteenth centuries. The early centuries of this encounter were violent indeed, as the invaders smashed Hindu and Buddhist temples and carried off vast quantities

MAPPING HISTORY

Map 9.3 The Growing World of Islam, 900–1500

Islam as a religion, a civilization, and an arena of commerce continued to grow even as the Arab Empire fragmented.

READING THE MAP: Where did Ibn Battuta's travels take him outside the worlds of Islam?

INTERPRETING THE MAP: Between 900 and 1500 Islam primarily spread along the Silk, Sea, and Sand Roads. To what extent does the map support this statement?

---

of Indian treasure. With the establishment of the Sultanate of Delhi in 1206 (see Map 9.4), Turkic rule became more systematic, although the Turks' small numbers and internal conflicts allowed only a very modest penetration of Indian society.

In the centuries that followed, substantial Muslim communities emerged in India, particularly in regions less tightly integrated into the dominant Hindu culture. Disillusioned Buddhists as well as low-caste Hindus and untouchables found the more egalitarian Islam attractive. So did peoples just beginning to make the transition to settled agriculture. Others benefited from converting to Islam by avoiding

Guided Reading Question

....

■ **COMPARISON**

What similarities and differences can you identify in the spread of Islam to India, Anatolia, West Africa, and Spain?

Map 9.4 The Sultanate of Delhi

Between 1206 and 1526 a number of Muslim dynasties ruled northern India as the Delhi sultanate, while an explicitly Hindu kingdom of Vijayanagar arose in the south after 1340. It drew on north Indian Muslim architectural features and made use of Muslim mercenaries for its military forces.

the tax imposed on non-Muslims. Sufis were particularly important in facilitating conversion, for India had always valued "god-filled men" who were detached from worldly affairs. Sufi holy men, willing to accommodate local gods and religious festivals, helped to develop a "popular Islam" that was not always so sharply distinguished from the more devotional (*bhakti*) forms of Hinduism.

Unlike the earlier experience of Islam in the Middle East, North Africa, and Persia, where Islam rapidly became the dominant faith, in India it was never able to claim more than 20 to 25 percent of the total population. Furthermore, Muslim communities were especially concentrated in the Punjab and Sind regions of northwestern India and in Bengal to the east. The core regions of Hindu culture in the northern Indian plain were not seriously challenged by the new faith, despite centuries of Muslim rule. One reason perhaps lay in the sharpness of the cultural divide between Islam and Hinduism. Islam was the most radically monotheistic of the world's religions, largely forbidding any representation of Allah, while Hinduism was surely among the most prolifically polytheistic, generating endless statues and images of the Divine in many forms. The Muslim notion of the equality of all believers contrasted sharply with the hierarchical assumptions of the caste system. Believing in sexual modesty, Muslims were deeply offended by the open eroticism of some Hindu religious art.

Although such differences may have limited the appeal of Islam in India, they also may have prevented it from being absorbed into the tolerant and inclusive embrace of Hinduism, as so many other religious ideas, practices, and communities had been. The religious exclusivity of Islam, born of its firm monotheistic belief and the idea of a unique revelation, set a boundary that the great sponge of Hinduism could not completely absorb.

Certainly, not all was conflict across that boundary. Many prominent Hindus willingly served in the political and military structures of a Muslim-ruled India. Mystical seekers after the Divine blurred the distinction between Hindu and Muslim, suggesting that God was to be found "neither in temple nor in mosque." "Look within your heart," wrote the great fifteenth-century mystic poet Kabir, "for there you will find both [Allah] and Ram [a famous Hindu deity]."[16] During the early sixteenth century, a new and distinct religious tradition emerged in India known as **Sikhism** (SIHK-iz'm), which blended elements of Islam, such as devotion to one universal

God, with Hindu concepts, such as karma and rebirth. "There is no Hindu and no Muslim. All are children of God," declared Guru Nanak (1469–1539), the founder of Sikhism.

Nonetheless, Muslims usually lived quite separately, remaining a distinctive minority within an ancient Indian civilization, which they now largely governed but which they proved unable to completely transform.

The Case of Anatolia

At the same time as India was being subjected to Turkic invasion, so too was Anatolia (now modern Turkey), where the largely Christian and Greek-speaking population was then governed by the Byzantine Empire (see Map 9.2 and Map 9.5). Here, as in India, the invaders initially wreaked havoc as Byzantine authority melted away beginning in

Map 9.5 The Ottoman Empire by the Mid-Fifteenth Century
As Turkic-speaking migrants bearing the religion of Islam penetrated Anatolia, the Ottoman Empire took shape, reaching into southeastern Europe and finally displacing the Christian Byzantine Empire. Subsequently, it came to control much of the Middle East and North Africa as well.

the eleventh century. Sufi practitioners likewise played a major role in the process of conversion. The outcome, however, was a far more profound cultural transformation than in India. By 1500, the population was 90 percent Muslim and largely Turkic-speaking, and Anatolia was the heartland of the powerful Turkic Ottoman Empire that had overrun Christian Byzantium and captured Constantinople in 1453. Why did the Turkic intrusion into Anatolia generate a much more thorough Islamization than in India?

One factor clearly lies in a very different demographic balance. The population of Anatolia—perhaps 8 million—was far smaller than India's roughly 48 million people, but far more Turkic-speaking peoples settled in Anatolia, giving them a much greater cultural weight than the smaller colonizing force in India. Furthermore, the disruption of Anatolian society was much more extensive. Massacres, enslavement, famine, and flight led to a sharp drop in the native population. The Byzantine state had been fatally weakened. Church properties were confiscated, and monasteries were destroyed or deserted. Priests and bishops were sometimes unable to serve their congregations. Christians, though seldom forced to convert, suffered many discriminations. They had to wear special clothing and pay special taxes, and they were forbidden to ride saddled horses or carry swords. Not a few Christians came to believe that these disasters represented proof that Islam was the true religion. Thus Byzantine civilization in Anatolia, previously focused on the

Guided Reading Question

■ **CHANGE**
In what ways was Anatolia changed by its incorporation into the Islamic world?

centralized institutions of church and state, was rendered leaderless and dispirited, whereas India's decentralized civilization, lacking a unified political or religious establishment, was better able to absorb the shock of external invasion while retaining its core values and identity.

The Turkic rulers of Anatolia built a new society that welcomed converts and granted them material rewards and opportunity for high office. Moreover, the cultural barriers to conversion were arguably less severe than in India. The common monotheism of Islam and Christianity, and Muslim respect for Jesus and the Christian scriptures, made conversion easier than crossing the great gulf between Islam and Hinduism. Such similarities lent support to the suggestion of some Sufi teachers that the two religions were but different versions of the same faith. Sufis also established schools, mills, orchards, hospices, and rest places for travelers and thus replaced the destroyed or decaying institutions of Christian Anatolia. All of this contributed to the thorough religious transformation of Anatolia and laid a foundation for the Ottoman Empire, which by 1500 had become the most impressive and powerful state within the Islamic world. It reached across Anatolia and the Black Sea, encompassed parts of Greece and southeastern Europe, and in the sixteenth century extended into the Arab lands of the Middle East and North Africa.

But the Islamization of Anatolia occurred within a distinctly Turkic context. A Turkic language, not Arabic, predominated. Some Sufi religious practices, such as ecstatic turning dances, actually derived from Central Asian Turkic shamanism. And Turkic tradition, common among pastoral peoples, offered a freer, more gender-equal life for women. This practice caught the attention of the Arab Moroccan visitor Ibn Battuta (1304–1368) during his travels among the Turks. He commented, "A remarkable thing that I saw . . . was the respect shown to women by the Turks, for they hold a more dignified position than the men. . . . The windows of the tent are open and her face is visible, for the Turkish women do not veil themselves."[17] He was not pleased.

The Case of West Africa

Still another pattern of Islamic expansion prevailed in West Africa. Here Islam accompanied Muslim traders across the Sahara rather than being brought by invading Arab or Turkic armies. Its gradual acceptance in the emerging civilization of West African states in the centuries after 1000 was largely peaceful and voluntary, lacking the incentives associated elsewhere with foreign conquest. Introduced by Muslim merchants from an already Islamized North Africa, the new faith was accepted primarily in the urban centers of the West African empires—Ghana, Mali, Songhay, Kanem-Bornu, and others (see Map 9.6). For African merchant communities, Islam provided an important link to Muslim trading partners, much as Buddhism had done in Southeast Asia. For the monarchs and their courts, it offered a source of literate officials to assist in state administration as well as religious legitimacy, particularly for those who gained the prestige conferred by a pilgrimage to Mecca. The most prominent such pilgrim was Mansa Musa, the ruler of Mali, who

Map 9.6 West Africa and the World of Islam

Both trans-Saharan commerce and Islam linked the civilization of West Africa to the larger Muslim world.

in 1324 undertook the hajj accompanied by a huge entourage and enormous quantities of gold. As a world religion with a single universal Creator-God, Islam had a religious appeal for societies that were now participating in a wider world.

By the sixteenth century, a number of West African cities had become major centers of Islamic religious and intellectual life, attracting scholars from throughout the Muslim world. **Timbuktu** boasted more than 150 lower-level Quranic schools and several major centers of higher education, with thousands of students from all over West Africa and beyond. Libraries held tens of thousands of books and scholarly manuscripts (see the "Manuscripts of Timbuktu" photo on page 299). Monarchs subsidized the construction of mosques as West Africa became an integral part of a larger Islamic world. Arabic became an important language of religion, education, administration, and trade, but it did not become the dominant language of daily life. Nor did West Africa experience the massive migration of Arab peoples that had promoted the Arabization of North Africa and the Middle East.

Islam remained the culture of urban elites and spread little into the rural areas of West Africa until the nineteenth century. No thorough religious transformation occurred in West Africa as it had in Anatolia. Although many rulers adopted Islam, they governed people who steadfastly practiced African religions and whose sensibilities

The Great Mosque at Jenne This mosque in the city of Jenne, initially constructed in the thirteenth century, illustrates the assimilation of Islam into West African civilization. (Antonello Lanzellotto/age-fotostock)

they had to respect if social peace were to prevail. Thus they made few efforts to impose the new religion on their rural subjects or to govern in strict accordance with Islamic law. During his mid-fourteenth-century travels in West Africa, Arab visitor Ibn Battuta was appalled that practicing Muslims in Mali permitted their women to appear in public almost naked and to mingle freely with unrelated men. "The association of women with men is agreeable to us," he was told, "and a part of good conduct to which no suspicion attaches. They are not like the women of your country."[18] Sonni Ali, a fifteenth-century ruler of Songhay, observed Ramadan and built mosques, but he also consulted traditional diviners and performed customary sacrifices. In such ways, Islam became Africanized even as parts of West Africa became Islamized.

The Case of Spain

The chief site of Islamic encounter with Christian Europe occurred in Spain, called **al-Andalus** by Muslims, which was conquered by Arab and Berber forces in the early eighth century during the first wave of Islamic expansion. By the tenth century, Muslim Spain was a vibrant civilization, often portrayed as a place of harmony and tolerance between its Muslim rulers and its Christian and Jewish subjects.

Certainly, Spain's agricultural economy was the most prosperous in Europe during this time, and its capital of Córdoba was among the largest and most splendid cities in the world. Muslims, Christians, and Jews alike contributed to a brilliant high culture in which astronomy, medicine, the arts, architecture, and literature flourished. Furthermore, social relationships among upper-class members of different faiths were easy and frequent. By 1000, perhaps 75 percent of the population had converted to Islam. Many of the remaining Christians learned Arabic, veiled their women, stopped eating pork, appreciated Arabic music and poetry, and sometimes married Muslims. One Christian bishop complained that Spanish Christians knew the rules of Arabic grammar better than those of Latin. During the reign of Abd al-Rahman III (r. 912–961), freedom of worship was declared as well as the opportunity for all to rise in the bureaucracy of the state.

But this so-called golden age of Muslim Spain was both limited and brief. Even assimilated or Arabized Christians remained religious infidels and second-class citizens in the eyes of their Muslim counterparts, and by the late tenth century toleration began to erode. The Córdoba-based regime fragmented into numerous rival states. Warfare with the remaining Christian kingdoms in northern Spain picked up in the tenth and eleventh centuries, and more puritanical and rigid forms of Islam entered Spain from North Africa. Under the rule of al-Mansur (r. 981–1002), an official policy of tolerance turned to one of overt persecution against Christians, which now included the plundering of churches and the seizure of their wealth, although he employed many Christian mercenaries in his armies. Social life also changed. Devout Muslims avoided contact with Christians; Christian homes had to be built lower than those of Muslims; priests were forbidden to carry a cross or a Bible, lest they offend Muslim sensibilities; and Arabized Christians were permitted to live only in particular places. Thus, writes one scholar, "the era of harmonious interaction between Muslim and Christian in Spain came to an end, replaced by intolerance, prejudice, and mutual suspicion."[19]

That intolerance intensified as the Christian reconquest of Spain gained ground after 1200. The end came in 1492, when Ferdinand and Isabella, the Catholic monarchs of a unified Spain, took Granada, the last Muslim stronghold on the Iberian Peninsula. Despite initial promises to maintain the freedom of Muslims to worship, in the opening decades of the sixteenth century the Spanish monarchy issued a series of edicts outlawing Islam in its various territories, forcing Muslims to choose between conversion or exile. Many Muslims were thus required to emigrate, often to North Africa or the Ottoman Empire, along with some 200,000 Jews expelled from Spain because they too refused to convert. In the early seventeenth century, even Muslim converts to Christianity were likewise banished from Spain. And yet cultural interchange persisted for a time. The translation of Arab texts into Latin continued under Christian rule, while Christian churches and palaces were constructed on the sites of older mosques and incorporated Islamic artistic and architectural features.

Thus Spain, unlike most other regions incorporated into the Islamic world, experienced a religious reversal as Christian rule was reestablished and Islam was painfully eradicated from the Iberian Peninsula. In world historical terms, perhaps the chief significance of Muslim Spain was its role in making the rich heritage of Islamic learning available to Christian Europe. As a cross-cultural encounter, it was largely a one-way street. European scholars wanted the secular knowledge—Greek as well as Arab—that had accumulated in the Islamic world, and they flocked to Spain to acquire it. That knowledge of philosophy, mathematics, medicine, optics, astronomy, botany, and more played a major role in the making of a new European civilization in the thirteenth century and beyond. Muslim Spain remained only as a memory.

> **PRACTICING HISTORICAL THINKING**
>
> "Islam had a revolutionary impact on every society that it touched." What evidence might support this statement, and what might challenge it?

The World of Islam as a New Civilization

As the religion spread and the Abbasid dynasty declined, the civilization of Islam, unlike that of China but similar to Western Christendom, operated without a dominant political center, bound more by a shared religious culture than by a shared state.

Twice that civilization was threatened from outside. The most serious intrusion came during the thirteenth century from the Mongols, whose conquest of Central Asia and Persia proved devastating while incorporating many Muslims within the huge Mongol domains. Less serious but more well known, at least in the West, were the Christian Crusades (1095–1291), which seized Jerusalem and established several small and temporary outposts along the eastern Mediterranean (see "Europe Outward Bound" in Chapter 10).

Despite these external threats and its various internal conflicts, Islamic civilization flourished and often prospered, embracing at least parts of virtually every other civilization in the Afro-Eurasian hemisphere. It was in that sense "history's first truly global civilization," although the Americas, of course, were not involved.[20] What held this Islamic world together? What enabled many people to feel themselves part of a single civilization despite its political fragmentation, religious controversies, and cultural and regional diversity?

Networks of Faith

At the core of that vast civilization was a common commitment to Islam. No group was more important in the transmission of those beliefs and practices than the ulama. These learned scholars were not "priests" in the Christian sense, for in Islam, at least theoretically, no person could stand between the believer and Allah. Rather, they served as judges, interpreters, administrators, prayer leaders, and reciters of the Quran, but especially as preservers and teachers of the sharia. Supported mostly by their local communities, some also received the patronage of sultans, or rulers, and were therefore subject to criticism for corruption and undue submission to state authority. In their homes, mosques, shrines, and Quranic schools, the ulama passed on the core teachings of the faith. Beginning in the eleventh century, formal colleges called **madrassas** offered more advanced instruction in the Quran and the sayings of Muhammad; grammar and rhetoric; sometimes philosophy, theology, mathematics, and medicine; and, above all else, law. Teaching was informal, mostly oral, and involved much memorization of texts. It was also largely conservative, seeking to preserve an established body of Islamic learning.

Guided Reading Question

■ **DESCRIPTION**

What makes it possible to speak of the Islamic world as a distinct and coherent civilization?

The ulama were an "international elite," and the system of education they created served to bind together an immense and diverse civilization. Common texts were shared widely across the world of Islam. Students and teachers alike traveled great distances in search of the most learned scholars. From Indonesia to West Africa, educated Muslims inhabited a "shared world of debate and reference."[21]

Paralleling the educational network of the ulama were the emerging religious orders of the Sufis. By the tenth century, particular Sufi *shaykhs* (shakes), or teachers, began to attract groups of disciples who were eager to learn their unique devotional practices and techniques of personal transformation. The disciples usually swore allegiance to their teacher and valued highly the chain of transmission by which those teachings and practices had come down from earlier masters. In the twelfth and thirteenth centuries, Sufis began to organize in a variety of larger associations, some limited to particular regions and others with chapters throughout the Islamic world. The Qadiriya order, for example, began in Baghdad but spread widely throughout the Arab world and into sub-Saharan Africa.

Sufi orders were especially significant in the frontier regions of Islam because they followed conquering armies or traders into Central and Southeast Asia, India, Anatolia, parts of Africa, and elsewhere. Their devotional teachings, modest ways of living, and reputation for supernatural powers gained a hearing for the new faith. Their emphasis on personal experience of the Divine, rather than on the law, allowed the Sufis to accommodate elements of local belief and practice and encouraged the growth of a popular or blended Islam. The veneration of deceased Sufi "saints," or "friends of God," particularly at their tombs, created sacred spaces that enabled Islam to take root in many places despite its foreign origins. But that flexibility also often earned Sufi practitioners the enmity of the ulama, who were sharply critical of any deviations from the sharia.

Like the madrassas and the sharia, Sufi religious ideas and institutions spanned the Islamic world and were yet another thread in the cosmopolitan web of Islamic civilization. Particular devotional teachings and practices spread widely, as did the writings of such famous Sufi poets as Hafiz and Rumi. Devotees made pilgrimages to the distant tombs of famous teachers, who, they often believed, might intercede with God on their behalf. Wandering Sufis, in search of the wisdom of renowned shaykhs, found fellow seekers and welcome shelter in the compounds of Sufi religious orders.

In addition to the networks of the Sufis and the ulama, many thousands of people, from kings to peasants, made the grand pilgrimage to Mecca—the hajj—no doubt gaining some sense of the umma. There men and women together, hailing from all over the Islamic world, joined as one people to rehearse the central elements of their faith. The claims of local identities based on family, clan, tribe, ethnicity, or state never disappeared, but now overarching them all was the inclusive unity of the Muslim community.

Networks of Exchange

The world of Islamic civilization cohered not only as a network of faith but also as an immense arena of exchange in which goods, technologies, food products, and ideas circulated widely. By 1000, large areas of the Afro-Eurasian world operated within a single cultural realm, practicing Islam or speaking Arabic. This huge region rapidly became a vast trading zone of hemispheric dimensions. In part, this was due to its central location in the Afro-Eurasian world and the breaking down of earlier political barriers between the Byzantine and Persian empires. Furthermore, commerce was valued positively within Islamic teaching, and laws regulating it figured prominently in the sharia, creating a predictable framework for exchange across many cultures. The pilgrimage to Mecca, as well as the urbanization that accompanied the growth of Islamic civilization, likewise fostered commerce. Baghdad, established in 756 as the capital of the Abbasid Empire, soon grew into a magnificent city of half a million people. The appetite of urban elites for luxury goods stimulated both craft production and the desire for foreign products.

Thus Muslim merchants, Arabs and Persians in particular, quickly became prominent and sometimes dominant players in all the major Afro-Eurasian trade routes of the third-wave era—in the Mediterranean Sea, along the revived Silk Roads, across the Sahara, and throughout the Indian Ocean basin. By the eighth century, Arab and Persian traders had established a commercial colony in Canton in southern China, thus linking the Islamic heartland with Asia's other giant and flourishing economy. Various forms of banking, partnerships, business contracts, and instruments for granting credit facilitated these long-distance economic relationships and generated a prosperous, sophisticated, and highly commercialized economy that spanned the Old World.

The vast expanse of Islamic civilization also contributed to ecological change as agricultural products and practices spread from one region to another, a process already under way in the earlier Roman and Persian empires. Among the food crops that circulated within and beyond the Islamic world were different varieties of sugarcane, rice, apricots, artichokes, eggplants, lemons, oranges, almonds, figs, and bananas. Equally significant were water-management practices, so important to the arid or semi-arid environments of many parts of the Islamic world. Persian-style reservoirs and irrigation technologies spread as far as Tunisia and Morocco, the northern fringes of the Sahara, Spain, and Yemen. All of this contributed to an "Islamic Green Revolution" of increased food production, as well as to population growth, urbanization, and industrial development across the Islamic world.

Technology too diffused widely within the realm of Islam. Muslim technicians made improvements on rockets, first developed in China, by developing one that carried a small warhead and another that was used to attack ships. Papermaking techniques entered the Abbasid Empire from China in the eighth century or earlier, with paper mills soon operating in Persia, Iraq, and Egypt. This revolutionary technology, which everywhere served to strengthen bureaucratic governments, passed from the Middle East into India and Europe over the following centuries. Everywhere it spurred the emergence of books and written culture at the expense of earlier orally based cultural expressions.

Ideas likewise circulated across the Islamic world. The religion itself drew heavily and quite openly on Jewish

Guided Reading Question

■ **CONNECTION**

In what ways was the world of Islam a "cosmopolitan civilization"?

A Muslim Astronomical Observatory Drawing initially on Greek, Indian, and Persian astronomy, the Islamic world after 1000 developed its own distinctive tradition of astronomical observation and prediction, reflected in this Turkish observatory constructed in 1557. Muslim astronomy later exercised considerable influence in both China and Europe. (From the "Sehinsahname of Murad III," ca. 1581/ Istanbul University Library, Istanbul, Turkey/Bridgeman Images)

and Christian precedents. Persia also contributed much in the way of bureaucratic practice, court ritual, and poetry, with Persian becoming a major literary language in elite circles. Scientific, medical, and philosophical texts, especially from ancient Greece, the Hellenistic world, and India, were systematically translated into Arabic, providing an enormous boost to Islamic scholarship and science for several centuries. In 830, the Abbasid caliph al-Mamun, himself a poet and scholar with a passion for foreign learning, established the **House of Wisdom** in Baghdad as an academic center for this research and translation. Stimulated by Greek texts, a school of Islamic thinkers known as Mutazalites ("those who stand apart") argued that reason, rather than revelation, was the "surest way to truth."[22] In the long run, however, the philosophers' emphasis on logic, rationality, and the laws of nature was subject to increasing criticism by those who held that only the Quran, the sayings of the Prophet, or mystical experience represented a genuine path to God.

But the realm of Islam was much more than a museum of ancient achievements from the civilizations that it encompassed. Those traditions mixed and blended to generate a distinctive Islamic civilization with many new contributions to the world of learning. (See Snapshot: Key Achievements in Islamic

SNAPSHOT Key Achievements in Islamic Science and Scholarship

Person/Dates	Achievement
al-Khwarazim (790–840)	Mathematician; spread use of Arabic numerals in Islamic world; wrote first book on algebra
al-Razi (865–925)	Discovered sulfuric acid; wrote a vast encyclopedia of medicine, drawing on Greek, Syrian, Indian, and Persian work and his own clinical observation
al-Biruni (973–1048)	Mathematician, astronomer, cartographer; calculated the radius of the earth with great accuracy; worked out numerous mathematical innovations; developed a technique for displaying a hemisphere on a plane
Ibn Sina (Avicenna) (980–1037)	Prolific writer in almost all fields of science and philosophy; especially known for *Canon of Medicine*, a fourteen-volume work that set standards for medical practice in Islamic and Christian worlds for centuries
Omar Khayyam (1048–1131)	Mathematician; critic of Euclid's geometry; measured the solar year with great accuracy; Sufi poet; author of *The Rubaiyat*
Ibn Rushd (Averroës) (1126–1198)	Translated and commented widely on Aristotle; rationalist philosopher; made major contributions in law, mathematics, and medicine
Nasir al-Din Tusi (1201–1274)	Founder of the famous Maragha observatory in Persia (data from Maragha probably influenced Copernicus); mapped the motion of stars and planets
Ibn Khaldun (1332–1406)	Greatest Arab historian; identified trends and structures in world history over long periods of time

Science and Scholarship, page 387.) Using Indian numerical notation, for example, Arab scholars developed algebra as a novel mathematical discipline. They also undertook much original work in astronomy and optics. They built on earlier Greek and Indian practice to create a remarkable tradition in medicine and pharmacology. Arab physicians such as al-Razi and Ibn Sina accurately diagnosed many diseases, such as hay fever, measles, smallpox, diphtheria, rabies, and diabetes. In addition, treatments such as using a mercury ointment for scabies, cataract and hernia operations, and filling teeth with gold emerged from Arab doctors. The first hospitals, traveling clinics, and examinations for physicians and pharmacologists were also developed within the Islamic world. In the eleventh and twelfth centuries, this enormous body of Arab medical scholarship entered Europe via Spain, and it remained at the core of European medical practice for many centuries.

REFLECTIONS

Past and Present: Choosing Our History

Prominent among the many uses of history is the perspective it provides on the present. Although historians sometimes worry that an excessive "present-mindedness" may distort our perception of the past, all of us look to history, almost instinctively, to comprehend the world we now inhabit. Given the obvious importance of the Islamic world in the international arena of the twenty-first century, how might some grasp of the early development of Islamic civilization assist us in understanding our present circumstances?

Certainly, that history reminds us of the central role that Islam played in the Afro-Eurasian world for a thousand years or more. From 600 to 1600 or later, it was a proud, cosmopolitan, often prosperous, and frequently powerful civilization that spanned Africa, Europe, the Middle East, and Asia. What followed were several centuries of European or Western imperialism that many Muslims found humiliating, even if some were attracted by elements of modern Western culture. In their recent efforts to overcome those centuries of subordination and exploitation, Muslims have found encouragement and inspiration in reflecting on the more distant and perhaps more glorious past. But they have not all chosen to emphasize the same past. Those labeled as "fundamentalists" have often viewed the early Islamic community associated with Medina, Mecca, and Muhammad as a model for Islamic renewal in the present. Others, often known as Islamic modernizers, have looked to the somewhat later achievements of Islamic science and scholarship as a foundation for a more open engagement with the West and the modern world.

The history of Islam also reveals a world of great diversity and debate. Sharp religious differences between Sunni and Shia understandings of the faith; differences in emphasis between advocates of the sharia and of Sufi spirituality; political conflicts among various groups and regions within the larger Islamic world; different postures toward women—all of this and more divided the umma and divide it still. Recalling that diversity is a useful reminder for any who would tag all Muslims with a single label.

A further dimension of that diversity lies in the many cultural encounters that the spread of Islam has spawned. Sometimes great conflict and violence have accompanied those encounters, as in the Crusades and in Turkic invasions of India and Anatolia. At other times and places, Muslims and non-Muslims have lived together in relative tranquillity and tolerance—in Spain, in West Africa, in India, and in the Ottoman Empire. Some commentaries on the current interaction of Islam and the West seem to assume an eternal hostility or an inevitable clash of civilizations. The record of the past, however, shows considerable variation in the interaction of Muslims and others. While the past certainly shapes and conditions what happens next, the future, as always, remains open. Within limits, we can choose the history on which we seek to build.

Second Thoughts

What's the Significance?

Muhammad, 361

Quran, 361

umma, 362

Pillars of Islam, 362

hijra, 363

sharia, 364

jizya, 367

Umayyad caliphate, 370

Abbasid caliphate, 371

ulama, 371

Sufism, 372

Sikhism, 378

Timbuktu, 381

al-Andalus, 382

madrassas, 384

House of Wisdom, 387

Big Picture Questions

1. How might you account for the immense religious and political/military success of Islam in its early centuries?
2. In what ways might Islamic civilization be described as cosmopolitan, international, or global?
3. "Islam was simultaneously a single world of shared meaning and interaction and a series of separate, distinct, and conflicting communities." What evidence could you provide to support both parts of this statement?
4. What changes did Islamic expansion generate in those societies that encountered it, and how was Islam itself transformed by those encounters?
5. **Looking Back:** What distinguished the early centuries of Islamic history from a similar phase in the history of Christianity and Buddhism?

Next Steps: For Further Study

Reza Aslan, *No God but God* (2005). A well-written and popular history of Islam by an Iranian immigrant to the United States.

G. W. Bowerstock, *The Crucible of Islam* (2017). Highlights the significance of Arab history and culture in the emergence of Islam.

Fred M. Donner, *Muhammad and the Believers* (2010). An innovative account of the first century of Islam by a leading scholar of that era.

John Esposito, ed., *The Oxford History of Islam* (1999). Up-to-date essays on various periods and themes in Islamic history. Beautifully illustrated.

Francis Robinson, ed., *Cambridge Illustrated History of the Islamic World* (1996). A series of essays by major scholars, with lovely pictures and maps.

Judith Tucker, *Gender and Islamic History* (1994). A brief overview of the changing lives of Islamic women.

Tim Mackintosh Smith, *The Man Who Walked across the World*, BBC FOUR, http://topdocumentaryfilms.com/man-who-walked-across-world/. A documentary travelogue tracing the many journeys of Ibn Battuta.

"Religions: Islam," http://www.bbc.co.uk/religion/religions/islam/. A BBC website providing information about all aspects of Islamic life and culture.

The Islamic World in the Seventh Century

The first seventy years of the Islamic era—roughly 610 to 680 C.E.—witnessed three major developments of enduring world historical significance: the emergence of a new religious tradition, a sharp and lasting division within the Islamic world, and the beginnings of a growing Arab Empire. The sources that follow provide a glimpse—both visual and documentary—into those processes.

SOURCE 9.1 Depicting Muhammad with the Angel Gabriel ▶

The three images that follow portray major events in the life of Muhammad. They are etched into the memory of Muslims everywhere, for they mark the beginnings of what became Islam. Representing these events artistically, and especially the figure of Muhammad, has long been controversial within Islamic societies. While not prohibited in the Quran, visual depictions of the Prophet have often been discouraged or even forbidden as a way of preventing idolatry. Nonetheless, Muhammad was on occasion portrayed in Persian and Turkish miniature painting, sometimes in full face, but often with his face obscured.

According to all Muslims, the central and defining experience in Muhammad's life occurred in the year 610 C.E. when he encountered for the first time an angel, usually identified as Gabriel, an event that marked the beginning of his revelations. While meditating in a cave outside Mecca, a towering and overpowering presence of the angel appeared to him, filling the entire horizon, squeezing the very breath from his body, and commanding him to "recite" or to "read." After repeated protests that "I am not a reciter/reader," Muhammad found himself speaking what became the first revelation of the Quran. Source 9.1, an early fourteenth-century Persian miniature painting, depicts this encounter between Muhammad and Gabriel.

■ What impression of this encounter does the artist seek to convey?

■ Traditional accounts of Muhammad's encounter with the angel stress the mysterious and overpowering "otherness" of the Divine Presence, which prompted Muhammad's initial fear and terror. What is the religious significance of such a depiction of the Divine? To what extent does this image convey that impression?

■ Muslims have traditionally stressed that their prophet was illiterate, based in part on his response to the angel: "I am not a reader." Why might it be important to Muslims to believe that Muhammad was illiterate?

Muhammad and the Angel Gabriel | ca. 1307

■ ■ ■

SOURCE 9.2 **Muhammad in Jerusalem** ▶

By far the most frequently portrayed event in the life of Muhammad was the *miraj*, the Prophet's Night Journey, said to have taken place in 619 or 620. The Quran refers briefly to God taking the Prophet "from the sacred place of worship to the far distant place of worship." This passage became the basis for a story, much embellished over the centuries, of deep meaning for Muslims. In this religious narrative, Muhammad was led one night by the angel Gabriel from Mecca to Jerusalem. For the journey he was given a *buraq*, a mythical winged creature with the body of a mule or donkey and the face of a woman. Upon arriving in Jerusalem, Muhammad led prayers for an assembly of earlier prophets including Abraham, Moses, and Jesus. (See the image "Muslims, Jews, and Christians" on page 362 for a fifteenth-century Persian painting illustrating this event.) Then, accompanied by many angels, Muhammad made his way through seven heavens, coming almost into the presence of God, where, according to the Quran, "he saw some of the greatest signs of his Lord."

Some believers have interpreted this literally as a miraculous event, while others have considered it a dream or vision. Source 9.2, dating from the early sixteenth century, is one of many representations of the Night Journey that emerged within Persian miniature painting.

- Looking closely at the image, what significance might one attach to the female head of the buraq, to the accompanying angels and their gifts, to the fiery halo around Muhammad's head, and to the image of the world below and slightly to the right of the buraq?

- What meaning might be derived from Muhammad's encounter with earlier prophets such as Abraham, Moses, and Jesus?

- How might the destination of the Night Journey (Jerusalem) have affected Muslim views of that city?

- How might Sufis have understood the Night Journey?

AQA MIRAK | *The Night Journey of Muhammad* | **16th century**

■ ■ ■

SOURCE 9.3 **Victory in Mecca** ▶

Widespread opposition to Muhammad's revolutionary message required almost a decade of struggle, military action, and negotiation before he was able to establish his control over most of Arabia. But finally in 630, Muhammad and some 10,000 soldiers triumphantly entered Mecca, almost completely without violence, and in a posture of reconciliation rather than revenge. In sharp contrast to traditional Arab practice, Muhammad issued a general amnesty for those who had opposed him. Then he turned his attention to the religious rationale of his entire movement. Riding his favorite camel, Muhammad circled the Kaaba seven times, shouting "Allahu Akbar" (God is greater), thus declaring the triumph of the believer's movement. Refusing to enter the Kaaba until it had been purified from its idolatry, Muhammad ordered its 360 idols and paintings removed. He then smashed each one, reciting a Quranic verse: "The truth has come and falsehood has vanished away." Muslim sources record that the Prophet invited his cousin and son-in-law Ali, the first male convert to the new faith, to stand on his shoulders to strike down the highest idols. Thus the Kaaba was cleansed and, in Muslim thinking, restored to its original purpose as a focal point for the worship of Allah alone.

Source 9.3, a fifteenth-century Persian image, portrays this dramatic event, showing Muhammad with Ali on his shoulders, both enveloped in holy fire, smashing the offensive idols while their followers look on.

■ What understanding of pre-Islamic Arab religion does this image reflect?

■ What fundamental Muslim teachings does this painting seek to convey? How do you understand the Muslim concern with idolatry?

■ Some traditions suggest that Muhammad ordered pictures of Mary and Jesus within the Kaaba to be left intact. What purpose might this tradition serve?

MIR HAVAND | *The Cleansing of the Kaaba* | ca. 1590

SOURCE 9.4 **Conflict and Division: The Emergence of Shia Islam**

Less than twenty-five years after Muhammad died, his beloved community, the umma, had descended into civil war, largely over the political issue of leadership. From this violent struggle emerged the lasting division of the Islamic world into Sunni and Shia versions of the faith. (See "Divisions and Controversies" in this chapter.) The Shia perspective on this conflict is reflected in a bitter poem attributed to Ali ibn Husayn, who was in the line of direct descent from the Prophet Muhammad. It was written as he went into battle against the dominant forces of the Umayyad dynasty in 680.

- The Shia outlook placed great emphasis on retaining the leadership of the Islamic community in the family line descending from Muhammad and his cousin and son-in-law Ali. How is this sensibility reflected in this poem?

- Another Shia ideal was that "the righteous should wage struggle against tyrants, even in the face of hopeless odds."[23] What evidence of this stance do you find in the poem?

ALI IBN HUSAYN | *Poem* | ca. 680

I am Ali, son of Husayn son of Ali; / We and the household of God are closer to the prophet

Than Shabath and Shamir the vile [military leaders of the opposing forces]. I strike you with the sword until it bends / the blows of a Hasimite [family of the prophet] youth, an 'Alid [in the family line of Ali, the fourth caliph and cousin and son-in-law of the Prophet] / And today I will not stop defending my father [Husayn, the great Shia martyr] / By God the son of the bastard [the local Umayyad governor] shall not rule over us.

Source: Quoted in Fred M. Donner, *Muhammad and the Believers* (Cambridge, MA: Harvard University Press, 2010), 179.

■ ■ ■

SOURCE 9.5 **Conquest**

Even as the Arab/Islamic world splintered internally, it was expanding externally. That expansion involved both military force and political agreements, as the two brief documents in Source 9.5 indicate. The first, from a Syrian Christian eyewitness known as Thomas the Presbyter, illustrates the violence of conquest in what is now Palestine in 634 C.E., just two years after the Prophet Muhammad's death. The second records an agreement between the invading Arab forces and the Christian people of Tiflis in the Caucasus region in 642–643.

■ Arab empire building has been described variously as extremely violent, generally tolerant, and motivated by the desire to convert people to Islam. In what ways might these documents support or challenge such characterizations?

■ What advantages and disadvantages does Source 9.5B hold for the people of Tiflis?

SOURCE 9.5A

Text of Thomas the Presbyter | 640

On Friday, 4 February [634 C.E.], at the ninth hour, there was a battle between the Romans [forces of the Byzantine Empire] and the Arabs of Muhammad in Palestine twelve miles east of Gaza. The Romans fled, leaving behind the patriarch Bryrdn, whom the Arabs killed. Some 4,000 poor villagers of Palestine were killed there, Christians, Jews and Samaritans. The Arabs ravaged the whole region. . . .

Source: Andrew Palmer (with contributions from Sebastian P. Brock and Robert G. Hoyland), *The Seventh Century in the West-Syrian Chronicles Including Two Seventh-Century Syriac Apocalyptic Texts* (Liverpool: Liverpool University Press, 1993), 18–19.

SOURCE 9.5B

Pact of Ibn Muslama and the People of Tiflis | 653

This is a statement from Habib ibn Muslama [commander of the invading Arab forces] to the inhabitants of Tiflis, . . . securing them safety for their lives, churches, convents, religious services, and faith, provided they acknowledge and pay tax to the amount of one *dinar* on every household. You are not to combine more than one household into one in order to reduce the tax and we are not to divide the same household into more than one in order to increase it. You owe us counsel and support against the enemies of Allah and his Prophet to the utmost of your ability, and are bound to entertain the needy Muslim for one night and provide him with food used by the "people of the book" and which it is legal for us to partake of. If a Muslim is cut off from his companions and falls into your hands, you are bound to deliver him to the nearest body of the "Believers." . . . If you return to the obedience of Allah and observe prayer, you are our brethren in faith; otherwise poll-tax is incumbent on you. In case an enemy of yours attacks and subjugates you while Muslims are too busy to come to your aid, the Muslims are not held responsible, nor is it a violation of the covenant with you.

Source: Al-Baladhuri, *The Origins of the Islamic State*, translated by P. K. Hitti (New York: Columbia University, 1916), 316–17.

SOURCE 9.6 Governing an Empire

Conquering an empire was one thing; governing it was another. In 658 C.E. the fourth caliph Ali sent a letter to Malik Ashtar, the newly appointed governor of Egypt, which was now part of a growing Arab Empire, outlining the principles of governance that he should follow. The high-minded nature of this letter provided a model for benevolent political leadership of an increasingly pluralistic empire, although few Arab or other rulers lived up to that high standard. In fact, Malik Ashtar was poisoned by a rival before he could take up his duties. Nonetheless, the letter has long stood, both in the Islamic world and beyond, as a charter for a moral approach to government.

- How might you define the principles of governance outlined in Ali's letter?

- To what extent does his letter reflect Islamic values?

- In what ways might it be seen as a response to a growing empire?

CALIPH ALI | *Letter to Malik Ashtar* | 658

Develop in your heart the feeling of love for your people. . . . Do not behave with them like a barbarian, and do not appropriate to yourself that which belongs to them. . . . Do not say: "I am your overlord and dictator, and that you should, therefore, bow to my commands," as that will corrupt your heart, weaken your faith in religion and create disorder in the state. . . .

Maintain justice in administration and impose it on your own self and seek the consent of the people, for the discontent of the masses sterilizes the contentment of the privileged few. . . . It is the common man who is the strength of the State and Religion. It is he who fights the enemy. So live in close contact with the masses and be mindful of their welfare. . . .

Never let men who have been companions of tyrants or shared their crimes be your counsellors. Keep close to you the upright, and the God fearing, and make clear to them that they are never to flatter you and never to give you credit for any good that you may not have done. . . .

Never select men for responsible posts either out of any regard for personal connections or under any influence, for that might lead to injustice and corruption. . . .

You should regard the proper upkeep of the land in cultivation as of greater importance than the collection of revenue, for revenue cannot be derived except by making the land productive. He who demands revenue without helping the cultivator to improve his land, inflicts unmerited hardship on the cultivator and ruins the state. . . .

Treat businessmen and artisans well. . . . Trade and industry are the real sources of profit to the state and the suppliers of consumer goods. . . . Visit every part of the country and establish personal contact with this class, and inquire into their condition. But bear in mind that a good many of them are intensely greedy. . . . They hoard grain and try to sell it at a high price and this is most harmful to the public. . . . Prevent them from hoarding, for the prophet of God had prohibited it. . . .

Fear God when dealing with the problem of the poor. . . . For God's sake, safeguard their rights, for on you rests the responsibility of protecting their interests. Assign for their uplift a portion of the state exchequer. . . . Meet the oppressed and the lowly periodically in an open conference and conscious of the divine presence there, have a heart-to-heart talk with them, . . . so that the representatives of the poor might state their grievances fearlessly and without reserve. . . .

Do not forget to set apart the best of your time for communion with God.

Source: Paul Salahuddin Armstrong, ed., "Caliph Ali's Letter to Malik Ashtar," https://paulsarmstrong.com/articles/caliph-ali-letter -to-malik-ashtar/.

DOING HISTORY

1. **Noticing visual sources:** Consider the first three visual sources together with the other images within the chapter. What general impression of the Islamic world emerges? What point of view, if any, is reflected in this selection of visual sources? Do they convey a positive, negative, or neutral impression of Islamic civilization?

2. **Considering Islamic unity and division:** What do these sources suggest about the factors that enhanced the unity of the Islamic world and those that divided it?

3. **Analyzing the usefulness of sources:** To what extent do these sources provide useful information about what really happened? And in what ways do they help us rather to understand the evolving Muslim view of Islam's history?

4. **Comparing narrative text and primary sources:** What do these sources add to the understanding of Islam you derived from the narrative text of this chapter?

Assessing the Prophet Muhammad

Clearly the Prophet Muhammad has been one of world history's outsized actors, whose life has resonated across many domains of human activity around the world for many centuries. In Voice 9.1, Francis Robinson, a prominent historian of Islam, reviews the evolving image of Muhammad in the Western world, while Voice 9.2 by Karen Armstrong, who has written a biography of the prophet, explores the meaning of Muhammad for Muslims.

- According to Robinson in Voice 9.1, in what different ways has Muhammed been understood in the Western world?

- How does Armstrong in Voice 9.2 understand Muhammad's personal significance for millions of ordinary Muslims?

- **Integrating Primary and Secondary Sources:** In what ways might the primary sources in this feature be used to support Muslim understandings of Muhammad as described in Voice 9.2?

VOICE 9.1

Francis Robinson on Western Attitudes to Muhammad | 1996

The changing image of the Prophet Muhammad is a touchstone of the changing western attitudes to Islam. For a thousand years he was the false prophet, the imposter. Hence the terrible fate which Dante contrived for him in the *Inferno* ... consigned to the ninth of ten gloomy ditches surrounding Satan's stronghold [hell], where, branded a spreader of scandal and discord, he was doomed to being split in twain continuously. From the eighteenth century a more complex picture begins to emerge. The historian Edward Gibbon in his *Decline and Fall of the Roman Empire* was able to admire the original genius of the Muhammad of Mecca, the moral leader, while questioning the motives of the Muhammad of Medina, the calculating politician. Some fifty years later, the historian Thomas Carlyle was able to make Muhammad his prophetic hero. . . . "He is by no means the truest of the Prophets, . . . but I do esteem

him a true one . . . a great soul." . . . [A] half century later the Victorian entrepreneur Thomas Holloway had little difficulty in having the Prophet's image affixed to the Chapel of his university college for women alongside other great teachers of humankind. In the twentieth century, attitudes range from the secular that would dismiss Muhammad along with Jesus as the misguided catalyst of religious enthusiasm to some recent Christian Roman Catholic scholars who have gone so far as to regard him as a religious genius and have wondered if he might not be a true prophet.

Source: Francis Robinson, ed., *Cambridge Illustrated History: Islamic World* (Cambridge: Cambridge University Press, 1996), xv.

VOICE 9.2

Karen Armstrong on Muslim Devotion to the Prophet | 1992

Muslims have continued to emphasize that Muhammad is merely an ordinary man like themselves, but over the centuries they have added a qualification. Yes, Muhammad is a man like other men, but he is "like a precious gem among stones." . . . Muhammad's life has become a "sign," like other signs that the Quran urges Muslims to see in the natural world. His prophetic career was a symbol, a theophany, which not only shows God's activity in the world, but illustrates the perfect human surrender to God. The development of the ideal of Muhammadan sanctity [holy behavior worthy of respect and imitation] has been an imaginative attempt to penetrate the meaning of his life and apply it to the circumstances of daily life. . . . Muhammad is therefore seen symbolically as the Perfect Man, the human archetype and the image of a perfect receptivity to God. . . . Muslims seek to imitate Muhammad in their daily lives in order to approximate as closely as possible to this perfection and so to come as close as they can to God himself.

Source: Karen Armstrong, *Muhammad: A Biography of the Prophet* (New York: Harper Collins, 1992), 262.

CHAPTER
10

The Worlds of Christendom

Contraction, Expansion, and Division

600–1450

Christian Contraction in Asia and Africa
Asian Christianity
African Christianity

Byzantine Christendom: Building on the Roman Past
The Byzantine State
The Byzantine Church and Christian Divergence
Byzantium and the World
The Conversion of Russia

Western Christendom: Rebuilding in the Wake of Roman Collapse
Political Life in Western Europe
Society and the Church
Accelerating Change in the West
Europe Outward Bound: The Crusading Tradition

The West in Comparative Perspective
Catching Up
Pluralism in Politics
Reason and Faith

Reflections: Remembering and Forgetting: Continuity and Surprise in the Worlds of Christendom

« **Charlemagne** This fourteenth-century manuscript painting depicts Charlemagne, king of the Franks, being crowned emperor by Pope Leo III surrounded by other churchmen. His coronation in 800 C.E. illustrates the close and sometimes-conflicted relationship of political and religious authorities in an emerging European civilization. His crowning also represents the futile desire of many in Western Europe to revive the old Roman Empire, even as a substantially new civilization was taking shape in the aftermath of the Roman collapse several centuries earlier.

Yao Hong, a Chinese woman, was about twenty years of age around 1990, when, distraught at discovering that her husband was having an affair, she became a Christian. As a migrant from a rural village to the huge city of Shanghai, Yao Hong found support and a sense of family in a Christian community. Interviewed in 2010, she observed, "Whether they know you or not, they treat you as a brother or sister. . . . [T]hey help out with money or material assistance or spiritual aid." Nor did she find the Christian faith alien to her Chinese culture. To the contrary, she felt conversion to Christianity as a patriotic act, even a way of becoming more fully modern. "God is rising here in China," she declared. "If you look at the United States or England, . . . [t]heir churches are rich, because God blesses them."[1] ■

Yao Hong is but one of many millions who have made Christianity a very rapidly growing faith in China over the past thirty years or so. In neighboring South Korea, practicing Christians now outnumber Buddhists. Even more impressively, the non-Muslim regions of Africa witnessed an explosive advance of Christianity during the twentieth century. By the early twenty-first century, over 60 percent of the world's Christians lived in Asia, Africa, or Latin America.

Interestingly enough, the sixth- and seventh-century world of Christendom revealed a broadly similar pattern. Christianity then enjoyed an Afro-Eurasian reach with flourishing communities in Anatolia, Arabia, Egypt, North Africa, Ethiopia,

403

Nubia, Syria, Armenia, Persia, India, and China, as well as Europe. But during the third-wave era, radical changes reshaped that Christian world. Its African and Asian outposts largely vanished, declined, or were marginalized as Christianity became primarily a European phenomenon for the next thousand years or more. Furthermore, this European Christian world became deeply divided. Its eastern half, known as the Byzantine Empire or Byzantium (bihz-ANN-tee-uhm), continued the traditions of the Greco-Roman world in the eastern Mediterranean basin until its conquest by the Muslim Ottoman Empire in 1453. Centered on the magnificent city of Constantinople, Byzantium gradually developed a particular form of Christianity known as Eastern Orthodoxy and a distinctive third-wave civilization.

In Western, or Latin, Christendom, encompassing what we now know as Western Europe, the setting was far different. There the Roman imperial order had largely vanished by 500 C.E., replaced by highly localized societies—fragmented, decentralized, and competitive—in sharp contrast to the unified state of Byzantium. In Western Europe, a Roman Catholic version of the faith gradually emerged, increasingly centered on the pope and with an independence from political authorities that the Eastern Orthodox Church did not possess. Moreover, the Western Church in particular and its society in general were far more rural than Byzantium and certainly had nothing to compare to the imperial splendor of Constantinople. However, slowly at first and then with increasing speed after 1000, Western Europe emerged as an especially dynamic, expansive, and innovative third-wave civilization, combining elements of its Greco-Roman-Christian past with the culture of Germanic and Celtic peoples to produce a distinctive hybrid, or blended, civilization.

Thus the story of global Christendom in the era of third-wave civilizations is one of contractions and expansions. As a religion, Christianity contracted sharply in Asia and Africa even as it expanded in Western Europe and Russia. As a civilization, Christian Byzantium flourished for a time, then gradually contracted and finally disappeared. The trajectory of civilization in the West traced an opposite path, at first contracting as the Roman Empire collapsed and later expanding as a new and blended civilization took hold in Western Europe.

SEEKING THE MAIN POINT

In what different ways did the history of Christianity and Christian civilizations unfold in various parts of the Afro-Eurasian world during the third-wave era?

Christian Contraction in Asia and Africa

It was the wholly unforeseen birth of Islam, an expanding Arab Empire, and a sophisticated transcontinental Muslim civilization that led to the contraction of Christendom in Asia and Africa. As a result, European civilization emerged as the principal center of the Christian faith.[2]

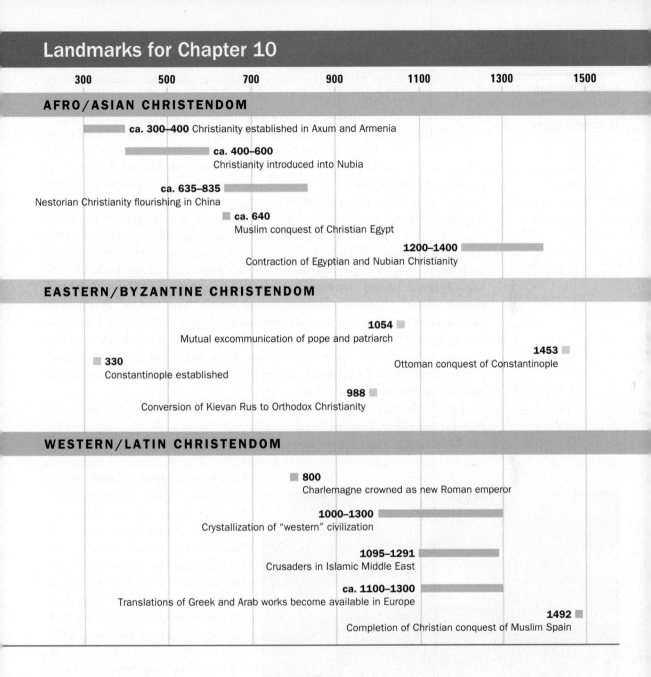

Landmarks for Chapter 10

| 300 | 500 | 700 | 900 | 1100 | 1300 | 1500 |

AFRO/ASIAN CHRISTENDOM

ca. 300–400 Christianity established in Axum and Armenia

ca. 400–600
Christianity introduced into Nubia

ca. 635–835
Nestorian Christianity flourishing in China

ca. 640
Muslim conquest of Christian Egypt

1200–1400
Contraction of Egyptian and Nubian Christianity

EASTERN/BYZANTINE CHRISTENDOM

1054
Mutual excommunication of pope and patriarch

330
Constantinople established

1453
Ottoman conquest of Constantinople

988
Conversion of Kievan Rus to Orthodox Christianity

WESTERN/LATIN CHRISTENDOM

800
Charlemagne crowned as new Roman emperor

1000–1300
Crystallization of "western" civilization

1095–1291
Crusaders in Islamic Middle East

ca. 1100–1300
Translations of Greek and Arab works become available in Europe

1492
Completion of Christian conquest of Muslim Spain

Asian Christianity

In Arabia, the homeland of Islam, the decimation of earlier Christian communities occurred most completely and most quickly, for within a century or so of Muhammad's death in 632, only a few Christian groups remained. During the eighth century, triumphant Muslims marked the replacement of the old religion by using pillars of a demolished Christian cathedral to construct the Grand Mosque of Sana'a in southern Arabia.

Guided Reading Question

■ COMPARISON

What variations in the experience of African and Asian Christian communities can you identify?

Elsewhere in the Middle East, other Jewish and Christian communities soon felt the impact of Islam. Expanding Muslim forces took control of Jerusalem in 638 and subsequently constructed the Muslim shrine known as the Dome of the Rock (687–691). In doing so, Muslim authorities appropriated for Islam a city long sacred to both Jews and Christians. In Syria and Persia, with more concentrated populations of Christians, the new Muslim rulers generally accommodated the religion of their new Christian subjects. In both areas, however, the majority of people turned to Islam voluntarily, attracted perhaps by its aura of success.

Treatment of Christians varied with the attitudes of local Muslim rulers. On occasion, churches were destroyed, villages plundered, fields burned, and Christians forced to wear distinctive clothing. By contrast, a wave of church building took place in Syria under Muslim rule, and Christians were recruited into the administration, schools, translation services, and even the armed forces of the Arab Empire. Thus the Nestorian Christian communities of Syria, Iraq, and Persia, sometimes called the Church of the East, survived the assault of Islam, but they did so as shrinking communities of second-class subjects, regulated minorities forbidden from propagating their message to Muslims. They also abandoned their religious paintings and sculptures, fearing to offend Muslims, who generally objected to any artistic representation of the Divine.

But farther east, a small and highly creative Nestorian Church, initiated in 635 by a Persian missionary monk, had taken root in China with the approval of the country's Tang dynasty rulers. Both its art and literature articulated the Christian message using Buddhist and Daoist concepts. The written texts themselves, known as the **Jesus Sutras**, refer to Christianity as the "Religion of Light from the West" or the "Luminous Religion." They describe God as the "Cool Wind," sin as "bad karma," and a good life as one of "no desire" and "no action." "People can live only by dwelling in the living breath of God," the Jesus Sutras declare. "All the Buddhas are moved by this wind, which blows everywhere in the world."[3] By the end of the Tang dynasty (907 C.E.), the Nestorian Church had substantially faded away. The contraction of this remarkable experiment owed little to Islam and more to the vagaries of Chinese politics. In the mid-ninth century, the Chinese state turned against all religions of foreign origin, Islam and Buddhism as well as Christianity (see "Losing State Support:

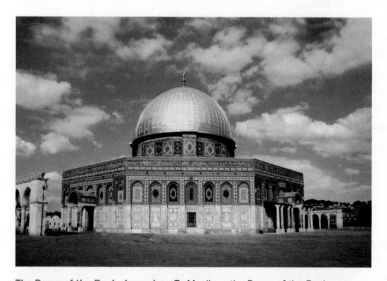

The Dome of the Rock, Jerusalem To Muslims, the Dome of the Rock was constructed on the site from which Muhammad ascended into the presence of Allah during his Night Journey. It was the first large-scale building in the Islamic world and drew heavily on Roman, Byzantine, and Persian precedents. Its location in Jerusalem marked the arrival of a competing faith to Jews and Christians, who had long considered the city sacred. (Aaron Horowitz/Getty Images)

The Crisis of Chinese Buddhism" in Chapter 8). Wholly dependent on the goodwill of Chinese authorities, this small outpost of Christianity withered.

African Christianity

The churches of Africa, like those of the Middle East and Asia, also found themselves on the defensive and declining in the face of an expanding Islam. Across coastal North Africa, widespread conversion to Islam over several centuries reduced to virtual extinction Christian communities that had earlier provided many of the martyrs and intellectuals of the early Church.

In Egypt, however, Christianity had become the religion of the majority by the time of the Muslim conquest around 640, and for the next 500 years or so, large numbers continued to speak Coptic and practice their religion as *dhimmis*, legally inferior but protected people paying a special

Nestorian Christianity in China This wall painting from western China, dating to the seventh or eighth century C.E., shows Nestorian priests in a procession on Palm Sunday. It provides visual evidence of a meaningful Christian presence in Tang dynasty China. (7th- or 8th-century wall painting from Gaochang [Khocho], Xinjiang, China/Pictures from History/Bridgeman Images)

cial tax, under relatively tolerant Muslim rulers. Many found Arab government less oppressive than that of their former Byzantine overlords, who considered Egyptian Christians heretics. By the thirteenth century, things changed dramatically as Christian Crusaders from Europe and Mongol invaders from the east threatened Egypt. In these circumstances, the country's Muslim rulers came to suspect the political loyalty of their Christian subjects. The mid-fourteenth century witnessed violent anti-Christian pogroms, destruction of churches, and the forced removal of Christians from the best land. Many felt like "exiles in their own country." As a result, most rural Egyptians converted to Islam and moved toward the use of Arabic rather than Coptic, which largely died out. But although Egypt was becoming an Arab and Muslim country, a substantial Christian minority persisted, especially among the literate in urban areas and in monasteries located in remote regions. In the early twenty-first century, Egyptian Christians still numbered about 10 percent of the population.

Even as Egyptian Christianity was contracting, a new center of African Christianity was taking shape during the fifth and sixth centuries in the several kingdoms of Nubia to the south of Egypt, where the faith had been introduced by Egyptian traders and missionaries. Parts of the Bible were translated into the Nubian language, while other writings appeared in Greek, Arabic, and the Ethiopian language of Ge'ez. A great cathedral in the Nubian city of Faras was decorated with magnificent murals, and the earlier practice of burying servants to provide for rulers in the afterlife stopped abruptly. At times, kings served as priests, and Christian bishops held state offices. By the mid-seventh century, both the ruling class and many commoners had become Christian. At the same time, Nubian armies twice defeated Arab incursions, and following these defeats an agreement with Muslim Egypt protected this outpost of Christianity for some 600 years. But pressures mounted in the thirteenth and fourteenth centuries as Egypt adopted a more hostile stance toward Christians, while Islamized peoples from the desert and Arab migrants pushed against Nubia. By 1500, **Nubian Christianity**, like its counterparts in coastal North Africa, had largely disappeared.

An important exception to these various contractions of Asian and African Christianity lay in Ethiopia. There the rulers of Axum had adopted Christianity in the fourth century, and it later took root among the general population as well. Over the centuries of Islamic expansion, Ethiopia became a Christian island in a Muslim sea, protected by its mountainous geography and its distance from major centers of Islamic power. Nonetheless, the spread of Islam largely cut Ethiopia off from other parts of Christendom and rendered its position in Northeast Africa precarious.

In its isolated location, **Ethiopian Christianity** developed some of its most distinctive features. One of these was a fascination with Judaism and Jerusalem, reflected in a much-told story about the visit of an Ethiopian Queen of Sheba to King Solomon. The story includes an episode in which Solomon seduces the queen, producing a child who becomes the founding monarch of the Ethiopian state. Since Solomon figures in the line of descent to Jesus, it meant that Ethiopia's Christian rulers could legitimate their position by tracing their ancestry to Jesus himself. Furthermore, Ethiopian monks long maintained a presence in Jerusalem's Church of the Holy Sepulcher, said to mark the site where Jesus was crucified and buried. Then, in the twelfth century, the rulers of a new Ethiopian dynasty constructed a remarkable cluster of about a dozen linked underground churches and buildings, apparently attempting to create a New Jerusalem on Christian Ethiopian soil, as the original city lay under Muslim control. Those churches are in use to this day in modern Ethiopia, where over 60 percent of the country's population retains an affiliation with this ancient Christian church.

The Church of St. George, Lalibela, Ethiopia Excavated from solid rock in the twelfth century, the churches of Lalibela were distinctive Christian structures, invisible from a distance and apparent only when looking down on them from ground level. Local legend has it that their construction was aided by angels. This one in the shape of a cross is named for Saint George, the patron saint of Ethiopia. (WtR/Shutterstock)

Byzantine Christendom: Building on the Roman Past

The contraction of the Christian faith and Christian societies in Asia and Africa left the two civilizations of western Eurasia, the **Byzantine Empire** and Western Europe, largely by default, as the centers of Christendom. At the end of the third century, the Roman Empire was divided into eastern and western halves in an effort to provide more effective governance in the face of mounting political instability. But this action launched a division of Christendom that has lasted into the twenty-first century.

Unlike most empires, Byzantium has no clear starting point. Its own leaders, as well as its neighbors and enemies, viewed it as simply a continuation of the Roman Empire, and it lasted for a thousand years after the collapse of Roman rule in the West. Housing the ancient civilizations of Egypt, Greece, Syria, and Anatolia, the eastern Roman Empire (Byzantium) was far wealthier, more urbanized, and more cosmopolitan than its western counterpart; it possessed a much more defensible capital in the heavily walled city of **Constantinople**; and it had a shorter frontier to guard. Byzantium also enjoyed access to the Black Sea and command of the eastern Mediterranean. With a stronger army, navy, and merchant marine as well as clever diplomacy, its leaders were able to deflect the Germanic and Hun invaders who had overwhelmed the western Roman Empire.

Much that was late Roman—its roads, taxation system, military structures, centralized administration, imperial court, laws, Christian Church—persisted in the East for many centuries. Like Tang dynasty China seeking to restore the glory of the Han era, Byzantium consciously sought to preserve the legacy of classical Greco-Roman civilization. Constantinople, established in 330 C.E., was to be a "New Rome," and people referred to themselves as "Romans." Fearing contamination by "barbarian" (non-Roman) customs, emperors forbade the residents of Constantinople to wear boots, trousers, clothing made from animal skins, and long hairstyles, all of which were associated with Germanic peoples, and insisted instead on Roman-style robes and sandals. But much changed as well over the centuries, marking the Byzantine Empire as the home of a distinctive civilization.

Guided Reading Question

■ **CONTINUITY AND CHANGE**

In what respects did Byzantium continue the patterns of the classical Roman Empire? In what ways did it diverge from those patterns?

The Byzantine State

Perhaps the most obvious change was one of scale, as the Byzantine Empire never approximated the size of its Roman predecessor (see Map 10.1). The western Roman Empire was permanently lost to Byzantium, despite Emperor Justinian's (r. 527–565) impressive but short-lived attempt to reconquer the Mediterranean basin. The rapid Arab/Islamic expansion in the seventh century resulted in the loss of Syria/Palestine, Egypt, and North Africa. Nonetheless, until roughly 1200, a more compact Byzantine Empire remained a major force in the eastern Mediterranean, controlling Greece, much of the Balkans (southeastern Europe), and Anatolia.

Map 10.1 The Byzantine Empire

The Byzantine Empire reached its greatest extent under Emperor Justinian in the mid-sixth century C.E. It later lost considerable territory to various Christian European powers as well as to Muslim Arab and Turkic invaders.

From that territorial base, the empire's naval and merchant vessels were active in both the Mediterranean and Black seas.

In its heyday, the Byzantine state was an impressive creation. Political author- ity remained tightly centralized in Constantinople, where the emperor claimed to govern all creation as God's worldly representative, styling himself the "peer of the Apostles" and the "sole ruler of the world." The imperial court tried to imi- tate the awesome grandeur of what it thought was God's heavenly court, but in fact it resembled ancient Persian imperial splendor. Aristocrats trained in Greek rhetoric and literature occupied high positions in the administration, participat- ing in court ceremonies that maintained their elite status. But this centralized state touched only lightly on the lives of most people, as it focused primarily on collecting taxes, maintaining order, and suppressing revolts. The Byzantine central authorities proved quite adaptable in their efforts to give local elites the auton- omy necessary to reduce tensions within the empire and to mount an effective defense of its borders.

Nonetheless, the ongoing inability of the empire to develop an orderly system for selecting new rulers sparked civil wars several times. Furthermore, periodic invasions by powerful neighbors—Huns, Persians, Arabs, Western Europeans, and Turks—weakened and diminished the empire even as it showed remarkable resilience and capacity for revival. After 1085 the empire entered a period of slow and ultimately terminal decline. Byzantine territory shrank, owing to incursions by aggressive Western European powers, by Catholic Crusaders, and by Turkic Muslim invaders. The end came in 1453 when the Turkic Ottoman Empire, then known as the "sword of Islam," finally took Constantinople. One eyewitness to the event wrote a moving lament to his fallen city:

> And the entire city was to be seen in the tents of the [Turkish] camp, the
> city deserted, lying lifeless, naked, soundless, without either form or beauty.
> O city, head of all cities, center of the four corners of the world, pride of the
> Romans, civilizer of the barbarians. . . . Where is your beauty, O paradise . . . ?
> Where are the bodies of the Apostle of my Lord . . . ? Where are the relics
> of the saints, those of the martyrs? Where are the remains of Constantine the
> Great and the other emperors? . . . Oh, what a loss![4]

The Byzantine Church and Christian Divergence

Intimately tied to the Byzantine state was the Eastern Orthodox Church, a relationship that became known as **caesaropapism**. Unlike in Western Europe, where the Roman Catholic Church maintained some degree of independence from political authorities, in Byzantium the emperor assumed something of the role of both "Caesar," as head of state, and the pope, as head of the Church. Thus he appointed the patriarch, or leader, of the Orthodox Church; sometimes made decisions about doctrine; called church councils into session; and generally treated the Church as a government department. "The [Empire] and the church have a great unity and community," declared a twelfth-century patriarch. "Indeed they cannot be separated."[5] A dense network of bishops and priests brought the message of the Church to every corner of the empire, while numerous monasteries accommodated holy men, whose piety, self-denial, and good works made them highly influential among both elite and ordinary people.

Eastern Orthodox Christianity had a pervasive influence on every aspect of Byzantine life. It legitimated the supreme and absolute authority of the emperor, for he was a God-anointed ruler, a reflection of the glory of God on earth. It also provided a cultural identity for the empire's subjects. Even more than being "Roman," they were orthodox, or "right-thinking," Christians for whom the empire and the Church were equally essential to achieving eternal salvation. Constantinople was filled with churches and the relics of numerous saints. And the churches were filled with icons—religious paintings, some of them artistic masterpieces, of Jesus, Mary, and numerous saints—that many believed conveyed the Divine Presence to the faithful.

Guided Reading Question

■ **COMPARISON**
How did Eastern Orthodox Christianity differ from Roman Catholicism?

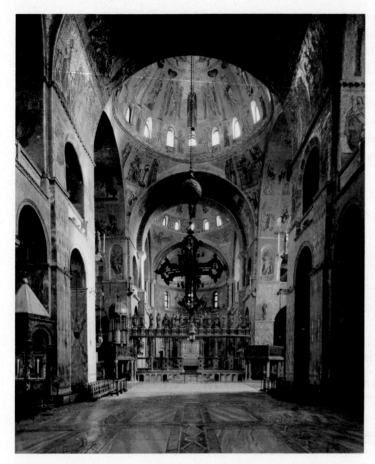

St. Mark's Basilica Consecrated in 1094, this ornate cathedral, although located in Venice, Italy, is a classic example of Byzantine architecture. Such churches represented perhaps the greatest achievement of Byzantine art and were certainly the most monumental expressions of Byzantine culture. (Erich Lessing/Art Resource, NY)

Complex theological issues about the Trinity and especially about the relationship of God and Jesus engaged the attention of ordinary people. For example, partisans of competing chariot-racing teams, known as the Greens and the Blues, vigorously debated theological issues as well as the merits of their favorite drivers.

In its early centuries and beyond, the Christian movement was rent by theological controversy and political division. But the most lasting and deepest division within the Christian world occurred as Eastern Orthodoxy came to define itself against an emerging Latin Christianity centered on papal Rome. Both had derived, of course, from the growth of Christianity in the Roman Empire and therefore had much in common—the teachings of Jesus; the Bible; the sacraments; a church hierarchy of patriarchs, bishops, and priests; a missionary impulse; and intolerance toward other religions. Despite these shared features, any sense of a single widespread Christian community was increasingly replaced by an awareness of difference, competition, and outright hostility that even a common fear of Islam could not overcome. In part, this growing religious divergence reflected the political separation and rivalry between the Byzantine Empire and the emerging kingdoms of Western Europe. As the growth of Islam in the seventh century submerged earlier centers of Christianity in the Middle East and North Africa, Constantinople and Rome alone remained as alternative hubs of the Church. But they were now in different states that competed with each other for territory and for the right to claim the legacy of imperial Rome.

Beyond such political differences were those of language and culture. Although Latin remained the language of the Church and of elite communication in the West, it was abandoned in the Byzantine Empire in favor of Greek, which remained the basis for Byzantine education. More than in the West, Byzantine thinkers sought to formulate Christian doctrine in terms of Greek philosophical concepts.

Differences in theology and church practice likewise widened the gulf between Orthodoxy and Catholicism. Disagreements about the nature of the Trinity, the source of the Holy Spirit, original sin, and the relative importance of faith and reason gave rise to much controversy. So too, for a time, did the Byzantine efforts to prohibit the use of icons, popular paintings of saints and biblical scenes that were usually painted on small wooden panels. Other more modest differences also occasioned mutual misunderstanding and disdain. Priests in the West shaved and, after 1050 or so, were supposed to remain celibate, while those in Byzantium allowed their beards to grow long and were permitted to marry. Orthodox ritual called for using bread leavened with yeast in the Communion, but Catholics used unleavened bread. Far more significant was the question of authority. Eastern Orthodox leaders sharply rejected the growing claims of Roman popes to be the sole and final authority for all Christians everywhere.

This rift in the world of Christendom grew gradually from the seventh century on, punctuated by various efforts to bridge the mounting divide between the Western and Eastern branches of the Church. A sign of this continuing deterioration occurred in 1054 when representatives of both churches mutually excommunicated each other, declaring in effect that those in the opposing tradition were not genuine Christians. The **Crusades**, launched in 1095 by the Catholic pope against the forces of Islam, made things worse. Western Crusaders, passing through the Byzantine Empire on their way to the Middle East, engaged in frequent conflict with Eastern Orthodox Christians, whom they regarded as "blasphemous, even heretical." During the Fourth Crusade in 1204, Western forces seized and looted Constantinople, and they ruled Byzantium for the next half century. According to one Byzantine account, "They sacked the sacred places and trampled on divine things . . . they tore children from their mothers . . . and they defiled virgins in the holy chapels, fearing neither God's anger nor man's vengeance."[6] After this, the rupture in the world of Christendom proved irreparable.

Byzantium and the World

Beyond its tense relationship with Western Europe, the Byzantine Empire, located astride Europe and Asia, also interacted intensively with its other neighbors. On a political and military level, Byzantium continued the long-term Roman struggle with the Persian Empire. That persisting conflict weakened both of them and was one factor in the remarkable success of Arab armies as they marched out of Arabia in the seventh century. Although Persia quickly became part of the Islamic world, Byzantium held out, even as it lost considerable territory to the Arabs. A Byzantine military innovation known as "Greek fire"—a potent and flammable combination of oil, sulfur, and lime that was launched from bronze tubes—helped hold off the Arabs. It operated as something like a flamethrower and subsequently passed into Arab and Chinese arsenals as well. Byzantium's ability to defend its core regions delayed for many centuries the Islamic advance into southeastern

Europe, which finally occurred at the hands of the Turkish Ottoman Empire in the fifteenth and sixteenth centuries.

Economically, the Byzantine Empire was a central player in the long-distance trade of Eurasia, with commercial links to Western Europe, Russia, Central Asia, the Islamic world, and China. Its gold coin, the bezant, was a widely used currency in the Mediterranean basin for more than 500 years, and wearing such coins as pendants was a high-status symbol in the less developed kingdoms of Western Europe. The luxurious products of Byzantine craftspeople—jewelry, gemstones, silver and gold work, linen and woolen textiles, purple dyes—were much in demand. Byzantium's silk industry, based on Chinese technology, supplied much of the Mediterranean basin with this precious fabric.

The cultural influence of Byzantium was likewise significant. Preserving much of ancient Greek learning, the Byzantine Empire transmitted this classical heritage to the Islamic world as well as to the Christian West. In both places, it had an immensely stimulating impact among scientists, philosophers, theologians, and other intellectuals. Some saw it as an aid to faith and to an understanding of the world, while others feared it as impious and distracting. Byzantine religious culture also spread widely among Slavic-speaking peoples in the Balkans and Russia. As lands to the south and the east were overtaken by Islam, Byzantium looked to the north. By the early eleventh century, steady military pressure had brought many of the Balkan Slavic peoples and the Turkic-speaking Bulgars under Byzantine control. Christianity and literacy accompanied this Byzantine offensive. Already in the ninth century, two Byzantine missionaries, Cyril and Methodius, had developed an alphabet, based on Greek letters, with which Slavic languages could be written. This Cyrillic script made it possible to translate the Bible and other religious literature into these languages and greatly aided the process of conversion.

The Conversion of Russia

The most significant expansion of Orthodox Christianity occurred among the Slavic peoples of what is now Ukraine and western Russia. In this culturally diverse region, which also included Finnic and Baltic peoples as well as Viking traders, a modest state known as **Kievan Rus** (KEE-yehv-ihn ROOS)—named after the most prominent city, Kiev—emerged in the ninth century. (See Map 10.3, page 420.) As in many of the new third-wave civilizations, the development of Rus was stimulated by trade, in this case along the Dnieper River, which linked Scandinavia and Byzantium. Loosely led by various princes, especially the prince of Kiev, Rus was a society of slaves and freemen, privileged people and commoners, dominant men and subordinate women. This stratification marked it as a third-wave civilization in the making.

Religion reflected the region's cultural diversity, as ancestral spirits, household deities, and various gods related to the forces of nature were worshipped. Small numbers of Christians, Muslims, and Jews were likewise part of the mix. Then, in 988,

Guided Reading Question

■ **CONNECTION**
In what ways was the Byzantine Empire linked to a wider world?

a decisive turning point occurred. The growing interaction of Rus with the larger world prompted **Prince Vladimir of Kiev** to affiliate with the Eastern Orthodox faith of the Byzantine Empire. The prince was searching for a religion that would unify the diverse peoples of his region while linking Rus into wider networks of communication and exchange.

As elsewhere in Europe, the coming of Christianity to Rus was a top-down process in which ordinary people followed their rulers into the Church. It was also a slow process, and elements of traditional religious sensibility long lingered among those who defined themselves as Christian. Perun, the god of thunder, continued to speak to some, and "magicians" sometimes led people astray in the eyes of church authorities. But building churches on the site where images of Perun and other gods once stood helped to anchor the new faith in its new land.

It was a fateful choice with long-term implications for Russian history, for it brought this fledgling civilization firmly into the world of Orthodox Christianity, separating it from both the realm of Islam and the Roman Catholic West. Like many new civilizations, Rus borrowed extensively from its older and more sophisticated Byzantine neighbor. Among these borrowings were Byzantine architectural styles, the Cyrillic alphabet, the extensive use of icons, a monastic tradition stressing prayer and service, and political ideals of imperial control of the Church, all of which became part of a transformed Rus. Orthodoxy also provided a more unified identity for this emerging civilization and religious legitimacy for its rulers. Centuries later, when Byzantium had fallen to the Turks, a few Russian church leaders proclaimed the doctrine of a "third Rome." The original Rome had abandoned the true Orthodox faith for Roman Catholicism, and the second Rome, Constantinople, had succumbed to Muslim infidels. Moscow was now the third Rome, the final protector and defender of Orthodox Christianity. Though not widely proclaimed in Russia itself, such a notion reflected the "Russification" of Eastern Orthodoxy and its growing role as an element of Russian national identity. It was also a reminder of the enduring legacy of a thousand years of Byzantine history, long after the empire itself had vanished.

Guided Reading Question

■ **CONNECTION**
How did links to Byzantium transform the new civilization of Kievan Rus?

Western Christendom: Rebuilding in the Wake of Roman Collapse

The western half of the European Christian world followed a rather different path than that of the Byzantine Empire. For much of the third-wave era, **Western Christendom** was distinctly on the margins of world history, partly because of its geographic location at the far western end of the Eurasian landmass. Thus it was at a distance from the growing routes of world trade — by sea in the Indian Ocean and by land across the Silk Roads to China and the Sand Roads to West Africa. Internally, Europe's geography made political unity difficult, for population centers were divided by mountain ranges and dense forests as well as by five major peninsulas and two large islands (Britain and Ireland). However, Europe's extensive coastlines and interior river systems facilitated exchange, while a moderate climate, plentiful rainfall, and fertile soils enabled a productive agriculture that could support a growing population.

Political Life in Western Europe

In the early centuries of this era, history must have seemed more significant than geography, for the Roman Empire was gone. Much that had characterized Roman civilization also weakened, declined, or disappeared in the several centuries before and after 476, the traditional date marking the collapse of Roman rule in the West when German general Odoacer overthrew the last Roman emperor. Any semblance of large-scale centralized rule vanished. Disease and warfare reduced Western Europe's population by more than 25 percent. Land under cultivation contracted, while forests, marshland, and wasteland expanded. Urban life too diminished sharply, as Europe reverted to a largely rural existence. Rome at its height was a city of 1 million people, but by the tenth century it numbered perhaps 10,000. Public buildings crumbled from lack of care. Outside Italy, long-distance trade dried up as Roman roads deteriorated, and money exchange gave way to barter in many places. Literacy lost ground as well. Germanic peoples, whom the Romans had viewed as barbarians — Goths, Visigoths, Franks, Lombards, Angles, Saxons — now emerged as the dominant peoples of Western Europe. In the process, Europe's center of gravity moved away from the Mediterranean toward the north and west.

Yet much that was classical or Roman persisted, even as a new order emerged in Europe. On the political front, a series of regional kingdoms — led by Visigoths in Spain, Franks in France, Lombards in Italy, and Angles and Saxons in England — arose to replace Roman authority. As these Germanic peoples migrated into or invaded Roman lands, many were deeply influenced by Roman culture, especially if they had served in the Roman army. On the funeral monument of one such person was a telling inscription: "I am a Frank by nationality, but a Roman soldier under arms."[7]

The prestige of things Roman remained high, even after the empire itself had collapsed. Now as leaders of their own kingdoms, the Germanic rulers actively embraced written Roman law, using fines and penalties to provide order and justice in place of feuds and vendettas. One Visigoth ruler named Athaulf (r. 410–415), who had married a Roman noblewoman, gave voice to the continuing attraction of Roman culture and its empire:

> At first I wanted to erase the Roman name and convert all Roman territory into a Gothic empire. . . . But long experience has taught me that . . . without law a state is not a state. Therefore I have more prudently chosen the different glory of reviving the Roman name with Gothic vigour, and I hope to be acknowledged by posterity as the initiator of a Roman restoration.[8]

Guided Reading Question

■ **CHANGE**

What replaced the Roman order in Western Europe?

Several of the larger, though relatively short-lived, Germanic kingdoms also had aspirations to re-create something of the unity of the Roman Empire. **Charlemagne** (SHAHR-leh-mane) (r. 768–814), ruler of the Carolingian Empire, occupying what is now France, Belgium, the Netherlands, and parts of Germany and Italy, erected an embryonic imperial bureaucracy, standardized weights and measures, and began to act like an imperial ruler. On Christmas Day of the year 800, he was crowned as a new Roman emperor by the pope, although his realm splintered shortly after his death (see Map 10.2). Later Otto I of Saxony (r. 936–973) gathered much of Germany under his control, saw himself as renewing Roman rule, and was likewise invested with the title of emperor by the pope. Otto's realm, later known as the **Holy Roman Empire**, was largely limited to Germany and soon proved little more than a collection of quarreling principalities. Though unsuccessful in reviving anything approaching Roman imperial authority, these efforts testify to the continuing appeal of the classical world, even as a new political system of rival kingdoms blended Roman and Germanic elements.

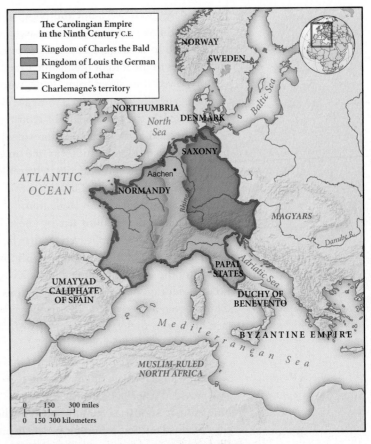

Map 10.2 Western Europe in the Ninth Century
Charlemagne's Carolingian Empire brought a temporary political unity to parts of Western Europe, but it was subsequently divided among his three sons, who then waged war on one another.

Society and the Church

Within these new kingdoms, a highly fragmented and decentralized society, widely known as **feudalism**, emerged with great local variation. In thousands of independent, self-sufficient, and largely isolated landed estates or manors, power—political, economic, and social—was exercised by a warrior elite of landowning lords. In the constant competition of these centuries, lesser lords and knights swore allegiance to greater lords or kings and thus became their vassals, frequently receiving lands and plunder in return for military service.

Such reciprocal ties between superior and subordinate were also apparent at the bottom of the social hierarchy, as Roman-style slavery gradually gave way to serfdom.

Unlike slaves, serfs were not the personal property of their masters, could not be arbitrarily thrown off their land, and were allowed to live in families. However, they were bound to their masters' estates as peasant laborers and owed various payments and services to the lord of the manor. One family on a manor near Paris in the ninth century owed four silver coins, wine, wood, three hens, and fifteen eggs per year. Women generally were required to weave cloth and make clothing for the lord, while men labored in the lord's fields. In return, the serf family received a small farm and such protection as the lord could provide. In a violent and insecure world adjusting to the absence of Roman authority, the only security available to many individuals or families lay in these communities, where the ties to kin, manor, and lord constituted the primary human loyalties. It was a world apart from the stability of life in imperial Rome or its continuation in Byzantium.

Also filling the vacuum left by the collapse of empire was the Church, later known as Roman Catholic, yet another link to the now-defunct Roman world. Its hierarchical organization of popes, bishops, priests, and monasteries was modeled on that of the Roman Empire and took over some of the empire's political, administrative, educational, and welfare functions. Latin continued as the language of the Church even as it gave way to various vernacular languages in common speech. In fact, literacy in the classical languages of Greek and Latin long remained the hallmark of educated people in the West.

Like the Buddhist establishment in China, the Church subsequently became quite wealthy, with reformers often accusing it of forgetting its central spiritual mission. It also provided a springboard for the conversion of Europe's many "pagan" peoples. Numerous missionaries, commissioned by the pope, monasteries, or already converted rulers, fanned out across Europe, generally pursuing a "top-down" strategy. Frequently it worked, as local kings and warlords found status and legitimacy in association with a literate and "civilized" religion that still bore something of the grandeur that was Rome. With "the wealth and protection of the powerful," ordinary people followed their rulers into the fold of the Church.[9] Christianity, like Buddhism in China, also bore the promise of superior supernatural powers, and its spread was frequently associated with reported miracles of healing, rainfall, fertility, and victory in battle.

But it was not an easy sell. Outright coercion was sometimes part of the process. More often, however, softer methods prevailed. The Church proved willing to accommodate a considerable range of earlier cultural practices, absorbing them into an emerging Christian tradition. For example, amulets and charms to ward off evil became medals with the image of Jesus or the Virgin Mary; traditionally sacred wells and springs became the sites of churches; and festivals honoring ancient gods became Christian holy days. December 25 was selected as the birthday of Jesus, for it was associated with the winter solstice, the coming of more light, and the birth or rebirth of various deities in pre-Christian European traditions. By 1100, most of Europe had embraced Christianity. Even so, for centuries priests and bishops had to warn their congregations against the worship of rivers, trees, and mountains, and for many people, ancient gods, monsters, trolls, and spirits still inhabited the land. The spreading Christian faith, like the new political framework of European civilization, was a blend of many elements. (For more on the rooting of Christianity in Western Europe, see Working with Evidence: The Remaking of Western Europe, page 438.)

Church authorities and the nobles/warriors who exercised political influence reinforced each other. Rulers provided protection for the papacy and strong encouragement for the faith. In return, the Church offered religious legitimacy for the powerful and the prosperous. "It is the will of the Creator," declared the teaching of the Church, "that the higher shall always rule over the lower. Each individual and class should stay in its place [and] perform its tasks."[10] But church and political authorities competed as well as cooperated, for they were rival centers of power in post-Roman Europe. Particularly controversial was the right to appoint bishops and the pope himself; this issue, known as the investiture conflict, was especially prominent in the eleventh and twelfth centuries. Was the right to make such appointments the responsibility of the Church alone, or did kings and emperors also have a role? In the compromise that ended the conflict, the Church won the right to appoint its own officials, while secular rulers retained an informal and symbolic role in the process.

Accelerating Change in the West

After various invaders—Huns, Magyars (Hungarians), and Vikings (see Map 10.3)—had been absorbed into settled society and in some cases had converted to Christianity, the pace of change in this emerging European civilization picked up considerably. In the several centuries after 1000, the greater security and stability that came with relative peace arguably opened the way to an accelerating tempo of change. The climate also seemed to cooperate. A generally warming trend after 750 reached its peak in the eleventh and twelfth centuries, enhancing agricultural production, especially in northern and highland regions.

During this new phase of European civilization, commonly called the High Middle Ages (1000–1300), the signs of expansion and growth were widely evident. The population of Europe grew from perhaps 35 million in 1000 to about 80 million in 1340. Many new lands were opened for cultivation in a process paralleling China's expansion to the south at the same time. Great lords, bishops, and religious orders organized new villages on what had recently been forest, marshes, or wasteland. Warmer weather during the summer months allowed farmers and pastoralists to herd their flocks into previously wild highland regions. Everywhere trees were felled at tremendous rates to clear agricultural land and to use as fuel or building material. By 1300, the forest cover of Europe had been reduced to about 20 percent of the land area. "I believe that the forest . . . covers the land to no purpose," declared a German abbot, "and hold this to be an unbearable harm."[11] These developments took a heavy toll on both the terrestrial and aquatic environments. Deforestation, overfishing, human waste, and the proliferation of new water mills and their associated ponds damaged freshwater ecosystems in many places. Lamenting the declining availability of fish, the French king Philip IV declared in 1289: "Today each and every river and waterside of our realm, large and small, yields nothing."[12]

Guided Reading Question

■ **CHANGE**
In what ways was European civilization changing after 1000?

Legend:
→ Viking invasions
→ Muslim invasions
→ Magyar invasions
▨ Muslim lands

MAPPING HISTORY

Map 10.3 Europe in the Middle Ages

By the eleventh century, the national monarchies that would organize European political life—France, Spain, England, Poland, and Germany—had begun to take shape. The earlier external attacks on Europe from Vikings, Magyars, and Muslims had largely ceased, although it was clear that European civilization was developing in the shadow of the Islamic world.

READING THE MAP: Trace the routes taken by the Vikings of Sweden to establish contact with the Byzantine Empire. What major waterways did they use?

MAKING CONNECTIONS: Comparing Maps 8.1 and 10.3, what differences do you notice between Chinese and European civilizations and their relationship with their neighbors?

A European Urban Market This image from a fourteenth-century Italian illuminated manuscript depicts a market scene in an urban setting. It illustrates two major elements of an emerging Western European civilization—urbanization and commercialization. (Biblioteca Nazionale, Turin, Italy/Mondadori Fortfolio/Electa/Paolo Manusardi/Bridgeman Images)

The increased production associated with this agricultural expansion stimulated a considerable growth in long-distance trade, much of which had dried up in the aftermath of the Roman collapse. One center of commercial activity lay in Northern Europe from England to the Baltic coast. The other major trading network centered on northern Italian towns such as Florence, Genoa, and Venice. Their trading partners were the more established civilizations of Islam and Byzantium, and the primary objects of trade included silks, drugs, precious stones, and spices from Asia. At great trading fairs, particularly those in the Champagne area of France near Paris, merchants from Northern and Southern Europe met to exchange the products of their respective areas, such as northern woolens for Mediterranean spices. Thus the self-sufficient communities of earlier centuries increasingly forged commercial bonds among themselves and with more distant peoples.

The population of towns and cities likewise grew on the sites of older Roman towns, at trading crossroads and fortifications, and around cathedrals all over Europe. In the early 1300s, London had about 40,000 people, Paris had approximately 80,000, and Venice by the end of the fourteenth century could boast perhaps 150,000. To keep these figures in perspective, Constantinople housed some 400,000 people in 1000, Córdoba in Muslim Spain about 500,000, and the Song dynasty capital of Hangzhou more than 1 million in the thirteenth century. These towns gave rise

Cecilia Penifader, an English Peasant and Unmarried Woman

Born in 1297 in a small English village, Cecilia Penifader was an illiterate peasant woman who seldom if ever traveled more than twenty miles beyond her birthplace. She was of no particular historical importance outside of her family and community. Nonetheless, her life, reconstructed from court records by historian Judith Bennett, provides a window into the conditions of ordinary rural people as a new European civilization was taking shape.[13]

From birth to death, Cecilia lived in Brigstock, a royal manor owned by the king of England or a member of the royal family. Free tenants such as Cecilia owed rents and various dues to the lord of the manor. Thus Cecilia occupied a social position above the serfs, unfree people who owed labor service to the lord, but infinitely below the clergy and nobility, to whom the lower orders of society owed constant deference.

But within the class of "those who work"—the peasantry—Cecilia was fortunate. She was born the seventh of eight children, six of whom survived to adulthood,

A European peasant woman such as Cecilia Penifader.

an unusual occurrence at a time when roughly half of village children died. Her family had substantially larger landholdings than most of their neighbors and no doubt lived in a somewhat larger house. Still, it was probably a single-room dwelling measuring about thirty by fifteen feet, with a dirt floor, and surely it was smoky, for chimneys were not a part of peasant homes.

Between 1315 and 1322, as Cecilia entered early adulthood, England and much of the rest of Europe experienced an immense famine, caused by several years of especially cold and wet weather that marked the end of centuries of favorable climatic conditions. During those years, Cecilia first entered the court records of Brigstock. In 1316, another peasant lodged a complaint against Cecilia and her father for ignoring his boundary stones and taking hay from his fields. Such petty quarrels and minor crimes proliferated as neighborliness broke down in the face of bad harvests and desperate circumstances. Furthermore, both of Cecilia's parents died during the famine years.

photo: Victoria & Albert Museum, London, UK/V&A Images, London/Art Resource, NY

to and attracted new groups of people, particularly merchants, bankers, artisans, and university-trained professionals such as lawyers, doctors, and scholars. Many of these groups, including university professors and students, organized themselves into guilds (associations of people pursuing the same line of work) to regulate their respective professions. Thus, from the rural social order of lord and peasant, a new more productive and complex division of labor was reshaping European society.

A further sign of accelerating change in the West lay in the growth of territorial states with more effective institutions of government commanding the loyalty, or at least the obedience, of their subjects. Since the disintegration of the Roman Empire, Europeans' loyalties had focused on the family, the manor, or the religious community, but seldom on the state. But in the eleventh through the thirteenth centuries, the nominal monarchs of Europe gradually and painfully began to consolidate their authority, and the outlines of French, English, Spanish, Scandinavian, and other states began to appear, each with its own distinct language and culture

Thus Cecilia was left a single woman in her early twenties, but the relative prosperity of her family allowed her to lead a rather independent life. In 1317, she acquired her first piece of land, probably with financial assistance from her father and her own earnings as a day laborer. In fact, Cecilia benefited from the famine because it forced desperate peasants to sell their land at reduced prices. As a result, Cecilia was able to accumulate additional land. By the time of her death in 1344, she was a fairly prosperous woman with a house and farmyard, seventy acres of pasture, and two acres of good farming land. She hired servants or day laborers to work her lands and depended considerably on her brothers, who lived nearby.

If class and family shaped Cecilia's life, so did gender. As a woman, she was unable to hold office in the manor; she was paid about one-third less than men when she worked as an unskilled day laborer; and she could not serve as an official ale-taster, responsible for the quality of the beverage, although women brewed the ale. Like all women, she suffered under a sexual double standard. Two of her brothers, one of whom was a priest, produced children out of wedlock, with no apparent damage to their reputations. But should Cecilia have done so, scandal would surely have ensued.

Unlike most women of her time, Cecilia never married. Did her intended perhaps die during the famine? Did she have a socially inappropriate lover? Did she have an intimate relationship with Robert Malin, a man to whom she left one-third of her estate? Or did she consider marriage a disadvantage? Married women and their property were legally under the control of their husbands, but as a free tenant and head of household, Cecilia bought and sold land on her own and participated as a full member in the deliberations of the local court, which regulated the legal affairs of the manor.

For a woman, the pros and cons of marriage depended very much on whom she married. As a medieval poem put it: "The good and bad happenstances that some women have had / Stands in the choice of a good husband or bad." So while Cecilia missed out on the social approval and support that marriage offered as well as the pleasures of intimacy and children, she also avoided the potential abuse and certain dependency that married life carried for women.

Cecilia's death in 1344 provoked sharp controversy within her family network over the familiar issues of inheritance, kinship, and land. She left her considerable property to the illegitimate son of her brother, to the daughter of her sister Agnes, and to the mysterious Robert Malin. Aggrieved parties, particularly her sister Christina and a nephew Martin, succeeded in having her will overturned.

QUESTION

In what ways did class, family, gender, and natural catastrophe shape Cecilia's life?

(see Map 10.3, page 420). Royal courts and fledgling bureaucracies were established, and groups of professional administrators appeared. In Italy, city-states flourished as urban areas grew wealthy and powerful, while the Germans remained divided among a large number of small principalities within the Holy Roman Empire.

These changes, which together represented the making of a new civilization, had implications for the lives of countless women and men. (See Zooming In: Cecilia Penifader, page 422.) Economic growth and urbanization initially offered European women substantial new opportunities. Women were active in a number of urban professions, such as weaving, brewing, milling grain, midwifery, small-scale retailing, laundering, spinning, and prostitution. In twelfth-century Paris, for example, a list of 100 occupations identified 86 as involving women workers, of which 6 were exclusively female. In England, women worked as silk weavers, hatmakers, tailors, brewers, and leather processors and were entitled to train female apprentices in some of these trades. However, much as economic and technological change in

China had eroded female silk production, by the fifteenth century artisan opportunities were declining for European women as well. Most women's guilds were gone, and women were restricted or banned from many others. Even brothels were run by men. In England, guild regulations now outlawed women's participation in manufacturing particular fabrics and forbade their being trained on new and larger weaving machines. Women might still spin thread, but the more lucrative and skilled task of weaving fell increasingly to men. Technological progress may have been one reason for this change. Water- and animal-powered grain mills replaced the hand-grinding previously undertaken by women, and larger looms making heavier cloth replaced the lighter looms that women had worked. Men increasingly took over these professions and trained their sons as apprentices, making it more difficult for women to remain active in these fields.

The Church had long offered some women an alternative to home, marriage, family, and rural life. As in Buddhist lands, substantial numbers of women, particularly from aristocratic families, were attracted to the secluded monastic life of poverty, chastity, and obedience within a convent, in part for the relative freedom from male control that it offered. Here was one of the few places where women might exercise authority as abbesses of their orders and obtain a measure of education. The twelfth-century abbess Hildegard of Bingen, for example, won wide acclaim for her writings on theology, medicine, botany, and music.

But by 1300, much of the independence that such abbesses and their nuns had enjoyed was curtailed and male control tightened, even as veneration of the Virgin Mary swept across Western Christendom. Restrictions on women hearing confessions, preaching, and chanting the Gospel were now more strictly enforced. The educational activities of monastic centers, where men and women could both participate, now gave way to the new universities, where only ordained men could study and teach. Furthermore, older ideas of women's intellectual inferiority, the impurity of menstruation, and their role as sexual temptresses were mobilized to explain why women could never be priests and must operate under male control.

Thus tightening male control of women took place in Europe as it did in Song dynasty China at about the same time. Accompanying this change was a new understanding of masculinity, at least in the growing towns and cities. No longer able to function as warriors protecting their women, men increasingly defined themselves as "providers"; a man's role was to brave the new marketplaces "to win wealth for himself and his children." In one popular tale, a woman praised her husband: "He was a good provider; he knew how to rake in the money and how to save it." By 1450, the English word "husband" had become a verb meaning "to keep" or "to save."[14]

Europe Outward Bound: The Crusading Tradition

Accompanying the growth of a new European civilization after 1000 were efforts to engage more actively with both near and more distant neighbors. This "medieval expansion" of Western Christendom took place as the Byzantine world was contracting under pressure from the West, from Arab invasion, and later from

Turkish conquest (see Map 10.1, page 410). The western half of Christendom was on the rise, while the eastern part was in decline. It was a sharp reversal of their earlier trajectories.

As Western Europe's population mounted, settlers cleared new land, much of it on the eastern fringes of Europe. The Vikings of Scandinavia, having raided much of Europe, set off on a maritime transatlantic venture around 1000 that briefly established a colony in Newfoundland in North America, and more durably in Greenland and Iceland. As Western economies grew, merchants, travelers, diplomats, and missionaries brought European society into more intensive contact with more distant peoples and with Eurasian commercial networks. By the thirteenth and fourteenth

The Crusades This fourteenth-century painting illustrates the Christian seizure of Jerusalem during the First Crusade in 1099. The crowned figure in the center is Godefroi de Bouillon, a French knight and nobleman who played a prominent role in the attack and was briefly known as the king of Jerusalem. (From "Le Roman de Godefroi de Bouillon" [vellum], 14th century/Bibliothèque Nationale de France, Paris, France/Bridgeman Images)

centuries, Europeans had direct, though limited, contact with India, China, and Mongolia. Europe clearly was outward bound.

Nothing more dramatically revealed European expansiveness and the religious passions that informed it than the Crusades, a series of "holy wars" that captured the imagination of Western Christendom for several centuries, beginning in 1095. In European thinking and practice, the Crusades were wars undertaken at God's command and authorized by the pope as Christ's representative on earth. Crusaders were required to swear a vow and in return received an indulgence, which removed the penalties for any confessed sins, and were also granted various material benefits, such as immunity from lawsuits and a moratorium on the repayment of debts. Any number of political, economic, and social motives underlay the Crusades, but at their core they were religious wars. Within Europe, the amazing support for the Crusades reflected an understanding of them "as providing security against mortal enemies threatening the spiritual health of all Christendom and all Christians."[15] Crusading drew on both Christian piety and the warrior values of the elite, with little sense of contradiction between these impulses.

The most famous Crusades were those aimed at wresting Jerusalem and the holy places associated with the life of Jesus from Islamic control and returning them to Christendom (see Map 10.4). Beginning in 1095, wave after wave of Crusaders from all walks of life and many countries flocked to the eastern Mediterranean,

Guided Reading Question

■ **CHANGE**
What was the impact of the Crusades in world history?

MAPPING HISTORY

Map 10.4 The Crusades

Western Europe's crusading tradition reflected the expansive energy and religious impulses of an emerging civilization. It was directed against Muslims in the Middle East, Sicily, and Spain as well as the Eastern Orthodox Christians of the Byzantine Empire. The Crusades also involved attacks on Jewish communities, probably the first organized mass pogroms against Jews in Europe's history.

READING THE MAP: Which of the Crusades were directed against other Christian peoples and which against Muslim lands?

INTERPRETING THE MAP: From the information provided by this map, how would you describe the role of Constantinople in the four Crusades to the eastern Mediterranean?

where they temporarily carved out four small Christian states, the last of which was recaptured by Muslim forces in 1291. Led or supported by an assortment of kings, popes, bishops, monks, lords, nobles, and merchants, the Crusades demonstrated a growing European capacity for organization, finance, transportation, and recruitment, made all the more impressive by the absence of any centralized direction for the project. They also demonstrated considerable cruelty. The seizure of Jerusalem in 1099 was accompanied by the slaughter of many Muslims and Jews as the Crusaders made their way to the tomb of Christ through streets littered with corpses and ankle deep in blood, according to no doubt exaggerated reports.

Crusading was not limited to targets in the Islamic Middle East, however. Those Christians who waged war for centuries to reclaim the Iberian Peninsula from Muslim hands were likewise declared "crusaders," with a similar set of spiritual and material benefits. So too were Scandinavian and German warriors who took part in wars to conquer, settle, and convert lands along the Baltic Sea. The Byzantine Empire and Russia, both of which followed Eastern Orthodox Christianity, were also on the receiving end of Western crusading, as were Christian heretics, Jews, and various enemies of the pope in Europe itself. Crusading, in short, was a pervasive feature of European expansion, which persisted as Europeans began their oceanic voyages in the fifteenth century and beyond.

Surprisingly perhaps, the Crusades had little lasting impact, either politically or religiously, in the Middle East. European power was not sufficiently strong or longlasting to induce much conversion, and the small European footholds there had come under Muslim control by 1300. The penetration of Turkic-speaking peoples from Central Asia and the devastating Mongol invasions of the thirteenth century were far more significant in Islamic history than were the temporary incursions of European Christians. In Europe, however, crusading in general and interaction with the Islamic world in particular had very significant long-term consequences. Spain, Sicily, and the Baltic region were brought permanently into the world of Western Christendom, while a declining Byzantium was further weakened by the Crusader sacking of Constantinople in 1204 and left even more vulnerable to Muslim Turkish conquest. In Europe itself, popes strengthened their position, at least for a time, in their continuing struggles with secular authorities. Tens of thousands of Europeans came into personal contact with the Islamic world, from which they picked up a taste for the many luxury goods available there, stimulating a demand for Asian goods. They also learned techniques for producing sugar on large plantations using slave labor, a process that had incalculable consequences in later centuries as Europeans transferred the plantation system to the Americas. Muslim scholarship, together with the Greek learning that it incorporated, also flowed into Europe, largely through Spain and Sicily.

If cross-cultural contacts born of crusading opened channels of trade, technology transfer, and intellectual exchange, they also hardened cultural barriers between peoples. The rift between Eastern Orthodoxy and Roman Catholicism deepened further and remains to this day a fundamental divide in the Christian world. Christian anti-Semitism was both expressed and exacerbated as Crusaders on their way to Jerusalem found time to massacre Jews, regarded as "Christ-killers," in a number of European cities, particularly in Germany. Such pogroms, however, were not sanctioned by the Church. A leading figure in the Second Crusade, Bernard of Clairvaux, declared, "It is good that you march against the Muslims, but anyone who touches a Jew to take his life, is as touching Jesus himself."[16] The Crusades also had other long-term influences. European empire building, especially in the Americas, continued the crusading notion that "God wills it." And more recently, over the past two centuries, as the world of the Christian West and that of Islam have collided, both sides have found many occasions

PRACTICING HISTORICAL THINKING

How did the historical development of the European West differ from that of Byzantium in the third-wave era?

for which images of the Crusades, however distorted, have proved politically popular or ideologically useful.

The West in Comparative Perspective

At one level, the making of Western civilization was unremarkable. Civilizations had risen, fallen, renewed themselves, and evolved at many times and in many places. The European case has received extraordinary scrutiny, not so much because of its special significance at the time, but because of its later role as a globally dominant region. However we might explain Europe's subsequent rise to prominence on the world stage, its development in the several centuries after 1000 made only modest ripples beyond its own region. Europe was surely distinctive, as are all civilizations, but it was not yet a major player in the global arena. Comparisons, particularly with China and the Islamic world, help to place these European developments in a world history context.

Catching Up

As the civilization of the West evolved, it was clearly less developed in comparison to Byzantium, China, India, and the Islamic world. Europe's cities were smaller, its political authorities weaker, its economy less commercialized, and its technology inferior. Muslim observers who encountered Europeans saw them as barbarians. An Arab geographer of the tenth century commented: "Their bodies are large, their manners harsh, their understanding dull, and their tongues heavy. . . . Those of them who are farthest to the north are the most subject to stupidity, grossness and brutishness."[17] Muslim travelers over the next several centuries saw more to be praised in West African kingdoms, where Islam was practiced and gold was plentiful.

Furthermore, thoughtful Europeans who directly encountered other peoples often acknowledged their own comparative backwardness. "In our time," wrote a twelfth-century European scholar, "it is in Toledo [a Spanish city long under Muslim rule] that the teaching of the Arabs . . . is offered to the crowds. I hastened there to listen to the teaching of the wisest philosophers of this world."[18] The Italian traveler Marco Polo in the thirteenth century proclaimed Hangzhou in China "the finest and noblest [city] in the world." In the early sixteenth century, Spanish invaders of Mexico were stunned at the size and wealth of the Aztec capital, especially its huge market, claiming that they "had never seen such a thing before."[19]

Curious about the rest of the world, Europeans proved quite willing to engage with and borrow from the more advanced civilizations to the east. Growing European economies, especially in the northwest, reconnected with the Eurasian trading system, with which they had lost contact after the fall of Rome. Now European elites eagerly sought spices, silks, porcelain, and sugar from afar even as they assimilated various technological, intellectual, and cultural innovations, as the Snapshot demonstrates. When the road to China opened in the thirteenth and fourteenth centuries, many Europeans, including the merchant-traveler Marco Polo, were more than willing to make the long and difficult journey, returning with amazing tales of splendor and abundance far

Guided Reading Question

■ **CHANGE**
In what ways did borrowing from abroad shape European civilization after 1000?

SNAPSHOT European Borrowing

Like people in other emerging civilizations of the third-wave era, Europeans borrowed extensively from their near and more distant counterparts. They adapted these imports, both technological and cultural, to their own circumstances and generated distinctive innovations as well.

Borrowing	Source	Significance
Horse collar	China / Central Asia via Tunisia	Enabled heavy plowing and contributed to European agricultural development
Stirrup	India/Afghanistan	Revolutionized warfare by enhancing cavalry forces
Gunpowder	China	Enhanced the destructiveness of warfare
Paper	China	Enabled bureaucracy; fostered literacy; prerequisite for printing
Spinning wheel	India	Sped up production of yarn, usually by women at home
Wheelbarrow	China	Laborsaving device for farm and construction work
Aristotle	Byzantium / Islamic Spain	Recovery of classical Greek thought
Medical knowledge/ treatments	Islamic world	Sedatives, antiseptics, surgical techniques, optics, and knowledge of contagious diseases enriched European medicine
Christian mysticism	Muslim Spain	Mutual influence of Sufi, Jewish, and Christian mysticism
Music/poetry	Muslim Spain	Contributed to tradition of troubadour poetry about chivalry and courtly love
Mathematics	India / Islamic world	Foundation for European algebra
Chess	India/Persia	A game of prestige associated with European nobility

beyond what was available in Europe. When Europeans took to the oceans in the fifteenth and sixteenth centuries, they were seeking out the sources of African and Asian wealth. Thus the accelerating growth of European civilization was accompanied by its reintegration into the larger Afro-Eurasian networks of exchange and communication.

In this willingness to borrow, Europe resembled several other third-wave civilizations of the time. Japan, for example, took much from China; West Africa drew heavily on Islamic civilization; and Russia actively imitated Byzantium. All of them were then developing civilizations, in a position analogous perhaps to the developing countries of recent times.

Technological borrowing required adaptation to the unique conditions of Europe and was accompanied by considerable independent invention as well. Together these processes generated a significant tradition of technological innovation that allowed Europe by 1500 to catch up with, and in some areas perhaps to surpass, China and the Islamic

European Technology Europeans' fascination with technology and their religious motivation for investigating the world are apparent in this thirteenth-century portrayal of God as a divine engineer, laying out the world with a huge compass. (Oesterreichische Nationalbibliothek, Vienna, Austria/Erich Lessing/Art Resource, NY)

world. That achievement bears comparison with the economic revolution of Song dynasty China (960–1279), although Europe began at a lower level and depended more on borrowing than did its Chinese counterpart. But in the several centuries surrounding 1000, at both ends of Eurasia, major processes of technological innovation were under way.

In Europe, technological breakthroughs first became apparent in agriculture as Europeans adapted to the very different environmental conditions north of the Alps in the several centuries following 500 C.E. They developed a heavy wheeled plow that could handle the dense soils of Northern Europe far better than the light, or "scratch," plow used in Mediterranean agriculture. To pull the plow, Europeans began to rely increasingly on horses rather than oxen and to use iron horseshoes and a more efficient collar, which probably originated in China or Central Asia and could support much heavier loads. In addition, Europeans developed a new three-field system of crop rotation, which allowed considerably more land to be planted at any one time. These were the technological foundations for a more productive agriculture that could support the growing population of European civilization, especially in its urban centers, far more securely than before.

Beyond agriculture, Europeans began to tap non-animal sources of energy in a major way, particularly after 1000. A new type of windmill, very different from an earlier Persian version, was widely used in Europe by the twelfth and thirteenth centuries. The water-driven mill was even more important. By the ninth century water mills were rapidly becoming more evident in Europe. In the early fourteenth century, a concentration of sixty-eight mills dotted a one-mile stretch of the Seine River near Paris. In addition to grinding grain, these mills provided power for sieving flour, tanning hides, making beer, sawing wood, manufacturing iron, and making paper. Devices such as cranks, flywheels, camshafts, and complex gearing mechanisms, when combined with water or wind power, enabled Europeans of the High Middle Ages to revolutionize production in a number of industries and to break with the ancient tradition of depending almost wholly on animal or human muscle as sources of energy. So intense was the interest of European artisans and engineers in tapping mechanical sources of energy that a number of them experimented with perpetual-motion machines, an idea borrowed from Indian philosophers.

Technological borrowing was also evident in the arts of war. Gunpowder was invented in China, but Europeans were probably the first to use it in cannons, in the early fourteenth century, and by 1500 they had the most advanced arsenals in the world. In 1517, one Chinese official, on first encountering European ships and weapons, remarked with surprise, "The westerns are extremely dangerous because of their artillery. No weapon ever made since memorable antiquity is superior to their cannon."[20] Advances in shipbuilding and navigational techniques—including the magnetic compass and sternpost rudder from China and adaptations of the Mediterranean or Arab lateen sail, which enabled vessels to sail against the wind—provided the foundation for European mastery of the seas.

Europe's passion for technology was reflected in its culture and ideas as well as in its machines. About 1260, the English scholar and Franciscan friar Roger Bacon wrote of the possibilities he foresaw, and in doing so, he expressed the confident spirit of the age:

> Machines of navigation can be constructed, without rowers . . . which are borne under the guidance of one man at a greater speed than if they were full of men. Also a chariot can be constructed, that will move with incalculable speed without any draught animal. . . . Also flying machines may be constructed so that a man may sit in the midst of the machine turning a certain instrument by means of which wings artificially constructed would beat the air after the manner of a bird flying . . . and there are countless other things that can be constructed.[21]

Pluralism in Politics

Unlike the large centralized states of Byzantium, the Islamic world, and China, this third-wave European civilization never regained the earlier unity it had under Roman rule. Rather, political life gradually crystallized into a system of competing states (France, Spain, England, Sweden, Prussia, the Netherlands, and Poland, among others) that has persisted into the twenty-first century and that the European Union still confronts. Geographic barriers, ethnic and linguistic diversity, and the shifting balances of power among its many states prevented the emergence of a single European empire, despite periodic efforts to re-create something resembling the still-remembered unity of the Roman Empire.

This multicentered political system shaped the emerging civilization of the West in many ways. It gave rise to frequent wars, enhanced the role and status of military men, and drove the "gunpowder revolution." Thus European society and values were militarized far more than in China, which gave greater prominence to scholars and bureaucrats. Intense interstate rivalry, combined with a willingness to borrow, also stimulated European technological development. By 1500, Europeans had gone a long way toward catching up with their more advanced Asian counterparts in agriculture, industry, war, and sailing.

The states within this emerging European civilization also differed from those to the east. Their rulers generally were weaker and had to contend with competing sources of power. Unlike the Orthodox Church in Byzantium, with its practice of caesaropapism, the **Roman Catholic Church** in the West maintained a degree

Guided Reading Question

■ **COMPARISON**
Why was Europe unable to achieve the kind of political unity that China experienced? What impact did this have on the subsequent history of Europe?

of independence from state authority that served to check the power of kings and lords. Moreover, European vassals had certain rights in return for loyalty to their lords and kings. By the thirteenth century, this meant that high-ranking nobles, acting through formal councils, had the right to advise their rulers and to approve new taxes.

This three-way struggle for power among kings, warrior aristocrats, and church leaders, all of them from the nobility, enabled urban-based merchants in Europe to achieve an unusual independence from political authority. Many cities where wealthy merchants exercised local power won the right to make and enforce their own laws and appoint their own officials. Some of them—Venice, Genoa, Pisa, and Milan, for example—became almost completely independent city-states. Elsewhere, kings granted charters that allowed cities to have their own courts, laws, and governments, while paying their own kind of taxes to the king instead of feudal dues. Powerful, independent cities were a distinctive feature of European life after 1100 or so. By contrast, Chinese cities, which were far larger than those of Europe, were simply part of the empire and enjoyed few special privileges. Although commerce was far more extensive in China than in the emerging European civilization, the powerful Chinese state favored the landowners over merchants, monopolized the salt and iron industries, and actively controlled and limited merchant activity far more than the new and weaker royal authorities of Europe were able to do.

The relative weakness of Europe's rulers allowed urban merchants more leeway and, according to some historians, opened the way to a more thorough development of capitalism in later centuries. It also led to the development of representative institutions or parliaments through which the views and interests of these contending forces could be expressed and accommodated. Intended to strengthen royal authority by consulting with major social groups, these embryonic parliaments did not represent the "people" or the "nation" but instead embodied the three great "estates of the realm"—the clergy (the first estate), the landowning nobility (the second estate), and urban merchants (the third estate).

Reason and Faith

A further feature of this emerging European civilization was a distinctive intellectual tension between the claims of human reason and those of faith. Christianity had developed in a world suffused with Greek rationalism. Some early Christian thinkers sought to maintain a clear separation between the new religion and the ideas of Plato and Aristotle. "What indeed has Athens to do with Jerusalem?" asked Tertullian (150–225 C.E.), an early church leader from North Africa. More common was the notion that Greek philosophy could serve as a "handmaiden" to faith, more fully disclosing the truths of Christianity. In the reduced circumstances of Western Europe after the collapse of the Roman Empire, however, the Church had little direct access to the writings of the Greeks, although some Latin translations and commentaries provided a continuing link to the world of classical thought.

But intellectual life in Europe changed dramatically in the several centuries after 1000, amid a rising population, a quickening commercial life, emerging towns and cities, and the Church's growing independence from royal or noble authorities. Moreover, the West was developing a legal system that provided a measure of independence for a variety of institutions—towns and cities, guilds, professional associations, and especially universities. An outgrowth of earlier cathedral schools, these European universities—in Paris, Bologna, Oxford, Cambridge, Salamanca—became "zones of intellectual autonomy" in which scholars could pursue their studies with some freedom from the dictates of religious or political authorities, although that freedom was never complete and was frequently contested.[22]

This was the setting in which a small group of literate churchmen began to emphasize, quite self-consciously, the ability of human reason to penetrate divine mysteries and to grasp the operation of the natural order. In the late eleventh century students in a monastic school in France asked their teacher, Anselm, to provide a proof for the existence of God based solely on reason, without using the Bible or other sources of divine revelation.

The new interest in rational thought was applied first and foremost to theology, the "queen of the sciences" to European thinkers. Logic, philosophy, and rationality would operate in service to Christ. Of course, some opposed this new emphasis on human reason. Bernard of Clairvaux, a twelfth-century French abbot, declared, "Faith believes. It does not dispute."[23] His contemporary and intellectual opponent, the French scholar William of Conches, lashed out: "You poor fools. God can make a cow out of a tree, but has he ever done so? Therefore show some reason why a thing is so or cease to hold that it is so."[24]

European intellectuals also applied their newly discovered confidence in human reason to law, medicine, and the world of nature, exploring optics, magnetism, astronomy, and alchemy. Slowly and never completely, the scientific study of nature, known as "natural philosophy," began to separate itself from theology. This mounting enthusiasm for rational inquiry stimulated European scholars to seek out original Greek texts, particularly those of Aristotle. They found them in the Greek-speaking world of Byzantium and in the Islamic world, where they had long ago been translated into Arabic. In the twelfth and thirteenth centuries, an explosion of translations from Greek and Arabic into Latin, many of them undertaken in Spain, gave European scholars direct access to the works of ancient Greeks and to the remarkable results of Arab scholarship in astronomy, optics, medicine, pharmacology, and more. One of these translators, Adelard of Bath (1080–1142), remarked that he had learned, "under the guidance of reason from Arabic teachers," not to trust established authority.[25]

It was the works of the prolific Aristotle, with his logical approach and "scientific temperament," that made the deepest impression. His writings became the basis for university education and largely dominated the thought of Western Europe in the five centuries after 1200. In the work of the thirteenth-century theologian Thomas Aquinas, Aristotle's ideas were thoroughly integrated into a logical and systematic

Guided Reading Question

■ **COMPARISON**
In what different ways did classical Greek philosophy and science have an impact in the West, in Byzantium, and in the Islamic world?

European University Life in the Middle Ages This fourteenth-century manuscript painting shows a classroom scene from the University of Bologna in Italy. Note the sleeping and disruptive students. Some things apparently never change. (bpk Bildagentur/Kupferstichkabinett, Staatliche Museen, Berlin, Germany/Photo: Joerg P. Anders/Art Resource, NY)

presentation of Christian doctrine. In this growing emphasis on human rationality, which some considered to be at least partially separate from divine revelation, lay one of the foundations of the later Scientific Revolution and the secularization of European intellectual life.

Surprisingly, nothing comparable occurred in the Byzantine Empire, where knowledge of the Greek language was widespread and access to Greek texts was easy. Although Byzantine scholars kept the classical tradition alive, their primary interest lay in the humanities (literature, philosophy, history) and theology rather than in the natural sciences or medicine. Furthermore, both state and church had serious reservations about Greek learning. In 529, the emperor Justinian closed Plato's Academy in Athens, claiming that it was an outpost of paganism. Its scholars dispersed into lands that soon became Islamic, carrying Greek learning into the Islamic world. Church authorities as well were suspicious of Greek thought, sometimes persecuting scholars who were too enamored with the ancients. Even those who did study the Greek writers did so in a conservative spirit, concerned with preserving and transmitting the classical heritage rather than with using it as a springboard for creating new knowledge. "The great men of the past," declared the fourteenth-century Byzantine scholar and statesman Theodore Metochites, "have said everything so perfectly that they have left nothing for us to say."[26]

In the Islamic world, Greek thought was embraced "with far more enthusiasm and creativity" than in Byzantium.[27] A massive translation project in the ninth and tenth centuries made Aristotle and many other Greek writers available in Arabic. That work contributed to a flowering of Arab scholarship, especially in the sciences and natural philosophy, between roughly 800 and 1200, but it also stimulated a debate about faith and reason among Muslim thinkers, many of whom greatly admired Greek philosophical, scientific, and medical texts. As in the Christian world, the issue was whether secular Greek thought was an aid or a threat to the faith. Western European church authorities after the thirteenth century had come to regard natural philosophy as a wholly legitimate enterprise and had thoroughly incorporated Aristotle into university education, but learned opinion in the Islamic world swung the other way. Though never completely disappearing from Islamic scholarship, the ideas of Plato and Aristotle receded after the thirteenth century in favor of teachings that drew more directly from the Quran or from mystical experience. Nor was natural philosophy a central concern of Islamic higher education, as it was in the West. The integration of political and religious life in the Islamic world, as in Byzantium, contrasted with their separation in the West, where there was more space for the independent pursuit of scientific subjects.

REFLECTIONS

Remembering and Forgetting: Continuity and Surprise in the Worlds of Christendom

Many of the characteristic features of Christendom that emerged during the era of third-wave civilizations have had a long life, extending well into the modern era. The crusading element of European expansion was prominent among the motives of Spanish and Portuguese explorers. Europe's grudging freedom for merchant activity and its eagerness to borrow foreign technology arguably contributed to the growth of capitalism and industrialization in later centuries. The endemic military conflicts of European states, unable to recover the unity of the Roman Empire, found terrible expression in the world wars of the twentieth century. The controversy about reason and faith resonates still, at least in the United States, in debates about the authority of the Bible in secular and scientific matters. The rift between Eastern Orthodoxy and Roman Catholicism remains one of the major divides in the Christian world. Modern universities and the separation of religious and political authority likewise have their origins in the European Middle Ages. Such a perspective, linking the past with what came later, represents one of the great contributions that the study of history makes to human understanding. We are limited and shaped by our histories.

Yet that very strength of historical study can be misleading, particularly if it suggests a kind of inevitability, in which the past determines the future. Knowing the outcome of the stories we tell can be a serious disadvantage, for it may rob the people we study of the freedom and uncertainty that they surely experienced. In 500 C.E., few people would have predicted that Europe would become the primary center of Christianity, while the African and Asian expressions of that faith withered away. As late as 1000, the startling reversal of roles between the Eastern and Western wings of Christendom that the next several centuries witnessed was hardly on the horizon. At that time, the many small, rural, unsophisticated, and endlessly quarreling warrior-based societies of Western Europe would hardly have borne comparison with the powerful Byzantine Empire and its magnificent capital of Constantinople. Even in 1500, when Europe had begun to catch up with China and the Islamic world in various ways, there was little to predict its remarkable transformation over the next several centuries and the dramatic change in the global balance of power that this transformation produced.

Usually students of history are asked to remember. But forgetting can also be an aid to historical understanding. To recapture the unexpectedness of the historical process and to allow ourselves to be surprised, it may be useful on occasion to forget — or at least set aside — what we know about what happened next and to see the world as contemporaries viewed it.

Second Thoughts

What's the Significance?

Jesus Sutras, 406
Nubian Christianity, 408
Ethiopian Christianity, 408
Byzantine Empire, 409
Constantinople, 409
caesaropapism, 411
Eastern Orthodox Christianity, 411
Crusades, 413
Kievan Rus, 414
Prince Vladimir of Kiev, 415
Western Christendom, 415
Charlemagne, 417
Holy Roman Empire, 417
feudalism, 417
Roman Catholic Church, 431

Big Picture Questions

1. What accounts for the different historical trajectories of the Byzantine and West European expressions of Christendom?

2. How did Byzantium and Western Europe interact with each other and with the larger world of the third-wave era?

3. In what respects was the civilization of the Latin West distinctive and unique, and in what ways was it broadly comparable to other third-wave civilizations?

4. **Looking Back:** How does the evolution of the Christian world in the third-wave era compare with that of Tang and Song dynasty China and of the Islamic world?

Next Steps: For Further Study

Bonnie S. Anderson and Judith P. Zinsser, *A History of Their Own* (2000). An overview of European women's history by two prominent scholars.

Edward Grant, *Science and Religion from Aristotle to Copernicus* (2004). Demonstrates the impact of Greek philosophy and science in Europe, with comparisons to Byzantium and the Islamic world.

Barbara A. Hanawalt, *The Middle Ages: An Illustrated History* (1999). A brief and beautifully illustrated introduction to the Middle Ages in European history.

Rowena Loverance, *Byzantium* (2004). A lavishly illustrated history of the Byzantine Empire, drawing on the rich collection of artifacts in the British Museum.

Diarmaid MacCulloch, *Christianity: The First Three Thousand Years* (2010). A recent and much-praised overview of the history of Christendom.

Christopher Tyerman, *Fighting for Christendom: Holy Wars and the Crusades* (2005). A very well-written, up-to-date history of the Crusades designed for nonspecialists.

"Byzantine Empire," http://www.history.com/topics/ancient-history/byzantine-empire. A History channel website that features a number of short, thoughtful videos about Byzantium.

"Middle Ages," http://www.learner.org/interactives/middleages/. An interactive website with text and images relating to life in Europe after the collapse of the Roman Empire.

The Remaking of Western Europe

Following the final collapse of the western part of the Roman Empire in the fifth century C.E., would-be kings and church leaders alike sought to maintain links with the older Greco-Roman-Christian traditions of classical Mediterranean civilization. In the absence of empire, however, new and far more decentralized societies emerged, led now by Germanic peoples and centered in Northern and Western Europe, considerably removed from the older centers of Rome and Athens. It was a hybrid civilization, combining Greco-Roman, Christian, and Germanic/Celtic elements, in a distinctive blending. The sources that follow illustrate how this blending created a new civilization at the western edge of Eurasia.

SOURCE 10.1 The Conversion of Clovis

Among the Germanic peoples of post-Roman Western Europe, none were of greater significance than the Franks, who occupied the region of present-day France (see Map 10.1, page 410). By the early sixth century, a loosely unified Frankish kingdom had emerged under the leadership of Clovis (r. 485–511), whose Merovingian dynasty ruled the area until 751. Clovis's conversion to Christianity, an important step in the mixing of German and Christian culture, was described about a century later by a well-known bishop and writer, Gregory of Tours (538–594).

- What issues are evident in the religious discussions of Clovis and his wife, Clotilda?

- Notice how Gregory modeled his picture of Clovis on that of Constantine, the famous Roman emperor whose conversion to Christianity in the fourth century gave official legitimacy and state support to the faith. What message did Gregory seek to convey in making this implied comparison?

GREGORY OF TOURS | *History of the Franks* | **late 6th century**

[Clovis] had a first-born son by queen Clotilda, and as his wife wished to consecrate him in baptism, she tried unceasingly to persuade her husband, saying: "The gods you worship are nothing, and they will be unable to help themselves or anyone else. For they are graven out of stone or wood or some metal. . . . They are endowed rather with the magic arts than with the power of the divine name. But he [God] ought rather to be worshipped who created by his word heaven and earth, the sea and all that is in them out of a state of nothingness . . . [and] by whose hand mankind was created. . . ."

But though the queen said this, the spirit of the king was by no means moved to belief, and he said: "It was at the command of our gods that all things were created and came forth, and it is plain that your God has no power and, what is more, he is proven not to belong to the family of the gods." Meantime the faithful queen made her son ready for baptism; [but], the boy, whom they named Ingomer, died after being baptized. . . . At this the king was violently angry, and reproached the queen harshly, saying: "If the boy had been dedicated in the name of my gods he would certainly have lived. . . ." To this the queen said: "I give thanks to the omnipotent God, creator of all, who has judged me not wholly unworthy, that he should deign to take to his kingdom one born from my womb . . . he will be fed by the vision of God. . . ."

The queen did not cease to urge him to recognize the true God and cease worshipping idols. But he could not be influenced in any way to this belief, until at last a war arose with the Alamanni [another Germanic people], in which he was driven by necessity to confess what before he had of his free will denied. It came about that as the two armies were fighting fiercely, there was much slaughter, and Clovis's army began to be in danger of destruction. He saw it and raised his eyes to heaven, and with remorse in his heart he burst into tears and cried: "Jesus Christ, whom Clotilda asserts to be the son of the living God . . . , if thou wilt grant me victory over these enemies . . . , I will believe in thee and be baptized. . . . I believe that they [my own gods] possess no power, since they do not help those who obey them. . . ." And when he said thus, the Alamanni turned their backs, and began to disperse in flight. And when they saw that their king was killed, they submitted to the dominion of Clovis, saying: "Let not the people perish further, we pray; we are yours now." And he stopped the fighting, and after encouraging his men, retired in peace and told the queen how he had had merit to win the victory by calling on the name of Christ. . . .

And so the king confessed all-powerful God in the Trinity, and was baptized in the name of the Father, Son and Holy Spirit, and was anointed with the holy ointment with the sign of the cross of Christ. And of his army more than 3,000 were baptized.

Source: Gregory Bishop of Tours, *History of the Franks*, translated by Ernest Brehaut (New York: Columbia University Press, 1916; copyright renewed 1944), bk. 2, selections from secs. 29, 30, 31.

■ ■ ■

SOURCE 10.2 Advice on Dealing with "Pagans"

In their dealings with the "pagan," or non-Christian, peoples and kings of Western Europe, church authorities such as missionaries, bishops, and the pope himself sometimes advocated compromise with existing cultural traditions rather than overt hostility to them. For example, Pope Gregory (r. 590–604) urged the bishop of England to adopt a strategy of accommodation with the prevailing religious practices of the Anglo-Saxon peoples of the island. Gregory's advice was included in a famous work about the early Christian history of England composed by a Benedictine monk known as the Venerable Bede and completed about 731.

■ What can we learn about the religious practices of the Anglo-Saxons from Bede's account?

■ In what specific ways did the pope urge toleration? Why did he advocate accommodation or compromise with existing religious practices? Keep in mind that the political authorities in England at the time had not yet become thoroughly Christian.

■ How might such an approach to conversion contribute to the emerging hybrid civilization in Western Europe?

POPE GREGORY | *Advice to the English Church* | 601

The temples of the idols in that nation [England] ought not to be destroyed; but let the idols that are in them be destroyed; let holy water be made and sprinkled in the said temples, let altars be erected, and relics placed. For if those temples are well built, it is requisite that they be converted from the worship of devils to the service of the true God; that the nation, seeing that their temples are not destroyed, may remove error from their hearts, and knowing and adoring the true God, may the more familiarly resort to the places to which they have been accustomed.

And because they have been used to slaughter many oxen in the sacrifices to devils, some solemnity must be exchanged for them on this account, as that on the day of the dedication, or the nativities of the holy martyrs, whose relics are there deposited, they may build themselves huts of the boughs of trees, about those churches which have been turned to that use from temples, and celebrate the solemnity with religious feasting, and no more offer beasts to the Devil, but kill cattle to the praise of God in their eating, and return thanks to the Giver of all things for their sustenance; to the end that, while some gratifications are outwardly permitted them, they may the more easily consent to the inward consolations of the grace of God. For there is no doubt that it is impossible to efface everything at once from their obdurate minds; because he who endeavors to ascend to the highest place, rises by degrees or steps, and not by leaps.

Source: The Venerable Bede, *The Ecclesiastical History of the English Nation*, edited by Ernest Rhys (London: J. M. Dent and Sons; New York: E. P. Dutton, 1910), 52–53.

■ ■ ■

SOURCE 10.3 Pagan Art and Christian Texts ▶

The mixing of Christian and pre-Christian cultural traditions during the conversion of Europe spawned remarkable hybrid works of art. Source 10.3 provides one example of the use of long-established Celtic and Anglo-Saxon artistic styles to decorate a copy of the Christian gospels in Latin. While most illuminated manuscripts were created by teams of artists and scribes, this one was the work of a single man named Eadfrith, Bishop of Lindisfarne. Over several decades between 698 and 721, he produced this manuscript at a monastery on remote Holy Island off the coast of northern England. Nowhere are Eadfrith's artistic skills more apparent than on the "incipit" pages, those containing the opening words of each gospel. Note the repeating designs, made up of elaborate patterns, swirls, birds, and animals, long used in Celtic and Germanic artistic expression.

■ What reaction to the Christian scriptures might Eadfrith hope to engender through this book?

■ In what ways does the Lindisfarne gospel reflect the new hybrid civilization that emerged in Western Europe after the fall of Rome?

■ Monks viewed the copying of holy works as acts of faith and piety. With this in mind, why might Eadfrith have so elaborately decorated his manuscript?

■ Compare this image to the Anglo-Saxon purse hinge from the pre-Christian Sutton Hoo burial site in southern England shown in the "Anglo-Saxon Treasure" photo in Chapter 3. What similarities can you identify between these two pieces of art?

Lindisfarne Gospel | 698–721

SOURCE 10.4 Germanic Law

As Germanic tribes conquered and then settled in regions of the former Roman Empire, they faced the practical challenge of ruling over kingdoms that incorporated both their followers and Romans. King Gundobad (r. 473–516), whose Germanic tribe, known as the Burgundians, had established a kingdom in what is now central France, sought to address this problem by creating two law codes—one for his own people based on their unwritten laws grounded in ancient customs, and a second for his conquered peoples or "Romans" based on Roman law. Germanic law prevailed in cases between "barbarians" and "Romans." While Gundobad's law code for his Germanic subjects sought to preserve Burgundian culture, the recording of customary law also represented a major shift because it embraced the Roman idea of written codified law and the role of rulers as lawmakers and judges. The selections that follow are drawn from Gundobad's law code for his Germanic subjects and give a sense of the values and organization of Burgundian society during this transitional period.

■ What does this law code tell us about the customs of the Germanic peoples who settled in Western Europe?

■ What social classes can you identify in Burgundian society?

■ How would you describe the status of women in Burgundian society?

■ To what extent is Gundobad the creator or enforcer of the law? To what extent is he constrained by the traditions and customs of his people? Why might Gundobad have opted for a written law code rather than maintaining unwritten traditions?

Burgundian Code | ca. 474 C.E.

II. Of Murders

1. If anyone presumes with boldness or rashness bent on injury to kill a native freeman of people of any nation or a servant of the king, in any case a man of barbarian tribe, let him make restitution for the committed crime not otherwise than by the shedding of his own blood.

2. [I]f violence shall have been done by anyone to any person so that he is injured by blows of lashes or by wounds and if he pursues his persecutor and overcome by grief and indignation kills him, proof of the deed shall be afforded by the act itself or by suitable witnesses who can be believed. Then the guilty party shall be compelled to pay to the relatives of the person killed half his wergeld [an amount paid as compensation to the family of someone who is slain based on that person's social rank] . . .

3. If a slave unknown to his master presumes to kill a native freeman, let the slave be handed over to death, and let the master not be made liable for damages.

4. If the master knows of the deed, let both be handed over for death.

VIII. Crimes Charged Against Freemen

1. If a native freeman either barbarian or Roman, is accused of a crime through suspicion let him render oath, and let him swear with his wife and sons and twelve relatives; if indeed he does not have wife and sons and he has mother or father, let him complete the designated number with father and mother. But if he has neither father nor mother, let him complete the oath with twelve relatives.

XXXIV. Of Divorces

1. If any woman leaves (puts aside) her husband to whom she is legally married, let her be smothered in mire.
2. If anyone wishes to put away his wife without cause, let him give her another payment such as he gave for her marriage price, and let the amount of the fine be 12 solidi [a form of currency].
3. If by chance a man wishes to put away his wife, and is able to prove one of these three crimes against her, that of adultery, witchcraft, or violation of graves, let him have full rights to put her away; and let the judge pronounce the sentence of law against her, just as should be done against criminals.
4. But if she admits to none of these three crimes, let no man be permitted to put away his wife for any other crime. But if he chooses, he may go away from the home, leaving all household property behind, and his wife with their children may possess the property of her husband.

XLV. [Of Trial by Combat]

We know that many of our people are corrupted through inability to establish a case and because of instinct of greed, so that they do not hesitate frequently to offer oaths about uncertain matters and likewise to perjure themselves about known matters. To break up this criminal practice, we decree by the present law that . . . [if the parties cannot agree] let the right of combat not be refused; . . . God being the judge.

Source: *The Burgundian Code*, translated by Katherine Fischer, in *Translations and Reprints from the Original Sources of History* (Philadelphia: University of Pennsylvania Press, 1949), 5:23, 29, 45–46, 52.

■ ■ ■

SOURCE 10.5 **Charlemagne's Palace Chapel** ▶

During the late eighth and early ninth centuries C.E., Charlemagne (r. 768–814) turned his powerful Frankish kingdom into a Christian empire that briefly incorporated much of continental Western Europe. Crowned Holy Roman Emperor on Christmas day 800 C.E. by Pope Leo III, Charlemagne was seemingly on the brink of reuniting the western portion of the Roman Empire under his rule. Instead, his empire quickly fragmented after his death. Nonetheless, during its height his empire was perhaps the fullest expression of the new hybrid Western European culture to that time.

Nowhere did Charlemagne display his understanding of his imperial status more clearly than in the chapel at his palace at Aachen. Several elements of the building were designed to evoke the majesty of previous Roman emperors, and particularly the first Christian emperor Constantine. The chapel was decorated with imported marble shipped in from Rome and elsewhere and was designed to echo two important Roman imperial churches—the Holy Sepulcher in Jerusalem and San Vitale in Ravenna. Moreover, Aachen itself was a former Roman site. Beyond these links to imperial Rome, Charlemagne also intended for the chapel to represent heavenly Jerusalem. Its octagonal design decorated in expensive marbles "heightened the celestial atmosphere," as did a fresco on the domed ceiling depicting the twenty-four elders adoring the throne of God, mentioned in the Bible's Book of Revelation (4:1–4). While most visitors hailed from the elite strata of society, even the most powerful nobles and churchmen of Charlemagne's realm were normally restricted to the lower floor, where religious ceremonies took place. Charlemagne observed proceedings from his throne on the second floor overlooking the main altar—visible in the center of Source 10.5. Positioned between Heaven and Earth in this holy setting, Charlemagne reminded all visitors of his unique status in society as God's anointed ruler on Earth. In the centuries that followed, Charlemagne's burial in the chapel and later coronations of Holy Roman Emperors in this space ensured that it became one of the most influential buildings in Western Europe.

- What specific elements of the chapel's structure and decoration might have evoked holy or otherworldly feelings in the viewer?

- What does the placement of Charlemagne's throne tell us about how he viewed his power and authority as emperor? Why do you think his throne is set back from the balcony edge? What might Charlemagne seek to convey from such a position?

- How might Charlemagne describe his chapel to a visitor?

Aachen Palace Chapel | completed 805 C.E.

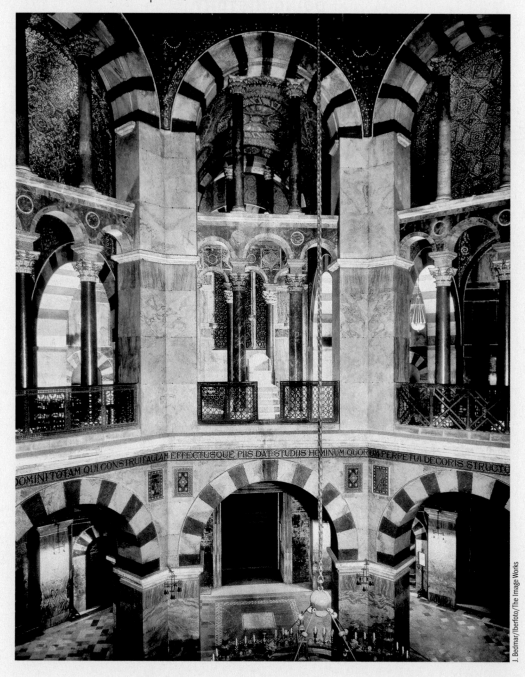

DOING HISTORY

1. **Describing cultural encounters:** What elements of cultural mixing do these sources highlight? What specific elements of ancient Roman, Christian, and Germanic/Celtic culture can you identify in each source?

2. **Thinking about legitimacy:** What strategies did Clovis, Gundobad, and Charlemagne use to bolster their legitimacy? How do their actions reflect or react to the evolving societies over which they ruled?

3. **Noticing point of view and assessing credibility:** From what point of view is each of the written sources created? Which elements of each source might historians find unreliable, and which would they find most useful?

The Legacy of Rome

The legacy of Rome in the hybrid Western European society that emerged from the fifth century has been the subject of much scholarly debate over the past thirty years. These two voices consider questions of survival and revival of the Roman past in the fifth to ninth centuries. In Voice 10.1, Wim Blockmans and Peter Hoppenbrouwers, both professors of medieval history at the University of Leiden, assess whether Roman civilization in Western Europe disappeared with the collapse of the empire. In Voice 10.2, Barry Cunliffe, a leading archeologist, looks at the controversy surrounding Charlemagne's effort to revive the title of "Roman Emperor."

- What major shifts in society do Blockmans and Hoppenbrouwers identify with the fall of the Roman Empire?

- What can Cunliffe's description of the dispute over Charlemagne's crowning as emperor tell us about the importance of the title "Roman Emperor" centuries after Rome's collapse in the West?

- **Integrating Primary and Secondary Sources:** How do these voices help you to better understand the primary sources in this feature?

VOICE 10.1

Blockmans and Hoppenbrouwers on the End of Roman Civilization | 2014

Did the fall of the Roman Empire in the West also mark the end of Roman civilization in the West? One is easily inclined to think it did because archaeology does not lie. What could better illustrate the end of a civilization than the astounding impoverishment of its material culture? Nothing crafted in the sixth and seventh centuries could equal the superb urban planning and construction of roads, harbours, aqueducts and drains of the Roman age, nothing compares to the magnificent public and private building of that time, to their refined house design, their decorations, their utensils, their tableware. . . .

Yet, there are three asides to be made here. The first is that this impoverishment of material culture cannot have been caused by barbarian invasions alone. . . . [T]here were other factors at stake. We have already pointed out two: the disappearance of classical city councils, responsible for public infrastructure and building, and the penetration of world-averse Christian ethics. . . .

The second aside is prompted by the consideration that loss of luxury and monumentality does not say all about average human well-being on a more elementary level. It was not all roses in the Roman world, and indeed proportionally more people may have been better fed in the early Middle Ages than they had during the later Roman Empire. And thirdly, neither did the demise of conveniences and comfort imply the death of Roman civilization in terms of ideals and ideas. On the contrary, in a sense, Rome's appeal proved to be eternal. Throughout the Middle Ages, and long after, Roman ideas on government and law, on science and literature continued to exert a compelling force on the imagination and activities of the upper strata of society in Western Europe.

Source: Wim Blockmans and Peter Hoppenbrouwers, *Introduction to Medieval Europe 300–1500*, 2nd ed. (London: Routledge, 2014), 40.

VOICE 10.2

Cunliffe on Charlemagne | 2008

On Christmas Day AD 800 in Rome, Charlemagne, king of the Franks and Lombards, was crowned *imperator et augustus* [a title given to Roman emperors] by Pope Leo III. It was an act of great symbolism designed to legitimize Charlemagne's claim to be the natural heir of old Rome—of the Latin-speaking, Christian West—an act not without its political dangers since it was done without the approval of the Byzantine emperor, who might have been expected to have views on the matter. The Byzantine rulers regarded themselves as the legitimate emperors of the Roman Empire and now the Frankish usurper was challenging their authority. It took twelve years of confrontation and bargaining before a compromise could be reached. Charlemagne was recognized as "emperor" by Constantinople but not as *Roman* emperor. Henceforth it was publicly accepted that there were two empires which could work together against common enemies, but only one—Byzantium—was "Roman."

Source: Barry Cunliffe, *Europe between the Oceans, 9000 BC–AD 1000* (New Haven, CT: Yale University Press, 2008), 445.

Moghul court painting, ca.1596/Pictures from History/Bridgeman Images

Pastoral Peoples on the Global Stage

CHAPTER 11

The Mongol Moment

1200–1450

The Long History of Pastoral Peoples
The World of Pastoral Societies
Before the Mongols: Pastoralists in History

Breakout: The Mongol Empire
From Temujin to Chinggis Khan: The Rise of the Mongol Empire
Explaining the Mongol Moment

Encountering the Mongols in China, Persia, and Russia
China and the Mongols
Persia and the Mongols
Russia and the Mongols

The Mongol Empire as a Eurasian Network
Toward a World Economy
Diplomacy on a Eurasian Scale
Cultural Exchange in the Mongol Realm
The Plague: An Afro-Eurasian Pandemic

Reflections: Changing Images of Pastoral Peoples

In late 2012, the Central Asian nation of Mongolia celebrated a "Day of Mongolian Pride," marking the birth of the country's epic hero Chinggis Khan 850 years earlier. Officials laid wreaths at a giant monument to the warrior leader; wrestlers and archers tested their skills in competition; dancers performed; over 100 scholars made presentations; traditional costumes abounded. For this small and somewhat remote country, seeking to navigate between its two giant neighbors, China and Russia, it was an occasion to express its own distinctive identity. And Chinggis Khan is central to that identity.

The 2012 celebrations marked a shift in Mongolian thinking about Chinggis Khan that has been under way since the 1990s. Under the country's earlier Soviet-backed communist government, the great Mongol leader had been regarded in very negative terms. After all, his forces had decimated Russia in the thirteenth century, and resentment lingered. But as communism faded in both Russia and Mongolia at the end of the twentieth century, the memory of Chinggis Khan made a remarkable comeback in the land of his birth. "He is like a god to us," said Bat-Erdene Batbayar, a Mongolian historian and political figure. "He is the founder of our state, the root of our history. The communists very brutally cut us off from our traditions and history. . . . Now we are becoming Mongols again."[1]

Increasingly, his bloody conquests were played down, and he was celebrated as a unifier of the Mongolian peoples, the creator of an empire tolerant of various faiths, and a promoter of economic and cultural ties among distant peoples. Vodka, cigarettes, a chocolate bar, two brands of beer, the country's most prominent rock band, and the central square of the capital city all bore his name, while his picture appeared on Mongolia's stamps and money. Rural young

« **Chinggis Khan and His Family** This late sixteenth-century Indian painting shows Chinggis Khan, the founder of the Mongol Empire, seated next to his primary wife, Borte Ujin, with his four sons seated to his left. At his death each of these sons inherited a portion of his vast empire, while his five daughters were strategically married to politically prominent men.

449

people on horseback sang songs in his honor, and their counterparts in urban Internet cafés constructed websites to celebrate his achievements. ■

All of this is a reminder of the enormous and surprising role that the Mongols played in the Eurasian world of the thirteenth and fourteenth centuries and of the continuing echoes of that long-vanished empire. More generally, the story of the Mongols serves as a useful corrective to the almost-exclusive focus that historians often devote to agricultural peoples and their civilizations, for the Mongols, and many other such peoples, were pastoralists who disdained farming while centering their economic lives around their herds of animals. Normally they did not construct elaborate cities, enduring empires, or monumental works of art, architecture, and written literature. Nonetheless, they left an indelible mark on the historical development of the entire Afro-Eurasian hemisphere, and particularly on the agricultural civilizations with which they so often interacted.

SEEKING THE MAIN POINT

What has been the role in world history of pastoral peoples in general and the Mongols in particular?

The Long History of Pastoral Peoples

On the arid margins of agricultural lands, where productive farming was difficult or impossible, an alternative kind of food-producing economy emerged around 4000 B.C.E., focused on the raising of livestock. Horses, camels, goats, sheep, cattle, yaks, and reindeer were the primary animals that separately, or in some combination, enabled the construction of herding or **pastoral societies**. Such societies took shape in the vast grasslands of inner Eurasia and sub-Saharan Africa, in the Arabian and Saharan deserts, in the subarctic regions of the Northern Hemisphere, and in the high plateau of Tibet. (See Snapshot: Varieties of Pastoral Societies, page 452.)

The World of Pastoral Societies

Guided Reading Question

■ **COMPARISON**
In what ways did pastoral societies differ from their agricultural counterparts?

Despite their many differences, pastoral societies shared several important features that distinguished them from settled agricultural communities and civilizations. Their generally less productive economies and their need for large grazing areas meant that they supported far smaller populations than did agricultural societies. People generally lived in small and widely scattered encampments or seasonal settlements made up of related kinfolk rather than in the villages, towns, and cities characteristic of agrarian civilizations. Beyond the family unit, pastoral peoples organized themselves in kinship-based groups or clans that claimed a common ancestry, usually through the male line. Related clans might on occasion come together as a tribe, which could also absorb unrelated people into the community. Although their values stressed equality and individual achievement, in some pastoral societies clans were ranked as noble or commoner, and considerable differences

Landmarks for Chapter 11

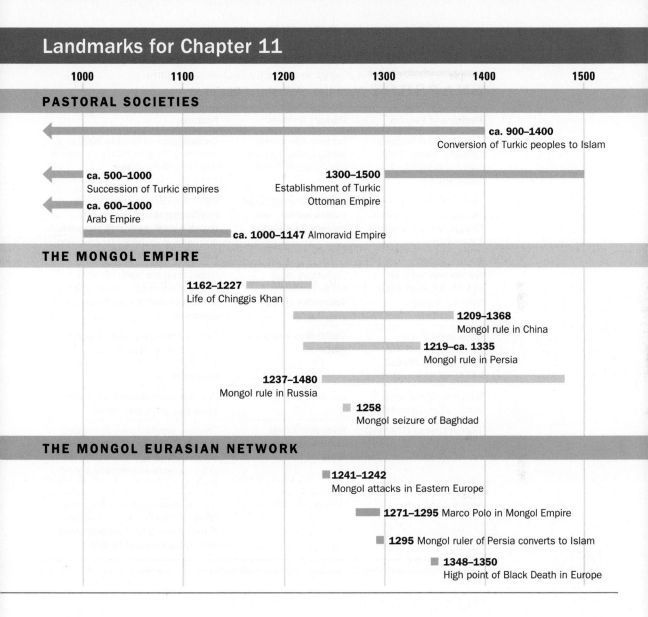

PASTORAL SOCIETIES

ca. 900–1400
Conversion of Turkic peoples to Islam

ca. 500–1000
Succession of Turkic empires

1300–1500
Establishment of Turkic
Ottoman Empire

ca. 600–1000
Arab Empire

ca. 1000–1147 Almoravid Empire

THE MONGOL EMPIRE

1162–1227
Life of Chinggis Khan

1209–1368
Mongol rule in China

1219–ca. 1335
Mongol rule in Persia

1237–1480
Mongol rule in Russia

1258
Mongol seizure of Baghdad

THE MONGOL EURASIAN NETWORK

1241–1242
Mongol attacks in Eastern Europe

1271–1295 Marco Polo in Mongol Empire

1295 Mongol ruler of Persia converts to Islam

1348–1350
High point of Black Death in Europe

emerged between wealthy aristocrats owning large flocks of animals and poor herders. Many pastoral societies held slaves as well.

Furthermore, pastoral peoples generally offered women a higher status, fewer restrictions, and a greater role in public life than their counterparts in agricultural civilizations. Everywhere pastoral women were involved in productive labor as well as having domestic responsibility for food and children. The care of smaller animals such as sheep and goats usually fell to women, although only rarely did women own or control their own livestock. Among the Mongols, the remarriage of a widow, often to a male relative of her husband, carried none of the negative connotations that it did among the Chinese, and women could initiate divorce. Mongol women frequently served as political advisers and were active in military

451

SNAPSHOT Varieties of Pastoral Societies

Region and Peoples	Primary Animals	Features
Inner Eurasian steppes (Xiongnu, Yuezhi, Turks, Uighurs, Mongols, Huns, Kipchaks)	Horses; also sheep, goats, cattle, Bactrian (two-humped) camel	Domestication of horse by 4000 B.C.E.; horseback riding by 1000 B.C.E.; site of largest pastoral empires
Southwestern and Central Asia (Seljuks, Ghaznavids, Mongol il-khans, Uzbeks, Ottomans)	Sheep and goats; used horses, camels, and donkeys for transport	Close economic relationship with neighboring towns; pastoralists provided meat, wool, milk products, and hides in exchange for grain and manufactured goods
Arabian and Saharan deserts (Bedouin Arabs, Berbers, Tuareg)	Dromedary (one-humped) camel; sometimes sheep	Camel caravans made possible long-distance trade; camel-mounted warriors central to early Arab/Islamic expansion
Grasslands of sub-Saharan Africa (Fulbe, Nuer, Turkana, Masai)	Cattle; also sheep and goats	Cattle were a chief form of wealth and central to ritual life; little interaction with wider world until nineteenth century
Subarctic Scandinavia, Russia (Sami, Nenets)	Reindeer	Reindeer domesticated only since 1500 C.E.; many also fished
Tibetan plateau (Tibetans)	Yaks; also sheep, cashmere goats, some cattle	Tibetans supplied yaks as baggage animals for overland caravan trade; exchanged wool, skins, and milk with valley villagers and received barley in return
Andean Mountains	Llamas and alpacas	Andean pastoralists in a few places relied on their herds for a majority of their subsistence, supplemented with horticulture and hunting

All data derived from Thomas J. Barfield, "Pastoral Nomadic Societies," in *Berkshire Encyclopedia of World History* (Great Barrington, MA: Berkshire, 2005), 4:1432–37.

affairs as well. A thirteenth-century European visitor, the Franciscan friar Giovanni DiPlano Carpini, recorded his impressions of Mongol women:

> Girls and women ride and gallop as skillfully as men. We even saw them carrying quivers and bows, and the women can ride horses for as long as the men; they have shorter stirrups, handle horses very well, and mind all the property. . . . They all wear trousers, and some of them shoot just like men.[2]

Certainly, literate observers from adjacent civilizations noticed and clearly disapproved of the freedom granted to pastoral women. Ancient Greek writers thought that the pastoralists with whom they were familiar were "women governed." To Han Kuan, a Chinese Confucian scholar in the first century B.C.E., China's northern pastoral neighbors "[made] no distinction between men and women."[3]

The most characteristic feature of pastoral societies was their mobility, as local environmental conditions largely dictated their patterns of movement. In some favorable regions, pastoralists maintained seasonal settlements, migrating, for instance, between highland pastures in the summer and less harsh lowland environments in the winter. Others lived more nomadic lives, moving their herds frequently in regular patterns to systematically follow the seasonal changes in vegetation and water supply. But even the most nomadic pastoralists were not homeless; they took their homes, often elaborate felt tents, with them. Whatever their patterns of movement, pastoralists shared a life based on turning grass, which people cannot eat, into usable food and energy through their animals.

Although pastoralists represented an alternative to the agricultural way of life that they disdained, they were almost always deeply connected to, and often dependent on, their farming neighbors. Few of these peoples could live solely from the products of their animals, and most of them actively sought access to the foodstuffs, manufactured goods, and luxury items available from nearby farming communities. Particularly among the pastoral peoples of inner Eurasia, this desire for the fruits of civilization periodically stimulated the creation of tribal confederations or states that could more effectively deal with the powerful agricultural societies on their borders.

Constructing a large state among pastoralists was no easy task. Such societies generally lacked the surplus wealth needed to pay for the professional armies and bureaucracies that everywhere sustained the states and empires of agricultural civilizations. And the fierce independence of widely dispersed pastoral clans and tribes as well as their internal rivalries made any enduring political unity difficult to achieve. Nonetheless, charismatic leaders, such as Chinggis Khan, were periodically able

Guided Reading Question

....

■ **CONNECTION**

In what ways did pastoral societies interact with their agricultural neighbors?

The Scythians An ancient horse-riding pastoral people during the second-wave era, the Scythians occupied a region in present-day Kazakhstan and southern Russia. Their pastoral way of life is apparent in this detail from an exquisite gold necklace from the fourth century B.C.E. (Historical Museum, Kiev, Ukraine/photo © Boltin Picture Library/Bridgeman Images)

to weld together a series of tribal alliances that for a time became powerful states. Despite their limited populations, such states had certain military advantages in confronting larger and more densely populated civilizations. They could draw on the horseback-riding and hunting skills of virtually the entire male population and some women as well. But what sustained these states was their ability to extract wealth, through raiding, trading, or extortion, from agricultural civilizations such as China, Persia, and Byzantium. Pastoralists interacted with their agricultural neighbors not only economically and militarily but also culturally, as they "became acquainted with and tried on for size all the world and universal religions."[4] At one time or another, Judaism, Buddhism, Islam, and several forms of Christianity all found a home somewhere among the pastoral peoples of inner Eurasia. So did Manichaeism, a religious tradition born in third-century Persia and combining elements of Zoroastrian, Christian, and Buddhist practice. Usually conversion was a top-down process as pastoral elites and rulers adopted a foreign religion for political purposes, sometimes changing religious allegiance as circumstances altered. Pastoral peoples, in short, did not inhabit a world totally apart from their agricultural and civilized neighbors.

As the pastoral peoples of the Inner Asian steppes learned the art of horseback riding, by roughly 1000 B.C.E., their societies changed dramatically. Now they could accumulate and tend larger herds of horses, sheep, and goats and move more rapidly over a much wider territory. New technologies, invented or adapted by pastoral societies, added to the mastery of their environment and spread widely across the Eurasian steppes, creating something of a common culture in this vast region. These innovations included complex horse harnesses, saddles with iron stirrups, a small compound bow that could be fired from horseback, various forms of armor, and new kinds of swords. Agricultural peoples were amazed at the centrality of the horse in pastoral life. As a Roman historian noted about the Huns, "From their horses, by day and night every one of that nation buys and sells, eats and drinks, and bowed over the narrow neck of the animal relaxes in a sleep so deep as to be accompanied by many dreams."[5]

Before the Mongols: Pastoralists in History

What enabled pastoral peoples to make their most visible entry onto the stage of world history was the military potential of horseback riding, and of camel riding somewhat later. Their mastery of mounted warfare made possible a long but intermittent series of pastoral empires across the steppes of inner Eurasia and parts of Africa. For 2,000 years, those states played a major role in Afro-Eurasian history and represented a standing challenge to and influence upon the agrarian civilizations on their borders.

One early large-scale pastoral empire was associated with the people known as the Xiongnu, who lived in the Mongolian steppes north of China. Provoked by Chinese penetration of their territory, the Xiongnu in the third and second centuries B.C.E. created a huge military confederacy that stretched from Manchuria deep into Central Asia (see map of Xiongnu Empire). "All the people who draw the bow have now become one family," declared **Modun** (r. 210–174 B.C.E.), the charismatic founder of the **Xiongnu Empire**. Tribute, exacted from other pastoral peoples and from China itself, sustained the Xiongnu Empire and forced the Han dynasty emperor Wen to acknowledge, unhappily, the equality of people he regarded as barbarians. "Our two great nations," he declared, "the Han and the Xiongnu, stand side by side."[6] Although it subsequently disintegrated under sustained Chinese counterattacks, the Xiongnu Empire provided a model and inspiration for later Turkic and Mongol empires.

The Xiongnu Empire

It was during the era of third-wave civilizations that pastoral peoples made their most significant mark on the larger canvas of world history. Arabs, Berbers, Turks, and Mongols—all of them of pastoral origin—created the largest and most influential empires of that era. The most expansive religious tradition of that time, Islam, derived from a largely pastoral people, the Arabs, and was carried to new regions by another pastoral people, the Turks. Most of the great civilizations of outer Eurasia—Byzantium, Persia, India, and China—had come under the control of previously pastoral people, at least for a time. But as pastoralists entered and shaped the arena of world history, they too were transformed by the experience.

The first and most dramatic of these incursions came from Arabs. In the Arabian Peninsula, the development of a reliable camel saddle somewhere between 500 and 100 B.C.E. enabled pastoral Bedouin (desert-dwelling) Arabs to fight effectively from atop their enormous beasts. With this new military advantage, they came to control the rich trade routes in incense running through Arabia. Even more important, these camel pastoralists served as the shock troops of Islamic expansion, providing many of the new religion's earliest followers and much of the military force that carved out the Arab Empire. Although intellectual and political leadership came from urban merchants and settled farming communities, the Arab Empire was in some respects a pastoralist creation that subsequently became the foundation of a new and distinctive civilization.

Even as the pastoral Arabs encroached on the world of Eurasian civilizations from the south, Turkic-speaking pastoralists were making inroads from the north. Never a single people, various Turkic-speaking clans and tribes migrated from their homeland in Mongolia and southern Siberia generally westward and entered the historical record as creators of a series of empires between 552 and 965 C.E., most of them lasting little more than a century. Like the Xiongnu Empire, they were fragile alliances of various tribes headed by a supreme ruler known as a *kaghan*, who was supported by a faithful corps of soldiers called "wolves," for the wolf was the mythical ancestor of **Turkic peoples**. From their base in the steppes, these Turkic states confronted the great civilizations to their south—China, Persia, Byzantium—alternately raiding them, allying with them against common enemies, trading with them, and extorting tribute payments from them. Turkic language and culture spread widely over much of Inner Asia, and elements of that culture entered

Guided Reading Question

■ **SIGNIFICANCE**
In what ways did the Xiongnu, Arabs, Turks, and Berbers make an impact on world history?

Seljuk Tiles Among the artistic achievements of Turkic Muslims were lovely ceramic tiles used to decorate mosques, minarets, palaces, and other public spaces. They contained intricate geometric designs, images of trees and birds, and inscriptions from the Quran. This one, dating from the thirteenth century, was used in a Seljuk palace, built as a summer residence for the sultan in the city of Konya in what is now central Turkey. (© Images & Stories/Alamy)

the agrarian civilizations. In the courts of northern China, for example, yogurt thinned with water, a drink derived from the Turks, replaced for a time the traditional beverage of tea, and at least one Chinese poet wrote joyfully about the delights of snowy evenings in a felt tent.[7]

A major turning point in the history of the Turks occurred with their conversion to Islam between the tenth and fourteenth centuries. This extended process represented a major expansion of the faith and launched the Turks into a new role as the third major carrier of Islam, following the Arabs and the Persians. It also brought the Turks into an increasingly important position within the heartland of an established Islamic civilization as they migrated southward into the Middle East. There they served first as slave soldiers within the Abbasid caliphate, and then, as the caliphate declined, they increasingly took political and military power themselves. In the **Seljuk Turkic Empire** of the eleventh and twelfth centuries, centered in Persia and present-day Iraq, Turkic rulers began to claim the Muslim title of *sultan* (ruler) rather than the Turkic *kaghan*. Although the Abbasid caliph remained the formal ruler, real power was exercised by Turkic sultans.

Not only did Turkic peoples become Muslims themselves, but they carried Islam to new areas as well. Their invasions of northern India solidly planted Islam in that ancient civilization. In Anatolia, formerly ruled by Christian Byzantium, they brought both Islam and a massive infusion of Turkic culture, language, and people, even as they created the Ottoman Empire, which by 1500 became one of the great powers of Eurasia. In both places, Turkic dynasties governed and would continue to do so well into the modern era. Thus Turkic people, many of them at least, had transformed themselves from pastoralists to sedentary farmers, from creators of steppe empires to rulers of agrarian civilizations, and from polytheistic worshippers of their ancestors and various gods to followers and carriers of a monotheistic Islam.

Broadly similar patterns prevailed in Africa as well. All across northern Africa and the Sahara, the introduction of the

The Seljuk Empire

camel, probably during the first millennium B.C.E., gave rise to pastoral societies. Much like the Turkic-speaking pastoralists of Central Asia, many of these peoples later adopted Islam, but at least initially had little formal instruction in the religion. In the eleventh century C.E., a reform movement arose among the Sanhaja Berber pastoralists living in the western Sahara; they had only recently converted to Islam and were practicing it rather superficially. The movement was sparked by a scholar, Ibn Yasin, who returned from a pilgrimage to Mecca around 1039 seeking to purify the practice of the faith among his own people in line with orthodox principles. That religious movement soon became an expansive state, the **Almoravid Empire**, which incorporated a large part of northwestern Africa and in 1086 crossed into southern Spain, where it offered vigorous opposition to Christian efforts to conquer the region.

The Almoravid Empire

For a time, the Almoravid state enjoyed considerable prosperity, based on its control of much of the West African gold trade and the grain-producing Atlantic plains of Morocco. The Almoravids also brought to Morocco the sophisticated Islamic culture of southern Spain, still visible in the splendid architecture of the city of Marrakesh, for a time the capital of the Almoravid Empire. By the mid-twelfth century, that empire had been overrun by its longtime enemies, Berber farming people from the Atlas Mountains. But for roughly a century, the Almoravid movement represented an African pastoral people who had converted to Islam, had come into conflict with their agricultural neighbors and built a short-lived empire, and had a considerable impact on neighboring civilizations in both North Africa and Europe.

Breakout: The Mongol Empire

Of all the pastoral peoples who took a turn on the stage of world history, the Mongols made the most stunning entry. Their thirteenth-century breakout from Mongolia gave rise to the largest land-based empire in all of human history, stretching from the Pacific coast of Asia to Eastern Europe (see Map 11.1). This empire joined the pastoral peoples of the inner Eurasian steppes with the settled agricultural civilizations of outer Eurasia more extensively and more intimately than ever before. It also brought the major civilizations of Eurasia—Europe, China, and the Islamic world—into far more direct contact than in earlier times. Both the enormous destructiveness of the process and the networks of exchange and communication that it spawned were the work of the Mongols, numbering only about 700,000 people. It was another of history's unlikely twists.

For all of its size and fearsome reputation, the Mongol Empire left a surprisingly modest cultural imprint on the world it had briefly governed. Unlike the Arabs, the Mongols bequeathed to the world no new language, religion, or civilization. Mongol religion centered on rituals invoking the ancestors that were performed around the family hearth. Rulers sometimes consulted religious specialists, known

MAPPING HISTORY

Map 11.1 The Mongol Empire
Encompassing much of Eurasia, the Mongol Empire was divided into four khanates after the death of Chinggis Khan.

READING THE MAP: Which of the four khanates included the traditional Mongol homeland?
MAKING CONNECTIONS: What does a comparison of this map with Map 7.1: The Silk Roads suggest about the limits of Mongol expansion?

as shamans, who might predict the future, offer sacrifices, and communicate with the spirit world, particularly with Tengri, the supreme sky god of the Mongols. There was little in this tradition to attract outsiders, and in any event the Mongols proved uninterested in spreading their own faith among subject peoples.

Although people with skills were put to work in ways useful to Mongol authorities, Mongols offered the majority of their conquered people little more than the status of defeated, subordinate, and exploited subjects. Unlike the Turks, whose languages and culture flourish today in many places far from the Turkic homeland in Central Asia, Mongol culture remains confined largely to Mongolia. The Mongol Empire proved to be "the last, spectacular bloom of pastoral power in Inner Eurasia."[8] After the decline and disintegration of the Mongol Empire, the tide turned against the pastoralists of inner Eurasia, who were increasingly swallowed up in the expanding Russian or Chinese empire. Nonetheless, while it lasted and for a few centuries thereafter, the Mongol Empire made an enormous impact throughout the entire Eurasian world.

From Temujin to Chinggis Khan: The Rise of the Mongol Empire

World historians are prone to focus attention on large-scale and long-term processes of change in explaining "what happened in history," but in understanding the rise of the Mongol Empire, most scholars have found themselves forced to look closely at the role of a single individual — **Temujin** (TEM-oo-chin) (1162–1227), later known as **Chinggis Khan** (universal ruler). The twelfth-century world into which he was born found the Mongols an unstable and fractious collection of tribes and clans, much reduced from a somewhat earlier and more powerful position in the shifting alliances in what is now Mongolia. "Everyone was feuding," declared a leading Mongol shaman. "Rather than sleep, they robbed each other of their possessions. . . . There was no respite, only battle. There was no affection, only mutual slaughter."[9]

The early life of Temujin showed few signs of a prominent future. The boy's father had been a minor chieftain of a noble clan, but he was murdered by tribal rivals before Temujin turned ten, and the family was soon deserted by other members of the clan. As social outcasts without livestock, Temujin's small family, headed by his resourceful mother, was forced to abandon pastoralism, living instead by hunting, fishing, and gathering wild foods. It was an enormous and humiliating drop in their social status. In these desperate circumstances, Temujin's remarkable character came into play. His personal magnetism and courage and his inclination to rely on trusted friends rather than ties of kinship allowed him to build up a small following and to ally with a more powerful tribal leader. This alliance received a boost from Chinese patrons, always eager to keep the pastoralists divided. Soon Temujin was recognized as a chief in his own right with a growing band of followers.

Temujin's rise to power within the complex tribal politics of Mongolia was a surprise to everyone, as it took place amid shifting alliances and betrayals. Temujin achieved a mounting string of military victories, aided by the indecisiveness of his enemies, a reputation as a leader generous to friends and ruthless to enemies, and the incorporation of warriors from defeated tribes into his own forces. In 1206, a Mongol tribal assembly recognized Temujin as Chinggis Khan, supreme leader of a now unified Great Mongol Nation. It was a remarkable achievement, but one little noticed beyond the highland steppes of Mongolia. That would soon change.

The unification of the Mongol tribes raised an obvious question: what was Chinggis Khan to do with the powerful army he had assembled? Without a common

Guided Reading Question

■ **DESCRIPTION**
Identify the major steps in the rise of the Mongol Empire.

A Mongol Failure: The Invasion of Japan

The Mongols are best known for the remarkable military victories that gave them one of the largest empires in history, but they experienced stunning defeats as well.[10] None was more dramatic than the failed invasion of Japan in 1281. The armada assembled by the Mongols for this campaign was one of the largest in history, comprising thousands of ships and as many as 140,000 sailors and soldiers. With little experience in naval warfare, the Mongols built their armada by drawing on the resources of their vassal state in Korea and their recently conquered subjects in China. But even with the aid of these seafaring peoples, this huge invasion fleet stretched the resources of the Mongols, who resorted to commuting the death sentences of criminals willing to serve in the fleet.

The invasion was the culmination of a deteriorating relationship between Japanese authorities and the Mongol ruler Khubilai Khan, grandson of Chinggis Khan and founder of the Chinese Yuan dynasty. In the 1260s,

Japanese samurai attacking a Mongol warship.

Japan's government ignored the khan's demands that it become a vassal state of the Mongol Empire. In 1274, the khan dispatched a raiding force against Japan that briefly landed on the main Japanese island of Kyushu. This force both scouted a suitable invasion route and put pressure on the Japanese to accept Mongol demands. In the years that followed, tensions increased, especially when the Japanese summarily beheaded Mongol envoys sent to demand their submission.

Following the final conquest of China in 1279, the khan shifted his attention to subjugating Japan. The massive invasion fleet sailed from ports in Korea and southern China with plans to combine off the shores of Japan. The fleet from Korea arrived first and attacked the mainland without waiting for the Chinese fleet. The Mongols sought to establish a beachhead at the site where Mongol

task, the new and fragile unity of the Mongols would surely dissolve into quarrels and chaos; and without external resources to reward his followers, Chinggis Khan would be hard-pressed to maintain his supreme position. Both considerations pointed in a single direction—expansion, particularly toward China, long a source of great wealth for pastoral peoples.

In 1209, the first major attack on the settled agricultural societies south of Mongolia set in motion half a century of a **Mongol world war**, a series of military campaigns, massive killing, and empire building without precedent in world history. In the process, Chinggis Khan, followed by his sons and grandsons (Ogodei, Mongke, and Khubilai), constructed an empire that contained China, Central Asia, Russia, much of the Islamic Middle East, and parts of Eastern Europe (see Map 11.1, page 458). "In a flash," wrote a recent scholar, "the Mongol warriors would defeat every army, capture every fort, and bring down the walls of every city they encountered. Christians, Muslims, Buddhists, and Hindus would soon kneel before the dusty boots of illiterate young Mongol horsemen."[11]

forces had briefly come ashore in 1274, but the heavily outnumbered Japanese forces were waiting for them behind recently constructed defensive walls. Unable to establish a beachhead, the Mongol fleet anchored in the harbor, where it was attacked by groups of Japanese warriors, known as samurai, in small open boats, like the one depicted in a contemporary scroll recounting the battle (see photo). In daring raids, often at night, the samurai boarded the much larger Mongol ships and engaged their crews in deadly close-quarters combat.

Under pressure, the Korean fleet withdrew and made its rendezvous with the Chinese fleet, which had arrived in the waters off Japan. The combined forces then moved against another Japanese island, where they engaged in a fierce all-night sea battle that once again pitted the large seagoing ships of the Mongol armada against heavily outnumbered groups of samurai in small raiding boats. It was at this moment that a typhoon, named the *kamikaze*, or "divine wind," by the Japanese defenders, struck, destroying perhaps 30 percent of the Korean fleet and between 60 and 90 percent of the Chinese flotilla. In the aftermath, the Mongol commanders abandoned the invasion, leaving behind thousands of shipwrecked soldiers and sailors on the beaches. Such was the role of natural events in confounding human plans.

The defeat had little impact on Khubilai Khan, whose empire recovered quickly from the setback. But the khan never again turned his attentions to Japan, instead seeking to expand his empire elsewhere, including the islands of Southeast Asia, the target of another ambitious but unsuccessful naval expedition in the 1290s. In Japan, the Mongol invasion had a much greater long-term impact. The destruction of the Mongol fleet through what was perceived as divine intervention strengthened Japanese conceptions of their island nation as the *shinkoku*, or "land of the gods." Memories of triumph over the Mongols continued to resonate into the twentieth century. At the end of World War II, when Japan was again faced with foreign invasion, Japanese suicide pilots who sought to stop the Allied advance took the name *kamikazes*, evoking the memory of the typhoon that had turned back the Mongol invasion centuries earlier.

QUESTION

How does the Mongols' military defeat at the hands of the Japanese shape your understanding of the Mongols and their empire?

Various setbacks marked the outer limits of the Mongol Empire—the Mongols' withdrawal from Eastern Europe (1242), their defeat at Ain Jalut in Palestine at the hands of Egyptian forces (1260), the failure of their invasion of Japan owing to typhoons, and the difficulty of penetrating the tropical jungles of Southeast Asia. (See Zooming In: A Mongol Failure, page 460.) But what an empire it was! How could a Mongol confederation, with a total population of less than 1 million people and few resources beyond their livestock, assemble an imperial structure of such staggering transcontinental dimensions?

Explaining the Mongol Moment

Like the Roman Empire but far more rapidly, the Mongol realm grew of its own momentum without any grand scheme or blueprint for world conquest. Each fresh victory brought new resources for making war and new threats or insecurities that seemed to require further expansion. As the empire took shape and certainly by the

A Mongol Warrior Horseback-riding skills, honed in herding animals and adapted to military purposes, were central to Mongol conquests, as illustrated in this Ming dynasty Chinese painting of a mounted Mongol archer. (Victoria & Albert Museum, London, UK/Bridgeman Images)

end of his life, Chinggis Khan had come to see his career in terms of a universal mission. "I have accomplished a great work," he declared, "uniting the whole world in one empire."[12] Thus the Mongol Empire acquired an ideology in the course of its construction.

What made this "great work" possible? The odds seemed overwhelming, for China alone outnumbered the Mongols 100 to 1 and possessed incomparably greater resources. Furthermore, the Mongols did not enjoy any technological superiority over their many adversaries. They did, however, enjoy the luck of good timing, for China was divided, with the Song dynasty having already lost control of its northern territory to the pastoral Jurchen people, while the decrepit Abbasid caliphate, once the center of the Islamic world, had shrunk to a fraction of its earlier size. But clearly, the key to the Mongols' success lay in their army. According to one scholar, "Mongol armies were simply better led, organized, and disciplined than those of their opponents."[13] In an effort to diminish a divisive tribalism, Chinggis Khan reorganized the entire social structure of the Mongols into military units of 10, 100, 1,000, and 10,000 warriors, an arrangement that allowed for effective command and control. Conquered tribes, especially, were broken up, and their members were scattered among these new units, which enrolled virtually all men and supplied the cavalry forces of Mongol armies. A highly prestigious imperial guard also recruited members across tribal lines.

An impressive discipline and loyalty to their leaders characterized Mongol military forces, and discipline was reinforced by the provision that should any members of a unit desert in battle, all were subject to the death penalty. More positively, loyalty was cemented by the leaders' willingness to share the hardships of their men. "I eat the same food and am dressed in the same rags as my humble herdsmen," wrote Chinggis Khan. "I am always in the forefront, and in battle I am never at the rear."[14] Such discipline and loyalty made possible the elaborate tactics of encirclement, retreat, and deception that proved decisive in many a battle. Furthermore, the enormous flow of wealth from conquered civilizations benefited all Mongols, though not equally. Even ordinary Mongols could now dress in linens and silks rather than hides and felt, could own slaves derived from the many prisoners of war, and had far greater opportunities to improve their social position in a constantly expanding empire.

To compensate for their own small population, the Mongols incorporated huge numbers of conquered peoples into their military forces. "People who lived in felt tents"—mostly Mongol and Turkic pastoralists—were conscripted en masse into the cavalry units of the Mongol army, while settled agricultural peoples supplied the infantry and artillery forces. As the Mongols penetrated major civilizations, with their walled cities and elaborate fortifications, they quickly acquired Chinese techniques and technology of siege warfare. Some 1,000 Chinese artillery crews, for example, took part in the Mongol invasion of distant Persia. Beyond military recruitment, Mongols demanded that their conquered people serve as laborers, building roads and bridges and ferrying supplies over long distances. Artisans, craftsmen, and skilled people generally were carefully identified, spared from massacre, and often sent to distant regions of the empire where their services were required. A French goldsmith captured by Mongol forces in Hungary wound up as a slave in the Mongol capital of Karakorum (kah-rah-KOR-um), where he constructed an elaborate silver fountain that dispensed wine and other intoxicating drinks.

A further element in the military effectiveness of Mongol forces lay in a growing reputation for a ruthless brutality and utter destructiveness. City after city was utterly destroyed. Chinggis Khan's policy was clear: "Whoever submits shall be spared, but those who resist, they shall be destroyed with their wives, children and dependents . . . so that the others who hear and see should fear and not act the same."[15] (See Working with Evidence, Source 11.3, page 487.) One scholar explained such policies in this way: "Extremely conscious of their small numbers and fearful of rebellion, Chinggis often chose to annihilate a region's entire population, if it appeared too troublesome to govern."[16] These policies also served as a form of psychological warfare, a practical inducement to surrender for those who knew of the Mongol terror. Historians continue to debate the extent and uniqueness of the Mongols' brutality, but their reputation for unwavering harshness proved a military asset.

Underlying the purely military dimensions of the Mongols' success was an impressive ability to mobilize both the human and material resources of their growing empire. Elaborate census-taking allowed Mongol leaders to know what was available to them and made possible the systematic taxation of conquered people. An effective system of relay stations, about a day's ride apart, provided rapid communication across the empire and fostered trade as well. The beginnings of a centralized bureaucracy with various specialized offices took shape in the new capital of Karakorum. There scribes translated official decrees into the various languages of the empire, such as Persian, Uighur, Chinese, and Tibetan.

Other policies appealed to various groups among the conquered peoples of the empire. Interested in fostering commerce, Mongol rulers often offered merchants 10 percent or more above their asking price and allowed them the free use of the relay stations for transporting their goods. In administering the conquered regions, Mongols held the highest decision-making posts, but Chinese and Muslim officials held many advisory and lower-level positions in China and Persia, respectively. In religious matters, the Mongols welcomed and supported many religious traditions—Buddhist, Christian, Muslim, Daoist—as long as they did not become the focus of political opposition. This policy of religious toleration allowed Muslims to seek converts among Mongol troops and afforded Christians much greater freedom than they had enjoyed under Muslim rule. One of Chinggis Khan's successors, Mongke, arranged a debate among representatives of several religious faiths, after which he concluded: "Just as God gave different fingers to the hand, so has He given different ways to men."[17] Such economic, administrative, and religious policies provided some benefits and a place within the empire—albeit subordinate—for many of its conquered peoples.

PRACTICING HISTORICAL THINKING

What accounts for the political and military success of the Mongols?

Encountering the Mongols in China, Persia, and Russia

The Mongol moment in world history represented an enormous cultural encounter between pastoralists and the settled civilizations of Eurasia. The process of conquest, the length and nature of Mongol rule, the impact on local people, and the extent of Mongol assimilation into the cultures of the conquered—all this and more varied considerably across the Eurasian domains of the empire. The experiences of China, Persia, and Russia provide brief glimpses into several expressions of this massive encounter of cultures.

China and the Mongols

Long the primary target for pastoral steppe dwellers in search of agrarian wealth, China proved the most difficult and extended of the Mongols' many conquests, lasting some seventy years, from 1209 to 1279. The invasion began in northern China, which had been ruled for several centuries by various dynasties of pastoral origin, and was characterized by destruction and plunder on a massive scale. Southern China, under the control of the native Song dynasty, was a different story, for there the Mongols were far less violent and more concerned with accommodating the local population. Landowners, for example, were guaranteed their estates in exchange for their support or at least their neutrality. By whatever methods, the outcome was the unification of a divided China, a treasured ideal among educated Chinese. This achievement persuaded some of them that the Mongols had indeed been granted the Mandate of Heaven and, despite their foreign origins, were legitimate rulers. One highly educated Chinese scholar wrote a short biography of a recently deceased Mongol official, praising him for curtailing the violence of Mongol soldiers, offering leniency to rebels, and providing tax relief and food during a famine. In short, he was behaving like a good Confucian Chinese official.

Having acquired China, what were the Mongols to do with it? One possibility, apparently considered by the Great Khan Ogodei (ERG-uh-day) in the 1230s, was to exterminate everyone in northern China and turn the country into pastureland for Mongol herds. That suggestion, fortunately, was rejected in favor of extracting as much wealth as possible from the country's advanced civilization. Doing so meant some accommodation to Chinese culture and ways of governing, for the Mongols had no experience with the operation of a complex agrarian society.

That accommodation took many forms. The Mongols made use of Chinese administrative practices and techniques of taxation as well as their postal system. They gave themselves a Chinese dynastic title, the Yuan, suggesting a new beginning in Chinese history. They transferred their capital from Karakorum in Mongolia to what is now Beijing, building a wholly new capital city there known as Khanbalik, the "city of the khan." Thus the Mongols were now rooting themselves solidly on the soil of a highly sophisticated civilization, well removed from their homeland on the steppes. **Khubilai Khan** (koo-buh-l'eye kahn), the grandson of Chinggis Khan and China's Mongol ruler from 1271 to 1294 who initiated the **Yuan dynasty**, ordered a set of Chinese-style ancestral tablets to honor his ancestors and posthumously awarded them Chinese names. Many of his policies evoked the values of a benevolent Confucian-inspired Chinese emperor, as he improved roads, built canals, lowered some taxes, patronized scholars and artists, limited the death penalty and torture, supported peasant agriculture, and prohibited Mongols from grazing their animals on peasants' farmland. (See Working with Evidence, Source 11.2, page 483, for various impressions of Khubilai Khan.) Mongol khans also made use of traditional Confucian rituals, supported the building of some Daoist temples, and were particularly attracted to a Tibetan form of Buddhism, which returned the favor with strong political support for the invaders.

Guided Reading Question

■ **CHANGE**

How did Mongol rule change China? In what ways were the Mongols changed by China?

Despite these accommodations, Mongol rule was still harsh, exploitative, foreign, and resented. Marco Polo, who was in China at the time, reported that some Mongol officials or their Muslim intermediaries treated Chinese "just like slaves," demanding bribes for services, ordering arbitrary executions, and seizing women at will—all of which generated outrage and hostility. The Mongols did not become Chinese, nor did they accommodate every aspect of Chinese culture. Deep inside the new capital, the royal family and court could continue to experience something of steppe life as their animals roamed freely in large open areas, planted with steppe grass. Many of the Mongol elite much preferred to live, eat, sleep, and give birth in the traditional tents that sprouted everywhere. In administering the country, the Mongols largely ignored the traditional Chinese examination system and relied heavily on foreigners, particularly Muslims from Central Asia and the Middle East, to serve as officials, while keeping the top decision-making posts for

Khubilai Khan This famous portrait of Khubilai Khan was probably painted by Aniko (1244–1306), a Nepalese artist and architect who designed a number of buildings for China's Mongol ruler. (Science History Images/Alamy)

themselves. Few Mongols learned Chinese, and Mongol law discriminated against the Chinese, reserving for them the most severe punishments. Furthermore, the Mongols honored and supported merchants and artisans far more than Confucian bureaucrats had been inclined to do.

In social life, the Mongols forbade intermarriage and prohibited Chinese scholars from learning the Mongol script. Mongol women never adopted foot binding and scandalized the Chinese by mixing freely with men at official gatherings and riding to the hunt with their husbands. The Mongol ruler Khubilai Khan retained the Mongol tradition of relying heavily on female advisers, the chief of which was his favorite wife, Chabi. Ironically, she urged him to accommodate his Chinese subjects, forcefully and successfully opposing an early plan to turn Chinese farmland into pastureland. Unlike many Mongols, biased as they were against farming, Chabi recognized the advantages of agriculture and its ability to generate tax revenue. With a vision of turning Mongol rule into a lasting dynasty that might rank with the splendor of the Tang, she urged her husband to emulate the best practices of that earlier era of Chinese history.

However one assesses Mongol rule in China, it was relatively brief, lasting little more than a century. By the mid-fourteenth century, intense factionalism among the Mongols, rapidly rising prices, furious epidemics of the plague, and growing peasant rebellions combined to force the Mongols out of China. By 1368, rebel forces had triumphed, and thousands of Mongols returned to their homeland in the steppes. For several centuries, they remained a periodic threat to China, but during the Ming dynasty that followed, the memory of their often-brutal and alien rule stimulated a renewed commitment to Confucian values and restrictive gender practices and an effort to wipe out all traces of the Mongols' impact.

Persia and the Mongols

A second great civilization conquered by the Mongols was Islamic Persia. There the Mongol takeover was far more abrupt than the extended process of conquest in China. A first invasion (1219–1221), led by Chinggis Khan himself, was followed thirty years later by a second assault (1251–1258) under his grandson **Hulegu** (HE-luh-gee), who became the first il-khan (subordinate khan) of Persia. Although Persia had been repeatedly attacked, from the invasion of Alexander the Great to that of the Arabs and Turkic peoples, nothing prepared it for the Mongols. In the eyes of Persian Muslims, the Mongols were infidels, and their stunning victory was a profound shock to people accustomed to viewing history as the progressive expansion of Islamic rule. Furthermore, Mongol military victory brought in its wake a degree of ferocity and slaughter that had no parallel in Persian experience. (See Working with Evidence, Source 11.3, page 487, for an account of the Mongol seizure of Bukhara.) The Persian historian Juvaini described it in fearful terms:

> Every town and every village has been several times subjected to pillage and massacre and has suffered this confusion for years so that even though there

be generation and increase until the Resurrection the population will not attain to a tenth part of what it was before.[18]

The sacking of Baghdad in 1258, which put an end to the Abbasid caliphate, was accompanied by the massacre of more than 200,000 people, according to Hulegu himself.

Beyond this human catastrophe lay the damage to Persian and Iraqi agriculture and to those who tilled the soil. Heavy taxes, sometimes collected twenty or thirty times a year and often under torture or whipping, pushed large numbers of peasants off their land. Furthermore, the in-migration of pastoral Mongols, together with their immense herds of sheep and goats, turned much agricultural land into pasture and sometimes into desert. As a result, a fragile system of underground water channels that provided irrigation to the fields was neglected, and much good agricultural land was reduced to waste. Some sectors of the Persian economy gained, however. Wine production increased because the Mongols were fond of alcohol, and the Persian silk industry benefited from close contact with a Mongol-ruled China. In general, though, even more so than in China, Mongol rule in Persia represented "disaster on a grand and unparalleled scale."[19]

Guided Reading Question

■ **COMPARISON**
How was Mongol rule in Persia different from that in China?

Nonetheless, the Mongols in Persia were themselves transformed far more than their counterparts in China. They made extensive use of the sophisticated Persian bureaucracy, leaving the greater part of government operations in Persian hands. During the reign of Ghazan (haz-ZAHN) (1295–1304), they made some efforts to repair the damage caused by earlier policies of ruthless exploitation by rebuilding damaged cities and repairing neglected irrigation works. Most important, the Mongols who conquered Persia became Muslims, following the lead of Ghazan, who converted to Islam in 1295. No such widespread conversion to the culture of the conquered occurred in China or in Christian Russia. Members of the court and Mongol elites learned at least some Persian, unlike most of their counterparts in China. A number of Mongols also turned to farming, abandoning their pastoral ways, while some married local people.

When the Mongol dynasty of Hulegu's descendants collapsed in the 1330s for lack of a suitable heir, the Mongols were not driven out of Persia as they had been from China. Rather,

The Mongols and Islam in Persia This image from the first half of the fourteenth century depicts a Mongol prince studying the Quran in what is likely a mosque tent. The arch at the left marks the *mihrab*, which points toward Mecca and indicates the direction that worshippers should face during ritual prayers. Above it is an inscription reading "Allah is the Ruler." The conversion of the Mongols in Persia to Islam was a crucial development in their rule over the region. (bpk Bildagentur/Staatsbibliothek zu Berlin, Stiftung Preussicher Kulturbesitz/Photo: Ellwardt/Art Resource, NY)

Mongol Rulers and Their Women The wives of Mongol rulers exercised considerable influence at court. This fourteenth-century painting shows Chinggis Khan's fourth son, Tului, the ruler of the Mongol heartland after his father's death, with his Christian wife Sorgaqtani. After her husband's early death from alcoholism, she maneuvered her children, including Khubilai Khan, into powerful positions and strongly encouraged them in the direction of religious toleration. (Bibliothèque Nationale de France, Paris, France/akg-images)

they and their Turkic allies simply disappeared, assimilated into Persian society. From a Persian point of view, the barbarians had been civilized, and Persians had successfully resisted cultural influence from their uncivilized conquerors. When the great Persian historian Rashid al-Din wrote his famous history of the Mongols, he apologized for providing information about women, generally unmentioned in Islamic writing, explaining that Mongols treated their women equally and included them in decisions of the court.[20] Now Persian rulers could return to their more patriarchal ways.

Russia and the Mongols

When the Mongol military machine rolled over Russia between 1237 and 1240, it encountered a relatively new third-wave civilization located on the far eastern fringe of Christendom. Whatever political unity this new civilization of Kievan Rus had earlier enjoyed was now gone, and various independent princes proved unable to unite even in the face of the Mongol onslaught. Although they had interacted extensively with pastoral people of the steppes north of the Black Sea, Mongol ferocity was stunning. City after city fell to Mongol forces, which were now armed with the catapults and battering rams adopted from Chinese or Muslim sources. What followed was described in horrific terms by Russian chroniclers, who reported mass slaughter of "men, women, and children, monks, nuns and priests" and the violation of "good women and girls in the presence of their mothers and sisters." From the survivors and the cities that surrendered early, laborers and skilled craftsmen were deported to other Mongol lands or sold into slavery. A number of Russian crafts were so depleted of their workers that they did not recover for a century or more.

If the violence of initial conquest bore similarities to the experiences of Persia, Russia's incorporation into the Mongol Empire was very different. To the Mongols, it was the Kipchak (KIP-chahk) Khanate, named after the Kipchak Turkic-speaking peoples north of the Caspian and Black seas, among whom the Mongols had settled. To the Russians, it was the "**Khanate of the Golden Horde**." By whatever name, the Mongols had conquered Russia, but they did not occupy it as they had China and Persia. Thus in Russia there were no garrisoned cities, permanently stationed administrators, or Mongol settlers. From the Mongol point of view, Russia had little to offer. Its economy was not nearly so sophisticated or productive as that of more established civilizations; nor was it located on major international trade routes. It was simply not worth the expense of occupying. Furthermore, the availability of extensive steppe lands for pasturing their flocks north of the Black and Caspian seas meant that the Mongols could maintain their preferred pastoral way of life, while remaining in easy reach of Russian cities when the need arose to send further military expeditions. They could dominate and exploit Russia from the steppes.

And exploit they certainly did. Russian princes received appointment from the khan and were required to send substantial tribute to the Mongol capital at Sarai, located on the lower Volga River. A variety of additional taxes created a heavy burden, especially on the peasantry, while continuing border raids sent tens of thousands of Russians into slavery. The Mongol impact was highly uneven, however. The Russian Orthodox Church flourished under the Mongol policy of religious toleration, for it received exemption from many taxes. Russian nobles who participated in Mongol raids earned a share of the loot. Some cities, such as Kiev, resisted the Mongols and were devastated, while others surrendered and collaborated and were left undamaged. Moscow in particular emerged as the primary collector of tribute for the Mongols, with one of its rulers, Ivan I, earning the nickname Ivan the Moneybags because of the riches that flowed to him from this position. Moscow's princes parlayed this position into a leading role as the nucleus of a renewed Russian state when Mongol domination receded in the fifteenth century.

The absence of direct Mongol rule had implications for the Mongols themselves, for they were far less influenced by or assimilated within Russian cultures than their counterparts in China and Persia had been. The Mongols in China had turned themselves into a Chinese dynasty, with the khan as a Chinese emperor. Some learned calligraphy, and a few came to appreciate Chinese poetry. In Persia, the

Guided Reading Question

■ **COMPARISON**
What was distinctive about the Russian experience of Mongol rule?

Mongol Russia This sixteenth-century painting depicts the Mongol burning of the Russian city of Ryazan in 1237. Similar destruction awaited many Russian towns that resisted the invaders. (Universal Images Group/Sovfoto/akg-images)

Mongols had converted to Islam, with some becoming farmers. Not so in Russia. There "the Mongols of the Golden Horde were still spending their days in the saddle and their nights in tents."[21] They could dominate Russia from the adjacent steppes without in any way adopting Russian culture. Even though they remained culturally separate from Christian Russians, eventually the Mongols assimilated to the culture and the Islamic faith of the Kipchak people of the steppes, and in the process they lost their distinct identity and became Kipchaks.

Despite this domination from a distance, "the impact of the Mongols on Russia was, if anything, greater than on China and Iran [Persia]," according to a leading scholar.[22] Russian princes, who were more or less left alone if they paid the required tribute and taxes, found it useful to adopt the Mongols' weapons, diplomatic rituals, court practices, taxation system, and military draft. Mongol policies facilitated, although not intentionally, the rise of Moscow as the core of a new Russian state, and that state made good use of the famous Mongol mounted courier service. Mongol policies also strengthened the hold of the Russian Orthodox Church and enabled it to penetrate the rural areas more fully than before. Some Russians, seeking to explain their country's economic backwardness and political autocracy in modern times, have held the Mongols responsible for both conditions, though most historians consider such views vastly exaggerated.

Divisions among the Mongols, the disruptive influence of plague, and the growing strength of the Russian state—centered now on the city of Moscow—enabled the Russians to break the Mongols' hold by the end of the fifteenth century. With the earlier demise of Mongol rule in China and Persia, and now in Russia, the Mongols had retreated from their brief but spectacular incursion into the civilizations of outer Eurasia. Nonetheless, they continued to periodically threaten these civilizations for several centuries, until their homelands were absorbed into the expanding Russian and Chinese empires. But the Mongol moment in world history was over.

The Mongol Empire as a Eurasian Network

During the third-wave era, Chinese culture and Buddhism provided a measure of integration among the peoples of East Asia; Christianity did the same for Europe, while the realm of Islam connected most of the lands in between. But it was the

Mongol Empire, during the thirteenth and fourteenth centuries, that brought all of these regions into a single interacting network, enabling the circulation of goods, information, disease, and styles of warfare all across Eurasia and parts of Africa.

Toward a World Economy

The Mongols themselves did not produce much of value for distant markets, nor were they active traders. Nonetheless, they consistently promoted international commerce, largely so that they could tax it and thus extract wealth from more developed civilizations. The Great Khan Ogodei, for example, often paid well over the asking price to attract merchants to his capital of Karakorum. The Mongols also provided financial backing for caravans, introduced standardized weights and measures, and gave tax breaks to merchants.

In providing a relatively secure environment for merchants making the long and arduous journey across Central Asia between Europe and China, the Mongol Empire brought the two ends of the Eurasian world into closer contact than ever before and launched a new phase in the history of the Silk Roads. Marco Polo was only the most famous of many European merchants, mostly from Italian cities, who made their way to China through the Mongol Empire. So many traders attempted the journey that guidebooks circulated with much useful advice about the trip. Merchants returned with tales of rich lands and prosperous commercial opportunities, but what they described were long-established trading networks of which Europeans had been largely ignorant.

The Mongol trading circuit was a central element in an even larger commercial network that linked much of the Afro-Eurasian world in the thirteenth century (see Map 11.2). Mongol-ruled China was the fulcrum of this vast system, connecting the overland route through the Mongol Empire with the oceanic routes through the South China Sea and Indian Ocean.

Guided Reading Question

....

■ **CONNECTION**
What kinds of cross-cultural interactions did the Mongol Empire generate?

Diplomacy on a Eurasian Scale

Not only did the Mongol Empire facilitate long-distance commerce, but it also prompted diplomatic relationships from one end of Eurasia to the other. As their invasion of Russia spilled over into Eastern Europe, Mongol armies destroyed Polish, German, and Hungarian forces in 1241–1242 and seemed poised to march on Central and Western Europe. But the death of the Great Khan Ogodei required Mongol leaders to return to Mongolia, and Western Europe lacked adequate pasture for Mongol herds. Thus Western Europe was spared the trauma of conquest, but fearing the possible return of the Mongols, both the pope and European rulers dispatched delegations to the Mongol capital, mostly led by Franciscan friars. They hoped to learn something about Mongol intentions, to secure Mongol aid in the Christian crusade against Islam, and, if possible, to convert Mongols to Christianity. These efforts were largely in vain, for no alliance or widespread conversion occurred. In fact, one of these missions came back with a letter for the pope from the Great Khan Guyuk, demanding that Europeans submit to him.

MAPPING HISTORY

Map 11.2 Trade and Disease in the Fourteenth Century

The Mongol Empire played a major role in the commercial integration of the Eurasian world as well as in the spread of the plague across this vast area.

READING THE MAP: Which circuits of trade played the greatest role in the spread of the plague?

INTERPRETING THE MAP: What does the map suggest about the regions—temperate, tropical (along the equator), subarctic—in which the plague spread most widely?

Perhaps the most important outcome of these diplomatic probings was the useful information about lands to the east that European missions brought back. Those reports contributed to a dawning European awareness of a wider world, and they have certainly provided later historians with much useful information about the Mongols. Somewhat later, in 1287, the il-khanate of Persia sought an alliance with European powers to take Jerusalem and crush the forces of Islam, but the

Persian Mongols' conversion to Islam soon put an end to any such anti-Muslim coalition.

Within the Mongol Empire itself, close relationships developed between the courts of Persia and China. They regularly exchanged ambassadors, shared intelligence information, fostered trade between their regions, and sent skilled workers back and forth. Thus political authorities all across Eurasia engaged in diplomatic relationships with one another to an unprecedented degree.

Cultural Exchange in the Mongol Realm

Accompanying these transcontinental economic and political relationships was a substantial exchange of peoples and cultures. Mongol policy forcibly transferred many thousands of skilled craftsmen and educated people from their homelands to distant parts of the empire, while the Mongols' religious tolerance and support of merchants drew missionaries and traders from afar. The Mongol capital at Karakorum was a cosmopolitan city with places of worship for Buddhists, Daoists, Muslims, and Christians. Chinggis Khan and several other Mongol rulers married Christian women. This relatively open Mongol outlook facilitated the exchange and blending of religious ideas. In Persia, for example, images of the Prophet Muhammad appeared, drawing on Chinese painting techniques and using Buddhist and Christian traditions as models. One such painting even portayed the birth of the Prophet in a distinctly Christian nativity scene. Actors and musicians from China, wrestlers from Persia, and a jester from Byzantium provided entertainment for the Mongol court. Persian and Arab doctors and administrators were sent to China, while Chinese physicians and engineers found their skills in demand in the Islamic world.

This movement of people facilitated the exchange of ideas and techniques, a process actively encouraged by Mongol authorities. A great deal of Chinese technology and artistic conventions—such as painting, printing, gunpowder weapons, compass navigation, high-temperature furnaces, and medical techniques—flowed westward. Acupuncture, for example, was poorly received in the Middle East because it required too much bodily contact for Muslim taste, even as Chinese techniques for diagnosing illness by taking the pulse of patients proved quite popular, as they involved minimal body contact. Muslim astronomers brought their skills and knowledge to China because Mongol authorities wanted "second opinions on the reading of heavenly signs and portents" and assistance in constructing the accurate calendars needed for ritual purposes.[23] Plants and crops likewise circulated within the Mongol domain. Lemons and carrots from the Middle East found a welcome reception in China, while the Persian il-khan Ghazan sent envoys to India, China, and elsewhere to seek "seeds of things which are unique in that land."[24] Europeans arguably gained more than most from these exchanges, for they had long been cut off from the fruitful interchange with Asia, and in comparison to the Islamic and Chinese worlds, they were less technologically developed. Now they could reap the benefits of new technology, new crops, and new knowledge of a wider world.

Debating Empire

The empires of the third-wave era—Chinese, Byzantine, Arab, and Mongol—have attracted considerable attention from historians, as have both earlier and later empires. And no wonder. Over the past 2,500 years, more people have lived in empires, where multiple distinct ethnic communities were ruled and often exploited by a dominant group, than in any other type of state or society.

Historians have long been intrigued by the various ways in which empires were born. The early Chinese and Egyptian empires, for example, took root in the heartland of already settled agricultural regions. The Persian, Greek, and Roman empires, by contrast, expanded from the edges of established agriculture civilizations, while the pastoralist empires of the Arabs, Mongols, and Turks found their origins in regions without much settled agriculture. More recently, European powers conquered and colonized regions thousands of miles from their home countries, creating the first overseas empires. But some civilizations developed for centuries without generating empires, such as those in ancient Sumer, in post-Roman Europe, and among the cities of the Maya and the Niger River valley. Was it because the rivalry of many small states or cities confounded efforts to develop larger imperial systems?

Other variations on the imperial theme have likewise surfaced in the work of historians. Empires were most frequently constructed through violence and conquest, but with important exceptions. The Athenian empire, for instance, started as a voluntary league. The European domains of the Habsburg Empire were largely brought together through family marriage strategies and inheritance. Some empires were constructed deliberately, like those of the Greek ruler Alexander the Great, the first Chinese emperor Qin Shihuangdi, and the Mongol leader Chinggis Khan. Others, like the Roman and Arab empires, grew more slowly in reaction to frontier insecurity or internal pressures. Autocrats frequently ruled over imperial enterprises, but democracies and republics have also created empires, including two of the largest, the ancient Roman and nineteenth-century British empires. Scholars have emphasized the durability of empires like that of Byzantium, which persisted for over a millennium, or its Ottoman successor, which survived for six centuries. But abortive or short-lived imperial adventures are also common, including that of the Mauryan dynasty in India, Axum in Northeast Africa, and Japan's East Asian empire in the early twentieth century. Explaining these variations provides grist for the mill of historical controversy.

So too does the collapse of empires. Historians have discovered that few imperial regimes have been toppled by internal rebellions of the oppressed. Even the largest rebellions, like the Yellow Turban in Han China or Spartacus's slaves in ancient Rome, were ultimately crushed. More commonly, empires fell or fragmented due to external invasion, as happened to the Aztec and Inca empires, or when the ruling elite split, as was the case following the deaths of Alexander the Great, Charlemagne, and Chinggis Khan. The end of the western Roman Empire has fostered endless controversy, with scholars emphasizing various factors: economic decline owing to war, corruption, and overreliance on slavery; penetration of the empire and its military forces by Germanic peoples; frequent turnover of emperors, often by murder; the invasion of the Huns; the coming of Christianity and the erosion of traditional values; environmental degradation; and many others. Scholars even disagree about when or if the empire ended. Was it in 476 C.E. when Emperor Romulus was overthrown by a German warlord? Or had the empire ceased to function as a state decades before Romulus was deposed? Still others date its demise to the

And almost alone among the peoples of Eurasia, they could do so without having suffered the devastating consequences of Mongol conquest. In these circumstances, some historians have argued, lay the roots of Europe's remarkable rise to global prominence in the centuries that followed. (See Controversies: Debating Empire, above, for a look at how historians think about empires.)

fall of Constantinople nearly 1,000 years later in 1453, arguing that the Roman Empire lived on in Byzantium.

Historians have also differed in their assessments of empire, in part reflecting the cultural attitudes of the times in which they wrote. The rapid expansion of European imperial enterprises in Africa and parts of Asia in the late nineteenth century coincided with the emergence of university history departments and professional historians in Europe and the United States. In this context, many Western historians produced studies of the remarkable accomplishments of empires through history, focusing on their military and administrative successes and exploring how imperial projects brought "civilization" to "traditional" societies. Historians identified the freer spread of ideas, goods, and people; the standardization of laws and currency; and the building of infrastructure and establishment of peace as advances for humankind as a whole—or, as Lord Curzon, a prominent imperial official and writer about empire, put it in 1894: "the British Empire is under Providence the greatest instrument for good that the world has seen."[25]

However, an increasingly negative assessment of empire gained influence among historians as the twentieth century progressed. Already in the nineteenth century some historians had emphasized the exploitative and oppressive aspects of modern European empires, which were built to feed the capitalist world's insatiable appetite for raw materials and markets. But the global spread of anticolonial ideologies and the breakup of European empires in the aftermath of World War II sparked a reassessment of imperial rule by historians and the emergence of the new fields of colonial and postcolonial studies in which the experiences of colonized peoples found voice. These historians put new emphasis on the massive bloodshed and oppression—enslavement, impoverishment, forced tribute and taxes, deportation—that frequently accompanied imperial conquest and rule. They also questioned the alleged "civilizing" missions of empires,

instead highlighting the repression or destruction of the cultures and societies of conquered peoples. Commenting on this more negative assessment of empire, one scholar has recently noted that "in our time 'imperialist' ranks second only to 'fascist' in the lexicon of political swear words."[26]

Over the past century, empires have been largely replaced by nation-states organized around the very different idea that sovereign countries should be composed of a single people or ethnic group. This transformation of the political landscape has sparked some nostalgic reflections on empires, perhaps none so influential or controversial as that of Niall Ferguson, a historian of the British Empire who recently argued that European empires were often better for their subjects than the local regimes they replaced. "It's hard to make the case . . . ," he declared, "that somehow the world would have been better off if the Europeans had stayed home. . . . Imperial guilt can lead to self-flagellation . . . [and] very simplistic judgements."[27] Other scholars, when comparing empires to modern nation-states, have found advantages to empires, especially their tolerance toward ethnic minorities within their boundaries.

The theme of empire resonates still among historians and the general public in the early twenty-first century. Is contemporary Russia seeking to re-create the old Russian Empire? Does Turkey want to replicate something of the Ottoman Empire? Does the global reach of the United States represent a new kind of empire, even if a declining one? The debates continue.

QUESTIONS TO CONSIDER

1. What variations in the experience of empires have historians noticed?
2. How might you account for their differing assessments of empire?

The Plague: An Afro-Eurasian Pandemic

Any benefits derived from participation in Mongol networks of communication and exchange must be measured alongside the hemispheric catastrophe known as the "**plague**" or the "pestilence" and later called the **Black Death**. Originating most likely in China, the bacteria responsible for the disease, known as *Yersinia pestis*, spread across the trade routes of the vast Mongol Empire in the early fourteenth century (see Map 11.2, page 472). Carried by rodents and transmitted by fleas to humans, the plague erupted initially in 1331 in northeastern China and had reached the Middle East and Western Europe by 1347. In 1409, the plague reached East Africa, probably by way of the famous Chinese maritime expeditions that encompassed the Indian Ocean basin.

Guided Reading Question

▪ **CHANGE**
Disease changes societies. How might this argument apply to the plague?

The disease itself was associated with swelling of the lymph nodes, terrible headaches, high fever, and internal bleeding just below the skin. Infected people generally died within a few days. In the densely populated civilizations of China, the Islamic world, and Europe as well as in the steppe lands of the pastoralists, the plague claimed enormous numbers of human victims, causing a sharp contraction in Eurasian population for a century or more. Chroniclers reported rates of death that ranged from 50 to 90 percent of the affected population, depending on the time and place. A recent study suggests that about half of Europe's people perished during the initial outbreak of 1348–1350.[28] A fifteenth-century Egyptian historian wrote that within a month of the plague's arrival in 1349, "Cairo had become an abandoned desert. . . . Everywhere one heard lamentations and one could not pass by any house without being overwhelmed by the howling."[29] The Middle East generally had lost perhaps one-third of its population by the early fifteenth century.[30] The intense first wave of the plague was followed by periodic visitations over the next several centuries. However, other regions of the Eastern Hemisphere, especially India and sub-Saharan Africa, were much less affected.

In those places where it struck hardest, the plague left thoughtful people grasping for language with which to describe a horror of such unprecedented dimensions. One Italian man, who had buried all five of his children with his own hands, wrote in 1348 that "so many have died that everyone believes it is the end of the world."[31] Another Italian, the Renaissance scholar Francesco Petrarch, was equally stunned by the impact of the Black Death; he wrote to a friend in 1349:

> When at any time has such a thing been seen or spoken of? Has what happened in these years ever been read about: empty houses, derelict cities, ruined estates, fields strewn with cadavers, a horrible and vast solitude encompassing the whole world? Consult historians, they are silent; ask physicians, they are stupefied; seek the answers from philosophers, they shrug their shoulders, furrow their brows, and with fingers pressed against their lips, bid you be silent. Will posterity believe these things, when we who have seen it can scarcely believe it?[32]

In the Islamic world, the famous historian Ibn Khaldun, who had lost both of his parents to the plague, also wrote about it in apocalyptic terms:

> Civilization in both the East and the West was visited by a destructive plague which devastated nations and caused populations to vanish. It swallowed up many of the good things of civilization and wiped them out. . . . It was as if the voice of existence had called out for oblivion and restriction, and the world responded to its call.[33]

Beyond its immediate devastation, the Black Death worked longer-term social changes in Europe, the region where the plague's impact has been most thoroughly studied. Labor shortages following the initial outburst provoked sharp conflict between scarce workers, who sought higher wages or better conditions, and the rich, who resisted those demands. A series of peasant revolts in the fourteenth century reflected this tension, which also undermined the practice of serfdom. That labor shortage also may have fostered a greater interest in technological innovation and created, at least for a time, more employment opportunities for women. Thus a resilient European civilization survived a cataclysm that had the power to destroy it. In a strange way, that catastrophe may have actually fostered its future growth.

Whatever its impact in particular places, the plague also had larger consequences. Ironically, that human disaster, born of the Mongol network, was a primary reason for the demise of that network in the fourteenth and fifteenth centuries. Population contracted, cities declined, and the volume of trade diminished all across the Mongol world. By 1350, the Mongol Empire itself was in disarray, and within a century the Mongols had lost control of Chinese, Persian, and Russian civilizations. The Central Asian trade route, so critical to the entire Afro-Eurasian world economy, largely closed.

This disruption of the Mongol-based land routes to the East, coupled with a desire to avoid Muslim

The Plague This illustration depicts a European doctor visiting a patient with the plague. Notice that the doctor and others around the bedside cover their noses to prevent infection. During the Black Death, doctors were often criticized for refusing to treat dying patients, as they feared for their own lives.

intermediaries, provided incentives for Europeans to take to the sea in their continuing efforts to reach the riches of Asia. Their naval technology gave them military advantages on the seas, much as the Mongols' skill with the bow and their mobility on horseback gave these pastoralists a decisive edge in land battles. As Europeans penetrated Asian and Atlantic waters in the sixteenth century, they took on, in some ways, the role of the Mongols in organizing and fostering world trade and in creating a network of communication and exchange over an even larger area. Like the Mongols, Europeans were people on the periphery of the major established civilizations; they too were economically less developed in comparison to Chinese and Islamic civilizations. Both Mongols and Europeans were apt to forcibly plunder the wealthier civilizations they encountered, and European empire building in the Americas, like that of the Mongols in Eurasia, brought devastating disease and catastrophic population decline in its wake.[34] Europeans, of course, brought far more of their own culture and many more of their own people to the societies they conquered, as Christianity, European languages, settler societies, and Western science and technology took root within their empires. Although their imperial presence lasted far longer and operated on a much larger scale, European actions at the beginning of their global expansion bore some resemblance to those of their Mongol predecessors. Perhaps they were, as one historian put it, "the Mongols of the seas."[35]

REFLECTIONS

Changing Images of Pastoral Peoples

Historians frequently change their minds, and long-term consensus on most important matters has been difficult to achieve. For example, until recently, pastoralists generally received bad press in history books. Normally they entered the story only when they were threatening or destroying established civilizations. In presenting a largely negative image of pastoral peoples, historians were reflecting the long-held attitudes of literate elites in the civilizations of Eurasia. Fearing and usually despising such peoples, educated observers in China, the Middle East, and Europe often described them as bloodthirsty savages or barbarians, bringing only chaos and destruction in their wake. Han Kuan, a Chinese scholar of the first century B.C.E., described the Xiongnu people as "abandoned by Heaven . . . in foodless desert wastes, without proper houses, clothed in animal hides, eating their meat uncooked and drinking blood."[36] To the Christian Saint Jerome (340–420 C.E.), the Huns "filled the whole earth with slaughter and panic alike as they flitted hither and thither on their swift horses."[37] Almost a thousand years later, the famous Arab historian Ibn Khaldun described pastoralists in a very similar fashion: "It is their nature to plunder whatever other people possess."[38]

Because pastoral peoples generally did not have written languages, the sources available to historians came from less-than-unbiased observers in adjacent agricultural civilizations. Furthermore, in the long-running conflict across the farming/pastoral frontier, agricultural civilizations ultimately triumphed. Over the centuries, some pastoralist or semi-agricultural peoples, such as the Germanic tribes of Europe and the Arabs, created new civilizations. Others, such as the Turkic and Mongol peoples, took over existing civilizations or were encompassed within established agrarian empires. By the early twentieth century, and in most places much earlier, pastoral peoples everywhere had lost their former independence and had often shed their pastoral life as well. Since "winners" usually write history, the negative views of pastoralists held by agrarian civilizations normally prevailed.

Reflecting more inclusive contemporary values, historians in recent decades have sought to present a more balanced picture of pastoralists' role in world history, emphasizing what they created as well as what they destroyed. These historians have highlighted the achievements of herding peoples, such as their adaptation to inhospitable environments; their technological innovations; their development of horse-, camel-, or cattle-based cultures; their role in fostering cross-cultural exchange; and their state-building efforts.

A less critical or judgmental posture toward the Mongols may also owe something to the "total wars" and genocides of the twentieth century, in which the mass slaughter of civilians became a strategy to induce enemy surrender. During the cold war, the United States and the Soviet Union were prepared, apparently, to obliterate each other's entire population with nuclear weapons in response to an attack. In light of this recent history, Mongol massacres may appear a little less unique. Historians living in the glass houses of contemporary societies are perhaps more reluctant to cast stones at the Mongols. In understanding the Mongols, as in so much else, historians are shaped by the times and circumstances of their own lives as much as by "what really happened" in the past.

Second Thoughts

What's the Significance?

pastoral societies, 450
Modun, 455
Xiongnu Empire, 455
Turkic peoples, 455
Seljuk Turkic Empire, 456
Almoravid Empire, 457
Temujin (Chinggis Khan), 459
Mongol world war, 460
Khubilai Khan, 465
Yuan dynasty (China), 465
Hulegu, 466
Khanate of the Golden Horde, 469
Black Death (plague), 475

Big Picture Questions

1. What accounts for the often-negative attitudes of settled societies toward the pastoral peoples living on their borders?

2. Why have historians often neglected pastoral peoples' role in world history? How would you assess the perspective of this chapter toward the Mongols? Does the chapter strike you as negative and critical of the Mongols, as bending over backward to portray them in a positive light, or as a balanced presentation?

3. In what different ways did Mongol rule affect the Islamic world, Russia, China, and Europe? In what respects did it foster Eurasian integration?

4. Why did the Mongol Empire last only a relatively short time?

5. **Looking Back:** In what ways did the Mongol Empire resemble previous empires (Arab, Roman, Chinese, or the Greek empire of Alexander, for example), and in what ways did it differ from them?

Next Steps: For Further Study

John Aberth, *The First Horseman: Disease in Human History* (2007). A global study of the history of disease, with a fine chapter on the Black Death.

Thomas Allsen, *Culture and Conquest in Mongol Eurasia* (2001). A history of cultural exchange within the Mongol realm, particularly between China and the Islamic world.

Thomas J. Barfield, *The Nomadic Alternative* (1993). An anthropological and historical survey of pastoral peoples on a global basis.

Carter Finley, *The Turks in World History* (2005). The evolution of Turkic-speaking people, from their nomadic origins to the twentieth century.

Carl Fredrik Sverdrup, *The Mongol Conquests* (2017). A thorough analysis of the military dimension of the Mongol experience.

Jack Weatherford, *Genghis Khan and the Making of the Modern World* (2010). A lively, well-written, and balanced account of the world the Mongols made and the legacy they left for the future.

"Horseback Riding and Bronze Age Pastoralism in the Eurasian Steppes," http://www .youtube.com/watch?v=QapUGZOObjA. An illustrated lecture on the origins of pastoralism by David W. Anthony, a prominent scholar.

"The Mongols in World History," http://afe.easia.columbia.edu/mongols. A wonderful resource on the Mongols generally, with a particular focus on their impact in China.

Perceptions of the Mongols

Questions about perception across the boundaries of culture, class, or gender loom large in any study of world history. Such issues certainly arise as historians seek to understand the Mongol phenomenon. How did the Mongols, and especially their rulers, understand themselves and the huge empire they had created? And how were the Mongols perceived by others, especially those they conquered or threatened? The sources that follow provide some raw material for reflecting on those questions.

SOURCE 11.1 The Self-Perception of Mongol Rulers

Both Chinggis Khan and his son and successor Ogodei engaged in some thoughtful self-reflection about their achievements as well as their mistakes, limitations, and needs. Source 11.1A derives from a personally revealing letter that Chinggis Khan wrote to an elderly Chinese Daoist master named Changchun seeking guidance on the "means of preserving life" and requesting a personal meeting with the teacher. Changchun did arrive at Chinggis Khan's camp, but confessed that "no medicine for immortality" existed. And in Source 11.1B, Ogodei ponders his own successes and failures toward the end of his reign. His reflections are contained in the major literary work that emerged among the Mongols themselves, known as *The Secret History of the Mongols.* Its unknown author was likely a member of the royal household.

- How does Chinggis Khan define his life's work? What is his image of himself? What does his request for a meeting with Changchun reveal about his own anxieties and his view of China?

- What does Ogodei regard as his greatest achievements and his most notable mistakes?

- What do these documents disclose about Mongol values and Mongol exercise of political authority?

SOURCE 11.1A

CHINGGIS KHAN | *Letter to Changchun* | 1219

Heaven has abandoned China owing to its haughtiness and extravagant luxury. But I, living in the northern wilderness, have not inordinate passions. I hate luxury and exercise moderation. I have only one coat and one food. I eat the same food and am dressed in the same tatters as my humble herdsmen. I consider the people my children, and take an interest in talented men as if they were my brothers. . . . At military exercises I am always in the front, and in time of battle am never behind. In the space of seven years I have succeeded in accomplishing a great work, and uniting the whole world into one empire. I have not myself distinguished qualities. But the government of the [Chinese] is inconstant, and therefore Heaven assists me to obtain the throne. . . .

All together have acknowledged my supremacy. It seems to me that since the remote time . . . such an empire has not been seen. . . . Since the time I came to the throne I have always taken to heart the ruling of my people; but I could not find worthy men to occupy [high offices]. . . . With respect to these circumstances I inquired, and heard that thou, master, hast penetrated the truth. . . . For a long time thou hast lived in the caverns of the rocks, and hast retired from the world; . . . [H]ave pity upon me, and communicate to me the means of preserving life. I shall serve thee myself. I hope that at least thou wilt leave me a trifle of thy wisdom.

Source: E. Bretschneider, *Medieval Researches for Eastern Asiatic Sources* (London, 1875), 1:37–39.

SOURCE 11.1B

The Secret History of the Mongols | ca. 1240

Then Ogodei Khan spoke these words: "Since my father the Khan passed away and I came to sit on his great throne, what have I done? I went to war against the people of Cathay [China] and I destroyed them. For my second accomplishment I established a network of post stations so that my words are carried across the land with great speed. Another of my accomplishments has been to have my commanders dig wells in the desert so that there would be pasture and water for the people there. Lastly I placed spies and agents among all the people of the cities. In all directions I've brought peace to the Nation and the people. . . .

"But also since my father passed away . . . , I allowed myself to be conquered by wine. This was one of my mistakes. Another of my mistakes was to listen to a woman with no principles and because of her take away the daughters who belonged to my Uncle Odchigin. Even though I'm the Khan, the Lord of the Nation, I have no right to go against established principle, so this was my mistake.

"Another mistake was to secretly harm Dokholkhu. If you ask, 'Why was this wrong?' I would say that to secretly harm Dokholkhu, a man who had served his proper lord, my father the Khan, performing heroic deeds in his service, was a mistake. Now that I've done this, who'll perform heroic deeds in my service? Then my last mistake was to desire too much, to say to myself, 'I'm afraid that all the wild game born under Heaven will run off toward the land of my brothers.' So I ordered earthen walls to be built to keep the wild game from running away, but even as these walls were being built I heard my brothers speaking badly of me. I admit that I was wrong to do this. Since the time of my father the Khan I've added four accomplishments to all that he'd done and I've done four things which I admit were wrong."

Source: Paul Kahn, *The Secret History of the Mongols: The Origin of Chingis Khan* (San Francisco: North Point Press, 1984), 192–93.

■ ■ ■

SOURCE 11.2 **Picturing Khubilai Khan**

After Chinggis Khan, the most well known of the Mongol emperors was his grandson, Khubilai Khan, whose main base lay in China, where he established the Yuan dynasty during the second half of the thirteenth century. He has been perceived and portrayed in various ways among the many peoples who encountered the Mongols. Three such images illustrate those different understandings of Khubilai Khan.

SOURCE 11.2A ▶

LIU GUANDAO │ *Khubilai on a Hunt* │ **1280**

The first, showing Khubilai Khan on a Mongol hunt accompanied by his wife and various attendants, was painted by the Chinese artist Liu Guandao under a commission from Khubilai himself. It portrays Khubilai dressed in a traditional red imperial robe and white lambskin coat.

- What marks this as a hunting scene?

- Why might Khubilai order this painting to show him on a hunt, though he was clearly aged and obese?

- What do the other people in the image contribute to the overall impression it makes?

- Does this image represent a Chinese or a Mongol perception of Khubilai Khan?

SOURCE 11.2B

Marco Polo and Khubilai Khan │ **15th century**

A second image derives from a European artist who provided illustrations for Marco Polo's *Book of the Marvels of the World*, in which he describes his close to twenty years in Mongol-ruled China. It shows Marco Polo and his father Nicolai presenting letters and gifts from the pope to Khubilai Khan upon their arrival in the early 1270s.

■ What relationship between the Polos and the Mongol ruler is suggested in this image? What do the postures of the khan and his attendants imply about how the pope's gifts were received?

■ Why did the artist depict the khan with European features and dress and seated on a European-style throne?

■ How does this portrayal differ from that of Liu Guandao? Which artist provides a more authentic depiction of the khan and his retainers? What factors might explain the differences?

From the *Livre des Merveilles du Monde*, ca. 1410–1412 (tempera on vellum)/Boucicaut Master (fl. 1390–1430), and workshop/Bibliothèque Nationale de France, Paris, France/Bridgeman Images

SOURCE 11.2C

Khubilai Khan in Council with His Courtiers and Scribes | 1590

A third image of Khubilai Khan derives from India, which the Mongols attacked but never conquered. Over the centuries, a number of Turkic/Mongol groups invaded India, the most successful of which were the Mughals, who claimed descent from the Mongols and Chinggis Khan. During the sixteenth century, these Turkic warriors constructed the Mughal Empire over much of India, which boasted a magnificient court and a sophisticated Islamic Persian culture. It was from artists at that court that this painting emerged, showing Khubilai Khan, in a black robe at the top of the image, in council with his courtiers and officials.

Werner Forman/Getty Images

- What is distinctive about the setting in which Khubilai Khan is placed in this image?

- Why might an artist at the Mughal court present Khubilai Khan in this elaborate imperial setting? How might you compare this painting with the other two images of Khubilai Khan?

- In what specific ways do these images reflect the expectations of the cultures that produced them?

■ ■ ■

SOURCE 11.3 A Persian View of the Conquest of Bukhara

Literate members of societies conquered by the Mongols sometimes expressed their understanding of these dramatic events in writing. Among the most well known was the thirteenth-century Persian historian Juvaini, himself a high official in the Mongol government ruling his Persian homeland. He composed an account of the creation of the Mongol Empire titled *The History of the World Conqueror*. In this excerpt from that work, he describes the Mongol conquest of the city of Bukhara, a major commercial and intellectual center of the Persian Islamic world located in what is now Uzbekistan.

- How might you describe Juvaini's posture toward the Mongols? What factors might have influenced his portrayal of them?

- What can we learn about the policies and strategies of the Mongols from Juvaini's account? What parts of this account seem most reliable?

- What aspects of Mongol behavior would be most offensive to Muslims?

- How did Chinggis Khan justify his conquest of Bukhara?

JUVAINI | *The History of the World Conqueror* | 1219

[Chinggis Khan's] troops were more numerous than ants or locusts, being in their multitude beyond estimation or computation.... When [our] forces reached the banks of the Oxus, the patrols and advance parties of the Mongol army fell upon them and left no trace of them.

On the following day . . . Chingis-Khan . . . entered to inspect the town and citadel. He rode into the Juma Mosque. . . . Chingis-Khan asked those present whether this was the palace of the Sultan; they replied it was the house of God. Then he too got down from his horse, and mounting two or three steps of the pulpit he exclaimed: "The countryside is empty of fodder, fill our horses' bellies." Whereupon they opened all the magazines in the town and began carrying off the grain. And they brought the cases in which the Qurans were kept out in the courtyard of the mosque, where they cast the Qurans right and left and turned the cases into mangers for their horses. After which they circulated cups and sent for the singing-girls of the town to sing and dance for them; while the Mongols raised their voices to the tunes of their own songs. . . . [T]he leaves of the Quran were trampled beneath the dirt beneath their own feet and their horses' hooves.

When Chingis-Khan left the town, he went to the festival muhalla and mounted the pulpit. . . . He then began a speech, in which, after describing the resistance and treachery of the Sultan, he addressed them as follows: "O People! know that you have committed great sins, and that the great ones among you have committed these sins. If you ask me what proof I have for these words, I say it is because I am the punishment of God. If you had not committed these great sins, God would not have sent a punishment like me upon you." When he had finished speaking in this strain, he continued his discourse with words of admonition, saying, "There is no need to declare your property that is on the face of the earth; tell me of that which is in the belly of the earth." . . . [A]lthough not subjecting them to disgrace or humiliation, they began to exact money from these men; and when they delivered it up they did not torment them by excessive punishment or demanding what was beyond their power to pay.

Chingis-Khan had given orders for the Sultan's troops to be driven out of the interior of the town and the citadel. . . . [H]e now gave orders for all quarters of the town to be set on fire; and since the houses were built entirely out of wood, within several days the greater part of the town had been consumed. . . . Then the people of Bukhara were driven against the citadel. And on either side the furnace of battle was heated. On the outside, mangonels [catapults] were erected, bows bent, and stones and arrows discharged, and, on the inside . . . pots of naphtha [a flammable liquid] were set in motion. It was like a red hot furnace. . . . For days they fought in this manner. . . . But finally . . . resistance was no longer in their power. . . . The moat had been filled with animate and inanimate and raised up with [the bodies of] levies [soldiers] and Bukharans. . . . [T]heir khans, leaders and notables . . . now became captives of abasement and were drowned in the sea of annihilation. . . . Of the Qanqli [Turkic defenders of the city] no male was spared who stood higher than the butt of a whip and more than thirty thousand were counted amongst the slain; whilst their small children, the children of their nobles and their womenfolk, slender as the cypress, were sold to slavery.

When the town and the citadel had been purged of rebels and the walls and outworks levelled with the dust, the inhabitants of the town, men and women, ugly and beautiful, were driven out onto the field of the *musalla* [an open space outside of a mosque]. Chingis-Khan spared their lives, but the youths and full-grown men that were fit for such service were pressed into a levy [body of soldiers] for the attack on Samarqand and Dabusiya.

Source: Juvaini, *The History of the World Conqueror*, translated by John Boyle (Manchester: Manchester University Press, 1958), 103–6.

■ ■ ■

SOURCE 11.4 **A European View of Mongol Life**

Although Western Europe was never conquered by the Mongols, European traders such as Marco Polo and various envoys from church or state authorities had contact with the Mongol Empire, especially in China. The accounts of these visitors provided Europeans with impressions of Mongol society. One of them, a Flemish Franciscan friar named William of Rubruck (1220–1293), left a detailed account of Mongol life in the mid-thirteenth century, which included observations about the domestic roles of men and women.

■ How does William of Rubruck portray the lives of Mongol women? What was the class background of the Mongol women he describes?

■ What do you think he would have found most upsetting about the position of women in Mongol society?

■ Based on this account, how might you compare the life of Mongol women to that of women in more established civilizations, such as China, Europe, or the Islamic world?

WILLIAM OF RUBRUCK | *Journey to the Land of the Mongols* | ca. 1255

The matrons [married women] make for themselves most beautiful [luggage] carts. . . . A single rich Mo'al or Tartar [Mongol] has quite one hundred or two hundred such carts with coffers. . . . And when they set up their houses, the first wife places her dwelling on the extreme west side, and after her the others according to their rank, so that the last wife will be in the extreme east; . . . The *ordu* [residence] of a rich Mo'al seems like a large town, though there will be very few men in it.

It is the duty of the women to drive the carts, get the dwellings on and off them, milk the cows, make butter and *gruit* [sour curd], and to dress and sew skins, which they do with a thread made of tendons. They divide the tendons into fine shreds, and then twist them into one long thread. They also sew the boots, the socks, and the clothing. They never wash clothes, for they say that God would be angered, and that it would thunder if they hung them up to dry. They will even beat those they find washing [their clothes]. Thunder they fear extraordinarily; and when it thunders they will turn out of their dwellings all strangers, wrap themselves in black felt, and thus hide themselves till it has passed away. Furthermore, they never wash their bowls, but when the meat is cooked they rinse out the dish in which they are about to put it with some of the boiling broth from the kettle, which they pour back into it. They [the women] also make the felt and cover the houses.

The men make bows and arrows, manufacture stirrups and bits, make saddles, do the carpentering on their dwellings and the carts; they take care of the horses, milk the mares, churn the *cosmos* or mare's milk, make the skins in which it is put; they also look after the camels and load them. Both sexes look after the sheep and goats, sometimes the men, other times the women, milking them.

As to their marriages, you must know that no one among them has a wife unless he buys her; so it sometimes happens that girls are well past marriageable age before they marry, for their parents always keep them until they sell them. . . . Among them no widow marries, for the following reason: they believe that all who serve them in this life shall serve them in the next, so as regards a widow they believe that she will always return to her first husband after death. Hence this shameful custom prevails among them, that sometimes a son takes to wife all his father's wives, except his own mother; for the *ordu* of the father and mother always belongs to the youngest son, so it is he who must provide for all his father's wives . . . and if he wishes it, he uses them as wives, for he esteems not himself injured if they return to his father after death. When then anyone has made a bargain with another to take his daughter, the father of the girl gives a feast, and the girl flees to her relatives and hides there. Then the father says: "Here, my daughter is yours: take her wheresoever you find her." Then he searches for her with his friends till he finds her, and he must take her by force and carry her off with a semblance of violence to his house.

Source: *The Journey of William of Rubruck* . . . , translated from the Latin and edited, with an introductory notice, by William Woodville Rockhill (London: Hakluyt Society, 1900), 56–57, 75–78.

DOING HISTORY

1. **Assessing sources:** What are the strengths and limitations of these sources for understanding the Mongols? Taking the positions of their authors or artists into account, what exaggerations, biases, or misunderstandings can you identify in these sources? What information seems credible, and what should be viewed more skeptically?

2. **Characterizing the Mongols:** Based on these sources and on the text of Chapter 11, write an essay arguing that the Mongols were more than destructive barbarians. How do your own values affect your understanding of the Mongol moment?

3. **Considering values and practice:** How would you describe the core values of Mongol culture? (Consider the leaders' goals, their attitudes toward conquered peoples, the duties of rulers, the views of political authority, and the role of women.) To what extent were these values put into practice in acquiring and ruling the Mongols' huge empire? And in what ways were these values undermined or eroded as that empire took shape?

4. **Assessing perceptions:** In what ways do the sources deriving from outside the Mongol world affirm or challenge the Mongols' own view of themselves?

Assessing the Mongol Impact

What has been the impact of the Mongol Empire? It is a question with which many historians have struggled. The answer, of course, is "it depends." It depends on whether historians are looking at the extraordinarily brutal process by which the empire was constructed or the later period of settled administration and adaptation to the cultures of conquered peoples. It also depends on whether they are interested in particular societies, such as China, or the larger interacting network of the Afro-Eurasian world. And finally, it depends on what aspect of Mongol life engages their attention—political, economic, or cultural, for example. In Voice 11.1, historian Jack Weatherford takes a global and quite positive view of the Mongol era, while Voice 11.2 by Paul S. Ropp focuses more explicitly on China and with a more critical posture.

- What does Voice 11.1 praise about the Mongols? What might he be leaving out of this account?

- What does Voice 11.2 criticize about Mongol rule in China? What might he be omitting?

- The author of Voice 11.1 has focused his research on the Mongols, while Voice 11.2 was written by a historian of China. How might these scholarly commitments have shaped their outlook on the Mongols?

- **Integrating Primary and Secondary Sources:** How might one or more of the primary sources support or challenge the conclusions of these historians?

VOICE 11.1

Jack Weatherford on the Mongols in World History | 2004

Genghis [Chinggis] Khan's empire connected and amalgamated the many civilizations around him into a new world order. . . . By the time of his death in 1227, he had connected them with diplomatic and commercial contacts that still remain unbroken.

As he smashed the feudal system of aristocratic privilege and birth, he built a new and unique system based on individual merit, loyalty, and achievement. He took the disjointed and languorous trading towns along the Silk Route and organized them into the world's largest free trade zone. He lowered taxes for everyone, and abolished them altogether for doctors, teachers, priests, and educational institutions. He established a regular census and created the first international postal system. . . . He widely distributed the goods he acquired in combat, so that they could make their way back into commercial circulation. He created an international law. . . . Genghis Khan insisted on laws holding rulers as equally accountable as the lowest herder. He granted religious freedom in his realms, though he demanded total loyalty from conquered subjects of all religions. He insisted on the rule of law and abolished torture. . . . He refused to hold hostages and, instead, instituted the novel practice of granting diplomatic immunity for all ambassadors and envoys. . . .

Source: Jack Weatherford, *Genghis Khan and the Making of the Modern World* (New York: Broadway Books, 2004), xix.

VOICE 11.2

Paul S. Ropp on the Mongol Impact on China's Economy | 2010

The Mongol conquest of China took a terrible economic toll. The Song [dynasty] iron industry was devastated and never fully regained Song levels of productivity. Intense warfare greatly reduced the population, and the spread of infectious diseases, such as bubonic plague, from Central Asia to China produced several terrible epidemics that killed millions in the fourteenth century (and eliminated one-fourth of Europe's population soon thereafter). The wars destroyed farmlands and irrigation works, and in places Mongol princes and generals turned rice-producing land into parks and pastures. The combined effect of war and disease greatly reduced the tax base. The Yuan government responded by printing more money, which only fueled inflation and undermined the economic health of the dynasty. . . .

The Mongols ambitiously undertook naval expeditions of conquest against Japan . . . and against the kingdom of Java. They also launched attacks on Vietnam and Burma. . . . These wars were a serious drain on the state's resources and only served to delay the economic recovery of the Yuan from the dislocation of their early years.

Source: Paul S. Ropp, *China in World History* (Oxford: Oxford University Press, 2010), 81–82.

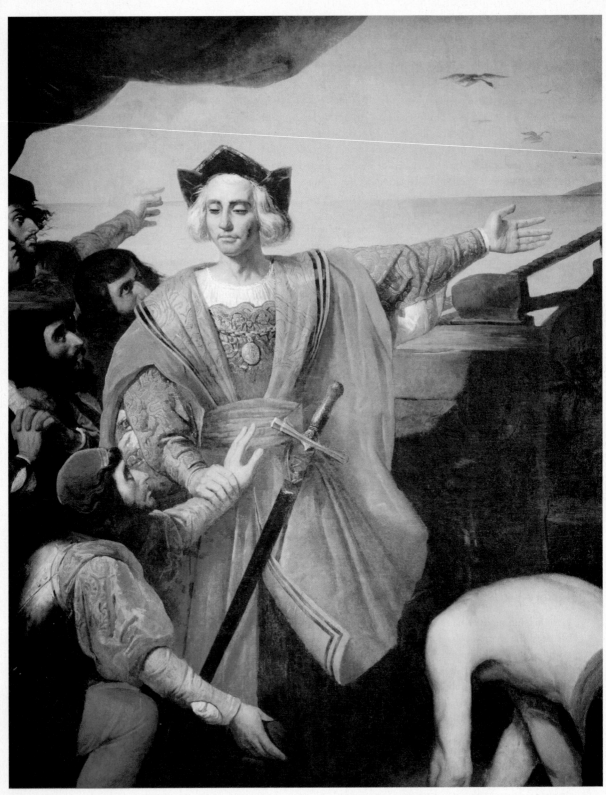

19th-century Spanish painting/Monastery of La Rabida, Huelva, Andalusia, Spain/Bridgeman Images

**Societies and Cultures of the
Fifteenth Century**
Paleolithic Persistence: Australia
and North America
Agricultural Village Societies: The
Igbo and the Iroquois
Pastoral Peoples: Central Asia and
West Africa

**Civilizations of the Fifteenth Century:
Comparing China and Europe**
Ming Dynasty China
European Comparisons: State
Building and Cultural Renewal
European Comparisons: Maritime
Voyaging

**Civilizations of the Fifteenth
Century: The Islamic World**
In the Islamic Heartland: The
Ottoman and Safavid Empires
On the Frontiers of Islam: The
Songhay and Mughal Empires

**Civilizations of the Fifteenth
Century: The Americas**
The Aztec Empire
The Inca Empire

Webs of Connection

**After 1500: Looking Ahead to the
Modern Era**

**Reflections: What If? Chance and
Contingency in World History**

The Worlds of the Fifteenth Century

By 2016, a number of American cities and the state of Vermont had transformed October 12 from a celebration of Columbus Day to a commemoration of Indigenous Peoples Day. Opposed in many places, such transformations of the holiday reflected a growing debate about the significance and legacy of Columbus. Was he "a perpetrator of genocide . . . , a slave trader, a thief, a pirate, and most certainly not a hero,"[1] as Winona LaDuke, president of the Indigenous Women's Network, declared in 1992, which marked the 500th anniversary of Columbus's arrival in the Americas? Or should Americans celebrate Columbus, as the Latino novelist and publisher Jonathan Marcantoni recommended in 2015, remembering "his achievement of connecting the Europeans with the Americas . . . because without it, the societies we love would not exist"?[2] ■

This sharp debate about Columbus reminds us that the past is endlessly contested and that it continues to resonate in the present. But it also reflects a broad agreement that the voyages of Columbus marked a decisive turning point, for better or worse, in world history and represent arguably the most important event of the fifteenth century.

It was not, however, the only globally significant departure of that century. If Columbus launched a European empire-building process in the Americas, other empires were also in the making during the fifteenth century. In 1383, a Central Asian Turkic warrior named Timur launched the last major pastoral invasion of adjacent civilizations. Then in 1405, an enormous Chinese fleet set out across the entire Indian Ocean basin, only to voluntarily withdraw twenty-eight years later,

《 The Meeting of Two Worlds This nineteenth-century painting shows Columbus on his first voyage to the New World. He is reassuring his anxious sailors by pointing to the first sight of land. In light of its long-range consequences, this voyage represents a major turning point in world history.

thus forgoing an empire in Asia. Four new empires gave the Islamic world a distinct political and cultural shape. One of them, the Ottoman Empire, put a final end to Christian Byzantium with the conquest of Constantinople in 1453, even as Spanish Christians completed the "reconquest" of the Iberian Peninsula from the Muslims in 1492. And in the Americas, the Aztec and Inca empires gave a final and spectacular expression to Mesoamerican and Andean civilizations before they were both swallowed up in the burst of European imperialism that followed the arrival of Columbus.

Because the fifteenth century was a hinge of major historical change on many fronts, it provides an occasion for a bird's-eye view of the world through an imaginary global tour. This excursion around the world will serve to briefly review the human saga thus far and to establish a baseline from which the enormous transformations of the centuries that followed might be measured. How, then, might we describe the world, and the worlds, of the fifteenth century?

SEEKING THE MAIN POINT

What predictions about the future might a global traveler in the fifteenth century have reasonably made?

Societies and Cultures of the Fifteenth Century

One way to describe the world of the fifteenth century is to identify the various types of human communities that it contained. Bands of gatherers and hunters, villages of agricultural peoples, newly emerging chiefdoms or small states, pastoral communities, established civilizations and empires—all of these social or political forms would have been apparent to a widely traveled visitor in the fifteenth century. Representing alternative ways of organizing human life, all of them were long established by the fifteenth century, but the balance among them in 1500 was quite different than it had been a thousand years earlier.

Paleolithic Persistence: Australia and North America

Despite millennia of agricultural advance, substantial areas of the world still hosted gathering and hunting societies, known to historians as Paleolithic (Old Stone Age) peoples. All of Australia, much of Siberia, the arctic coastlands, and parts of Africa and the Americas fell into this category. These peoples were not simply relics of a bygone age, for they too had a history, although most history books largely ignore them after the age of agriculture arrived. Nonetheless, this most ancient way of life still had a sizable and variable presence in the world of the fifteenth century.

Consider, for example, Australia. That continent's many separate groups, some 250 of them, still practiced a gathering and hunting way of life in the fifteenth century, a pattern that continued well after Europeans arrived in the late eighteenth century. Over many thousands of years, these people had assimilated various material items or cultural practices from outsiders—outrigger canoes, fishhooks, complex netting techniques, artistic styles, rituals, and mythological ideas—but despite the presence of farmers in nearby New Guinea, no agricultural practices penetrated the Australian mainland. Was it because large areas of Australia were unsuited for

Guided Reading Question

....

■ **COMPARISON**
In what ways did the gathering and hunting people of Australia differ from those of the northwest coast of North America?

Landmarks for Chapter 12

	1375	1400	1425	1450	1475	1500	1525

CHINA

1368–1644
Ming dynasty

1402–1424
Emperor Yongle relocates capital to Beijing;
Forbidden City constructed

1405–1433 Chinese maritime voyages

EUROPE

1337–1453
Hundred Years' War

ca. 1350–1500
European Renaissance

1415–1497
Portuguese exploration
of West African coast

1492–1498
Columbus's voyage to the Americas;
da Gama's voyage to India

1492
Christian reconquest of
Muslim Spain completed

ISLAMIC WORLD

1453
Ottoman seizure of Constantinople

1464
Founding of Songhay Empire in West Africa

1501
Founding of Safavid
Empire in Persia

1526
Founding of Mughal Empire in India

THE AMERICAS

1345–1528
Aztec Empire

ca. 1400–1450
Iroquois League established

1438–1533
Inca Empire

the kind of agriculture practiced in New Guinea? Or did the peoples of Australia, enjoying an environment of sufficient resources, simply see no need to change their way of life?

Despite the absence of agriculture, Australia's peoples had mastered and manipulated their environment, in part through "firestick farming," the practice of deliberately setting fires, which they described as "cleaning up the country." These controlled burns cleared the underbrush, thus making hunting easier and encouraging the growth of certain plant and animal species. In addition, native Australians exchanged goods among themselves over distances of hundreds of miles, created elaborate mythologies and ritual practices, and developed sophisticated traditions of sculpture and rock painting. They accomplished all of this on the basis of an economy and technology rooted in the distant Paleolithic past.

A very different kind of gathering and hunting society flourished in the fifteenth century along the northwest coast of North America among the Chinookan, Tulalip, Skagit, and other peoples. With some 300 edible animal species and an abundance of salmon and other fish, this extraordinarily bounteous environment provided the foundation for what scholars sometimes call "complex" or "affluent" gathering and hunting cultures. What distinguished the northwest coast peoples from those of Australia were permanent village settlements with large and sturdy houses, considerable economic specialization, ranked societies that sometimes included slavery, chiefdoms dominated by powerful clan leaders or "big men," and extensive storage of food.

Although these and other gathering and hunting peoples persisted in the fifteenth century, both their numbers (an estimated 1 percent of the world's population by 1500) and the area they inhabited had contracted greatly as the Agricultural Revolution unfolded across the planet. That relentless advance of the farming frontier continued in the centuries ahead as the Russian, Chinese, and European empires encompassed the lands of the remaining Paleolithic peoples.

Agricultural Village Societies: The Igbo and the Iroquois

Far more numerous than gatherers and hunters but still a small percentage of the total world population were those many peoples who, though fully agricultural, had avoided incorporation into larger empires or civilizations and had not developed their own city- or state-based societies. Living usually in small village-based communities and organized in terms of kinship relations, such people predominated during the fifteenth century in much of North America; in most of the tropical lowlands of South America and the Caribbean; in parts of the Amazon River basin, Southeast Asia, and Africa south of the equator; and throughout Pacific Oceania. Historians have often treated them as marginal to the cities, states, and large-scale civilizations that predominate in most accounts of the global past. Viewed from within their own circles, though, these societies were at the center of things, each with its own history of migration, cultural transformation, social conflict, incorporation of new people, political rise and fall, and interaction with strangers.

East of the Niger River in the heavily forested region of West Africa lay the lands of the **Igbo** (EE-boh) peoples. By the fifteenth century, their neighbors, the Yoruba and Bini, had begun to develop small states and urban centers. But the Igbo, whose dense population and extensive trading networks might well have given rise to states, declined to follow suit. The deliberate Igbo preference was to reject the kingship and state-building efforts of their neighbors. They boasted on occasion that "the Igbo have no kings." Instead, they relied on other institutions to maintain social cohesion beyond the level of the village: title societies in which wealthy men received a series of prestigious ranks, women's associations, hereditary ritual experts serving as mediators, and a balance of power among kinship groups. It was a "stateless society," famously described in Chinua Achebe's *Things Fall Apart*, the most widely read novel to emerge from twentieth-century Africa.

But the Igbo peoples and their neighbors did not live in isolated, self-contained societies. They traded actively among themselves and with more distant peoples, such as the large African kingdom of Songhay (sahn-GEYE) far to the north. Cotton cloth, fish, copper and iron goods, decorative objects, and more drew neighboring peoples into networks of exchange. Common artistic traditions reflected a measure of cultural unity in a politically fragmented region, and all of these peoples seem to have changed from a matrilineal to a patrilineal system of tracing their descent. Little of this registered in the larger civilizations of the Afro-Eurasian world, but to the peoples of the West African forest during the fifteenth century, these processes were central to their history and their daily lives. Soon, however, all of them would be caught up in the transatlantic slave trade and would be changed substantially in the process.

Across the Atlantic in what is now central New York State, other agricultural village societies were also undergoing major change during the several centuries preceding their incorporation into European trading networks and empires. The Iroquois-speaking peoples of that region had only recently become fully agricultural, adopting maize- and bean-farming techniques that had originated centuries earlier in Mesoamerica. As this productive agriculture took hold by 1300 or so, the population grew, the size of settlements increased, and distinct peoples emerged. Frequent warfare also erupted among them. Some scholars have speculated that as agriculture, largely seen as women's work, became the primary economic activity, "warfare replaced successful food getting as the avenue to male prestige."[3]

Whatever caused it, this increased level of conflict among **Iroquois** peoples triggered a remarkable political innovation around the fifteenth century: a loose alliance or confederation among five Iroquois-speaking peoples—the Mohawk, Oneida, Onondaga, Cayuga, and Seneca (see Map 12.5, page 515). Based on an agreement known as the Great Law of Peace, the Five Nations, as they called themselves, agreed to settle their differences peacefully through a confederation council of clan leaders, some fifty of them altogether, who had the authority to adjudicate

Guided Reading
Question
....
■ CHANGE
What kinds of changes were transforming the societies of the West African Igbo and the North American Iroquois as the fifteenth century unfolded?

Iroquois Women This seventeenth-century French engraving depicts two Iroquois women preparing a meal. Among the Iroquois, women controlled both agriculture and property and had a significant voice in public affairs. (From "Historiae Canadensis" by Father Francisco Creuxio, 1664/De Agostini Picture Library/Bridgeman Images)

disputes and set reparation payments. Operating by consensus, the Iroquois League of Five Nations effectively suppressed the blood feuds and tribal conflicts that had only recently been so widespread. It also coordinated its peoples' relationship with outsiders, including the Europeans, who arrived in growing numbers in the centuries after 1500.

The Iroquois League gave expression to values of limited government, social equality, and personal freedom, concepts that some European colonists found highly attractive. One British colonial administrator declared in 1749 that the Iroquois had "such absolute Notions of Liberty that they allow no Kind of Superiority of one over another, and banish all Servitude from their Territories."[4] Such equality extended to gender relationships, for among the Iroquois, descent was matrilineal (reckoned through the woman's line), married couples lived with the wife's family, and women controlled agriculture and property. While men were hunters, warriors, and the primary political officeholders, women selected and could depose those leaders.

Wherever they lived in 1500, over the next several centuries independent agricultural peoples such as the Iroquois and Igbo were increasingly encompassed in expanding economic networks and conquest empires based in Western Europe, Russia, China, or India, as had many other such peoples before them.

Pastoral Peoples: Central Asia and West Africa

Pastoral peoples had long impinged more directly and dramatically on civilizations than did gathering and hunting or agricultural village societies. The Mongol incursion, along with the enormous empire to which it gave rise, was one in a long series of challenges from the steppes, but it was not quite the last. As the Mongol Empire disintegrated, a brief attempt to restore it occurred in the late fourteenth and early fifteenth centuries under the leadership of a Turkic warrior named **Timur**, born in what is now Uzbekistan and known in the West as Tamerlane (see Map 12.1, page 501).

With a ferocity that matched or exceeded that of his model, Chinggis Khan, Timur's army of pastoralists brought immense devastation yet again to Russia and Persia, and also to India. Timur himself died in 1405, while preparing for an invasion of China. Conflicts among his successors prevented any lasting empire, although his

Guided Reading Question

....

■ **SIGNIFICANCE**
What role did Central Asian and West African pastoralists play in their respective regions?

descendants retained control of the area between Persia and Afghanistan for the rest of the fifteenth century. That state hosted a sophisticated elite culture combining Turkic and Persian elements, particularly at its splendid capital of Samarkand, as its rulers patronized artists, poets, traders, and craftsmen. Timur's conquest proved to be the last great military success of pastoral peoples from Central Asia. In the centuries that followed, their homelands were swallowed up in the expanding Russian and Chinese empires, as the balance of power between steppe pastoralists of inner Eurasia and the civilizations of outer Eurasia turned decisively in favor of the latter.

Modern Fulbe Herdsmen This photo shows modern Fulbe herdsmen from Nigeria tending to perhaps their most distinctive animal, long-horned cattle. Wealth in many pastoralist groups is reckoned through the size of cattle herds. (Eye Ubiquitous/Newscom)

In Africa, pastoral peoples stayed independent of established empires several centuries longer than those of Inner Asia, for not until the late nineteenth century were they incorporated into European colonial states. The experience of the **Fulbe** (FULB), West Africa's largest pastoral society, provides an example of an African herding people with a highly significant role in the fifteenth century and beyond. From their homeland in the western fringe of the Sahara along the upper Senegal River, the Fulbe had migrated gradually eastward in the centuries after 1000 C.E. (see Map 12.3, page 506). Unlike the pastoral peoples of Inner Asia, they generally lived in small communities among agricultural peoples and paid various grazing fees and taxes for the privilege of pasturing their cattle. Relations with their farming hosts often were tense because the Fulbe resented their subordination to agricultural peoples, whose way of life they despised. That sense of cultural superiority became even more pronounced as the Fulbe, in the course of their eastward movement, slowly adopted Islam. Some of them in fact dropped out of a pastoral life and settled in towns, where they became highly respected religious leaders. In the eighteenth and nineteenth centuries, the Fulbe were at the center of a wave of religiously based uprisings, or jihads, that greatly expanded the practice of Islam and gave rise to a series of new states ruled by the Fulbe themselves.

Civilizations of the Fifteenth Century: Comparing China and Europe

Beyond the foraging, farming, and pastoral societies of the fifteenth-century world were its civilizations, those city-centered and state-based societies that were far larger and more densely populated, more powerful and innovative, and much more unequal in terms of class and gender than other forms of human community. Since the First Civilizations had emerged between 3500 and 1000 B.C.E., both the geographic space they encompassed and the number of people they embraced had grown substantially. By the fifteenth century, about 30 percent of the world's land was controlled by states and a considerable majority of the world's population lived within one or another of these civilizations. But most of these people, no doubt, identified more with local communities than with a larger civilization. What might an imaginary global traveler notice about the world's major civilizations in the fifteenth century?

Ming Dynasty China

Such a traveler might well begin his or her journey in China. That civilization had been greatly disrupted by a century of Mongol rule, and its population had been sharply reduced by the plague. During the **Ming dynasty** (1368–1644), however, China recovered (see Map 12.1). In the early decades of that dynasty, the Chinese attempted to eliminate all signs of foreign rule, discouraging the use of Mongol names and dress while promoting Confucian learning and orthodox gender roles based on earlier models from the Han, Tang, and Song dynasties. Emperor Yongle (YAHNG-leh) (r. 1402–1424) sponsored an enormous *Encyclopedia* of some 11,000 volumes. With contributions from more than 2,000 scholars, this work sought to summarize or compile all previous writing on history, geography, philosophy, ethics, government, and more. Yongle also relocated the capital to Beijing, ordered the building of a magnificent imperial residence known as the Forbidden City, and constructed the Temple of Heaven, where subsequent rulers performed Confucian-based rituals to ensure the well-being of Chinese society. Two empresses wrote instructions for female behavior, emphasizing traditional expectations after the disruptions of the previous century. Culturally speaking, China was looking to its past.

Politically, the Ming dynasty reestablished the civil service examination system that had been neglected under Mongol rule and went on to create a highly centralized government. Power was concentrated in the hands of the emperor himself, while a cadre of eunuchs (castrated men) personally loyal to the emperor exercised great authority, much to the dismay of the official bureaucrats. The state acted vigorously to repair the damage of the Mongol years by restoring millions of acres to cultivation; rebuilding canals, reservoirs, and irrigation works; and planting, according to some estimates, a billion trees in an effort to reforest China. As a result, the economy rebounded, both international and domestic trade flourished, and the population grew. During the fifteenth century, China had recovered and was perhaps the best governed and most prosperous of the world's major civilizations.

China also undertook the largest and most impressive maritime expeditions the world had ever seen. Since the eleventh century, Chinese sailors and traders

Guided Reading Question

....

■ **DESCRIPTION**

How would you define the major achievements of Ming dynasty China?

MAPPING HISTORY

Map 12.1 Asia in the Fifteenth Century

The fifteenth century in Asia witnessed the massive Ming dynasty voyages into the Indian Ocean, the last major eruption of pastoral power in Timur's empire, and the flourishing of the maritime city of Malacca.

READING THE MAP: Which major cities did the Ming dynasty voyages visit?

MAKING CONNECTIONS: Compare Map 12.1 with Map 11.1. Which part of the Mongol Empire did Timur's empire most closely resemble? OR Compare Map 12.1 with Map 13.3. How did the Chinese empire evolve after the Qing dynasty replaced the Ming?

had been a major presence in the South China Sea and in Southeast Asian port cities, with much of this activity in private hands. But now, after decades of preparation, an enormous fleet, commissioned by Emperor Yongle himself, was launched in 1405, followed over the next twenty-eight years by six more such expeditions. On board more than 300 ships of the first voyage was a crew of some 27,000, including 180 physicians, hundreds of government officials, 5 astrologers, 7 high-ranking or grand eunuchs, carpenters, tailors, accountants, merchants, translators, cooks, and thousands of soldiers and sailors. Visiting many ports in Southeast Asia, Indonesia, India, Arabia, and East Africa, these fleets, captained by the Muslim eunuch **Zheng He** (JUHNG-huh), sought to enroll distant peoples and states in the Chinese tribute system (see Map 12.1). Dozens of rulers accompanied the fleets back to China, where they presented tribute, performed the required rituals of submission, and received in return abundant gifts, titles, and trading opportunities. Officially described as "bringing order to the world," Zheng He's expeditions served to establish Chinese power and prestige in the Indian Ocean and to exert Chinese control over foreign trade in the region. The Chinese, however, did not seek to conquer new territories, establish Chinese settlements, or spread their culture, though they did intervene in a number of local disputes.

The most surprising feature of these voyages was how abruptly and deliberately they were ended. After 1433, Chinese authorities simply stopped such expeditions and allowed this enormous and expensive fleet to deteriorate in port. "In less than a hundred years," wrote a recent historian of these voyages, "the greatest navy the world had ever known had ordered itself into extinction."[5] Part of the reason involved the death of the emperor Yongle, who had been the chief patron of the enterprise. Many high-ranking officials had long seen the expeditions as a waste of resources because China, they believed, was the self-sufficient "middle kingdom," the center of the civilized world, requiring little from beyond its borders. In their eyes, the real danger to China came from the north, where barbarians constantly threatened. Finally, they viewed the voyages as the project of the court eunuchs, whom these officials despised. Even as these voices of Chinese officialdom prevailed, private Chinese merchants and craftsmen continued to settle and trade in Japan, the Philippines, Taiwan, and Southeast Asia, but they did so without the support of their government. The Chinese state quite deliberately turned its back on what was surely within its reach—a large-scale maritime empire in the Indian Ocean basin.

European Comparisons: State Building and Cultural Renewal

At the other end of the Eurasian continent, similar processes of demographic recovery, political consolidation, cultural flowering, and overseas expansion were under way. Western Europe, having escaped Mongol conquest but devastated by the plague, began to regrow its population during the second half of the fifteenth century. As in China, the infrastructure of civilization proved a durable foundation for demographic and economic revival.

Politically too, Europe joined China in continuing earlier patterns of state building. In China, however, this meant a unitary and centralized government that encompassed almost the whole of its civilization, while in Europe a decidedly fragmented system of many separate, independent, and highly competitive states made for a sharply divided Western civilization (see Map 12.2). Many of these states—Spain, Portugal, France, England, the city-states of Italy (Milan, Venice, and Florence), various German principalities—learned to tax their citizens more

Map 12.2 Europe in 1500

By the end of the fifteenth century, Christian Europe had assumed its early modern political shape as a system of competing states threatened by an expanding Muslim Ottoman Empire.

efficiently, to create more effective administrative structures, and to raise standing armies. A small Russian state centered on the city of Moscow also emerged in the fifteenth century as Mongol rule faded away. Much of this state building was driven by the needs of war, a frequent occurrence in such a fragmented and competitive political environment. England and France, for example, fought intermittently for more than a century in the Hundred Years' War (1337–1453) over rival claims to territory in France. Nothing remotely similar disturbed the internal life of Ming dynasty China.

**Guided Reading
Question**

■ **COMPARISON**

What political and cultural differences stand out in the histories of fifteenth-century China and Western Europe? What similarities are apparent?

A renewed cultural blossoming, the **European Renaissance**, likewise paralleled the revival of all things Confucian in Ming dynasty China. In Europe, however, that blossoming celebrated and reclaimed a classical Greco-Roman tradition that earlier had been lost or obscured. Beginning in the vibrant commercial cities of Italy between roughly 1350 and 1500, the Renaissance reflected the belief of the wealthy male elite that they were living in a wholly new era, far removed from the confined religious world of feudal Europe. Educated citizens of these cities sought inspiration in the art and literature of ancient Greece and Rome; they were "returning to the sources," as they put it. Their purpose was not so much to reconcile these works with the ideas of Christianity, as the twelfth- and thirteenth-century university scholars had done, but to use them as a cultural standard to imitate and then to surpass. The elite patronized great Renaissance artists such as Leonardo da Vinci, Michelangelo, and Raphael, whose paintings and sculptures were far more naturalistic, particularly in portraying the human body, than those of their medieval counterparts. Some of these artists looked to the Islamic world for standards of excellence, sophistication, and abundance. (See Working with Evidence: Islam and Renaissance Europe, page 527.)

Although religious themes remained prominent, Renaissance artists now included portraits and busts of well-known contemporary figures and scenes from ancient mythology. In the work of those scholars known as humanists, reflections on secular topics such as grammar, history, politics, poetry, rhetoric, and ethics complemented more religious matters. For example, Niccolò Machiavelli's (1469–1527) famous work *The Prince* was a prescription for political success based on the way politics actually operated in a highly competitive Italy of rival city-states rather than on idealistic and religiously based principles. His slim volume was filled with ruthless advice, including the observation that "the ends justify the means" when ruling a state and that it was safer for a sovereign to be feared than loved by his subjects. But the teachings in *The Prince* were controversial, with many critics at the time rejecting its amoral analysis of political life and its assertion that rulers should—indeed must—set aside moral concerns to rule effectively.

While the great majority of Renaissance writers and artists were men, among the remarkable exceptions to that rule was Christine de Pizan (1363–1430), the daughter of a Venetian official who lived mostly in Paris. Her writings pushed against the misogyny of many European thinkers of the time. In her *City of Ladies*, she mobilized numerous women from history, Christian and pagan alike, to demonstrate that women too could be active members of society and deserved an education equal to that of men. "No matter which way I looked at it," she wrote, "I could find no evidence from my own experience to bear out such a negative view of female nature and habits. Even so . . . I could scarcely find a moral work by any author which didn't devote some chapter or paragraph to attacking the female sex."[6]

Heavily influenced by classical models, Renaissance figures were more interested in capturing the unique qualities of particular individuals and in describing the world as it was than in portraying or exploring eternal religious truths. In its

The Waldseemüller Map of 1507 Just fifteen years after Columbus landed in the Western Hemisphere, this map, which was created by the German cartographer Martin Waldseemüller, reflected a dawning European awareness of the planet's global dimensions and the location of the world's major landmasses. (bpk, Bildagentur/Staatsbibliothek zu Berlin, Stiflung Preussicher Kulturbesitz/Photo: Ruth Schacht/ Art Resource, NY)

focus on the affairs of this world, Renaissance culture reflected the urban bustle and commercial preoccupations of Italian cities. Its secular elements challenged the otherworldliness of Christian culture, and its individualism signaled the dawning of a more capitalist economy of private entrepreneurs. A new Europe was in the making, one more different from its own recent past than Ming dynasty China was from its pre-Mongol glory.

European Comparisons: Maritime Voyaging

A global traveler during the fifteenth century might be surprised to find that Europeans, like the Chinese, were also launching outward-bound maritime expeditions. Initiated in 1415 by the small country of Portugal, those voyages sailed ever farther down the west coast of Africa, supported by the state and blessed by the pope (see Map 12.3). As the century ended, two expeditions marked major breakthroughs, although few suspected it at the time. In 1492, Christopher Columbus, funded by Spain, Portugal's neighbor and rival, made his way west across the Atlantic hoping to arrive in the East and, in one of history's most consequential mistakes, ran into the Americas. Five years later, in 1497, Vasco da Gama launched a voyage

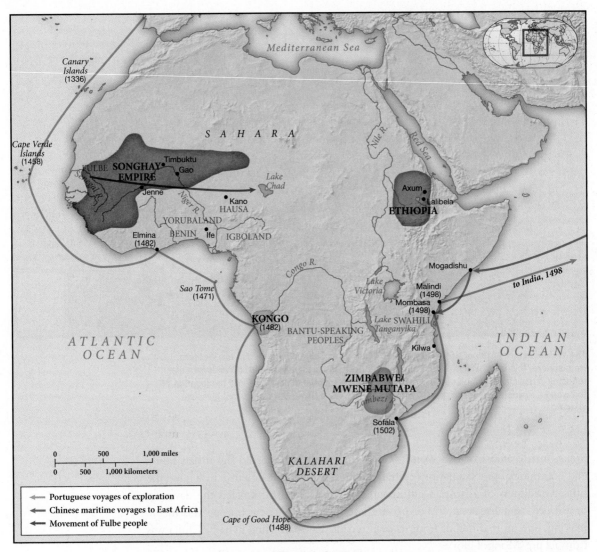

Map 12.3 **Africa in the Fifteenth Century**

By the fifteenth century, Africa was a panorama of political and cultural diversity, encompassing large empires, such as Songhay; smaller kingdoms, such as Kongo; city-states among the Yoruba, Hausa, and Swahili peoples; village-based societies without states at all, as among the Igbo; and pastoral peoples, such as the Fulbe. Both European and Chinese maritime expeditions touched on Africa during that century, even as Islam continued to find acceptance in the northern half of the continent.

that took him around the tip of South Africa, along the East African coast, and, with the help of a Muslim pilot, across the Indian Ocean to Calicut in southern India.

The differences between the Chinese and European oceangoing ventures were striking, most notably perhaps in terms of size. Columbus captained three ships and a crew of about 90, while da Gama had four ships, manned by perhaps 170 sailors. These were minuscule fleets compared to Zheng He's hundreds of ships and a crew in the many thousands. "All the ships of Columbus and da Gama combined," according to a recent account, "could have been stored on a single deck of a single vessel in the fleet that set sail under Zheng He."[7]

Motivation as well as size differentiated the two ventures. Europeans were seeking the wealth of Africa and Asia—gold, spices, silk, and more. They also were in search of Christian converts and of possible Christian allies with whom to continue their long crusading struggle against threatening Muslim powers. China, by contrast, faced no similar threat in the Indian Ocean basin, needed no military allies, and required little that these regions produced. Nor did China possess an impulse to convert foreigners to its culture or religion, as the Europeans surely did. Furthermore, the confident and overwhelmingly powerful Chinese fleet sought neither conquests nor colonies, while the Europeans soon tried to monopolize by force the commerce of the Indian Ocean and violently carved out huge empires in the Americas.

The most striking difference in these two cases lay in the sharp contrast between China's decisive ending of its voyages and the continuing, indeed escalating, European effort, which soon brought the world's oceans and growing numbers of the world's people under its control. This is why Zheng He's voyages were so long neglected in China's historical memory. They led nowhere, whereas the initial European expeditions, so much smaller and less promising, were but the first steps on a journey to world power. But why did the Europeans continue a process that the Chinese had deliberately abandoned?

In the first place, Europe had no unified political authority with the power to order an end to its maritime outreach. Its system of competing states, so unlike China's single state, ensured that once begun, rivalry alone would drive the Europeans to the ends of the earth. Beyond this, much of Europe's elite had an interest in overseas expansion. Its budding merchant communities saw opportunity for profit; its competing monarchs eyed the revenue from taxing overseas trade or from seizing overseas resources; the Church foresaw the possibility of widespread conversion; impoverished nobles might imagine fame and fortune abroad. In China, by contrast, support for Zheng He's voyages was very shallow in official circles, and when the emperor Yongle passed from the scene, those opposed to the voyages prevailed within the politics of the court.

Finally, the Chinese were very much aware of their own antiquity, believed strongly in the absolute superiority of their culture, and felt with good reason that, should they desire something from abroad, others would bring it to them. Europeans too believed themselves unique, particularly in religious terms as the possessors of Christianity, the "one true religion." In material terms, though, they were seeking out the greater riches of the East, and they were highly conscious that Muslim power blocked easy access to these treasures and posed a military and religious threat to Europe itself. All of this propelled continuing European expansion in the centuries that followed.

Guided Reading Question

■ **COMPARISON**
In what ways did European maritime voyaging in the fifteenth century differ from that of China? What accounts for these differences?

The Chinese withdrawal from the Indian Ocean actually facilitated the European entry. It cleared the way for the Portuguese to penetrate the region, where they faced only the eventual naval power of the Ottomans. Had Vasco da Gama encountered Zheng He's massive fleet as his four small ships sailed into Asian waters in 1498, world history may well have taken quite a different turn. As it was, however, China's abandonment of oceanic voyaging and Europe's embrace of the seas marked different responses to a common problem that both civilizations shared—growing populations and land shortage. In the centuries that followed, China's rice-based agriculture was able to expand production internally by more intensive use of the land, while the country's territorial expansion was inland toward Central Asia. By contrast, Europe's agriculture, based on wheat and livestock, expanded primarily by acquiring new lands in overseas possessions, which were gained as a consequence of a commitment to oceanic expansion.

Civilizations of the Fifteenth Century: The Islamic World

Beyond the domains of Chinese and European civilization, our fifteenth-century global traveler would surely have been impressed with the transformations of the Islamic world. Stretching across much of Afro-Eurasia, the enormous realm of Islam experienced a set of remarkable changes during the fifteenth and early sixteenth centuries, as well as the continuation of earlier patterns. The most notable change lay in the political realm, for an Islamic civilization that had been severely fragmented since at least 900 now crystallized into four major states or empires (see Map 12.4). At the same time, a long-term process of conversion to Islam continued the cultural transformation of Afro-Eurasian societies both within and beyond these new states.

In the Islamic Heartland: The Ottoman and Safavid Empires

The most impressive and enduring of the new Islamic states was the **Ottoman Empire**, which lasted in one form or another from the fourteenth to the early twentieth century. It was the creation of one of the many Turkic warrior groups that had migrated into Anatolia, slowly and sporadically, in the several centuries following 1000 c.e. By the mid-fifteenth century, these Ottoman Turks had already carved out a state that encompassed much of the Anatolian peninsula and had pushed deep into southeastern Europe (the Balkans), acquiring in the process a substantial Christian population. During the sixteenth century, the Ottoman Empire extended its control to much of the Middle East, coastal North Africa, the lands surrounding the Black Sea, and even farther into Eastern Europe.

Map 12.4 Empires of the Islamic World
The most prominent political features of the vast Islamic world in the fifteenth and sixteenth centuries were four large states: the Songhay, Ottoman, Safavid, and Mughal empires.

The Ottoman Empire was a state of enormous significance in the world of the fifteenth century and beyond. In its huge territory, long duration, incorporation of many diverse peoples, and economic and cultural sophistication, it was one of the great empires of world history. In the fifteenth century, only Ming dynasty China and the Incas matched it in terms of wealth, power, and splendor. The empire represented the emergence of the Turks as the dominant people of the Islamic world, ruling now over many Arabs, who had initiated this new faith more than 800 years before. In adding "caliph" (successor to the Prophet) to their other titles, Ottoman sultans claimed the legacy of the earlier Abbasid Empire. They sought to bring a renewed unity to the Islamic world, while also serving as protector of the faith, the "strong sword of Islam."

The Ottoman Empire also represented a new phase in the long encounter between Christendom and the world of Islam. In the Crusades, Europeans had

Guided Reading Question

■ **COMPARISON**
What differences can you identify among the four major empires in the Islamic world of the fifteenth and sixteenth centuries?

1453 in Constantinople

On May 29, 1453, forces of the Muslim Ottoman sultan Mehmed II seized control of the great Christian city of Constantinople, an event that marked the final end of the Roman/Byzantine Empire and the ascendency of the Ottoman Empire. In retrospect, this event acquired a certain air of inevitability about it, for the Byzantine Empire had been retreating for almost two centuries before the steady advance of the Ottomans. By 1453, that once-great empire, heir to all things Roman, had shrunk to little more than the city

Ottoman Turks storm the walls of Constantinople in 1453.

itself, with only some 50,000 inhabitants and 8,000 active defenders compared to a vast Ottoman army of 60,000 soldiers. And little was left of the fabled wealth of the city. But what later observers see as inevitable generally occurs only with great human effort and amid vast uncertainty about the outcome. So it was in Constantinople in 1453.

Constantine XI, the last Byzantine emperor, was well aware of the odds he faced. Yet his great city, protected by water on two sides and a great wall on a third, had repeatedly withstood many attacks and sieges. Further-

more, until the very end, he had hoped for assistance from Western Christians, even promising union with the Roman Church to obtain it. But no such help arrived, at least not in sufficient quantities to make a difference, though rumors of a fleet from Venice persisted. The internal problems of the Western powers as well as the long-standing hostility between Eastern Orthodoxy and Roman Catholicism ensured that Constantinople would meet its end alone.

On the Ottoman side, enormous effort was expended with no assurance of success. In 1451, a new sultan came to the throne of the Ottoman Empire, Mehmed II, only nineteen years old and widely regarded as not very promising. Furthermore, some among the court officials had reservations about an attack on Constantinople. But the young sultan seemed determined to gain the honor promised in Islamic prophesies, going back to Muhammad himself, to the one who conquered the city. Doing so

photo: © ullstein bild/The Image Works

taken the aggressive initiative in that encounter, but the rise of the Ottoman Empire reversed their roles. The **Ottoman seizure of Constantinople** in 1453 marked the final demise of Christian Byzantium and allowed Ottoman rulers to see themselves as successors to the Roman Empire. (See Zooming In: 1453 in Constantinople, above.) It also opened the way to further expansion, and in 1529 a rapidly expanding Ottoman Empire laid siege to Vienna in the heart of Central Europe. The political and military expansion of Islam, at the expense of Christendom, seemed clearly under way. Many Europeans spoke fearfully of the "terror of the Turk."

In the neighboring Persian lands to the east of the Ottoman Empire, another Islamic state was also taking shape in the late fifteenth and early sixteenth could also rid him of a potential rival to the Ottoman throne, who had taken refuge in Constantinople.

And so preparations began for an assault on the once-great city. The Ottomans assembled a huge fleet, gathered men and materials, and constructed a fortress to control access to Constantinople by water. In late 1452, Mehmed secured the services of a Hungarian master cannon builder named Orban, who constructed a number of huge cannons, one of which could hurl a 600-pound stone ball over a mile. These weapons later had a devastating effect on the walls surrounding Constantinople. Interestingly enough, Orban had first offered his services to the Byzantine emperor, who simply could not afford to pay for this very expensive project.

In early April of 1453, the siege began, and it lasted for fifty-seven days. As required by Islamic law, Mehmed offered three times to spare the emperor and his people if they surrendered. Constantine apparently considered the offer seriously, but he finally refused, declaring, "We have all decided to die with our own free will." After weeks of furious bombardment, an ominous silence descended on May 28. Mehmed had declared a day of rest and prayer before the final assault the next day. That evening, the Byzantine emperor ordered a procession of icons and relics about the city and then entered the ancient Christian church of Hagia Sophia, seeking forgiveness for his sins and receiving Holy Communion.

And then, early the next day, the final assault began as Ottoman forces breached the walls of Constantinople and took the city. The Christians bravely defended their city, and Constantine discarded his royal regalia and died fighting like a common soldier. A later legend suggested that angels turned Constantine into marble and buried him in a nearby cave from which he would eventually reappear to retake the city for Christendom.

Islamic law required that soldiers be permitted three days of plundering the spoils, but Mehmed was reluctant, eager to spare the city he longed for as his capital. So he limited plundering to one day. Even so, the aftermath was terrible. According to a Christian eyewitness, "The enraged Turkish soldiers . . . gave no quarter. When they had massacred and there was no longer any resistance, they were intent on pillage and roamed through the town stealing, disrobing, pillaging, killing, raping, taking captive men, women, children, monks, priests."[8] When Mehmed himself entered the city, praying at the Christian altar of Hagia Sophia, he reportedly wept at seeing the destruction that had occurred.

Constantinople was now a Muslim city, capital of the Ottoman Empire, and Hagia Sophia became a mosque. A momentous change had occurred in the relationship between the world of Islam and that of Christendom.

QUESTIONS

What factors contributed to Mehmed's victory? Under what circumstances might a different outcome have been possible?

centuries—the Safavid (SAH-fah-vihd) Empire. Its leadership was also Turkic, but in this case it had emerged from a Sufi religious order founded several centuries earlier by Safi al-Din (1252–1334). The long-term significance of the **Safavid Empire**, which was established in the decade following 1500, was its decision to forcibly impose a Shia version of Islam as the official religion of the state. Over time, this form of Islam gained popular support and came to define the unique identity of Persian (Iranian) culture.

This Shia empire also introduced a sharp divide into the political and religious life of heartland Islam, for almost all of Persia's neighbors practiced a Sunni form of the faith. For a century (1534–1639), periodic military conflict erupted between the Ottoman and Safavid empires, reflecting both territorial rivalry and sharp religious differences. In 1514, the Ottoman sultan wrote to the Safavid ruler in the most bitter of terms:

> You have denied the sanctity of divine law . . . you have deserted the path of salvation and the sacred commandments . . . you have opened to Muslims the gates of tyranny and oppression . . . you have raised the standard of irreligion and heresy. . . . [Therefore] the *ulama* and our doctors have pronounced a sentence of death against you, perjurer and blasphemer.[9]

This Sunni/Shia hostility has continued to divide the Islamic world into the twenty-first century.

On the Frontiers of Islam: The Songhay and Mughal Empires

While the Ottoman and Safavid empires brought both a new political unity and a sharp division to the heartland of Islam, two other states performed a similar role on the expanding African and Asian frontiers of the faith. In the West African savannas, the **Songhay Empire** rose in the second half of the fifteenth century. It was the most recent and the largest in a series of impressive states that operated at a crucial intersection of the trans-Saharan trade routes and that derived much of their revenue from taxing that commerce. Islam was a growing faith in Songhay but was limited largely to urban elites. This cultural divide within Songhay largely accounts for the religious behavior of its fifteenth-century monarch Sonni Ali (r. 1465–1492), who gave alms and fasted during Ramadan in proper Islamic style but also enjoyed a reputation as a magician and possessed a charm thought to render his soldiers invisible to their enemies. Nonetheless, Songhay had become a major center of Islamic learning and commerce by the early sixteenth century. A North African traveler known as Leo Africanus remarked on the city of **Timbuktu**:

> Here are great numbers of [Muslim] religious teachers, judges, scholars, and other learned persons who are bountifully maintained at the king's expense. Here too are brought various manuscripts or written books from Barbary [North Africa] which are sold for more money than any other merchandise. . . . Here are very rich merchants and to here journey continually large numbers of negroes who purchase here cloth from Barbary and Europe. . . . It is a wonder to see the quality of merchandise that is daily brought here and how costly and sumptuous everything is.[10]

The Mughal (MOO-guhl) Empire in India bore similarities to Songhay, for both governed largely non-Muslim populations. Much as the Ottoman Empire initiated a new phase in the interaction of Islam and Christendom, so too did the **Mughal Empire** continue an ongoing encounter between Islamic and Hindu civilizations. Established in the early sixteenth century, the Mughal Empire was the

Ottoman Janissaries Originating in the fourteenth century, the Janissaries became the elite infantry force of the Ottoman Empire. Complete with uniforms, cash salaries, and marching music, they were the first standing army in the region since the days of the Roman Empire. When gunpowder technology became available, Janissary forces soon were armed with muskets, grenades, and handheld cannons. This Turkish miniature painting dates from the sixteenth century. (Topkapi Palace Museum, Istanbul, Turkey/Album/Art Resource, NY)

creation of yet another Islamized Turkic group that invaded India in 1526. Over the next century, the Mughals (a Persian term for Mongols) established unified control over most of the Indian peninsula, giving it a rare period of political unity and laying the foundation for subsequent British colonial rule. During its first 150 years, the Mughal Empire, a land of great wealth and imperial splendor, undertook a remarkable effort to blend many Hindu groups and a variety of Muslims into an effective partnership. The inclusive policies of the early Mughal emperors showed that Muslim rulers could accommodate their overwhelmingly Hindu subjects in somewhat the same fashion as Ottoman authorities provided religious autonomy for their Christian minority.

Together these four Muslim empires—Ottoman, Safavid, Songhay, and Mughal—brought to the Islamic world a greater measure of political coherence, military power, economic prosperity, and cultural brilliance than it had known since the early centuries of Islam. This new energy, sometimes called a "second flowering of Islam," impelled the continuing spread of the faith to yet new regions.

The most prominent of these was oceanic Southeast Asia, which for centuries had been intimately bound up in the world of Indian Ocean commerce, while borrowing elements of both Hindu and Buddhist traditions. By the fifteenth century, that trading network was largely in Muslim hands, and the demand for Southeast Asian spices was mounting as the Eurasian world recovered from the devastation of Mongol conquest and the plague. Growing numbers of Muslim traders, many of them from India, settled in Java and Sumatra, bringing their faith with them. Eager to attract those traders to their port cities, a number of Hindu or Buddhist rulers along the Malay Peninsula and in Indonesia converted to Islam, while transforming themselves into Muslim sultans and imposing Islamic law. Thus, unlike in the Middle East and India, where Islam was established in the wake of Arab or Turkic conquest, in Southeast Asia, as in West Africa, it was introduced by traveling merchants and solidified through the activities of Sufi holy men.

The rise of **Malacca**, strategically located on the waterway between Sumatra and Malaya, was a sign of the times (see Map 12.1, page 501). During the fifteenth century, it was transformed from a small fishing village to a major Muslim port city. A Portuguese visitor in 1512 observed that Malacca had "no equal in the world. . . . Commerce between different nations for a thousand leagues on every hand must come to Malacca."[11] That city also became a springboard for the spread of Islam throughout the region. In the eclectic style of Southeast Asian religious history, the Islam of Malacca demonstrated much blending with local and Hindu/Buddhist traditions, while the city itself, like many port towns, had a reputation for "rough behavior." An Arab Muslim pilot in the 1480s commented critically: "They have no culture at all. . . . You do not know whether they are Muslim or not."[12] Nonetheless, Malacca, like Timbuktu on the West African frontier of an expanding Islamic world, became a center for Islamic learning, and students from elsewhere in Southeast Asia were studying there in the fifteenth century. As the core regions of Islam were consolidating politically, the frontier of the faith continued to move steadily outward.

> **PRACTICING HISTORICAL THINKING**
>
> In what ways did the civilizations of China, Europe, and the Islamic world in the fifteenth century seem to be moving in the same direction, and in what respects were they diverging from one another?

Civilizations of the Fifteenth Century: The Americas

Across the Atlantic, centers of civilization had long flourished in Mesoamerica and in the Andes. The fifteenth century witnessed new, larger, and more politically unified expressions of those civilizations, embodied in the Aztec and Inca empires. Both were the work of previously marginal peoples who had forcibly taken over and absorbed older cultures, giving them new energy, and both were decimated in the sixteenth century at the hands of Spanish conquistadores and their diseases (see Map 12.5).

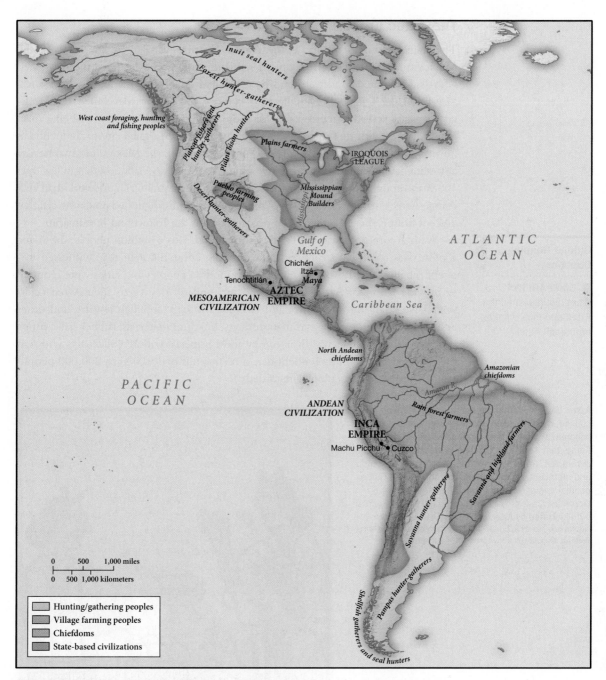

Map 12.5 The Americas in the Fifteenth Century

The Americas before Columbus represented a world almost completely separate from Afro-Eurasia. It featured similar kinds of societies, though with a different balance among them, but it largely lacked the pastoral economies that were so important in the Eastern Hemisphere.

The Aztec Empire

The state known to history as the **Aztec Empire** was largely the work of the Mexica (meh-SHEEH-kah) people, a semi-nomadic group from northern Mexico who had migrated southward and by 1325 had established themselves on a small island in Lake Texcoco. Over the next century, the Mexica developed their military capacity, served as mercenaries for more powerful people, negotiated elite marriage alliances with those people, and built up their own capital city of Tenochtitlán (te-nawch-tee-tlahn). In 1428, a Triple Alliance between the Mexica and two nearby city-states launched a highly aggressive program of military conquest that in less than 100 years brought more of Mesoamerica within a single political framework than ever before. Aztec authorities, eager to shed their rather undistinguished past, now claimed descent from earlier Mesoamerican peoples such as the Toltecs and Teotihuacán.

With a core population recently estimated at 5 to 6 million people, the Aztec Empire was a loosely structured and unstable conquest state that witnessed frequent rebellions by its subject peoples. Conquered peoples and cities were required to provide labor for Aztec projects and to regularly deliver to their Aztec rulers impressive quantities of textiles and clothing, military supplies, jewelry and other luxuries, various foodstuffs, animal products, building materials, rubber balls, paper, and more. The process was overseen by local imperial tribute collectors, who sent the required goods on to Tenochtitlán, a metropolis of 150,000 to 200,000 people, where they were meticulously recorded.

Guided Reading Question

·····························

■ **COMPARISON**
What distinguished the Aztec and Inca empires from each other?

Aztec Women Within the home, Aztec women cooked, cleaned, spun and wove cloth, raised their children, and undertook ritual activities. Outside the home, they served as officials in palaces, priestesses in temples, traders in markets, teachers in schools, and members of craftworkers' organizations. This domestic image comes from the sixteenth-century Florentine Codex, which was compiled by the Spanish but illustrated by Aztec artists. (Facsimile detail from Book IV of Florentine Codex, "General History of the Things of New Spain"/Museo del Templo Mayor, Mexico City, Mexico/De Agostini Picture Library/Bridgeman Images)

That city featured numerous canals, dikes, causeways, and bridges. A central walled area of palaces and temples included a pyramid almost 200 feet high. Surrounding the city were "floating gardens," artificial islands created from swamplands that supported a highly productive agriculture. Vast marketplaces reflected the commercialization of the economy. A young Spanish soldier who beheld the city in 1519 declared, "Gazing on such wonderful sights, we did not know what to say, or whether what appeared before us was real."[13]

Beyond tribute from conquered peoples, ordinary trade, both local and long-distance, permeated Aztec domains. The extent of empire and rapid population growth stimulated the development of markets and the production of craft goods, particularly in the fifteenth century. Virtually every settlement, from the capital city to the smallest village, had a marketplace that hummed with activity during weekly market days. The largest was that of Tlatelolco, near the capital city, which stunned the Spanish with its huge size, its good order, and the immense range of goods available. Hernán Cortés, the Spanish conquistador who defeated the Aztecs, wrote that "every kind of merchandise such as can be met with in every land is for sale there, whether of food and victuals, or ornaments of gold and silver, or lead, brass, copper, tin, precious stones, bones, shells, snails and feathers."[14] Professional merchants, known as *pochteca*, were legally commoners, but their wealth, often exceeding that of the nobility, allowed them to rise in society and become "magnates of the land."

Among the "goods" that the pochteca obtained were slaves, many of whom were destined for sacrifice in the bloody rituals so central to Aztec religious life. Long a part of Mesoamerican and many other world cultures, human sacrifice assumed an unusually prominent role in Aztec public life and thought during the fifteenth century. Tlacaelel (1398–1480), who was for more than half a century a prominent official of the Aztec Empire, is often credited with crystallizing the ideology of state that gave human sacrifice such great importance.

In that cyclical understanding of the world, the sun, central to all life and identified with the Aztec patron deity Huitzilopochtli (wee-tsee-loh-pockt-lee), tended to lose its energy in a constant battle against encroaching darkness. Thus the Aztec world hovered always on the edge of catastrophe. To replenish its energy and thus postpone the descent into endless darkness, the sun required the life-giving force found in human blood. Because the gods had shed their blood ages ago in creating humankind, it was wholly proper for people to offer their own blood to nourish the gods in the present. The high calling of the Aztec state was to supply this blood, largely through its wars of expansion and from prisoners of war, who were destined for sacrifice. The victims were "those who have died for the god." The growth of the Aztec Empire therefore became the means for maintaining cosmic order and avoiding utter catastrophe. This ideology also shaped the techniques of Aztec warfare, which put a premium on capturing prisoners rather than on killing the enemy. As the empire grew, priests and rulers became mutually dependent, and "human sacrifices were carried out in the service of politics."[15] Massive sacrificial

Guided Reading Question

■ **DESCRIPTION**
How did Aztec religious thinking support the empire?

rituals, together with a display of great wealth, served to impress enemies, allies, and subjects alike with the immense power of the Aztecs and their gods.

Alongside these sacrificial rituals was a philosophical and poetic tradition of great beauty, much of which mused on the fragility and brevity of human life. Such an outlook characterized the work of Nezahualcoyotl (1402–1472), a poet and king of the city-state of Texcoco, which was part of the Aztec Empire:

> Truly do we live on Earth?
> Not forever on earth; only a little while here.
> Although it be jade, it will be broken.
> Although it be gold, it is crushed.
> Although it be a quetzal feather, it is torn asunder.
> Not forever on earth; only a little while here.[16]

The Inca Empire

While the Mexica were constructing an empire in Mesoamerica, a relatively small community of Quechua-speaking people, known to us as the Incas, was building the Western Hemisphere's largest imperial state along the entire spine of the Andes Mountains. Much as the Aztecs drew on the traditions of the Toltecs and Teoti-huacán, the Incas incorporated the lands and cultures of earlier Andean civilizations: Chavín, Moche, Wari, and Tiwanaku. The **Inca Empire**, however, was much larger than the Aztec state; it stretched some 2,500 miles along the Andes and contained perhaps 10 million subjects. Whereas the Aztec Empire controlled only part of the Mesoamerican cultural region, the Inca state encompassed practically the whole of Andean civilization during its short life in the fifteenth and early sixteenth centuries. In the speed of its creation and the extent of its territory, the Inca Empire bears some similarity to that of the Mongols.

Both the Aztec and Inca empires represent rags-to-riches stories in which quite modest and remotely located people very quickly created by military conquest the largest states ever witnessed in their respective regions, but the empires themselves were quite different. In the Aztec realm, the Mexica rulers largely left their conquered people alone, if the required tribute was forthcoming. No elaborate administrative system arose to integrate the conquered territories or to assimilate their people to Aztec culture.

The Incas, on the other hand, erected a rather more bureaucratic empire. At the top reigned the emperor, an absolute ruler regarded as divine, a descendant of the creator god Viracocha and the son of the sun god Inti. Each of the some eighty provinces in the empire had an Inca governor. In theory, the state owned all land and resources, though in practice state lands, known as "lands of the sun," existed alongside properties owned by temples, elites, and traditional communities. At least in the central regions of the empire, subjects were grouped into hierarchical units of 10, 50, 100, 500, 1,000, 5,000, and 10,000 people, each headed by local officials, who were appointed and supervised by an Inca governor or the emperor.

Guided Reading Question

■ **DESCRIPTION**
In what ways did Inca authorities seek to integrate their vast domains?

A separate set of "inspectors" provided the imperial center with an independent check on provincial officials.

Births, deaths, marriages, and other population data were carefully recorded on *quipus*, the knotted cords that served as an accounting device. A resettlement program moved one-quarter or more of the population to new locations, in part to disperse conquered and no doubt resentful people and sometimes to reward loyal followers with promising opportunities. Efforts at cultural integration required the leaders of conquered peoples to learn Quechua (keh-choo-wah). Their sons were removed to the capital of Cuzco for instruction in Inca culture and language. Even now, millions of people from Ecuador to Chile still speak Quechua, and it is the official second language of Peru after Spanish.

But the sheer human variety of the Incas' enormous empire required great flexibility. In some places Inca rulers encountered bitter resistance; in others local elites were willing to accommodate Incas and thus benefit from their inclusion in the empire. Where centralized political systems already existed, Inca overlords could delegate control to native authorities. Elsewhere they had to construct an administrative system from scratch. Everywhere they sought to incorporate local people into the lower levels of the administrative hierarchy. While the Incas required their subject peoples to acknowledge major Inca deities, these peoples were then largely

Machu Picchu Machu Picchu, high in the Andes Mountains, was constructed by the Incas in the fifteenth century on a spot long held sacred by local people. Its 200 buildings stand at some 8,000 feet above sea level, making it a "city in the sky." It was probably a royal retreat or religious center, rather than a location serving administrative, commercial, or military purposes. The outside world became aware of Machu Picchu only in 1911, when it was popularized by a Yale University archeologist. (fStop/Superstock)

free to carry on their own religious traditions. The Inca Empire was a fluid system that varied greatly from place to place and over time. It depended as much on the posture of conquered peoples as on the demands and desires of Inca authorities.

Like the Aztec Empire, the Inca state represented an especially dense and extended network of economic relationships within the "American web," but these relationships took shape in quite a different fashion. Inca demands on their conquered people were expressed, not so much in terms of tribute, but as labor service, known as *mita*, which was required periodically of every household. What people produced at home usually stayed at home, but almost everyone also had to work for the state. Some labored on large state farms or on "sun farms," which supported temples and religious institutions; others herded, mined, served in the military, or toiled on state-directed construction projects.

Those with particular skills were put to work manufacturing textiles, metal goods, ceramics, and stonework. The most well known of these specialists were the "chosen women," who were removed from their homes as young girls, trained in Inca ideology, and set to producing corn beer and cloth at state centers. Later they were given as wives to men of distinction or sent to serve as priestesses in various temples, where they were known as "wives of the Sun." In return for such labor services, Inca ideology, expressed in terms of family relationships, required the state to arrange elaborate feasts at which large quantities of food and drink were consumed and to provide food and other necessities when disaster struck. Thus the authority of the state penetrated and directed Inca society and economy far more than did that of the Aztecs.

If the Inca and Aztec civilizations differed sharply in their political and economic arrangements, they resembled each other more closely in their gender systems. Both societies practiced what scholars call "gender parallelism," in which "women and men operate in two separate but equivalent spheres, each gender enjoying autonomy in its own sphere."[17] In both Mesoamerican and Andean societies, such systems had emerged long before their incorporation into the Aztec and Inca empires. In the Andes, men reckoned their descent from their fathers and women from their mothers, while Mesoamericans had long viewed children as belonging equally to their mothers and fathers. Parallel religious cults for women and men likewise flourished in both societies. Inca men venerated the sun, while women worshipped the moon, with matching religious officials. In Aztec temples, both male and female priests presided over rituals dedicated to deities of both sexes. Particularly among the Incas, parallel hierarchies of male and female political officials governed the empire, while in Aztec society, women officials exercised local authority under a title that meant "female person in charge of people." Social roles were clearly defined and different for men and women, but the domestic concerns of women — childbirth, cooking, weaving, cleaning — were not regarded as inferior to the activities of men. Among the Aztecs, for example, sweeping was a powerful and sacred act with symbolic significance as "an act of purification and a preventative against evil elements penetrating the center of the Aztec universe, the home."[18]

In the Andes, men broke the ground, women sowed, and both took part in the harvest.

This was gender complementarity, not gender equality. Men occupied the top positions in both political and religious life, and male infidelity was treated more lightly than was women's unfaithfulness. As the Inca and Aztec empires expanded, military life, limited to men, grew in prestige, perhaps skewing an earlier gender parallelism. The Incas in particular imposed a more rigidly patriarchal order on their subject peoples. In other ways, the new Aztec and Inca rulers adapted to the gender systems of the people they had conquered. Among the Aztecs, the tools of women's work, the broom and the weaving spindle, were ritualized as weapons; sweeping the home was believed to assist men at war; and childbirth was regarded by women as "our kind of war."[19] Inca rulers replicated the gender parallelism of their subjects at a higher level, as the *sapay Inca* (the Inca ruler) and the *coya* (his female consort) governed jointly, claiming descent respectively from the sun and the moon.

Webs of Connection

Few people in the fifteenth century lived in entirely separate and self-contained communities. Almost all were caught up, to one degree or another, in various and overlapping webs of influence, communication, and exchange.[20] Perhaps most obvious were the webs of empire, large-scale political systems that brought together a variety of culturally different people. Christians and Muslims encountered each other directly in the Ottoman Empire, as did Hindus and Muslims in the Mughal Empire. And no empire tried more diligently to integrate its diverse peoples than the fifteenth-century Incas.

Inca Agricultural Practice This sixteenth-century drawing by Felipe Guaman Poma, an Inca nobleman, illustrates the cooperation of Inca men and women in agriculture. The men are loosening the soil with a "foot-plow," while the women plant the seeds. (Werner Forman/Getty Images)

Religion too linked far-flung peoples, and divided them as well. Christianity provided a common religious culture for peoples from England to Russia, although the great divide between Roman Catholicism and Eastern Orthodoxy endured, and in the sixteenth century the Protestant Reformation would shatter permanently the Christian unity of the Latin West. Although Buddhism had largely vanished from its South Asian homeland, it remained a link among China, Korea, Tibet, Japan, and parts of Southeast Asia, even as it splintered into a variety of sects and practices. More than either of these, Islam actively brought together its many peoples. In the hajj, the pilgrimage to Mecca, Africans, Arabs, Persians, Turks, Indians, and many others joined as one people as they rehearsed together the events that gave birth to their common faith. And yet divisions and conflicts persisted within the vast realm of Islam, as the violent hostility between the Sunni Ottoman Empire and the Shia Safavid Empire so vividly illustrates.

Guided Reading
Question

■ **CONNECTION**
In what different ways did the peoples of the fifteenth century interact with one another?

Long-established patterns of trade among peoples occupying different environments and producing different goods were certainly much in evidence during the fifteenth century, as they had been for millennia. Hunting societies of Siberia funneled furs and other products of the forest into the Silk Road trading network traversing the civilizations of Eurasia. In the fifteenth century, some of the agricultural peoples in southern Nigeria were receiving horses brought overland from the drier regions of Africa to the north, where those animals flourished better. The Mississippi River in North America and the Orinoco and Amazon rivers in South America facilitated a canoe-borne commerce along those waterways. Coastal shipping in large seagoing canoes operated in the Caribbean and along the Pacific coast between Mexico and Peru. In Pacific Polynesia, the great voyaging networks across vast oceanic distances that had flourished especially since 1000 were in decline by 1500 or earlier, leading to the abandonment of a number of islands.

The great long-distance trading patterns of the Afro-Eurasian world, in operation for a thousand years or more, continued in the fifteenth century, although the balance among them was changing (see Map 12.6). The Silk Road overland network, which had flourished under Mongol control in the thirteenth and fourteenth centuries, contracted in the fifteenth century as the Mongol Empire broke up and the devastation of the plague reduced demand for its products. The rise of the Ottoman Empire also blocked direct commercial contact between Europe and China, but oceanic trade from Japan, Korea, and China through the islands of Southeast Asia and across the Indian Ocean picked up considerably. Larger ships made it possible to trade in bulk goods such as grain as well as luxury products, while more sophisticated partnerships and credit mechanisms greased the wheels of commerce. A common Islamic culture over much of this vast region likewise smoothed the passage of goods among very different peoples, as it also did for the trans-Saharan trade.

After 1500: Looking Ahead to the Modern Era

While ties of empire, culture, commerce, and disease surely linked many of the peoples in the world of the fifteenth century, none of those connections operated on a genuinely global scale. Although the densest webs of connection had been woven within the Afro-Eurasian zone of interaction, this huge region had no enduring ties with the Americas, and neither of them had sustained contact with the peoples of Pacific Oceania. That situation was about to change as Europeans in the sixteenth century and beyond forged a set of genuinely global relationships that generated sustained interaction among all of these regions. That huge process and the many outcomes that flowed from it marked the beginning of what world historians

MAPPING HISTORY

Map 12.6 Religion and Commerce in the Afro-Eurasian World

By the fifteenth century, the many distinct peoples and societies of the Eastern Hemisphere were linked to one another by ties of religion and commerce. Of course, most people were not directly involved in long-distance trade, and many people in areas shown as Buddhist or Islamic on the map practiced other religions. While much of India, for example, was ruled by Muslims, the majority of its people followed some form of Hinduism. And although Islam had spread to West Africa, that religion had not penetrated much beyond the urban centers of the region.

READING THE MAP: Where were Buddhists concentrated in the Indian Ocean region? In which areas were Muslims most prominent?

INTERPRETING THE MAP: What does this map suggest about the places where cross-cultural contacts and interactions among the three major faiths during the fifteenth century might most likely occur?

commonly call the modern age—the more than five centuries that followed the voyages of Columbus starting in 1492.

Over those five centuries, the previously separate worlds of Afro-Eurasia, the Americas, and Pacific Oceania became inextricably linked, with enormous consequences for everyone involved. Global empires, a global economy, global cultural exchanges, global migrations, global disease, global wars, and global environmental changes have made the past 500 years a unique phase in the human journey. Those webs of communication and exchange—the first defining feature of the modern era—have progressively deepened, so much so that by the end of the twentieth century few if any people lived beyond the cultural influences, economic ties, or political relationships of a globalized world.

Several centuries after the Columbian voyages, and clearly connected to them, a second distinctive feature of the modern era took shape: the emergence of a radically new kind of human society, first in Europe during the nineteenth century and then in various forms elsewhere in the world. The core feature of such societies was indus-trialization. That revolutionary economic process was accompanied by a host of other transformations: accelerating technological innovation; the massive consumption of energy and raw materials; a scientific outlook on the world; an unprecedented increase in human population (see the Snapshot); rapid urbanization; widespread commercial-ization; more powerful and intrusive states; the growing prominence and dominance of Europeans on the world stage; and a very different balance of global power.

This was the revolution of modernity, comparable in its pervasive consequences only to the Agricultural Revolution of some 10,000 years ago. It usually meant a self-conscious and often uneasy awareness of living and thinking in new ways that deliberately departed from tradition. Sorting out what was gained and what was lost during the modern transformation has been a persistent and highly controversial thread of human thought over the past several centuries. And it is a central concern of historians who trace the contours of the human journey in the centuries after 1500.

SNAPSHOT   World Population Growth, 1000–2000

Data from David Christian, *Map of Time* (Berkeley: University of California Press, 2004), 343.

REFLECTIONS

What If? Chance and Contingency in World History

Seeking meaning in the stories they tell, historians are inclined to look for deeply rooted or underlying causes for the events they recount. And yet, is it possible that, at least on occasion, historical change derives less from profound and long-term sources than from coincidence, chance, or the decisions of a few that might well have gone another way?

Consider, for example, the problem of explaining the rise of Europe to a position of global power in the modern era. What if the Great Khan Ogodei had not died in 1241, requiring the Mongol forces then poised for an assault on Germany to return to Mongolia? It is surely possible that Central and Western Europe might have been overrun by Mongol armies as so many other civilizations had been, a prospect that could have drastically altered the trajectory of European history. Or what if the Chinese had decided in 1433 to continue their huge maritime expeditions, creating an empire in the Indian Ocean basin and perhaps moving on to "discover" the Americas and Europe? Such a scenario suggests a wholly different future for world history than the one that in fact occurred. Or what if the forces of the Ottoman Empire had taken the besieged city of Vienna in 1529? Might they then have incorporated even larger parts of Europe into their expanding domain, requiring a halt to Europe's overseas empire-building enterprise?

None of this necessarily means that the rise of Europe was merely a fluke or an accident of history, but it does raise the issue of "contingency," the role of unforeseen or small events in the unfolding of the human story. An occasional "what if" approach to history reminds us that alternative possibilities existed in the past and that the only certainty about the future is that we will be surprised.

Second Thoughts

What's the Significance?

Igbo, 497

Iroquois, 497

Timur, 498

Fulbe, 499

Ming dynasty, 500

Zheng He, 502

European Renaissance, 504

Ottoman Empire, 508

Ottoman seizure of Constantinople, 510

Safavid Empire, 511

Songhay Empire, 512

Timbuktu, 512

Mughal Empire, 512

Malacca, 514

Aztec Empire, 516

Inca Empire, 518

Big Picture Questions

1. Assume for the moment that the Chinese had not ended their maritime voyages in 1433. How might the subsequent development of world history have been different? What value is there in asking this kind of "what if" or counterfactual question?

2. How does this chapter distinguish among the various kinds of societies contained in the world of the fifteenth century? What other ways of categorizing the world's peoples might work as well or better?

3. What common patterns might you notice across the world of the fifteenth century? And what variations in the historical trajectories of various regions can you identify?

4. **Looking Back:** What would surprise a knowledgeable observer from 500 or 1000 C.E., were he or she to make a global tour in the fifteenth century? What features of that earlier world might still be recognizable?

Next Steps: For Further Study

Terence N. D'Altroy, *The Incas* (2002). A history of the Inca Empire that draws on recent archeological and historical research.

Alan Covey, *How the Incas Built their Heartland* (2006). An interdisciplinary examination of the processes and strategies that allowed the Inca to create their empire.

Edward L. Dreyer, *Zheng He: China and the Oceans in the Early Ming Dynasty* (2006). The most recent scholarly account of the Ming dynasty voyages.

Halil Inalcik and Donald Quataert, *An Economic and Social History of the Ottoman Empire, 1300–1914* (1994). A classic study of the Ottoman Empire.

Robin Kirkpatrick, *The European Renaissance, 1400–1600* (2002). A beautifully illustrated history of Renaissance culture as well as the social and economic life of the period.

Charles C. Mann, *1491: New Revelations of the Americas before Columbus* (2005). A review of Western Hemisphere societies and academic debates about their pre-Columbian history.

J. R. McNeill and William H. McNeill, *The Human Web* (2003). A succinct account of the evolving webs or relationships among human societies in world history.

Michael Smith, *The Aztecs* (2003). A history of the Aztec Empire, with an emphasis on the lives of ordinary people.

Khan Academy, "An Introduction to the Ming Dynasty (1368–1644)," https://www .khanacademy.org/humanities/art-asia/imperial-china/ming-dynasty/a/an -introduction-to-the-ming-dynasty-13681644. A collection of brief essays, images, and videos about Ming dynasty China.

Joel Westerbrook, Executive Producer, "Inca: Secrets of the Ancestors," Time-Life, Lost Civilizations, 1995, https://www.youtube.com/watch?v=3GrcN24PqmE. A thoughtful video exploring this largest of pre-Columbian states.

Islam and Renaissance Europe

The Renaissance era in Europe, roughly 1350 to 1500, represented the crystallization of a new third-wave civilization at the western end of Eurasia. In cultural terms, its writers and artists sought to link themselves to the legacy of the pre-Christian Greeks and Romans. But if Europeans were reaching back to their classical past, they were also reaching out — westward to the wholly new world of the Americas, southward to Africa, and eastward to Asia generally and the Islamic world in particular. The European Renaissance, in short, was shaped not only from within but also by its encounters with a wider world.

Interaction with the world of Islam was, of course, nothing new. Centuries of Muslim rule in Spain, the Crusades, and the expansion of the Ottoman Empire were markers in the long relationship of conflict, cooperation, and mutual influence between Christendom and the realm of Islam. Politically, that relationship was changing in the fifteenth century. The Christian reconquest of Spain from Muslim rule was completed by 1492. At the other end of the Mediterranean Sea, the Turkish Ottoman Empire was expanding into the previously Christian regions of the Balkans (southeastern Europe), seizing the ancient capital of the Byzantine Empire, Constantinople, in 1453, while becoming a major player in European international politics.

Despite such conflicts, commerce flourished across political and religious divides. European bulk goods such as wool, timber, and glassware, along with silver and gold, were exchanged for high-value luxury goods from the Islamic world or funneled through it from farther east. These included spices, silks, carpets, tapestries, brocades, art objects, precious stones, gold, dyes, and pigments. In 1384, a Christian pilgrim from the Italian city of Florence wrote: "Really all of Christendom could be supplied for a year with the merchandise of Damascus."[21] Along with goods, Arab and Muslim learning — in medicine, astronomy, philosophy, architecture, mathematics, business practices, and more — also flowed into the Christian West. These various engagements with the Islamic world all found expression in Renaissance Italy, as the sources that follow illustrate.

SOURCE 12.1 **Portrait of Mehmed II** ▶

The year 1453 marked a watershed in the long relationship between Christendom and the Islamic world, for it was in that year that the Ottoman sultan Mehmed II decisively conquered the great Christian city of Constantinople, bringing the thousand-year history of Byzantium to an inglorious end. To many Europeans, that event was a catastrophe and Mehmed was the "terror of the world." Others, however, saw opportunity. Less than a year after that event, the northern Italian city of Venice signed a peace treaty with the Ottoman sultan, declaring, "It is our intention to live in peace and friendship with the Turkish emperor."[22] Some even expressed admiration for the conquering Muslim ruler. George of Trebizond, a Greek-speaking Renaissance scholar, described Mehmed as "a wise king and one who philosophizes about the greatest matters."[23]

For his part, Mehmed admired both classical and contemporary European culture, even as his armies threatened European powers. This cosmopolitan emperor stocked his library with Western texts and decorated the walls of his palace with Renaissance-style frescoes. Seeing himself as heir to Roman imperial authority, he now added "Caesar" to his other titles. And in 1480, he had his portrait painted by the leading artist of Venice, Gentile Bellini, who had been sent to the Ottoman court as a cultural ambassador of his city.

Source 12.1 shows Bellini's portrait of the emperor sitting under a marble arch, a symbol of triumph that evokes his dramatic conquest of Constantinople. The three golden crowns on the upper left and right likely represent the lands recently acquired for the Ottoman Empire, and the inscription at the bottom describes Mehmed as "Conqueror of the World."

- What overall impression of the sultan does this portrait convey?

- Why might this Muslim ruler want his portrait painted by a Christian artist from Venice?

- Why might Bellini and the city government of Venice be willing—even eager—to undertake the assignment, less than thirty years after the Muslim conquest of Constantinople?

GENTILE BELLINI | *Portrait of Mehmed II* | 1480

National Gallery, London, UK/Bridgeman Images

∎ ∎ ∎

SOURCE 12.2 Machiavelli on the Turkish State

The increasing power of the Ottoman Empire inspired fear and admiration among Christian observers, along with a growing interest in how the Turkish sultan governed his state. Niccolò Machiavelli (1469–1527), the diplomat, historian, and political theorist from Florence, offered his assessment of Ottoman government in his most famous treatise, *The Prince*, when he compared the Turkish state to that of France, one of the most powerful kingdoms in Western Europe.

■ How would you characterize Machiavelli's view of the Ottoman state? Does he see it clearly as superior or inferior to that of France, or just different?

■ Does religion enter into Machiavelli's analysis?

■ Many at the time criticized Machiavelli's *Prince* for its amoral analysis of political life and its assertion that rulers must set aside concerns about morality to rule effectively. Is there anything in this passage that supports this interpretation of Machiavelli's thought?

NICCOLÒ MACHIAVELLI | *The Prince* | 1513

Examples of these two kinds of government in our own time are the Turk and the King of France. All the Turkish monarchy is governed by one ruler, the others are his servants, and dividing his kingdom into "sangiascates" [administrative units], he sends to them various administrators, and charges or recalls them at his pleasure. But the King of France is surrounded by a large number of ancient nobles, recognized as such by their subjects, and loved by them; they have their prerogatives, which the king cannot deprive them of without danger to himself. Whoever now considers these two states will see that it would be difficult to acquire the state of the Turk; but having conquered it, it would be very easy to hold it.

The causes of the difficulty of occupying the Turkish kingdom are, that the invader could not be invited by princes of that kingdom, nor hope to facilitate his enterprise by the rebellion of those around [the Turkish sultan], as will be evident from reasons given above. Because, being all slaves, and bound, it will be more difficult to corrupt them, and even if they were corrupted, little effect could be hoped for, as they would not be able to carry the people with them for the reasons mentioned. Therefore, whoever assaults the Turk must be prepared to meet his united forces, and must rely more on his own strength than on the disorders of others [i.e., rebellious subjects of the Turkish ruler]; but having once conquered him, and beaten him in battle so that he can no longer raise armies, nothing else is to be feared except the family of the prince, and if this is extinguished [i.e., if all members of the Turkish ruler's family are killed], there is no longer any one to be feared, the others having no credit with the people; and as the victor before the victory could place no hope in them, so he need not fear them afterwards. The contrary is the case in the kingdoms governed like that of France, because it is easy to enter them by winning over some baron of the kingdom, there being always some malcontents, and those desiring innovations. These can, for the reasons stated, open the way to you and facilitate victory; but afterwards, if you wish to keep possession, infinite difficulties arise, both from those who have aided you and from those you have oppressed. Nor is it sufficient to extinguish the family of the prince, for there remain those nobles who will make themselves the head of new changes, and being neither able to content them nor exterminate them, you will lose the state whenever an occasion arises.

Source: Niccolò Machiavelli, *The Prince*, translated by Luigi Ricci (London: Grant Richards, 1903), 15–16.

■ ■ ■

SOURCE 12.3 **Venetian Trade in the Middle East** ▶

Venice had long been the primary point of commercial contact between Europe and the East and the source of the much-desired luxury goods that its merchants obtained from Alexandria in Egypt. At that time, Muslim Egypt was ruled by the Mamluks, a warrior caste of slave origins who had checked the westward advance of the Mongols in 1260 and had driven the last of the European Crusaders out of the Middle East in 1291. Venetian traders, however, were more interested in commerce than in religion, and by the fifteenth century they enjoyed a highly profitable relationship with the Mamluk rulers of Egypt and Syria, despite the periodic opposition of the pope and threats of excommunication. Thus it is not surprising that the Renaissance artists of Venice were prominent among those who reflected the influence of the Islamic world in their work. By the late fifteenth century, something of a fad for oriental themes surfaced in Venetian pictorial art.

Source 12.3, painted by an anonymous Venetian artist in 1511, expresses this intense interest in the Islamic world. The setting is Damascus in Syria, then ruled by the Egyptian Mamluk regime. The local Mamluk governor of the city, seated on a low platform with an elaborate headdress, is receiving an ambassador from Venice, shown in a red robe and standing in front of the governor. Behind him in black robes are other members of the Venetian delegation, while in the foreground various members of Damascus society—both officials and merchants—are distinguished from one another by variations in their turbans. Behind the wall lies the city of Damascus with its famous Umayyad mosque, formerly a Roman temple to Jupiter and later a Christian church, together with its three minarets. The city's lush gardens and its homes with wooden balconies and rooftop terraces complete the picture of urban Islam.

- What impressions of the city and its relationship with Venice does the artist seek to convey?

- How are the various social groups of Damascus distinguished from one another in this painting? What does the very precise visual description of these differences suggest about Venetian understanding of urban Mamluk society?

- What does the total absence of women suggest about their role in the public life of Damascus?

- How would you know that this is a Muslim city? What role, if any, does religion play in this depiction of the relationship between Christian Venice and Islamic Damascus?

The Venetian Ambassador Visits Damascus | 1511

Musée du Louvre, Paris, France/Bridgeman Images

■ ■ ■

SOURCE 12.4 Greek and Islamic Philosophers in Renaissance Art ▶

Beyond political and commercial relationships, Europeans had long engaged with the Islamic world intellectually as well. Source 12.4 illustrates that engagement in a work by Girolamo da Cremona, a fifteenth-century Italian painter known for his "illuminations" of early printed books. Created in 1483 (only some forty years after the invention of the printing press in Europe), it served as the frontispiece for one of the first printed versions of Aristotle's writings, translated into Latin, along with commentaries by the twelfth-century Muslim scholar Ibn Rushd (1126–1198), better known in the West as Averroes.

Aristotle, of course, was the great Greek philosopher of the fourth century B.C.E. whose writings presented a systematic and rational view of the world, while commenting on practically every branch of knowledge. The legacy of Greek thought in general and Aristotle in particular passed into both the Christian and Islamic worlds. Ibn Rushd, who wrote voluminous commentaries on Aristotle's works and much else as well, lived in Muslim Spain, where he argued for the compatibility of Aristotelian philosophy and the religious perspectives of Islam. While that outlook faced growing opposition in the Islamic world, Aristotle's writings found more fertile ground among European scholars in the new universities of the twelfth and thirteenth centuries, where they became the foundation of university curricula and nourished the growth of "natural philosophy." In large measure it was through translations of Ibn Rushd's Arabic commentaries on Aristotle that Europeans regained access to the thinking of that ancient philosopher. A long line of European scholars defined themselves as "Averroists."

The painting in Source 12.4 is presented as a parchment leaf, torn to disclose two worlds behind Aristotle's text. At the top in a rural setting, Aristotle, dressed in a blue robe, is speaking to Ibn Rushd, clad in a yellow robe with a round white turban. The bottom of the painting depicts the world of classical Greek mythology. The painted jewels, gems, and pearls testify to the great value placed on such illuminated and printed texts.

■ What overall impression of Renaissance thinking about the classical world and the world of Islam does this painting convey?

■ Notice the gestures of the two men at the top as well as the pen in Ibn Rushd's hand and the book at his feet. How might you describe the relationship between the men?

■ What made it possible for at least some European Christians of the Renaissance era to embrace both the pagan Aristotle and the Islamic Ibn Rushd?

Aristotle and Averroes | 1483

Aristotle, "Opera." Frontispiece. Illumination attributed to Girolamo da Cremona and assistants, Venice, Italy, 1483. Gothic type, PML 21194/The Pierpont Morgan Library, New York, NY, USA/The Morgan Library & Museum/Art Resource, NY

SOURCE 12.5 A Papal Call for Crusade

Violent conflict was also a feature of Christian/Muslim relations during the Renaissance, particularly on the Iberian Peninsula, where Christian forces had triumphed by the 1490s. In the eastern Mediterranean, the growing power of the Turks led to several less successful military campaigns or Crusades by Christian powers, several of which were organized by the papacy. In this selection dating from 1343, Pope Clement VI seeks support to send a fleet to counter Turkish navel raids against Christian communities in what are now Greece and the Aegean Islands.

■ What specific strategies does Clement pursue to recruit the faithful to his cause?

■ How might you describe Clement's posture toward Islam?

■ How does this call to crusade compare to earlier Crusader movements to seize the Holy Lands?

POPE CLEMENT VI | *Call for Crusade* | **September 30, 1343**

Those who launch themselves against the Catholic faith and strive to destroy the Christian religion must be resisted by the faithful with valour and steadfastness. The faithful themselves, fired by ardour for the orthodox faith, and armed to the fullest extent by its virtues, must oppose their hateful design with a rampart of determination, and forbid their evil undertakings with a firm defence. In this way, arrayed in mental and bodily armour, and directed by the light of faith, they may, with the assistance of God for whom they fight, cast down the insurgents, who lack [such] spiritual protection and are blinded by the shadows of unbelief.

To our sorrow, recent proof has confirmed what we have been hearing for some time now about groups of those unbelieving pagans, called . . . the Turks, who thirst for blood of Christian people and seek the destruction of the Catholic faith. For some time past they have mobilised the strength of their nation and used a great number of armed vessels to invade by sea Christian territories in the region of *Romania* [Greece and the Aegean Islands], and other neighbouring places in the hands of the faithful. Raging atrociously against the Christians and their lands and islands, they have taken to roaming the seas, as they are doing at present, despoiling and depopulating the settlements . . . and what is worse, seizing the Christians themselves as booty and subjecting them to horrible and perpetual slavery, selling them like animals and forcing them to deny their Catholic faith.

[The pope then declares his plan to create a fleet to counter the Turks.]

And so that the faithful may respond the more willingly, in so far as they know that they will receive the greater grace for their labours . . . we grant to those faithful who proceed with the flotilla or in another fashion in support of the Christians . . . and who remain on campaign for a year . . . and also those who die while engaged on this matter, or receive wounds in the field . . . forgiveness of their sins, for which they are truthfully contrite and which they have confessed orally. . . .

We grant the same indulgence of their sins to those who do not take part in person, but who send suitable soldiers at their own expense in accordance with their means and standing . . . and also to those who offer as much from their own goods for the matter, as they would have spent going there, staying there for a year, and coming back. . . .

Source: Norman Housley, *Documents on the Later Crusades 1274–1580* (New York: St. Martin's Press, 1996), 79–81.

DOING HISTORY

1. **Making comparisons:** What range of postures toward the Islamic world do these sources convey? How might you account for the differences among them?

2. **Imagining reactions:** How might Clement VI in Source 12.5 react to the other four sources in this feature?

3. **Analyzing sources:** While all of these sources deal with the Islamic world, with what different aspects of that world are they concerned?

4. **Considering European identity:** What role did the Islamic world play in the emerging identity of European civilization?

Christian/Muslim Relations during the Renaissance

The relationship between Christian and Islamic civilizations during the Middle Ages and Renaissance has been the subject of considerable attention from historians, who have emphasized both hostility and competition and peaceful cross-cultural contacts and exchanges between the two faiths. In Voice 12.1, Jerry Brotton, a specialist on the Renaissance, explores how trade and cultural exchange between Christians and Muslims profoundly shaped the European Renaissance. In Voice 12.2, Bernard Lewis, an expert in Islamic history, examines the reasons behind Christians' and Muslims' hostility toward one another during their first millennium of interaction.

- What reasons do these two sources identify for the intense cultural interaction between Christian and Islamic societies during the Renaissance?

- What do Brotton and Lewis agree on? And on what matters do they disagree?

- **Integrating Primary and Secondary Sources:** Which sources in this collection might Brotton and Lewis draw upon to support their assertions?

VOICE 12.1

Jerry Brotton on the Role of Cross-cultural Exchange in the European Renaissance | 2002

The Renaissance Bazaar [Brotton's book] describes the historical period starting in the early 15th century when eastern and western societies vigorously traded art, ideas, and luxury goods in a competitive but amicable exchange that shaped what we now call the European Renaissance. The eastern bazaar is a fitting metaphor for the fluid transactions that occurred throughout the 15th and 16th centuries, when Europe began to define itself by purchasing and emulating the opulence and cultured sophistication of the cities, merchants, scholars and empires of the Ottomans, the Persians, and the Egyptian Mamluks. The flow of spices, silks, carpets, porcelain, majolica, porphyry, glassware, lacquer, dyes, and pigments from the eastern bazaars of Muslim Spain, Mamluk Egypt, Ottoman Turkey, Persia, and the Silk Road between China and Europe provided the inspiration and materials for the [Renaissance] art and architecture

of Bellini, van Eyck, Dürer, and Alberti. The transmission of Arabic understanding of astronomy, philosophy, and medicine also profoundly influenced thinkers and scientists like Leonardo da Vinci, Copernicus, Vesalius, and Montaigne, whose insights into the workings of the human mind and body, as well as the individual's relationship to the wider world, are often still seen as the foundation of modern science and philosophy. It was the complex impact of these exchanges between east and west that created the culture, art, and scholarship that have been popularly associated with the Renaissance.

Source: Jerry Brotton, *The Renaissance Bazaar: From the Silk Road to Michelangelo* (Oxford: Oxford University Press, 2002), 1.

VOICE 12.2

Bernard Lewis on Hostility between Christians and Muslims | 1995

Between Islam and Christendom there was inevitably great and continuing hostility, but it was not due, in accordance with currently fashionable notions, to misperception and misunderstanding. On the contrary, the two understood each other very well, far better than either of them, in their other encounters could understand the more remote civilizations of Asia and, later, pre-Columbian America. As well as a shared or, rather, disputed mission and domain, Islam and Christendom had a great shared inheritance, which drew on common sources: the science and philosophy of Greece, the law and government of Rome, the ethical monotheism of Judaea, and beyond all of them, the deeply rooted cultures of the ancient Middle East. Christians and Muslims around the Mediterranean could find a common language in both the figurative and the literal senses. They could communicate, they could argue, if only to disagree; they could translate, as they did, both ways. All of this would have been difficult, if not impossible, between Christians or Muslims, on the one hand, and exponents of the civilizations of India or China, on the other.

Source: Bernard Lewis, *Cultures in Conflict: Christians, Muslims and Jews in the Age of Discovery* (Oxford: Oxford University Press, 1995), 14.

Notes

Prologue

1. See David Christian, *Maps of Time* (Berkeley: University of California Press, 2004).
2. Voltaire, *Treatise on Toleration*, chap. 22.
3. See David Christian, "World History in Context," *Journal of World History* 14, no. 4 (December 2003): 437–58.

Chapter 1

1. Richard Rainsford, "What Chance, the Survival Prospects of East Africa's Last Hunting and Gathering Tribe the Hadzabe, in a Gameless Environment?," Information about Northern Tanzania, March 1997, http://www.ntz.info/gen/b00473.html.
2. What follows comes from Sally McBreatry and Alison S. Brooks, "The Revolution That Wasn't: A New Interpretation of the Origin of Modern Human Behavior," *Journal of Human Evolution* 39 (2000): 453–563.
3. Charles V. Langlois and Charles Seignobos, *Introduction to the Study of History*, translated by G. G. Berry (New York: Holt, 1898), 17.
4. David Christian, Cynthia Stokes Brown, and Craig Benjamin, *Big History: Between Nothing and Everything* (New York: McGraw-Hill, 2014), 2.
5. William H. McNeill, "History and the Scientific Worldview," *History and Theory* 37, no. 1 (1998): 12.
6. Christian et al., *Big History*, 4.
7. David Christian, *Maps of Time: An Introduction to Big History* (Berkeley: University of California Press, 2004), 1–5.
8. Fred Spier, *Big History and the Future of Humanity* (West Sussex: Wiley-Blackwell, 2011), 132; Christian, *Maps of Time* (Berkeley: University of California Press, 2004), 143.
9. Richard B. Lee, *The Dobe Ju/'hoansi* (New York: Harcourt Brace, 1993), 58.
10. J. C. Beaglehole, *The Journals of Captain James Cook* (Cambridge: Hakluyt Society, 1968), 1:399.
11. Inga Clendinnen, *Dancing with Strangers* (Cambridge: Cambridge University Press, 2005), 159–67.
12. Steven Pinker, *The Better Angels of Our Nature* (New York: Viking, 2011), 47–52.
13. Marshall Sahlins, *Stone Age Economics* (London: Tavistock, 1972), 1–39.
14. Christopher Ehret, *The Civilizations of Africa* (Charlottesville: University of Virginia Press, 2002), chap. 2.
15. Marija Gimbutas, *The Language of the Goddess* (San Francisco: HarperCollins, 1989), 316–18.
16. Neil Roberts, *The Holocene: An Environmental History* (Oxford: Blackwell, 1998), 116.
17. Nina V. Federoff, "Prehistoric GM Corn," *Science* 302 (November 2003): 1158.
18. Andrew Sherrat, "The Secondary Exploitation of Animals in the Old World," *World Archeology* 15, no. 1 (1983): 90–104.

19. Tom Standage, *A History of the World in Six Glasses* (New York: Walker, 2005), chaps. 1, 2; Li Zhengping, *Chinese Wine* (Cambridge: Cambridge University Press, 2011), 1–3.
20. Yuval Noah Harari, *Sapiens: A Brief History of Humankind* (New York: HarperCollins, 2015), chap. 5.
21. Anatoly M. Khazanov, *Nomads and the Outside World* (Madison: University of Wisconsin Press, 1994), 15.
22. Ian Hodder, "Women and Men at Catalhoyuk," *Scientific American* 15, no. 1 (2005): 35–41.
23. Marija Gimbutas, *The Language of the Goddess* (New York: Harper and Row, 1989), xix.
24. "Cultural Information," Jinta Desert Art, accessed May 9, 2017, http://www.jintaart.com.au/culinfo.html.
25. Josephine Flood, "Linkage between Rock-Art and Landscape in Aboriginal Australia," in *The Figured Landscape of Rock-Art*, edited by Christopher Chippindale and George Nash (Cambridge: Cambridge University Press, 2004), 197.

Chapter 2

1. Bryan Nelson, "Becoming One with Nature," Mother Nature Network, http://www.mnn.com/earth-matters/wilderness-resources/photos/7-people-who-gave-up-on-civilization-to-live-in-the-wild-0.
2. Charles C. Mann, *1491: New Revelations of the Americas before Columbus* (New York: Alfred A. Knopf, 2005), 174–91.
3. Jonathan Mark Kenoyer, *Ancient Cities of the Indus Valley Civilization* (Oxford: Oxford University Press, 1998), 83–84.
4. David Christian, *A History of Russia, Central Asia and Mongolia* (Oxford: Blackwell, 1998), 114.
5. Robert Carneiro, "A Theory of the Origin of the State," *Science* 169 (1970): 733–38.
6. Susan Pollock, *Ancient Mesopotamia* (Cambridge: Cambridge University Press, 1999), 48.
7. *The Epic of Gilgamesh*, translated and edited by Benjamin R. Foster (New York: W. W. Norton, 2001), 10, tablet 1: 226–32.
8. James Legge, trans., *The Chinese Classics* (London: Henry Frowde, 1893), 4:171–72.
9. Margaret Ehrenberg, *Women in Prehistory* (London: British Museum, 1989), 107.
10. Sherry Ortner, "Is Female to Male as Nature Is to Culture?," in *Women, Culture, and Society*, edited by Michelle Rosaldo and Louise Lamphere (Stanford, CA: Stanford University Press, 1974), 67–88.
11. Gerda Lerner, *The Creation of Patriarchy* (New York: Oxford University Press, 1986), 70.
12. I Samuel 8: 11–17.
13. Steven Pinker, *The Better Angels of Our Nature* (New York: Viking, 2011), chaps. 2, 3.

14. Hammurabi, *The Code of Hammurabi King of Babylon,* edited by Robert Francis Harper (Chicago: University of Chicago Press, 1904), http://oll.libertyfund.org/titles/1276#Harper_0762_26.

15. Adolf Erman, *The Literature of the Ancient Egyptians,* translated by Aylward M. Blackman (London: Methuen, 1927), 136–37.

16. Henri Frankfort et al., *Before Philosophy: The Intellectual Adventure of Ancient Man* (Baltimore: Penguin Books, 1963), 39, 138.

17. Quoted in Peter Stearns et al., *World Civilizations* (New York: Longman, 1996), 1:30.

18. See Clive Ponting, *A Green History of the World* (New York: St. Martin's Press, 1991), chap. 5.

19. K. J. W. Oosthoek, "The Role of Wood in World History," Environmental History Resources, 1998, http://www.eh-resources.org/wood.html#_ednref1.

20. James B. Pritchard, ed., *Ancient Near Eastern Texts Relating to the Old Testament* (Princeton, NJ: Princeton University Press, 1969), 647–48.

21. Miriam Lichtheim, *Ancient Egyptian Literature* (Berkeley: University of California Press, 1975), 1:25–27.

22. M. J. Rowlands et al., eds., *Center and Periphery in the Ancient World* (Cambridge: Cambridge University Press, 1987), 59.

23. Marvin Harris, ed., *Cannibals and Kings* (New York: Vintage, 1978), 102.

24. Kenoyer, *Ancient Cities of the Indus Valley Civilization,* 84.

25. Gregory L. Possehl, *The Indus Civilization: A Contemporary Perspective* (Walnut Creek, CA: AltaMira Press, 2002), 114.

PART 2

1. Colin Ronan and Joseph Needham, *The Shorter Science and Civilization in China* (Cambridge: Cambridge University Press, 1978), 58.

Chapter 3

1. Cullen Murphy, *Are We Rome? The Fall of an Empire and the Fate of America* (Boston: Houghton Mifflin, 2007).

2. J. M. Cook, *The Persian Empire* (London: J. M. Dent, 1983), 76.

3. George Rawlinson, trans., *The Histories of Herodotus* (London: Dent, 1910), 1:131–40.

4. Erich F. Schmidt, *Persepolis I: Structures, Reliefs, Inscriptions,* Oriental Institute Publications 68 (Chicago: University of Chicago Press, 1953), 63.

5. Quoted in Anthony N. Penna, *The Human Footprint* (Oxford: Wiley-Blackwell, 2010), 151.

6. Quoted in Thomas R. Martin, *Ancient Greece from Prehistoric to Hellenistic Times* (New Haven, CT: Yale University Press, 1996), 86.

7. Christian Meier, *Athens* (New York: Metropolitan Books, 1993), 93.

8. Arrian, *The Campaigns of Alexander,* translated by Aubrey de Selincourt, revised by J. R. Hamilton (London: Penguin, 1971), 395–96.

9. Stanley Burstein, *The Hellenistic Period in World History* (Washington, DC: American Historical Association, 1996), 12.

10. Norman F. Cantor, *Antiquity* (New York: HarperCollins, 2003), 25.

11. Paul Halsall, "Early Western Civilization under the Sign of Gender," in *A Companion to Gender History,* edited by Teresa A. Meade and Merry E. Wiesner-Hanks (London: Blackwell, 2004), 293–94.

12. Keith W. Taylor, *The Birth of Vietnam* (Berkeley: University of California Press, 1983), 334.

13. Roger Boesche, *The First Great Political Realist: Kautilya and His Arthashastra* (Lanham, MD: Lexington Books, 2002), 17.

14. Stanley Wolpert, *A New History of India* (New York: Oxford University Press, 1993), 90.

15. Zhengyuan Fu, *Autocratic Tradition and Chinese Politics* (New York: Cambridge University Press, 1993), 188.

Chapter 4

1. "Birthday of Confucius celebrated with grand ceremony. . . ," Embassy of the People's Republic of China in Australia, September 29, 2009, http://au.china-embassy.org/eng/xw/t608286.htm.

2. Quoted in Arthur Waley, *Three Ways of Thought in Ancient China* (Garden City, NY: Doubleday, 1956), 159–60.

3. Nancy Lee Swann, trans., *Pan Chao: Foremost Woman Scholar of China* (New York: Century, 1932), 111–14.

4. Kam Louie and Morris Low, *Asian Masculinities* (London: Routledge, 2003), 3–6.

5. Quoted in Huston Smith, *The Illustrated World's Religions* (San Francisco: HarperCollins, 1994), 123.

6. Robert Marks, *China: Its Environment and History* (Lanham, MD: Rowman and Littlefield, 2012), 94–95.

7. Lao-tzu, *Tao Te Ching,* translated by James Legge, in *Sacred Books of the East* (Oxford: The Clarendon Press, 1891), 39:122.

8. Catherine Clay et al., *Envisioning Women in World History* (New York: McGraw-Hill, 2009), 1:67–77.

9. Quoted in Karen Andrews, "Women in Theravada Buddhism," Institute of Buddhist Studies, accessed November 21, 2017, http://www.bhikkhuni.net/women-in-theravada-buddhism/.

10. A. L. Basham, *The Wonder That Was India* (London: Sidgwick and Jackson, 1967), 309.

11. Isaiah 1:11–17.

12. Plato, *Apologia,* translated by Benjamin Jowett (1891).

13. Hippocrates, *On the Sacred Disease,* translated by Francis Adams, Internet Classics Archive, accessed February 2, 2012, http://classics.mit.edu/Hippocrates/sacred.html.

14. Karl Jaspers, *The Origin and Goal of History* (New Haven, CT: Yale University Press, 1953).

15. See, for example, Robert N. Bellah, "What Is Axial about the Axial Age?" *European Journal of Sociology* 46, no. 1 (2005): 69–89.

16. Jaspers, *The Origin and Goal of History,* 6.

17. See Iain Provan, *Convenient Myths* (Waco, TX: Baylor University Press, 2013), 2–3, 41.

18. Galatians 3:28.

19. Ephesians 5:22–23; 1 Corinthians 14:35.

20. "The Martyrdom of Saints Perpetua and Felicitas," *Frontline,* "From Jesus to Christ," PBS, April 1998, http://www.pbs.org/wgbh/pages/frontline/shows/religion/maps/primary/perpetua.html.

21. Robert Sider, "Early Christians in North Africa," *Coptic Church Review* 19, no. 3 (1998): 2.

22. Quoted in Mary Ann Rossi, "Priesthood, Precedent, and Prejudice: On Recovering the Women Priests of Early Christianity," *Journal of Feminist Studies* 7, no. 1 (1991): 73–94.

23. Chai-Shin Yu, *Early Buddhism and Christianity* (Delhi: Motilal Banarsidass, 1981), 211.

24. Peter Frankopan, *The Silk Roads: A New History of the World* (New York: Vintage, 2017), 9.

Chapter 5

1. Quoted in Lydia Polgreen, "Business Class Rises in Ashes of Caste System," *New York Times*, September 10, 2010.

2. Po Chu-I, "After Passing the Examination," in *More Translations from the Chinese*, by Arthur Waley (New York: Alfred A. Knopf, 1919), 37.

3. Quoted in Michael Lowe, *Everyday Life in Early Imperial China* (New York: Dorset, 1968), 38.

4. Li Shen, "Old Style," Selected Poems from T'ang Dynasty, accessed May 25, 2017, http://www.shigeku.org/xlib /lingshidao/hanshi/tang1.htm.

5. Orlando Patterson, *Slavery and Social Death* (Cambridge, MA: Harvard University Press, 1982).

6. A. L. Basham, *The Wonder That Was India* (London: Sidgwick and Jackson, 1967), 152.

7. Sarah Pomeroy et al., *Ancient Greece* (New York: Oxford University Press, 1999), 63, 239.

8. R. Zelnick-Abramovitz, *Not Wholly Free* (Leiden: Brill, 2005), 337, 343.

9. I Peter 2:18.

10. Quoted in Brent D. Shaw, *Spartacus and the Slave Wars: A Brief History with Documents* (Boston: Bedford/St. Martin's, 2001), 145.

11. Shaw, 143.

12. Milton Meltzer, *Slavery: A World History* (New York: Da Capo Press, 1993), 189.

13. Judith Bennett, *History Matters: Patriarchy and the Challenge of Feminism* (Philadelphia: University of Pennsylvania Press, 2006), chap. 4.

14. Quoted in Bret Hinsch, *Women in Early Imperial China* (Oxford: Rowman and Littlefield, 2002), 155.

15. Nancy Lee Swann, trans., *Pan Chao: Foremost Woman Scholar of China* (New York: Century, 1932), 111–14.

16. Quoted in Valerie Hansen, *The Open Empire* (New York: Norton, 2000), 183–84; see also Thomas Barfield, *The Perilous Frontier* (Cambridge: Blackwell, 1989), 140.

17. Aristotle, *Politica*, translated by H. Rackham, Loeb Classical Library, no. 264 (Cambridge, MA: Harvard University Press, 1932), 1254b10–14.

18. Sarah B. Pomeroy, *Spartan Women* (Oxford: Oxford University Press, 2002), 63.

19. Anton Powell, "Dining Groups, Marriage, Homosexuality," in *Sparta*, edited by Michael Whitby (New York: Routledge, 2002), 93.

20. Quoted in "The Destruction of Pompeii, 79 AD," EyeWitness to History, 1999, www.eyewitnesstohistory.com/pompeii.htm.

Chapter 6

1. "Morales Becomes Head of a Pluri-national State Blessed by Aymara Gods," *MercoPress*, January 22, 2010, http://en. mercopress.com/2010/01/22/morales-becomes-head-of-a-pluri-national-state-blessed-by-aymara-gods.

2. Roderick J. McIntosh, *Ancient Middle Niger* (Cambridge: Cambridge University Press, 2005), 10.

3. Roderick J. McIntosh, *The Peoples of the Middle Niger* (Oxford: Blackwell, 1998), 177.

4. Richard E. W. Adams, *Ancient Civilizations of the New World* (Boulder, CO: Westview Press, 1997), 53–56; T. Patrick Culbert, "The New Maya," *Archeology* 51, no. 5 (1998): 47–51.

5. George L. Cowgill, "The Central Mexican Highlands . . . ," in *The Cambridge History of the Native Peoples of the Americas*, vol. 2, pt. 1, "Mesoamerica," edited by Richard E. W. Adams and Murdo J. MacLeod (Cambridge: Cambridge University Press, 2000), 289.

6. Scott Norris, "Mummy of Tattooed Woman Discovered in Peru Pyramid," *National Geographic News*, May 16, 2006, http://news .nationalgeographic.com/news/2006/05/mummy-peru.html.

7. Gordon F. McEwan, *The Inca: New Perspectives* (New York: W. W. Norton, 2008), 39–41.

8. Christopher Ehret, *The Civilizations of Africa* (Charlottesville: University of Virginia Press, 2002), 175.

9. David Schoenbrun, "Gendered Themes in Early African History," in *A Companion to Gender History*, edited by Teresa Meade and Merry Wiesner-Hanks (Oxford: Blackwell, 2004), 253–56.

10. See Jan Vansina, *Paths in the Rainforest* (Madison: University of Wisconsin Press, 1990), 95–99.

11. David Hurst Thomas, *Exploring Ancient Native America* (New York: Routledge, 1999), 137–42.

12. Brian M. Fagan, *Ancient North America* (London: Thames and Hudson, 2005), 475.

13. Quoted in Lynda Norene Shaffer, *Native Americans before 1492* (Armonk, NY: M. E. Sharpe, 1992), 70.

14. Steven R. Fischer, *A History of the Pacific Islands* (New York: Palgrave Macmillan, 2013), 37. This section draws heavily on Fischer, chaps. 1, 2; Ian Campbell, *Worlds Apart* (Cambridge: Cambridge University Press, 2011), chaps. 1, 2; and Matt K. Matsuda, *Pacific Worlds* (Cambridge: Cambridge University Press, 2012), chaps. 1, 2.

15. Campbell, *Worlds Apart*, 48.

16. Terry L. Hunt, "Rethinking the Fall of Easter Island," *American Scientist* 94, no. 5 (September/October 2006), 412–19.

17. David W. Phillipson, *Foundations of an African Civilization: Aksum and the Northern Horn 100 BC–AD 1300* (Woodbridge, Suffolk: James Currey, 2012), 143.

Chapter 7

1. Nayan Chanda, *Bound Together* (New Haven, CT: Yale University Press, 2007), 35–36.

2. William J. Bernstein, *A Splendid Exchange* (New York: Grove Press, 2008), 58–66; Proverbs 7:17–18.

3. Quoted in Patricia Buckley Ebrey, *The Inner Quarters* (Berkeley: University of California Press, 1993), 150.

4. Seneca the Elder, *Declamations* (Cambridge: Harvard University Press, 1999), 1:374–75.

5. Liu Xinru, "Silks and Religion in Eurasia, A.D. 600–1200," *Journal of World History* 6, no. 1 (1995): 25–48.

6. Boccaccio, *The Decameron*, translated by M. Rigg (London: David Campbell, 1921), 1:5–11.

7. Kenneth McPherson, *The Indian Ocean* (Oxford: Oxford University Press, 1993), 15.

8. Janet L. Abu-Lughod, *Before European Hegemony* (Oxford: Oxford University Press, 1989), 269.

9. McPherson, *Indian Ocean*, 97.

10. This section draws heavily from Craig A. Lockard, *Southeast Asia in World History* (Oxford: Oxford University Press, 2009), chaps. 2, 3. See also Victor Lieberman, *Strange Parallels* (Cambridge: Cambridge University Press, 2009), chaps. 1, 7.

11. Kenneth R. Hall, *Maritime Trade and State Development in Early Southeast Asia* (Honolulu: University of Hawaii Press, 1985), 101.

12. M. C. Horton and T. R. Burton, "Indian Metalwork in East Africa: The Bronze Lion Statuette from Shanga," *Antiquities* 62 (1988): 22.

13. Ross Dunn, *The Adventures of Ibn Battuta* (Berkeley: University of California Press, 1986), 124.

14. Christopher Ehret, *The Civilizations of Africa* (Charlottesville: University of Virginia Press, 2002), 255.

15. Richard W. Bulliet, *The Camel and the Wheel* (New York: Columbia University Press, 1990), 8. This feature largely derives from this book.

16. Nehemia Levtzion and Jay Spaulding, eds., *Medieval West Africa: Views from Arab Scholars and Merchants* (Princeton, NJ: Marcus Wiener, 2003), 5.

17. David Schoenbrun, "Gendered Themes in Early African History," in *A Companion to Gender History*, edited by Teresa Meade and Merry Wiesner-Hanks (Oxford: Blackwell, 2004), 263.

18. Quoted in John Iliffe, *Africans: The History of a Continent* (Cambridge: Cambridge University Press, 1995), 75–76.

19. J. R. McNeill and William McNeill, *The Human Web* (New York: W. W. Norton, 2003), 160.

20. Li Rongxi, trans., *A Biography of the Tripitaka Master of the Great Ci'en Monastery of the Great Tang Dynasty* (Berkeley, CA: Numata Center for Buddhist Translation, 1995), 31.

Chapter 8

1. Tom Phillips, "China's Xi Jinping Says Paris Climate Deal Must Not Be Allowed to Fail," *The Guardian*, January 18, 2017.

2. Quoted in Mark Elvin, *The Retreat of the Elephants* (New Haven, CT: Yale University Press, 2004), 19.

3. Mark Elvin, *The Pattern of the Chinese Past* (London: Eyre Methuen, 1973), 55.

4. Samuel Adshead, *Tang China: The Rise of the East in World History* (New York: Palgrave, 2004), 30.

5. William McNeill, *The Pursuit of Power* (Chicago: University of Chicago Press, 1984), 50.

6. See "The Attractions of the Capital," in *Chinese Civilization: A Sourcebook*, edited by Patricia Buckley Ebrey (New York: Free Press, 1993), 178–85.

7. Marco Polo, *The Travels of Marco Polo*, translated by Henry Yule (Toronto: General, 1993), 2:185.

8. Jack Kelly, *Gunpowder: Alchemy, Bombards, and Pyrotechnics: The History of the Explosive That Changed the World* (New York: Basic Books, 2005), 4. Much of this feature is derived from this book.

9. J. R. McNeill and William H. McNeill, *The Human Web* (New York: W. W. Norton, 2003), 123.

10. Quoted in Francesca Bray, *Technology and Gender: Fabrics of Power in Late Imperial China* (Berkeley: University of California Press, 1997), 116.

11. Patricia Buckley Ebrey, *The Inner Quarters* (Berkeley: University of California Press, 1993), 207.

12. Ebrey, 37–43.

13. Ebrey, 6.

14. Burton Watson, trans., *Records of the Grand Historian of China*, rev. ed. (New York: Columbia University Press, 1993), 2:144–45, as quoted in Thomas J. Barfield, "Steppe Empires, China, and the Silk Route," in *Nomads in the Sedentary World*, edited by Anatoly M. Khazanov and Andre Wink (New York: Routledge, 2001), 237.

15. Quoted in Edward H. Shafer, *The Golden Peaches of Samarkand* (Berkeley: University of California Press, 1963), 28.

16. Susan Mann, "Women in East Asia," in *Women's History in Global Perspective*, edited by Bonnie Smith (Urbana: University of Illinois Press, 2005), 2:53–56.

17. Quoted in McNeill, *Pursuit of Power*, 40.

18. John K. Fairbank et al., *East Asia: Tradition and Transformation* (Boston: Houghton Mifflin, 1978), 353.

19. Arnold Pacey, *Technology in World Civilization* (Cambridge, MA: MIT Press, 1991), 50–53.

20. McNeill, *Pursuit of Power*, 24–25.

21. Quoted in Arthur F. Wright, *Studies in Chinese Buddhism* (New Haven, CT: Yale University Press, 1990), 16.

22. Arthur F. Wright, *Buddhism in Chinese History* (Stanford, CA: Stanford University Press, 1959), 36–39.

23. Quoted in Wright, 67.

24. Quoted in Eric Zurcher, *The Buddhist Conquest of China* (Leiden: E. J. Brill, 1959), 1:262.

25. Quoted in Robert Marks, *China: Its Environment and History* (Lanham, MD: Rowman and Littlefield, 2012), 139–40.

26. Edwin O. Reischauer, *Ennin's Travels in Tang China* (New York: Ronald Press, 1955), 221–24.

27. "Ma Yuan — Song Dynasty," China Online Museum, http://www.chinaonlinemuseum.com/painting-ma-yuan-6.php.

28. David Hinton, *Existence: A Story* (Boulder, CO: Shambhala, 2016), 3.

Chapter 9

1. "Religion in Sierra Leone," *The Economist*, May 31, 2014.

2. Reza Aslan, *No God but God* (New York: Random House, 2005), 14.

3. Quoted in Karen Armstrong, *A History of God* (New York: Ballantine Books, 1993), 146.

4. Quran 1:5 and 41:53.

5. Quran 9:71.

6. "Prophet Muhammad's Farewell Sermon," IslamiCity, accessed November 28, 2014, http://www.islamicity.com/articles/Articles.asp?ref=ic0107-322.

7. Quoted in Fred M. Donner, *Muhammad and the Believers* (Cambridge, MA: Harvard University Press, 2010), 114. The preceding section draws on chapter 3.

8. Richard Bulliet, *Conversion to Islam in the Medieval Period* (Cambridge, MA: Harvard University Press, 1979), 33.

9. Quoted in Bertold Spuler, *The Muslim World*, vol. 1, *The Age of the Caliph* (Leiden: E. J. Brill, 1960), 29.

10. Bernard Lewis, *Islam and the West* (New York: Oxford University Press, 1993), 157.

11. Quoted in Patricia Crone, "The Rise of Islam in the World," in *Cambridge Illustrated History of the Islamic World*, edited by Francis Robinson (Cambridge: Cambridge University Press, 1996), 14.

12. Many of these stories are summarized from accounts in Imam Jamal Rahman, *Sacred Laughter of the Sufis* (Woodstock, VT: Skylight Paths, 2014).

13. Quran 4:34.

14. Quoted in Judith Tucker, "Gender and Islamic History," in *Islamic and European Expansion*, edited by Michael Adas (Philadelphia: Temple University Press, 1993), 46.

15. Ria Kloppenborg and Wouter Hanegraaf, eds., *Female Stereotypes in Religious Traditions* (Leiden: E. J. Brill, 1995), 111.

16. Quoted in William T. de Bary, ed., *Sources of Indian Tradition* (New York: Columbia University Press, 1958), 2:355–57.

17. Quoted in Nikki R. Keddie, "Women in the Middle East since the Rise of Islam," in *Women's History in Global Perspective*, edited by Bonnie G. Smith (Urbana: University of Illinois Press, 2005), 81.

18. Ross Dunn, *The Adventures of Ibn Battuta* (Berkeley: University of California Press, 1986), 300.

19. Jane I. Smith, "Islam and Christendom," in *The Oxford History of Islam*, edited by John L. Esposito (Oxford: Oxford University Press, 1999), 317–21.

20. Richard Eaton, "Islamic History as Global History," in Adas, *Islamic and European Expansion*, 12.

21. Francis Robinson, "Knowledge, Its Transmission and the Making of Muslim Societies," in Robinson, *Cambridge Illustrated History of the Islamic World*, 230.

22. Robinson, 215.

23. Donner, *Muhammad and the Believers*, 179.

Chapter 10

1. Louisa Lim, "In the Land of Mao, a Rising Tide of Christianity," *All Things Considered*, NPR, July 19, 2010, http://www.npr.org/templates/story/story.php?storyId=128546334.

2. This section relies heavily on Diarmaid MacCulloch, *Christianity: The First Three Thousand Years* (New York: Viking, 2010), chap. 8.

3. Quoted in Ray Riegert and Thomas Moore, eds., *The Lost Sutras of Jesus* (Berkeley, CA: Ulysses Press, 2006), 103.

4. Quoted in Deno John Geanakoplos, *Byzantium: Church, Society, and Civilization Seen through Contemporary Eyes* (Chicago: University of Chicago Press, 1984), 389.

5. Quoted in Geanakoplos, *Byzantium*, 143.

6. Quoted in Geanakoplos, *Byzantium*, 369.

7. Quoted in Patrick J. Geary, *Before France and Germany* (New York: Oxford University Press, 1988), 79.

8. Quoted in Stephen Williams, *Diocletian and the Roman Recovery* (London: Routledge, 1996), 218.

9. Peter Brown, *The Rise of Western Christendom* (London: Blackwell, 1996), 305.

10. Quoted in John M. Hobson, *The Eastern Origins of Western Civilization* (New York: Cambridge University Press, 2004), 113.

11. Clive Ponting, *A Green History of the World* (New York: St. Martin's, 1991), 121–23.

12. Quoted in Richard C. Hoffman, "Economic Development and Aquatic Ecosystems in Medieval Europe," *American Historical Review* 101, no. 3 (1996): 648.

13. Judith M. Bennett, *A Medieval Life* (Boston: McGraw-Hill, 1998).

14. Bonnie Anderson and Judith Zinsser, *A History of Their Own* (Oxford: Oxford University Press, 2000), 1:393–94.

15. Christopher Tyerman, *Fighting for Christendom: Holy Wars and the Crusades* (Oxford: Oxford University Press, 2004), 16.

16. Quoted in Elizabeth Hallam, *Chronicles of the Crusades* (New York: Welcome Rain, 2000), 127.

17. Quoted in Peter Watson, *Ideas* (New York: Harper, 2006), 319.

18. Quoted in Jean Gimple, *The Medieval Machine* (New York: Holt, 1976), 178.

19. Quoted in Stuart B. Schwartz, ed., *Victors and Vanquished* (Boston: Bedford/St. Martin's, 2000), 147.

20. Quoted in Carlo Cipolla, *Before the Industrial Revolution* (New York: Norton, 1976), 207.

21. Quoted in S. Lilley, *Men, Machines, and History* (New York: International, 1965), 62.

22. See Toby Huff, *The Rise of Early Modern Science* (Cambridge: Cambridge University Press, 1993).

23. Quoted in Edward Grant, *Science and Religion from Aristotle to Copernicus* (Westport, CT: Greenwood Press, 2004), 158.

24. Quoted in L. Thorndike, *A History of Magic and Experimental Science* (New York: Columbia University Press, 1923), 2:58.

25. Quoted in Edward Grant, *God and Reason in the Middle Ages* (Cambridge: Cambridge University Press, 2001), 70.

26. Quoted in Grant, *Science and Religion*, 228–29.

27. Marcia L. Colish, *Medieval Foundations of the Western Intellectual Tradition* (New Haven, CT: Yale University Press, 1997), 128.

Chapter 11

1. Jehangir S. Pocha, "Mongolia Sees Genghis Khan's Good Side," *New York Times,* May 10, 2005.

2. Giovanni Carpini, *The Story of the Mongols*, translated by Erik Hildinger (Boston: Braden, 1996), 54.

3. Quoted in Peter B. Golden, "Nomads and Sedentary Societies in Eurasia," in *Agricultural and Pastoral Societies in Ancient and Classical History*, edited by Michael Adas (Philadelphia: Temple University Press, 2001), 73.

4. Anatoly Khazanov, "The Spread of World Religions in Medieval Nomadic Societies of the Eurasian Steppes," in *Nomadic Diplomacy, Destruction and Religion from the Pacific to the Adriatic*, edited by Michael Gervers and Wayne Schlepp (Toronto: Joint Center for Asia Pacific Studies, 1994), 11.

5. Quoted in J. Otto Maenchen-Helfer, *The World of the Huns* (Berkeley: University of California Press, 1973), 14.

6. Carter Finley, *The Turks in World History* (Oxford: Oxford University Press, 2005), 28–37.

7. Finley, 40.

8. David Christian, *A History of Russia, Central Asia, and Mongolia* (London: Blackwell, 1998), 1:385.

9. Quoted in Christian, 389.

10. Stephen Turnbull, *The Mongol Invasions of Japan, 1274 and 1281* (Oxford: Osprey, 2010). This feature is derived largely from this book.

11. Jack Weatherford, *Genghis Khan and the Making of the Modern World* (New York: Crown, 2004), 86.

12. Chinggis Khan, "Letter to Changchun," in E. Bretschneider, *Mediaeval Researches from Eastern Asiatic Sources* (London: Kegan, Paul, Trench, Trübner, 1875), 1:37–39.

13. Thomas T. Allsen, *Mongol Imperialism* (Berkeley: University of California Press, 1987), 6.

14. Chinggis Khan, "Letter to Changchun," 38.

15. Quoted in Weatherford, *Genghis Khan*, 111.

16. Thomas J. Barfield, *The Nomadic Alternative* (Englewood Cliffs, NJ: Prentice Hall, 1993), 166.

17. Quoted in Christian, *History of Russia*, 1:425.

18. Quoted in David Morgan, *Medieval Persia* (London: Longman, 1988), 79.

19. Morgan, 82.

20. Guity Nashat, "Women in the Middle East," in *A Companion to Gender History*, edited by Teresa A. Meade and Merry E. Wiesner-Hanks (London: Blackwell, 2004), 243.

21. Charles J. Halperin, *Russia and the Golden Horde* (Bloomington: Indiana University Press, 1985), 126.

22. Charles H. Halperin, "Russia in the Mongol Empire in Comparative Perspective," *Harvard Journal of Asiatic Studies* 43, no. 1 (1983): 261.

23. Thomas Allsen, *Culture and Conquest in Mongol Eurasia* (Cambridge: Cambridge University Press, 2001), 211.

24. Quoted in Allsen, 121.

25. George Nathaniel Curzon, *Problems of the Far East* (London: Longmans, Green, 1894), vi.

26. Yuval Noah Harari, *Sapiens: A Brief History of Humankind* (New York: HarperCollins, 2015), 191.

27. William Skidelsky, "Niall Ferguson: 'Westerners Don't Understand How Vulnerable Freedom Is,'" *The Observer*, February 19, 2011, accessed May 22, 2017, https://www.theguardian.com/books/2011/feb/20/niall-ferguson-interview-civilization.

28. John Aberth, *The First Horseman: Disease in Human History* (Upper Saddle River, NJ: Pearson/Prentice Hall, 2007), 18.

29. Quoted in John Aberth, *The Black Death: The Great Mortality of 1348–1350* (Boston: Bedford/St. Martin's, 2005), 84–85.

30. Michael Dols, *The Black Death in the Middle East* (Princeton, NJ: Princeton University Press, 1977), 212, 223.

31. Quoted in John Aberth, *A Knight at the Movies: Medieval History on Film* (New York: Routledge, 2003), 225.

32. Quoted in Aberth, *Black Death*, 72.

33. Quoted in Dols, *Black Death in the Middle East*, 67.

34. Andre Gunder Frank, *ReOrient: Global Economy in the Asian Age* (Berkeley: University of California Press, 1998), 256.

35. Arnold Pacey, *Technology in World Civilization* (Cambridge, MA: MIT Press, 1990), 62.

36. Quoted in Golden, "Nomads and Sedentary Societies," 72–73.

37. Quoted in Gregory Guzman, "Were the Barbarians a Negative or Positive Factor in Ancient and Medieval History?" *Historian* 50 (August 1988): 558–72.

38. Quoted in Barfield, *Nomadic Alternative*, 3.

Chapter 12

1. Winona LaDuke, "We Are Still Here: The 500 Years Celebration," *Sojourners*, October 1991.

2. Jonathan Marcantoni, "Columbus Day . . . Is Complicated," October 9, 2015, http://www.latinorebels.com/2015/10/09/in-defense-of-columbus-day/.

3. Brian Fagan, *Ancient North America* (London: Thames & Hudson, 2005), 503.

4. Quoted in Charles C. Mann, *1491: New Revelations of the Americas before Columbus* (New York: Alfred A. Knopf, 2005), 334.

5. Louise Levanthes, *When China Ruled the Seas* (New York: Simon & Schuster, 1994), 175.

6. Christine de Pisan, *The Book of the City of Ladies*, translated by Rosalind Brown-Grant (New York: Penguin Books, 1999), pt. 1, p. 1.

7. Frank Viviano, "China's Great Armada," *National Geographic*, July 2005, 34.

8. Quoted in C. R. N. Routh, *They Saw It Happen in Europe: An Anthology of Eyewitnesses' Accounts of Events in European History, 1450–1600* (Oxford: Blackwell, 1965), 386.

9. Quoted in John J. Saunders, ed., *The Muslim World on the Eve of Europe's Expansion* (Englewood Cliffs, NJ: Prentice Hall, 1966), 41–43.

10. Leo Africanus, *History and Description of Africa* (London: Hakluyt Society, 1896), 824–25.

11. Quoted in Craig A. Lockhard, *Southeast Asia in World History* (Oxford: Oxford University Press, 2009), 67.

12. Quoted in Patricia Risso, *Merchants and Faith* (Boulder, CO: Westview Press, 1995), 49.

13. Quoted in Stuart B. Schwartz, ed., *Victors and Vanquished* (Boston: Bedford/St. Martin's, 2000), 8.

14. Quoted in Michael E. Smith, *The Aztecs* (London: Blackwell, 2003), 108.

15. Smith, 220.

16. Quoted in Miguel Leon-Portilla, *Aztec Thought and Culture*, translated from the Spanish by Jack Emory Davis (Norman: University of Oklahoma Press, 1963), 7.

17. For a summary of this practice among the Aztecs and Incas, see Karen Vieira Powers, *Women in the Crucible of Conquest* (Albuquerque: University of New Mexico Press, 2005), chap. 1.

18. Powers, 25.

19. Louise Burkhart, "Mexica Women on the Home Front," in *Indian Women of Early Mexico*, edited by Susan Schroeder et al. (Norman: University of Oklahoma Press, 1997), 25–54.

20. The "web" metaphor is derived from J. R. McNeill and William H. McNeill, *The Human Web* (New York: W. W. Norton, 2003).

21. Quoted in Rosamund E. Mack, *Bazaar to Piazza* (Berkeley: University of California Press, 2002), 1.

22. Jerry Brotton, *The Renaissance Bazaar: From the Silk Road to Michaelangelo* (Oxford: Oxford University Press, 2006), 51.

23. Brotton, 51.

Acknowledgments

Chapter 1

Source 1.2: "The Rainbow Serpent Awakens" from http://www.expedition360.com/australia_lessons_literacy/2001/09/dreamtime_stories_the_rainbow.html. Used by permission of BullyFish Books LLC.

Source 1.4: Excerpts from *Time Before Morning: Art and Myth of the Australian Aborigines,* pages 215–219, by Louis A. Allen. Copyright © 1975 by Louis A. Allen. Reprinted by permission of HarperCollins Publishers.

Chapter 2

Excerpt beginning "Come then, Enkidu to ramparted Uruk" from *The Epic of Gilgamesh,* translated by Benjamin R. Foster. Copyright © 2001 by W. W. Norton & Company. Used by permission of W. W. Norton & Company, Inc. This selection may not be reproduced, stored in a retrieval system, or transmitted in any form or by any means without the prior written permission of the publisher.

Excerpt beginning "He has come unto us" from Adolf Erman, *The Literature of the Ancient Egyptians,* by Adolf Erman, translated by Aylward M. Blackman. Copyright © 1927 by Methuen Publishing Ltd, 1927. Reproduced by permission of Taylor & Francis Books UK.

Excerpt beginning "In those Days" from James B. Pritchard, editor, *Ancient Near Eastern Texts Relating to the Old Testament* by James Bennett Pritchard. Reproduced with permission of Books on Demand in the format Book via Copyright Clearance Center.

Chapter 4

Source 4.5: "Sunita the Outcaste" (Thag 12.2), translated from the Pali by Thanissaro Bhikkhu. Access to Insight (Legacy Edition). November 30, 2013, http://www.accesstoinsight.org/tipitaka/kn/thag/thag.12.02.than.html. Used by permission of Thanissaro Bhikkhu.

Chapter 5

Source 5.4: From *Daily Life in Ancient Rome: A Sourcebook,* by Brian Harvey. Copyright © 2016 Hackett. Reprinted with permission of Hackett Publishing Company, Inc. All rights reserved.

Voice 5.1: From Mary Beard, "Pompeii Exhibition" *The Telegraph,* April 10, 2017. © Telegraph Media Group Limited 2017.

Chapter 8

Excerpt beginning "A tumbled confusion" from Mark Elvin, *The Retreat of the Elephants* (New Haven, CT: Yale University Press, 2004). Copyright © 2004 by Mark Elvin. Used by permission of Yale University Press.

Excerpt beginning "Ever since the Western horsemen" from *The Golden Peaches of Samarkand: A Study of T'ang Exotics,* by Edward H. Schafer, © 1985 by the Regents of the University of California. Published by the University of California Press.

Source 8.4A: Li Po, "Zazen on Ching-t'ing Mountain" from *Crossing the Yellow River: Three Hundred Poems from the Chinese,* translated by Sam Hamill. Copyright © 2000 by Sam Hamill. Reprinted with the permission of The Permissions Company, Inc., on behalf of Tiger Bark Press, www.tigerbarkpress.com.

Source 8.4B: Li Po, "Drinking Alone with the Moon," from *The Jade Mountain.* Print usage: Translated by Witter Bynner, translation copyright © 1929, renewed 1957 by Penguin Random House LLC. Used by permission of Alfred A. Knopf, an imprint of the Knopf Doubleday Publishing Group, a division of Penguin Random House LLC. All rights reserved. Any third party use of this material, outside of this publication, is prohibited. Interested parties must apply directly to Penguin Random House LLC for permission. Electronic usage: Translated by Witter Bynner, translation copyright © 1929, renewed 1957 by Penguin Random House LLC. Used by permission of the Witter Bynner Foundation.

Source 8.4C: Wang Wei, "My Retreat at Mount Zhongnan," from *The Jade Mountain.* Print usage: Translated by Witter Bynner, translation copyright © 1929, renewed 1957 by Penguin Random House LLC. Used by permission of Alfred A. Knopf, an imprint of the Knopf Doubleday Publishing Group, a division of Penguin Random House LLC. All rights reserved. Any third party use of this material, outside of this publication, is prohibited. Interested parties must apply directly to Penguin Random House LLC for permission. Electronic usage: Translated by Witter Bynner, translation copyright © 1929, renewed 1957 by Penguin Random House LLC. Used by permission of the Witter Bynner Foundation.

Source 8.4D: Du Fu, "A View of Taishan," from *The Jade Mountain.* Print usage: Translated by Witter Bynner, translation copyright © 1929, renewed 1957 by Penguin Random House LLC. Used by permission of Alfred A. Knopf, an imprint of the Knopf Doubleday Publishing Group, a division of Penguin Random House LLC. All rights reserved. Any third party use of this material, outside of this publication, is prohibited. Interested parties must apply directly to Penguin Random House LLC for permission. Electronic usage: Translated by Witter Bynner, translation copyright © 1929, renewed 1957 by Penguin Random House LLC. Used by permission of the Witter Bynner Foundation.

Chapter 9

Source 9.4: From *Muhammad and the Believers: At the Origins of Islam* by Fred M. Donner, Cambridge, Mass.: The Belknap Press of Harvard University Press, Copyright © 2010 by Fred M. Donner.

Source 9.6: From Caliph Ali, Letter to Malik Ashtar, 658 C.E., in Paul Salahuddin Armstrong (ed.), "Caliph Ali's Letter to Malik Ashtar." Used by permission of Paul Salahuddin.

Chapter 11

Source 11.1B: From Paul Kahn, *The Secret History of the Mongols: The Origins of Chingis Khan* (San Francisco: North Point Press, 1984). Copyright © 1984 by Paul Kahn. Reprinted by permission of the author.

Chapter 12

Excerpt beginning "Truly do we live on Earth" from *Aztec Thought and Culture: A Study of the Ancient Nahuatl Mind,* by Miguel Leon-Portilla. Reproduced with permission of the University of Oklahoma Press in the format Republish in a book via Copyright Clearance Center.

Source 12.5: From Norman Housely, *Documents of the Later Crusades, 1274–1580,* published 1996 by St. Martin's Press, reproduced with permission of Palgrave Macmillan.

Glossary

Abbasid caliphate An Arab dynasty of caliphs (successors to the Prophet) who governed much of the Islamic world from its capital in Baghdad beginning in 750 C.E. After 900 C.E. that empire increasingly fragmented until its overthrow by the Mongols in 1258.

Alexander the Great A ruler of Macedonia who unified the Greek city-states and during a ten-year military expedition (334–323 B.C.E.) conquered Egypt, the Persian Empire, and part of northwest India, creating a vast Greek empire.

Alexandria A cosmopolitan Egyptian city established by Hellenistic rulers, with a population of half a million people; a major avenue for the spread of Greek culture and learning.

Almoravid Empire Emerging out of an Islamic reform movement among the Sanhaja Berber pastoralists in the eleventh century, the Almoravid Empire incorporated a large part of northwestern Africa and southern Spain. The empire collapsed by the mid-twelfth century.

American web A term used to describe the network of trade that linked parts of the pre-Columbian Americas; although less densely woven than the Afro-Eurasian trade networks, this web nonetheless provided a means of exchange for luxury goods and ideas over large areas.

al-Andalus Arabic name for Spain, most of which was conquered by Arab and Berber forces between 711 and 718 C.E. Muslim Spain represented a point of encounter between the Islamic world and Christian Europe.

Angkor Wat The largest religious structure in the premodern world, this temple was built by the powerful Angkor kingdom (located in modern Cambodia) in the twelfth century C.E. to express a Hindu understanding of the cosmos centered on a mythical Mount Meru, the home of the gods in Hindu tradition. It was later used by Buddhists as well.

Arabian camel Introduced to North Africa and the Sahara in the early centuries of the Common Era, this animal made trans-Saharan commerce possible by 300 to 400 C.E.

Aristotle A Greek philosopher (384–322 B.C.E.); student of Plato and teacher of Alexander the Great.

Ashoka The most famous ruler of India's Mauryan Empire (r. 268–232 B.C.E.), who converted to Buddhism and tried to rule peacefully and with tolerance.

Aspasia A foreign resident in Athens (ca. 470–400 B.C.E.) who was famed for her learning and wit. She was the partner of the statesman Pericles.

Athenian democracy A radical form of direct democracy in which most of the free males of Athens were able to vote in the Assembly and officeholders were chosen by lot.

Augustus A title that implied divine status for Octavian (r. 27 B.C.E.–14 C.E.), who emerged as sole ruler of the Roman state at the end of an extended period of civil war.

Austronesian migrations The last phase of the great human migration that established a human presence in every habitable region of the earth. Austronesian-speaking people settled the Pacific islands and Madagascar in a series of seaborne migrations that began around 3,500 years ago.

Axum Second-wave era kingdom of East Africa in present-day Eritrea and northern Ethiopia with a highly productive plow-based farming system; an early adopter of Christianity. (pron. AX-uhm)

Aztec Empire Major state that developed in what is now Mexico in the fourteenth and fifteenth centuries; dominated by the semi-nomadic Mexica, who had migrated into the region from northern Mexico.

Banpo An early agricultural village in northern China dating to around 6,000 years ago. It consisted of approximately 45 thatched buildings that housed an estimated 500 people. Archeological evidence suggests millet, pigs, and dogs had been domesticated, and diets were supplemented with wild plants, animals, and fish.

Ban Zhao A major female Confucian author of China (45–116 C.E.) whose works explore the implications of Confucian thinking for women. (pron. bahn jow)

Bantu migration Gradual movement of Bantu-speaking peoples, beginning in ca. 3000 B.C.E., from their homeland in what is now southern Nigeria and the Cameroons into most of eastern and southern Africa by ca. 400 C.E. The agricultural techniques and ironworking technology of Bantu-speaking farmers gave them an advantage over the gathering and hunting peoples they encountered.

Bhagavad Gita A great Hindu epic text that conveyed the message that ordinary people could find spiritual fulfillment by selflessly performing the ordinary duties of their lives. (pron. BUH-guh-vahd GEE-tuh)

bhakti movement Meaning "worship," this Hindu movement began in south India and moved northward between 600 and 1000 C.E.; it involved the intense adoration of and identification with a particular deity through songs, prayers, and rituals. (pron. BAHK-tee)

Black Death A massive pandemic that swept through Eurasia in the early fourteenth century, spreading along the trade routes within and beyond the Mongol Empire and reaching the Middle East and Western Europe by 1347. Associated with a massive loss of life.

bushido The "way of the warrior," referring to the martial values of the Japanese samurai, including bravery, loyalty, and an emphasis on death over surrender. (pron. boo-shee-doh)

Byzantine Empire The surviving eastern Roman Empire and one of the centers of Christendom during the medieval centuries. The Byzantine Empire was founded at the end of the third century, when the Roman Empire was divided into eastern and western halves, and survived until its conquest by Muslim forces in 1453.

caesaropapism A political-religious system in which the secular ruler is also head of the religious establishment, as in the Byzantine Empire.

Cahokia The dominant center of an important Mississippi valley mound-building culture, located near present-day St. Louis, Missouri; flourished from about 900 to 1250 C.E.

Caral The largest of some twenty-five urban centers that emerged in the Norte Chico region along the central coast of Peru from 3000 B.C.E. to 1800 B.C.E.

Çatalhüyük An early agricultural village and archeological site in what is now Turkey; flourished between 7400 and 6000 B.C.E. With a settled population of several thousand people, the village displayed few signs of class or gender inequality. (pron. cha-TAHL-hoo-YOOK)

Central Asian / Oxus civilization A major First Civilization that emerged around 2200 B.C.E. in Central Asia in the Oxus or Amu Darya River valley in what is now northern Afghanistan and southern Turkmenistan. An important focal point for a Eurasian-wide system of intellectual and cultural exchange, it faded away by about 1700 B.C.E.

Chaco Phenomenon Name given to a major process of settlement and societal organization that occurred in the period 860–1130 C.E. among the peoples of Chaco canyon, in what is now northwestern New Mexico; the society formed is notable for its settlement in large pueblos and for the building of hundreds of miles of roads, the purpose of which is not known.

Charlemagne Ruler of the Carolingian Empire (r. 768–814) who staged an imperial revival in Western Europe. (pron. SHAHR-leh-mane)

Chavín An Andean town strategically located between the western coast and eastern rain forests that was the center of a large Peruvian religious movement from around 900 to 200 B.C.E. (pron. cha-BEEN)

chiefdom A societal grouping governed by a chief who typically relies on generosity, ritual status, or charisma rather than force to win obedience from the people.

China's economic revolution A major rise in prosperity that took place in China under the Song dynasty (960–1279), which was marked by rapid population growth, urbanization, economic specialization, the development of an immense network of internal waterways, and a great increase in industrial production and technological innovation.

China's scholar-gentry class A term used to describe members of China's landowning families, reflecting their wealth from the land and the privileges that they derived as government officials.

Chinese Buddhism Buddhism was China's only large-scale cultural borrowing before the twentieth century; it entered China from India in the first and second centuries C.E. but only became popular in 300 to 800 C.E. through a series of cultural accommodations. At first supported by the state, Buddhism suffered persecution during the ninth century but continued to play a role in Chinese society alongside Confucianism and Daoism.

chu nom A variation of Chinese writing developed in Vietnam that became the basis for an independent national literature; "southern script."

Church of the East An early theologically and organizationally distinct Christian church based in Syria and Persia but with followers in southern India and Central Asia.

Clovis culture The earliest widespread and distinctive culture of North America, dating to about 13,000 years ago; named for a particular kind of projectile point, initially found near the city of Clovis, New Mexico.

Code of Hammurabi A series of laws publicized at the order of King Hammurabi of Babylon that reveals much about the social order of Mesopotamian civilization. (pron. hahm-moo-RAH-bee)

Confucianism The Chinese philosophy first enunciated by Confucius, advocating the moral example of superiors as the key element of social order.

Constantinople New capital for the eastern half of the Roman Empire; Constantinople's highly defensible and economically important site helped ensure the city's cultural and strategic importance for many centuries.

Crusades A term used to describe the "holy wars" waged by Western Christendom, especially against the forces of Islam in the eastern Mediterranean from 1095 to 1291 and on the Iberian Peninsula into the fifteenth century.

Further Crusades were also conducted in non-Christian regions of Eastern Europe from about 1150 on. Crusades could be declared by only the pope; participants swore a vow and received in return an indulgence removing the penalty for confessed sins.

Daoism A Chinese philosophy / popular religion that advocates a simple and unpretentious way of living and alignment with the natural world, founded by the legendary figure Laozi. (pron. dow-ism)

Dreamtime A complex worldview of Australia's Aboriginal people that held that living humans exist in a vibration or echo of ancestral happenings.

Eastern Orthodox Christianity Branch of Christianity that developed in the eastern part of the Roman Empire and gradually separated, mostly on matters of practice, from the branch of Christianity dominant in Western Europe; noted for the subordination of the Church to political authorities, a married clergy, the use of leavened bread in the Eucharist, and a sharp rejection of the authority of Roman popes.

Egypt One of the earliest civilizations in world history, with a three-thousand-year history as an intact state ruled by pharaohs. It became part of an international political system that included Babylon and Mesopotamia.

Empress Wu China's only female ruler (r. 690–705 C.E.), who patronized scholarship and worked to elevate the position of women.

Epic of Gilgamesh Mesopotamia's ancient epic poem dating to around 2000 B.C.E.

Ethiopian Christianity Emerging in the fourth century with the conversion of the rulers of Axum, this Christian church proved more resilient than other early churches in Africa. Located in the mountainous highlands of modern Ethiopia, it was largely cut off from other parts of Christendom and developed traditions that made it distinctive from other Christian churches.

European Renaissance A "rebirth" of classical learning that is most often associated with the cultural blossoming of Italy in the period 1350–1500 and that included not just a rediscovery of Greek and Roman learning but also major developments in art, as well as growing secularism in society. It spread to Northern Europe after 1400.

Fertile Crescent Region sometimes known as Southwest Asia that includes the modern states of Iraq, Syria, Israel/Palestine, Jordan, and southern Turkey; the earliest home of agriculture and some of the first civilizations.

feudalism A highly fragmented and decentralized society in which power was held by the landowning warrior elite. In this highly competitive system, lesser lords and knights swore allegiance to greater lords or kings and thus became their vassals, frequently receiving lands and plunder in return for military service.

foot binding The Chinese practice of tightly wrapping girls' feet to keep them small, prevalent in the Song dynasty and later; an emphasis on small size and delicacy was central to views of female beauty.

Fulbe West Africa's largest pastoral society, whose members gradually adopted Islam and took on a religious leadership role that led to the creation of a number of new states by the nineteenth century. (pron. FULB)

Ghana An early and prominent state within West African civilization. With a reputation for great riches, Ghana flourished between 750 and 1076 and was later absorbed into the larger Kingdom of Mali.

Göbekli Tepe A ceremonial site in southeastern Turkey comprising twenty circles made up of large carved limestone pillars. The site, which dates to almost 12,000 years ago, was built by gatherers and hunters who lived at least part of the year in settled villages. (pron. goh-BEHK-lee TEH-peh)

Great Zimbabwe A powerful state in the southern African interior that apparently emerged from the growing trade in gold to the East African coast; flourished between 1250 and 1350 C.E.

Greco-Persian Wars A half century of intermittent conflict (499–449 B.C.E.) between the Greek city-states and the Persian Empire. During two major Persian invasions of Greece, in 490 B.C.E. and 480 B.C.E., the Persians were defeated on both land and sea.

Greco-Roman slavery In the Greek and Roman world, most slaves were captives from war, slave raiding, and piracy (and their descendants); manumission was common. Among the Greeks, household service was the most common form of slavery, but slavery was entrenched in all areas of Roman society except the military.

Greek rationalism A secularizing system of scientific and philosophic thought that developed in classical Greece in the period 600 to 300 B.C.E.; it emphasized using human reason to understand the world in nonreligious terms.

gunpowder A Chinese invention that came about during the ninth century. A mix of saltpeter, sulfur, and charcoal, it was originally created by Daoist alchemists seeking to discover an elixir of immortality. Ultimately, though, it revolutionized global military affairs.

Gupta Empire An era of Indian civilization from 320 to 550 C.E. that witnessed considerable political unity, cultural flourishing, and thriving trade.

Han dynasty The Chinese dynasty (206 B.C.E.–220 C.E.) that emerged after the Qin dynasty collapsed, establishing political and cultural patterns that lasted into the twentieth century.

hangul A phonetic alphabet developed in Korea in the fifteenth century in a move toward greater cultural independence from China. (pron. HAHN-gool)

Hangzhou China's capital during the Song dynasty, with a population at its height of more than a million people.

Hellenistic era The period from 323 to 30 B.C.E. in which Greek culture spread widely in the Middle East and parts of India in the cities and kingdoms ruled by Alexander's political successors.

helots The dependent, semi-enslaved class of ancient Sparta whose social discontent prompted the militarization of Spartan society.

hijra The "journey" of Muhammad and his original followers from Mecca to Yathrib (later Medina) in 622 C.E.; the journey marks the starting point of the Islamic calendar. (pron. HIJJ-ruh)

Holy Roman Empire A loose confederation of regional states, centered on what is now Germany but stretching from Denmark to Rome and the borders of France to Poland. From its beginning in the early ninth century, it was headed by an emperor, but in practice regional states proved effective in limiting his power.

Hopewell culture A common name for the Mississippi valley mound-building culture, after an archeological site in Ohio. Significant for the wide variety of artifacts found in elaborate burial mounds.

House of Wisdom An academic center for research and translation of foreign texts that was established in Baghdad in 830 C.E. by the Abbasid caliph al-Mamun.

Hulegu Grandson of Chinggis Khan who became the first il-khan (subordinate khan) of Persia. (pron. HE-luh-gee)

Igbo People whose lands were east of the Niger River in what is now southern Nigeria in West Africa. They built a complex society that rejected kingship and centralized statehood, while relying on other institutions to provide social coherence. (pron. EE-boh)

Inca Empire The Western Hemisphere's largest imperial state in the fifteenth and early sixteenth centuries. Built by a relatively small community of Quechua-speaking people (the Incas), the empire stretched some 2,500 miles along the Andes Mountains, which run nearly the entire length of the west coast of South America, and contained perhaps 10 million subjects.

Indus Valley civilization A major civilization that emerged in what is now Pakistan during the third millennium B.C.E., in the valleys of the Indus and Saraswati rivers, noted for the uniformity of its elaborately planned cities over a large territory.

Iroquois Iroquois-speaking peoples in what is now New York State; around the fifteenth century they formed a loose alliance based on the Great Law of Peace, an agreement to settle disputes peacefully through a council of clan leaders.

jatis The thousands of occupationally based social groups, each associated with a *varna*, that became the primary cells of social life in the Indian caste system.

Jesus of Nazareth A peasant/artisan "wisdom teacher" and Jewish mystic (ca. 4 B.C.E.–29 C.E.) whose life, teachings, death, and alleged resurrection gave rise to the new religion of Christianity.

Jesus Sutras The written product of Nestorian Christians living in China, these texts articulate the Christian message using Buddhist and Daoist concepts.

jizya Special tax paid by *dhimmis* (protected but second-class subjects) in Muslim-ruled territory in return for freedom to practice their own religion.

Judaism The monotheistic religion developed in the Middle East by the Hebrews, emphasizing a sole personal god (Yahweh) with concerns for social justice.

Khanate of the Golden Horde The Russian name for the incorporation of Russia into the Mongol Empire in the mid-thirteenth century; known to Mongols as the Kipchak Khanate.

Khubilai Khan Grandson of Chinggis Khan who ruled China from 1271 to 1294. (pron. koo-buh-l'eye kahn)

Kievan Rus A culturally diverse civilization that emerged around the city of Kiev in the ninth century C.E. and adopted Christianity in the tenth, thus linking this emerging Russian state to the world of Eastern Orthodoxy.

Legalism A Chinese philosophy distinguished by an adherence to clear laws with vigorous punishments.

madrassas Formal colleges for higher instruction in the teachings of Islam as well as in secular subjects like law, established throughout the Islamic world beginning in the eleventh century.

Mahayana Buddhism "Great Vehicle," the popular development of Buddhism in the early centuries of the Common Era, which gives a much greater role to supernatural beings and to compassion and proved to be more popular than original (Theravada) Buddhism.

maize An ancient version of corn, first domesticated in southern Mexico by 4000 to 3000 B.C.E. This ancestor of corn was a mountain grass that looks nothing like today's corn or maize. Selective adaptation of this plant over thousands of years allowed for the development of sustainable agriculture in Mesoamerica and elsewhere.

Malacca Muslim port city that came to prominence on the waterway between Sumatra and Malaya in the fifteenth century C.E.; it was the springboard for the spread of a syncretic form of Islam throughout the region.

Mali A prominent state within West African civilization; it was established in 1235 C.E. and flourished for several centuries. Mali monopolized the import of horses and metals as part of the trans-Saharan trade; it was a large-scale producer of gold; and its most famous ruler, Mansa Musa, led a large group of Muslims on the pilgrimage to Mecca in 1324–1325.

mana and *tapu* Religious concepts in Oceania; people or objects became sacred through a spiritual energy or power (mana) that was kept pure with ritual restrictions (tapu), which came into English as "taboo."

Mauryan Empire The first and largest of India's short experiments with a large-scale political system (326–184 B.C.E.), it encompassed all but the southern tip of the Indian subcontinent. (pron. MORE-yuhn)

Maya civilization A major civilization of Mesoamerica known for the most elaborate writing system in the Americas and other intellectual and artistic achievements; flourished from 250 to 900 C.E.

megafaunal extinction The dying out of a number of large animal species, including the mammoth and several species of horses and camel. Occurred around 11,000 years ago, at the end of the Ice Age in North America. The extinction may have been caused by excessive hunting or by the changing climate of the era.

Meroë City in southern Nubia that was the center of Nubian civilization between 300 B.C.E. and 100 C.E.; had a reputation for great riches and was culturally distinct from Egypt. (pron. MER-oh-ee)

Ming dynasty Chinese dynasty (1368–1644) that succeeded the Yuan dynasty of the Mongols; noted for its return to traditional Chinese ways and restoration of the land after the destructiveness of the Mongols.

Moche An important regional civilization of northern Peru, governed by warrior-priests; flourished from around 100 to 800 C.E. (pron. MOH-chee)

Modun Great ruler of the Xiongnu Empire (r. 210–174 B.C.E.) who exacted tribute from other Central Asian pastoral peoples as well as China itself, forcing Han dynasty emperor Wen to acknowledge the Xiongnu Empire as an equal.

Mohenjo Daro / Harappa Major cities of the Indus Valley civilization, both of which flourished around 2000 B.C.E. (pron. moe-hen-joe DAHR-oh) / (pron. hah-RAHP-uh)

Mongol world war Term used to describe half a century of military campaigns, massive killing, and empire building pursued by Chinggis Khan and his successors in Eurasia after 1209.

Mound Builders Members of a number of cultures that developed east of the Mississippi River in what is now the United States and that are distinguished by their large earthen mounds; most widespread between 200 B.C.E. and 1250 C.E.

Mughal Empire A successful state founded by Muslim Turkic-speaking peoples who invaded India and provided a rare period of relative political unity (1526–1707); their rule was noted for efforts to create partnerships between Hindus and Muslims. (pron. MOO-guhl)

Muhammad (570–632 C.E.) The Prophet and founder of Islam whose religious revelations became the Quran, bringing a radically monotheistic religion to Arabia and the world.

Neolithic Revolution The "new stone age," referring to the introduction of agriculture in societies that had long survived with a gathering and hunting economy.

Niger Valley civilization Distinctive city-based civilization that flourished from about 300 B.C.E. to about 900 C.E. in the floodplain of the middle Niger and that included major cities like Jenne-jeno; the Niger Valley civilization is particularly noteworthy for its apparent lack of centralized state structures, having been organized instead in clusters of economically specialized settlements.

Norte Chico A region along the central coast of Peru, home to an early civilization that developed from 3000 B.C.E. to 1800 B.C.E.

Nubia A region to the south of Egypt in the Nile Valley, noted for its development of a separate civilization with an alphabetic writing system and a major ironworking industry by 500 B.C.E.

Nubian Christianity Emerging in the fifth and sixth centuries in the several kingdoms of Nubia to the south of Egypt, this Christian church thrived for six hundred years but had largely disappeared by 1500 C.E., by which time most of the region's population practiced Islam.

Olmec civilization An early civilization that developed along the coast of the Gulf of Mexico around 1200 B.C.E. and possibly created the first written language in the Americas.

"the original affluent society" Term coined to describe Paleolithic societies, which are regarded as affluent not because they had so much but because they wanted or needed so little.

Ottoman Empire Major Islamic state centered on Anatolia that came to include the Balkans, parts of the Middle East, and much of North Africa; lasted in one form or another from the fourteenth to the early twentieth century.

Ottoman seizure of Constantinople The city of Constantinople, the capital and almost the only outpost left of the Byzantine Empire, fell to the army of the Ottoman sultan Mehmed II "the Conqueror" in 1453, an event that marked the end of Christian Byzantium.

Paleolithic era The long period during which human societies sustained themselves through gathering, hunting, and fishing without the practice of agriculture. Such ways of living persisted well after the advent of agriculture in many places.

Paleolithic settling down The process by which some Paleolithic peoples moved toward permanent settlement in the wake of the last Ice Age. Settlement was marked by increasing storage of food and accumulation of goods, as well as growing inequalities in society.

pastoral society Based on an alternative kind of food-producing economy focused on the raising of livestock, pastoral societies emerged in the Afro-Eurasian world where settled agriculture was difficult or impossible. Pastoral peoples often led their animals to seasonal grazing grounds rather than settling permanently in a single location.

patriarchy A social system in which women have been made subordinate to men in the family and in society; often linked to the development of plow-based agriculture, intensive warfare, and private property.

Paul, Saint An early convert and missionary (ca. 6–67 C.E.) and the first great popularizer of Christianity, especially to Gentile (non-Jewish) communities.

pax Romana The "Roman peace," a term typically used to denote the stability and prosperity of the early Roman Empire, especially in the first and second centuries C.E.

Peloponnesian War The Greek civil war (431–404 B.C.E.) that followed the Greco-Persian Wars, with Sparta defending city-state independence against Athenian dominance; the war left the Greeks in a state of distrust and disunity.

Perpetua Christian martyr (181–203 C.E.) from an upper-class Roman family in Carthage. Her refusal to renounce her faith made her an inspiration for other early Christians.

Persian Empire A major empire of the second-wave era that expanded from the Iranian plateau to incorporate the Middle East from Egypt to India; flourished from around 553 to 330 B.C.E.

Pillars of Islam The five core requirements of the Quran: the belief in one God, regular prayer, charitable giving, fasting during Ramadan, and a pilgrimage to Mecca (if financially and physically possible).

Plato A Greek philosopher (429–348 B.C.E.) who famously sketched out a design for a good society in *The Republic*.

pochteca Professional merchants among the Aztecs who undertook large-scale trading expeditions in the fifteenth century C.E. (pron. pohch-TEH-cah)

Pohnpei Micronesian island dubbed the "Venice of the Pacific" where a complex urban construction made of coral and stone served as the ceremonial, administrative, and burial center.

Qin Shihuangdi Literally "first emperor from the Qin"; Shihuangdi (r. 221–210 B.C.E.) forcibly reunited China and established a strong state that governed, often brutally, according to a Legalist philosophy. (pron. chin shee-HUANG-dee)

Quran Also transliterated as Qur'án and Koran, this is the most holy text of Islam, which records the words of God through revelations given to the Prophet Muhammad.

ritual purity and pollution The idea that members of higher Indian castes must adhere to strict regulations limiting or forbidding their contact with "polluted" objects and members of lower castes to preserve their own caste standing and personal purity.

Roman Catholic Church Western European branch of Christianity that gradually defined itself as separate from Eastern Orthodoxy, with a major break occurring in 1054 C.E. that still has not been overcome. By the eleventh century, Western Christendom was centered on the pope as the ultimate authority in matters of doctrine. The Church struggled to remain independent of established political authorities.

Safavid Empire Major Turkic empire established in Persia in the early sixteenth century and notable for its efforts to convert its people to Shia Islam. (pron. SAH-fah-vid)

Sand Roads A term used to describe the routes of the trans-Saharan trade, which linked interior West Africa to the Mediterranean and North African world.

Sea Roads The world's largest sea-based system of communication and exchange before 1500 C.E. Centered on India, it stretched from southern China to eastern Africa.

secondary products revolution The series of technological changes that began ca. 4000 B.C.E. as people in the Eastern Hemisphere began to use their domesticated animals in new ways, such as for their milk, wool, and manure. Also involved learning to ride horses and camels and using animals to pull carts, plows, and chariots.

Seljuk Turkic Empire An empire of the eleventh and twelfth centuries, centered in Persia and present-day Iraq. Seljuk rulers adopted the Muslim title of *sultan* (ruler) as part of their conversion to Islam.

shamans Persons believed to be especially skilled at dealing with the spirit world, often by means of trances induced by psychoactive drugs.

sharia Islamic law, dealing with political, economic, social, and religious life. It literally translates as "a path to water," which is considered the source of all life. (pron. shah-REE-ah)

Shotoku Taishi Japanese statesman (572–622) who launched the drive to make Japan into a centralized bureaucratic state modeled on China; he is best known for issuing the Seventeen Article Constitution in 604 C.E., which lays out the principles of this reform.

Siddhartha Gautama (the Buddha) The Indian prince whose exposure to human suffering led him to develop a path to Enlightenment, which became the basis for the emerging religious tradition of Buddhism; lived ca. 566–ca. 486 B.C.E. (pron. sidd-ARTH-uh gow-TAHM-uh)

Sikhism Religious tradition of northern India founded by Guru Nanak (1469–1539); combines elements of Hinduism and Islam and proclaims the brotherhood of all humans and the equality of men and women.

Silk Roads Land-based trade routes that linked many regions of Eurasia. They were named after the most famous product traded along these routes.

Silla kingdom The first ruling dynasty to bring a measure of political unity to the Korean peninsula (688–900). (pron. SHEE-lah)

Socrates The first great Greek philosopher (469–399 B.C.E.), whose constant questioning of conventional thinking led to his death at the hands of an Athenian jury.

Song dynasty The Chinese dynasty (960–1279) that rose to power after the Tang dynasty. During the Song dynasty, an explosion of scholarship gave rise to Neo-Confucianism, and a revolution in agricultural and industrial production made China the richest and most populated country on the planet.

Songhay Empire Major Islamic state of West Africa that formed in the second half of the fifteenth century. (pron. song-GAH-ee)

Spartacus A Roman gladiator who led the most serious slave revolt in Roman history in 73 B.C.E.

Srivijaya A Malay kingdom that dominated the critical choke point in Indian Ocean trade at the Straits of Malacca between 670 and 1025 C.E. Like other places in Southeast Asia, Srivijaya absorbed various cultural influences from India. (pron. SREE-vih-juh-yuh)

Sufism An understanding of the Islamic faith that saw the worldly success of Islamic civilization as a distraction and deviation from the purer spirituality of Muhammad's time. By renouncing the material world, meditating on the words of the Quran, chanting the names of God, using music and dance, and venerating Muhammad and various "saints," Sufis pursued an interior life, seeking to tame the ego and achieve spiritual union with Allah.

Sui dynasty Ruling dynasty of China (589–618) that effectively reunited the country after several centuries of political fragmentation. This unity was solidified through the extension of canals economically linking northern

and southern China, but harsh leadership and futile efforts to conquer Korea eventually prompted the overthrow of the dynasty.

Sumer The region in the southern reaches of Mesopotamia between the Tigres and Euphrates rivers, mostly in present-day Iraq. Home to an early civilization that arose around 3500 B.C.E. to 3000 B.C.E., this area likely gave rise to the world's earliest written language.

Swahili civilization An East African civilization that emerged in the eighth century C.E. as a set of commercial city-states linked into the Indian Ocean trading network. Combining African Bantu and Islamic cultural patterns, these competing city-states accumulated goods from the interior and exchanged them for the products of distant civilizations.

Tang dynasty Ruling dynasty of China (618–907) noted for its openness to foreign cultural influences. Together with its successor, the Song dynasty, it represented a golden age of arts and literature and established patterns of Chinese life that endured into the twentieth century.

Temujin (Chinggis Khan) Birth name of the Mongol leader better known as Chinggis Khan (1162–1227), or "universal ruler," a name he acquired after unifying the Mongols. (pron. TEM-oo-chin)

Teotihuacán The largest city of pre-Columbian America, with a population between 125,000 and 150,000; seemingly built to a plan in the Valley of Mexico, Teotihuacán flourished between 300 and 600 C.E., during which time it governed or influenced much of the surrounding region. The name Teotihuacán is an Aztec term meaning "city of the gods." (pron. tay-uh-tee-wah-KAHN)

Theravada Buddhism "Teaching of the Elders," the early form of Buddhism according to which the Buddha was a wise teacher but not divine; emphasizes practices rather than beliefs. (pron. THAIR-ah-VAH-dah)

Timbuktu A major commercial city of West African civilization and a noted center of Islamic scholarship and education by the sixteenth century.

Timur Turkic warrior, also known as Tamerlane, whose efforts to restore the Mongol Empire in the late fourteenth and early fifteenth centuries devastated parts of Persia, Russia, and India. His successors created a vibrant elite culture drawing on both Turkic and Persian elements, especially in the city of Samarkand. Timur's conquests represent the last major military success of Central Asian pastoral peoples.

Tonga Islands Polynesian state with a central royal court, specialized craftsmen, and widespread military and commercial influence in the central Pacific.

"three obediences" In Chinese Confucian thought, the notion that a woman is permanently subordinate to male control: first to her father, then to her husband, and finally to her son.

trans–Saharan slave trade A fairly small-scale commerce in enslaved people that flourished especially from 1100 to 1400, exporting West African slaves across the Sahara for sale in Islamic North Africa.

tribute system A set of practices that required a show of subordination from all non-Chinese authorities and the payment of tribute—products of value from their countries—to the Chinese emperor. In return, China would grant trading rights to foreigners and offer gifts even more valuable than the tribute itself.

Turkic peoples Turkic speakers from Central Asia, originally nomads, who spread westward, creating a series of nomadic empires between 552 and 965 C.E. Having converted to Islam between the tenth and fourteenth centuries, Turkic peoples carried that faith into new lands, most notably the Christian Byzantine Empire, and became a politically powerful presence in the Islamic world.

ulama Islamic religious scholars, both Sunni and Shia, who shaped and transmitted the core teachings of Islamic civilization.

Umayyad caliphate Family of caliphs who ruled the Islamic world from 661 to 750 C.E., expanding the Arab Empire and creating a ruling class of Arab military aristocrats. (pron. oo-MEYE-ahd)

umma The community of all believers in Islam, bound by common belief rather than territory, language, or tribe. (pron. OOM-mah)

Upanishads Indian mystical and philosophical works written between 800 and 400 B.C.E. (pron. oo-PAHN-ee-shahds)

Uruk The largest city of ancient Mesopotamia, with a population around 50,000 in the third millennium B.C.E. (pron. OOH-rook)

varnas The four inherited ranked social classes of the Indian caste system.

Vedas The earliest religious texts of India, a collection of ancient poems, hymns, and rituals that were transmitted orally before being written down ca. 600 B.C.E. (pron. VAY-duhs)

Venus figurines Paleolithic carvings of the female form, often with exaggerated breasts, buttocks, hips, and stomachs.

vertical integration Control of a variety of ecological zones (and thus a variety of crops and animals) in areas with diverse climates and competing cities, chiefdoms, and states; common in Mesoamerican and Andean civilizations.

Vladimir of Kiev Grand prince of Kiev whose conversion to Orthodox Christianity in 988 C.E. led to the incorporation of an emerging Russian state into the sphere of Eastern Orthodoxy.

Wang Mang A Han court official who usurped the throne and ruled from 8 C.E. to 23 C.E.; noted for his Confucian-inspired reform movement that included the breakup of large estates.

Wari and Tiwanaku Two states that flourished between 400 and 1000 C.E. in the interior highlands of the Andean region. At their height, they possessed urban capitals with populations in the tens of thousands and productive agricultural systems. (pron. wah-ree)

West African civilization A series of important states that developed in the region stretching from the Atlantic coast to Lake Chad in the period 500 to 1600 C.E. Developed in response to the economic opportunities of trans-Saharan trade (especially control of gold production), it included the states of Ghana, Mali, Songhay, and Kanem, as well as numerous towns and cities.

Western Christendom Western European branch of Christianity, also known as Roman Catholicism, that gradually defined itself as separate from Eastern Orthodoxy, with a major break occurring in 1054 C.E.; characterized by its relative independence from the state and its recognition of the authority of the pope.

Xiongnu Empire An imperial creation of nomadic steppe peoples who inhabited lands north of China. In the third and second centuries B.C.E., this empire stretched from Manchuria to Central Asia, establishing a model for later Turkic and Mongol empires.

Yap An island in western Micronesia that developed ceremonial tributary relationships with surrounding islands based in part on fear of Yapese sorcery.

Yellow Turban Rebellion A massive Chinese peasant uprising around 184 B.C.E. that was inspired by Daoist teachings; it aimed to establish a new golden age of equality, harmony, and common ownership of property.

Yuan dynasty (China) Mongol dynasty initiated by Khubilai Khan that ruled China from 1271 to 1368.

Zheng He Great Chinese admiral who commanded a huge fleet of ships in a series of voyages in the Indian Ocean that began in 1405. Intended to enroll distant peoples and states in the Chinese tribute system, those voyages ended abruptly in 1433 and led to no lasting Chinese imperial presence in the region. (pron. JUHNG-huh)

Zoroastrianism Persian monotheistic religion founded by the prophet Zarathustra and emphasizing free will and the choice between good and evil. (pron. zohr-oh-ASS-tree-ahn-i'zm)

Index

A Note about the Index: Names of individuals are in **boldface**. Letters in parentheses following pages refer to the following:

(d) documents in the docutext portion of the book

(v) visual sources in the docutext portion of the book

(i) illustrations, including photographs and artifacts

(f) figures, including charts and graphs

(m) maps

(t) tables

Aachen, Charlemagne at, 444, 445*(v)*
Abbasid caliphate, 371
    Mongols and, 376, 462
    Ottomans and, 509
    Persians and, 369
    Silk Roads trade and, 279
    women in, 374
Aboriginal Australians
    culture of, 51*(d)*
    Dreamtime of, 17, 44–49, 48*(v)*, 50*(v)*
    religious rituals of, 22–23, 142
    society and art of, 17, 17*(i)*
Abraham (Hebrews), 361, 362*(i)*
Abu Bakr (caliph), 369
Abyssinia. *See* Axum; Ethiopia
academy
    of Plato, 161, 434
    of Wu Di, 189
accounting systems, in First Civilizations, 73
Achaemenid dynasty (Persia), 102
Achebe, Chinua (writer), 497
A.D., 4
adaptation, 3, 32, 255
Adelard of Bath, 433
administration. *See* government; specific locations
Adulis, East Africa, 234
Advice to the English Church (Gregory), 440*(d)*
Aegean region, population of, 105. *See also* specific locations
Aeschylus (Greece), 108
Afghanistan
    Greece and, 109
    Turkic peoples and, 499

Africa. *See also* Afro-Eurasia; specific locations
    in 15th century, 506*(m)*
    camels in, 456–457
    Christianity in, 167, 168–169, 403, 404, 407–408
    civilizations of, 231–237
    early humans in, 3, 10–16
    environment in, 231
    Islam in, 407
    migration and, 10–16
    plague in, 476
    population of, 228, 230*(t)*
    second-wave era in, 231–237, 232*(m)*
    slavery and, 66
    trade in, 497, 522
Afro-Asia
    culture and, 23
    interactions and exchange in, 80
Afro-Eurasia
    from 600 to 1450, 357–358
    Arab Empire in, 365–376
    Christianity in, 171, 403–404
    civilizations in, 63
    disease transmission in, 284
    farming in, 32
    Islam and, 270, 358–388, 508
    Mongols and, 450, 471
    plague in, 475–478
    trade in, 280, 281, 288–289, 522–524, 523*(m)*
afterlife, in Egypt, 75
agents of change, in third-wave era, 270
age of warring states. *See* warring states period
Agricultural Revolution, 3–4, 26–30, 35, 37–41. *See also* agriculture
    in Africa, 231
    in Americas, 253
    civilizations and, 62
    Göbekli Tepe and, 25
    horticulture and, 30
    locations of, 30–33
agricultural societies
    village societies, 496–498
    women in, 204
agriculture. *See also* Agricultural Revolution; farms and farming; hunting; irrigation; technology

in Africa, 248, 295
in Americas, 250
ancient, 10
in Arab world, 366
in Australia, 494–496
in Axum, 234
Bantu, 247, 248
in China, 321
climate warming and, 419
culture of, 34–37
in Egypt, 76, 77
in Europe, 420–421, 508
exploration and, 508
in Fertile Crescent, 30–31
in First Civilizations, 74
gender roles and, 67–68
globalization of, 28–29*(m)*, 33–37
Green Revolution and, 386
Inca, 521*(i)*
Islamic, 386
land clearing and, 419
language diffusion and, 34
Maya, 238
in Meroë, 233
in Mesopotamia, 76
Moche, 243
Mongols and, 467, 473
Neolithic, 26–33
Paleolithic, 26
pastoralism and, 28–29*(m)*, 37–39
in Roman Empire, 123
transition to, 30
in Vietnam, 334
village societies and, 496–498
in Wari and Tiwanaku, 246
in Yemen, 360
Ahura Mazda (Persian god), 102, 104, 156, 156*(i)*
Ain Ghazal, Jordan, statues of, 33*(i)*
Ain Jalut, Battle of, 461
air pollution, Roman and Chinese, 122
Aisha (Islamic scholar), 375–376
Akkad and Akkadians, 54, 66*(i)*, 75*(m)*, 77
Alaric (Germanic leader), 126
alchemy, gunpowder from, 322, 323
alcohol
    in Agricultural Revolution, 36
    Mongols and, 467

Alexander the Great (Macedonia), 100, 108–110, 109*(m)*, 110*(i)*
  cultural diffusion by, 161, 279
  India and, 126
  Zoroastrianism and, 156–157
Alexandria, Egypt, 110–111
  trade and, 288
algebra, 388
Ali (caliph), 369, 395, 396*(v)*
  "Letter to Malik Ashtar," 399*(d)*
Ali ibn Husayn, 397*(d)*
Allah, 360, 361–362. *See also* Islam; Muhammad; Muslims
Almoravid Empire, 457, 457*(m)*
Alopen (Persia), 167
alpacas, 32, 38
alphabet. *See also* writing and writing systems
  Cyrillic, 414, 415
  Korean *hangul,* 333
  Pallava, 290
Amazon River region, 301. *See also* specific locations
America(s). *See also* North America; South America; Western Hemisphere; specific locations
  in 15th century, 515*(m)*
  agriculture in, 32–33
  civilizations in, 514–521
  commerce in, 300–302
  diseases in, 285
  domesticated animals in, 228
  empires in, 477
  human migrations to, 17–18
  pastoralists in, 228
  percentage of world's population in, 228
  slavery in, 212
  trade in, 257, 522
  transcontinental comparisons with, 228–230
American web, 301, 301*(m)*
Amitabha (Buddhist deity), 343
Amu Darya (Oxus) river region, 61
Anasazi people. *See* Ancestral Pueblo people
Anatolia. *See also* Ionia; Ottoman Empire; Turkey
  Byzantine Empire and, 409
  Christianity in, 167
  Greece and, 107, 109
  Islam and, 379–380
  Turkic peoples in, 456, 508
ancestors
  in Bantu religions, 249
  in Chinese culture, 142

  in Dreamtime Australia, 17, 44–49
  in Japanese culture, 337
  Roman "ways of," 112
  in Southeast Asia, 293
Ancestral Pueblo people (Anasazi), 250–251
ancient world, perceptions of outsiders in, 130–137
al-Andalus, 382. *See also* Spain
Andes Mountains region. *See also* specific locations
  agriculture in, 32, 33
  Chavín culture of, 59, 242–243
  civilizations of, 58–59, 237, 242–246, 242*(i)*
  exchange and communication in, 301
  Inca in, 59, 242, 518–520
  Machu Picchu in, 519*(i)*
  Moche civilization in, 243–245
  pastoralism in, 228, 452*(t)*
  Tiwanaku in, 245–246
  Wari in, 245–246
  writing in, 72*(t)*
Andromache (Greek character), 209
Angkor, Khmer kingdom of, 290, 293
Angkor Wat, 292, 292*(i)*
Angles, 416
Anglo-Saxons, 123*(i)*, 124, 439, 440, 441*(v)*
Angola. *See* Kongo, kingdom of
animals. *See also* domestication
  in Americas, 18
  domestication of, 10, 26, 32, 38*(i)*
  extinction of, 18, 19
  globalization of, 37
  in pastoral societies, 37–38
An Lushan rebellion (China), 344
Anselm (Christian philosopher), 433
anthrax, Black Death and, 285
anti-Semitism. *See also* Jews and Judaism
  Crusades and, 427
Aotearoa (New Zealand), 19
Apedemek (Meroë god), 233
Appian (historian), 202, 203
Aquinas, Thomas, 433–434
Arabia. *See also* Arabs and Arab world
  Christianity in, 405
  Islam and, 269, 358–365, 360*(m)*
  kingdoms in, 360
  pastoralists in, 452*(t)*
  religions in, 360
  seaborne trade and, 287
Arabian camels, 296–297
Arabian Desert, societies of, 450
Arabic language, 365, 368, 407
  in Spain, 383

  text translations into, 163–164, 387, 433
Arabs and Arab world. *See also* intellectual thought; Islam
  Arab Empire and, 270, 289, 365–376, 366*(m)*
  Bedouins and, 358–360
  Byzantine Empire and, 409, 411
  camels and, 296–297
  China and, 330
  Crusades and, 424–425
  on Europeans, 428
  government of, 398–399*(d)*
  historians on, 474
  Islam in 7th century, 391–399
  learning from, 527
  men in, 374–376
  Nubia and, 233, 408
  Ottomans and, 509
  pastoralists and, 455
  scholarly translations and, 435
  Spain and, 382
  wars in, 365–367
  women in, 374–376
Aramaic language, 167
Are We Rome? (book), 99
aristocracy. *See also* elites; nobility
  in China, 117
  in Japan, 336, 337
  in Korea, 333
  in Oxus civilization, 61
  in Vietnam, 334
Aristotle (Greece), 161, 166*(t)*
  European thought and, 432, 433–434, 533, 534*(v)*
  on slaves, 198, 199
  on Spartans, 211
  on women, 208
armada, Mongol, 460
armed forces. *See* military; navy; specific battles and wars
Armenia, Christianity in, 167
arms and armaments. *See* weapons
Armstrong, Karen
  on Buddha and biography, 184–185*(d)*
  on Muslim devotion to the Prophet, 401*(d)*
Arrian (historian), 110
art(s). *See also* specific arts and artists
  in African village societies, 497
  Chavín, 243
  European depiction of Asia, 309, 309*(v)*
  Indian, 2
  Maya, 238
  in Meroë, 233, 233*(i)*
  of Moche craftsmen, 243–244

pagan, 440, 441*(v)*
Paleolithic, 8*(i)*
in Pompeii, 216*(v)*
in Renaissance, 504
of Seljuk Turks, 456*(i)*
of Teotihuacán, 241
Arthashastra, 126
artifacts
Hopewell, 252
from Pompeii, 224*(d)*
artisans, women as, 424
Aryan peoples, in India, 194, 195
ascetics, Hindu, 150*(i)*
Ashoka (India), 110, 126, 128, 153, 171
Buddhism and, 282
al-Ashtar, Malik (Egypt), 398–399, 399*(d)*
Asia. *See also* Afro-Asia; Eurasia; Indus River region; specific locations
in 15th century, 501*(m)*
Buddhism in, 342*(m)*
Christianity in, 404, 405–407
Europeans and, 309, 309*(v)*
pastoralists in, 452*(t)*
Aspasia (Athens), 209
assemblies, in Athens, 106
assimilation
in China, 119–120, 197, 345
in India, 155
in Roman Empire, 119–120
Assyria and Assyrians, 54, 75*(m)*, 77
Egypt and, 81
Israel and, 157
veils for women in, 69
Astarte (goddess), 78
astrolabe, 288
astronomy
of Chaco peoples, 251
in China, 316*(i)*
Islamic, 388
in Mongol world, 473
Thales on, 160
Athaulf (Visigoths), 416
Athens, 106, 159. *See also* Greece
Academy in, 161
civilization of, 104
democracy in, 107, 108
disease in, 284
empire of, 474
government of, 106, 107
Greco-Persian Wars and, 107–108
patriarchy in, 208–212
slavery in, 199
Socrates on, 160
Sparta and, 108
women in, 208–212, 209*(i)*

Atlantic Ocean region, exploration in, 505–506. *See also* specific locations
atman (individual soul), 150
atom, Democritus on, 160
Attar (Sufi poet), 376
Augustine (Saint), 168, 201
Augustus (Rome), 115
Australia. *See also* Aboriginal Australians; Dreamtime
in 15th century, 494
Cook, James, in, 21
environment in, 22
migrations into, 16–17
Paleolithic lifestyle in, 21, 494–496
population of, 230*(t)*
Austronesian migrations and languages, 18–19, 19*(m)*, 34, 255, 287
authority (power). *See also* government; state (nation)
in agricultural societies, 40
in Europe, 432
in First Civilizations, 70–71
Averroës (**Ibn Rushd**, Muslim scholar), 387*(t)*, 533, 534*(v)*
Axial Age, 162–163
Axum, 232*(m)*, 233, 234–235, 260–265. *See also* Ethiopia
Christianity in, 169, 234–235, 235*(i)*, 262, 263*(d)*, 267*(d)*, 288, 408
coins in, 234, 235, 265*(v)*
columns of, 261, 261*(v)*
empire of, 260, 261*(d)*
gold trade and, 264*(d)*
government of, 234
trade and, 234
world and, 260–265
Azerbaijan, 38–39
Aztec Empire, 516–518, 520–521. *See also* Teotihuacán
Incas and, 300
Spain and, 428
Tenochtitlán and, 241
women in, 516*(i)*, 520–521

Babylon and Babylonians, 54, 75*(m)*, 77
Egypt and, 81
Greek thought and, 160
Hittites and, 80
Babylonian Exile, of Jews, 103, 157
Bach Dang River, Battle of, 334*(i)*
Bacon, Roger (scholar), 431
Bactria, 110, 111
Baghdad
Abbasid capital in, 371, 375, 386
Mongol sack of, 467

Bah, Wurie (Sierra Leone), 357
Balkan region
Byzantine Empire and, 409, 414
Islam and, 527
Ottoman Empire and, 508
Baltic region, 421, 427
Banpo, China, 35
Bantu speakers, 247–250
migration of, 34, 34*(m)*, 232*(m)*
Swahili and, 293
Ban Zhao (Chinese writer), 145–146, 205
barbarians
Byzantine Empire and, 409
in China, 123, 135, 318, 327, 330
Germanic peoples as, 416
idea of, 138–139*(d)*
slaves as, 201
battles. *See* war(s) and warfare; specific battles and wars
Bayard, Bat-Ardene (historian), 449
B.C.E., 4
Beard, Mary, on Pompeii artifacts, 224*(d)*
Bede (Venerable), 439
Bedouins, 358–360, 455
Beijing. *See also* China
capital in, 500
Temple of Heaven in, 500
"believers," in Islam, 367, 369
Bellini, Gentile, 528, 529*(v)*
Bengal region, India, 378
Bennett, Judith (historian), 422
Bentley, Jerry, 138–139*(d)*
Berbers
Almoravids and, 457
Islam and, 368
pastoralists and, 455
Spain and, 382
Bering Strait, migrations across, 17
Bernard of Clairvaux (Saint), 427, 433
Bhagavad Gita, 154–155
bhakti movement (India), 154–155
Bible. *See also* New Testament; Old Testament
Cain and Abel in, 38
"big history," 13
big men
in Melanesia, 256
of North American northwest coast, 496
Bini people, 497
birth control, in Sparta, 210–211
al-Biruni (Islam), 387*(t)*
bishops. *See also* popes
Roman Catholic, 172

Black Death, 285, 475. *See also* plague

"blackness," slavery and, 66

black people. *See* Africa

Black Sea region, 409, 410, 508

Blockmans, Wim, and **Peter Hoppenbrouwers,** on end of Roman civilization, 447(*d*)

Blombos Cave, South Africa, 12

boats. *See* navigation; ships and shipping

Bodhi (enlightenment) tree, 151

bodhisattvas, 343

   of Compassion (Korea), 180, 181(*v*)

   Silk Roads' impact on, 284

Bolivia, second-wave civilization in, 227

Bologna, Italy, university in, 433

Book of the Marvels of the World (Polo), 485(*v*)

books

   Chinese burning of, 73

   in Islamic world, 386

borders, 117. *See also* frontiers

Borneo, 257

Borno Kingdom, Leo Africanus on, 311(*d*)

Borobudur, Java, 291(*i*), 292

Boudica (Celtic queen), 114(*i*)

Bouillon, Godefroi de (France), 425

Bound Together (Chanda), 275

boys. *See also* men

   in Sparta, 210

Brahman (World Soul), 150

Brahmins (Indian priests), 149, 150, 152, 154, 194, 195, 195(*t*), 196

Britain. *See* British Empire; England (Britain)

British Empire, historians on, 475

bronze

   in Agricultural Revolution, 36

   in China, 80

   from Shang China, 60(*i*)

   spread of metallurgy and, 79

Brotton, Jerry, on cross-cultural exchange in European Renaissance, 537(*d*)

bubonic plague. *See* plague

Buddha (Siddhartha Gautama), 142, 151–152, 151(*i*), 166(*t*)

   in ancient stories, 179

   classical Indian, 178(*v*)

   Great Stupa and, 217(*v*)

   Greco-Indian, 176–177, 177(*v*)

   historians on, 184–185(*d*)

   Jesus compared with, 164–165

   outcast and, 181, 182(*d*)

   representations of, 176–183

Buddhism, 142, 173, 521

   Asian, 342(*m*)

   Borobudur, Java, and, 291(*i*), 292

   changes in, 284

   China and, 119, 120–121, 141, 182, 183(*v*), 207, 283, 318, 340, 341–345, 406

   Chinese traveler in India and, 305, 306–307(*d*)

   Christianity and, 164–172

   classical Indian, 178(*v*)

   doctrinal changes in, 284

   Greek culture and, 111, 176–177, 177(*v*)

   Hinduism and, 152, 155

   India and, 119, 151–154, 171

   interpretations of, 172

   in Japan, 336–337, 341

   in Korea, 151(*i*), 333, 341

   Mahayana, 153, 154, 165, 172, 173, 284, 340(*i*), 343

   pastoralists and, 454

   spread of, 165–171, 170(*m*), 282–284, 291

   Theravada, 153, 172, 173, 343

   women in, 152

   Xuanzang on, 306(*d*)

Bukhara, Mongol seizure of, 487–488(*d*)

Bulgars, Byzantine culture and, 414

bureaucracy. *See also* government; political systems; specific locations

   Carolingian, 417

   in China, 121, 124, 145, 188, 189–191, 321

   in Europe, 423

   Inca, 518–519

   in India, 126

   in Mongol Empire, 463, 467

   in Persia, 103, 467

   in Vietnam, 334

Burgundian Code, 442–443(*d*)

Burgundy, kingdom of, 442

burial mounds, Hopewell, 251–252

burials. *See also* pyramids

   in China, 60–61

   Egyptian, 77

   in Korea, 332

   Moche, 243

   in Nubia, 231

   Paleolithic, 24

   in pastoral societies, 39

   of rulers, 73

bushido (Japanese way of the warrior), 336

Byzantine Empire (Byzantium), 122, 409–411, 410(*m*)

   Arabs and, 365

   Christianity and, 404, 409–415, 412(*i*)

Crusades and, 413–414, 424–425, 427

Egypt and, 407

Greek learning and, 161

historians on, 474, 475

intellectual thought in, 414, 434–435

invasions of, 411

Islam and, 360, 413–414

Ottoman Empire and, 379, 379(*m*), 527

Russian architecture and, 415

trade in, 279, 414

world and, 413–414

Byzantium (city), 413. *See also* Byzantine Empire; Constantinople

Caesar, Julius (Rome), 115

Caesar Augustus. *See* Augustus

caesaropapism, 411, 431

Cahokia, 40(*i*), 41, 252, 253, 301

calendars, in Mesopotamia, 73

California, 24

caliphs, 369–371

   Abbasid, 371, 456

   Ottoman, 509

   Umayyad, 370–371

Call for Crusade (Clement VI), 535(*d*)

Cambodia, 290

Cambridge University, 433

camels, 296(*i*)

   in Africa, 456–457

   Arabian, 296–297

   of pastoral peoples, 38

   saddles for, 455

   Silk Roads trade and, 279

   trans-Saharan trade and, 230, 237

Cameroon(s), Bantu and, 34, 247

Campbell, Ian (historian), 253

Canada. *See* North America

canals

   Aztec, 517

   in China, 318–319, 323

   in Persian Empire, 103–104

cannibalism, of Chaco peoples, 251

cannons, in Europe, 430

Canton, 341

Caral, Peru, 58–59, 58(*i*), 59(*i*)

caravans

   Arabian camels in, 296–297, 296(*i*)

   llama, 302

   in Mesoamerica, 302

   Mongol support of, 471

   Persian, 104

   on Silk Roads, 279

Caribbean region, trade in, 301

Carneiro, Robert (anthropologist), 62–63

Carolina Islands, 257

Carolingian Empire, 417, 417*(m)*
Carpini, Giovanni DiPlano (Franciscan friar), impressions of Mongol women, 452
Carthage
  destruction of, 200
  Punic Wars and, 112
  Roman Empire and, 114
carts, from Mohenjo Daro, 87, 88*(v)*
caste system. *See also* classes
  Hinduism and, 150
  in India, 126, 150, 152, 154, 188, 193–197, 194*(i)*, 378
  jati as, 196–197
  Xuanzang on, 306*(d)*
Çatalhüyük, Turkey, 39
cathedral schools, 433
Catholicism. *See* Roman Catholic Church
cave paintings, 16. *See also* rock art
Cayuga people, 497
Celtic peoples, 404, 440, 441*(v)*
census, Mongol, 463
Central Africa. *See* Africa; specific locations
Central America, 230*(t)*, 237. *See also* Mesoamerica
Central Asia. *See also* Silk Roads
  Buddhism in, 282–283
  China and, 317–318, 330
  civilizations in, 61
  Islam in, 365
  migration to India from, 125
  Mongols and, 384, 460
  pastoralists in, 452*(t)*, 498–499
  silk in, 281
  trade in, 477
  Turkic peoples in, 380, 427
  Xiongnu in, 454
ceramics, Roman, 121–122
cereal grains, 32
Chaco canyon, New Mexico, 251
Chaco Phenomenon, 251
Chad, Lake, 297
Chalcedon, Council of (451 C.E.), 172
Champagne, trading fairs in, 421
Champa kingdom, Vietnam, 290, 292
Chan Buddhism. *See* Buddhism
Chanda, Nayan (journalist), 275
Chang'an, China, 332, 335
change
  agents of, 270
  continuity and, 212–213
  reasons for, 345–346
chariots, 80, 81, 412
Charlemagne (Franks), 402*(i)*, 417, 417*(m)*

Cunliffe on, 447*(d)*
  palace chapel of, 444, 445*(v)*
Chavín culture, 59, 242–243, 518
Chavín de Huántar, village of, 242–243
chiefs and chiefdoms, 40–41, 70
  Bantu, 249
  human society and, 19
  in India, 149
child marriage, in India, 150
children, of slaves, 200–201
China. *See also* Buddhism; bureaucracy; Mao Zedong; peasant(s)
  ancestor veneration in, 142
  Asian empire and, 493–494
  astronomy in, 316*(i)*
  bronze in, 80
  Buddha from, 182, 183*(v)*
  Buddhism in, 119, 120–121, 141, 283, 340, 341–345
  bureaucracy in, 121, 124, 145, 321
  canals in, 318–319, 323
  Christianity in, 141, 167, 403, 406–407, 407*(i)*
  civilizations in, 60–61
  civil service system in, 121
  classes in, 65, 188–193
  classical era in, 118*(m)*
  climate change and, 317
  collapse of empire in, 122–125
  commerce in, 432
  communism in, 141
  Confucianism in, 144–146
  consolidation of, 118–122
  cultural exchange from, 473
  culture of, 140*(i)*, 141, 142–148, 340–341, 346
  Daoism in, 141, 146–148
  economy in, 325, 338–341, 471, 500
  elites in, 189–191
  empire of, 117, 118–122
  Eurasia and, 338–341
  Europe and, 428–429
  examination system in, 121, 124, 146, 189–191, 190*(i)*
  expansion of, 501–502
  exploration by, 501–502, 507–508
  families in, 145–146
  filial piety in, 145*(i)*
  foot binding in, 325
  gender and gender issues in, 145–146, 500
  golden age in, 318–324
  government of, 70, 117, 500
  gunpowder in, 322–323, 322*(i)*
  "Heaven" in, 119

India and, 290, 305, 306–307*(d)*, 340, 341
  Indian Ocean trade and, 288–289
  industry in, 322–324
  influence of, 317–318, 331
  Islam and, 365
  Japan and, 335–338, 335*(m)*
  kings in, 71
  Korea and, 117, 319, 331–333
  landlord class in, 191
  landscape painting in, 147*(i)*
  language in, 121
  laws in, 144
  Legalism in, 142–144
  under Mao, 128
  men in, 146
  merchants in, 192–193
  as middle kingdom, 327, 346
  monasteries in, 343–344, 345
  Mongols and, 460, 462, 463, 469
  Nestorian Christianity in, 406, 407*(i)*
  nomads and, 117, 207, 318, 324, 326–330
  patriarchy in, 205–208
  peasants in, 66, 122, 192, 199, 205, 206, 323
  plague and, 475, 476
  Polo and, 307–308*(d)*, 315*(d)*, 321, 428–429
  population of, 321
  printing in, 322
  prosperity of, 339
  religions in, 119, 140*(i)*, 141–148, 330
  revival of, 288
  Roman Empire and, 111–112
  rural areas in, 280
  scholar-officials in, 148, 189–191, 348–354, 349*(v)*, 350*(v)*, 351*(v)*, 353, 354*(v)*, 355*(d)*
  second-wave trade and, 279
  silk in, 280–281, 467
  slavery in, 198–199
  society in, 188–193, 197
  state in, 188, 189–191
  taxation in, 323–324
  technology of, 338–339, 339*(t)*, 340, 346
  Temple of Heaven in, 500
  as third-wave civilization, 317–318
  trade and, 288–289, 340–341, 432, 500
  tribute system in, 327–330
  unity in, 124
  Vietnam and, 116, 117, 333–335, 334*(i)*
  warring states period in, 73, 115–117, 142
  waterways in, 313

China (*continued*)
women in, 145–146, 206*(i)*, 207*(i)*, 324–326, 500
world prominence of, 317
writing in, 72*(t)*
Xiongnu and, 118*(m)*, 123, 135–137*(d)*, 455
Yellow Turban Rebellion in, 122, 148, 192, 192*(m)*
Chincha people, Peru, 301
Chinggis Khan (Mongols), 448*(i)*, 453–454, 459–460, 462
celebration of, 449–450
military organization of, 462
Persian invasion by, 466
self-perception of, 481, 482*(d)*
Chinookan peoples, 496
chosen people, Jews as, 361
Christ. See Jesus of Nazareth
Christendom, 403–404, 435–436. *See also* Christianity
Crusades and, 424–428
Christianity. *See also* Christendom; Crusades; Eastern Orthodox Christianity; Jesus of Nazareth
in Africa, 168–169, 404, 407–408
in Arabia, 360
in Asia, 404, 405–407
in Axum, 169, 234–235, 235*(i)*, 262, 263*(d)*, 267*(d)*
Buddhism compared with, 164–172
Byzantine Empire and, 404, 409–415
in China, 167, 307, 403, 406–407
Crusades and, 424–428
culture and, 418–419
doctrine of, 172, 434
in Egypt, 168, 407
in Ethiopia, 169, 234, 235, 408
Europe and, 404, 409–428, 507
hierarchy in, 171–172, 173, 364
in India, 167
Islam and, 363, 364, 367, 405–406, 537, 537*(d)*
Jews and, 427
monotheism of, 142, 155, 362*(i)*
Muslims and, 357
in Nubia, 233, 407–408
Ottoman Empire and, 379, 508
pagan art and texts of, 440, 441*(v)*
pastoralists and, 454
plague and, 285
in Renaissance, 504
Roman Catholicism *vs.* Eastern Orthodoxy, 411–413
in Roman Empire, 118, 119, 170–171
in Russia, 414–415

silk and, 281
slavery and, 201
in Southwest Asia and Africa, 167
in Spain, 382, 383
spread of, 165–171, 170*(m)*, 230, 288, 403–404
trade and, 289
women in, 119, 166–167, 171, 424
Zoroastrianism and, 157
Christian-Muslim hostility, Lewis on, 537*(d)*
Christine de Pizan (writer), 504
Chumash peoples (California), 24
chu nom (Vietnamese writing), 335
churches
of Charlemagne, 444, 445*(v)*
of the East, 167, 172, 406
government and, 419
of the Holy Sepulcher (Jerusalem), 408
of St. George (Ethiopia), 408*(i)*
Cicero (Rome), 211
cities and towns. *See also* city-states; state (nation); urbanization; specific locations
Aztec, 516–517
in East Africa, 294
in Egypt, 76–77
emergence of, 4
in Europe, 432, 504
in First Civilizations, 59–60, 63–65
guilds in, 422
in Indus River region, 60, 65
in Mesopotamia, 76–77
Mongol, 463
in Niger Valley civilization, 236
of Norte Chico, 59
population of European, 421–422
along Silk Road, 282–283
citizenship
in Athens, 106–107
Greek, 105, 106
in Roman Empire, 114, 119–120
City of Ladies (Christine de Pizan), 504
"City of Timbuktu, The" (Leo Africanus), 310–311*(d)*
cityscape, of Mohenjo Daro, 84, 85*(v)*
city-states
Greek, 105–106, 159
in Italy, 124, 423, 432
of Maya, 239
Sumer as, 76
Swahili, 294
Texcoco as, 518
civilization(s), 4. *See also* culture; empire(s); First Civilizations;

government; second-wave civilizations; society; third-wave civilizations
of Africa, 231–237
alternatives to, 247–257
in Americas, 514–521
of Andes Mountains region, 58–59, 237, 242–246
balance in writing about, 258
in China, 60–61, 499–502
emergence of, 53–58, 63–74
equality in, 65–69
in Europe, 502–508
globalization of, 92–95
in India, 125–126
Indus Valley, 60, 84–89, 91*(d)*
Islam and, 383–388, 508–514
Maya, 238–239
of Mesoamerica, 237–246, 238*(m)*
of Mesopotamia, 53–58, 63–74
Moche, 243–245
of Nubia, 58
slavery and, 66, 66*(i)*, 198–199
Swahili, 293–295
use of term, 81–82
West African, 295–300
Western, 162
civil service system. *See also* bureaucracy; examination system
in China, 121, 146, 207, 500
civil wars
among Muslims in Arab Empire, 369
in Rome, 115
clans, in pastoral societies, 38, 450–451
classes. *See also* caste system
in Arab Empire, 367
in China, 188–193
in Europe, 432
in First Civilizations, 65–69
gender and, 67
in India, 193–197
classical civilizations
intellectual thought and, 434
in Western Europe, 159–164
classical era
in China, 118*(m)*
in Greece, 104, 105*(m)*, 159–164
in India, 178*(v)*
"Cleansing of the Kaaba, The" (Mir Havand), 396*(v)*
Cleisthenes (Athens), 107
Clement VI (Pope), *Call for Crusade,* 535*(d)*
clergy
Christian, 172
as first estate, 432
Islam and, 364

climate. *See also* environment; global warming; Ice Age
  in Africa, 231
  agriculture and, 27, 30
  changes in, 317
  collapses of empires and, 123
  human population and, 13
  Maya and, 239
  of Peru, 58
  warming after 750, 419
clitorectomy, Islamic, 375
Clovis (Franks), conversion of, 438–439*(d)*
Clovis points and culture, 18
coal and coal industry, in China, 322
codes of law. *See* law codes
coins
  in Axum, 234, 235, 265, 265*(v)*
  Byzantine bezant as, 414
  Persian, 103
colonies and colonization. *See also* America(s); British Empire; empire(s); exploration; imperialism; independence; specific locations
  in Pacific Ocean region, 19, 19*(m)*
  of Wari and Tiwanaku, 246
color, slavery and, 66
Columbian exchange, 530
Columbus, Christopher
  Americas and, 492*(i)*
  voyages of, 505
commerce. *See also* slaves and slavery; slave trade; trade
  in Afro-Eurasia, 523*(m)*
  China and, 340–341, 507
  Islam and, 527
  in Italy, 504
  Mongol, 463, 471
Common Era, agriculture in, 34
common people
  in First Civilizations, 65–66
  in India, 194
communication. *See also* trade
  Mongol, 457, 463
  on Sea Roads, 286
  in second- and third-wave civilizations, 95
  trade and, 477
  webs of, 276, 301–302, 301*(m)*
Communist Party, in China, 141
communities. *See* villages; specific locations
compass, 288, 431
complex hunting and gathering cultures, 496

concubines, in China, 206
conflict. *See* war(s) and warfare; specific battles and wars
Confucianism. *See also* Neo-Confucianism
  in China, 117, 124, 141, 144–146, 207, 319, 341, 500
  Daoism and, 147–148
  in Japan, 337
  Korea and, 332
  scholar-officials and, 188
  in Vietnam, 334–335
  on women, 205, 325
Confucius (Chinese philosopher), 140*(i)*, 142, 144, 166*(t)*
conquistadores, 514
Constantine (Rome), conversion to Christianity, 170, 171*(i)*
Constantinople
  Byzantine Empire and, 404, 409, 410
  Council of (553 c.e.), 172
  Crusader sack of, 413, 427
  fall of (1453), 411, 528
  as "New Rome," 409
  Ottoman seizure of, 510–511, 528
  plague in, 285
  population of, 421
constitution(s), in Japan, 335
consumption, trade and, 276
Conteh, Kelfala (Sierra Leone), 357
continents
  cultural comparisons by, 228–230
  populations in second-wave era and beyond, 228, 230*(t)*
  separation of, 228–230
continuous revelation, in Bantu religions, 250
convents. *See* nuns
conversion. *See also* Christianity
  to Buddhism, 282
  of Clovis (Franks), 438–439*(d)*
  to Islam, 361, 367–369, 377–378
  of pastoralists, 454
Cook, James (British explorer), 21
copper, 36
Coptic Christianity and language, 169, 233, 234, 407
Córdoba, Spain, 382–383, 421
Corinth, 106
corn (maize), 26, 32, 250–251, 300
Cortés, Hernán (Spain), 517
cosmology, of Dreamtime, 44–49
cotton and cotton industry. *See also* textiles and textile industry
  in India, 127
Council of Elders (Sparta), 107

councils (Christian)
  of Constantinople, 172
  of Nicaea, 172
court (royal)
  Byzantine, 410
  in Europe, 423
  Japanese, 337
  Persian, 103
coya (Inca ruler female consort), 521
crafts
  Aztec, 517
  Russian, 469
Crassus, Marcus Licinius (Rome), 203
creation
  Australian Aboriginal, 17, 44–49, 44*(d)*, 45–46*(d)*, 48–49*(d)*, 48*(v)*, 50*(v)*
  Jews on, 158–159
Crixus (Roman rebel), 202
crops. *See also* food(s)
  in Africa, 32, 248
  domestication of, 27, 30
  in Mesopotamia, 76
  in Pacific Oceania, 255
  spread of, 288
  in sub-Saharan Africa, 295
  trade and, 386
cross-cultural interactions. *See also* communication; culture(s); globalization; technology; trade
  in Andes region, 301–302
  in China, 80, 338–341
  in Crusades, 427–428
  in empires, 270
  in European Renaissance, 537*(d)*
  in First Civilizations, 78–81
  Islamic, 376–383
  in Mesoamerica, 301–302, 520–521
  in Mongol Empire, 454, 473–474
  in Spain, 383
  transregional interaction and, 269–271
  in West Africa, 296–300
  in Western Hemisphere, 300–302
crucifixions, of Roman prisoners, 203
Crusades, 413, 424–428, 425*(i)*, 426*(m)*
  Byzantine Empire and, 411
  Eastern and Western Christianity and, 413
  impact of, 427
  Jerusalem and, 425–426
  Muslims and, 384, 407
  Ottomans and, 509–510, 527
  papal call for, 535, 535*(d)*
cult(s)
  Chavín, 243
  goddess, 39
  Indian devotional, 150
  of Isis and Osiris, 168

cult(s) (*continued*)
of kingship, 102
in Pompeii, 220
religious, 118
cultural borrowings
by Japan, 429
Mongols and, 473–474
by Roman Catholic Church, 418
by Russia, 429
by West Africa, 429
culture(s). *See also* cross-cultural
interaction; diversity; language(s);
religion(s)
of 15th century, 494–499
of agriculture, 34–37
ancient, 13–14
Australian Aboriginal, 51*(d)*
in Axial Age, 162–163
Christianity and, 412, 418
continental comparisons of, 228–230
defined, 10
environment and, 74–76
extinction of, 9
foreign accounts of, 138–139
interactions among, 269–271
Paleolithic, 19–25
religion and, 521–522
Sea Roads spread of, 290–293
Silk Roads spread of, 282–284
Cunliffe, Barry, on Charlemagne,
447*(d)*
currency, silk as, 281
Curzon (Lord), on British Empire, 475
Cuzco, Peru, 519
Cyril (Byzantine missionary), 414
Cyrillic alphabet, 414, 415
Cyrus (Persia), 102, 103

da Gama, Vasco (explorer), 505–506
Damascus, Syria, 370, 375
dao (the way), 147, 208, 343
Daodejing (Laozi), 147, 148
Daoism
in China, 141, 146–148, 207, 208, 322,
323, 343
Confucianism and, 140*(i)*, 147–148
women in, 325
Darius I (Persia), 102, 104, 156*(i)*
dating systems, 4–5, 12
Davis, Natalie Zemon (historian), on
Leo Africanus's audiences, 315*(d)*
Day of Judgment, in Egypt, 77
death and death rates
in Australian Dreamtime, 48*(v)*
in Paleolithic society, 21
from plague, 476

Deeb, Semon, 44
deforestation
in Europe, 419
in Greece, 106
human society and, 19
in Indus Valley civilization, 60
in Meroë, 233
in Mesopotamia, 76
in Rome, 121
deities. *See* gods and goddesses; religion(s);
specific deities
Delhi, Sultanate of, 377–378, 378*(m)*
democracy, in Athens, 107, 108
Democritus (Greece), 160
Denmark. *See* Scandinavia
depressions. *See* economy
deserts, in Africa, 231
dharma (Buddha's teaching), as *dao,*
196, 343
dhimmis (protected subjects), 378, 407
dhow, 287*(i)*, 288
Diamond Sutra, 340, 340*(i)*
diffusion
of agriculture, 33
of languages, 34
Dionysus (god), 159, 161, 222
diplomacy, Mongols in Eurasia and,
471–473
diseases. *See also* plague; specific
conditions
in 14th century, 472*(m)*
in Africa, 231
in Americas, 285, 514
in Chinese and Roman empires, 122
in early communities, 35
spread of, 284–285
diversity
in Hellenistic world, 110–111
in India, 125, 127, 149
in Pacific Oceania, 255
divinity. *See also* gods and goddesses
of Buddha, 165
of Jesus, 165, 172
Jewish conception of, 158
division of labor, gender and, 21
divorce
in 21st century, 96
in Korea, 332
in Mesopotamia, 68
in Mongol society, 451
in San society, 21
doctors. *See* medicine
Dome of the Rock (Jerusalem), 406,
406*(i)*
domestication. *See also* Agricultural
Revolution

of animals, 10, 26, 30, 34, 37–38,
38*(i)*, 228
pastoralism and, 37–38, 38*(i)*
of plants, 10, 26, 30, 34, 37–38, 38*(i)*
Dreamtime (Australia), 17, 44–49, 48*(v)*,
50*(v)*, 51*(d)*
Drinking Alone with the Moon (Li Po), 352*(d)*
Du Fu (China), 353*(d)*
Dunhuang, China, 282, 283*(i)*
dynasties. *See* specific dynasties

Eadfrith (Bishop of Lindisfarne), 440,
441*(v)*
East Africa. *See also* specific locations
agriculture in, 248
Axum and, 234
plague in, 476
Sea Roads and change in, 293–295
Swahili and, 293–295, 294*(m)*
trade in, 288
East Asia, Buddhism in, 144–146
Easter Island. *See* Rapa Nui
Eastern Europe. *See also* Christianity;
Eastern Orthodox Christianity;
specific locations
Mongols and, 460, 471
Ottomans and, 508
Eastern Hemisphere, 36, 54, 285, 300,
476, 523*(m)*
Eastern Orthodox Christianity, 172, 521.
See also Russian Orthodox Church
in Byzantine Empire, 404, 411
Crusades and, 427
Roman Catholic Church and,
411–413, 427
eastern Roman Empire, 122, 409. *See also*
Byzantine Empire
eastern woodlands (North America)
Mound Builders of, 251–253
peoples of, 250
Eastern world, churches of, 167, 406
East Indies. *See* Indonesia
ecology. *See also* environment
in Mesoamerica, 237
Moche, 245
in Polynesia, 253–254
economic revolution, in China, 321
economic systems. *See* agriculture;
gathering and hunting peoples;
industrialization; pastoralists and
pastoral societies
economy. *See also* industrialization; labor;
trade
animal husbandry and, 37
in Australia, 496
Aztec, 516

of Byzantine Empire, 414
Chinese, 325, 338–341, 471, 491*(d)*, 500
Chumash, 24
European, 428–429
globalization of, 302–303
Inca, 520
in India, 126, 127
Maya, 238
in Meroë, 233
Moche, 243
in Mongol Empire, 471
in Niger River civilzation, 236–237
of Norte Chico, 59
Paleolithic, 22
Persian, 467
of Pompeii, 224–225*(d)*
in Russia, 469
in Southeast Asia, 290
ecosystems, in Europe, 419
education. *See also* literacy; scholars and scholarship; universities and colleges
in China, 146, 189
Islamic, 375–376, 384
for women, 146, 375–376
egalitarian societies, 20–21
Egypt, 232*(m)*. *See also* Alexandria; Coptic Christianity; Nile River region; pharaohs
afterlife in, 75
agriculture in, 76
Alexander the Great in, 109–110
Christianity in, 168, 407
cities in, 76–77
civilization of, 58, 77
empire of, 80–81, 80*(m)*, 81
environment of, 74–76
foreign migrations into, 80–81
government of, 70
Greece and, 79–80
Islam and, 368, 407
Jewish exodus from, 157
Mamluks in, 531
Mesopotamia and, 74–81
Mongol defeat by, 461
Nile–Red Sea canal in, 103–104
nobility in, 77
Nubia and, 62, 79, 79*(i)*, 231, 233*(i)*
pyramids in, 75
slavery in, 66
technology in, 81
trade in, 78–81
women in, 69
writing in, 52*(i)*, 71–73, 72*(t)*
Ehrenberg, Margaret (archeologist), 68

Ehret, Christopher, on trade in coming of Christianity to Axum, 267*(d)*
elites. *See also* aristocracy; caste system; classes; nobility
in Arab Empire, 367
in Byzantine Empire, 410
Chaco, 251
in China, 146, 189–191
in India, 148–149
in Korea, 332, 333
in North American eastern woodlands, 253
in Paleolithic society, 24
Roman, 200
in Southeast Asia, 291
trade and, 276
in Vietnam, 333, 334
women and, 204–205, 206*(i)*, 208–209, 325
El Niño, Moche society and, 245
emancipation, of slaves, 198
emperors. *See* specific empires and emperors
empire(s). *See also* colonies and colonization; imperialism
of Alexander the Great, 108–111, 109*(m)*
American, 477, 493, 514–521
Arab (Islamic), 270, 289, 365–376, 366*(m)*
Axumite, 260, 261*(d)*
Byzantine, 409–414, 410*(m)*
in China, 111–112, 117, 118–122, 493–494
collapse of, 122–125, 474–475
cross-cultural interactions in, 270
defined, 100
early, 99–100
Egyptian, 80*(m)*, 81
Eurasian, 100
historians on, 474–475
in India, 125–127, 125*(m)*
Islamic, 508–514, 509*(m)*
Mongol, 457–464, 458*(m)*
Persian, 100, 102–104
Roman, 99–100, 111–112
second-wave, 128–129
in South Asia, 125–128, 125*(m)*
of third-wave civilizations, 474–475
of United States, 128
in Wari and Tiwanaku, 246
in West Africa, 297–300
Encyclopedia (China), 500
energy, European, 430
engineering, 238, 319
England (Britain). *See also* British Empire
development of, 422

Hundred Years' War and, 503
India and, 128
religious practices in, 439, 440*(d)*
taxation in, 502
trade and, 421
women in, 423
Enkidu (friend of Gilgamesh), 64, 76
Enlightenment (Buddhism), 151, 151*(i)*, 153
environment. *See also* agriculture; climate
in Africa, 231
Buddhist monasteries and, 344
in China, 121, 122, 500
collapse of empires and, 123
in Egypt, 74–76
of Greece, 106
of Indus Valley civilization, 60
Islamic agriculture and, 386
in Mesopotamia, 74–76
of Moche, 244–245
in North America, 250
Paleolithic, 22
in Roman Empire, 121–122
in sub-Saharan Africa, 295
in Western Europe, 419
epic literature
Epic of Gilgamesh, 64, 75–76
in India, 154
Shahnama as, 368
epidemics
plague as, 285
Silk Road spread of, 284
epilepsy, Hippocrates on, 160
equality
in early civilizations, 65–69
gender, 67
Muslims on, 378
era of warring states (China). *See* warring states period (China)
Eritrea, 231
Axum in, 168, 234
erosion, of soil, 106, 121, 123
estates (land)
in China, 191
in Roman Empire, 122, 201
estates (classes), in European states, 432
ethics, Greek thought on, 159, 161
Ethiopia. *See also* Axum
agriculture in, 231
Christianity in, 169, 234, 235, 408
Church of St. George in, 408*(i)*
seaborne trade and, 287
ethnicity. *See also* race and racism
slavery and, 201
Euphrates River region, 54. *See also* Tigris-Euphrates river valley

Eurasia. *See also* Afro-Eurasia; Asia;
    Europe and Europeans
  China and, 338–341
  Christianity in, 409–415
  cross-cultural interaction in, 79
  diseases spread along Silk Road in,
    284
  empires in, 100
  gunpowder in, 323
  migrations into, 16
  Mongol Empire and, 450, 470–478
  nomads in, 326–327
  pastoralists in, 450, 452(t), 455
  population of, 230(t)
  second-wave civilizations in, 125,
    227–228
  Silk Roads in, 278–285, 278(m)
  trade networks in, 522
  Turkic peoples in, 455–456
Euripides (Greece), 108, 209
Europe and Europeans. *See also* Chris-
    tianity; colonies and colonization;
    Eastern Europe; empire(s); Eurasia;
    Western Europe; Western world
  in 1500, 503(m)
  Asia and, 309, 309(v)
  China and, 307–308(d)
  Christianity in, 404, 409–428
  culture and, 429(t)
  diseases and, 285
  exploration and, 505–507
  global rise of, 474
  government and, 502–503
  Greek thought and, 161–164
  gunpowder and weapons in, 338–339
  Islamic goods and, 427
  Mongols and, 471, 472–473, 488,
    489(d)
  Muslims and, 365, 428
  Ottomans and, 508
  paper in, 338
  plague and, 476, 477
  political hierarchy in, 419
  population of, 419
  power and, 432
  printing in, 338
  Renaissance and, 504–505, 527–536
  Roman Empire in, 112
  state building in, 502–505
  technology and, 429–430, 430(i), 431
  trade in, 421
  urban areas in, 421(i)
evolution, human direction of, 26
examination system
  in China, 121, 124, 146, 189–191,
    190(i), 321

  in Korea, 333
  in Vietnam, 334
exchange. *See also* trade
  in Indian Ocean region, 287–289,
    288(t)
  Islamic networks of, 385–388
  in Paleolithic Australia, 17
  on Sea Roads, 285–295
  on Silk Roads, 280(t)
  webs of, 275–278, 301, 301(m)
exodus, of Jews, 157
expansion. *See also* imperialism; migration
  by Axum, 234–235
  Bantu, 247
  of China, 501–502
  Crusades and, 424–428
  European, 478
  Greek, 106
  in Islamic world, 365–373, 397–398,
    398(d), 409, 456
  of Western Christendom, 424–428
expeditions, Chinese, 501–502
exploration. *See also* expansion;
    navigation
  Chinese, 501–502, 507–508
  Christianity and, 507
  by Columbus, 492(i), 493
  European, 478
extinction
  of animals, 18, 19
  environment and, 22

fairs, trading, 421
faith. *See* religion(s)
families. *See also* kinship
  in China, 145–146, 344
  in Korea, 332
  in Southeast Asia, 293
  women in, 204
famines
  in early societies, 35
  in Europe (1315–1322), 422
Faras, Nubia, cathedral in, 407–408
farms and farming. *See also* agriculture
  in Africa, 31–32
  Bantu, 248
  in China, 122, 192
  civilization and, 26
  foragers and, 37
  Inca, 520
  Neolithic, 26–30
  Paleolithic peoples and, 496
Farsi (Persian) language, 368, 387
Fatwa (Pygmy) people, 248
Faxian (Chinese traveler), 126
Ferdinand and **Isabella** (Spain), 383

Ferdowsi (Persian poet), 368
Ferguson, Niall, 475
Fertile Crescent, 30, 31(m), 32
festivals, Christian, 418
feudalism, 417–418. *See also* Middle Ages
Fiji, 257
filial piety, in China, 145, 145(i)
firestick farming, in Australia, 496
First Civilizations, 53–82. *See also* second-
    wave civilizations; third-wave
    civilizations
  agriculture in, 74
  characteristics of, 54–62
  cities in, 63–65
  common elements of, 63
  Indian Ocean commerce and, 287
  interactions among, 78–81
  Mesopotamia, Egypt, and, 74–81
  Norte Chico as, 242
  origins of, 62–63
  patriarchy in, 69
  slavery in, 66, 198
  states in, 69–74
  trade in, 85
  urbanization and, 76–77
  writing and accounting in, 71–73
First Crusade, 425(i)
First Emperor. *See* Qin Shihuangdi
first estate, clergy as, 432
"first man," in Rome, 115
fishing, environment and, 419
Five Nations (Iroquois League), 497–498
Flohr, Miko, on Pompeii economy,
    224–225(d)
flooding
  in China, 122
  of Nile River, 77
  in Old Testament, 78
Florence, Italy
  Islamic learning and, 421
  trade in, 421
Florentine Codex, Aztec women in,
    516(i)
Flores man, 22
food(s). *See also* agriculture; crops; farms
    and farming; gathering and hunting
    peoples
  in Bantu Africa, 248
  in Islamic world, 386
  in Pacific Oceania, 255
foot binding, in China, 325
foragers. *See* gathering and hunting peoples
Forbidden City (Beijing), 500
force. *See* authority (power)
forced labor. *See* slaves and slavery
forests

in China, 318
land clearing and, 419
in West Africa, 295
Fotudeng (Buddhist monk), 283
Fourth Crusade (1204), 413
France
in Carolingian Empire, 417
development of, 422
humans in, 16
Hundred Years' War and, 503
Islam and, 365
taxation in, 502
Franks, 124, 416. *See also* Charlemagne
freedom(s). *See* independence
freemen, in Rome, 200
French language, 121
frescoes, from Pompeii, 218*(v)*
frontiers. *See also* borders
of Byzantine Empire, 409, 410
of empires, 123, 474
Fulbe people, 499, 499*(i)*
Funan, state of, 290
fundamentalism. *See* religious
fundamentalism
funerals. *See also* burials
in Korea, 332

Gabriel (angel), Muhammad and, 391,
392*(v)*, 393, 394*(v)*
Gama, Vasco da (explorer),
505–506, 507
Ganesan, Chezi K. (India), 187
Ganges River region, 125, 193
Gao, 297, 299
Garnet, Jacques, "'Learned Culture' of
Song Dynasty China," 355*(d)*
gathering and hunting peoples, 9–10,
20*(i)*. *See also* agriculture;
hunting
of Africa, 247, 248
of Americas, 18, 496
of Australia, 17, 496
human societies and, 19–20, 27
gays and lesbians. *See* homosexuality
Ge'ez (Semitic language), 169, 407
Gelasius (Pope), 171
gender and gender issues. *See also* men;
patriarchy; women
in agricultural societies, 39, 204
in Bantu societies, 249
in China, 145–146, 205–208, 500
hierarchies and, 66–68, 298–299
Inca and Aztec, 520–521
in Islam, 374–376
in Moche society, 245
in Niger Valley civilization, 236*(i)*

in Oceania, 256
in Paleolithic society, 20–21
parallelism as (Africa), 249
in pastoral societies, 39
in patriarchal societies, 204–205
in Rome, 113
in second-wave era, 95, 188
in third-wave era, 95, 270–271
Turkic peoples and, 380
in West African societies, 298–299
Genesis (Bible), 158–159
genital mutilation. *See* clitorectomy
Genoa, trade in, 421
Gentiles (non-Jews), 165
gentry, in Vietnam, 334
geography
of Africa, 231
of Andes region, 242
civilizations and, 62
of Europe, 415–416
George (Saint), 408, 408*(i)*
George of Trebizond (Renaissance
scholar), 528
Germania (Tacitus), 133–134*(d)*
Germanic peoples
art of, 13*(i)*
Byzantine Empire and, 409
kingdoms of, 416
law of, 442–443*(d)*
Roman Empire and, 124
Roman views of, 416
Western European societies and, 404,
416–417
Germany
Mongols and, 471
taxation in, 502
Ghana, 237, 297
Islam in, 380
silk in, 281
wealth of, 298
al-Ghazali (Islamic scholar), 375
Ghazan (Mongols), 467
gifts. *See* tribute
Gilbert, Erik, and Jonathan Reynolds,
on transregional nature of early
Christianity, 267*(d)*
Gilgamesh (Mesopotamian ruler). *See*
Epic literature
Gimbutas, Marija, 39
Girolamo da Cremona (Italian artist),
533, 534*(v)*
glaciers, in Ice Age, 16
gladiators (Rome), 203
globalization
in 15th century, 523–524
of agriculture, 28–29*(m)*, 33–37

of civilization, 92–95
economic, 302–303
of trade, 286, 298
Global South, 95
global warming, after Ice Age, 23–24, 30
glyphs, in Teotihuacán, 241
Göbekli Tepe, Turkey, 24, 25, 25*(i)*
Gobir, 297, 299
gods and goddesses. *See also* religion(s)
Aztec, 517
in China, 118
cults of, 39
Greek, 142, 161
Hebrew, 69, 142, 157–158
Hindu, 150, 154–155
Inca, 518
in Islam, 360, 368
Moche, 244
Mongol, 458
monotheism and, 155
in Oceania, 257
in Rome, 118
women's roles and, 69
gold
African trade in, 457
in Agricultural Revolution, 36
Axum and, 264*(d)*, 265, 265*(v)*
in West Africa, 296–297, 298
Gold Coast (Ghana). *See* Ghana
golden age
in China, 318–324
of Greek culture, 108
Golden Horde, Khanate of, 469. *See also*
Kipchak Khanate
goods. *See* products; trade
Gosch, Stephen, and **Peter Stearns,**
on travelers' accounts, 138*(d)*
gospels, pagan art and, 440, 441*(v)*
Goths, 416
government. *See also* state (nation); specific forms
of agricultural villages, 40
in ancient civilizations, 70–71
of Arab Empire, 398–399, 399*(d)*
in Arab world, 367, 371
Aristotle on, 161
in Athens, 106
of Axum, 234
Aztec, 518
of Byzantine Empire, 409, 410
Carolingian, 417
chiefdoms as, 40–41
of China, 61, 117, 124, 148, 189–191,
206–207, 500
church and, 419
in Europe, 423, 502–503

government (*continued*)
  of Greece, 105–106
  of Igbo peoples, 497
  Inca, 518–520
  Iroquois, 497–498
  of Japan, 335, 336
  of Korea, 333
  of Maya, 239
  Mongol, 453–454, 463–464
  in Paleolithic society, 21–22
  of Persian Empire, 102
  Plato on, 161
  of Roman Empire, 115, 121, 124
  of Sparta, 107
  of Swahili city-states, 294
  of Vietnam, 334
  in West Africa, 381–382
  women and Athenian, 208
graffiti, of Pompeii, 219–220(d)
grains
  domestication of, 32
  mills for, 430
Granada, Spain, 383
Grand Mosque of Sana'a (Arabia), 405
grasslands, pastoralists in, 450, 452(t), 453
"Greater Discourse to Sakuludayin, The," 179(d)
Great Khans. *See* Mongols and Mongol Empire
Great Law of Peace, 497
Great Mongol Nation, 459. *See also* Mongols and Mongol Empire
Great Mosque (Jenne), 382
Great Stupa of Sanchi, 127(i)
Great Vehicle (Mahayana) Buddhism, 153, 154
Great Wall (China), 117, 123, 327
Great Zimbabwe state, 294(m), 295
Greco-Indian Buddha, 176–177, 177(i)
Greco-Persian Wars, 107–108, 160–161
Greco-Roman traditions, 120
  in Byzantine Empire, 404, 409
  Renaissance and, 504
  slavery and, 199–203
Greece. *See also* Athens; Greco-Roman traditions
  Byzantine Empire and, 409
  citizenship in, 105, 106
  classical era in, 159–164
  culture of, 142, 159–164, 433
  Egyptian influence on, 79–80
  as empire, 100, 104–107, 108
  environment of, 106
  Golden Age of, 108
  Hellenistic, 109(m), 110–111
  intellectual thought in, 159–164

  medicine in, 160
  perception of Persia in, 130, 131(d)
  Persian wars with, 107–108
  rationalism in, 159–161
  Rome and, 120
  Scythians depicted in, 131–132(d), 132(v)
  slavery in, 66, 198
Greek Church. *See* Eastern Orthodox Christianity
Greek culture and language
  in Byzantine Empire, 410
  in eastern Church, 233, 412
  intellectual thought and, 433
Greek fire, 413
Green Revolution, 386
Gregory I (Pope), 439
  Advice to the English Church, 440(d)
Gregory of Tours, *History of the Franks,* 438–439(d)
Guatemala, 301
guilds, 422, 424
Gundobad (Burgundy), 442–443(d)
gunpowder, 322–323, 322(i), 338–339, 430–431
gunpowder revolution, 339
guns, in China, 323
Gupta Empire (India), 100, 125(m), 126
Guru Nanak. *See* Nanak (Indian guru)
Gutenberg, Johannes, 338
Guyuk (Great Khan), 471

Habsburgs (Austria), 474
hadiths (Muslim traditions), women in, 375
Hafiz (Sufi poet), 372, 385
Haiti, slavery in, 203
Haitian Revolution, 203
hajj (pilgrimage), 356(i), 362, 385
  Islam connected through, 522
  of Musa, Mansa, 380–381
hallucinogenic drugs, 243
Hammurabi (Mesopotamia), 65–66, 71, 73, 198
Han dynasty (China), 100, 117, 500
  Buddhism and, 119, 120, 341, 343
  collapse of, 122–123, 206–207
  diseases spread in, 284
  disorder after, 318
  government and, 121, 191
  Korea and, 331
  migration of farmers and, 340
  slavery and, 198–199
  trade in, 279
  tribute system and, 327, 329

Han Fei (China), 144
hangul (Korean language), 333
Hangzhou, China, 321, 421, 428
Han Kuan (Chinese scholar), 452, 478
Han Xizai (China), 353, 354(v)
Han Yu (China), 344
Harappa, 64, 87(v)
Harijan. *See* untouchables
Harris, Marvin (anthropologist), 81
Hatshepsut (Egyptian queen), 69
Hawaii
  settler impact on, 253
  society in, 19, 256
Hazda people (Tanzania), 9
health and health care. *See* diseases; medicine
"heaven," Chinese tradition of, 119
Hebrews, 69, 78, 157–159. *See also* Jews and Judaism
Heian-kyo (Kyoto), Japan, 335
Heian period (Japan), 337
Hellenes, Greeks as, 105
Hellenistic era, 109(m), 110–111. *See also* Greece
helots, in Greece, 210
Herculaneum, 215
herding, pastoralism and, 450
heresy, after Crusades, 427
Herodotus (Greek historian)
  on Greco-Persian Wars, 160–161
  on Persia, 130–131
  on Persian Empire, 103
hetaera (companion), 209
hierarchies. *See also* caste system; classes
  in Christianity, 171–172, 173, 364
  in Europe, 419
  in First Civilizations, 65–68
  gender, 66–68, 298–299
  in Inca society, 518–519
  in Mohenjo Daro, 86, 87(v)
  in Oceania, 256
  in second- and third-wave civilizations, 94–95
  in Western Europe, 417–418
higher education. *See* universities
High Middle Ages, 419
highways. *See* roads and highways
Hildegard of Bingen (abbess), 424
Hinduism, 149–151, 173. *See also* India
  ascetics of, 150(i)
  Buddhism and, 152, 155
  caste system in, 150, 152, 197
  in India, 126, 149–151, 154–155, 512–513
  Islam and, 378

Muslims and, 380
spread of, 292
Hinton, David (translator), 351–352
"'Public Service' and 'Mountain Seclusion,'" 355(d)
Hippocrates (Greece), 160
Hispaniola. *See* Haiti
Histories, The (Herodotus), 131(d)
History and Description of Africa, The (Leo Africanus), 310–311(d)
history and historiography
balance in writing of, 258
"big history" and, 13
on Buddha, 184–185(d)
chance and, 525
Christendom and, 435–436
divisions of history and, 10
on historical change, 345–346
of Islam, 388–389
on Mongols, 491(d)
pastoralists and, 476–478
religion and, 173–174
time periods and, 4–5, 12–13
world history and, 12–13
writing of, 258
History of the Franks (Gregory of Tours), 438–439(d)
History of the World Conqueror, The (Juvaini), 487–488(d)
Hittites, 80
hoe-based agriculture, 30, 67, 68
Holy Land. *See* Middle East; specific locations
Holy Roman Empire, 417
Holy Sepulcher, Church of (Jerusalem), 408
Holy Spirit, in Christianity, 413
holy wars, Crusades as, 425
hominids, 3, 10
Homo sapiens, 3, 10
homosexuality, in Athens and Sparta, 211
Honkoji Copy of the Kangnido Map, Korea, The, 312, 313(v)
Hopewell culture, 251–253
Hoppenbrouwers, Peter, and **Wim Blockmans,** on end of Roman civilization, 447, 447(d)
Horace (Rome), 121
Horn of Africa, 234
horses
Bedouin and, 455
domestication of, 38
horse collar, in Europe, 430
pastoralists and, 326–327, 454
spread of, 279
horticulture, 30

household religion, in Pompeii, 220, 221(v)
House of Wisdom (Baghdad), 387
housing, in agricultural settlements, 31
"How Death Came: The Purukapali Myth," 48–49(d)
Huitzilopochtli (Aztec god), 517
Huizong (China), 348, 349(v)
Hulegu (Mongol il-khan), 466
humanists, 504
humans. *See also* migration
emergence of, 3
prehistory and, 12
human sacrifice. *See* sacrifices
"Humped Cattle Seal from Mohenjo Daro, A," 86(v)
Hundred Years' War, 503
Hungary
Magyars and, 419
Mongols and, 471
Huns, 411, 419, 454, 478
hunting. *See also* gathering and hunting peoples
in Aboriginal rock art, 49, 50(v)
by Clovis peoples, 18
human and animal migration and, 27
in Pacific Oceania, 253
husband, use of term, 424
Hwang-ho River, 122

Iberian Peninsula, 383, 427. *See also* Portugal; Spain
Ibn Battuta (Arab scholar), 294, 299, 380, 382
Ibn Husayn, Ali, "Poem," 397(d)
Ibn Khaldun (historian), 387(t), 476, 478
Ibn Muslama, Habib, pact with people of Tiflis, 398–399(d)
Ibn Rushd (**Averroës,** scholar), 387(t), 533, 534(v)
Ibn Sina (**Avicenna,** scientist), 387(t), 388
Ice Age, 16, 18
Agricultural Revolution and, 27, 30
climate and, 16
warming after, 23–24
icons, Byzantine, 411–412, 415
ideas. *See* intellectual thought; philosophy
identities
of Germanic peoples, 124
Greek cultural, 106
Muslim, 385
ideology
Aztec, 517–518
Mongol, 462

idols, Muhammad on, 395, 396(v)
Igbo people, 40, 496–497
il-khans, in Persia, 466, 471–472
illuminated manuscripts. *See* manuscripts
imams (Islamic leaders), 369
immigrants and immigration. *See* migration
imperialism. *See also* colonies and colonization
of Axum, 234–235
empires and, 485
Inca Empire, 59, 242, 246, 518–520, 521(i)
Aztecs and, 300
roads of, 302(i)
women in, 520–521
independence
India and, 128
for Vietnam, 334, 334(i)
India, 128. *See also* Indus River region; Pakistan; South Asia
Buddhism and, 119, 151–154, 171, 282, 284, 341
caste system in, 126, 150, 154, 188, 193–197, 194(i)
China and, 290, 330, 341
Chinese Buddhist in, 305, 306–307(d)
Christianity in, 167
classical Buddha in, 178, 178(v)
culture of, 148–155
empires in, 125–127, 125(m)
European exploration and, 506
Greece and, 109, 110
Hinduism in, 126, 149–151, 154–155, 512–513
independence and, 128
Islam and, 365, 376–380
Khubilai Khan in, 486(v)
mothers in, 186(i)
paper in, 338
religion and culture in, 126, 142, 148–155
seaborne trade and, 287
slavery in, 199
society in, 126, 148–155, 193–197, 195(t)
spread of culture from, 290–292
textiles in, 127
trade in, 126, 288
women in, 86, 149, 150
"Indianization," of Southeast Asia, 293
Indian Ocean region. *See also* specific locations
China and, 340–341, 502,
civilizations in, 287–28
commercial network

Indian Ocean region (*continued*)
　East Africa trade and, 293
　Islam and, 360
　Sea Roads across, 286–287
　Srivijaya kingdom and trade in, 209
　Swahili civilization and, 293–295
　trade in, 234, 287–289, 288(*t*), 522
indigenous people. *See* native peoples;
　　specific groups
individualism, in Renaissance, 504–505
Indochina. *See* Cambodia; Vietnam
Indo-European peoples
　diffusion of languages, 279
　Greeks as, 104
　horse domestication and chariots of, 80
　Persians as, 102
　Sumer and, 79
Indonesia
　China and, 339
　Islam in, 368
　languages of, 255
　migration from, 16
　seaborne trade and, 287–288
　volcanic eruption in, 13
indulgences, Crusades and, 425
Indus River region, 60
　Arab armies in, 365
　civilization of, 84–89, 85(*v*), 86, 86(*v*),
　　87(*v*), 88(*v*), 89(*v*), 125
　dancing girl from, 88, 89(*v*)
　First Civilization in, 59, 61
　Harappa in, 64
　interactions by, 78
　Mohenjo Daro in, 64, 84–87, 85(*v*),
　　86(*v*), 87(*v*), 88(*v*)
　seal from, 85, 86(*v*)
　slavery in, 66
　state in, 91(*d*)
　writing in, 72(*t*)
industrialization, modern age and, 524
industrial pollution. *See* pollution
industry. *See also* industrialization
　in China, 322–324
　in India, 126
"Indus Valley Girl, An," 89(*v*)
infidels
　Mongols as, 466–467

innovation. *See also* industrialization;
　　technology
　in second- and third-wave civilizations,
　　93–94
　technological, 429
intellectual thought. *See also* science(s);
　　Scientific Revolution
　in Byzantine Empire, 414
　in Europe, 432–435
　Greek, 159–164, 208, 533, 534(*v*)
　in Islamic world, 299(*i*), 386–387, 512,
　　514, 527, 533, 534(*v*)
　Maya, 238
　in Renaissance, 504
　of second-wave era, 166(*t*)
　transmission of, 270
　women and, 424
intermarriage
　in Hellenistic world, 111
　in Mongol world, 111
Inti (Inca sun god), 518
invasions. *See* specific countries
inventions. *See* innovation; technology
Ionia, Greek settlements in, 107, 160
Iran. *See also* Persia
　Islam and, 368
Iraq. *See also* Fertile Crescent;
　　Mesopotamia
　Islam and, 368
　Mongols and, 467
　Seljuk Turks in, 456
iron and iron industry
　in Africa, 247
　in Agricultural Revolution, 36
　in China, 122, 322
Iroquois peoples, 497–498, 498(*i*)
irrigation
　in Caral, 58
　civilization and, 62
　in Indus river valleys, 60
　Islamic, 386
　in Meroë, 233
　Moche, 243
　Persian, 467
　in Wari, 246
Isabella (Spain), 383
Isaiah (Jewish prophet), 158
Ishtar (god), 69
Isis (god), 233
Isis and **Osiris** (gods), cult of, 168
Islam. *See also* Mongols and Mongol Empire;
　　Muhammad; Muslims; Ottoman
　　Empire; Quran; Shia Muslims; Sufis
　　and Sufism; Sunni Muslims
　in 7th century, 391–399
　900–1500, 377(*m*)

　in Africa, 407
　Afro-Eurasia and, 357–388
　of Almoravids, 457
　in Anatolia, 379–380
　Arabs and, 363
　Byzantine Empire and, 360, 413–414
　Christianity and, 387, 405–406, 537(*d*)
　civilization of, 383–388, 508–514
　connections among, 521–522
　conversion to, 361, 367–369
　Crusades and, 427
　culture and, 368–369, 376–383
　divisions in, 369–373
　empires of, 398–399(*d*), 508–514,
　　509(*m*)
　expansion of, 365–373, 397–398,
　　398(*d*), 409, 456
　forms of, 357–358
　Fulbe people and, 499
　Greek influence on, 163–164
　hajj in, 356(*i*)
　historic role of, 388–389
　homeland of, 358–360
　India and, 376–379, 512–513
　Indian Ocean commerce and, 289
　intellectual thought and, 299(*i*),
　　386–387, 512, 514, 527
　Judaism and, 386
　laws of, 364, 372–373, 382
　learning from, 299(*i*), 533, 534(*v*)
　luxury goods from, 427
　in Malacca, 514
　men in, 374–376
　Mongols and, 376, 384, 462, 467,
　　467(*i*), 472–473
　monotheism of, 142
　mullahs in, 372–373, 372(*i*)
　networks of Islamic faith and, 384–385
　Nubia and, 233
　paper in, 338
　pastoralists and, 454, 455
　patriarchy in, 375
　Persia and, 368, 413, 466, 467(*i*)
　Renaissance Europe and, 527–536
　scholarship in, 364(*i*), 375–376, 384,
　　386–387, 434
　sciences in, 386, 387(*t*)
　"second flowering of," 514
　slavery and, 212
　society of, 362, 367–369
　in Southeast Asia, 293
　in Spain, 365, 368, 382–383
　Sunni-Shia rift in, 369
　Swahili civilization and, 294–295
　as third-wave civilization, 269
　trade and, 289, 300, 385–388

Turks and, 456
  in West Africa, 357, 380–382, 381(m)
  women in, 374–376, 375(i)
  Zoroastrianism and, 157
Islamic empire. See Arabs and Arab world;
    Islam; Muslims
Islamic law. See sharia
islands, in Pacific Ocean region, 17, 253
Island Southeast Asia, 253, 255, 257
Israel. See also Fertile Crescent
  ancient kingdom of, 157, 158(m)
Istanbul. See Constantinople
Italian language, 121
Italy. See also Roman Empire; Rome
  city-states in, 124, 423, 432
  Rome and, 112
  taxation in, 502
  trade in, 421
Ivan I (Russia), 469

Janissaries, in Ottoman Empire, 513(i)
Japan. See also samurai (Japan)
  aristocracy in, 336, 337
  Buddhism in, 341
  China and, 328, 335–338, 335(m)
  Confucianism in, 337
  culture in, 335–338
  government of, 335, 336
  Jomon society in, 24
  military of, 336
  Mongols and, 460–461, 460(i)
  paper in, 338
  religions in, 336–337
  samurai in, 172, 336, 336(i)
  society in, 336, 337
  women in, 337
  writing in, 336, 337
Jasaw Chan K'awiil I (Maya), 226(i)
Jaspers, Karl, 162–163
jati, caste as, 196–197
Java
  Borobudur in, 291(i), 292
  Buddhist monument in, 292
  Indian culture in, 291–292, 514
  Muslims in, 514
Jenne, 297, 299
  Great Mosque at, 382
Jenne-jeno, 236, 236(i)
Jericho, 35
Jerome (Saint), on Huns, 478
Jerusalem
  Church of the Holy Sepulcher in, 408
  Crusades and, 425–426, 425(i)
  Dome of the Rock in, 406, 406(i)
  Ethiopian Christianity and, 408
  Mongols and, 472

Muslim control of (in 638), 406
  temple in, 103
Jesus of Nazareth, 164, 166(t)
  Buddha compared with, 164–165
  dating of birth, 171
  nature of, 172
Jesus Sutras, 406
Jews and Judaism, 157–159. See also anti-
    Semitism; Arabs and Arab world;
    Hebrews; Israel; Palestine
  Arab Empire and, 367
  in Arabia, 360
  Christianity and, 120, 165
  Crusades and, 427
  Ethiopia and, 408
  expelled from Spain, 383
  Greek culture and, 110
  Islam and, 363, 364, 367, 386, 406
  monotheism of, 142, 155, 362(i)
  pastoralists and, 454
  in Persian Empire, 103
  pogroms against, 426
  in Russia, 414
  trade and, 289
  Zoroastrianism and, 157
Jie people (nomads), 283
jihad (struggle), 363, 367, 499
Jin Empire (Jurchen, China), 320(m), 329
jizya (Islamic tax), 367
jobs. See economy; labor; workers
Jomon society, 24
Jordan. See also Fertile Crescent
  Ain Ghazal statues in, 33(i)
Joseon dynasty (Korea), 331
Journey to the Land of the Mongols (William
    of Rubruck), 489(d)
Judah, state of, 157
Judaism. See Jews and Judaism
judgment day, in Zoroastrianism,
    156, 157
junks (ships), 288
Jurchen people, 320, 329, 462
justice, Xuanzang on, 306–307(d)
Justinian (Byzantine Empire), 409, 434
Juvaini (Persian historian)
  History of the World Conqueror, The,
    487–488(d)
  on Mongols, 466–467

Kaaba (shrine), 282, 360, 370(i)
Kabir (Indian poet), 378
kaghan (Turkic ruler), 455
Kaifeng, China, 323, 324(i)
Kalahari Desert region, 231
Kamasutra, 150
kami (Japanese sacred spirits), 337

kamikaze (divine wind), Mongol invasion
    of Japan and, 461
Kaminaljuyú (Maya city), 241
Kanem, 297, 299
Kanem-Bornu, Islam in, 380
Kano, 297, 299
Karakorum (Mongol capital), 463,
    471, 473
Kargbo, Hassan (Sierra Leone), 357
karma, 150, 152, 196
Kazakhstan, Scythians in, 453(i)
Kenoyer, Jonathan (archeologist), 85,
    91(d)
Kenya, Bantu society in, 248–249
Kerala, India, Christianity in, 288
Kerwin, Dale, 51(d)
Khadija (wife of Muhammad), 361
khanates
  of the Golden Horde, 469
  in Mongol Empire, 458(m)
Khanbalik (China). See Beijing
khans (Mongol). See specific rulers
Khayyam, Omar (mathematician), 387(t)
Khitan people, 329
Khmer kingdom, Angkor as, 290
Khotan, Central Asia, 282
Khubilai Khan (China), 460
  picturing, 483, 484(v), 485(v), 486(v)
  Polo, Marco and, 485(v)
al-Khwarazim (mathematician), 387(t)
Kiev, 414, 469
Kievan Rus, 414, 468. See also Russia
Kilwa, East Africa, 294
kings and kingdoms. See also pharaohs
    (Egypt); specific rulers
  in Arabia, 360
  in China, 115–117
  cults of, 102
  of First Civilizations, 69–70, 73–74, 77
  Germanic, 124, 416
  Hellenistic, 110–111
  in Korea, 331, 332(m)
  powers of, 70
  in Western Europe, 416
kinship. See also families
  in agricultural village societies,
    496, 497
  Bantu, 248–249
  Paleolithic, 20
  in pastoral societies, 38
  state and, 69
kinship groups, pastoralists a[s]
Kipchak Khanate, 469
Kipchak people, Mon[gol]
kivas, 250–251
Kong Dejun (

Kong Fuzi. *See* Confucius
Kongo, Kingdom of, 506*(m)*
Koran. *See* Quran
Korea. *See also* South Korea
  Bodhisattva of Compassion in, 180,
    181*(v)*
  Buddhism in, 151*(i)*, 333, 341
  China and, 117, 319, 328, 328*(i)*,
    331–333
  kingdoms of, 331, 332*(m)*
  Mongols and, 461
  paper in, 338
  women in, 332
  world map of, 312, 313*(v)*
Koryo dynasty (Korea), 331
Krishna (Indian god), 154
Kshatriya (warrior) caste, 111, 194, 195,
  195*(t)*, 196
Kumbi Saleh, 297, 299
Kumsong, Korea, 331–332
Kush (Nubian kingdom), 79

labor. *See also* division of labor; workers
  Inca, 520
  Maya, 238
  plague and, 477
  plantation, 417
  trade and, 276
  women as, 423–424
Labrador, longhouses in, 24
LaDuke, Winona (Indigenous Women's
  Network), on Columbus, 493
Lady of Cao (Moche culture), 244–245,
  245*(i)*
Lagash, 71
Lalibela, Ethiopia, Church of St. George
  in, 408*(i)*
Lamu, East Africa, 294
land, cultivation in Europe, 419
land bridges, in Ice Age, 16
landowners
  in China, 191
  feudal, 417
landscape painting, in China, 147*(i)*
language(s). *See also* alph~~_____~~ and

Ge'ez, 169, 407
Greek, 110
  in India, 290
Latin, 120, 121
  in Mongol Empire, 463
  in Pacific Oceania, 255
Persian (Farsi), 387
Quechua, 519
spread of, 34
Swahili, 294
Turkic-speakers and, 455
vernacular, 418
in Vietnam, 334
Laozi (Daoism), 140*(i)*, 142, 147, 166*(t)*
Lapita pottery, 257
Larner, John (historian), on Polo travels,
  315*(d)*
last judgment, 157
Lateran Accords (1929), 80
latifundia (estates), 201
Latin America. *See* America(s); slave trade
Latin Christendom. *See* Roman Catholic
  Church; Western world
Latin language
  in Roman Catholic Church, 412, 418
  Roman Empire and, 120, 121
Latins, Rome and, 112
law(s). *See also* law codes; sharia
  in China, 144, 207
  Germanic, 442–443*(d)*
  Islamic, 364, 372–373, 382
  Roman, 121, 416
  in West, 433
law codes. *See also* law(s); sharia
  (Islamic law)
  of Hammurabi, 65–66, 71, 73
  patriarchy in, 68–69
  in Rome, 112, 121
Laws of Manu (India), 150, 204
lead, pollution from, 122
League of Five Nations (Iroquois),
  497–498
"'Learned Culture' of Song Dynasty
  China" (Garnet), 355*(d)*
learning. *See* education; intellectual
  thought
Lee, Richard (anthropologist), 21
Legalism (China), 117, 142–144
legal systems. *See also* law(s)
  European, 433
legions (Rome), 120
Leo III (Pope), Charlemagne and,
  403*(i)*, 444
Leo Africanus (North African traveler),
  310–311*(d)*, 315*(d)*, 512
Leonardo da Vinci (artist), 504

Lerner, Gerda (historian), 69
lesbians. *See* homosexuality
Lessons for Women (Ban Zhao), 145
"Letter to Changchun" (Chinggis Khan),
  482*(d)*
"Letter to Malik Ashtar" (Caliph Ali),
  399*(d)*
Lewis, Bernard, on Christian-Muslim
  hostility, 537*(d)*
libraries
  in Alexandria, 110
  Islamic, 364*(i)*, 381
  in Timbuktu, 299*(i)*
life expectancy, Paleolithic, 22
lifestyle. *See also* cities and towns;
  settlement(s)
  in 15th century, 494–499
  in Arab Empire, 374–376
  of Chaco peoples, 251
  in China, 148, 191
  in Mohenjo Daro, 87, 88*(v)*
  Nubian, 79
  Paleolithic, 3, 19–25
  in Pompeii, 217*(v)*
  of Roman slaves, 201–202
  of serfs, 418
Limpopo River region, 295
Lindisfarne Gospel, 440, 441*(v)*
lineage systems
  in Africa, 249
  in agricultural village societies, 39, 40
Li Po (Chinese poet), 352*(d)*
Li Shen (China poet), poem by, 192
literacy. *See also* education
  Byzantine, 414
  for elites, 71
  of pastoralist, 478
  for women, 209
literature
  epic, 64, 75–76, 154, 368
  Persian, 368
  in Vietnam, 335
Liu Guandao, "Khubilai on a Hunt,"
  483, 484*(v)*
Liu Zongyuan (Chinese official), 318
llamas, 32, 38, 300, 302
Lombards, 416
London, 421
long-distance trade. *See* trade
longhouses, 24
Lord of Sipan (Moche culture),
  244–245
Luba people (Central Africa), 249, 249*(i)*
luxury goods
  Silk Roads trade of, 279–280, 282
  trade and, 386, 427

Macedonia, Greece and, 108
Machiavelli, Niccolò (Italian diplomat), 504
   Prince, The, 530*(d)*
   on Turkish state, 529–530, 530*(d)*
machines, European, 431
Machu Picchu, 519*(i)*
Madagascar, 18, 19*(m),* 255, 287
madrassas (Islamic schools), 375, 384
Magdalene, Mary, 166
magnetic compass, 288, 339
Magyars (Hungarians), invasions by, 419
Mahabharata (epic poem), 154
Mahavira (Jainism), 166*(t)*
Mahayana Buddhism, 153, 154, 165, 172, 173, 284, 340*(i),* 343
Mahiya, Gudo (Hazda people), 9, 37
Maitreya Buddha (China), 183*(v)*
maize. *See* corn (maize)
Malacca
   maritime city of, 501*(m),* 514
   Straits of, 294
malaria, 284
Malaya, 290
Malaysia, languages of, 255
Mali (West African kingdom), 237, 297, 298, 299, 380
Mamluks (Egypt), 531
mammals, 18, 27, 30, 32
mana (spiritual energy), in Oceania, 256
Manchuria
   China and, 329
   Xiongnu in, 454
Mandate of Heaven (China), 71, 119, 146, 334
Manichaeism, 454
manners, Xuanzang on, 306–307*(d)*
manors, feudal, 418
Mansur (caliph, r. 754–775), 374–375
al-Mansur (Spain, r. 981–1002), 383
manufacturing, Inca, 520
manumission. *See also* slaves and slavery
   in Rome, 202
manuscripts
   illuminated, 440
   of Timbuktu, 299*(i)*
Maori people, 256
Mao Zedong (China), 128
   Confucianism and, 141
maps, of Korea, 312, 313*(v)*
Marduk (Babylonian god), 71
maritime culture, in Malacca, 514
maritime voyages. *See also* Exploration; Sea Roads; Zheng He
   Chinese, 288–289, 500–502, 507

European, 505–507
   in Pacific Oceania, 253–254
markets
   Aztec, 517
   in China, 339
   in Europe, 421*(i)*
   global, 339
Marrakesh, 457
marriage. *See also* gender and gender issues
   in India, 150, 196
   in Islam, 374
   in Japan, 337
   in Korea, 332
   in Mongol society, 451
   patriarchy and, 67
   in San society, 21
   in Sparta, 210
   Xuanzang on, 306*(d)*
martyrs, Christian, 167, 168–169
Marvelous Races of the East, The, 309*(v)*
Mary (mother of Jesus), 167, 424
masculinity, European concept of, 424
mathematics. *See also* science(s)
   Maya, 238
   Pythagoras on, 160
matrilineal descent, 497
Mauryan Empire (India), 100, 125*(m),* 126
Maya civilization, 238–239. *See also* Teotihuacán
   Olmec influence on, 62
   Temple of Great Jaguar, 74, 226*(i)*
   Teotihuacán and, 241
   trade and, 301–302
   writing systems of, 72*(t),* 73, 238
Ma Yuan (China), 350, 351*(v)*
McIntosh, Roderick (archeologist), 236
McNeill, William (historian), 12, 339–340
measles, 284
Mecca, 360, 362
   Gabriel at, 391
   hajj to, 356*(i),* 362, 380, 385
   Islam and, 363
   Muhammad's victory in, 395, 396*(v)*
Medes, Persians and, 103
medicine. *See also* diseases; specific conditions
   European, 433
   Greek, 160
   Islamic, 388
Medina, 363, 364
Mediterranean region. *See also* Roman Empire; specific locations
   Byzantine Empire and, 409, 410
   Christian states in, 426
   Egyptian influence in, 79–80

Greeks and, 106, 110–111
   Islamic trade in, 360
   plague in, 284–285
   Rome and, 112–114, 113*(m)*
   Sand Roads to, 295
megafaunal extinction, 18
Mehmed II (Ottomans), 528, 529*(v)*
Melanesia, 253, 255, 257
men. *See also* gender and gender issues; patriarchy
   in Athens and Sparta, 208–212
   in Aztec society, 520–521
   in China, 146
   in Christianity, 166–167, 171, 173
   in Inca society, 520–521
   in Islam, 374–376
   in Korea, 332, 333
   patrilineal descent and, 39
   roles in Middle Ages, 424
   in Roman society, 114
   in third-wave era, 270
   in West African society, 298–299
Mercantoni, Jonathan (novelist), 493
merchants. *See also* trade
   in Africa, 294, 380
   Aztec, 517
   in China, 192–193
   in Europe, 432
   in India, 195
   in Mesoamerica, 302
   Mongols and, 463, 471
   Muslim, 386
   as third estate, 432
   trade and, 276, 282, 288
Meroë, Kingdom of, 231–233, 233*(i),* 234
Meroitic script, 233
Mersankh (Egyptian wife), 52*(i)*
Merv, Central Asia, 282
Mesoamerica
   agriculture in, 32
   civilizations of, 237–246, 238*(m),* 514–521
   exchange and communication in, 301–302
   government of, 70
   Maya in, 238–239
   Olmec civilization in, 74
   Teotihuacán in, 64
   trade and communication in,
Mesopotamia, 75*(m).* See also
   chiefdoms in, 40
   cities in, 76–77
   civilizations of, 5
   deforestation
   Egypt co

Mesopotamia (*continued*)
environment in, 74–76
government of, 70
seaborne trade and, 287
trade in, 78–81
Uruk in, 63–64
women in, 68–69
writing in, 72*(t)*, 73
Messiah, 157
metallurgy
in Agricultural Revolution, 36
in Americas, 228
in China, 339
spread of, 79, 279
metals
in Greece, 106
in Rome, 121
Methodius (Byzantine missionary), 414
Metochites, Theodore (Byzantine Empire), 435
Mexica (Aztec) people, 516, 518. *See also* Aztec Empire
Mexico. *See also* Aztec Empire; Maya civilization; Mesoamerica; North America; Olmec civilization; Teotihuacán, Mexico
civilization in, 237
Teotihuacán in, 64
Michelangelo (artist), 504
micro-blades, 23
Micronesia, 254–255
Middle Ages
Europe during, 419–428, 420*(m)*
High Middle Ages and, 419
Middle East. *See also* Fertile Crescent; Islam; Ottoman Empire; Persian Empire
agriculture in, 32
Christianity in, 405–406
Crusades and, 426–427, 426*(m)*
Indian Ocean trade and, 289
Islam and, 358–360
Mongols and, 460
monotheism in, 142, 155–159
Ottomans in, 508

into Egypt, 80–81
into Eurasia, 16
Germanic, 416
human, 13–19, 27
into Pacific Ocean region, 18–19
by Turks, 456
Miletus, Greece, 209
military. *See also* navy; war(s) and warfare; weapons; specific battles and wars
in Axum, 234
Byzantine, 413, 414
chariots, bronze, and, 80
Chinese gunpowder and, 322–323
European, 503
horses and, 455
Janissaries as, 513*(i)*
in Japan, 336
in Mauryan Empire, 126
of Mexica, 516
in Mississippi chiefdoms, 252
Mongol, 454, 459–460, 462, 462*(i)*, 463
in Rome, 115
in Sparta, 107
mills, in Europe, 424, 430
Ming dynasty (China), 500–502, 501*(m)*
miniature paintings, 391, 513*(i)*
mining. *See* coal; gold
miraj (Prophet's Night Journey), 393
Mir Havand, "Cleansing of the Kaaba, The," 396*(v)*
missions and missionaries
Byzantine, 414
in Europe, 418
Hindu, 292
in Japan, 418
Mississippi River region, eastern woodlands peoples of, 251–252
mita (labor tribute), 520
Mithra (god), 120
moa bird (New Zealand), 19, 253
Moai (stone figures), 256*(i)*
mobility. *See also* migration
of pastoral societies, 453
Moche civilization, 59, 243–245, 244*(i)*, 518
Lord of Sipan and Lady of Cao in, 244–245
modern era, origins of, 522–524
modernity, discontent with, 53
modernization, Islamic, 388
Modun (Xiongnu), 455
Mohawk people, 497
Mohenjo Daro, 64
cart and oxen from, 87, 88*(v)*
cityscape of, 84, 85*(v)*
man from, 86, 87*(v)*

moksha (liberation), 150, 151, 154
Mombasa, Portugal and, 294
monarchs and monarchies. *See also* kings and kingdoms; specific rulers
in China, 61
in Europe, 422–423
in Nubia, 231–233
Persian, 102
monasteries and monasticism. *See also* nuns
Buddhist, 153, 172, 282–283, 340, 343–344, 345
in Ethiopia, 408
women and, 424
money. *See* currency
Mongke (Mongol Empire), 460
Mongolia. *See also* Chinggis Khan (Mongols); Mongols and Mongol Empire
celebration of Chinggis Khan in, 449–450
Turkic empires in, 329
Xiongnu in, 454–455
Mongols and Mongol Empire, 270, 457–464, 458*(m)*
assessment of, 491, 491*(d)*
Baghdad sacked by, 467
China and, 460, 462, 463, 464–466, 469, 491*(d)*, 500
Chinggis Khan and, 448*(i)*, 449, 459–460
cultural exchange and, 457–459, 473–475
diplomacy and, 471–473
disease spread from, 285
economy in, 471
as Eurasian network, 470–478
European view of, 488, 489*(d)*
government of, 463–464
gunpowder and, 323
historians on, 474–475
Islam and, 376, 384, 466, 467, 470
Japan and, 460–461, 460*(i)*
khanates in, 458*(m)*
Khubilai Khan and, 483, 484*(v)*, 485*(v)*, 486*(v)*
Kipchak people and, 470
military of, 454, 460–461, 462, 462*(i)*, 463
Moscow and, 415, 469, 503
perceptions of, 481–489
Persia and, 384, 466–468, 469–470
plague and, 476, 477
population of, 463
reasons for growth of, 461–464
religion and, 457–458, 463–464
Russia and, 460, 468–470, 470*(i)*

Secret History of the Mongols, The, 481, 482*(d)*
self-perception of rulers of, 481, 482*(d)*
technology and, 462
trade and, 279, 463, 522
warfare of, 460–461, 468–469
warriors of, 462*(i)*
women and, 450–451, 468*(i)*
in world history, 491*(d)*
world war of, 460
Xiongnu Empire and, 455
monks. *See* monasteries and monasticism
monotheism. *See also* polytheism
    in Arab world, 360
    of Christianity, 170
    of Islam, 361
    of Judaism, 157–158
    in Middle East, 142, 155–159
    of Zoroastrianism, 142, 155–157
monsoons, 287
Monte Albán, 241
monumental construction
    in Axum, 234, 261, 262*(v)*
    in Caral, 58
    in Göbekli Tepe, 25, 25*(i)*
    for kings, 73–74
    Olmec heads as, 73*(i)*, 74
    in Wari and Tiwanaku, 246
Morales, Evo (Bolivia), 227
morality, Confucian, 145
Morocco
    Almoravids in, 457
    diplomat from, in West Africa, 310–311*(d)*
    Islam and, 386
mortality rates. *See* death and death rates
Moscow
    Mongols and, 469, 470, 503
    as third Rome, 415
Moses (prophet), 362*(i)*
mosques. *See also* Dome of the Rock; Islam
    Grand Mosque of Sana'a, 405
    in West Africa, 381, 382
    women in, 374
mothers, in India, 186*(i)*
Mound Builders, 251–253
Mountain and Me, The (Li Po), 352*(d)*
mountains. *See* specific mountain regions
movable type, 338
movement of peoples. *See* expansion; migration
Mozambique, trade and, 293
Mughal Empire (India), 486*(v)*, 512, 513
Muhammad (Islam), 361–365. *See also* Islam; Muslims
    Arab Christians and, 167–168

assessments of, 401*(d)*
Gabriel and, 391, 392*(v)*, 393, 394*(v)*
on idolatry, 395, 396*(v)*
in Jerusalem, 393, 394*(v)*
as religious leader, 364
representations of, 391
successor to, 369
mullahs, in Islam, 372–373, 372*(i)*
multiculturalism, in U.S., 99
munitions. *See* weapons; specific weapons
murals, in Teotihuacán, 241
Murasaki Shikibu, Lady (Japan), 337, 337*(i)*
Musa, Mansa (Mali), 380–381
Museum (Alexandria), 110
music, in China, 121*(i)*, 330
Muslims. *See also* Arabs and Arab world; Islam; Mughal Empire; Shia Muslims; Sunni Muslims
    Christianity and, 357, 405–406
    Crusades and, 426, 426*(m)*
    empires of, 513–514
    European exploration and, 507
    Islamic societies and, 364–365, 367–369
    monotheism of, 362*(i)*
    Ottoman Empire and, 413–414, 527
    plague and, 285
    in Russia, 414
    in Spain, 382–383
Mussolini, Benito (Italy), 128
Mutazalites (Islamic thinkers), 387
My Retreat at Mount Zhongnan (Wang Wei), 352–353*(d)*
mystery religions, in Pompeii, 222, 223*(v)*
mysticism. *See also* Sufis and Sufism
    in Islamic practice, 371–372
mythology
    of Australian Aboriginal people, 44–49, 48*(v)*, 50*(v)*
    on Mesopotamian deforestation, 76

Nadar people (India), 187
Nalanda (monastic complex), 305
Nanak (Indian guru), 379
Nara, Japan, 335
Naram-Sin (Akkad), 66
Nasruddin (Mullah), 372–373, 372*(i)*
Natchez people, 252
nations. *See* state (nation); specific locations
native peoples. *See also* specific groups
    Columbus Day and, 493
natural philosophy. *See* science(s)
nature. *See also* agriculture; climate; environment

in Chinese poetry, 351
Daoism on, 147–148
women's roles and, 68
navigation
    in China, 322, 339
    compass and, 288
    trade and, 287, 288
navy. *See also* military
    Chinese, 501–502, 507
    Roman, 112
Neanderthals, 22
Neo, Terentius (Pompeii), 216*(v)*
Neo-Confucianism, 319
Neolithic era, 10, 26–33
Neolithic (New Stone Age) Revolution, 26–30. *See also* Agricultural Revolution
Nestorian Christianity, 172, 406, 407*(i)*
New Britain, 257
New Guinea, 253, 255, 494
New Jerusalem, in Ethiopia, 408
New Kingdom Egypt, 80
"New Rome," Constantinople as, 409
New Stone Age. *See* Neolithic era
New Testament, 166–167, 172. *See also* Bible
New World. *See* America(s); plantations; specific locations
New York (state), agricultural villages in, 497–498
New Zealand, 253
    Maori in, 256
    settlement of, 19
Nezahualcoyotl (Texcoco), 518
Ngo Quyen (Vietnam), 334*(i)*
Nicaea, Council of (325 C.E.), 172
Nigeria
    Bantu and, 34, 247
    Fulbe people from, 499, 499*(i)*
    Igbo people of, 40, 496–497
    Nok culture of, 36*(i)*
Niger Valley region, civilizations of, 231, 232*(m)*, 235–237, 236*(i)*
Night Journey of Muhammad, 393, 394*(v)*
Night Revels of Han Xizai, The, 353, 354*(v)*
Nile River region, 54, 74, 76, 231. *See also* Egypt
    flooding in, 77
    Meroë in, 231–233
Ningzong (China), 350
nirvana, 152
nobility. *See also* aristo
    in Egypt, 77
    in Europe, 4
    as secon

Nok culture (Nigeria), 36(i)
nomads. See also pastoralists and pastoral
    societies
    Bedouins as, 358–360
    China and, 117, 207, 318, 324,
      326–330
    collapse of empires and, 123
    plague and, 285
    settlements and, 16
Norte Chico civilization, 58–59, 58(i),
    59(i), 242
North Africa
    camel caravans in, 296
    Carthage in, 112
    Christianity in, 168, 407, 408
    Islam and, 365, 368, 407
    Ottoman Empire and, 508
    Sand Roads to, 295
    society and inequality in, 187–212
North America. See also America(s)
    agriculture in, 33
    eastern woodlands societies of, 250
    gathering and hunting peoples in, 496
    migrations to, 17, 18
    population of, 230(t)
    second-wave civilizations in,
      250(m)
    southwestern peoples of, 250–253
Northern Europe, trade in, 421
Norway. See Scandinavia
Nubia, 232(m)
    Christianity in, 233, 407–408
    civilization of, 58, 62
    Egypt and, 62, 79, 79(i), 81, 233(i)
    Meroë and, 231–233
numerals, from India, 388
nuns
    Buddhist, 152, 172
    Christian, 424
    patriarchies and, 204

obelisks, in Axum, 234
obsidian, trade in, 257
Oceania, 4(m), 253–257

Ohio River region, Hopewell mounds
    in, 252
Old Kingdom (Egypt), 75
Old Stone Age. See Paleolithic era
Old Testament, 70, 78–79
Olmec civilization, 62, 72(t), 73(i), 238
Olympic Games, ancient, 106
Olympus, Mount, 159
On a Mountain Path in Spring, 351(v)
Oneida people, 497
Onondaga people, 497
Orinoco River region, 301
Orthodox Christianity. See Eastern
    Orthodox Christianity
Osiris (Egyptian god), 77, 233
Otto I (Saxony, Holy Roman
    Empire), 417
Ottoman Empire, 379–380, 379(m), 404,
    508–512, 513. See also Crusades;
    Turkey
    Christianity and, 379, 508
    Constantinople seized by, 510–511
    Islam in, 413–414, 527
    Janissaries in, 513(i)
    Machiavelli on, 529–530, 530(d)
    Muslims and, 413–414, 527
    Safavid Empire and, 508–512
    trade and, 522
    Turkic creation of, 456
Ottoman Turks. See Ottoman Empire;
    Turks
outcasts, Buddha and, 181, 182(d)
Outer Eurasia, 278–279
overland trade. See Silk Roads; trade
Oxford, university in, 433
Oxus Valley region, 61, 61(i)

Pacific Oceania. See Oceania; Pacific
    Ocean region
Pacific Ocean region
    chiefdoms in, 41
    human migration and, 18–19, 19(m)
Pact of Ibn Muslama and the People of Tiflis,
    398(d)
pagans (non-Christians), 439, 440, 440(d),
    441(v)
Pagan state, 292
painting. See also art(s); rock art
    in China, 147(i)
    Persian and Turkish miniatures, 391
    from Pompeii, 216(v)
    in Renaissance, 504
Pakistan. See also India; Indus River
    region
    civilizations of, 59–60
    Islam and, 368

palaces, of Charlemagne, 444, 445(v)
Palembang, Srivijaya kingdom, 291
Paleolithic era, 3, 10, 19–25. See also
    gathering and hunting peoples
    agriculture in, 26
    art in, 8(i)
    in Australia, 21, 494–496
    economy and environment in, 22
    human migrations in, 10–19
    in Ice Age, 16
    lifestyle transitions in, 23–24
    religion in, 22–23
    settling down in, 24
    societies in, 19–25
    uses of, 41–42
Palestine. See also Fertile Crescent; Israel;
    Middle East
    Egypt and, 80(m), 81
Pali language, 153
Pallava alphabet, in Southeast Asia,
    290
pandemics, 475–478
papacy. See popes; specific popes
paper, 338, 386
Paris
    population of, 421
    university in, 433
    women workers in, 423
parliament. See government
Parthenon (Athens), 108
Parthian dynasty (Persia), 157
pastoralists and pastoral societies,
    37–39, 450–457. See also
      Mongols and Mongol Empire;
      nomads
    in Africa, 499
    agriculture and, 28–29(m), 37–39
    animals of, 37–38, 38(i)
    Arabs and, 455
    Berbers and, 455
    in Central Asia, 452(t), 498–499
    culture diffusion by, 80
    in Eurasia, 279
    global spread of, 28–29(m)
    history of, 454–457
    images of, 478–479
    Mongols and, 455, 469
    as nomads, 37, 38, 327, 453
    region and peoples of, 452(t)
    religion and, 454, 455
    Turks and, 455, 498
    varieties of, 452(t)
    in West Africa, 498–499
    in Western Hemisphere, 228
    women and, 38–39, 204, 451–452
pater familias, 114

patriarch, of Eastern Orthodox Christianity, 411
patriarchy
in Athens and Sparta, 208–212
in China, 205–208
in Christian Church, 172
comparison of, 204–212
defined, 67
Inca, 521
in India, 149
in Islam, 375
practice of, 68–69
in second-wave civilizations, 212–213
slavery and, 198
social hierarchies and, 67
women and, 67, 198, 204–205
patrician class, in Rome, 112
patrilineal descent, 39, 497
Paul (Saint), 165–166, 166(t)
pax Romana, 115, 119
peasant(s). *See also* land; serfs and serfdom
in China, 66, 122, 192, 199, 205, 206, 323
revolts by, 477
in Rome, 122
in Russia, 469
women's lives as, 422–423
Peloponnesian War (431–404 B.C.E.), 108
Penifader, Cecilia (English peasant), 422–423, 422(i)
people of the book, Muslims as, 364(i)
Pericles (Athens), 107, 209
Perpetua (Christian martyr), 167, 168–169, 168(i)
perpetual-motion machines, 430
Persepolis (Persia), 104, 104(i)
Persia. *See also* Iran; Persian Empire; Sassanid Empire
Bukhara conquest and, 487–488(d)
China and, 330
Christianity in, 167, 406
Greco-Persian Wars and, 107–108
Greek perception of, 130, 131(d)
il-khans in, 466, 471–472
invasions by, 410
Islam and, 368–369, 387, 467(i)
Mongols and, 384, 466–468, 467(i), 469–470
Safavid Empire in, 511–512
Seljuk Turks in, 456
Turkic peoples and, 499
Zoroastrianism in, 142, 155–157, 368
Persian Empire, 100, 102–104, 103(m). *See also* Persia; Safavid Empire
Byzantine Empire and, 413
India and, 126

Jews in, 103
miniature painting in, 391
as second-wave empire, 279
Zoroastrianism in, 155–157, 156(i)
Persian Gulf region, 287
Peru. *See also* Inca Empire
Caral civilization in, 58–59, 58(i), 59(i)
Chavín culture of, 242–243
Chincha people of, 301
Moche civilization in, 243
Quechua language in, 519
Perun (god), 415
Petrarch, Francesco (scholar), on Black Death, 476
pharaohs (Egypt), 71, 73, 75, 77
Pharisees, 110
Philip II (Macedonia), 108
Philip IV (France), 419
philosopher-king, Plato on, 161
philosophy. *See also* Aristotle; culture; Enlightenment; intellectual thought
Greek, 159–161, 533, 534(v)
in second- and third-wave civilizations, 93–94, 166(t)
Phoenicians, 78
physicians. *See* medicine
pilgrimage, hajj as, 356(i), 362
Pillars of Islam, 362–363
piracy, in Vietnam, 290
place notation, in Maya math, 238
plague, 477(i). *See also* Black Death; diseases
as Afro-Eurasian pandemic, 475–478
spread of, 270, 284, 285
plantations, labor for, 427
plants, 10, 27, 30, 34
Plato (Greece), 160(i), 161, 166(t)
Academy of, 161, 434
European thought and, 432
on homosexuality, 211
plebeians, in Rome, 112
plow, 228, 234, 430
gender hierarchies and, 67–68
pluralism, in European politics, 431–432
Plutarch (historian), 203
pochteca (Aztec merchants), 302, 517
Po Chu-I (China), 190
"Poem" (Ali Ibn Husayn), 397(d)
poets and poetry. *See also* literature
in China, 192
in Japan, 337
Sufi, 385
from Tang dynasty, 351–353(d)

pogroms
anti-Christian, 407
against Jews in Crusades, 426, 427
Pohnpei, Micronesia, 254–255
Poland, Mongols and, 471
political systems. *See also* empire(s); specific systems
in agricultural villages, 40
in China, 121, 143–144
empires as, 100
in India, 126–127
in Indus Valley region, 91(d)
in Japan, 336
in Rome, 112, 121
politics. *See also* government; specific issues
in China, 61
in Egypt, 77
Iroquois, 497–498
pluralism in European, 431–432
in Renaissance, 504
in Sparta, 210
trade and, 276
in Western Europe, 416–417
pollution. *See also* environment
lead, 122
Polo, Marco (Italian traveler)
China and, 307–308(d), 315(d), 321, 428–429
Khubilai Khan and, 485(v)
in Mongol Empire, 471
polygamy, among San people, 21
polygyny, in Islam, 374
Polynesia
Americas and, 17
chiefdoms in, 41
settlement of, 253–254
Tonga Islands in, 255
trade networks in, 522
women in, 256
polytheism. *See also* monotheism
in Persia, 156
Quran and, 361, 362
in Roman Empire, 171
Pompeii
artifacts from, 224(d)
banquet in, 217(v)
destruction of, 215, 216(v)
economy of, 224–225(d)
frescoes from, 218(v)
graffiti of, 219–220(d)
household religion in, 220
mosaic from, 120(i)
mystery religions i
Roman world se
wall paintin
Pompey (R

popes, 172. *See also* specific popes
  Eastern Orthodox Christianity and,
    411, 413
  political rulers and, 419
population. *See also* food
  of Aegean region, 105
  agriculture and, 26, 35, 94*(f)*
  of Anatolia, 379
  Aztec, 516
  in China, 321
  civilizations and, 62, 63
  distribution of world, 228
  European, 419, 421–422
  exploration and, 508
  Maya, 239
  of Medina, 363
  Mongol, 463
  Paleolithic growth in, 20
  of Persian Empire, 102
  plague deaths and, 476
  of Roman Empire, 122–123, 167
  of Teotihuacán, 64, 240
  world, 524*(t)*
  in writing about world history, 258
porcelain, 285. *See also* pottery
Portugal
  exploration by, 505
  taxation in, 502
Portuguese language, 121
Possehl, Gregory (archeologist), 89, 91*(d)*
postclassical era. *See* third-wave
    civilizations
potatoes, 300
pottery, 24, 257
power (authority). *See* authority (power)
prehistory, 12
prejudice. *See* race and racism
priesthood, Christian, 172
Prince, The (Machiavelli), 504, 530*(d)*
princes, in Russia, 469
printing
  China and, 322, 338, 340
  seals for imprinting and, 85, 86*(v)*
  spread of, 338

property ownership
  by gender, 68
  in Rome, 114–115
  slaves and, 198, 202
prophets
  Jewish (Hebrew), 158, 166*(t)*
  Muhammad as, 361–365, 368
protected peoples, in Islam, 407
protest(s). *See* revolts and rebellions;
    revolution(s)
Psalms of the Sisters (India), 204
Ptolemaic empire (Egypt), 111
"'Public Service' and 'Mountain Seclu-
    sion'" (Hinton), 355*(d)*
public works, in Chinese and Roman
    empires, 118
Pueblo Bonito, 251
pueblo peoples. *See* Ancestral Pueblo
    people
pueblos, 251
Punic Wars, 112
punishment, Legalists on, 144
Punjab, Islam in, 378
Pure Land Buddhism, 343
purification rituals, in India, 196
Purusha (Indian god), 194, 195*(t)*
Pwa Saw (Pagan queen), 293
pyramids
  Aztec, 516
  in Caral, 58
  in Egypt, 75
  in Teotihuacán, 240, 240*(i)*
  ziggurats as, 63
Pythagoras (Greece), 160

Qadiriya order (Sufi), 385
Qin dynasty (China), 100, 117, 128, 144
Qin Shihuangdi (China), 73, 98*(i)*, 117,
    128, 144, 346
Quanzhou, China, 340
Quechua language, 519
queen(s). *See also* specific rulers
  in Egypt, 69
  of Sheba, 408
quipu (Inca counting device), 58,
    302, 519
Quran
  "believers" in, 367
  education in, 384
  laws based on, 364
  Muhammad's revelations in,
    361–362, 391
  women and, 374, 375*(i)*
Quraysh (Arabian tribe), 360, 361,
    363, 375

Rabia (female Sufi), 376
race and racism
  caste system and, 193
  slavery and, 201
Raherka (Egyptian inspector of scribes),
    52*(i)*
Rainbow Serpent (Australian mythology),
    17*(i)*, 46*(d)*
Ramadan, 370*(i)*, 382
Ramayana (epic poem), 154, 290
Ramisht (Persian merchant), 282
Rapa Nui (Easter Island), 19
  settlement of, 253–254
  stone figures of, 256*(i)*
  trade in, 257
rape, in Mesopotamia, 68
Raphael (artist), 504
rationalism, Greek, 159–161
al-Razi (Arab physician), 387*(t)*, 388
reason, faith and, 432–435
rebellions. *See* revolts and rebellions
rebirth
  in Buddhism, 343
  in Indian religions, 150, 152, 196
reconquest (Spain), 383, 527
Record of the Western Regions (Xuanzang),
    305, 306–307*(d)*
Records of the Grand Historian (Sima Qian),
    136*(d)*
Red River region, in Vietnam, 333
Red Sea region, trade in, 104, 234
reform(s), in China, 191
reincarnation, in Hinduism, 150
relay trade, Mongol, 463
relics, Buddhist, 127*(i)*
religion(s). *See also* cult(s); gods and
    goddesses; philosophy; shamans;
    specific groups
  of Aboriginal Australians, 22–23,
    142
  in Afro-Eurasia, 523*(m)*
  Aztec, 517
  of Bantu-speaking peoples, 249–250
  change and, 173–174
  of Chavín culture, 242–243
  in China, 119, 140*(i)*, 141–148, 330,
    341–345
  connections from, 521–522
  exploration and, 507
  government and, 71
  of Greek city-states, 159
  historians and, 173–174
  Inca, 519–520
  in India, 126, 127, 148–155
  industrialization and, 524

221*(v)*
222, 223*(v)*
en in, 215–223
from, 216*(v)*
ome), 115

in Japan, 336–337
in Korea, 332
in Mesoamerica, 237–247
from Middle East, 358–360
in Mongol Empire, 457–458, 463–464
of Norte Chico, 59
in Oceania, 256–257
in Ottoman Empire, 511–512
in Pacific Oceania, 255
in Paleolithic era, 22–23
in Pompeii, 220, 221*(v)*, 222, 223*(v)*,
    224–225*(d)*
reason and, 432–435
in Rome, 119
in Russia, 414–415, 469
in Safavid Empire, 511–512
in second- and third-wave civilizations,
    93–94
silk and, 281
in Southeast Asia, 290
in Spain, 382
spread of, 165–172, 276–278
in Western Europe, 418
women in, 39, 208
religious fundamentalism, Islamic, 388
religious toleration
    by Mongols, 464, 469
    in Spain, 383
religious wars. *See* Crusades; jihad
Renaissance (Europe), 504–505
    arts in, 531
    cross-cultural exchange in, 537*(d)*
    Islam and, 527–535
reproduction, women and, 208
republic, in Rome, 112, 115
Republic, The (Plato), 161
resistance. *See* revolts and rebellions
resources. *See also* trade
    in Andes Mountains region, 246
    in Niger River region, 237
reunification, of China, 117, 343
revelations
    continuous, in Bantu religions, 250
    in Islam, 361–363
revolts and rebellions. *See also*
    revolution(s)
    in China, 122, 148, 192, 205, 344
    collapse of empires and, 474
    in Haiti, 203
    by Muslims, 370
    by peasants, 477
    by slaves, 202–203
    in Vietnam, 334
revolution(s). *See also* revolts and rebellions
    economic, in China, 321

Reynolds, Jonathan, and Erik Gilbert,
    on transregional nature of early
    Christianity, 267*(d)*
rice, 321, 340
Rightly Guided Caliphs (632-661),
    369, 370
rights, of slaves, 198, 199
ritual purity and pollution (India), 196
rituals
    Aztec, 517–518
    in India, 149, 152, 154, 155
    Moche, 243
river valley civilizations. *See* specific
    locations
roads and highways. *See also* Sand Roads;
    Sea Roads; Silk Roads; trade
    of Chaco, 251
    of Inca, 302*(i)*
    in Mesoamerica, 302
    in Persian Empire, 104
    of Wari, 246
Robinson, Francis (Islamic scholar), on
    Western attitudes to Muhammad,
    401*(d)*
rock art
    Australian Aboriginal, 17, 17*(i)*, 44, 47,
        48*(v)*, 50*(v)*
    cave paintings and, 16
    Paleolithic, 8*(i)*
rockets
    Chinese development of, 323
    Muslims and, 386
Roman Catholic Church, 172, 431, 521.
    See also Crusades; missions and
    missionaries
    Eastern Orthodoxy and, 404,
        411–413, 427
    intellectual thought and, 432–435
    Roman world and, 418
    vs. state, 125, 431–432
    in Western Europe, 415–428
Roman Empire, 112–115, 113*(m)*. *See also*
    Byzantine Empire; Greco-Roman
    traditions
    Axum and, 234
    Charlemagne and, 403*(i)*
    Chinese Empire and, 111–112
    Christianity in, 119, 167, 168,
        170–172
    civil wars in, 115
    collapse of, 122–125, 416, 474–475
    consolidation of, 118–122
    creation of, 112–115
    diseases spread in, 122, 284
    eastern and western, 409

economy of, 201
Germanic peoples and, 124,
    133–134*(d)*
government of, 115, 121
Greece and, 120, 161
lead pollution in, 122
legacy of, 447, 447*(d)*
military in, 115
Mussolini and, 128
Pompeii as window on, 215–223
on Sarmatians, 134–135, 135*(v)*
second-wave trade and, 279
slavery in, 66, 115, 198–203, 200*(i)*
trade in, 288
United States and, 99–100
western and eastern, 122
Western Europe after, 416–417
Romanian language, 121
Rome. *See* Roman Empire
Rome (city), siege of (410 C.E.), 126
Romulus (Rome), 474
Ropp, Paul S., on Mongols, 491*(d)*
"Royal Priest of Harappa, A," 87*(v)*
royal road, in Persian Empire, 104
Rufinus (Christian monk), 262, 263*(d)*
rulers. *See* kings and kingdoms; monarchs
    and monarchies; specific rulers and
    locations
Rumi (Sufi poet), 385
runaway slaves, in Rome, 202–203
rural areas. *See also* agriculture; farms and
    farming; villages
    in China, 280
Russia. *See also* Kievan Rus
    Byzantine religion and, 414
    Christianity in, 414–415
    Crusades and, 427
    Mongols and, 460, 468–470, 503
    religion in, 469
Russian Orthodox Church. *See also* East-
    ern Orthodox Christianity
    Mongols and, 469, 470
Russification, of Eastern Orthodoxy, 415
Ryazan, Russia, Mongols and, 470*(i)*

sacks of cities. *See* specific locations
sacred writings. *See* Bible; Quran;
    Scriptures
sacrifices
    Aztec, 517–518
    in China, 61
    in India, 149, 152, 15[...]
    in Mesoamerica, 2[...]
    by Moche peo[...]
    in Teotihua[...]

saddles, camel, 455
Safavid Empire, 511–512, 513
    Ottoman Empire and, 508–512
Safi al-Din (Safavids), 511
Sahara Desert region, 231, 235. *See also*
    sub-Saharan Africa
    pastoralists in, 452*(t)*
    plants and animals in, 32
    Sand Roads across, 295–300
Sailendra kingdom, Java, 291–292
St. Mark's Basilica (Venice), 412*(i)*
Saka pastoralists, in Azerbaijan, 38–39
Salamanca, university in, 433
salinization of soil, 76, 123
salt, 276
salvation, in Buddhism, 153–154, 343
Samarkand, Central Asia, 282, 284, 499
Samoa, 257
samsara (rebirth/reincarnation), 150
samskara (ritual), 195*(t)*
Samuel (prophet), 70
samurai (Japan), 172, 336, 336*(i)*
Sand Roads, 295–300, 298*(m)*
Sanhaja Berber pastoralists, 457
San peoples, society of, 8*(i)*, 20*(i)*, 21
Sanskrit language, 153
    in Southeast Asia, 290
    translations of texts from, 282
Sanxingdui, China, 62
sapay Inca (Inca ruler), 521
Sarai, Mongol capital at, 469
Saraswati River region, 59
Sarmatians, Romans on, 134–135, 135*(v)*
Sassanid Empire (Persia), 157, 360, 365
satraps (Persia), 102
Saudeleur dynasty (Micronesia), 255
savanna grasslands, in Africa, 295, 297
savior, in Zoroastrianism, 156, 157
Saxons, 416
Scandinavia
    development of, 422
    pastoralists in, 452*(t)*
Schmidt, Klaus (archaeologist)~~...~~

science(s). *See also* Scientific Revolution;
    technology
    in China, 322
    in historic dating, 12
    Islamic, 386, 387*(t)*
Scientific Revolution, human rationality
    and, 434
scratch plow, in Europe, 430
scribes
    in Egypt, 52*(i)*
    in Mongolia, 463
script, Arabic, 368
Scriptures, Hebrew, 69, 157
sculpture. *See also* art(s); Mohenjo Daro
    Ain Ghazal statues as, 33*(i)*
    from Indus Valley civilization, 88, 89*(v)*
    Olmec, 73*(i)*, 74
    of Rapa Nui, 256*(i)*
    Venus figurines as, 16, 23, 23*(i)*
Scythians, 131–132, 132*(v)*, 453*(i)*
seaborne trade, 285, 302. *See also* Indian
    Ocean region; ships and shipping
seals (imprinting), 85, 86*(v)*
Sea Roads, 285–295, 286*(m)*
secondary products revolution, 36
Second Crusade, 427
second estate, nobility as, 432
"second flowering of Islam," 514
second-wave civilizations, 92–95, 128,
    142, 188. *See also* classical era
    in Africa, 231–237, 247–250
    in Americas, 227
    change and continuity in, 212–213
    culture and religion in, 142–174
    in Eurasia, 227–228
    legacies of, 128
    in North America, 250–253, 250*(m)*
    patriarchy in, 204–212
    Silk Roads and, 279
    slavery in, 198–203
    in South Asia, 125–127
    thinkers and philosophies of, 166*(t)*
Secret History of the Mongols, The, 481,
    482*(d)*
secularism, in China, 146
sedentary lifestyle, 27
Seleucid empire (Persia), 111
self-perception, Mongol, 481, 482*(d)*
Seljuk Turks, 456, 456*(i)*, 456*(m)*
Senate, in Rome, 115
Seneca people, 497
Seneca the Younger (Rome), 281
Seokguram Grotto, 151*(i)*
Septimus Severus (Rome), 168
serfs and serfdom, 417–418. *See also*
    peasant(s)

peasant revolts and, 477
    in post-Roman Europe, 212
settlement(s). *See also* agriculture; colonies
    and colonization; migration
    ancient, 12
    by China, 502
    Greek, 106
    Neolithic, 27
    in North America, 250
    in Pacific Oceania, 253
    Paleolithic, 16, 24, 26
settling down, Paleolithic, 24
Seventeen Article Constitution
    (Japan), 335
sex and sexuality
    in Greece, 211–212
    in India, 150
    in Islam, 374
    in San society, 21
    women and, 424
Shahnama (The Book of Kings,
    Ferdowsi), 368
shamans
    Australian Aboriginal, 22–23
    Chavín, 243
    Maya, 239
    Mongol, 458
    in Oceania, 257
Shanga, East Africa, 294
Shang dynasty (China), 60, 60*(i)*, 62, 115.
    See also China
sharecroppers, in China, 192
sharia (Islamic law), 364
    Sufis and, 371–372
    ulama and, 371
shaykhs (Sufi teachers), 384–385, 389
Sheba, Queen of, 408
Shia Muslims, 369–370
    emergence of, 397*(d)*
    empire of, 511–512
    women and, 376
Shihuangdi. *See* Qin Shihuangdi
Shi Le (Jie), 283
ships and shipping. *See also* navy; Sea
    Roads
    15th-century trade and, 522
    Chinese, 322, 340, 501, 502
    European, 430–431
    human migration and, 16, 17, 18–19,
        19*(m)*
    in Indian Ocean, 287*(i)*, 288
    Mongol armada and, 460–461
    technology of, 287
Shiva (Hindu god), 154, 291, 292
Shotoku Taishi (Japan), 335
shrine, from Pompeii, 221*(v)*

~~...38~~
~~...ple, 243~~
~~...an, 240~~

Sicily, Crusades and, 426*(m)*
Siddhartha Gautama (Buddha), 142, 151, 151*(i)*, 166*(t)*. *See also* Buddha
Sierra Leone, 357
Sikhs and Sikhism, 378–379
silk and silk industry
    in China, 280–281
    Islamic, 281*(i)*
    Mongols and, 467
    spread of, 281
Silk Roads, 270, 278–285, 278*(m)*
    in 15th century, 522
    cultural exchange along, 282–284
    disease spread along, 284–285
    Dunhuang, China, and, 282
    economic exchange along, 280*(t)*
    goods transported along, 279–282
    Mongols and, 471
    Muslims and, 386
    pastoral nomads and, 327
    Sogdians and, 282
    travels on, 274*(i)*
Silla kingdom (Korea), 331
Sima Guang (Chinese historian), 325
Sima Qian, on Xiongnu people, 135–137*(d)*
Skagit peoples, 496
skin color, slavery and, 66
slaves and slavery. *See also* slave trade
    Africa and, 66, 299
    Aztecs and, 517
    in China, 198–199
    civilization and, 66, 66*(i)*, 198–199
    existence of, 212
    as Greco-Roman tradition, 199–203
    Hammurabi on, 198
    in India, 199
    Islam and, 212
    in Korea, 333
    as labor, 198, 199, 201, 203
    Mongols and, 469
    in pastoral societies, 451
    plantations and, 427
    in Pompeii, 217*(v)*
    revolts by, 202–203
    Roman Empire and, 66, 115, 198–203, 200*(i)*
    serfdom and, 417–418
    warfare and, 66*(i)*
    women as, 198, 199
slave trade, 530
    trans-Saharan, 299–300
Slavs, Byzantine religion and, 414
smallpox, 284
smelting, in Meroë, 233
social classes. *See* classes; specific classes

social hierarchies. *See* hierarchies
society. *See also* cities and towns; civilization(s); classes; culture(s); families; women
    in 15th century, 494–499
    agricultural, 10, 30–33, 37–41
    ancient, 4, 20–22
    in Australia, 21
    Bantu, 248
    Black Death and, 477
    in China, 147–148, 188–193, 197
    civilization as, 82, 93
    in Eurasia and North Africa, 187–212
    feudal, 417–418
    in First Civilizations, 64–65
    hierarchies in, 419
    Hopewell, 252
    in India, 126, 148–155, 193–197, 195*(t)*
    industrialization and, 524
    Islamic, 362, 367–369
    in Japan, 336, 337
    of Mongol Empire, 462
    in Pacific Ocean region, 19, 253–257
    Paleolithic, 19–25
    pastoral, 37–39, 450–457
    pattern changes in, 187–188
    Roman, 114
    in Western Europe, 438
Socrates (Greece), 108, 159–160, 166*(t)*
Sofala, East Africa, 294
Sogdians (Central Asia), 282
soil, 76, 106, 121, 123
solar system. *See* astronomy
soldiers. *See* military
Solomon (Hebrew king), 408
Solon (Athens), 107
Somalia, 287, 293
Song dynasty (China), 124, 190*(i)*, 319–321, 320*(m)*, 324*(i)*, 500
    Buddhism and, 345
    gunpowder and, 322–323
    Mongols and, 462
    patriarchy under, 208
    trade and, 288
    tribute system and, 329
    women in, 324–326
Songhay Empire (West Africa), 237, 297, 506*(m)*, 512, 513
    Igbo trade with, 497
    Islam in, 380, 382
Sonni Ali (Songhay ruler), 382
Son of Heaven (China), 61, 71, 119
Sophocles (Greece), 108
South (Global). *See* Global South
South Africa, exploration and, 506

South America. *See also* America(s); civilization(s); Mesoamerica
    migrations to, 17
    population of, 230*(t)*
    rivers in, 301
    trade in, 257
South Asia. *See also* Indus River region
    civilizations in, 60, 150
    empires in, 125–128, 125*(m)*
South China Sea, trade in, 288
Southeast Asia. *See also* specific locations
    ca. 1200 C.E., 290*(m)*
    cultures in, 335
    economy in, 290
    elites in, 291
    Hinduism in, 149, 292
    "Indianization" of, 293
    Islam in, 293, 514
    Island, 253, 255, 257
    religions in, 521–522
    sea roads and, 289–293
    trade and, 286–287, 288, 522
Southeast Ceremonial Complex, 253
South Korea. *See also* Korea
    Christianity in, 403
Southwest Asia, 30, 167, 452*(t)*. *See also* Asia
southwestern North America, peoples of, 250–253
sovereignty, of nation-states, 475
Spain
    Almoravids in, 457
    Aztecs and, 428
    Crusades and, 426*(m)*, 427
    development of, 422
    exploration by, 505–506
    humans in, 16
    Islam and, 365, 368, 382–383, 527, 533
    Jews in, 382, 383
    Maya and, 239
    reconquest in, 383
    religions in, 382, 383
    Rome and, 112
    taxation in, 502
Spanish America. *See* America(s); Spain
Spanish language, 121
Sparta, 106
    Athenian war with, 108
    civilization of, 104
    government of, 107
    patriarchy in, 208–21
    Socrates on, 160
    women in, 20
Spartacus (sl
specializati

spice trade, 285
  in Srivijaya, 290
spirits and spirituality. *See also* religion(s)
  Paleolithic, 22–23
Srivijaya kingdom, Sumatra, 290–291
standards of living. *See* lifestyle
state (nation). *See also* civilization(s);
    empire(s); government
  in China, 60–61, 188, 189–191
  civilizations and, 63
  development of, 422–423
  in Europe, 502–503
  in Indus Valley, 60, 91*(d)*
  in Mesopotamia and Egypt, 76–77
  pluralism in European, 431
  rise of, 69–74
  Roman Catholicism and, 125, 431–432
  Russian, 469
  in Southeast Asia, 290
state building
  commerce and, 290
  in Europe, 502–505
status. *See also* classes
  in agricultural village societies, 39
Stearns, Peter, and Peter Gosch, on
    travelers' accounts, 138*(d)*
steppe nomads, 324, 326–327, 330
  Mongol Empire and, 457, 469
  pastoralist as, 454
sternpost rudder, 431
"Stone Model of a Cart Pulled by Two
    Oxen," 88*(v)*
Straits of Malacca, 294
Strong, John, on Buddha's life, 184*(d)*
stupas, Buddhist, 153
sub-Saharan Africa. *See also* Africa; Sahara
    Desert region
  agriculture in, 31–32, 295
  pastoralists in, 450
  trade in, 512
succession
  Mongol, 467
  to Muhammad, 369

sultans and sultanates, 456
  of Delhi, 377, 378*(m)*
Sumatra, 13, 290, 514
Sumer, 54–62, 75*(m)*, 76–77
  writing in, 72*(t)*, 79
Sunga dynasty (India), 186*(i)*
"Sunita the Outcast," 182*(d)*
Sunni Muslims, 369–370, 389
  in Ottoman Empire, 511
  Persia's neighbors as, 511
  women and, 375–376
supercontinents, 228
Supe River region, 58
supernatural. *See also* religion(s)
  Bantu, 249–250
  Christian, 418
  in Persia, 156
  in Roman and Chinese empires, 118
  rulers and, 71
Susa (Persia), 104
Sutton Hoo, grave site at, 123*(i)*
Swahili civilization (East Africa), 293–295,
    294*(m)*
Swahili language, 294
Sweden. *See* Scandinavia
symbolic behavior and language, 12
Syria
  Christianity in, 167, 406
  Egypt and, 80*(m)*, 81
  Islam and, 368, 370
Syriac language, 167

Tacitus (historian), on Germans,
    133–134*(d)*
Talas River, Battle of, 365
Tale of Genji, The (Murasaki Shikibu),
    337, 337*(i)*
Tamerlane (Timur) (warrior), 493, 498,
    501*(m)*
Tang dynasty (China), 124, 319–321,
    320*(m)*, 330, 343, 500
  Buddhism under, 340
  examination system in, 190
  Nestorian Christianity under, 406,
    407*(i)*
  poetry from, 351–353*(d)*
  Silla kingdom and, 331
  trade and, 279, 288
  Turkic empires and, 329
  Vietnam and, 334
  women in, 207, 280, 324
tanka (Japanese poetry), 337
tapu (taboo), in Oceania, 256
Tartars. *See* Mongols and Mongol Empire
Ta-Seti, Nubian kingdom of, 62
tatau (tattoo), 255

taxation
  in China, 323–324
  in Europe, 502–503
  Islamic jizya as, 367
  in Japan, 335
  Mongols and, 463, 469
  in Persia, 103
technology. *See also* industrialization;
    science(s); tools
  agriculture and, 30, 35–36
  ancient, 10–12, 20
  in Australia, 17
  borrowings of, 429–430
  Chinese, 338–339, 339*(t)*, 340,
    346
  Clovis, 18
  in Egypt, 81
  European, 429–430, 430*(i)*, 431
  in Islamic world, 386
  in Mesoamerica, 237
  in modern world, 524
  Mongols and, 462, 473
  in Paleolithic societies, 16, 20
  pastoralists and, 454
  in second- and third-wave civiliza-
    tions, 94
  in secondary products revolution, 36
  spread of, 279
  women workers and, 424
Temple of Heaven (Beijing, China), 500
temples. *See also* mosques; ziggurats
  Chavín, 243
  of Feathered Serpent (Teoti-
    huacán), 240
  in Göbekli Tepe, 25
  of Great Jaguar (Maya), 74, 226*(i)*
  Hellenistic, 111
  Hindu, 292, 292*(i)*
  in Jerusalem, 103
Temujin. *See* Chinggis Khan
tenant farmers, 192
Ten Commandments, 158
Tengri (Mongol god), 458
Tenochtitlán, 516–517
Teotihuacán, Mexico, 64, 64*(i)*, 240–241,
    240*(m)*, 516, 518
  commerce in, 302
  Olmec influence on, 62
terra-cotta warriors, in China, 98*(i)*
Tertullian (Carthage), 168, 432
Texcoco, 516, 518
textiles and textile industry
  in Agricultural Revolution, 35–36
  in China, 206, 325, 339
  India and, 127
Text of Thomas the Presbyter, 398*(d)*

Thales (Greece), 160
theater, Roman, 120(i)
Thebes, 106
Theodosius (Rome), 171
theology, in eastern and western Christianity, 172, 412–413
Theravada Buddhism, 153, 172, 173, 343
Things Fall Apart (Achebe), 497
third estate (merchants), 432
third Rome, Moscow as, 415
third-wave civilizations, 93, 268–271
    China as, 317–318, 474
    economic globalization in, 302–303
    empires of, 474–475
    Eurasian, 470–471
    European, 429
    Indian Ocean exchange and, 288–289
    Islam and, 269, 386
    pastoral peoples in, 455
    Russia as, 414–415, 468
    Southeast Asia commerce and, 289–293
    transregional interaction by, 269–271
    Western Christendom in, 415–428
Thomas the Presbyter, text of, 398(d)
Thoreau, Henry David (author), 53
three obediences, the, 205
Tibet
    China and, 328
    pastoralists in, 450, 452(t)
Tiflis, Christians and Muslims in, 367, 397–398, 398(d)
Tigris-Euphrates river valley, 54
Tikal (Maya city), 74, 226(i), 239, 241
Timbuktu, 297, 299, 299(i), 381, 512
time, historical periods and, 4–5
Timur (Tamerlane) (Turkic warrior), 493, 498, 501(m)
title societies, 40, 497
Tiwanaku civilization (Andes), 59, 227, 245–246, 518
Tlacaelel (Aztec official), 517
Tlatelolco, Aztec market in, 517
toga (Rome), 120
toleration. *See* religious toleration
Toltec civilization, 516, 518
tombs. *See* burials
Tonga, 255, 256, 257
tools, 3, 10–12, 23, 61(i). *See also* technology
towns. *See* cities and towns
trade. *See also* Exchange; merchants; roads and highways
    in 14th century, 472(m)
    in Africa, 497

    in Afro-Eurasia, 280, 281, 288–289, 522–524, 523(m)
    in Americas, 300–302, 301(m)
    in Arab world, 366
    Austronesian, 18–19
    in Axum, 234
    Aztec, 517
    in Byzantine Empire, 414
    China and, 288–289, 340–341, 432, 500
    civilizations and, 62
    communication and, 477
    connections through, 522
    culture and, 275–277
    in East Africa, 293–295
    in Egypt, 78–81
    European, 416, 428–429
    in First Civilizations, 85
    in gold, 264(d), 296–297
    Hellenistic, 110
    Hopewell, 252
    in India, 126
    in Indian Ocean region, 234, 286–287
    intercontinental, 230
    Islam and, 289, 300, 360, 380, 527
    of Meroë, 233
    in Mesopotamia, 78–81
    Mongols and, 457
    in Niger River region, 236–237
    in Northern Europe, 421
    northern nomads and, 327
    in Oceania, 257
    plague and, 477
    Sand Roads and, 295–300
    Sea Roads and, 285–295
    in second-wave civilizations, 95
    Silk Roads and, 270, 278–285
    state building and, 290
    in Sudan, 296
    Swahili, 293–295
    in third-wave civilizations, 95, 270
    trans-Saharan, 230, 237, 296–297
    travelers' tales about, 305–313
    in Venice, 531, 532(v)
    West African, 380–381
    in Western Europe, 415
trading fairs, 421
Trajan's Column, 135(v)
trans-African trade, 295–300. *See also* trade
translations, of texts, 163–164, 282, 387, 433, 435
transoceanic trade routes. *See* Sea Roads
transportation
    in Americas, 300
    animals for, 37

    in China, 323
    Sea Roads costs of, 287
transregional interaction
    Sea Roads and, 285–286
    in third-wave era, 269–271
trans-Saharan trade, 230, 298
    camels in, 230, 237, 296–297
    in slaves, 299–300
travel. *See also* trade
    accounts as historical sources, 138(d)
    Asia depictions and, 305–313
    on Silk Roads, 274(i)
Travels of Marco Polo, The (Polo), 307–308(d)
treaties. *See* specific treaties
trees, land clearing and, 419
tribes and tribalism. *See also* kinship
    in pastoral societies, 38
tribute
    to Aztecs, 516
    in China, 327–329, 502
    Korea-China and, 329, 331
    in Russia, 469
    in Xiongnu Empire, 455
Trinity doctrine (Christianity), 172, 413
Triple Alliance, of Mexica people, 516
Trojan Women, The (Euripides), 209
tropical regions, of Africa, 231
Trump, Donald, environment and, 317
Trung sisters (Trung Trac and Trung Nhi, Vietnam), 116, 116(i)
Tu'i Tonga, 255
Tulalip peoples, 496
Tunisia, 386
Turkey. *See also* Anatolia; Fertile Crescent
    ancient societies in, 24, 39
    Göbekli Tepe in, 24, 25, 25(i)
    Islam and, 368
Turkic peoples. *See also* Turks
    arts of, 456(i)
    Byzantine Empire and, 411, 414
    in Central Asia, 498–499
    Chinese culture and, 330
    civilizations of, 478
    Crusades and, 427
    in Eurasia, 455–456
    gender relations and, 380
    Islam and, 365, 376
    Kipchak-speaking, 469
    in Mongolia, 329
    Ottoman Empire and, ?, 379(m), 508
    Safavid, 511
    Timur (Tame...
    Xiongnu E...
Turkmen...

Turks. *See also* Ottoman Empire; Turkic peoples
  Byzantine Empire and, 411, 425
  Islam and, 456
  miniature painting in, 391
  Ottoman, 508–511, 527
  pastoralists and, 455
  Seljuk, 456
Tusi, Nasir al-Din (astronomer), 387*(t)*
twice-born people, in India, 194

Uighur peoples, 329
ulama (Islamic scholars), 371–372, 384
  Sufis on, 372–373
Umayyad caliphate (Arab Empire), 370
umma (Islamic community), 362, 364*(i)*, 369, 397
unification, of China, 117
Unified Silla Kingdom (Korea), 331
United States. *See also* North America
  climate change and, 317
  empire of, 128
universities and colleges, European, 433
untouchables, 126, 187, 195, 195*(t)*, 196
Upanishads (India), 142, 149–150, 166*(t)*
upper classes, 65. *See also* classes
Upper River during Qing Ming Festival (China), 324*(i)*
urban areas. *See also* cities and towns
  collapse of empires and, 124
  in East Africa, 294
  in Europe, 421–422
  in First Civilizations, 63–65
  Islam in, 385–386
  markets in, 421*(i)*
  in Mesopotamia, 76–77
  in Niger Valley civilization, 235–237
  in third-wave era, 270
  in Wari and Tiwanaku, 245–246
  women in, 204, 423
urbanization. *See also* cities and towns; globalization; industrialization
  industrialization

veils
  in Islamic societies, 374
  in Mesopotamia, 69
veneration, of Virgin Mary, 424
Venice, Italy
  Ottomans and, 528
  population of, 421
  trade in, 285, 421, 531, 532*(v)*
Venus figurines, 16, 23, 23*(i)*
vernacular languages, in Europe, 418
vertical integration, in Meosamerica, 237
Vesuvius, Mount, eruption of, 215
Victoria, Lake, 249
Vietnam
  China and, 116, 117, 328, 333–335
  environment in, 333*(m)*
  Funan in, 290
  independence for, 334
  papermaking in, 338
  rice from, 321, 340
  trade in, 290
View of Taishan, A (Du Fu), 353*(d)*
Vikings, 414, 419
villages. *See also* cities and towns
  agricultural, 35, 39–40, 496–498
  in Jenne-jeno, 236
  in North America, 250–251, 496
violence. *See* revolution(s)
Viracocha (Inca god), 518
Virgin Mary (mother of Jesus). *See* Mary
virtue, Aristotle on, 161
Vishnu (Hindu god), 154, 155
Visigoths, 124, 416
Vladimir (Kiev), 415
volcanoes, in Sumatra, 13
voyages. *See* exploration; maritime voyages; Sea Roads

Waldseemüller, Martin (German cartographer), map of 1507 by, 505*(i)*
"Wall Painting of Mohenjo Daro Reconstruction," 85*(v)*
Wang Changling (China), 349, 350*(v)*
Wang Mang (China), 191
Wang Wei (China), 352–353*(d)*
war(s) and warfare. *See also* revolution(s); weapons; specific battles and wars
  in Arab world, 365–367
  civilizations and, 62
  gender roles and, 68
  of Iroquois, 497
  Maya and, 239
  in Mesoamerica, 302
  Mongol, 460, 468–469
  in Oceania, 256
  religious, 383

  slavery and, 66*(i)*
  technology and, 430–431
Wari civilization (Andes region), 59, 245–246, 518
warring states period (China), 73, 115–117, 142, 345
warriors
  in Europe, 419
  gender roles and, 68
  Mongol, 463*(i)*
  in Sparta, 210
al-Wasiti (Arab artist), 287*(i)*, 375*(i)*
water. *See also* irrigation; waterways
  Islamic management of, 386
water mills, 430
waterways. *See also* canals; oceans
  Aztec, 517
  in China, 323
wealth
  in China, 321, 324, 339, 344
  of Meroë, 233
  Moche, 243
  Mongol, 462
  of Roman Catholic Church, 418
  slavery and, 199–200
  trade and, 285
weapons. *See also* gunpowder; war(s) and warfare
  European, 338–339, 430–431
  Greek fire as, 413
weather. *See* climate
Weatherford, Jack, on Mongols, 491*(d)*
weaving
  in Agricultural Revolution, 35–36
  women and, 325, 424
Wen (China), 455
Wendi (China), 119, 343
Wen-hsiang (Chinese writer), 280
wen/wu (Chinese qualities), 146
West, Barbara, 51*(d)*
West Africa. *See also* Niger Valley region
  agriculture in, 248
  Almoravid Empire and, 457
  Christianity in, 357
  civilizations in, 235–237, 297–300
  commerce in, 236–237
  empires in, 297–300
  Igbo society in, 497
  Islam and, 357, 368, 380–382, 381*(m)*
  Moroccan diplomat in, 310–311*(d)*
  pastoral peoples in, 498–499
  Sand Roads to, 295–300
  slavery and, 299
  societies of, 497
  trade and, 380–381
  women in, 382

Western Christendom, 415, 427. *See also* Roman Catholic Church

Western Europe. *See also* Europe and Europeans; religion(s); Roman Catholic Church; Western world; specific locations
 Byzantine Empire and, 412–413
 Christianity in, 415–428
 civilizations in, 159–164, 419–424
 culture of, 124
 Germanic kingdoms in, 416–417
 invasions of, 419
 in Middle Ages, 419–428
 plague in, 476
 political life in, 416–417
 Roman Catholic Church and, 404
 Roman Empire and, 124, 438–447
 society in, 438
 urban areas in, 421–422
 world economy and, 303

Western Hemisphere. *See also* America(s); empire(s)
 agriculture in, 32
 cross-cultural interactions in, 300–302
 human migrations to, 17
 pastoral societies in, 228

western Roman Empire, 409, 474. *See also* Roman Empire

Western world. *See also* colonies and colonization; Europe and Europeans; Western Europe
 China and, 330
 comparative perspective on, 428–435
 empires in, 477–478
 Greek thought in, 161–164

Western Zhou dynasty (China), Mandate of Heaven in, 71

Wheeler, Mortimer (archeologist), 88–89

whiskey. *See* alcohol

widows
 in Japan, 337
 in Korea, 332
 in Mongol society, 451

Willendorf Venus, 23*(i)*

William of Conches (French scholar), 433

William of Rubruck (Franciscan friar), 488
 Journey to the Land of the Mongols, 489*(d)*

Wilson, Andrew, on Pompeii economy, 224–225*(d)*

wind power, 430

witches, Bantu belief in, 249–250

"Woman of Athens, A," 209*(i)*

women. *See also* gender and gender issues; queen(s)
 in Angkor, 293
 in Athens, 208–212
 Aztec, 516*(i)*, 520–521
 Bantu, 249, 249*(i)*
 in Buddhism, 152
 in China, 145–146, 205–208, 280, 324–326, 500
 in Christianity, 119, 166–167, 171–172
 in Egypt, 69
 in elites, 204–205
 Inca, 520–521
 in India, 149, 150
 in Indus Valley civilization, 88, 89*(v)*
 Iroquois, 498*(i)*
 Islamic, 374–376, 375*(i)*
 in Japan, 337
 in Korea, 332
 lifestyle of peasants, 422–423
 in monastic life, 424
 Mongol, 450–451, 468*(i)*
 as Nubian monarchs, 231
 in Oceania, 256
 in pastoral societies, 38–39, 451–452
 patriarchy and, 67, 198, 204–205
 religion and, 39
 in Roman society, 114
 in second-wave civilizations, 188
 as slaves, 198, 199
 in Song China, 324–326
 in Sparta, 208–212, 210*(i)*
 in third-wave era, 270–271
 Turkic, 380
 in urban areas, 423
 in Vietnam, 334–335
 weaving and, 424
 in West Africa, 298–299, 382
 in Western Europe, 418
 as workers, 423–424

workers. *See also* labor; migration
 women as, 423–424

world history. *See also* history and historiography
 balance in writing about, 258
 as field of study, 12–13

world wars, Mongol, 460

writing and writing systems, 12, 13. *See also* alphabet
 in Andes Mountains region, 300
 Chinese, 121
 in Egypt, 52*(i)*, 71–73, 72*(t)*
 in First Civilizations, 71–73
 Islamic, 386
 in Japan, 336, 337
 of Maya, 238

Meroitic, 233
 Sumerian, 72*(t)*, 79
 in Teotihuacán, 241
 travel, 138*(d)*, 315*(d)*
 in Vietnam, 335

Wu (Chinese Empress), 207

Wudi (China), 121, 189

Xia dynasty (China), 60, 115

Xian, China, terra-cotta army in, 98*(i)*

Xi Jinping (China), 317

Xinjiang, China, 39

Xiongnu people, 279
 China and, 118*(m)*, 123, 135–137*(d)*, 329, 455
 Empire of, 455, 455*(m)*
 as pastoral society, 454–455, 478

Xuanzang (Chinese monk), 305, 306–307*(d)*

Yahweh (deity), 69, 142, 157–158, 360

yams, 248

Yangzi River region, 282, 318, 340

Yao Hong (Chinese Christian), 403

Yap, Micronesia (island), 257

Yellow River, 122

Yellow Turban Rebellion (China), 122, 148, 192, 192*(m)*

Yemen, agriculture in, 360, 386

"Yhi Brings Life to the World," 45–46*(d)*

Yi Jing (Chinese monk), 291

yin/yang, 148

Yongle (China), 500, 501, 502

Yoruba people, 497

Yuan Chen (Chinese poet), 330

Yuan dynasty (China), 460

Yucatán area, 239, 301–302

Zambezi River, 295

Zapotec people, 241

Zarathustra (**Zoroaster**, Persia), 155, 156, 166*(t)*

zero, Maya concept of, 238

Zheng He (China), 501–502, 507

Zhou dynasty (China), 60, 61, 71, 115

Zhuangzi (Chinese philosopher), 166*(t)*

ziggurats, 62

Zimbabwe, 249. *See also* Great Zimb

Zoroaster. *See* Zarathustra

Zoroastrianism
 in Arabia, 360
 Buddhism and, 282
 Islam and, 367, 3
 monotheism
 pastoralists
 in Persi

ROCKY MTS.

Mississippi R.

APPALACHIAN MTS.

ATLANTIC
OCEAN

Gulf of
Mexico

Tropic of Cancer

PACIFIC OCEAN

Niger R.

Equator

Amazon R.

A N D E S   M T S.

Tropic of Capricorn

ATLANTIC
OCEAN

abwe

284

08

of, 155–157

and, 454

a, 142, 155–157, 156(i)

URAL MTS.

Volga R.

Ob R.

ALPS

GOBI

Yellow R.

SYRIAN
DESERT

Mediterranean Sea

HIMALAYA MTS.

Yangzi R.

SAHARA

Ganges R.

Tropic of Cancer

Nile R.

Arabian
Sea

Bay of
Bengal

South
China
Sea

PACIFIC OCEAN

Congo R.

INDIAN OCEAN

Equator

Zambezi R.

Tropic of Capricorn

KALAHARI
DESERT

Vegetation Zones

- Tundra
- Northern forest
- Temperate forest
- Temperate grassland
- Desert and dry shrub
- Mediterranean shrub
- Mountain grassland
- Tropical grassland
  and savanna
- Tropical forest
- Permanent ice cover

About the Authors

Robert W. Strayer (Ph.D., University of Wisconsin) brings wide experience in world history to the writing of *Ways of the World*. His teaching career began in Ethiopia, where he taught high school world history for two years as part of the Peace Corps. At the university level, he taught African, Soviet, and world history for many years at the College at Brockport: State University of New York, where he received the Chancellor's Awards for Excellence in Teaching and for Excellence in Scholarship. In 1998 he was visiting professor of world and Soviet history at the University of Canterbury in Christchurch, New Zealand. Since moving to California in 2002, he has taught world history at the University of California, Santa Cruz; California State University, Monterey Bay; and Cabrillo College. He is a long-time member of the World History Association and served on its Executive Committee. He has also participated in various AP World History gatherings, including two years as a reader. His publications include *Kenya: Focus on Nationalism, The Making of Mission Communities in East Africa, The Making of the Modern World, Why Did the Soviet Union Collapse?*, and *The Communist Experiment.*

Eric W. Nelson (D.Phil., Oxford University) is a professor of history at Missouri State University. He is an experienced teacher who has won a number of awards, including the Missouri Governor's Award for Teaching Excellence in 2011 and the CASE and Carnegie Foundation for the Advancement of Teaching Professor of the Year Award for Missouri in 2012. His publications include *Layered Landscapes: Early Modern Religious Space across Faith and Cultures, The Legacy of Iconoclasm: ____s War and the Relic Landscape of Tours, Blois and Vendôme,* and *The Jesu-____he Monarchy: Catholic Reform and Political Authority in France.*